Studies in Tectonic Culture

Contents

Foreword

In a recent novel by Phillip Lopate the somewhat intrepid attempt of the leading character to write a doctoral dissertation on Gottfried Semper ends with a nervous breakdown. The erstwhile graduate student never quite recovers. He first withdraws into a dreary shop in which he sells Persian carpets, then into an emotional aporia in which he is no longer able to connect with friends and family or to divert his failing business from bankruptcy. Like some whorl in an Oriental arabesque, his life circles feverishly in an eddy of nondirectional space; ultimately he loses the capacity to make the simplest decision and retreats into the calm of a psychological stupor.[1]

Architectural theory can be a heady experience, as a few adventurous souls have taken the occasion to discover. It is perhaps for this reason that so many of our architectural educators have gone to such lengths to exclude it from the architectural curriculum, to shunt the student out of harm's way, as it were. When schools of architecture do offer the pretense of engaging in weighty matters of philosophical import, it is generally limited to carefully diluted readings of Heidegger or Foucault or Derrida (certainly no one from the discipline of architecture), and these measured doses are taken sparingly in the privacy of the design studio where they can be shielded from contact with that other nemesis to "creative" design—architectural history. Hence in a rather perverse and arcane way, theory in these instances becomes a pretext to ignore, or at least to downplay, architecture's legitimate intellectual development. One of the merits of this book by Kenneth Frampton is that it seeks to redress this bias or imbalance.

It may seem axiomatic to define architecture simply as the "poetics of construction," but Frampton does precisely this. In a time when the profession increasingly gravitates toward pedantic gamesmanship and neo–avant-gardism, it is salutary to recall that architecture was once rendered as a more substantial art. It is also refreshing to be reminded that architecture can be evaluated by an entirely different set of criteria, involving the appreciation of craft and an expressive emphasis on what Frampton terms its tectonic and tactile dimension. But this focus on architecture's tangible materiality, which must be distinguished from cruder efforts at artistic materialism, is at the same time fraught with certain dangers. How do we follow Frampton and Giorgio Grassi in stressing this art's tectonic basis (and consequently de-emphasizing the supposed nihilism of its technology) without at the same time undermining architecture's capacity for representational values? How do we articulate a building's corporeal presence without diminishing the allusive poetics of its form?

The partial answer to this dilemma can be found, I think, at the point where the author's historical panorama begins: in the late eighteenth and first half of the nineteenth century. The better architects of this period—from Jacques-Germain Soufflot to John Soane to Henri Labrouste—would hardly have viewed this issue as a dilemma in the first place. Karl Friedrich Schinkel, for example, accepted it as apodictic that an edifice conveys cultural meaning on various levels: not only in the capacity of tectonic form to portray its constructional logic but also in the efficacy of the building to function inconographically and didactically. Thus while the exposed brick piers and castellated cornice of his Bauakademie (structurally necessary to anchor the interior system of fireproof vaults) pay homage to the innovative tectonic system, the building comes to be defined on another level by the terra-cotta tapestry that Schinkel wove into the surrounds of the doors and principal windows, in which he depicted, through a series of narrative panels, the mythological and constructional history of this art.

It is also easy to overlook the fact that the giant Ionic colonnade of the Altes Museum was rationalized by Schinkel simply as a hierarchic plastic response to its location on the Lustgarten, opposite the honorific mass of the royal palace. The principal facade of the building, however, was the recessed wall of this urban stoa, on which were painted four colossal murals, two of which were one story high and six in length, portraying his intensively artistic vision of the cosmological and cultural history of mankind. Even seemingly ancillary details, such as the ornamental railings of the upper vestibule of the fountain placed in front, were scrupulously crafted to expound his grander vision of allegory. It was only through the rationalist filter of an Augustus Welby Pugin or Eugène Emmanuel Viollet-le-Duc that the modern concern with enhancing or articulating the logic of construction began to overshadow these others forms of tectonic expression.

But this graphic impulse did not entirely expire. Carl Bötticher elevated this tendency to another level of theoretical refinement with his distinction between the *Kernform* (core form) and *Kunstform* (symbolic art form), that is, by interpreting the degree of curvature of a Greek entablature molding more abstractly as an artistic response to the intensity of the load placed upon it. Friedrich Theodor Vischer and Robert Vischer circumscribed this animistic thesis of Bötticher (and Schopenhauer) with the psychological notion of "empathy," which they defined as the mostly unconscious projection of human emotion, of our "mental-sensory self," into sensuous form. Only later in the century, in fact around 1900, did architects (forever condemned, it seems, to search beyond their own discourse for ideological inspiration) again take an interest in exploring the potent empathetic expressiveness of what Frampton now calls ontological form. This notion of empathy for Robert Vischer (and later, in 1886, for Heinrich Wölfflin) was in no way a merely figurative reading of form. It presumed both our physiological and emotional engagement with the world and therefore was corporeal and emotive rather than conceptual or intellectual.

It is this empathetic sensitivity to form and its material expression—the nineteenth-century Germanic notion of *Formgefühl*—that elevates Frampton's tectonic thesis well above the plane of vulgar materialism and leads it back to its complementary touchstone of representation. The author does not wish to deprive architecture of other levels of iconic expression but rather to reinvest a design with a now largely understated layer of meaning, one perhaps more primitive or primordial in its sensory apprehension. When he brings this theoretical perspective to his analyses of such twentieth-century architects as Auguste Perret, Frank Lloyd Wright, Mies van der Rohe, Louis Kahn, Jørn Utzon, and Carlo Scarpa, Frampton at the same time posits elements of a new paradigm by which we might once again draw history and theory closer to one another—or rather, view one more properly as the critical engagement of the other. He seeks in this way to reaffirm that very ancient connection between the artificer and the artifice, between the designer's initial conception and design's hard-won ingenuity. In such a view ornament indeed becomes, as he interprets Scarpa's work, a "kind of writing," but it is now an embellishment more germane and indeed intrinsic to the tectonic process. It is manifest in the creative act rather than in its figurative appropriation.

In one of the more astute architectural analyses of the nineteenth century, written in 1898, the Munich architect Richard Streiter, after surveying the major directions of nineteenth-century Germanic theory from Bötticher to Otto Wagner, decided that architecture could only renew itself by becoming emphatically "realist," which he defined as the most scrupulous fulfillment of the demands of function, convenience, health, and *Sachlichkeit,* in addition to taking into account the local materials, landscape, and historically conditioned ambiance of a building's milieu. This prescription of Streiter is not so different from Frampton's almost quixotic task to unite vitality with calm, in order "to create a still yet vital point within the whirlwind." It seems that about every 100 years or so we have to be reminded of the cogency of our sensuous discourse with the world. This book, with its rich and palmate array of ideas, may not put an end to the affected disenchantment that so often insinuates itself into our "post-postmodern" architectural discourse (as some, sadly, are already referring to it), but it will certainly give a tangible start to this art's deepening and further elaboration.

Harry Francis Mallgrave

Acknowledgments

These studies have their origin in the inaugural Francis Craig Cullivan lecture that I had the honor to give in 1986 at Rice University in Houston, Texas. In this regard I have to thank the faculty of architecture at Rice University, without whom this book would never have been started. I wish also to extend my particular gratitude to Professor Anderson Todd of Rice for his patience and tireless support and to Alan Balfour who, while chairman of the same faculty, was able to arrange for further financial assistance. In terms of the actual production I would also like to acknowledge my profound debt to John Cava of the University of Oregon at Eugene, for his constant and invaluable help during the seemingly endless period of research and preparation that preceded the publication of this text. I have also to thank Claudia Schinkievicz, who not only translated this text into German but also effected its initial publication in German in 1993. While the present text is virtually the same, subsequent minor corrections and refinements have been made and new insights have inevitably emerged. Particular acknowledgments have to be given to Harry Mallgrave and Duncan Berry for their invaluable help in the development of the material embodied in chapter 3. I must also thank Karla Britton and Karen Melk for their untiring assistance in the countless reworkings to which this text has been subjected, not to mention the various students of the Graduate School of Architecture, Planning and Preservation at Columbia University who have on occasion assisted with the preparation of certain study models. There are a number of other scholars and architects who indirectly, through their work, have played a key role in the conceptual development of this book. Among these particular credit should be accorded to Stanford Anderson, Robert Bartholomew, Barry Bergdoll, Rosemarie Bletter, Massimo Cacciari, Peter Carter, Peter Collins, Francesco Dal Co, Hubert Damisch, Guy Debord, Kurt Forster, Marco Frascari, Scott Gartner, Roula Geraniotis, Vittorio Gregotti, Wolfgang Herrmann, Eleftherios Ikonomou, Richard Francis Jones, Aris Konstantinidis, Sergio Los, Robin Middleton, Ignasí de Sola-Morales, Fritz Neumeyer, Bruno Reichlin, Colin Rowe, Eduard Sekler, Manfredo Tafuri, and Giuseppe Zambonini. It should go without saying that there are countless others to whom I am also equally indebted and whose specific contributions are acknowledged, as it were, in the footnotes. Last, but not least, I would like to salute the production staff and editorial direction of the MIT Press and above all the Graham Foundation in Chicago, whose timely grant enabled us to proceed with the publication of this present book.

We don't ask to be eternal beings. We only ask that things do not lose all their meaning.

Antoine de Saint-Exupéry

Studies in Tectonic Culture

1 Introduction:
Reflections on the Scope of the Tectonic

The history of contemporary architecture is inevitably multiple, multifarious even; a history of the structures that form the human environment independently of architecture itself; a history of the attempts to control and direct those structures; a history of the intellectuals who have sought to devise policies and methods for those attempts; a history of new languages which, having abandoned all hope of arriving at absolute and definitive words, have striven to delimit the area of their particular contribution.

Obviously the intersection of all those manifold histories will never end up in unity. The realm of history is, by nature, dialectical. It is that dialectic that we have tried to pin down, and we have done what we could not to smooth over conflicts which are cropping up again today in the form of worrisome questions as to what role architecture itself should or can have. It is useless to try to reply to such questions. What needs to be done, instead, is to trace the entire course of modern architecture with an eye to whatever cracks and gaps break up its compactness, and then to make a fresh start, without, however, elevating to the status of myth either the continuity of history or those separate discontinuities.
Manfredo Tafuri and Francesco Dal Co, L'architettura contemporanea, *1976*

The great French architectural theorist Eugène-Emmanuel Viollet-le-Duc would compile his magnum opus of 1872, his *Entretiens sur l'architecture,* without once using the term space in a modern sense.[1] Twenty years later nothing could be further from the structuralism of Viollet-le-Duc's thought than the primacy given to space as an end in itself in August Schmarsow's *Das Wesen der architektonischen Schöpfung (The Essence of Architectural Creation),* first published in 1894.[2] Like many other theorists before him, Schmarsow would advance the primitive hut as the primordial shelter, only this time he would see it as a spatial matrix, or what he would call the *Raumgestalterin,* the creatress of space.[3]

To a greater extent perhaps than any other late nineteenth-century theorist, including the sculptor Adolf von Hildebrand, who gave primacy to kinetic vision, and Gottfried Semper, from whom Schmarsow derived his thesis, Schmarsow came to see the evolution of architecture as the progressive unfolding of man's feeling for space, what he called *Raumgefühl.* Between 1893 and 1914 Schmarsow's identification of space as the driving principle behind all architectural form coincides with the evolving space-time models of the universe as these were successively adduced by Nikolai Ivanovich Lobachevsky, Georg Riemann, and Albert Einstein. As we know, such paradigms would come to be deployed early in this century to rationalize in various ways the appearance of dynamic spatial form in the field of avant-gardist art.[4] This conjunction was reinforced through the experience of speed and the actual transformation of space-time in an everyday sense, due to the mechanical inventions of the last half of the century: the familiar Futurist technology of the train, the transatlantic liner, the car, and the plane.

Space has since become such an integral part of our thinking about architecture that we are practically incapable of thinking about it at all without putting our main emphasis on the spatial displacement of the subject in time. This quintessentially modern viewpoint has clearly underlain innumerable texts treating the intrinsic nature of modern architecture, ranging from Sigfried Giedion's *Space, Time and Architecture* of 1941 to Cornelis van de Ven's *Space in Architecture* of 1978. As van de Ven shows, the idea of space established a new concept that not only overcame eclecticism through a relativizing of style, but also gave priority to the spatio-plastic unity of interior and exterior space and to the nonhierarchical assimilation of all instrumental forms, irrespective of their scale or mode of address, into one continuous space-time experience.

Without wishing to deny the volumetric character of architectural form, this study seeks to mediate and enrich the priority given to space by a reconsideration of the constructional and structural modes by which, of necessity, it has to be achieved. Needless to say, I am not alluding to the mere revelation of constructional technique but rather to its expressive potential. Inasmuch as the tectonic amounts to a poetics of construction it is art, but in this respect the artistic dimension is neither figurative nor abstract. It is my contention that the unavoidably earthbound nature of building is as tectonic and tactile in character as it is scenographic and visual, although none of these attributes deny its spatiality. Nevertheless we may assert that the built is first and foremost a construction and only later an abstract discourse based on surface, volume, and plan, to cite the "Three Reminders to Architects" in Le Corbusier's *Vers une architecture* of 1923.[5] One may also add that building, unlike fine art, is as much an everyday experience as it is a representation and that the built is a thing rather than a sign, even if, as Umberto Eco once remarked, as soon as one has an object of "use" one necessarily has a sign that is indicative of this use.

From this point of view, we may claim that type form—the received "what" deposited by the lifeworld—is as much a precondition for building as craft technique, however much it may remain open to inflection at different levels. Thus we may claim that the built invariably comes into existence out of the constantly evolving interplay of three converging vectors, the *topos,* the *typos,* and the *tectonic.* And while the tectonic does not necessarily favor any particular style, it does, in conjunction with site and type, serve to counter the present tendency for architecture to derive its legitimacy from some other discourse.

This reassertion of the tectonic derives in part from Giorgio Grassi's critical polemic as this was advanced in his essay "Avant Garde and Continuity" of 1980, in which he wrote:

As far as the architectural vanguards of the Modern Movement are concerned, they invariably follow in the wake of the figurative arts. . . . Cubism, Suprematism, Neo-plasticism, etc., are all forms of investigation born and developed in the realm of the figurative arts, and only as a second thought carried over into architecture as well. It is actually pathetic to see the architects of that "heroic" period, and the best among them, trying with difficulty to accommodate themselves to these "isms"; experimenting in a perplexed manner because of their fascination with the new doctrines, measuring them, only later to realize their ineffectuality.[6]

Despite the retardataire implications of this Lukacsian critique, Grassi's observation nonetheless challenges the prestige that still seems to attach itself to the figurative in architecture. This challenge comes at a time when architecture appears to oscillate uneasily between a deconstructive aestheticization of its traditional modus operandi and a reassertion of its liberative capacity as a critical form. It is perhaps a measure of Grassi's professional alienation that his work remains somewhat hermetic and indeed paradoxically removed, when built, from the poetics of craft construction. This is all the more inexplicable given the care that he takes in developing the constructional details of his work (fig. 1.1). No one perhaps has made a more judicious assessment of the contradictory aspects of Grassi's architecture than the Catalan critic Ignasí de Sola Morales:

Architecture is posited as a craft, that is to say, as the practical application of established knowledge through rules of the different levels of intervention. Thus, no notion of architecture as problem-solving, as innovation, or as invention ex novo, is present in showing the permanent, the evident, and the given character of knowledge in the making of architecture.

. . . The work of Grassi is born of a reflection upon the essential resources of discipline, and it focuses upon specific media which determine not only aesthetic choices but also the ethical content of its cultural contribution. Through these channels of ethical and political will, the concern of the Enlightenment . . . becomes enriched in its most critical tone. It is not solely the superiority of reason and the analysis of form which are indicated, but rather, the critical role (in the Kantian sense of the term), that is, the judgement of values, the very lack of which is felt in society today. . . . In the sense that his architecture is a metalanguage, a reflection on the contradictions of his own practice, his work acquires the appeal of something that is both frustrating and noble.[7]

Etymology

Greek in origin, the term tectonic derives from the word *tekton,* signifying carpenter or builder. The corresponding verb is *tektainomai.* This in turn is related to the Sanskrit *taksan,* referring to the craft of carpentry and to the use of the axe. Remnants of a similar term can be found in Vedic poetry, where it again refers to carpentry. In Greek it appears in Homer, where it alludes to the art of construction in general. The poetic connotation of the term first appears in Sappho, where the *tekton,* the carpenter, assumes the role of the poet. In general, the

1.1
Giorgio Grassi, restoration and reconstruction of the Roman theater of Sagunto, Valencia, 1985. Cross section.

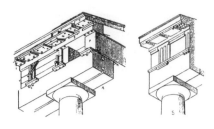

1.2
Auguste Choisy, the derivation of the Doric order from timber construction, from *Histoire de l'architecture,* 1899.

term refers to an artisan working in all hard materials except metal. In the fifth century B.C. this meaning undergoes further evolution, from something specific and physical, such as carpentry, to a more generic notion of making, involving the idea of *poesis.* In Aristophanes it would seem that the notion is even associated with machination and the creation of false things, a transformation that would appear to correspond to the passage from pre-Socratic philosophy to Hellenism. Needless to say, the role of the *tekton* leads eventually to the emergence of the master builder or *architekton.*[8] That the term would eventually aspire to an aesthetic rather than a technological category has been remarked on by Adolf Heinrich Borbein in his 1982 philological study:

Tectonic becomes the art of joinings. "Art" here is to be understood as encompassing tekne, *and therefore indicates tectonic as assemblage not only of building parts but also of objects, indeed of artworks in a narrower sense. With regard to the ancient understanding of the word, tectonic tends toward the construction or making of an artisanal or artistic product. . . . It depends much more upon the correct or incorrect applications of the artisanal rules, or the degree to which its usefulness has been achieved. Only to this extent does tectonic also involve judgment over art production. Here, however, lies the point of departure for the expanded clarification and application of the idea in more recent art history: as soon as an aesthetic perspective—and not a goal of utility—is defined that specifies the work and production of the* tekton, *then the analysis consigns the term "tectonic" to an aesthetic judgement.*[9]

The first architectural use of the term in German dates from its appearance in Karl Otfried Müller's *Handbuch der Archäologie der Kunst* (Handbook of the Archaeology of Art), published in 1830, wherein he defines *tektonische* as applying to a series of art forms "such as utensils, vases, dwellings and meeting places of men, which surely form and develop on the one hand due to their application and on the other due to their conformity to sentiments and notions of art. We call this string of mixed activities tectonic; their peak is architecture, which mostly through necessity rises high and can be a powerful representation of the deepest feelings." In the third edition of his study Müller remarks on the specifically junctional or "dry" jointing implications of the term. "I did not fail to notice that the ancient term *tektones,* in specialized usage, refers to people in construction or cabinet makers, not however, to clay and metal workers; therefore, at the same time, it takes into account the general meaning, which lies in the etymology of the word."[10]

In his highly influential *Die Tektonik der Hellenen* (The Tectonic of the Hellenes), published in three volumes between 1843 and 1852, Karl Bötticher would make the seminal contribution of distinguishing between the *Kernform* and the *Kunstform;* between the core form of the timber rafters in a Greek temple and the artistic representation of the same elements as petrified beam ends in the triglyphs and metopes of the classical entablature (fig. 1.2). Bötticher interpreted the term tectonic as signifying a complete system binding all the parts of the Greek temple into a single whole, including the framed presence of relief sculpture in all its multifarious forms.

Influenced by Müller, Gottfried Semper would endow the term with equally ethnographic connotations in his epoch-making theoretical departure from the Vitruvian triad of *utilitas, fermitas,* and *venustas.* Semper's *Die vier Elemente der*

Baukunst (Four Elements of Architecture), published in 1851, indirectly challenged the neoclassic primitive hut as posited by the Abbé Laugier in his *Essai sur l'architecture* of 1753.[11] Based in part on an actual Caribbean hut that he saw in the Great Exhibition of 1851, Semper's primordial dwelling was divided into four basic elements: (1) the earthwork, (2) the hearth, (3) the framework/roof, and (4) the lightweight enclosing membrane. On the basis of this taxonomy Semper would classify the building crafts into two fundamental procedures: the *tectonics* of the frame, in which lightweight, linear components are assembled so as to encompass a spatial matrix, and the *stereotomics* of the earthwork, wherein mass and volume are conjointly formed through the repetitious piling up of heavyweight elements. That this last depends upon load-bearing masonry, whether stone or mud brick, is suggested by the Greek etymology of stereotomy, from *stereos,* solid, and *tomia,* to cut. This tectonic/stereotomic distinction was reinforced in German by that language's differentiation between two classes of wall; between *die Wand,* indicating a screenlike partition such as we find in wattle and daub infill construction, and *die Mauer,* signifying massive fortification.[12] This distinction will find a certain correspondence in Karl Gruber's 1937 reconstruction of a typical German medieval city, which illustrates the difference between heavyweight battlements built of masonry and lightweight residential fabric framed in wood and filled with wattle and daub (*Fachwerkbau*) (fig. 1.3).[13]

This distinction between light and heavy reflects a more general differentiation in terms of material production, wood construction displaying an affinity for its tensile equivalent in terms of basketwork and textiles, and stonework tending toward its substitution as a compressive material by brickwork or *pisé* (rammed earth) and later by reinforced concrete. As Semper was to point out in his *Stoffwechseltheorie,* the history of culture manifests occasional transpositions in which the architectonic attributes of one mode are expressed in another for the

1.3
Karl Gruber, reconstruction of a typical medieval city, 1937.

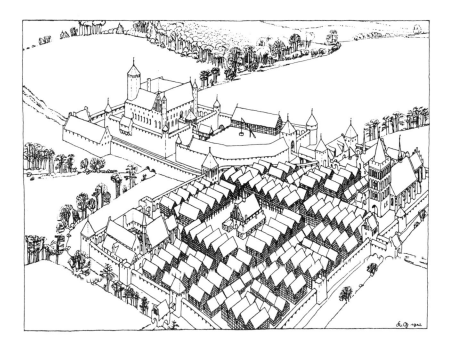

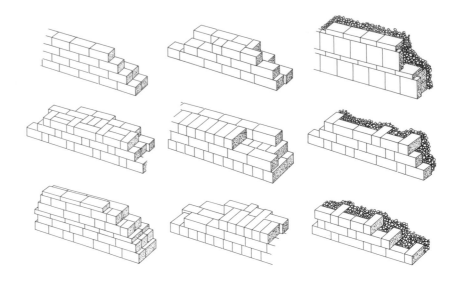

sake of retaining traditional symbolic value, as in the case of the Greek temple, where stone is cut and laid in such a way as to reinterpret the form of the archetypal timber frame. In this regard we need to note that masonry, when it does not assume the form of a conglomerate as in *pisé* construction, that is to say when it is bonded into coursework, is also a form of weaving, to which all the various traditional masonry bonds bear testimony (fig. 1.4).[14] The woven overlapping thin tiles or *bóveda* of traditional Catalan vaulting point to the same end (fig. 1.5).

The general validity of Semper's *Four Elements* is borne out by vernacular building throughout the world, even if there are cultures where the woven vertical screen wall does not exist or where the woven wall is absorbed, as it were, into the roof and frame, as in, say, the North American Mandan house (fig. 1.6). In African tribal cultures the enclosing vertical screen covers a wide range of expression, from primitive infill walls, plastered on the inside only, as in the Gogo houses of Tanzania (fig. 1.7), to precisely woven wall mats that line the exterior of the chief's hut, as we find in Kuba culture. Moreover according to climate, custom, and available material the respective roles played by tectonic and stereotomic form vary considerably, so that the primal dwelling passes from a condition in which the earthwork is reduced to point foundations, as in the boulder footings of the traditional Japanese house (fig. 1.8), to a situation in which ste-

1.4
Methods of Roman brick bonding.

1.5
Antoni Gaudí, brick and Catalan vaulting in the Casa Vicens, Barcelona, 1878–1880.

1.6
Mandan house, American Indian, section.

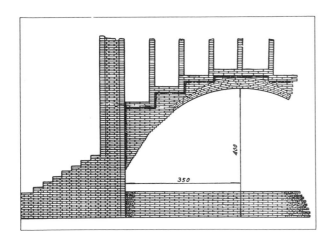

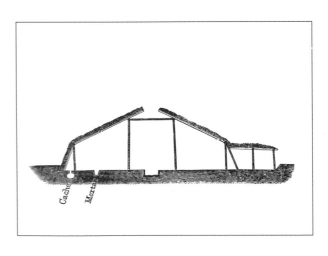

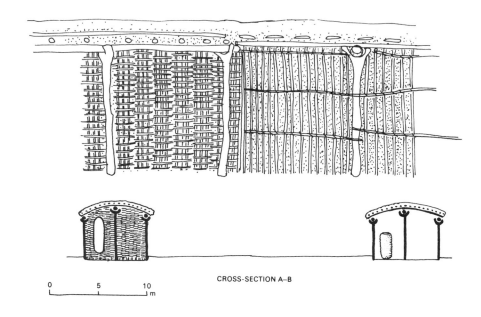

CROSS-SECTION A–B

0   5   10
m

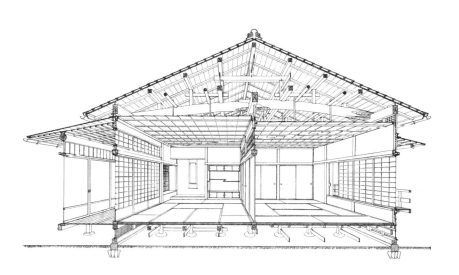

1.7
Gogo houses of Tanzania, detail of infill walls.

1.8
Traditional Japanese one-story house.

reotomic walls are extended horizontally to become floors and roofs, made up of the same material although reinforced with brushwood or basketwork (fig. 1.9). Alternatively the basic cell is covered by a vault of the same material, both techniques being equally prevalent in North African, Cycladic, and Middle Eastern cultures.

It is characteristic of our secular age that we should overlook the cosmic associations evoked by these dialogically opposed modes of construction; that is to say the affinity of the frame for the immateriality of sky and the propensity of mass form not only to gravitate toward the earth but also to dissolve in its substance. As the Egyptian architect Hassan Fathy was to point out, this is never more evident than in mud brick construction, where the walls tend to fuse with the earth once they fall into ruin and disuse. However, untreated wood is equally

7

ephemeral when exposed to the elements, as opposed to a well-bedded stone foundation that tends to endure across time and thus to mark the ground in perpetuity.[15]

Topography

No one has argued more persuasively as to the cosmogonic implications of the earthwork than the Italian architect Vittorio Gregotti, who in 1983 wrote:

The worst enemy of modern architecture is the idea of space considered solely in terms of its economic and technical exigencies indifferent to the ideas of the site.

. . . Through the concept of the site and the principle of settlement, the environment becomes [on the contrary] the essence of architectural production. From this vantage point, new principles and methods can be seen for design. Principles and methods that give precedence to the siting in a specific area. This is an act of knowledge of the context that comes out of its architectural modification. The origin of architecture is not in the primitive hut, or the cave or the mythical "Adam's House in Paradise."

Before transforming a support into a column, a roof into a tympanum, before placing stone on stone, man placed the stone on the ground to recognize a site in the midst of an unknown universe: in order to take account of it and modify it. As with every act of assessment this one required radical moves and apparent simplicity. From this point of view, there are only two important attitudes to the context. The tools of the first are mimesis, organic imitation and the display of complexity. The tools of the second are the assessment of physical relations, formal definition and interiorization of complexity.[16]

It is difficult to find a more didactic modern example of this last than the acknowledged masterwork of the Greek architect Dimitris Pikionis. I have in mind his Philopapou hillside park, laid in place during the second half of the 1950s on a site adjacent to the Acropolis in Athens (fig. 1.10). In this work, as Alexander Tzonis and Liane Lefaivre have remarked, Pikionis created a topographic continuum that was removed from any kind of technological exhibitionism. This serpentine causeway, passing across an undulating rock-strewn site, constituted, in essence, a stone tapestry, bonded into the ground through irregularly coursed pavers, furnished with occasional seats, and studded here and there with iconic signs.[17] Collaged rather than designed, it reinterprets the *genius loci* as a mythic

1.9
Traditional construction from the towns of Mzab in Algeria:
 1. masonry foundation walls
 2. mud brick
 3. *timchent* rendering
 4. smooth rendering
 5. palmwood lintel
 6. clay gargoyle
 7. *timchent* roof finish
 8. small stone vaults
 9. *timchent* rendering
10. palm branch beams
11. stone arch
12. palm nervures centering

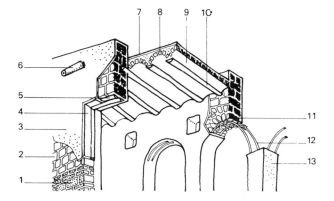

1.10
Dimitris Pikionis, detail of park paving, Philopapou Hill, Athens, 1951–1957.

narrative, part Byzantine, part pre-Socratic, a promenade to be experienced as much by the body as by the eyes. That this was always central to Pikionis's sensibility is evident from a 1933 essay entitled "A Sentimental Topography":

We rejoice in the progress of our body across the uneven surface of the earth and our spirit is gladdened by the endless interplay of the three dimensions that we encounter with every step. . . . Here the ground is hard, stony, precipitous, and the soil is brittle and dry. There the ground is level; water surges out of mossy patches. Further on, the breeze, the altitude and the configuration of the ground announce the vicinity of the sea.[18]

Pikionis's work testifies to the fact that the earthwork tends to transcend our received perceptions about both aesthetics and function, for here the surface of the ground is kinetically experienced through the gait, that is to say through the locomotion of the body and the sensuous impact of this movement on the nervous system as a whole. There is moreover, as Pikionis reminds us, the "acoustical" resonance of the site as the body negotiates its surface. One recalls at this juncture Steen Eiler Rasmussen's *Experiencing Architecture* and the remarkable chapter entitled "Hearing Architecture," where he notes the all but imperceptible acoustical character of built form.[19] Rasmussen reminds us that the spatial reflection or absorption of sound immediately affects our psychological response to a given volume, so that we may find it warm or cold according to its particular resonance rather than its appearance. Similar psycho-acoustical effects have been remarked on by Ulrich Conrads and Bernhard Leitner in a 1985 essay in which they comment on the spiritual aura evoked by the reverberation time of the Taj Mahal and, rather coincidentally, on the way in which Mediterranean vernacular forms appear to be suited to the articulation of certain diphthongs and vowels and not others, with the result that such dwellings prove unsuitable as vacation homes for people speaking northern languages.[20] That even formal integrity may depend in part on acoustical effect is confirmed by Luis Barragán's San Cristóbal horse farm realized in the suburbs of Mexico City in 1967, wherein the central reflecting pool and the sound of its water fountain jointly assure the unity of the whole.

Corporeal Metaphor

The capacity of the being to experience the environment bodily recalls the notion of the corporeal imagination as advanced by the Neapolitan philosopher Giambattista Vico in his *Scienza nuova* of 1730. Against the rationalism of Descartes, Vico argued that language, myth, and custom are the metaphorical legacy of the species brought into being through the self-realization of its history, from the first intuitions deriving from man's primordial experience of nature to the long haul of cultural development running across generations. In his 1985 study Michael Mooney had this to say about Vico's conception of this metaphorical process:

In a moment of stirring oratory, Vico held, when the beauty of a conceit overwhelms the spirit as its truth impresses the mind, both speaker and listener are caught up in a rush of ingenuity, each making connections that were not made before, their spirits fused by the freshness of the language, their minds and finally their wills made one. So here, too, analogously to be sure, the first dim seeing of Jove is an event in which body through language becomes conscious, the poetry of a thundering sky evoking in response the poetry of giants made men, struck dumb with awe.

What occurs is an exchange in metaphor, the image of providence in a thundering heaven passing into the bodies of awestruck men. The physical universe of deus artifex, *itself a poem, everywhere written in conceits, becomes in the bodies of clustered men a poet, henceforth a maker of self; the passive ingenuity of the universe comes to life in the mind (however unrefined it yet is) and the spirit (however passionate and violent it may be) of man, and man, now standing erect, becomes the* artifex *of his own existence.*[21]

Vico's concept of the enactment and reenactment of man through history is not only metaphorical and mythical but also corporeal, in that the body reconstitutes the world through its tactile appropriation of reality. This much is suggested by the psycho-physical impact of form upon our being and by our tendency to engage form through touch as we feel our way through architectonic space. This propensity has been remarked on by Adrian Stokes, in discussing the impact of time and touch on the weathering of stone.

Hand-finish is the most vivid testimony of sculpture. People touch things according to their shape. A single shape is made magnificent by perennial touching. For the hand explores, all unconsciously to reveal, to magnify an existent form. Perfect sculpture needs your hand to communicate some pulse and warmth, to reveal subtleties unnoticed by the eye, needs your hand to enhance them. Used, carved stone, exposed to the weather, records on its concrete shape in spatial, immediate, simultaneous form, not only the winding passages of days and nights, the opening and shutting skies of warmth and wet, but also the sensitiveness, the vitality even, that each successive touching has communicated.[22]

That such a purview stands in total opposition to all our more recent attempts to impose upon cultural experience a consciously distanced and exclusively semiotic character has been remarked on by Scott Gartner.

The philosophical alienation of the body from the mind has resulted in the absence of embodied experience from almost all contemporary theories of meaning in architecture. The overemphasis on signification and reference in architectural theory has led to a construal of meaning as an entirely conceptual phenomenon. Experience, as it relates to understanding, seems reduced to a matter of the visual registration of coded messages—a function of the eye which might well rely on the printed page and dispense with the physical presence of architecture altogether. The body, if it figures into architectural theory at all, is often reduced to an aggregate of needs and constraints which are to be accommodated by methods of design grounded in behavioral and ergonomic analysis. Within this framework of thought, the body and its experience do not participate in the constitution and realization of architectural meaning.[23]

Metaphor, rather than being solely a linguistic or rhetorical trope, constitutes a human process by which we understand and structure one domain of experience in terms of another of a different kind.[24] This concept surely lies behind Tadao Ando's characterization of the *Shintai* as a sentient being that realizes itself through lived-in space.

Man articulates the world through his body. Man is not a dualistic being in whom spirit and the flesh are essentially distinct, but a living corporeal being active in the world. The "here and now" in which this distinct body is placed is what is first taken as granted, and subsequently a "there" appears. Through a perception of that distance, or rather the living of that distance, the surrounding space becomes manifest as a thing endowed with various meanings and values. Since man has an asymmetrical physical structure with a top and a bottom, a left and a right, and a front and a back, the articulated world, in turn, naturally becomes a heterogeneous space. The world that appears to man's senses and the state of man's body become in this way interdependent. The world articulated by the body is a vivid, lived-in space.

The body articulates the world. At the same time, the body is articulated by the world. When "I" perceive the concrete to be something cold and hard, "I" recognize the body as something warm and soft. In this way the body in its dynamic relationship with the world becomes the shintai. *It is only the* shintai *in this sense that builds or understands architecture. The* shintai *is a sentient being that responds to the world.*[25]

This concept parallels similar arguments advanced by Schmarsow and later by Merleau-Ponty,[26] particularly Schmarsow's thesis that our concept of space is determined by the frontalized progression of the body through space in depth. Similar spatio-corporeal connotations are evident in Adolphe Appia's disquisition on the interplay between body and form on the stage, in his *L'Oeuvre d'art vivant* of 1921.[27] A similar phenomenological awareness is also evident in Alvar

1.11
Alvar Aalto, Säynätsalo Town Hall, 1949–1952. Plan, section through council chamber, and longitudinal section.

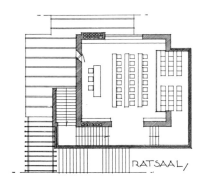

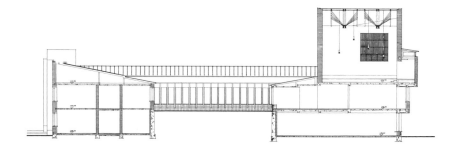

1.12
Alvar Aalto, Säynätsalo Town Hall, stair to the council chamber.

1.13
Ogre's Night at the turn of the year, Kyushu. Ritual raising and burning of the *hashira*.

Aalto's Säynätsalo Town Hall (1952) where, from entry to council chamber, the subject encounters a sequence of contrasting tactile experiences (fig. 1.11). Thus, from the stereotomic mass and relative darkness of the entry stair (fig. 1.12), where the feeling of enclosure is augmented by the tactility of the brick treads, one enters into the bright light of the council chamber, the timber-lined roof of which is carried on fanlike, wooden trusses that splay upward to support concealed rafters above a boarded ceiling. The sense of arrival occasioned by this tectonic display is reinforced by various nonretinal sensations, from the smell of polished wood to the floor flexing under one's weight together with the general destabilization of the body as one enters onto a highly polished surface.

Ethnography

Semper's theory of tectonics was profoundly rooted in the emerging science of ethnography. Like Sigfried Giedion after him, Semper tried to reground the practice of architecture in what Giedion would call "the eternal present," in his 1964 study of this title. This search for a timeless origin is directly evoked in the Prolegomenon to *Der Stil* where, in a manner uncannily reminiscent of Vico, Semper writes of the cosmogonic drive as an archaic impulse continually changing across time (fig. 1.13).

Surrounded by a world full of wonder and forces, whose law man may divine, may want to understand but never decipher, which reaches him only in a few fragmentary harmonies and which suspends his soul in a continuous state of unresolved tension, he himself conjures up the missing perfection in play. He makes himself a tiny world in which the cosmic law is evident within strict limits, yet complete in itself and perfect in this respect; in such play man satisfies his cosmogonic instinct.

His fantasy creates these images, by displaying, expanding, and adapting to his mood the individual scenes of nature before him, so orderly arranged that he believes he can discern in the single event the harmony of the whole and for short moments has the illusion of having escaped reality. Truly this enjoyment of nature *is not very different from the enjoyment of art, just as the beauty of nature . . . is assigned to the general beauty of art as a lower category.*

However, this artistic enjoyment of nature's beauty is by no means the most naive or earliest manifestation of the artistic instinct. On the contrary, the former is undeveloped in simple, primitive man, whereas he does already take delight in nature's creative law as it gleams through reality in the rhythmical sequence of space and time movements, is found once more in the wreath, the bead necklace, the scroll, the circular dance and the rhythmic tone that attends it, the beat of an oar, and so on. These are the beginnings out of which music and *architecture* grew; *both are the highest purely cosmic nonimitative arts, whose legislative support no other art can forgo.*[28]

Although we cannot dwell here on all the ethnographic evidence that may be summoned in support of Semper's thesis, I will cite nonetheless two examples that testify to the way in which the two basic modes of building, the compressive mass and the tensile frame, have been deployed throughout time in such a way as to create a lifeworld that is cosmogonically encoded.

The first instance is taken from Pierre Bourdieu's 1969 study of the Berber house, in which he demonstrates how the entire domain is organized in terms of sectional displacement and material finish in such a way as to distinguish the *upper/dry/human* from the *lower/wet/animal* parts of the dwelling (fig. 1.14). On the opposing transverse axis the same space is ordered about a main entrance, invariably oriented toward the east, and a weaving loom that, in being set opposite the open door and the rising sun, is analogously seen as the sun of the interior. On the basis of this cosmic cross axis the house and its surroundings are divided into a homological hierarchy in which every value is counterbalanced by its opposite. Thus, the attributes of the external world are reversed on the interior; the southern exterior wall becomes the "northern" interior wall, and so on.

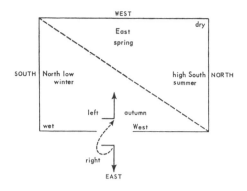

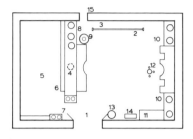

1.14
Berber house, seasonal orientation and internal/external inversion according to the cardinal points:

1. threshold
2. loom
3. rifle
4. *thigejdity*
5. stable
6. trough for oxen
7. water pitchers
8. jars of dried vegetables, etc.
9. hand mill
10. jars of grain
11. bench
12. *kanun*
13. large water jar
14. chest
15. back door

Associated with dawn, spring, fertility, and birth, the loom, before the "eastern" interior wall, is regarded as the female place of honor and is seen as the spiritual nexus of the dwelling. It is balanced by the male object of honor, namely the rifle, that is stacked close to the loom. That this symbolic system is reinforced by the construction itself is confirmed by Bourdieu's testimony.

In front of the wall opposite the door stands the weaving loom. This wall is usually called by the same name as the outside front wall giving onto the courtyard (tasga), or else the wall of the weaving-loom or opposite wall, since one is opposite it when one enters. The wall opposite this is called the wall of darkness, or of sleep, or of the maiden, or of the tomb. . . . One might be tempted to give a strictly technical explanation to these oppositions since the wall of the weaving-loom . . . receives the most light and the stone-flagged stable is, in fact, situated at a lower level than the rest. The reason given for the last is that the house is most often built perpendicularly with the contour lines in order to facilitate the flow of liquid-manure and dirty water. A number of signs suggest, however, that these oppositions are the center of a whole cluster of parallel oppositions, the necessity of which is never completely due to technical imperatives or functional requirements. In addition to all this, at the center of the dividing wall, between "the house of human beings" stands the main pillar, supporting the governing beam and all the framework of the house. Now this governing beam which connects the gables and spreads the protection of the male part of the house to the female part . . . is identified explicitly with the master of the house, whilst the main pillar on which it rests, which is the trunk of a forked tree . . . is identified with the wife . . . and their interlocking represents the act of physical union.[29]

Bourdieu proceeds to show how this same symbolic system differentiates in a categorical way between the lower and upper parts of the house; that is, between the sunken, stone-flagged stable regarded as a space of darkness, fertility, and sexual intercourse and the upper dry, light space of human appearance, finished in polished cow dung.

Our second example is drawn from Japanese culture, in which weaving and binding emerge from archaic time as the primary element in a number of agrarian renewal and ground-breaking rites that still survive today throughout the country (fig. 1.15). In an essay on these rituals, Gunter Nitschke shows how Japanese archaic land-taking/agricultural rites are invariably initiated by knotted or bound signs, known generically as *musubi*, from *musubu*, to bind (fig. 1.16).[30] Nitschke argues that building/binding as a cyclical activity takes priority over religion in the archaic creation of order out of chaos, citing by way of evidence the etymological origin of the word religion in the Latin verb *ligare*, to bind. In contrast to the Western monumental tradition with its dependence on the relative permanence of stereotomic mass, the archaic Japanese world was symbolically structured through ephemeral tectonic material, knotted grasses or rice straw ropes known as *shime-nawa*, literally "bound ropes" (fig. 1.17), or more elaborately through bound pillars of bamboo and reed called *hashira* (fig. 1.18). As Nitschke and others have shown, these Shinto prototectonic devices exercised a decisive influence on the evolution of Japanese sacred and domestic architecture through its various incarnations, from the earliest Shimmei shrines dating from the first century through to the seventeenth-century *shoin* and *chaseki* versions of Heian wooden construction. Due to the relative perishability of untreated wood, Japanese honorific structures were everywhere subject to cyclical rebuilding, the most famous instance being the monumental Naiku and Geku precincts at Ise that, with their attendant buildings, are rebuilt in their entirety every twenty years. On these occasions a new shrine is built on the adjacent site of a previous shrine, this sacred domain having lain dormant over the intervening twenty-year period (fig. 1.19).

Aside from the evident differences separating stereotomic and tectonic construction in archaic building culture, two common factors may be seen as obtaining in both of these examples. The first is the primacy accorded to the woven as a place-making agent in so-called primitive cultures; the second is the universal presence of a nonlinear attitude toward time that guarantees, as it were, the cyclical renewal of an eternal present. This premodern seasonal perception of the temporal finds reflection in the fact that as late as a century and a half ago the

1.15
Ritual tools on display in the course of a Shinto ground-breaking ceremony.

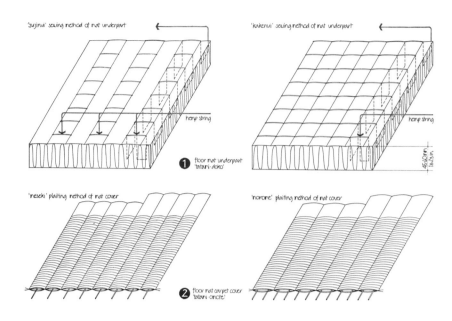

1.20
Diagram showing typical methods of *tatami* mat construction.

up and greatly developed by August Schmarsow in a 1893 lecture, in which he specifically rejected the decorative attributes of the "art of dressing" (Bekleidungskunst) in favor of architecture's abstract capacity to "create space" (Raumgestalterin). The history of architecture is now to be analyzed as a "feeling for space" (Raumgefühl). Schmarsow's proposal was effectively canonized by the Dutch architect Hendrik Berlage in his important lecture of 1904, in which he defined architecture as the "art of spatial enclosure." In the addendum he attached to the publication of his lecture Berlage argued that the nature of the wall was surface flatness, and such constructive parts as the pillar and capitals should be assimilated into it without articulation. Semper's figurative masking of reality is transposed in Berlage's conception into a literal mask, in which surface ornamentation, materials, and structural components represent, as it were, their own constructive and nonconstructive roles as surface decoration. [33]

This dialogue between the constructive and the nonconstructive would be denied by Adolf Loos in his somewhat biased interpretation of Semper's *Bekleidungstheorie,* which may explain why structure and construction play such a negligible role in his architecture. In his 1898 essay entitled "Das Prinzip der Bekleidung" (The Principle of Cladding) Loos stresses the primacy of cladding over all other considerations. [34] Even so, he will still insist on the authenticity of material, so that contrary to Renaissance practice he will argue against the use of stucco to imitate stone or, even more ironically, against the "graining" of wood so as to resemble wood of a higher quality. Loos's habitual application of thin marble revetment on the grounds that it was the cheapest wallpaper in the world, since it would never need to be replaced, tended to remove him, as his work would suggest, from Semper's initial preoccupation with the articulation of the frame and its infill. Like the dissimulating rhetoric of the *Gesamtkunstwerk* to which he was so opposed, Loos embraced an atectonic strategy in that his spatially dynamic *Raumplan* could never be clearly expressed in tectonic terms. Indeed, this masking of the actual fabric so that its substance cannot be discerned is perhaps the sole attribute linking Loos to his rival, the Secessionist architect Josef Hoffmann. The fact that Loos revered tradition makes this affinity all the more paradoxical, particularly since the aura of tradition emanating from his marble cladding served to conceal as much as to reveal the harsh reality lying beyond the confines of the bourgeois house. At the same time, as Mallgrave remarks, Peter Behrens's 1910 dismissal of Semper as a positivist will prove quite decisive for modern building culture in that, strongly influenced by the counterthesis of Alois Riegl, the central preoccupations of German architects will shift away from the tectonic to the abstractly atectonic, bordering on the graphic, thereby assisting in that transformation which Robert Schmutzler will call the crystallization of the Jugendstil.[35]

Tectonic/Atectonic

In a 1973 essay entitled "Structure, Construction, and Tectonics," Eduard Sekler defined the tectonic as a certain expressivity arising from the statical resistance of constructional form in such a way that the resultant expression could not be accounted for in terms of structure and construction alone.[36] Sekler proceeded

1.21
Details of traditional and modern *amado* sliding wooden shutters.

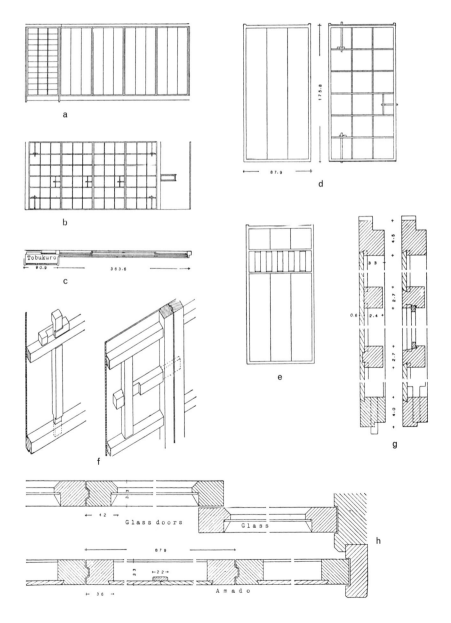

to show how similar combinations of structure and construction could become the occasion for a subtle variation in expression, as in the various corner details that appear in the American work of Mies van der Rohe. He went on to note that a given expression may be at variance with either the order of the structure or the method of construction, citing as an example the concealed flying buttresses of the Baroque. However, when structure and construction appear to be mutually interdependent, as in, say, Paxton's Crystal Palace of 1851, the tectonic potential of the whole would seem to derive from the eurythmy of its parts and the articulation of its joints. Even here, however, statical capacity and representational form can be said to diverge, albeit imperceptibly, since Paxton's modular cast-iron columns of standard diameter are brought to sustain different loads by varying their wall thickness.

In a subsequent essay dealing with Josef Hoffmann's masterwork, the Stoclet House, built in Brussels in 1911 (fig. 1.22), Sekler would introduce the counter-concept of the *atectonic,* as made manifest in this instance by the cable moldings deployed throughout.

At the corners or any other places of juncture where two or more of these parallel mouldings come together, the effect tends towards a negation of the solidity of the built volumes. A feeling persists as if the walls had not been built up in a heavy construction but consisted of large sheets of thin material, joined at the corners with metal bands to protect the edges. . . . The visual result is very striking and atectonic in the extreme. "Atectonic" is used here to describe a manner in which the expressive interaction of load and support in architecture is visually neglected or obscured. . . . There are many other atectonic details at the Stoclet House. Heavy piers have nothing of adequate visual weight to support but carry a thin, flat roof as at the entrance and over the loggia on the roof terrace. . . . In this connection it is equally significant that windows are set flush into the fa-

1.22
Josef Hoffmann, Stoclet House, Brussels,
1911. Main hall.

1.23
Peter Behrens, AEG turbine factory, Berlin,
1909.

cades, even slightly protruding, not in recesses which would betray the thickness of the wall.[37]

Similar weightless effects can be found in a great deal of German architectural production at the beginning of this century, most notably perhaps in Peter Behrens's AEG turbine factory built in Berlin in 1909. Here, the massive Egyptoid corner bastions stop short of supporting the roof that otherwise appears to rest on them. In this unique work, tectonic and atectonic patently coexist; in the first instance, the ontologically tectonic, pin-jointed steel frames that run down Berlichingenstrasse, in the second the representationally atectonic corner bastions, of in situ concrete that, while supporting their own weight, pointedly fail to carry the oversailing cantilever of the roof (fig. 1.23).

It is ironic that this architectonic ambivalence should emerge in Behrens's symbolization of technological power, particularly since he envisaged architecture as serving power throughout history—the thesis advanced in his essay "What Is Monumental Art?" of 1908. Perhaps this psycho-cultural ambivalence arises directly out of his rather willful (*Kunstwollen*) attempt to render the factory shed as a kind of crypto-classical barn in order to signify what Ernst Jünger would later call the *Gestalt* of the worker—the "will to power" of the workers who had already been transformed from an agrarian labor force into a highly skilled proletariat, indentured in the service of the industrial *Kartel*.[38]

Technology

There is perhaps no twentieth-century philosopher who has responded more profoundly to the cultural impact of technology than Martin Heidegger, and while there can be little doubt that there are reactionary aspects of his thought, his work amounts to a fundamental break with positivism; above all, perhaps, through his notion of "thrownness," the idea that each generation has to confront its own destiny within the long trajectory of history.[39] At the same time he has articulated a number of specific insights that are of relevance to the arguments advanced here. The first of these concerns the topographic concept of the bounded domain or place, as opposed to the space endlessness of the megalopolis. This was first broached by him in an essay entitled "Building, Dwelling, Thinking" of 1954:

What the word for space Raum, Rum, *designates is said by its ancient meaning.* Raum *means a place cleared or freed for settlement and lodging. A space is something that has been made room for, something that is cleared and free, namely within a boundary, Greek* peras. *A boundary is not that at which something stops, but, as the Greeks recognized, the boundary is that from which something begins its presencing. . . . Space is in essence that for which room has been made, that which is let into its bounds. That for which room is made is always granted and hence is joined, that is, gathered, by virtue of a location. . . . Accordingly spaces receive their being from locations and not from "space." . . . The space that is thus made by positions is space of a peculiar sort. As distance or "stadion" [in Greek] it is what the same word* stadion *means in Latin, a* spatium, *an intervening space or interval. Thus nearness and remoteness between men and things can become mere distance, mere intervals of intervening space. . . . What is more the mere dimensions of height, breadth, and depth can be abstracted from space as intervals. What is so abstracted we represent as the pure manifold of the three dimensions. Yet the room made by this manifold is also no longer determined by distances; it is no longer a* spatium, *but now no more than* extensio—extension. *But from space as* extensio *a further abstraction can be made, to analytic-algebraic relations. What these relations make room for is the possibility of the purely mathematical construction of manifolds with an arbitrary number of dimensions. The space provided for in this mathematical manner may be called "space," the "one" space as such. But in this sense "the" space, "space," contains no spaces and no places.*[40]

The implications of this for tectonic form are perhaps self-evident, namely the need for human institutions to be integrated with the topography in such a way as to offset the rapacity of development as an end in itself. For Heidegger the problem with technology does not reside in the benefits that it affords but in its emergence as a quasi-autonomous force that has "stamped" the epoch with its *Gestalt.* It is not primarily the environmentally degrading aspects of industrial technique that concern him, but rather the fact that technology has the tendency to transform everything, even a river, into a "standing reserve," that is to say, at one and the same time, into a source of hydroelectric power and an object of tourism.

For Heidegger the rootlessness of the modern world begins with the translation of the Greek experience into the edicts of the Roman imperium, as though the literal translation of Greek into Latin could be effected without their having had the same experience. Against this misunderstanding that culminates for him in the productionist philosophy of the machine age, Heidegger returns us, like his master Eduard Husserl, to the phenomenological presence of things in themselves.

That which gives things their constancy and pith but is also at the same time the source of their particular mode of sensuous pressure—colored, resonant, hard, massive—is the matter in things. In this analysis of the thing as matter, form is already co-posited. What is constant in a thing, its consistency, lies in the fact that matter stands together with a form. The thing is formed matter.[41]

To the extent that architecture remains suspended between human self-realization and the maximizing thrust of technology, it must of necessity become engaged in discriminating among different states and conditions; above all perhaps among the durability of a thing, the instrumentality of equipment, and the worldliness of human institutions. The tectonic presents itself as a mode by which to express these different states and thereby as a means for accommodating, through inflection, the various conditions under which different things appear and sustain themselves. Under this precept different parts of a given building may be rendered differently according to their ontological status. In a 1956 essay entitled "On the Origin of the Work of Art," Heidegger conceives of architecture as having the capacity not only of expressing the different materials from which it is made but also of revealing the different instances and modes by which the world comes into being.

In fabricating equipment—e.g. an axe—stone is used and used up. It disappears into usefulness. The material is all the better and more suitable the less it resists perishing in the equipmental being of equipment. By contrast the temple-work, in setting up a world, does not cause the material to disappear, but rather causes it to come forth for the very first time and to come into the Open of the work's world. The rock comes to bear and rest and so first becomes rock; metals come to glitter and shimmer, colors to glow, tones to sing, the word to speak. All this comes forth as the work sets itself back into the massiveness and heaviness of stone, into the firmness and pliancy of wood, into the hardness and luster of metal, into the lighting and darkening of color, into the clang of tone and into the naming power of the word.[42]

This essay contains further insights that are of pertinence to the tectonic. The first turns on the related but etymologically distinct notion of *techne,* derived from the Greek verb *tikto,* meaning to produce. This term means the simultaneous existence of both art and craft, the Greeks failing to distinguish between the two. It also implies knowledge, in the sense of revealing what is latent within a work; that is to say it implies *aletheia,* or knowing in the sense of an ontological revealing. This revelatory concept returns us to Vico's *verum, ipsum, factum,* to that state of affairs in which knowing and making are inextricably linked; to a condition in which *techne* reveals the ontological status of a thing through the disclosure of its epistemic value. In this sense one may claim that knowledge and hence beauty are dependent upon the emergence of "thingness." All of this is categorically opposed to connoisseurship, where works of art are offered solely for aesthetic enjoyment or where alternatively by virtue of their curatorial preservation they are withdrawn from the world. Of this last Heidegger writes, "World-withdrawal and world-decay can never be undone. The works are no longer the same as they once were. It is they themselves, to be sure, that we encounter there, but they themselves are gone by."[43]

Heidegger asserts a fertile and necessary opposition between the *artifice* of the world and the *natural* condition of the earth, realizing that the one is symbiotically conditioned by the other and vice versa. *Measure* and *boundary* are two terms by which he tries to articulate this relationship. His thinking in this regard, combined with his later emphasis on dwelling, caring, and letting-be, have led a number of commentators to see him as a pioneer of "eco-philosophy."[44] Technology was disturbing to Heidegger inasmuch as he saw it as being devoid of any respect for the intrinsic nature of things. He considered that neither nature nor history nor man himself would be able to withstand the unworldliness of technology if it were released on a planetary scale.

Tradition and Innovation

The notion of mediating instrumental reason through an appeal to tradition, as an evolving matrix from within which the lifeworld is realized both materially and conceptually, is echoed by the Italian school of thought known as *pensiero debole*.[45] One of the key precepts in "weak thought" is the a priori value attached to the fragmentary. This seems to be particularly relevant to the practice of architecture in that the *métier* has no hope of being universally applied in the sense that technoscience achieves such an application. One has only to look at the spontaneous megalopolitan proliferation of our times to recognize the incapacity of the building industry, let alone architecture, to respond in any effective way. Where technology, as the maximization of industrial production and consumption, merely serves to exacerbate the magnitude of this proliferation, architecture as craft and as an act of place creation is excluded from the process.[46]

Seen from this standpoint, the radically new, as an end in itself, loses its claim to perpetual validity, particularly when it is set against the "thrownness" of history. This *Geschick* as Heidegger calls it embodies not only a material condition, specific to a given time and place, but also the legacy of a particular historical tradition that, however much it may be assimilated, is always in the process of transforming itself through what Hans Georg Gadamer has characterized as the "fusion of horizons."[47] For Gadamer, critical reason and tradition are inextricably linked to each other in a hermeneutical circle in which the prejudices of a given cultural legacy have to be continually assessed against the implicit critique of "other" traditions. As Georgia Warnke has written: "it is not that Gadamer no longer identifies the dialectical or dialogical process with the possibility of an advance on the part of reason; it is rather that Gadamer refuses to foreclose this advance by projecting a point of absolute knowledge at which no further dialogic encounters can develop that rationality."[48]

Such a transformational concept is necessarily opposed to the triumph of one universal method. It is, by definition, unstable and specific in a fragmentary sense. Unlike technoscience that regards the past as a series of obsolete moments along the ever-upward trajectory of hypothetical progress, the so-called human sciences cherish the lived past as an *Erlebnis* that is open to being critically reintegrated into the present. As Warnke puts it:

The way in which we anticipate the future defines the meaning that the past can have for us, just as the way in which our ancestors projected the future determines our own range of possibilities. Thus for Gadamer, Vico's formula entails that we understand history not simply because we make it but also because it has made us; we belong to it in the sense that we inherit its experience, project a future on the basis of the situation the past has created for us and act in light of our understanding of this past whether such understanding is explicit or not.[49]

This formulation seems to be echoed in the famous apodictic statement of the Portuguese architect Alvaro Siza that "architects don't invent anything, they transform reality."[50] Unlike fine art, all such transformations have to be rooted in the opacity of the lifeworld and come to their maturity over an unspecified period of time. The way in which such transformations are at once, however imperceptibly, transformed in their turn means that neither a hypostasized past nor an idealized future carries the conviction that they once had in the heyday of the Enlightenment. The decline of utopia denies the validity of the *novum* as an end in itself. As the Italian philosopher Gianni Vattimo puts it in his book *The End of Modernity,* once progress in either science or art becomes routine it is no longer new in the sense that it once was. He remarks, after Arnold Gehlen, that "progress seems to show a tendency to dissolve itself, and with it the value of the new as well, not only in the effective process of secularization, but even in the most extremely futuristic utopias."[51] While the crisis of the neo-avant-garde derives directly from this spontaneous dissolution of the new, critical culture attempts to sustain itself through a dialectical play across a historically determined reality in every sense of the term. One may even claim that, critique aside, critical culture attempts to compensate, in a fragmentary manner, for the manifest disenchantment of the world. The transformed, transforming real is thus constituted not only by the material circumstances obtaining at the moment of intervention but also by a critical intersubjective deliberation upon or about these conditions, both before and after the design and its realization. Material constraints aside, innovation is, in this sense, contingent upon a self-conscious rereading, remaking, and re-collection of tradition (*Andenken*), including the tradition of the new, just as tradition can only be revitalized through innovation. It is in this sense that we may come to conceive of Gehlen's *posthistoire* as the domain of the "bad infinite," to borrow Gadamer's phrase.[52]

Such a hermeneutical model presupposes a continual intersubjective self-realization on the part of the species and a kind of "cantonal" decentralization of power and representation in the field of politics, not to mention the imperative of raising the general level of education throughout society. Under such circumstances we might begin to entertain a possible convergence between Jürgen Habermas's ideal speech situation, his concept of undistorted communication, and Gianni Vattimo's formulation of hermeneutical legitimation as this ought to be applied to the realization of an architectural project. Of this last we find Vattimo writing in terms that seem uncommonly close to those of Habermas:

If therefore, in architecture, as also in philosophy, in existence in general, we renounce any metaphysical, superior, transcendent legitimation (of the kind reaching ultimate truths, redemption of humanity, etc.), all that is left is to understand legitimation as a form of the creation of horizons of validity through dialogue, a dialogue both with the traditions to which we belong and with others.[53]

Irrespective of the inroads of the media, that is to say, of the distortions of mass communication that condition such a large sector of everyday life in the late twentieth century, Habermas's "ideal speech situation" seems to be a prerequisite for an intelligent cultivation of the environment, for as every architect knows, without good clients it is impossible to achieve an architecture of quality.[54] Apart from this, architectural practice has little choice but to embrace what one may call a double hermeneutic, one that, first, seeks to ground its practice in its own tectonic procedures, and second, turns to address itself to the social and to the inflection of what Hannah Arendt termed "the space of public appearance."[55] Vittorio Gregotti reflects on these two aspects in the following terms:

In the course of [the last] thirty years, during which the obsession with history emerged and developed, the belief has taken root that architecture cannot be a means for changing social relationships; but I maintain that it is architecture itself that needs, for its very production, the material represented by social relations. Architecture cannot live by simply mirroring its own problems, exploiting its own tradition, even though the professional tools required for architecture as a discipline can be found only within that tradition.[56]

Elsewhere Gregotti returns to the problem of land settlement, to his earlier preoccupation with the territory of architecture,[57] effectively touching on what may be the ultimate consequence of global mobilization: the simple fact that we have yet to arrive at any pattern of "motopian" land settlement that could be possibly regarded as *rational.*[58]

I believe that if there is a clear enemy to fight today, it is represented by the idea of an economic/technical space indifferent in all directions. This is now such a widespread idea that it seems almost objective. . . . It is a question of a shrewd, modernistic enemy capable of accepting the latest, most fashionable proposal, especially any proposal capable of selling every vain formalistic disguise, favorable only to myth, redundancy or uproar, as a genuine difference.[59]

With remarkable perspicacity Gregotti implies the manner in which tectonic detail may be combined with traditional type forms, modified in light of today's needs but free from gratuitous novelty, in such a way as to articulate the qualitative *difference* separating irresponsible speculation from critical practice. The difficulty of realizing this *répétition différente* is at no point underestimated by Gregotti.[60]

After Auguste Perret's famous slogan "Il n'y a pas de détail dans la construction," Gregotti maintains that detailing should never be regarded as an insignificant technical means by which the work happens to be realized. The full tectonic potential of any building stems from its capacity to articulate both the poetic and the cognitive aspects of its substance. This double articulation presupposes that one has to mediate between technology as a productive procedure and craft technique as an anachronistic but renewable capacity to reconcile different productive modes and levels of intentionality. Thus the tectonic stands in opposition to the current tendency to deprecate detailing in favor of the overall image. As a value it finds itself in opposition to the gratuitously figurative, since to the degree that our works are conceived as having a long duration "we must produce things that look as if they were always there."[61]

In the last analysis, everything turns as much on exactly *how* something is realized as on an overt manifestation of its form. This is not to deny spatial ingenuity but rather to heighten its character through its precise realization. Thus the presencing of a work is inseparable from the manner of its foundation in the ground and the ascendancy of its structure through the interplay of support, span, seam, and joint—the rhythm of its revetment and the modulation of its fenestration. Situated at the interface of culture and nature, building is as much about the ground as it is about built form. Close to agriculture, its task is to modify the earth's surface in such a way as to take care of it, as in Heidegger's concept of *Gelassenheit* or letting be. Hence the notion of "building the site," in Mario Botta's memorable phrase, is of greater import than the creation of freestanding objects, and in this regard building is as much about the topos as it is about technique. Furthermore, despite the privatization of modern society, architecture, as opposed to building, tends to favor the space of public appearance rather than the privacy of the *domus*.[62] At the same time, it is as much about place-making and the passage of time as it is about space and form. Light, water, wind, and weathering, these are the agents by which it is consummated. Inasmuch as its continuity transcends mortality, building provides the basis for life and culture. In this sense, it is neither high art nor high technology. To the extent that it defies time, it is anachronistic by definition. Duration and durability are its ultimate values. In the last analysis it has nothing to do with immediacy[63] and everything to do with the unsayable. What was it Luis Barragán said? "All architecture which does not express serenity fails in its spiritual mission."[64] The task of our time is to combine vitality with calm.

2   Greco-Gothic and Neo-Gothic:
The Anglo-French Origins of Tectonic Form

Ornament is the secret that Baukunst keeps to allow the Tekton to display the values of which he is guardian. And to conclude this point, it may be useful to remember one of Mies's more felicitous aphorisms. When the architect states that architecture begins where two bricks are carefully joined together, our attention should not fall on the curious, reductive image of the "two bricks," but on what is required for their joining to create something architecturally significant: "carefully" is the key word here. Planning, building, and Baukunst imply continual care. And such attention demands dedication, "idleness," and time—irrevocable decisions, as Nietzsche instructs. To build is thus to provide protection for the possibility of the event; it is a rejection of the "new" and a love of tradition. Baukunst, finally, is the art of time.
Francesco Dal Co, Figures of Architecture and Thought, *1990*

The roots of the Greco-Gothic ideal go back to the seventeenth century inasmuch as they are ultimately traceable to Claude Perrault's retranslation of Vitruvius published in French in 1673, and to his *Ordonnance des cinq espèces de colonnes selon la méthode des anciens* of a decade later. Perrault's Cartesian doubt was to have a lasting impact on French architecture since he repudiated the mythic proportions of the Renaissance, along with the almost divine status accorded to the five orders, asserting instead a theory of positive and arbitrary beauty that was to have a subversive impact on the French classical tradition. The tectonic implications of Perrault's position are evident from his contention that style belongs to the realm of arbitrary beauty, whereas symmetry, richness of materials, and precision of execution are the only indisputable constituents of a positive and universal form of beauty. Where we may elect to regard style as atectonic by virtue of its representational emphasis, positive beauty may be seen to be tectonic inasmuch as it is based on material substance and geometrical order.

Perrault's cultural universalism was further developed by Michel de Fremin in his *Mémoires critiques d'architecture* of 1702. Fremin was the first author to challenge the truism that familiarity with the five orders was necessarily an indication of architectural competence. He was also one of the earliest theorists to regard the Gothic as being fundamental to the development of a structural architecture. In advocating a synthesis of Gothic intercolumnar and Greek trabeated form, the Abbé de Cordemoy would follow Fremin's lead in his *Nouveau traité de tout l'architecture* of 1706, which was significantly subtitled *l'art de bâtir utile aux entrepreneurs et aux ouvriers* (the art of building useful for contractors and craftsmen). In his seminal essay of 1962, "The Abbé de Cordemoy and the Graeco-Gothic Ideal," Robin Middleton stresses the critical importance of Cordemoy in the evolution of French classical tradition:

Interpreting the old Roman theorist [Vitruvius] with unusual rigor, impelled by the conviction that antique architecture was more pure in form than the architecture of the Renaissance cared to admit, Cordemoy proposed an architecture of simplified geometric forms, set one in relation to another, to result in a unified whole. But while he insisted on the unity of the whole, he demanded that each element should retain an air of independence—"le dégagement," he called this quality. He vigorously condemned the bas relief effect of contemporary architecture and rejected scornfully the numerous motifs that were scattered over the surfaces of

buildings, blurring their outlines with continuous and uneasy modelling. He at-
tacked especially the court facade of the Louvre. Three superimposed orders
were, he considered, excessive, even if sanctioned by antique example. He liked
plain masonry surfaces. And, in accord with Fremin, he discouraged the use of
ornament. He went even further; he declared that pedestals, applied orders of
columns and pilasters should be dispensed with, although he conceded that pi-
lasters could be used in antis or to express the external junction of walls. When
pilasters were to be used, however, he insisted (and here once again he showed
his allegiance to Perrault) there was to be no diminution in their width from top
to bottom. He desired, above all, a simplified rectangular architecture. He dis-
liked acute angles and all curves. He approved only of rectangular door and win-
dow openings. He liked roof lines to be horizontal. Demanding the use of flat
roofs or, as a more practical alternative, Mansart roofs, he sought to do away
with the pediment altogether.[1]

It is necessary to mention that Cordemoy insisted on the hierarchical principles
of propriety in architecture, arguing that all utilitarian structures should be left entirely devoid of ornament, thereby serving to express the difference in cultural
stature between everyday building and works of institutional and symbolic import. It is difficult to adequately represent the cultural complexity of the synthesis that Fremin, Cordemoy, and Laugier successively sought to achieve in their
drive to promote a hypothetical Greco-Gothic architecture embodying the character of *dégagement,* that is, columnar articulation within the ordinance of Neo-
platonic form. All three theorists wanted to eliminate the elliptical vault and the
flying buttress from the syntax of architecture along with the organic excesses
of Gothic tracery and detailing—what Fremin called *un amas confus de figures*
monstrueuses et déréglées. The touchstone for all of them was the freestanding
column that was common to both the Gothic cathedral and the Greek temple.

Dégagement plays an absolutely fundamental role in Abbé Laugier's characterization of the ideal Greco-Gothic church as this appears in his *Essai sur l'archi-*
tecture of 1753.

Let us choose the most common form, that of the Latin Cross. I place all around
the nave, transept and choir the first Order of isolated columns standing on low
socles; they are coupled like those of the portico of the Louvre in order to give
more width to the intercolumniations. On these columns I place a straight archi-
trave terminated by an ogee of moderate projection and erect over this a second
Order, consisting, like the first one, of free-standing and coupled columns. This
second Order has its complete straight entablature and, directly over it without
any sort of attic, I erect a plain barrel vault without transverse ribs. Then, around
the nave, crossing, and choir, I arrange columned aisles which form a true peri-
style and are covered by flat ceilings placed on the architraves of the first Or-
der. . . . This is then my idea and here are the advantages: (1) A building like this
is entirely natural and true; everything is reduced to simple rules and executed
according to great principles: no arcades, no pilasters, no pedestals, nothing
awkward or constrained. (2) The whole plain wall is nowhere to be seen, there-
fore nothing is superfluous, nothing is bulky, nothing is offensive. (3) The win-
dows are placed in the most suitable and most advantageous position. All
intercolumniations are glazed, above and below. There are no more plain lu-
nettes cutting into the vault as in ordinary churches, but ordinary large windows.
(4) The two Orders placed one above the other bring nave, crossing and choir to

a height which is in no way irregular and does not require columns of an exorbitant scale. (5) The vault, although barrel vault, loses all heaviness through this height, especially since it has no transverse ribs which would appear to weigh down heavily. (6) Splendor and magnificence could easily be added to the dégagement, *simplicity, elegance and dignity of such a building.*[2]

In the frontispiece of his *Essai sur l'architecture,* Laugier was to state this paradigm in more aboriginal terms, inasmuch as the hut was of skeletal timber construction and its roof was pitched rather than vaulted. It was ideologically significant of course that this last was more compatible with the form of the

2.1

The primitive hut. Frontispiece from the second edition of Abbé Laugier's *Essai sur l'architecture,* engraved by Ch. Eisen, 1755.

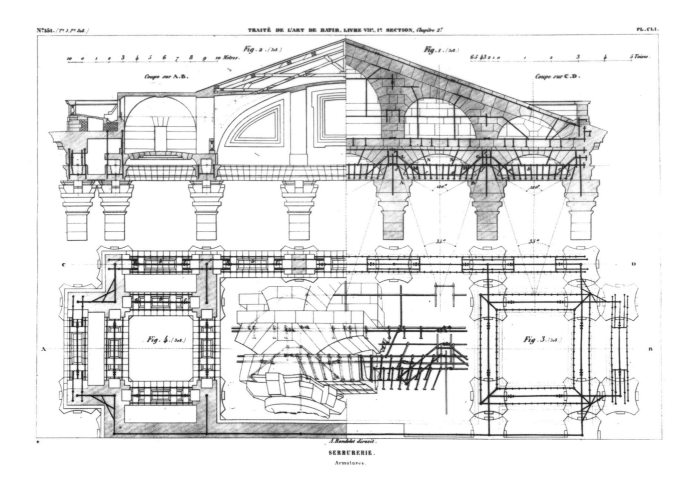

SERRURERIE.
Armatures.

carrying the main loads at the crossing of the church and the representative semicircular arches employed throughout the internal volume (fig. 2.6).

Where the Greco-Gothic movement was almost exclusively French, the Gothic revival of the nineteenth century was Anglo-French in that it arose out of the careers of two figures who were mutually influential: the Comte Charles de Montalembert, who published his Catholic tract *De l'état actuel de l'art religieux en France* in 1839, and the Anglo-French Augustus Welby Northmore Pugin (son of the French émigré Augustus Charles Pugin), who published his pro-Catholic cultural polemic in 1836 under the title *Contrasts: Or a Parallel between the Noble Edifices of the Fourteenth and Fifteenth Centuries and Similar Buildings of the Present Day; Showing the Present Decay of Taste.* There were other contemporary Anglo-French intellectuals who pursued similar goals, notably the Cambridge polymath Robert Willis, who, influenced like Pugin by A. F. Frézier's study of medieval stereotomy, advanced his own thesis in 1842 "On the Construction of Vaults in the Middle Ages," and the French scholar Arcisse de Caumont, who in 1824 published his pioneering archaeological study *Sur l'architecture du Moyen Âge.*[5]

With the exception of a didactic comparison between Gothic and Romanesque, one that will favor the former for its aspirational height, Pugin's *Contrasts* gives little indication as to how ecclesiastical architecture might be renewed. It is a pro-Catholic diatribe against a degenerate present rather than an architectural thesis, and it is only after Pugin has achieved a number of works himself—some twenty churches in the space of five years—that he is able to give more cogent advice as to the manner in which a truly Catholic architecture might be revived. This comes with his *True Principles of a Christian or Pointed Architecture* published in 1841, in which he characterizes the reductive form of the typical nineteenth-century church or chapel as little more than a room full of seats facing the street (fig. 2.7).

The critical but regressive nature of Pugin's *Contrasts* is evident from his desire to turn the clock back. Catholic convert at the age of 23 and henceforth desirous of being affiliated with Cardinal Newman's Oxford Movement, Pugin was never able to exorcise his nostalgia for the golden age of Christendom. Like Henri Saint-Simon in his influential book *The New Christianity* of 1825, Pugin was to regard himself as an untimely witness to the decay of European Christian culture, not only the decay induced by the Reformation in all its forms but also the inner decay of the Catholic Church as a sociocultural institution. While Pugin was critical of Catholicism in its decline, he was against those emerging forms

2.5
Jacques-Germain Soufflot, Ste.-Geneviève, pronaos. Rondelet's cutaway elevation and isometric reveals only too clearly the extent to which the masonry is reinforced by a wrought-iron armature as well as by stone anchors that are hidden behind the sculptured pediment.

2.6
Jacques-Germain Soufflot, Ste.-Geneviève, partial section through base of dome.

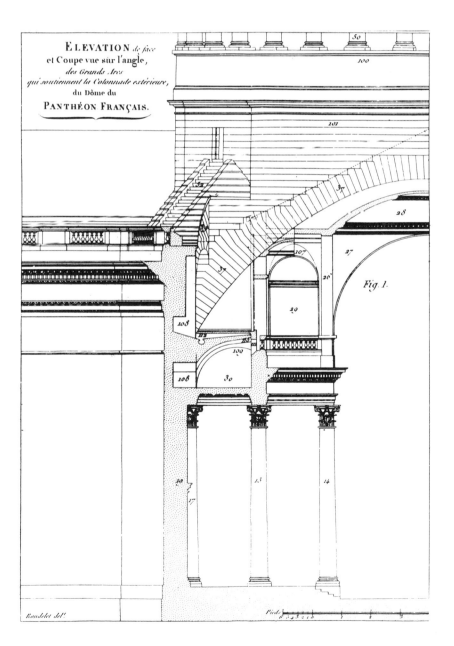

ELEVATION de face
et Coupe vue sûr l'angle,
des Grands Arcs
qui soutiennent la Colonnade extérieure,
du Dôme du
PANTHÉON FRANÇAIS.

Fig. 1.

Rondelet del.

of modern social welfare advanced by such utilitarian reformers as Sir Robert Peel, founder of the police force, and Jeremy Bentham, the inventor of the Panopticon. Pugin's opposition to any kind of authoritarian secular reform also served to distance him from Saint-Simon, since the latter, as the founder of the Napoleonic Ecole Polytechnique, favored a technocratically administered welfare state as opposed to Pugin's ideal of a benevolent theocracy.

While convinced of the possibility of recovering a lost harmony through architecture, Pugin is initially unable to articulate this project in any detail. In 1835, while designing the neo-Gothic details for Charles Barry's Palace of Westminster, Pugin can do little more than rant against Catholic decadence in the first edition of *Contrasts.* His polemic is sharpened considerably in the second edition of 1841, when he criticizes a whole range of utilitarian practices, from Benjamin's Panopticon to the habit of dissecting the bodies of the poor in the name of medical research (fig. 2.8). Pugin's ultimate contrast, drawn between the generic cities of 1440 and 1840, enables him to reject as barbarous the brick-faced, vaulted, iron-framed, fireproof mill construction of the late eighteenth century.[6]

Opposed to the rhetorical architecture of the Counter-Reformation and hence as anti-Baroque as the Jesuit, Greco-Gothic movement, Pugin was incapable of countenancing the slightest trace of what he called classical paganism in architectural form. For Pugin architecture was a religious and ethical affair, and his passionate commitment to the moral rigor of early Christendom was to lead him into constant conflict with the more worldly members of the British Catholic hierarchy. However, despite the contentious nature of his polemic, his evident talent assured him a wide patronage and enabled him to realize nearly a hundred buildings, many of them churches, before his untimely death in 1852 (fig. 2.9).

While Pugin's ability as an antiquarian draftsman recommended him to Barry as a Gothic delineator for the Palace of Westminster, he was not trained as an architect in the usual sense. This lack of schooling makes it all the more remarkable that, after leaving Barry in 1837, he was able to build with such conviction and assurance. Part of this was no doubt due to the training he had received at an early age from his father, and part was also probably due, as Phoebe Stanton has suggested, to his familiarity with A. F. Frézier's *La Théorie et la pratique de la coupe des pierres et des bois pour la construction des voûtes* (1737–1739). Pugin's *True Principles* of 1841 was based on two fundamental axioms that, aside from serving as the guiding precepts for his own practice, were to be followed throughout the rest of the century as the protofunctionalist principles of the Gothic Revival. These precepts, which also served as the basic underpinning of the Arts and Crafts movement, read as follows: "First, that there should be no features about a building which are not necessary for convenience, construction or propriety; second, that all ornament should consist of the enrichment of the essential construction of the building."[7] Pugin distinguished applied ornament from the decorative elaboration of tectonic features and argued for the precise significance of the smallest detail in this last regard. He was convinced that tectonic form should be largely determined by the nature of the material and that all these conditions had been best met in the English Gothic manner of the fifteenth century, irrespective of whether the work in hand was a cathedral or an almshouse. In the course of this thesis Pugin will pass from a warm appraisal of the Gothic to a deprecation of the Greek temple, above all for its misapplication of stone to forms deriving from timber construction.

Grecian architecture is essentially wooden *in its construction; it originated in wooden buildings and never did its professors possess either sufficient imagination or skill to conceive any departure from the original type. . . . This is at once the most ancient and most barbarous mode of building that can be imagined; it is heavy and, as I before said, essentially wooden; but is it not extraordinary that when the Greeks commenced building in stone, the properties of this material did not suggest to them some different and improved mode of construction?*

Pugin proceeds to contrast this lack of development with the architects of the Middle Ages who "with stone scarcely larger than ordinary bricks, threw their lofty vaults from slender pillars across a vast intermediate space, and that at an

2.7
A. W. N. Pugin, plate from *True Principles,* 1841. The utilitarian chapel as a decorated shed.

2.8
A. W. N. Pugin, plate from *Contrasts,* 1841.

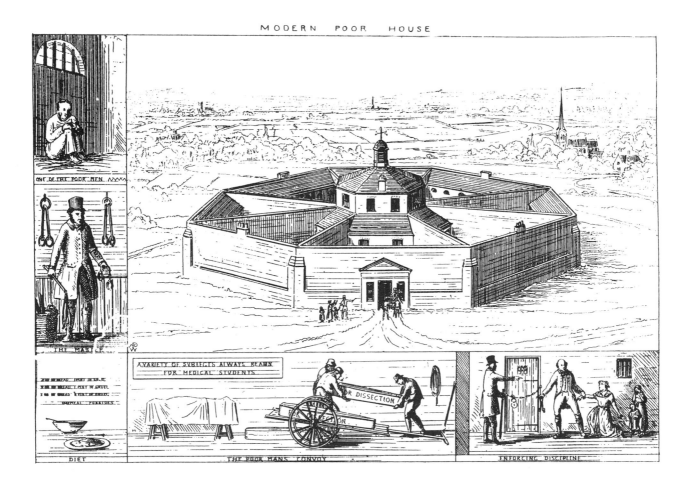

amazing height, where they had every difficulty of lateral pressure to contend with. This leads me to speak of buttresses, a distinguishing feature of Pointed Architecture."[8]

From this contrast between trabeated and vaulted stereotomic form, we may assume that Pugin was at least familiar with some of the Greco-Gothic arguments advanced by Cordemoy and Laugier. Like the Greco-Gothicists, Pugin is convinced that a column should be a freestanding, load-bearing support, but unlike them he proceeds to praise the tectonic virtues of the pointed arch and the flying buttress and to point out that in St. Paul's cathedral, London, Christopher Wren, far from dispensing with flying buttresses, merely built a screen wall to conceal them (compare Soufflot's Ste.-Geneviève) (fig. 2.10).

Pugin's subsequent appraisal of the Gothic groin vault follows a similar line of reasoning, in which he argues in favor of its lightness, its techno-aesthetic unity (its ribs wedged into position by a central boss), and its aspirational height. This last is contrasted to the decadence of the English Decorated style as this appears in Henry VII's chapel in Westminster, with its structurally redundant fan vaulting and its vulgarly rhetorical stone pendants. He applies a similar logic to

2.9
A. W. N. Pugin, Church of St. Augustine, Ramsgate, 1842.

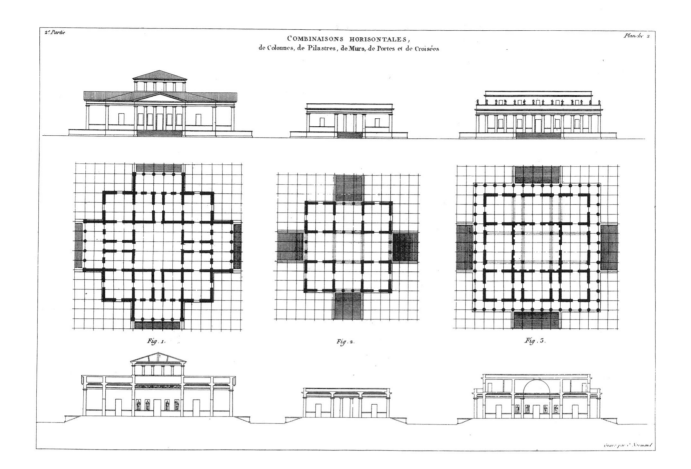

COMBINAISONS HORISONTALES,
de Colonnes, de Pilastres, de Murs, de Portes et de Croisées

Fig. 1.   Fig. 2.   Fig. 3.

Greco-Gothic and Neo-Gothic

45

barrel-vaulted roof, made up of lightweight iron sheets, with its roof loads carried on a skeleton of fretted, openwork iron ribs. This assembly rested in part on a central line of cast-iron columns and in part on brackets corbeling out from the masonry perimeter. It is of the utmost importance, as Herman Hertzberger has remarked, that the arcuated iron ribs go around the corner at the end of the long volume, thereby unifying the space and forestalling a reading of the library structure as two parallel lines of vaults (fig. 2.22).[12] Not least among the expressive subtleties of this encased armature is the way its structural module is reflected on the exterior. Iron tie rods, connected to the foot of each iron rib, extend through the thick masonry walls to terminate in circular cast-iron anchor plates, visible on the facade (fig. 2.23). A similar permeation of the thick masonry case by a metallic tectonic can be found elsewhere in the fabric, above all in the cast-iron beams that support the floor above the entry colonnade and the sundry rails, radiators, and light fittings that furnish the reading room.

Labrouste would amplify this approach in his Bibliothèque Nationale begun in 1854. In this instance "encasement" was unavoidable, since the respective wrought-iron armatures of the stacks and the reading room itself had to be installed within the existing masonry shell of the Palais Mazarin. The exact manner in which this operation was carried out is significant, from the grillwork and catwalks of the cast-iron book stacks to the sixteen cast-iron columns carrying the armature of the wrought-iron reading room roof. In the first instance, we have a dematerialized top-lit "engine room" space of astonishing lightness and precision; in the second we are presented with shell vaults covering a nine-square plan. These last comprise cupolas, built up out of terra-cotta panels and pierced by oculi. While providing light for the reading room, their assembly rests on a grid of riveted latticework iron arches that in turn take their support from the slender cast-iron columns. It is of the utmost import that *each* of these columns is a freestanding element, including those lining the perimeter, for this fur-

2.19
Henri Labrouste, Bibliothèque Ste.-Geneviève, Paris, 1838–1850. Transverse section.

2.20
Henri Labrouste, Bibliothèque Nationale, Paris, 1854–1875. Plan, section, and details.

2.21
Henri Labrouste, Bibliothèque Nationale, perspective.

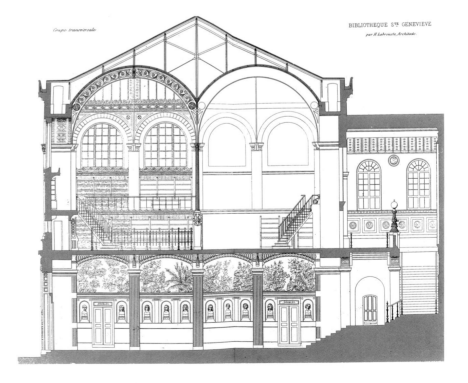

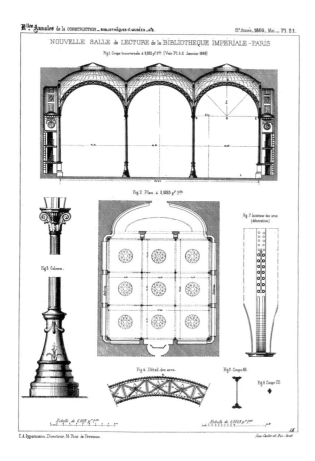

NOUVELLE SALLE de LECTURE de la BIBLIOTHÈQUE IMPÉRIALE - PARIS

Fig 1. Coupe transversale à 0.005 p.r 1m (Voir Pl. 1-2. Janvier 1869)

Fig 2. Plan à 0.0023 p.r 1m

Fig 3. Colonne.

Fig 7. Intérieur des arcs (décoration)

Fig 4. Détail des arcs.

Fig 5. Coupe AB.

Fig 6. Coupe CD.

Echelle de 0.005 p.r 1m

Echelle de 0.0023 p.r 1m

C. A. Oppermann, Directeur, 56 Rue de Provence.   Imp. Casse 53 Rue Jacob

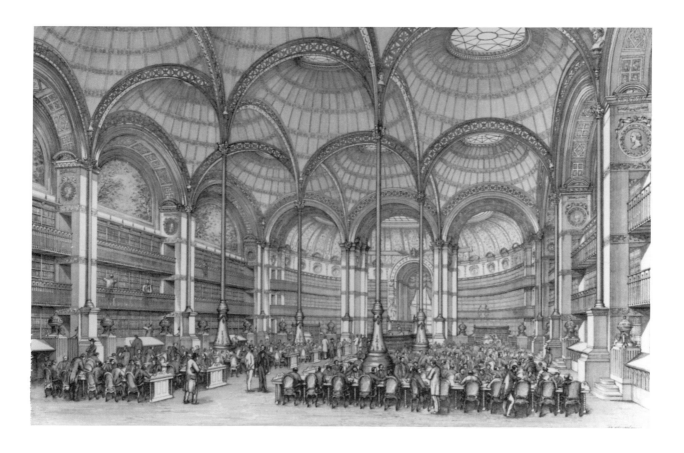

Other than a common Saint-Simonian passion for the application of objective analysis to the history of architecture, François Auguste Choisy and Viollet-le-Duc had little in common. However, this intellectual background plus a brief shared experience in the Franco-Prussian War seem to have prompted Viollet-le-Duc to acknowledge Choisy in the last volume of the *Entretiens,* above all for Choisy's work on the optical corrections employed in the Parthenon. Choisy, for his part, emulated Viollet-le-Duc to the letter, particularly in his first book, *L'Art de bâtir chez les Romains,* published in 1873. Apart from being written by an engineer, this was the first architectural history to explain the origin of tectonic form in terms of the materials available, the structural systems employed, and the state of craft production. Choisy's subsequent fieldwork in Turkey led, a decade later, to his second historical opus, *L'Art de bâtir chez les Byzantines* published in 1883. By then he was already established as a technocratic academic, first in the Ecole des Ponts and Chaussées and after 1881 in the Ecole Polytechnique. The next sixteen years of research and writing resulted in his magnum opus, his two-volume *Histoire de l'architecture* published in 1899.

The overriding thesis of Choisy's *Histoire* was simple enough. He tried to show how each great civilization arrived at its apogee when, subject to geographical and material conditions, its essence was expressed collectively in tectonic form. Once the prime point of synthesis had been achieved, however, there was a tendency for the culture to decay through excessive formal variation until it became little more than a parody of the original. In two successive maps Choisy attempts to show how Romanesque and Gothic building cultures were diffused along different trade routes in France between the tenth and thirteenth centuries.

2.29
Anatole de Baudot, *salle des fêtes,* c. 1910. Plan and interior.

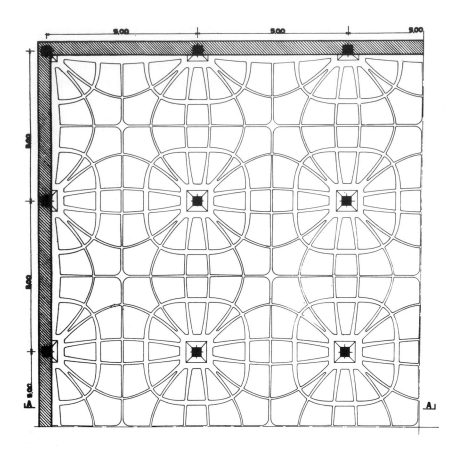

Choisy's isometric representational method had an inherent disadvantage, in that it tended to inhibit a sufficiently precise analysis of the structural articulation of the given tectonic form. This was particularly true of skeletonal structures that did not submit as well to his method as those of load-bearing masonry construction.[27] It was as though all the examples that he analyzed were forged out of the same homogeneous substance, as we find this, say, in brick, mud, rammed earth, or reinforced concrete construction. Choisy's accompanying text, however, was more analytical and sophisticated, and this more than made up for the slightly schematic nature of his illustrations. It is clear for example from his discussion of the origins of the Doric that he was aware of the German debate on the aboriginal structural authority of the Greek orders as this had been challenged by Heinrich Hübsch in his book *In welchem Style sollen wir bauen*? (1828). All in all Choisy sees little pragmatic justification for the Vitruvian thesis that the Doric order was derived from trabeated wooden construction. His skepticism in this regard seems to have been bolstered by the technologically inconsistent detailing that had been found in a number of Greek temples. From this Choisy concludes that it took many years before the pragmatics of masonry construction could be successfully reconciled with the aboriginal image of a trabeated construction in wood. In the end, he opted for a subtle reconciliation of the two theories, namely, that while the order may well have derived from timber construction it also derived from the technical demands of building in masonry.[28]

The enduring influence of Choisy's *Histoire* was due as much to the revelatory aspect of his didactic isometric projections as to the precision of his analytical text (fig. 2.31). Realizing that conventional orthographic and perspectival methods were inadequate and misleading, Choisy opted for a comparative method and a mode of projection by which the essence of the construct could be both represented and classified. Resorting to a projective graphic technique previously reserved for the representation of iron castings and machine tools, he aspired to an objective characterization of his subject matter, and it was exactly these typified abstractions that led to his extensive influence on the architects of the machine age, from Le Corbusier to Louis Kahn. Restricted by his method from entering fully into the pragmatics of any specific technology, Choisy presented tectonic tropes as complete entities wherein the space form was inseparable from the mode of construction and where subcomponents were presented as set pieces derived from the influences of climate, material, and cross-cultural interaction. In this way, as Cornelis van de Ven has argued, Choisy attempted to bridge between the typological plan forms of Durand and the structural rationalism of Viollet-le-Duc.[29] Apart from Auguste Perret, who was his follower in many ways, Choisy seems to have been the last theorist of the Greco-Gothic ideal, as we may judge from his two-volume encyclopedic history that devoted a third of the first volume and a third of the second to Greek and Gothic architecture respectively. In one upward-looking isometric after another, in which the corporeal volume was depicted as being homogeneous with its columnar supports, Choisy seems to have anticipated reinforced concrete as the sole technique that would prove capable of overcoming the age-old schism and fusing into a single entity the two great lines of Western building culture.

2.30
Pier Luigi Nervi, Gatti wool factory, Rome, 1953. Partial plan.

2.31
Auguste Choisy, Beauvais cathedral, from *Histoire de l'architecture,* 1899.

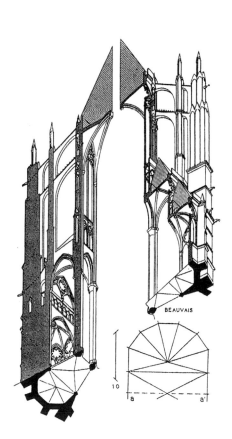

3 The Rise of the Tectonic: Core Form and Art Form in the German Enlightenment, 1750–1870

Two examples illustrate the cultural conjunction of nature and architecture within the panoramic scope of Schinkel's view. Just when he was preparing the final plan for the museum, he also started to work on a painting, View of Greece in Its Flowering, *which betrays a deep conceptual affinity with the museum vestibule. Comparably elevated onto the porch of a Greek temple under construction, the viewer looks out onto a large ancient town that descends from the slopes toward a gulf. A wide awning shields from the sun the workmen and sculptors on the right, while the crowns of tall trees shade a landscaped terrace to the left. These natural and artificial umbrellas, enhanced by subtle color correspondences, complement one another and bracket the field of vision. The main activity in the painting, the construction of a great monument, centers on a sturdy scaffolding in the middle of the picture: the scaffolding is, of course, a temporary device, required merely for construction, but its prominence and pivotal role surely signify the activity of building as much as its material result. Construction is indeed the very building of social and cultural fact. This image of ancient building also lends its framework to Schinkel's example of modern architecture. The general conditions have changed, but the similarity of Schinkel's images—the temple in ancient culture, the museum in modern—also reveals a telling distinction. A comparable double row of Ionic columns, a narrative frieze appropriately transferred from sculpture to wall painting, and spectators rather than workmen at once liken the Berlin museum to ancient architecture and contrast the modern consumption of that culture to the image of its ancient production. Subsuming and transcending all of these distinctions is, of course, the fact that nature no longer provides the foil of culture but has yielded that role to the cityscape.*
Kurt Forster, "Schinkel's Panoramic Planning of Central Berlin," 1983

From 1750 onward the antique Greek world exercised a fundamental hold over the German imagination, from the time of J. J. Winckelmann's appraisal of the serenity of the Apollo Belvedere to J. C. F. Hölderlin's poetic preoccupation with Greece; a country that he, like Winckelmann, never visited. Hölderlin's hypersensitive career epitomizes many of the dilemmas that confronted the intellectuals of the *Sturm und Drang* period, above all their intense nostalgia for the spirit and life of a lost golden age, for an age that was as divorced from the historical experience of Germany as it was distant from the political and moral aims of the *Aufklärung.* Thus, while Friedrich Schiller admitted the unsurpassable greatness of Greek art, he nonetheless believed that the liberative aims of the Enlightenment would be better served by a dramatic art form that would be ethically superior to Greek tragedy. In 1792, he wrote: "In this branch alone our civilization will perhaps be able to make good the theft which it has committed on art as a whole."[1]

In his seminal *Geschichte der Kunst des Altertums* (History of Ancient Art) of 1764, Winckelmann was the first to introduce the notion of cyclical growth and decay into the history of civilization, a paradigm that would be transformed into a dialectical system by Hegel in his aesthetic lectures given between 1818 and 1829.[2] Winckelmann divided Greek art into four periods, the archaic period, the sublime moment of Phidias, the idealism of Praxiteles, and, finally, the deliquescence of Hellenism. He believed that the naturalistic beauty of Greek art arose out of two basic causes: the temperate nature of the Greek climate and the liberative political order of the Greek state.[3] Winckelmann's appraisal of this dichotomous legacy seems to have indirectly affected the character of the Prussian Enlightenment, dividing it as it did into two related but antithetical impulses: the expressivist and the rationalist.

The former can be traced as a recurrent theme that runs through the writing of Herder and Goethe. Both men felt that a Germanic culture comparable to that of ancient Greece could only arise out of the intrinsic character of the people, the climate, and the nordic landscape. As Charles Taylor has written: "We are here at the point of modern Nationalism. Herder thought that each people had its own peculiar guiding theme or manner of expression, unique and irreplaceable, which should never be suppressed and which could never simply be replaced by any attempt to ape the manners of others, as many educated Germans tried to ape French *philosophes*."[4] Herder's concern for autochthonous culture partially accounts for Goethe's initial preference for the Germanic character of Gothic architecture over the alien rationality of Greek classicism, before he moved to Weimar in 1775 and embraced Palladianism as the touchstone of progressive culture.[5] Thus for all his youthful enthusiasm for Strassbourg's cathedral, as this appears in his essay "Von deutscher Baukunst, D. M. Erwin von Steinbach" of 1772, published in Herder's *Von deutsches Art und Kunst,* Goethe's cultivated preference for the classical at the end of the eighteenth century would parallel the teachings of the art historian Aloys Hirt, who was so convinced of the spiritual superiority of Greek culture as to strive for its full embodiment in the emerging Prussian state.

Notwithstanding its classicizing proclivities, German idealistic philosophy saw the Enlightenment as a radical break for which one had to evolve a new set of ethical and cultural values appropriate to a rational and scientific age. The most prominent figure after Kant to advance this position was Hegel, who attempted to formulate a dialectical view of world culture. In Hegel's protean scheme, architecture emerges as a primordial manifestation within the changing spectrum of cultural form. For Hegel, beauty in art, as opposed to natural beauty, derives from the extent to which the evolving spirit and its corresponding form are interrelated; his three stages of cultural development arose out of the different degrees to which this synthesis of form and content was achieved. In this system, architecture first makes itself manifest as an apotheosis of *symbolic* form, a stage that was epitomized by the Egyptian pyramids, whose construction is expressed through the mute character of massive monumental form. Hegel saw such an art as essentially oriental, as opposed to the subsequent occidental apotheosis of Greek art, with its sensuous, sculptural representation of anthropomorphic form. This moment of *classical* balance between art and life and presumably between form and spirit begins to disintegrate with the eventual demise of the Greek city-state. For Hegel this collapse will have the ultimate consequence of engendering *romantic* art, wherein form and content veer apart, due in large measure to the dematerializing aspirations of Christianity.

In the Hegelian system, art comprises a dichotomy consisting of the idea and its material embodiment. Subject to the changing nature of the dominant form, the history of art passes through the same three successive stages of symbolic, classical, and romantic. Within this overview, sculpture is seen as the liberative, anthropomorphic embodiment of human individuality, as opposed to the universality of symbolic art as this appeared when architecture was the primary artistic manifestation. The romantic period is initiated by the advent of Gothic architecture; only later does it develop into the dominant expressive modes of painting, music, and poetry.

Painting, music and poetry are three preeminently romantic arts (although Gothic architecture is essentially romantic). This is so for two reasons. Firstly, romantic art is concerned with action and conflict, not repose. Architecture cannot represent action at all, sculpture very little. . . . Secondly, the material media of painting, music and poetry are more ideal, more removed from the purely material plane of architecture and sculpture. Painting uses only two dimensions and presents merely the appearance of matter without its reality. Music abstracts from space altogether and subsists in time only. . . . Poetry, lastly, has for its medium the wholly subjective and inward forms of the sensuous image. Romantic art has the germ of its dissolution within itself. Art is according to its very notion the union of spiritual content and outward form. Romantic art has to some extent already ceased to be art, by virtue of the fact that it breaks up the harmonious accord of the two sides that are present in classical art.[6]

In viewing his own time as quintessentially romantic, Hegel predicts the ultimate disappearance of art. Architecture seems to be specially privileged within his tripartite system, however, as each of the three phases has its equivalent expression in architectonic form. Thus, while the quintessence of the symbolic epoch in architecture would remain the achievement of Egyptian civilization, Hegel opposes to this the classical apotheosis of the Greek temple as the sanctuary of an anthropomorphic godhead together with the politically liberative form of the *polis*. This last is seen as totally antithetical to the Gothic, which Hegel regards as epitomizing the introspective dematerializing obsessions of romanticism.

The cruciform shape, the spires, the general trend of the building upwards into vast and aspiring heights,—all is symbolical. Yet the spirit of this symbolism is throughout romantic. These forests of spires and points rising one above the other, the upward-pointed arches and windows, the vast height of the buildings, represent the upward aspirations of the soul which has withdrawn from the outward world into its own self-seclusion. The essential feature of romantic art is, as we have seen, precisely this withdrawal of the soul from the external and sensuous world into the subjectivity of its own inner soul-life. And this in general is what the Christian Church represents. The Greek temple with its walks and colonnades is open to the world. It invites ingress and egress. It is gay and pleasant. It is flat, low, and wide, not, like the Christian Church, narrow and high. This flatness and horizontal extension represent extension outward into the external world. All these features are reversed in the Gothic Church. The pillars are not outside but inside. The whole is entirely enclosed, forming an abode of the soul shut off in self-seclusion from the outside world. The sun enters in a glimmer through the stained-glass windows. Everyone comes and goes, prays upon his knees and moves away. . . . The absorption of all this life as in these infinite silent spaces, represents, in sensuous fashion,the infinity of the spirit and its aspirations. What is emphasized here, then, is the inner soul-life, cut off from the world, the subjectivity which is the essential principle of romantic art.[7]

The term "classical romanticism" thus comes to imply a good deal more than a stylistic characterization, for it expresses precisely that synthesis of Greek and Christian cultures with which intellectuals such as Hegel and the architect Karl Friedrich Schinkel would attempt to sublimate their nostalgia for a lost golden age, through their separate formulation and representation of Prussia as a rational, Christian nation. Schinkel's architecture comes to fruition in that post-Napoleonic moment of reconciliation between the rational and the ideal, wherein

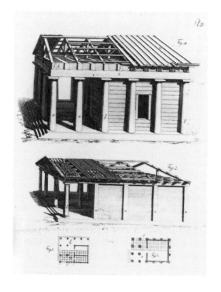

3.1
Aloys Hirt, plate from *Die Baukunst nach den Grundsätzen der Alten*, 1809.

public works are projected and realized in order to embody the enlightened institutions of the modern, liberal state.

Given the prevailing Greek influence, the emergence of the tectonic idea in Prussia was bound up with an attempt to reinterpret the antique world in modern form, as we may judge from the title of Aloys Hirt's influential book *Die Baukunst nach den Grundsätzen der Alten* (Architecture According to the Basic Principles of the Ancients) that appeared in 1809 (fig. 3.1). In 1793, sixteen years prior to the publication of Hirt's book, David Gilly founded the Bauschule in Berlin. Gilly's son, Friedrich, and the art historian Hirt were among the first members of the faculty of this school, later known as the Bauakademie, the former passing from the status of student to teacher by the time he was twenty.

Before coming to Berlin in 1788, the elder Gilly had practiced in Pomerania, both as an architect and a pedagogue, founding his private architectural school in Stettin in 1783. French building technology exercised a strong influence first on Gilly and later on his son, with the latter studying French construction methods during his stay in Paris in 1798, shortly before his premature death two years later (fig. 3.2). Father and son seem to have been equally preoccupied with French framing techniques dating back to the time of Philibert Delorme, and David Gilly would exploit a French timber roofing method, known in German as *Bohlendach,* in a military gymnasium that he built in Berlin in 1800. Gilly the elder possessed what others of his generation lacked, namely, a feeling for simplicity and practical economy in building. These values were evident in his numerous publications and in the character of his teaching in the Bauschule. In this he was later influenced by the typological, modular economy of J. N. L. Durand, whose *Précis des leçons d'architecture données à l'Ecole Polytechnique* was published from 1802 to 1805. Durand's influence on the Bauschule curriculum brought it closer to the practical engineering standpoint of the Ecole Polytechnique than to the emerging postrevolutionary rhetoric of the Ecole des Beaux-Arts.

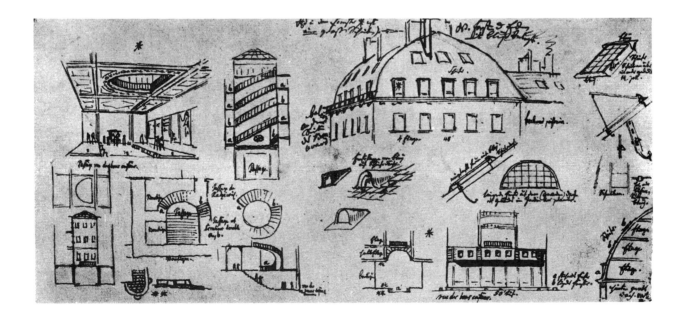

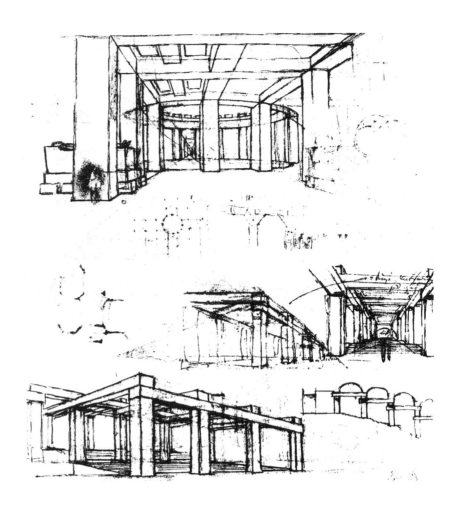

The younger Gilly was fired by the idea of an emergent Germanic identity, as is evident from his design for the monument to Frederick the Great in Leipziger Platz, Berlin. Despite his hypersensitivity and the rich legacy that he left to the Bauschule (fig. 3.3), Friedrich Gilly was as much a constructor as his father, as is evident from the last design of his life, his project for the Hundebrücke in Berlin, to be executed later in a different and more rhetorical form by Schinkel (figs. 3.4, 3.5).[8] As Hermann Pundt has remarked:

Where Gilly's Hundebrücke design comprised three spans of cast iron mounted on simple abutments and on hydraulically profiled stone bases, Schinkel's Schlossbrücke projected for the same site in 1822 was entirely rendered in masonry. We are already witness here to the way in which Schinkel would transform the legacy of Friedrich Gilly and turn even the commission for a bridge into an occasion for a representative urban monument.[9]

Schinkel, for his part, would remain suspended throughout his career between the conflicting demands of ontological and representational tectonic form. The representational aspect predominates in his Singakademie of 1821, where an interior peristyle is created through the encasement of freestanding timber stanchions in such a way as to simulate a Doric colonnade (fig. 3.6). A similar but more ontologically valid tectonic will appear in the castellated brick cornice of his building for the Bauakademie, completed in Berlin in 1836 (figs. 3.7, 3.8).

3.2
Friedrich Gilly, studies (rue des Bons Enfants), Paris, 1798. Gilly notes the details of roof lights, stairwells, and the *Bohlendach* roof construction.

3.3
Friedrich Gilly, design for a mausoleum, c. 1798.

3.4
Friedrich Gilly, Hundebrücke, Lustgarten, Berlin, 1800.

3.5
Karl Friedrich Schinkel, Schlossbrücke, Berlin, 1824.

3.6
Karl Friedrich Schinkel, Singakademie, Berlin, 1821.

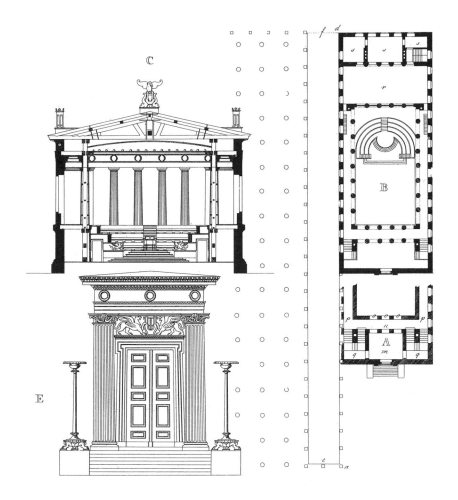

The lower line of projecting corbels in this cornice alludes to the size and spacing of the rafter system supporting the roof, and may thus be read as the metaphoric representation of the real structure hidden within. It is significant that the Bauakademie was the most astylistic of Schinkel's works in that its "utilitarian" form was all but totally free of historical allusion. It was indebted in this regard to British industrial mill construction of the last quarter of the eighteenth century.

Goethe's uncertainty as to the necessary destiny of German architecture—his lifelong vacillation between the Classic and the Gothic culminating in his mature appreciation of the neo-Gothic (see his later reworking of *Von deutsche Baukunst* of 1823)[10]—had the effect of initiating a more general quest for a reconciliatory "third style" appropriate to the modern age and the embodiment of the emerging German state. This hypothetical third style was first formulated in Hübsch's essay *In welchem Style sollen wir bauen*? (In What Style Should We Build?) of 1828, in which he advanced the so called "round-arch style" as an antithesis to both the Grecophilia of Hirt's academic classicism and the *Spitzbogenstil* of the Gothic that Hübsch distanced himself from much like the Greco-Gothicists, in part because of its grotesque complexity and in part for its inapplicability to secular tasks. In the spirited debate that ensued, Hübsch's thesis was first taken up by Rudolf Wiegmann, who initially criticized Hübsch for his historicizing materialism and then defended him as he recognized the emerging *Rundbogenstil* as the interrupted, underevolved Romanesque or Byzantine manner of the thirteenth century as this had been eclipsed before its prime by

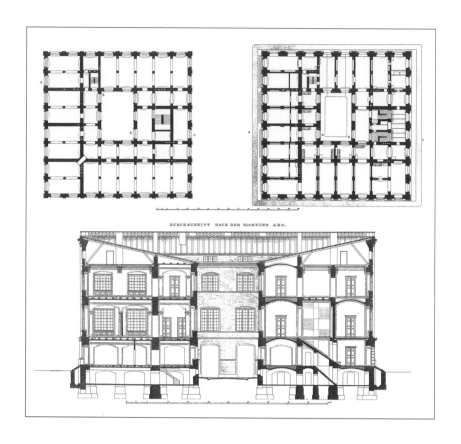

DURCHSCHNITT NACH DER RICHTUNG ABC.

3.7
Karl Friedrich Schinkel, Bauakademie, Berlin,
1836. Note that the centers of the rafters correspond to the centers of the indented corbels on the cornice of the building.

3.8
Karl Friedrich Schinkel, Bauakademie.

3.9
Page from Schinkel's diary of July 16–18, 1826: factories and mills at Manchester, England.

3.10
Page from Schinkel's diary, 1826.

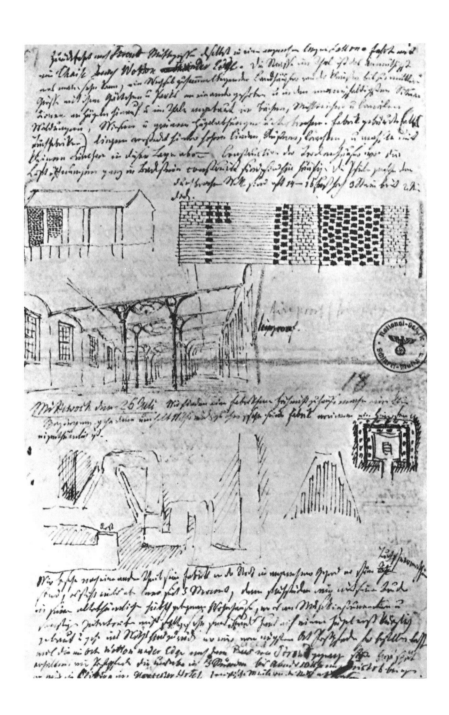

the Gothic. This was virtually the same argument that Gottfried Semper would advance in his defense of his neo-Romanesque Nikolaikirche projected for Hamburg in 1845.[11]

Despite his passing affinity in the 1830s for the technostatics of Hübsch's *Rundbogenstil,* Schinkel was drawn to the stylistic potential of the new technology, particularly as he encountered this on his visit to Britain in 1826, when, as his travel diaries indicate, he was more interested in advanced iron technology and mill construction than in the civic aspects of contemporary English architecture (figs. 3.9, 3.10). Having become professor of building at the Berlin Bauakademie, formerly the Bauschule, Schinkel went to England as an official Prussian emissary in the company of his friend and colleague Peter Christian Beuth.[12] Their joint brief was to study not only museums but also British industrial production. Beuth's interest lay in the field of "industrial design," long before such a profession existed, as we may judge from his founding of the Technischer Gewerbeschule in 1821 and from his joint editorship with Schinkel of a pattern book for applied artists and craftsmen, published in the same year under the title *Vorbilden für Fabrikanten und Handwerker.*[13] They later became jointly involved in writing the program of the Bauakademie that was designed to accommodate both an architectural school and Beuth's Gewerbeinstitut. It is interesting to note that at midcentury the building's ground-floor show windows were filled with what were presumably ideal production items from the point of view of high-quality design, as we may judge from Eduard Gartner's painting of the Bauakademie, dating from 1868.

Despite his reservations about the tectonic status of iron, designs for exposed ferro-vitreous construction appear with increasing frequency in the pages of Schinkel's *Architektonisches Lehrbuch* from the 1820s on.[14] This unfinished textbook, his sole pedagogical legacy, becomes an ever more fertile catalogue of the various ways in which one might impart tectonic significance to engineering technique (fig. 3.11). Thus the *Lehrbuch* contains many examples of differently articulated structural assemblies, rendered in different materials. In the main, these sketches are ontological rather than representational in character, that is

3.11
Karl Friedrich Schinkel, plate from the *Architektonisches Lehrbuch,* 1826. This seems to be an adaptation of a system of Catalan or Roussillon vaulting in flat tile.

3.12
Karl Friedrich Schinkel, plate from the *Architektonisches Lehrbuch.*

3.13
Karl Friedrich Schinkel, plate from the *Architektonisches Lehrbuch.*

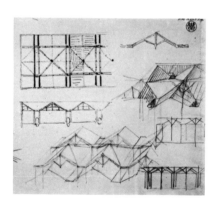

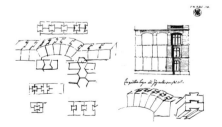

3.22
Karl Friedrich Schinkel, Friedrich Werder
Church, alternative Roman interior.

3.23
Karl Friedrich Schinkel, Schauspielhaus, Berlin, 1821.

3.24
Karl Friedrich Schinkel, Schauspielhaus, side
elevation. Note how the four applied pilasters
in the center allude to the portico on the front
of the building. The underlying modular grid
comes from Durand.

3.25
Karl Friedrich Schinkel, Altes Museum, Berlin, 1830.

3.26
Karl Friedrich Schinkel, Altes Museum. Once again a Durandesque modular grid appears categorically on the rear elevation. The sculpture is by Gottfried Schaden throughout.

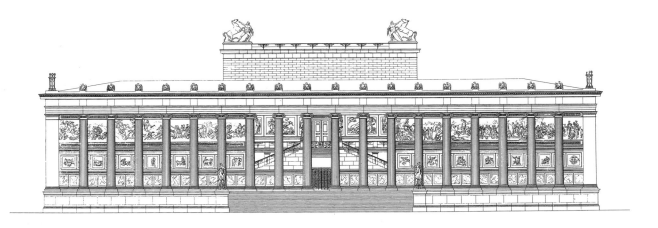

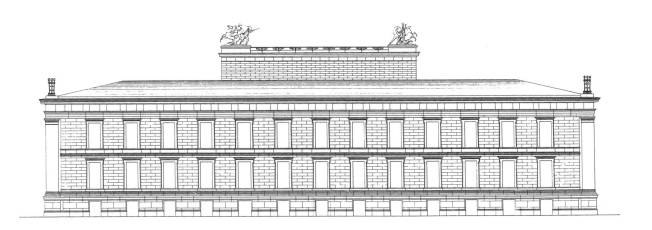

3.27
Karl Friedrich Schinkel, Altes Museum.

"Beauty is the visible proof of the inner intelligence of nature"[20] have much in common. They both reflect Schelling's natural philosophy, his view that the presence of God emanates from every part of the universe. Thus, Schinkel's thought manifests a doubly articulated dualism, that is to say, not only the reconciliation of the ideal and the real but also of the *typos* with the *topos.* Beyond this, Schinkel was to remain indebted to Durand for his way of representing the institutions of the state. In one of his rare theoretical statements, "Das Prinzip der Kunst in der Architektur" (The Principle of Art in Architecture), he wrote:

1. *To build (bauen) is to join different materials into a whole, corresponding to a definite purpose.*

2. *This definition, encompassing a building in both its spiritual and material aspects, clearly demonstrates that purposiveness is the fundamental principle of all building.*

3. *The material edifice, which now presumes a spiritual aspect, is here the subject of my consideration.*

4. *The purposiveness of every building can be considered under three aspects: these are:*
   a) *Purposiveness of spatial distribution or of the plan;*
   b) *Purposiveness of construction or of the joining together of materials appropriate to the plan.*
   c) *Purposiveness of ornament or of the decoration.*[21]

The Rise of the Tectonic

Later in the same theoretical statement he qualifies the criteria of fitness as this applies to construction and ornamentation by stressing the importance of using the best possible material and of revealing not only the quality of the material but also the quality of craftsmanship with which the various components are assembled together. This concern for craft precision and material richness surely derives from Perrault's concept of positive beauty. At the same time, the idea of purposiveness or *Zweckmässigkeit* in Schinkel's work derives in some measure from the philosophy of Kant. As Ikonomou and Mallgrave have written,

Kant advanced the notion of form in a more substantial way in his Kritik der Urtheilskraft *(Critique of judgment), 1790, which considered the process of how we judge forms to be aesthetically pleasing or beautiful. Parallel to his earlier "forms of intuition" and "forms of thought" . . . Kant now proposed a new principle governing the faculty of aesthetic judgment, one that he hoped would provide it with a measure of universality and at the same time allow it to remain subjective. This principle was the notion of "purposiveness" (Zweckmässigkeit)—for Kant the sense of internal harmony that we presume to exist in the world, the bias, as it were, that we bring to the aesthetic act. Purposiveness is the heuristic rule or standard by which we relate to the forms of nature and art.*[22]

Schinkel would link his interpretation of this concept to hierarchical notions of culture as these are set forth in the writings of Johann Gottlieb Fichte. In his book *Die Bestimmung des Menschen* (The Vocation of Man), published in 1800, Fichte gave primacy to public action and to the cultivation of ethical value. In the light of this, Schinkel insisted that not all buildings were of equal stature and that the presence, location, and choice of ornament should directly express the level of the work. Whereas French influences are detectable here, above all the theories of Cordemoy and Laugier, it is possible to argue that this hierarchical sense of order was latent in the German language, with its capacity to distinguish among *Architektur, Baukunst,* and *Bauen.* Schinkel's ability to discriminate among different levels of building has been remarked on by Kurt Forster in his analysis of the varying syntax employed in the complex that Schinkel built along the banks of the Kupfergraben opening off the Spree in Berlin (fig. 3.28).

Not only the warehouse exhibited such specific characteristics; each one of Schinkel's buildings along the riverfront projected its distinctive role into a panoramic ensemble. The columnar front and acroteria privileged the museum as a monumental building in neo-antique fashion, while the pedimented facade of the customs office reduced its ornamentation and surface treatment to revetted facades. Its twin to the rear, the office block, received only a stuccoed elevation and the exterior of the warehouse was left in unfaced brick. This calibrated sequence of architectural forms and building materials injects into the optical perspective a dimension of rhetorical and historic "depth." Ashlar, revetment, stucco and brick mark rungs on a descending scale of architectural values, each one appropriate—and characteristic—for a particular type of structure. Schinkel differentiated each building stylistically without falling into the trap of purely eclectic justification. The passage from trabeation to arcuation belongs as much to this hierarchy as do the colorist qualities of the different building materials.[23]

Taking as his point of departure the *édifices publiques* of Durand's *Précis des leçons,* Schinkel develops his Neuer Packhof warehouse (see fig. 3.14) as a combination of two types given by Durand, the *halle* and the *maison commune,*

3.28
View of Schinkel's buildings from the Schlossbrücke: Altes Museum in the foreground, the
three Packhof buildings behind.

although, as in Eduard Metzger's later *Rundbogenstil* Staatsbibliothek for Munich (1831–1842), there lies behind this synthesis the prototype of the early
Florentine palace as we find this, say, in the Palazzo Riccardi dating from the
mid-fifteenth century. The warehouse was one of Schinkel's most technostati-
cally articulated works in that the intervals between the five stringcourses of its
facade (one for each floor) diminish incrementally as the building rises upward
and the cumulative load on the structure reduces. This diminishment is accompanied by a slight batter in the building's load-bearing brick face, which corresponds to a reduction in the thickness of the structural walls. The round-arched
window openings also diminish slightly in width as they move upward from floor
to floor, inducing a kind of perspectival monumentality, while a line of semicircular openings running above the first stringcourse indicates the presence and the
status of the undercroft. Similar indications and technostatic diminishments also
occur in the Bauakademie, which likewise is of load-bearing brickwork and derives from mill building typology (see figs. 3.7, 3.8). In this instance, however, the
upward diminishment between the first- and second-floor studio windows is in
both height and width, while the ground-floor fenestration and triadic basement
and attic lights are correspondingly suppressed, thereby indicating their inferior
status (see fig. 3.8). This differential is reinforced by further elaboration in the
detailing of the first- and second-floor studio lights, framed by mullions and a
transom in iron, covered by a flat brick arch and embellished with acroteria and
decorative spandrel panels in terra-cotta. Unlike the Packhof warehouse, the interior of the Bauakademie was systematically subdivided into rooms of varying
size by load-bearing cross walls, and these structural lines were expressed on
the facade as vertical piers,thereby entailing a certain suppression of the stringcourses marking the floors. Despite all this subtle inflection, the British historian
James Ferguson, writing at midcentury, would find the building to be misscaled
for having been rendered in brick rather than in stone.[24]

Soon after Schinkel's death in 1841, Hirt's neo-Greek theory[25] came to be replaced as the primary ideological text of the Bauakademie by Karl Bötticher's
Die Tektonik der Hellenen (The Tectonic of the Hellenes), published in three volumes between 1843 and 1852. First attending the Bauakademie as a student in
1827 and thereafter studying with both Beuth and Schinkel, Bötticher became a
member of the faculty after his qualification as an architect in 1844. Influenced
by Hübsch's structural rationalism and by Hirt's unwavering faith in the symbolic

superiority of Greek form, but simultaneously denying both the materialism of the former and the traditionalism of the latter, Bötticher sought to resolve the dichotomy between classicism and romanticism through the specific hieratic procedures exemplified in Schinkel's Neuer Packhof and Bauakademie. Taking Schinkel's *Architektonisches Lehrbuch* as his point of departure, Bötticher sought a synthesis between the ontological status of the structure and the representational role of the ornament. Antithetical to all forms of eclecticism, be it Gothic Revival or neo-Renaissance, and equally susceptible to both the rational (Kant) and the antirational (Herder) lines in Enlightenment thought, Bötticher respectively assimilated the representational to the Greek and the ontological to the Gothic.

Influenced through the writings of Christian Weisse by Arthur Schopenhauer's thesis that architecture could only express its essential form and significance through the dramatic interaction of support and load (*Stütze und Last*),[26] Bötticher insisted on the corporeality of architecture and on the interstitial spatiality of its ligaments at every conceivable scale. Taking his cue in part from Herder's tactile sculptural aesthetic and in part from Schinkel's articulated method, Bötticher maintained that the symbolic revetment of a work must never be allowed to obscure its fundamental, constructional form. Thus as Mitchell Schwarzer has written:

Bötticher's attempt to harmonize the muscular passion of architectural materiality and statics with the objectivity of art was quite different from Kant and Schiller's concept of Architektonik *beauty as the marshalling of the subjective senses towards an objective reality. . . . [Bötticher] proposed that the beauty of architecture was precisely the explanation of mechanical concepts. As much as its artistic demands related to the imagination, the constructive demands of the Tektonik argued against the autonomy of architectural from extrinsic ends.*[27]

Bötticher envisaged a kind of reciprocally expressive joint that comes into being through the appropriate interlocking of constructional elements. At once articulate and integrated, these joints were seen as *Körperbilden,* not only permitting constructions to be achieved but also enabling these assemblies to become the symbolic components of an expressive system. In addition to this syntactical/constructional concept, Bötticher, as we have noted, distinguished between the *Kernform* and the *Kunstform,* the latter having the task of representing the constructional and/or institutional status of the former. He wrote: "The concept of each part can be thought of as being realized by two elements: the core-form and the art-form. The core-form of each part is the mechanically necessary and statically functional structure; the art-form, on the other hand, is only the characterization by which the mechanical-statical function is made apparent."[28] According to Bötticher, the shell of the *Kunstform* should be capable of revealing and augmenting the essence of the constructional nucleus. At the same time, he insisted that one must always try to distinguish and express the difference between the constructional form and its enrichment, irrespective of whether this last manifests itself as cladding or ornament. He wrote that the art form "is only a covering and a symbolic attribute of the part—*decoration, κοσμος.*"[29]

Bötticher was as much influenced by Schelling's natural philosophy as was Schinkel, above all by Schelling's view that architecture transcends the mere pragmatism of building by virtue of assuming symbolic significance. For Schelling and Bötticher alike, the inorganic had no symbolic meaning and hence

structural form could only acquire symbolic status by virtue of its capacity to engender analogies between tectonic and organic form. Direct imitation of natural form was to be avoided, however, for like Schelling, Bötticher held the view that architecture was an imitative art only to the extent that it imitated itself. Nevertheless, unlike Schinkel, Bötticher tended to distance himself theoretically from an opportunistic borrowing of historical form.

A fuller development of Bötticher's theory came with his 1846 *Schinkelfest* address entitled "The Principles of the Hellenic and Germanic Way of Building," in which, after praising the tradition of the Bauakademie and above all Schinkel as the initiator of "architectural science," Bötticher proceeded to posit, in somewhat Hegelian manner, the future possibility of an unnamed third style capable of engendering a new cultural entity, synthesizing thereby the dual Germanic legacy of the Gothic and the Greek.[30] For Bötticher the true tectonic tradition, what he refers to as the "eclecticism of the spirit," resides not in the appearance of any one style but rather in the essence that lies behind the appearance. While he condones the adaptation of traditional stylistic formats to new situations, he is categorically against any form of arbitrary stylistic selection, such as the *Rundbogenstil* advocated by Hübsch. Bötticher will argue that any new spatial system or future style will have to be brought into being by a new structural principle, and not the other way round. Thus, in a manner that anticipates Viollet-le-Duc, we find him writing:

Our contention that the manner of covering determines every style and its ultimate development is confirmed by the monuments of all styles. Equally evident is the truth that from the earliest and roughest attempts to cover spaces by using stone, to the culmination represented by the Spitzbogen *vault, and down to the present time, all the ways in which stone could possibly be used to span a space have been exploited, and they have completely exhausted the possible structural applications of this material. No longer can stone alone form a new structural system of a higher stage of development. The reactive, as well as relative, strength of stone has been completely exhausted. A new and so far unknown system of covering (which will of course bring in its train a new world of art-forms) can appear only with the adoption of an unknown material, or rather a material that so far has not been used as a guiding principle. It will have to be a material with physical properties that will permit wider spans, with less weight and greater reliability, than are possible when using stone alone. With regard to spatial design and construction, it must be such as will meet any conceivable spatial or planning need. A minimal quantity of material should be needed for the walls, thus rendering the bulky and ponderous buttresses of the* Spitzbogenstil *completely superfluous. The whole weight of the covering system would be confined to vertical pressure, that is, to the reactive strength of walls and supports. Of course, this does not mean that the indirect use of stone vaulting, especially the system of ribbed and stellar vaulting, will be excluded; on the contrary, the latter will be widely used. But it does mean that, for those parts on which the whole system rests, another material will be used, one that makes it possible to transfer their structural function to other parts in which a different principle operates. It makes no difference whether the members to be replaced are buttresses or members that support the ceiling, such as ribs, bands, etc.*

Such a material is iron, which has already been used for this purpose in our century. Further testing and greater knowledge of its structural properties will ensure that iron will become the basis for the covering system of the future and that structurally it will in time come to be as superior to the Hellenic and medieval systems as the arcuated medieval system was to the monolithic trabeated system of antiquity. Disregarding the fragile wooden ceiling (which in any case cannot serve as a comparison) and using mathematical terms, one can say that iron is indeed the material whose principle, yet unutilized, will introduce into architecture the last of the three forces, namely, absolute strength.[31]

As in the later theory of Viollet-le-Duc, Bötticher foresees the essential complementary role to be played by the absolute strength of iron tie rods, thereby enabling the relative strength of stone vaulting to greatly increase its capacity to span. Yet unlike the French structural rationalist, he insists that the tectonic expressivity of such an unprecedented system will have to model its representational form on some kind of reinterpretation of the principles of Hellenic architecture. Through this assertion, based on attributing some measure of symbolic universality to the classical, Bötticher already anticipates the semiotic transformations of the Jugendstil in its crystallizing phase, particularly as one encounters this at the turn of the century in the work of Otto Wagner.[32] Implicitly acknowledging the difficulty of superimposing traditional stereotomic symbolism onto unprecedented lightweight, skeletonal structure, Bötticher looked to the organic as a fundamental form force by which to synthesize the mechanical and the natural and in so doing to reinterpret and transform the received iconography of classic form. Thus he will argue in the 1846 address:

Pictorial art cannot represent an idea as such, but must represent it through a symbol and thus embody it. Architecture follows the same method. It takes its symbols and art-forms only from those natural objects that embody an idea analogous to the one inherent in the members of the architectural system. Therefore, an idea for which no analogue exists in the external world cannot be represented by pictorial art nor for that matter by architecture. The essence of pictorial art and its relation to nature rests in this interaction between concept and object, between invention and imitation.[33]

In 1825, after having studied mathematics in the University of Göttingen, Gottfried Semper appears to have attended architectural classes at the Munich Academy of Fine Arts before fleeing to France in 1826 as the result of a duel. In Paris he studied with Franz Christian Gau, who may have introduced him to the controversy then raging over the original polychromatic rendering of Greek temples.[34] Between 1830 and 1833 Semper traveled in Italy and Greece to see for himself, returning to Germany in 1834 to become architectural director at the Royal Academy in Dresden on Gau's recommendation. His first major commissions following from this appointment were the first Dresden Opera House, completed in 1841, and the Picture Gallery, erected between 1847 and 1854. His participation in the 1848–1849 revolution brought him to exile himself first in France, then in England, where he became part of the Crystal Palace circle around Henry Cole and Richard Redgrave, and then to Zurich where he became head of the Polyteknikum in 1855.

The theoretical elaboration of Semper's *Die vier Elemente der Baukunst* (The Four Elements of Architecture), largely written in 1850, parallels in certain respects some of the arguments advanced by Bötticher in his *Die Tektonik der Hellenen,* the first volume of which Semper did not read until after 1852, following the publication of his *Four Elements* in 1851. The notion of the seminal role played by the internal carpet wall in the evolution of classical architecture seems to have been developed independently by both men. Close to such anthropological insights lay the tectonic theories of Karl Otfried Müller, whose work Semper studied assiduously in 1834 in preparation for his lectures at the Dresden Academy. Another early influence on Semper was the ethnographer Gustav Klemm, who as Royal Librarian was attached to the imperial court at Dresden during the period of Semper's tenure there. That Klemm was seminal for Semper is suggested by his *Allgemeine Kultur-Geschichte des Menschheit* (General Cultural History of Mankind), published in nine volumes between 1843 and 1851, the fourth volume of which accorded particular import to a description of a Pacific Island hut that Klemm had derived from a late eighteenth-century account of a German explorer who had accompanied Captain Cook to the South Seas. Klemm's gloss on this account gave prominence to the same elements as would later make up Semper's model of the primordial dwelling. While Semper would only refer to Klemm on two occasions, he was nonetheless also indebted to him for his theory of cultural transformation in which southern passive races are succeeded by northern nomadic, active, warlike tribes, with the aboriginal dwelling becoming modified according to climate and the racial origin of the nomads as they settle down. As Harry Mallgrave has observed, this pacifying process will give rise to "southern" building types in masonry that, for Semper, formed the historical beginning of architecture, attaining their apotheosis, so to speak, in the dynastic order of Egypt, wherein a warm climate and geographical isolation will allow architecture to develop into a courtyard style of building. The core of the temple complex, for instance, was the hidden *sekos* or tabernacle from which evolved a series of processional yards, formerly open and later covered either with canvas or with a permanent roof. One may see this as similar to the transposition in which a tectonic hut eventually becomes transformed into the stereotomic Greek *megaron* surrounded by columns.[35]

Corroborated by evidence of the Caribbean hut that he saw in the Crystal Palace Exhibition of 1851, Semper's four elements represent a fundamental break with the Vitruvian triad of *utilitas, firmitas, venustas* (fig. 3.29). The empirical fact of this primordial shelter prompted Semper to propose an anthropological countertesis to Laugier's primitive hut of 1753. In its place, he proposed a more articulated model comprising (1) a hearth, (2) an earthwork, (3) a framework/roof, and (4) an enclosing membrane.

While challenging the authority of Laugier's primitive hut, Semper gave primacy to the tensile frame and its infill as opposed to the compressive earthwork or load-bearing mass. Thus, while Schinkel and Semper made exclusive use of load-bearing masonry in their architecture, they nonetheless conceived of their form as a phenomenally transparent grid, structured about a hierarchical articulation of discrete parts. Nevertheless what Semper added to this hieratic assembly was an emphasis upon the earthwork as a stereotomic, topographic mass upon which the more ephemeral form of the tectonic frame literally took its ground.

This emphasis on the earthwork had a number of consequences. On the one hand, it complemented the universal nomadic textile culture that Semper regarded as the ultimate *Urkunst*; on the other hand, as Rosemarie Bletter has remarked, it gave new importance to a nonspatial element, namely the hearth, which was an inseparable part of the earthwork.[36] For Semper, this last was the

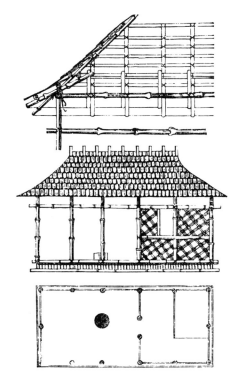

3.29
Gottfried Semper, illustration from *Der Stil in den technischen und tektonischen Künsten*, 1860–1863. The Caribbean hut in the Great Exhibition of 1851.

irreducible *raison d'être* of architecture in that it incorporated in a single element the public and spiritual nexus of the built domain. At the same time, his four elements were possessed of significant etymological ramifications. Thus the Latin term *reredos* was open to a dichotomous reading; on the one hand it signified the back of an altar, on the other the back of a hearth. Meanwhile the term hearth itself carried with it certain civic implications inasmuch as the Latin root *aedificare,* from which the word *edifice* derives, means literally to make a hearth. The institutional connotations of both hearth and edifice are further amplified by the verb *to edify,* which means to educate, strengthen, and instruct. Semper went on to rationalize a great deal of his ethnographic theory on a similar etymological basis. Thus, he would distinguish the massiveness of the fortified wall, as indicated by the word *die Mauer,* from the light, screenlike enclosure signified by the term *die Wand.* Both terms imply enclosure, but the latter is related to the German word for dress, *Gewand,* and to the verb *winden,* which means to embroider. Semper maintained that the earliest basic structural artifact was the knot, from which follows the primary nomadic building culture of the tent and its textile fabric.[37] Here again, one encounters significant etymological connotations of which Semper was fully aware, above all the curious archaic conjunction of *knot* and *joint,* the former being indicated by *der Knoten* and the latter by *die Naht.* In modern German, both words are connected to the concept *die Verbindung,* binding. Thus, for Semper, the most significant basic tectonic element was the joint or the knot (fig. 3.30). As Joseph Rykwert has written,

By a curious use of word-play, Semper foreshadows his later reference to the knot as the essential work of art quite early in the textile chapter, when he considers the term Naht: *the seam, the joining. It is, he says, an expedient, a* Nothbehelf *for the joining of two planes of similar or dissimilar material. But the very juxtaposition of* Noth *and* Naht *suggests a connection.*[38]

Of Semper's characterization of the knot as "the oldest tectonic, cosmogonic symbol," Rykwert notes that

the word-play might have seemed so facile as to be meaningless; though the connection between Naht *and* knot (Knoten, Noeud, nodus) *seemed to him in some way related to the Greek* ἀνακὴ *force, necessity. Presumably he had made himself familiar with the articles* Knoten, Naht *etc. in Jakob and Wilhelm Grimm's German dictionary. However, he found the answer to his problem after he had written this passage in the work on Linguistics by Albert Höfer, a disciple of von Humboldt. Höfer justified the word-play, and pointed out the relation of such words to the Indo-European root* noc, *Latin* nec-o, nexus, necessitas, nectere, νέω *(to spin).*[39]

Semper's emphasis on the joint implies that a fundamental syntactical transition is expressed as one passes from the stereotomic base of a building to its tectonic frame, and that such transitions are of the very essence of architecture.

3.30
Gottfried Semper, typical knot forms used in traditional fabrics, illustrated in the first volume of *Der Still in den technischen und tektonischen Künsten.*

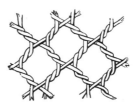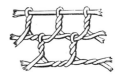

In his later two-volume *Der Stil in den technischen und tektonischen Künsten, oder praktische Aesthetik* (Style in the Technical and Tectonic Arts, or Practical Aesthetics, 1860–1863), Semper assigned certain tectonic crafts to each of the four elements: textiles pertained to the art of enclosure and thus to the side walls and roof, carpentry to the basic structural frame, masonry to the earth-work, and metallurgy and ceramics to the hearth. In the same text, Semper also outlined his *Stoffwechseltheorie,* that is to say his theory of symbolic conserva-tion, in which the mythical-cum-spiritual values attaching to certain structural elements cause them to be translated into petrified compressive forms, even when they were originally of tensile construction. Semper cited sacred Greek ar-chitecture as exemplifying the persistence of certain symbolic motifs that had been transformed from a nomadic wooden framework with textile covering to the permanence of stone. According to Semper, this would explain the transpo-sition of textile motifs into the polychromatic ornamental dressings of the tri-glyphs and metopes in the Doric order. Contrary to the Abbé Laugier, Semper did not feel that such forms arose from the petrification of timber construction, of beam ends and rafters, but rather from features used to tie down the textile fabric covering the roof.

In reference to his own historical period, however, Semper felt that the cheap industrial simulation of one material by another, above all through casting, stamping, and molding, paradoxically undermined the principle of symbolic con-servation, largely because these substitutions were expedient and secular and were thus conceptually indifferent to the symbolic continuity essential to the re-creation of tectonic form. The various synthetic substances and processes ex-hibited at the 1851 Great Exhibition had been an object lesson for Semper, for here he had seen cast iron and gutta-percha employed for the simulation of stone and wood respectively.

In his essay *Wissenschaft, Industrie und Kunst* (Science, Industry, and Art) of 1852, Semper argued that the general crisis of style had arisen out of three dif-ferent causes, first the alienation of the arts from their original motifs, second the devaluation of material and labor, and third the loss of the ability of the art form to exercise a specific function in relation to the historical moment. Semper sought to counter this degeneration by reasserting the ethnographic origins of the various manufacturing procedures, together with their material references and corresponding forms. In this respect he emphasized the task of the form and the process of fabrication over the specific nature of any given material. Thus, while he regarded clay as the primary molding material or *Urstoff,* this did not prevent him from seeing facing brick or tile as a "dressing," a kind of petri-fied fabric and hence a transformation of nomadic textile forms into a more per-manent material.

Taking something of his taxonomic discourse from the writings of Alexander von Humboldt, Semper, like Hübsch, wanted to transcend the classical paradigm successively advanced by Winckelmann, Hirt, and Bötticher. Like Hübsch he en-visaged a return to the "interrupted" style of the Romanesque; to the same style that the American architect H. H. Richardson would assume as his point of de-parture in 1870. This swerve away from the classical led Semper to ground his theory in the universality of making, placing the burden of tectonic proof on the evolution of the crafts and the industrial arts. As Rykwert has written:

There are, therefore, in Semper's system, two primary archetypes: The hearth and the cloth, the Urherd *and the* Urtuch. *They were the first mark of settlement and the first fabrication; but although they seem to have the same reality for Semper as the* Urpflanze *(original plant) had for Goethe (1788), yet they were not reducible to a single root phenomenon as Goethe would presumably have wanted them, nor do the other root-actions, that of jointing and of heaping, ever merge into each other, but they always, even when they overlap, retain their character, through representation and symbolization.*[40]

For Semper, the ultimate cultural model was linguistic, and in this too, like Bötticher, he was indebted to Wilhelm von Humboldt's insistence that language is not just a description of things but rather a vocalization of action. Linguists of Humboldt's generation saw speech as displaying the will of the people, almost as a Hegelian manifestation of collectivity. In much the same vein, Semper saw artistic culture as an evolving language in which certain root forms and operations are transposed over time.

Semper was a late romantic to the degree that he inherited the epistemological and political project of the *Aufklärung,* and in this regard his participation in the unsuccessful liberal revolution of 1849 is symptomatic. He was Hegelian to the extent that he saw Greek classical architecture as sculptural rather than tectonic in its manner of deploying stone. At the same time he challenged Hegel's triadic scheme of symbolic, classic, and romantic by insisting that the monumental art of architecture derives its formal elaboration from the so-called industrial arts and above all from the craft of textiles, to which Semper would devote the entire first volume of *Der Stil,* according some 480 pages to textiles as opposed to the 200 for ceramics, 132 for carpentry, and 120 for masonry that together make up the second volume. Semper recognized the material and technological ramifications of his four elements by grounding them in different material properties and in correspondingly different crafts. In this vein he would discriminate between the elasticity of textiles, the softness of ceramics, the ductility of carpentry, and the hardness of masonry. Semper saw the articulation of craft capacity in relation to these materials as the evolution of technical skill, in which the hand gradually increases its ability to work a given material to the full extent of its expressive scope.

The emphasis that Semper placed on textiles assumed the form of an obsession, and in one text after another, from his first London lecture of 1853 to his lecture "Über Baustyle" given in Zurich in 1869, he would demonstrate, through anthropological evidence, the symbolic primacy of textile sheathing, as opposed to the corporeality of the form to which it is applied, either as surface decoration or as a shallow, three-dimensional relief. Semper revealed himself a romantic in the Hegelian sense inasmuch as his *Bekleidung* theory became a mode for the progressive dematerialization of architecture, liberating the mind from the stereotomic obtuseness of matter and focusing it instead on a reticulation of surface and thus on a dematerialization that, as in the Crystal Palace, aspired to the dissolution of form into light.[41]

In his "Theorie des Formell-Schönen" (Theory of Formal Beauty) of 1856, he will no longer classify architecture with painting and sculpture as a plastic art but rather with dance and music as a cosmic art, as an ontological, world-making art evocative of nature in action rather than as the static substance of two- and three-dimensional form. Semper regarded the performing arts as cosmic not only because they were symbolic but also because they embodied man's underlying erotic-ludic urge, that is to say the impulse to decorate according to a rhythmic law.

This anthropological insight exposes the conceptual schism running through the entire body of Semperian theory. This split manifests itself, at many different scales, as a representational/ontological division that may be seen as an irreducible aspect of architecture. I am alluding here to the difference between the representational face of a building's surface and the phenomenological (ontic) depth of its space. And while the two may be more easily reconciled in a pantheistic world, this becomes problematic in a secular age, as August Schmarsow was prompt to recognize in his fundamental critique of Semper's *Bekleidung* theory which he saw, in 1893, as having placed an undue emphasis on the representational facade. This stress, for Schmarsow, was at the expense of the experiential body of the building considered as a whole.

Notwithstanding the rationally articulated structural logic of his early work as epitomized in his first Dresden Opera House of 1841, Semper would acknowledge in 1869 that an authentic style of the epoch had failed to emerge and that until such time as it did one would have to make do with the old styles as best one could. It is just this acceptance of eclecticism, made in the name of pragmatic reality and the representation of the bourgeois state, that made him so vulnerable to criticism in the last quarter of the nineteenth century; first from Konrad Fiedler, who saw his architecture as uninspired historicism, overburdened by erudition, second from Otto Wagner, who saw Semper as lacking sufficient courage to push his own tectonic insights to their logical conclusion, namely that a new style must depend of necessity on a new means of construction,[42] and last but not least from Schmarsow, who, however indebted, would regard Semper's architecture as unduly mesmerized by incrusted surface expression and as insufficiently concerned with spatial depth. Semper for his part felt that architecture had lost its cosmic dimension due to secularization and that this loss left his own time with no alternative but to reproduce historical forms, preferably those of the Renaissance that, for him, were symbolic of democracy.

It was left to the next generation of Semperians to pursue the technical and tectonic consequences of his theoretical corpus, together with the legacy of his scientific, architectural realism. Of the many who followed him in this regard, two in particular merit our attention; first the Austrian Otto Wagner, whose work came closest to demonstrating a precise relationship between an articulated skin and the development of a building in depth, and second Georg Heuser, who, in a number of essays written between 1881 and 1894, would assert that architectural realism was more a matter of principle than of style.[43] Heuser believed that architecture could only ultimately evolve through constructive rather than decorative innovation. As if to prove the point, he developed an entire typology of composite, rolled and plated iron supports that according to him could be used for different constructive *and* expressive ends, depending on the situation. While he shared Semper's antipathy to excessive dematerialization, as this had already been demonstrated, so to speak, by the Crystal Palace and by all the ferro-vitreous structures that followed in its wake, he tried to evolve the substance of an iron architecture that had its own corporeal being. To this end he attempted to adduce a strictly tectonic, one might say paleotechnological, equivalent of the classical orders. While Heuser was aware that such built-up elements could only realize their full cultural potential if they were assimilated by the society in everyday practice, he seems to have been among the first to acclaim the riveted steel frame as the new industrial vernacular of the machine age.

If there is a single heir at the turn of the century to the line of Gilly, Schinkel, Bötticher, and Semper, then it is surely Wagner, who, despite the limitations of his practice, attempted to apply the tectonic legacy of the *Aufklärung* to the modernizing realities of the twentieth-century metropolis. This much is already manifest in the pages of his major theoretical text, *Moderne Architektur,* first published in 1896 and later reissued, in slightly modified versions, in 1898, 1902, and 1914. The changed title of the last edition—*Die Baukunst unserer Zeit*—testifies to Wagner's allegiance to the so-called realist approach of such writers as Hermann Muthesius (*Stilarchitektur und Baukunst,* 1902) and Karl Scheffler (*Moderne Baukunst,* 1907). The term *Baukunst* (building art) indicated an approach that was more *sachlich,* in the sense that it responded objectively to the socio-technical building task of everyday life rather than to the ideals of high art. Nevertheless, despite his mature affinity for the real, Wagner never relinquished his aspirations for the ideal, not even at the peak of his career as an engineer/architect in the service of the Viennese *Stadtbahn,* as we may judge from the 1914 edition of *Moderne Architektur,* published some four years before his death in 1918. Here a series of capitalized aphorisms dotted throughout the text highlight the major tenets of his theoretical position, particularly in the seminal fourth chapter dedicated to "Construction" in which we may read the following six apodictic statements:

Every architectural form has risen in construction and has successively become an art-form. It is therefore certain that new purposes must give birth to new methods of construction and by this reasoning also to new forms. The architect always has to develop the art-form, but only the structural calculation and the expense will therefore speak a language unsympathetic to man, while on the other hand, the architect's mode of expression will remain unintelligible if in the creation of the art-form he does not start from construction. Well conceived construction not only is the prerequisite of every architectural work, but also, and this cannot be repeated often enough, provides the modern creative architect with a number of positive ideas for creating new forms—in the fullest meaning of this word. Without the knowledge and experience of construction, the concept "architect" is unthinkable.[44]

While all of this supported Bötticher's thesis that a new *Kunstform* could only arise out of a new *Werkform,*[45] it makes no reference to Semper's *Bekleidung* theory, which Wagner assumed for its capacity to synthesize lightweight panel construction in both stone and metal. At this juncture, Wagner seems to have embraced the metaphor of the mask of which Semper had written in *Der Stil,* with a certain ambiguity: "Masking does not help, however, when *behind* the mask the thing is false."[46] By masking Semper did not intend falsehood, but rather the creation of a tectonic veil through which and by which it would be possible to perceive the spiritual significance of the constructional form, as it lay suspended, as it were, between the pragmatic world of fact and the symbolic world of value. No one has perhaps written more perceptively of Wagner's contribution in this regard than Fritz Neumeyer:

Like the then floating garment that clothes the female body in ancient Greek sculpture, revealing as much beauty as it conceals, Wagner's treatment of the structure and construction exploits a similar kind of delicate, sensuous play that was probably only evident to a connoisseur of a certain age and experience. Exactly this principle gives the interior of the Postsparkasse its quality of silk-like transparency. The glass veil is lifted up on iron stilts that carefully cut into its skin and gently disappear. Semper's theory of "dressing" could find no more ingenious interpretation because here an artist, not a theoretician, generously appealed to it to mask his own interests and obsessions.[47]

Influenced by the *fin-de-siècle* theory of empathy, *Einfühlung,* by which the "form force" of an artwork becomes by association an analogue for corporeal movement and states of bodily being, Wagner found his way back to Bötticher's double articulation of the tectonic, in which the classical legacy of the *Kunstform* would come to be inseminated by the dynamism of the *Werkform* as an inorganically articulated structural invention.[48]

4   Frank Lloyd Wright
and the Text-Tile Tectonic

What, then, could a young radical of the Chicago School learn from the Japanese Imperial exhibit of 1893? Nothing less than a highly provocative clue to a fresh concept of Western architecture: the interplay of solid structure with unprecedented quantities of light and atmosphere. Roofs, walls, and, above all, fenestration could be liberated from bondage to a rigid formalism, could be divorced from their hitherto ambiguous function, in the Western tradition, as boundary lines for preconceived canons of proportion. The Ho-o-den demonstrated that uninterrupted strip fenestration with suppressed sills under eaves restored to their proper place as shades were the means whereby a house could be, so to speak, turned inside out. Given these new directions, the "style" would come naturally—especially to anyone already predisposed. . . . A good house, Wright instinctively realized, must not be rigid; it must consciously acknowledge the earth beneath it and invite the air around it, and yet display its very human need for protection from a nature which is not always benign. In the Ho-o-den, Wright beheld an unfamiliar architectural heritage which approximated the vision in his mind. Here was the germ of continuous plastic fenestration that could be bent around corners, that need recognize no formalistic allegiance to canons of design, that could open the interior to the outdoors anywhere and everywhere, and that would produce by its inherent horizontality and by its awning-like overhangs that level domestic line which Wright intuitively admired and had determined to develop as the main theme of his house architecture.

Within a year of this event, he began to discard the sash window in favor of the casement, to prepare his work for the final change from fenestration in spots to fenestration in strips. Once done, the change automatically obliterated the severity and resistance of wall, fostered the free running treatment of sills and bases, and resulted in the victory of the horizontal as the dominant characteristic of a great style that was, indeed, to make history.
Grant Carpenter Manson, Frank Lloyd Wright to 1910, *1958*

The fact that Frank Lloyd Wright (1867–1959) always referred to Louis Sullivan as his *lieber Meister* testifies to the strong hold that the German culture exercised over Chicago during the last quarter of the nineteenth century. By the time of the Columbian Exposition of 1893, Germans constituted a third of the city's population. In 1898, a survey of distinguished citizens of German origin listed seventeen prominent architects including August Bauer, Frederick Baumann, and Dankmar Adler. It is equally significant that Adler and Sullivan's Schiller Theatre of 1893 would be built for the performance of German plays in the original, just as their canonical Auditorium Building of 1884 was largely devoted to opera, primarily of course to Richard Wagner's musical drama. At this time Chicago published two daily newspapers in German and had numerous German clubs and associations. By 1898 Louis Sullivan had been Adler's design partner for almost a decade. Caught between his Beaux-Arts education and this omnipresent German environment, Sullivan had almost as many German as French books in his library, even if he understood little of the language. Thus, as Barry Bergdoll has written,

While neither Sullivan nor Wright read or understood German they were surrounded by people who did and who took an active interest in redefining the bases of architectural practice. In their own office in the Auditorium tower two of the principals were native Germans, Dankmar Adler and Paul Mueller, the young engineer from Stuttgart who later built many of Wright's most important designs. Sullivan, it should be remembered, had been exposed to German metaphysical philosophy already before joining Adler through his friend, the elusive John Edel-

man, who had spoken German since childhood and according to Sullivan's autobiography reinforced Sullivan's sympathy with American transcendentalist philosophy by long discourses on German Romantic philosophy. In addition the entire office seems to have been interested in Wagner's music, the Auditorium building itself resonant with overtones of the Germanic notion of the Gesamt-kunstwerk *and the possibility of dramatic art to lift the spectator to a higher realm of awareness.*[1]

Bergdoll proceeds to show that the influence of the German theorist Gottfried Semper on late nineteenth-century Chicago architecture was as intense as it was diffuse. It entered the architectural discourse from different quarters and was thus subject to varied interpretations. Two architects in particular seem to have been largely responsible for the dissemination of Semper's views. These were the German émigré Frederick Baumann and the American John Wellborn Root.

Baumann would contribute to the development of the Chicago School in different ways. In the first place, he would establish himself as a technician through his formula for constructing isolated pier foundations made available in his pamphlet of 1873, *The Art of Preparing Foundations for All Kinds of Buildings with Particular Illustration of the Method of Isolated Piers.* In the second place, he would play a major public role in the interpretation of German architectural theory in translating Friedrich Adler's *Schinkelfest* address of 1869 and in paraphrasing Semper's theories, the latter in his address "Thoughts on Architecture" presented to the American Institute of Architects convention in 1890 and his lecture "Thoughts on Style" delivered to the AIA convention in 1892. As Roula Geraniotis has remarked:

The reasons why Baumann was so impressed by Semper are obvious: Semper was a profound thinker and a keen architectural critic, who had enjoyed a brilliant career as a designing architect. It is important to note that Semper's influence had reached Baumann directly through one of his former students; from 1869 to 1874 the foreman at the architectural office of Frederick Baumann and Eduard Baumann in Chicago was Carl Maximilian Heinz, who had studied architecture under Gottfried Semper at the Eidgenössisches Polytechnikum (today's ETH) in Zurich. It is known that Semper was literally adored by his students and there is no doubt that Baumann shared fully the fascination that the young Heinz had felt for his master.[2]

Baumann was not the sole figure to introduce Semper to the Chicago architectural scene. In late 1889 and again early in 1890, *Inland Architecture* published John Wellborn Root's translation of Semper's 1869 essay "Über Baustyle." The closeness of theory and practice at this moment is borne out by the fact that Root made the translation in collaboration with his friend, the German émigré Fritz Wagner, who happened to be an architect specializing in terra-cotta facing. It would be hard to imagine more appropriate translators, since terra-cotta was a Semperian material par excellence and it was exactly this material that Root would use in cladding his steel-framed Rand McNally Building, completed in 1890[3] (not to mention Sullivan's acknowledged mastery over this material).

Two aspects of Semper's theory were of special importance for Baumann and for the development of the Chicago School in all its subsequent manifestations: first, Semper's insistence that the archetypal origin of all built form was textile production, with the knot serving as the primordial joint, and second, his contention that the art of building is anthropologically indebted to the applied arts for many of its motifs.[4] These hypotheses led to Semper's theory of *Bekleidung,* wherein clothing is seen as extending itself across time into forms of large-scale enclosure. For Semper, screenlike walls in permanent construction were reminiscent of tented nomadic textile form. As far as he was concerned terra-cotta facing and even brickwork were the tectonic transpositions of woven fabric. While neither Wright nor Sullivan made any reference to Semper, we have every reason to suppose that they were aware of his theory, given that Chicago was so impregnated with German cultural values and ideas. In any event, Sullivan would have heard Baumann's paper delivered to the Illinois State Association of Architects in 1887, wherein he paraphrased Semper's definition of style, namely that "style is the coincidence of a structure with the conditions of its origins."[5]

Among the more fertile encounters in the prehistory of the modern movement is the meeting of the Welshman Owen Jones with Semper's close associate, the young French architect Jules Goury. At the time of their encounter in Athens in 1831, Goury had already traveled with Semper for over a year, the object of their tour being to study the polychromatic decoration in Greek architecture. This concern for documenting aboriginal ornamentation later led Jones and Goury to make a similar study of the Alhambra, their joint results being published in two volumes in 1836 and 1865 under the title *Plans, Elevations, Sections and Details of the Alhambra.*

Following Victor Hugo, Jones and Goury saw the Alhambra as a "palace that the genies have gilded like a dream filled with harmony," and their documentation of this complex helped to further the vision of an exotic heterotopia that ran as a promise of cultural redemption throughout the rest of the century.[6] Jones, Sullivan, and Wright, all anti-establishment figures of Celtic origin, followed each other in this search for an "other" culture with which to overcome the spiritual bankruptcy of the eclectic battle of styles. Jones's *Grammar of Ornament,* published in 1856, served as a polemical guide for the pursuit of this transcultural overcoming; its colonialist sweep through the world of ornament demonstrated by implication the relative inferiority of the European, Greco-Roman-medieval legacy compared to the riches of the Orient, the former being represented by insipid, palely tinted plates, compared to the multicolored illustrations featuring exotic oriental or savage ornament. Over two-thirds of *The Grammar of Ornament* was devoted to these relatively remote cultures, and the plates depicting such ornamental systems were beautifully printed in chromolithography at considerable expense (figs. 4.1, 4.2). Jones's magnum opus led almost directly to Sullivan's own polychromatic ornament—to his richly colored incantatory decor, abstracted from natural form and pattern, that was already fully elaborated by the time of his Chicago Stock Exchange interior of 1894. This efflorescent enrichment reached its apotheosis in the midwestern banks that he designed toward the end of his career between 1906 and 1919. It is significant that almost all of these buildings were faced in rough-cut, tinted, pressed brick, a material that Sullivan regarded as a kind of textile. Thus he wrote in 1910:

Manufacturers, by grinding the clay or shale course and by the use of cutting wires, produced on its face a new and most interesting texture, a texture with a nap-like effect, suggesting somewhat an Anatolian rug. . . . When [tinted bricks are] laid up promiscuously, especially if the surface is large and care is taken to

4.1
Owen Jones, Islamic ornament, plate from
The Grammar of Ornament, 1856.

4.2
Owen Jones, Celtic ornament, plate from *The
Grammar of Ornament.*

avoid patches of any one color, the general tone suggests that of a very old Oriental rug.[7]

Wright made exactly the same analogy when writing about his textile block system in 1927: "A building for the first time may be lightly fabricated, complete, of mono-material—literally woven into a pattern or design as was the oriental rug."[8] This textile metaphor was present in Wright's thought almost from the beginning; certainly it is already there in his second address to the Architectural League of Chicago delivered in June 1900, entitled simply "The Architect."

Sullivan first came across the work of Jones through the Philadelphia architect Frank Furness. Furness had been influenced by Jones in part through *The Grammar of Ornament,* which he seems to have read first in French translation, and in part through contact with Jacob Gray Mould, who had been apprenticed to Jones.[9] Furness evolved an orientalized Gothicism that was certainly as evocative of Moorish culture as the Alhambresque villas that Jones himself had realized in Kensington Palace Gardens, London, in the late 1840s. Sullivan entered into Furness's employ in 1873 at exactly the moment when the latter's orientalized neo-Gothic attained its maturity in his design for the Pennsylvania Academy of Fine Arts (fig. 4.3). While Sullivan unquestionably used sources other than Jones's *Grammar* as the model and the method for his own ornament, above all his assiduous study of botanical form as this appears in Asa Gray's *Botany,*[10] there is little doubt that many of Sullivan's philosophical ideas find their origin in the various scholarly glosses that accompanied Jones's compendium. Among these one may cite Jones's own recognition of the cultural exhaustion of the West, condemned to the eternal repetition of the same depleted syntax, and his insistence that we need to return to nature as the Egyptians and the Greeks did rather than in the manner adopted by the Chinese and the

Goths.[11] We may also note that passage in Jones's introduction where he follows Semper in insisting on the primacy of tectonic form and urging that one decorate construction rather than construct decoration, a principle that Sullivan did not always adhere to.[12] *The Grammar of Ornament* also contains J. O. Westwood's suggestion that Celtic art had its origin in the East, from which it may have been brought back by Irish missionaries; an incidental fact that must have been extremely stimulating to Sullivan's imagination, given his Irish background.[13] In a chapter dealing with the derivation of ornament from nature, Jones lays out the essence of Sullivan's own ornamental program:

We think it impossible that a student fully impressed with the law of the universal fitness of things in nature, with the wonderful variety of form, yet all arranged around some few fixed laws, the proportionate distributions of areas, the tangential curvature of lines, and the radiation from the parent stem, whatever type he may borrow from nature, if he will dismiss from his mind the desire to imitate it, but will only seek to follow still the path which it so plainly shows him, we doubt

4.3
Frank Furness, Pennsylvania Academy of
Fine Arts, Philadelphia, 1871–1876. Elevation.

4.4
Louis Sullivan, plate from *A System of Architectural Ornament According with a Philosophy of Man's Power,* 1924.

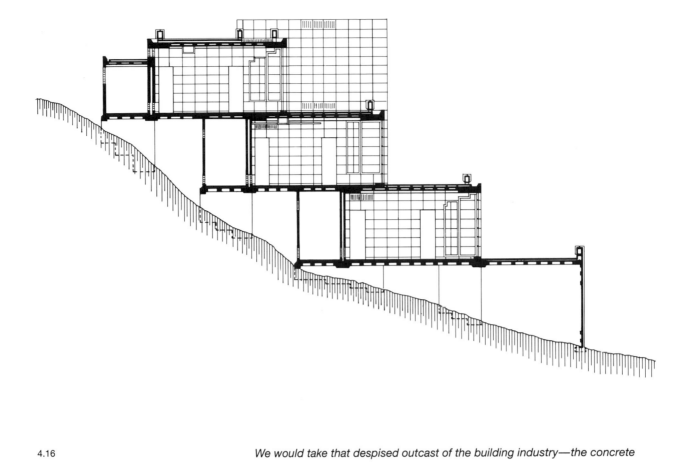

4.16
Frank Lloyd Wright, Alice Millard house, "La Miniatura," Pasadena, California, 1923.

4.17
Frank Lloyd Wright, patent double-wall, light-weight block system.

4.18
Frank Lloyd Wright, San Marcos in the Desert, near Chandler, Arizona, 1927. Section.

We would take that despised outcast of the building industry—the concrete block—out from underfoot or from the gutter—find a hitherto unsuspected soul in it—make it live as a thing of beauty—textured like the trees. Yes, the building would be made of the "blocks" as a kind of tree itself standing at home among the other trees in its own native land. All we would have to do would be to educate the concrete block, refine it and knit it together with steel in the joints and so construct the joints that they could be poured full of concrete after they were set up and a steel strand laid in them. The walls would thus become thin but solid reinforced slabs and yield to any desire for form imaginable. And common labor could do it all. We would make the walls double of course, one wall facing inside and the other wall facing outside, thus getting continuous hollow spaces between, so the house would be cool in summer, warm in winter and dry always [fig. 4.17].[31]

Immediately after this passage Wright referred to himself as the "weaver," thereby stressing, once again, his conception of the textile block as an all-enveloping woven membrane. In practice he suppressed at every turn those latent "unwoven" structural members that contributed to its equilibrium; that is to say, those reinforced concrete beams and columns that were essential to the overall stability of these tessellated walls. This discreet suppression is emphasized by the fact that in almost all of the concrete block houses the floor depths do not coincide with the modular dimension of the system. This displacement is very clear in the Xanadu-like project for San Marcos in the Desert, where the actual floor slab is evidently shallower than the block depth (fig. 4.18).

With its patterned, perforated, glass-filled apertures, La Miniatura already embodied the essential syntax of the textile block system that was employed, with

109

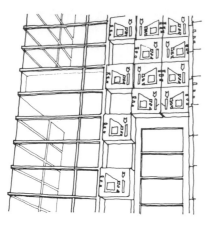

4.19
Frank Lloyd Wright, Samuel Freeman House,
Los Angeles, 1924. Sketch of corner.

4.20
Frank Lloyd Wright, National Life Insurance
Offices, Chicago, 1920–1925.

subtle variations, in each of the subsequent block houses. With the exception of the Freeman House, Los Angeles, of 1924, where the textile blocks run into open glass corners and where the muntins seem to extend directly from the joints between the blocks (fig. 4.19), Wright's later California block houses, the Ennis and Storer houses, add little to the basic syntax of La Miniatura. The full potential of this singular innovation, the extension, that is, of a tessellated semi-solid membrane into a mitered glass corner, comes into its own with Wright's National Life Insurance Offices, projected for Chicago in 1924, informally dedicated to Sullivan in the year of his demise (fig. 4.20). Conceived nearly thirty years after Wright's Luxfer Prism office project of 1895 but only seven years after Willis Polk had achieved the Hallidie Building, San Francisco, as the first curtain-walled, high-rise structure in the world, Wright elaborated this thirty-one-story skyscraper slab as a woven glass and sheet metal fabric suspended from a concrete core. The exceptional brilliance of this particular synthesis is made clear in Wright's description of 1928.

The exterior walls, as such, disappear—instead are suspended, standardized sheet-copper screens. The walls themselves cease to exist as either weight or thickness. Windows become in this fabrication a matter of a unit in the screen fabric, opening singly or in groups at the will of the occupant. All windows may be cleaned from the inside with neither bother nor risk. The vertical mullions (copper shells filled with non-conducting material), are large and strong enough only to carry from floor to floor and project much or little as shadow on the glass may or may not be wanted. Much projection enriches the shadow. Less projection dispels the shadows and brightens the interior. These protecting blades of copper act in the sun like the blades of a blind.

The unit of two feet both ways is, in this instance, emphasized on every alternate vertical with additional emphasis on every fifth. There is no emphasis on the horizontal units. The edge of the various floors being beveled to the same section as is used between the windows, it appears in the screen as such horizontal division occurring naturally on the two-foot unit lines.

. . . Being likewise fabricated on a perfect unit system, the interior partitions may all be made up in sections, complete with doors, ready to set in place and designed to match the general style of the outer wall screen. These interior partition-units thus fabricated may be stored ready to use, and any changes to suit tenants made over night with no waste of time and material.

The increase of glass area over the usual skyscraper fenestration is only about ten per cent (the margin could be increased or diminished by expanding or contracting the copper members in which it is set), so the expense of heating is not materially increased. Inasmuch as the copper mullions are filled with insulating material and the window openings are tight, being mechanical units in a mechanical screen, this excess of glass is compensated.

The radiators are cast as a railing set in front of the lower glass unit of this outer screen wall, free enough to make cleaning easy.[32]

This entire project can be seen in retrospect as a projection at a mammoth scale of the 1897 patent for the Luxfer Prism electro-glazing process as devised by W. H. Winslow, wherein four-by-four-inch glass lenses, interlaced in two directions with copper filaments, could be fused into glazed panels suitable for the construction of clerestories and roof lights. It is interesting to note that Wright would receive forty-one design patents for decorative patterns to be cast into the Luxfer Prism lenses. Far from this scale, Wright would conceive of the concrete treelike superstructure of his National Life Insurance project as supporting its crystalline envelope in two different ways, first as a composite cantilever about a single support line (fig. 4.21) and second as an independent twin-stem column system, supporting symmetrically cantilevered floors that are linked by a slab of shallower depth spanning between the points of contraflexure (fig. 4.22). In this work Wright moves toward a particularly dense synthesis of ontological and representational tectonic form. The essential continuity and articulation of Wright's late masterwork, his S. C. Johnson Administration Building of 1936, is already anticipated in this dramatic combination of structural and membranous form (fig. 4.23).

As M. F. Hearn has suggested, the National Life Insurance project was particularly significant for the way in which it extended Wright's debt to the Orient to a

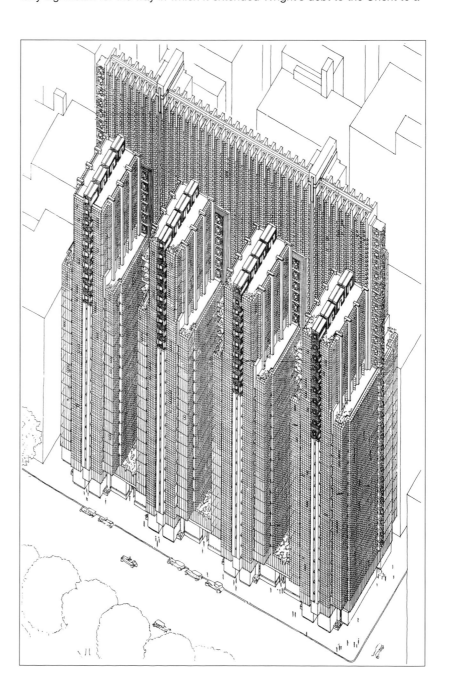

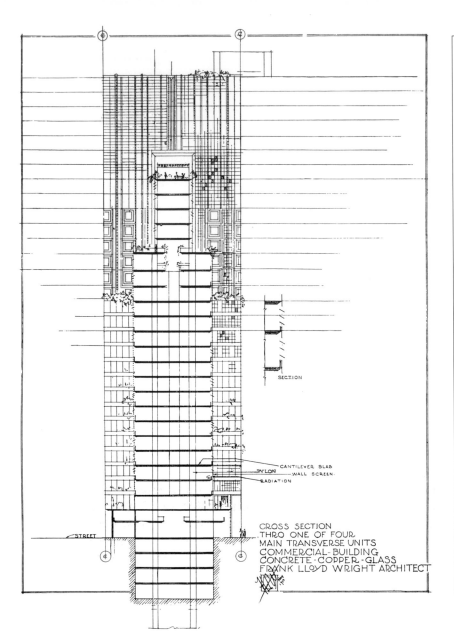

CROSS SECTION
THRO ONE OF FOUR
MAIN TRANSVERSE UNITS
COMMERCIAL·BUILDING
CONCRETE·COPPER·GLASS
FRANK LLOYD WRIGHT ARCHITECT

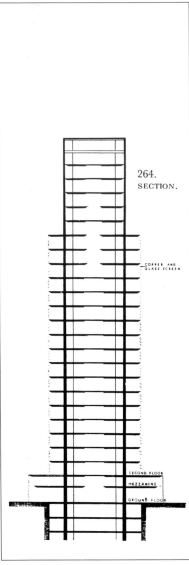

264.
SECTION.

4.21
Frank Lloyd Wright, National Life Insurance
Offices, section.

4.22
Frank Lloyd Wright, National Life Insurance
Offices, section.

4.23
Frank Lloyd Wright, Johnson Wax Administration Building, Racine, 1936–1939. Typical column section.

more structural level. After noting that Wright's previous skyscraper proposal—the twenty-story 1912 San Francisco Call Tower—had been predicated on what by then was already a fairly conventional reinforced concrete frame, Hearn goes on to suggest an oriental prototype for the treelike, high-rise form that he would adopt twelve years later.

Although the Imperial Hotel deeply involved Wright in concern about structural earthquake-proofness, the scheme for that project was unrelated to the one for the insurance company, except that they both employed the cantilever principle. Indeed, the basic idea for each seems to have been transported in different directions across the Pacific Ocean to the opposite shore: the inspiration for the "pincushion" of concrete posts that was poured into the swampy mud in order to ground the foundation platform of the hotel, heretofore not attributed, can be identified in the writings of Wright's hero in architectural theory, Viollet-le-Duc; conversely, the rigid-core skyscraper seems to have been inspired by an indigenous Japanese structure.

As is well known, Wright had espoused a special interest in and regard for the architecture of Japan since seeing the Ho-o-den at the Columbian Exposition in Chicago in 1893. There can be no doubt that, during the years when he resided primarily in Japan (1917–1922), while working on the Imperial Hotel, he was both interested and attentive when he had the opportunity to see something new to him in Japanese architecture. (He acknowledged, for instance, that he got the idea for the heated floors of his Usonian houses from Baron Okuda's "Korean room," with its warm-air ducts beneath the floor.) Therefore, when the occasion for an excursion to major sites of Japanese religious architecture arose, he would certainly have welcomed it. One of the most likely candidates for such an experience would have been the oldest sanctuary in Japan, the Horyu-ji shrine near Nara, preserved from the seventh and eighth centuries. Waiting there for Wright's attention was a feature in the pagoda that had been consciously adopted from China to help the tower withstand the shock of earthquakes: a rigid central member, or "heart pillar," acting as a mast.[33]

The wheel comes full circle when one learns that the pagoda has its ultimate origin in the Indian stupa, the central spine of which was seen as an *axis mundi* or cosmic pillar, identified in Buddhist philosophy as the Tree of Enlightenment.[34] In confirmation of this origin Wright would go on to project his 1946 research tower for Johnson Wax as a "pagoda," complete with a concrete core and cantilevered floors.

Wright's last purpose-made concrete block house, built in 1929 in Tulsa, Oklahoma, for his cousin Richard Lloyd Jones, already appears as a transitional work, since here the hitherto finely woven fabric of the textile block is abandoned in favor of a larger block formation, laid up as piers (figs. 4.24, 4.25). Wright's unrealizable Egyptoid ideal of elevations without windows[35] is relinquished here in favor of an alternating pattern of piers and slots that is as solid as it is void (fig. 4.26). This passage from the sixteen-inch-square block pattern of the Freeman House to the fifteen-by-twenty-inch plain-faced, stack-bonded block pattern of the Lloyd Jones House produces a paradoxical decrease in the apparent mass; the true scale being lost through the suppression of floor heights.[36] Apart from permitting a consistent alignment between block courses and window transoms, the larger block has many advantages, from the saving of labor in laying to the filling of the hollow cores with cement and steel rods to

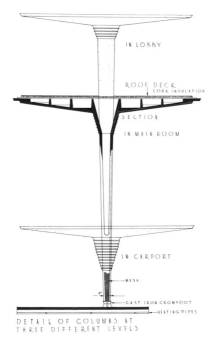

IN LOBBY

ROOF DECK
CORK INSULATION

SECTION

IN MAIN ROOM

IN CARPORT

MESH

CAST IRON CROWFOOT
HEATING PIPES

DETAIL OF COLUMNS AT
THREE DIFFERENT LEVELS

produce an integrated reinforced concrete pier, or the use of similar voids for the purpose of ventilation and other services.

Wright's return to his midwestern roots led to the final phase of his textile tectonic, the self-styled Usonian house that endured in his work as a continuous type right up to his death in 1959. The brick and timber Usonian house emerged as a type in the Malcolm Willey House projected for Minneapolis in 1932, a prototype that was built in modified form two years later. That Wright was aware of the breakthrough that this work represented is borne out by the following passages written in the same year:

Now came clear an entirely new sense of architecture, a higher conception of architecture . . . space enclosed. . . . This interior conception took architecture away from sculpture, away from painting and entirely away from architecture as it had been known in the antique. The building now became a creation of interior space in light. And as this sense of the interior space as the reality of the building began to work, walls as walls fell away.[37]

While this is not the place to enter into the development of the Usonian house, it is nonetheless important to note that once again the prototype was conceived as having woven walls. Double-sided and triple-layered, these walls were of lightweight construction, with timber boards affixed to a continuous plywood core so as to produce horizontal recesses, as opposed to the projecting cover battens of Wright's Forest Style (fig. 4.27). Woven at more than one scale, the Usonian house was also conceived as a three-dimensional gridded cage in which two-foot-by-four-foot and four-foot-square horizontal modular units

4.24
Frank Lloyd Wright, Richard Lloyd Jones House, Tulsa, Oklahoma, 1929. Glazing detailing in block surround.

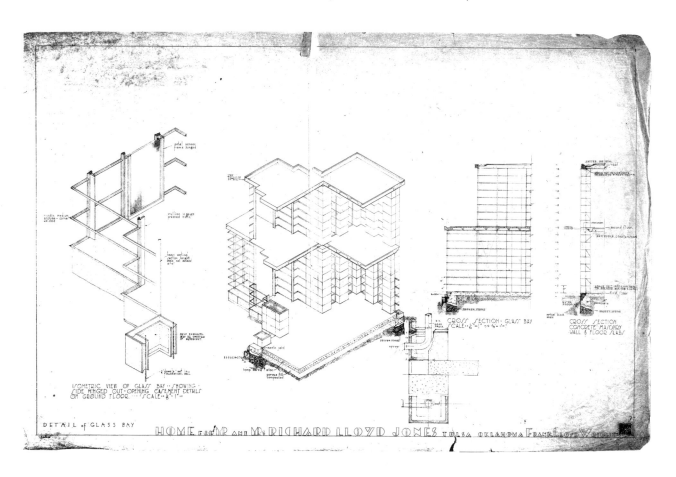

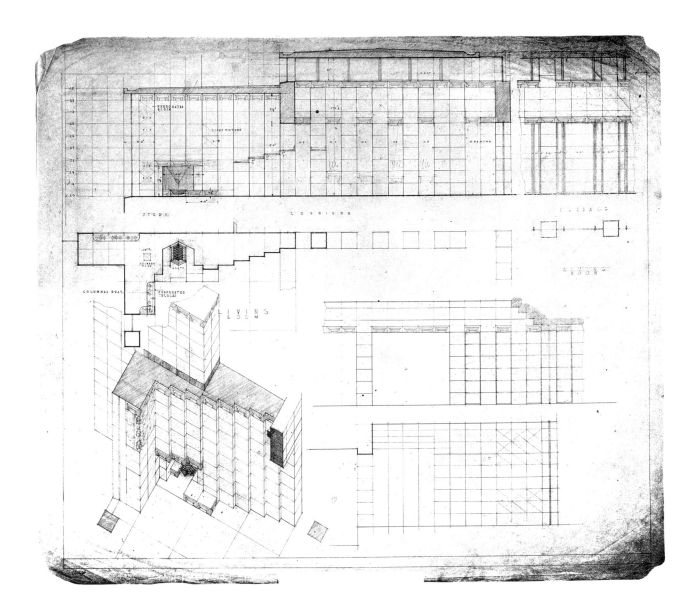

4.25
Frank Lloyd Wright, Richard Lloyd Jones
House, fireplace detail.

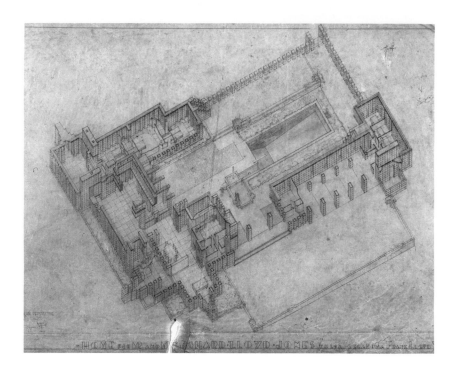

4.26
Frank Lloyd Wright, Richard Lloyd Jones House, axonometric.

4.27
Frank Lloyd Wright, Usonian house, typical wall section.

yielded spatial layers that were interwoven with a thirteen-inch vertical interval, governing the module of the horizontal recesses, window transoms, door heights, and built-in furniture. The walls were given a thick warp and woof in which, as Wright put it in the sixth point of his famous *Architectural Forum* manifesto of 1938, "furniture, pictures and bric-a-brac are unnecessary except as the walls can be made to include them or be them."[38] That the typical Usonian dwelling consisted of a three-dimensional matrix made up of interlocking locational fixes and layers is borne out by Wright's provision of three separate plan cuts; one at floor level, one at doorhead or clerestory height, and finally one at roof level. As John Sergeant remarked in his study of the Usonian house, Wright's millwork is interwoven here like basketry.[39]

As far as was feasible, Wright eliminated field labor and reduced wastage in the cutting of timber by adopting a module that corresponded with standard mill dimensions, for example the typical eight-by-four-foot sheet. At the same time, he attempted to exploit the thermal flywheel effect of the in situ concrete slab that tended in any event to be warmer in winter and cooler in summer than the average wooden floor. It is significant that Wright chose to identify this system with the gravity heating systems that he claimed he had first encountered in Japan in 1919. With serpentine, small-bore heating pipes cast into the slab, a typical Usonian dwelling, even when boosted with fire, would be comfortable in the winter rather than overheated, and Wright openly admitted that in severe weather people would simply have to put on more clothes. In high summer the ubiquitous clerestory window system provided ample cross ventilation as did the chimney flues, while the deep overhangs shielded the large areas of full glass from sun penetration in the middle of the day. Many liberative spatial sequences were built into the volume of a typical Usonian house, including ample continuous wall storage (the thick-wall concept), continuous seating, and the close physical and visual proximity of the kitchen to the dining/living area. In the canonical

Herbert Jacobs House, built in Madison, Wisconsin, in 1939, subtle zones of microspace are distributed throughout the house for every conceivable activity (fig. 4.28).

From the beginning Wright conceived of the Usonian system as a kit of parts that had to be assembled according to a particular sequence. His growing recognition of the socioeconomic need for many people to build their own house led him to standardize many of the details in the Usonian system, and these, quite naturally, were repeated with variations from one house to the next. Borrowing its sequence and method of assembly from traditional Japanese house construction, the typical Usonian dwelling was built in a particular order. At each of its stages, this sequence can be seen as incorporating one of Semper's four elements. One would first cast the floor slab and build the masonry chimney and thus arrive at the first two elements of Semper's primordial paradigm, the earthwork and the hearth. This was followed by the Semperian third element, the framework and the roof. The whole was then enclosed through the application of the screenlike fourth element, the infill wall or *Wand.*

Wright will resort to a similar textile metaphor in his master work of the mid-thirties, the S. C. Johnson Administration Building opened at Racine, Wisconsin, in 1939. In this instance the introspective, woven paradigm of the Larkin Building of 1904 will come to be overlaid, as it were, by a gossamer network of glass tubing (fig. 4.29); that is to say, by an interstitial element that will appear throughout as though it were a transformed refractory material, almost on the point of changing into the raked brickwork by which it was borne aloft as a kind of anti-cornice. We are once again close to Semper's *Stoffwechseltheorie,* as where glass is fused into copper sheet as in the National Life Insurance project or where "positive" muntins grow out of the "negative" mortar joints as in the Samuel Freeman house. Housed under a roof composed of 19-foot-diameter three-story-high mushroom columns tied together as a network, this mosquelike workroom, lit from above through tubular glass laylights, is a tectonic tour de force by any standard, as the following account by Jonathan Lipman makes clear.

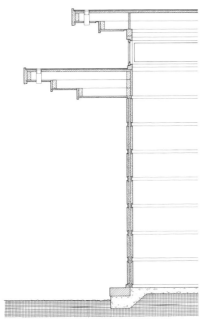

Wright called the columns "dendriform"—tree-shaped—and he borrowed from botany to name three of their four segments, stem, petal and calyx. The base of each column is a seven-inch-high, three-ribbed shoe, which he called a crow's foot. On it rests the shaft, or stem, nine inches wide at the bottom and widening two and a half degrees from the vertical axis. The taller columns are mostly hollow, the walls being only three and a half inches thick. Capping is a wider hollow, ringed band, which Wright referred to as a calyx. On the calyx sits a twelve-and-a-half-inch thick hollow pad Wright called a petal. Two radical concrete rings and continuous concrete struts run through it. Both stem and calyx are reinforced with expanded steel mesh, and the petal is reinforced with both mesh and bars.[40]

Once again, as in Wright's concrete block houses of the twenties, we are presented with the notion of steel rods literally binding the piece together. This concept of the building as a woven fabric is metaphorically reinforced in this instance by hollow glass tubing that in running around the perimeter of the building posits itself almost as the translucent counterthesis to the solid steel rods reinforcing the structure. As Wright was to put it:

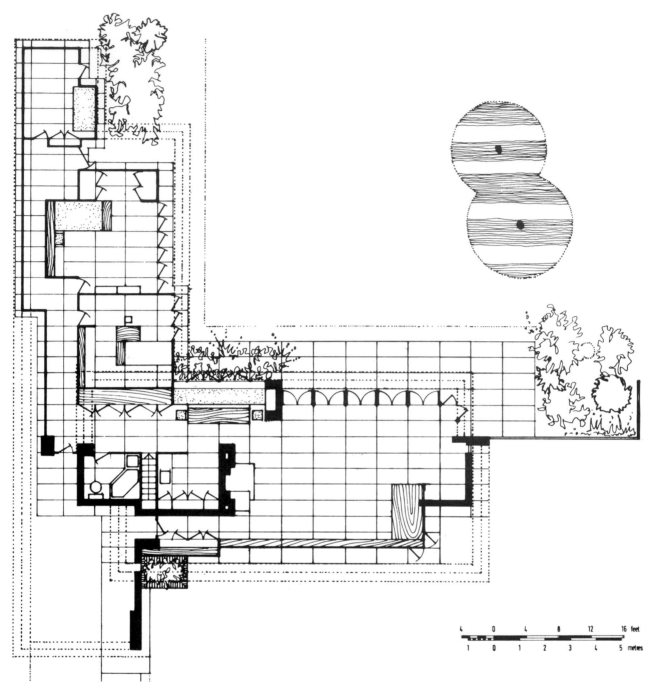

4.28
Frank Lloyd Wright, Herbert Jacobs House,
Madison, Wisconsin, 1936. Plan.

4.29
Frank Lloyd Wright, Johnson Wax Administration Building, glass tubing.

4.30
Frank Lloyd Wright, Johnson Wax Administration Building, prototypical solution to glass
block "anti-cornice"; eventually rejected in
favor of glass tubing.

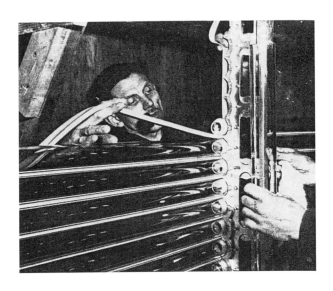

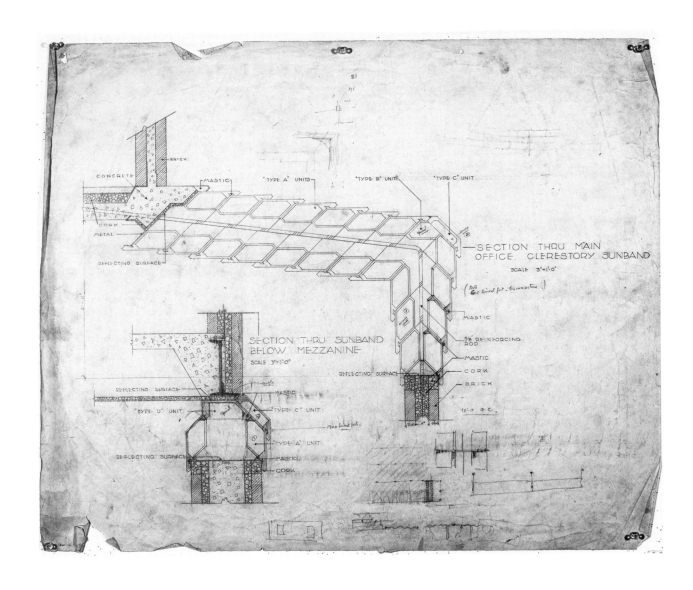

SECTION THRU MAIN
OFFICE CLERESTORY SUNBAND

SCALE 3"=1'-0"

SECTION THRU SUNBAND
BELOW MEZZANINE

SCALE 3"=1'-0"

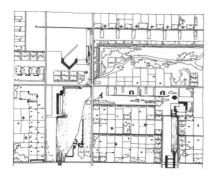

4.31
Frank Lloyd Wright, Broadacre City: sketch plan of the Civic Center surrounded by a "plaid" of farms and Usonian houses.

Glass tubing laid up like bricks in a wall composes all the lighting surfaces. Light enters the building where the cornice used to be. In the interior the box-like structure has vanished completely. The walls carrying the glass ribbing are of hard red brick and red Kasota sandstone. The entire fabric is reinforced concrete, cold-drawn mesh being used for the reinforcement.[41]

An earlier incarnation of this clerestory system assumed the form of interlocking hollow glass blocks that would have provided a more prominent translucent clerestory running around the top of the brick perimeter (fig. 4.30). As realized, the tubular glass hollow anti-cornice, artificially lit at night, effects a magical de-materialization in which solid material becomes void and vice versa, the work being illuminated at night by sweeping, streamlined bands of glowing glass and by equally radiant laylights woven out of the same Pyrex tube.

Apart from his masterworks dating from 1936, Fallingwater and the Johnson Wax Building, Wright's architecture, however structurally consequent, became increasingly arbitrary as the years wore on, even descending, at times, into self-parody bordering on kitsch. Here and there a particular commission, such as the Guggenheim Museum, New York, or the Beth Shalom Synagogue in Philadelphia, achieved a certain tectonic conviction. In the main, however, what remained of Wright's former New World vision was best expressed in the Usonian houses. This Usonian moment in Wright's long career reached its apotheosis during the New Deal in the decade 1934 to 1944, when he realized some twenty-five Usonian dwellings in the course of a decade. Built all over the country, these were not designed for a plutocracy but for an American exurban middle class to whom Wright's message had always been addressed. From the "Small House with Lots of Room in It" of 1901, designed for the *Ladies Home Journal*, to the canonical Herbert Jacobs House of 1936, the underlying liberal vision is always there. Along with the Usonian house went, in theory at least, a similar consciously cultivated and differentiated vision of society as had already been outlined in Peter Kropotkin's *Factories, Fields and Workshops* of 1898. The Usonian house, formulated by Wright when he was already sixty-three, is inseparable from the underlying thesis of his Broadacre City, first broached in his Kahn Lectures given at Princeton University in 1930 and subsequently published as a socioeconomic exurban polemic in *The Disappearing City* of 1932. Broadacre City and the Usonian house shared a similar hypothetical socioeconomic basis in Wright's idealized, egalitarian vision of an acre of ground being reserved for every citizen at birth. The two paradigms, Usonia and Broadacre, were mutually related, since the oversailing horizontal roofs and outriding walls of the typical house would have layered each dwelling into the horizontal land settlement pattern of Wright's motopian plan. Wright's Broadacre City, first exhibited in 1934 (fig. 4.31), may be seen in this light as his ultimate "oriental rug," that is to say as a transcultural, ecological tapestry writ large as an oriental paradise garden woven as a counterpoint to the Cartesian land grid of the North West Ordinance of 1785. This was the Wrightian textile tectonic literally projected over the face of the earth, evoking an Edenic condition in which culture and agriculture would once again be one and the same.

5   Auguste Perret
and Classical Rationalism

The French tradition . . . was based on the correspondence between classical rules and building practice, and through this correspondence they became so automatic as to pass for natural laws. Perret, steeped in this tradition, was naturally led to identify concrete framework (which was a fact of construction) with the framework as it was to appear on the outside of the building, and to transfer to the first the needs and associations of the second. Hence the desire for symmetry and the continued suggestion of the architectural orders, if not as formal presences, at least as terms of comparison. . . . He probably believed that he had discovered the constructional system best suited to the realization of traditional works, since the unity of its elements was real and not apparent, as in the classical orders composed of several blocks of hewn stone. . . . Perret's faith in the universal rules of architecture, although unfounded in our eyes, cannot be discounted as a mere personal quirk, and must be considered within its historical framework. The association between Classicism and the science of building was all the more tenacious in that, after losing its ideological bases in the second half of the eighteenth century, it had been limited to the practical and organizational sphere; the form of the calculations and the habits of the building site still largely reflected the old parallelism, and even the normal terminology used with regard to reinforced concrete—pillar, plinth, architrave, corbel, portal, span—was that of the classical orders.

A whole century of experiment had approved and reinforced this convention from which all advances in modern engineering were born. Perret lived in the midst of it, he was the heir of Durand, of Labrouste, Dutert, Eiffel; his particular merit was to have sensed that this glorious tradition, impoverished by eclecticism, still had a margin of unexplored possibilities to help resolve the problem of our time, and to have developed these possibilities courageously. In doing this, however, he ruined the last chances of structural classicism, and revealed definitively that the path ended in an impasse, because the initial premises were rooted in an outdated mode of thought.

Leonardo Benevolo, Storia dell'architettura moderna, *1960*

As we may judge from the title of the only study of Auguste Perret (1874–1954) in English, *Concrete: The Vision of a New Architecture* published by Peter Collins in 1959, Perret's architectural career was inextricably bound up with the articulation of reinforced concrete frame construction, as though it were the ultimate structural demiurge of the century. While *béton armé* was an unprecedented technique, concrete as such was not, since its use dated from the Roman deployment of *opus caementicum* in foundation work and in the hearting of stone walls. More importantly, plain concrete, combined with brick casing, was used by the Romans to create vaults of considerable span such as the 145-foot-diameter dome of the Pantheon in Rome. Unlike Gothic buildings, such spans depended upon the strength of the monolithic shell itself, rather than on the thrust and counterthrust of arch and buttress. However, with Louis Vicat's perfection of hydraulic cement around 1800, concrete began to be used in a new way, and this led, through the French tradition of constructing low buildings out of rammed earth or *pisé,* to the idea of casting one-off small concrete forms in timber molds, as in Joseph Monier's prefabricated, wire-reinforced flower pots and sewer pipes, put into regular production around 1850. The subsequent Wayss and Freytag monopoly over the Monier system, the patent of which they purchased from him in 1884, did not, in the long run, prevent the French from maintaining their lead in the field, which became decisive with François Hennebique's perfection of reinforced concrete construction in 1897 (fig. 5.1).

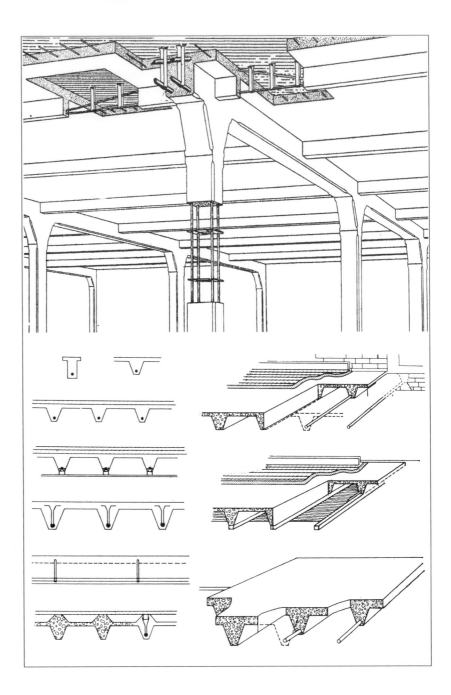

Significantly enough, the contractor Hennebique was to start his building career
as a restorer of Gothic structures, during which time he acquired considerable
archaeological knowledge. In 1880, however, Hennebique familiarized himself
with reinforced concrete in an effort to devise more economical systems of fireproof flooring, made of concrete and steel. It is characteristic of his methodical
and cautious approach that he did not patent his various fireproof concrete
flooring methods until 1892. His real breakthrough, however, came five years
later, with his patent use of iron stirrups for their capacity to resist shear stress
on reinforced concrete beams. Hennebique was to propagate his reinforced concrete system by training contractors in its application under license. Such was
the status of this new technique that to be certified as an "Hennebique con-

tractor" was a mark of great prestige. This is the grounds on which Perret's contractor-father, Claude-Marie Perret, was persuaded, at the urging of his son, to employ the Hennebique system for the framing out of the apartments built at 25 bis rue Franklin, Paris.[1]

Perret's career has its origin in two antithetical experiences: the stimulating and challenging reality of his father's building business and the privileged education that he received in the Ecole des Beaux-Arts, above all from his theory teacher Julien Guadet, whose encyclopedic *Eléments et théories de l'architecture* was published in 1902.[2] This age-old opposition between practice and theory in architectural education was to be decided quite precipitously in Perret's case in favor of practice, for while he dutifully entered the Ecole des Beaux-Arts in 1891 and gained seven *médailles* and the Prix des Architectes Américains during his course of study there, he left abruptly in 1897 without submitting a project for his final diploma.

For Perret, reinforced concrete was the perfect homogeneous system with which to reconcile the two-hundred-year-old schism lying at the very heart of the Greco-Gothic ideal, that is to say, to combine the asperities of Platonic form with the tectonic expressivity of structural rationalism. Three seminal buildings testify to Perret's synthetic approach, as he passes from a brilliant adaptation of the precepts of Viollet-le-Duc to the more idealized forms of classicized rationalism in which he would, nonetheless, remain committed to the primacy of the frame. The three buildings in succession are the Casino at St.-Malo (1899), an apartment block at 25 bis rue Franklin, Paris (1903), and a four-story parking garage completed in the rue Ponthieu, Paris, in 1905.

The general availability of reinforced concrete as a universal technique, which came into being with Paul Christophe's *Le Béton armé et ses applications* of 1902, serves to separate the first of these buildings from the other two, since the casino was built from load-bearing stonework and a timber superstructure. Perret's adoption of reinforced concrete as the primary if not the sole material of his practice would distance him from the more articulate constructed modes of structural rationalism advocated by Viollet-le-Duc. Like Frank Lloyd Wright, who attempted fair-faced, reinforced concrete construction at virtually the same time, Perret knew that this material did not lend itself to the poetic manifestation of construction as an articulate syntax. Nor could its mode of resisting gravity be made precisely expressive, at least not in the Greco-Gothic approach of Perret, who, save for utilitarian work, always chose to dispense with the typical haunched beam of the Hennebique frame, preferring to express his trabeated joints as having a uniform section throughout. This architectonic repression of the moment of maximum stress appeared even when Hennebique himself acted as consultant, as in the rue Franklin apartment; such a formal choice, made surely at the behest of the architect, seems all the more ironic given Hennebique's personal taste for an orientalized Gothic, as is evident from his own house completed in Bourg-la-Reine in 1904, where the haunched brackets of the cantilevered roofs, terraces, and balconies are fairly prominent, as are the fretted precast concrete balconies and the water tower minaret (fig. 5.2).

Where Perret's St.-Malo casino remains a structural rationalist exercise in a manner uncannily close to the work of his American contemporary Frank Furness, 25 bis rue Franklin is a polemical celebration of the reinforced concrete frame,

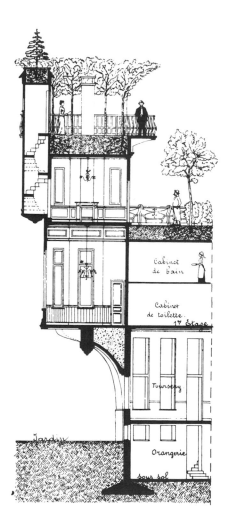

5.2
François Hennebique, his own house in Bourg-la-Reine, 1904. Section.

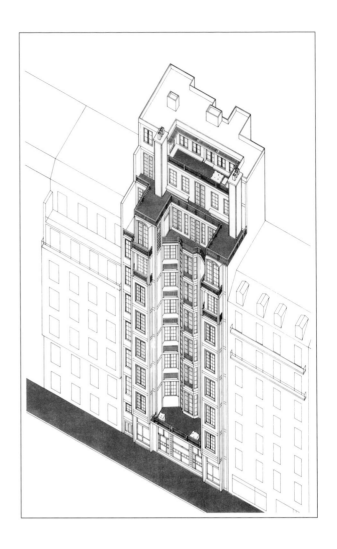

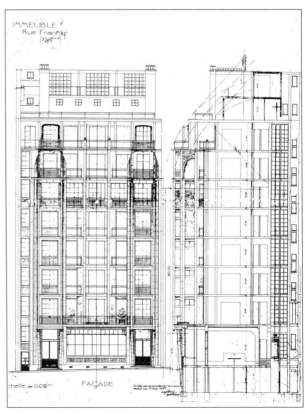

124

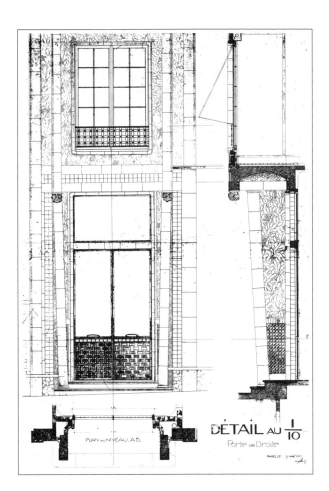

5.3
Auguste Perret, 25 bis rue Franklin, Paris,
1902–1903. Axonometric.

5.4
Auguste Perret, 25 bis rue Franklin, elevation
and sectional setback in relation to 1903 by-
law limits.

5.5
Auguste Perret, 25 bis rue Franklin, sunflower
ceramic infill and terra-cotta cladding to the
framework. Note the carpentry-like boss applied to the cantilever.

for here the frame is *seen* in its entirety, much like a traditional half-timbered skeleton, rather than being masked under an overriding stone revetment, as was the standard practice of the period (figs. 5.3, 5.4). Apart from the elimination of the haunch, the frame itself is directly expressed as an assertion of the basic structure, particularly since a distinction between frame and infill is maintained throughout. However, concrete as such is not apparent since the skeleton is faced throughout with Alexandre Bigot's patent ceramic tiles. Given that this revetment discriminates between frame and infill (fig. 5.5), we may say that the overall expression is representational not only because of the articulation of the frame but also because of a certain referential ambiguity in its detailing. I am alluding to the decorative newels that terminate the vertical members of the cantilevered bays at the first floor. The carpentry look of these elements encourages a reading of the frame as though it were made out of wood, an analogical treatment that surely derived in some measure from Auguste Choisy's *Histoire de l'architecture* of 1899. We need to remark here on Choisy's subscription to the theory that the classical Greek entablature was a transposition of archaic temple prototypes in timber, the skeletonal form being retained in order to sustain symbolic continuity (see fig. 2.31).[3] This, together with similar theories advanced by Guadet, is surely the fundamental basis of Perret's lifelong obsession with the expression of the skeleton or *charpente*. As he was to put it in his *Contribution à une théorie de l'architecture* of 1952: "In the beginning architecture is only

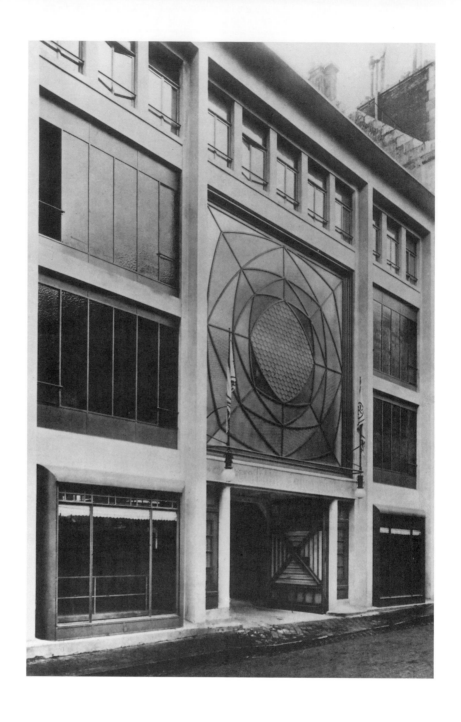

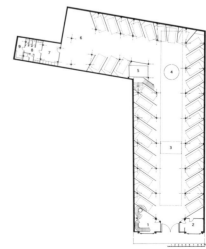

5.6
Auguste Perret, Garage Marboeuf, front facade.

5.7
Auguste Perret, Garage Marboeuf, 51 rue Ponthieu, Paris, 1905. Ground-floor plan.

wooden framework. In order to overcome fire one builds in hard material. And the prestige of the wooden frame is such that one reproduces all the traits, including the heads of the nails."[4] Perret's stress on the *charpente* evokes the same high status accorded to the carpenter or *tekton* as in the antique Greek world.

In spite of the symmetry of its plan, one can hardly interpret 25 bis rue Franklin as a crypto-classical work, for as we have already seen the building would appear to be more Gothic in its affinities than Greek. However, Perret will soon change his attitude in this regard with the rue Ponthieu garage, built by the newly constituted firm of Perret Frères in 1905 (figs. 5.6, 5.7). In this work, the exposed concrete frame is manipulated in such a way as to allude to traditional classical elements; above all, the giant order implied by the two projecting piers situated on either side of the central aisle and the fourth-floor attic clerestory, which, together with its rudimentary projecting cornice, appears to be a conscious simulation of a classical entablature. This Greek feeling is mediated by the neo-Gothic, proto–Art Deco "rose window" that fills the spandrel of the central nave. On balance, however, despite the utilitarian character of the aisles, dedicated to the storage of automobiles, the work makes an overall allusion to the French classical tradition. Peter Collins's acute analysis of the facade tends to confirm this affinity.

The wider spacing of the central bay, the sharp projection of the principal columns, the quickened rhythm of the topmost story and the variations in the depths of beams, have all been introduced or exploited as deliberate aesthetic devices for producing contrasting proportions of a calculated emotional value, whilst the entasis of the main columns and the method of joining the beams to them with intermediate frames or alettes *betokened a regard for the finer subtleties of trabeated articulation seldom seen since the* ancien régime.[5]

Despite the exposed fair-faced concrete and the direct presence of the frame itself, the facade is tectonically manipulated. We need look no further for this than to the orthogonal form of exterior trabeation, as opposed to the haunched column supports carrying the beams of the reinforced concrete skeleton within (fig. 5.8). We may note here that Perret, like Schinkel, introduced hierarchical in-

5.8
Auguste Perret, Garage Marboeuf, interior.
Note the haunched beam-column junctions.

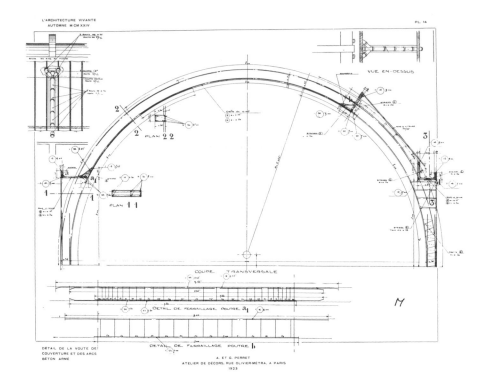

VUE EN-DESSUS

PLAN 2 2

PLAN 1 1

COUPE TRANSVERSALE

DÉTAIL DE FERRAILLAGE POUTRE

DÉTAIL DE FERRAILLAGE POUTRE

DÉTAIL DE LA VOUTE DE
COUVERTURE ET DES ARCS
BÉTON ARMÉ

A. ET G. PERRET
ATELIER DE DÉCORS, RUE OLIVIER-MÉTRA, A PARIS
1923

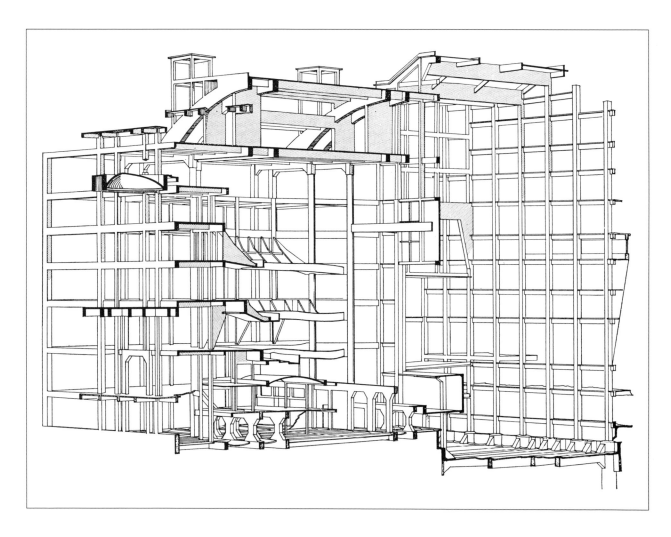

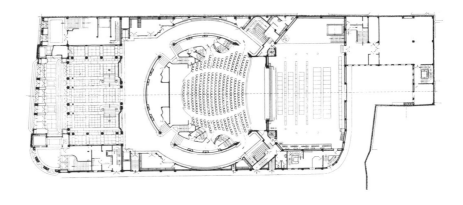

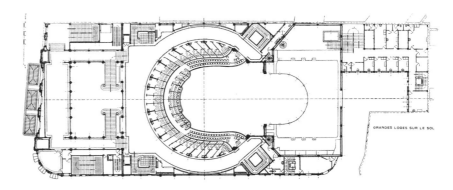

5.9
Auguste Perret, scene painting studios, rue
Olivier-Métra, Paris, 1923. Section.

5.10
Auguste Perret, Théâtre des Champs-
Elysées, axonometric.

5.11
Auguste Perret, Théâtre des Champs-
Elysées, ground floor.

5.12
Auguste Perret, Théâtre des Champs-
Elysées, Paris, 1911–1913. Mezzanine level.

flections into his work that varied with the sociocultural status of the institution,
this declension at times extending to different parts of the same structure. Thus,
in the rue Ponthieu garage, the industrial sash glazing, filled with obscured
glass, expresses the utilitarian nature of the galleries on either side of the central
aisle, while the rose window, held in place by glazing bars of virtually the same
section, represents the honorific space of public appearance; that is to say, the
opening through which both pedestrians and automobiles appear. One should
note that this kind of differentiation stands in strong contrast to the solely utilitarian work of the firm, where reinforced concrete frames or vaults were simply
expressed as such and hence struck straight from timber formwork, as in the
vaulted single-story warehouses built at Casablanca in 1915 or the scene
painting studio erected in the rue Olivier-Métra, Paris, in 1923 (fig. 5.9). The rue
Ponthieu is a transitional work in which Perret's struggle to find a satisfactory
expression for a building of this type is suggested by an alternative crypto–Art
Nouveau facade, where the main concrete piers are flanked with brick *alettes*
and where the spandrels are filled with hexagonal glass blocks, similar in kind to
those used by Perret on the rear of the rue Franklin apartment.

Perret's structurally classicist mode is further elaborated in the ABABA Palladian
parti adopted for the entrance foyer of the Théâtre des Champs-Elysées,
completed in the Avenue Montaigne, Paris, at the end of 1913.[6] This rhythm is
extended into the plan in depth, inasmuch as four pairs of columns are used to
support the bowstring trusses carrying the roof (fig. 5.10). These columns also
serve to carry a series of circumferential galleries opening onto the circular void
of the main auditorium (figs. 5.11, 5.12, 5.13). Within the foyer itself, this ABABA

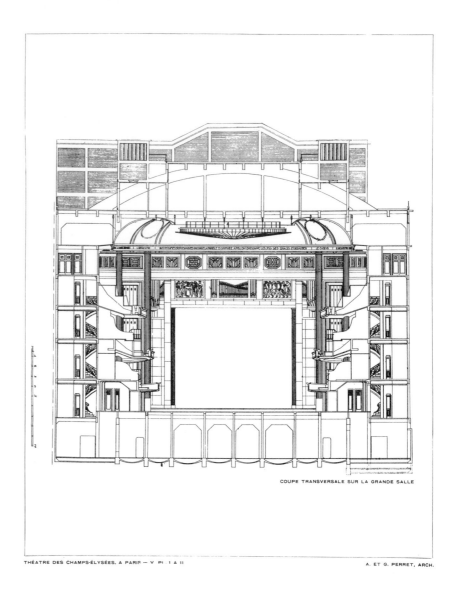

COUPE TRANSVERSALE SUR LA GRANDE SALLE

bay system generates a peristyle of sixteen columns that orchestrates the space of the entrance hall and thereafter projects its presence onto the front facade in terms of representational pilasters (fig. 5.14). This structural system, represented as a tartan grid on the floor and the ceiling, is articulated all round the perimeter of the space in order to separate the columnar structure from the enclosing walls (fig. 5.13). The resulting slots articulate the full peristyle as an a/ABABA/a scheme, with the facade expressing the diminutive "a" bay as an *alette* and the larger B bay as a coupled pilaster. This syncopated modeling is flanked by two giant, coupled pilasters that, running the full height of the facade, effectively close the composition. Following Henri Labrouste, all these pilasters are terminated by thin golden bands instead of capitals. Otherwise, throughout the facade Perret seems to adhere to the precepts of *modénature* developed by François Mansart. He observes the principles of *vraisemblance,* that is to say, he places his pilasters at the corner in order to *represent* their hypothetical load-bearing capacity, following the model of Mansart's Maisons-Laffitte, Château des Maisons of 1642.

5.13
Auguste Perret, Théâtre des Champs-
Elysées, section through main auditorium.

5.14
Auguste Perret, Théâtre des Champs-
Elysées, front facade.

Once again, as in 25 bis rue Franklin, exposed concrete is not employed for the honorific parts of the structure, the facade and the foyer being veneered in stone and plaster. On the side and end elevations, however, it is left as struck from the timber *coffrage,* the bays being filled in with large expanses of brickwork. Thus, where the corpus of the theater becomes utilitarian, as in the backstage volume, Perret returns to standard fireproof concrete frame construction, as we find this in the textile mills built by Hennebique in Tourcoing and Lille in 1895 and 1896 respectively.

The final fusion of classical rationalism with the Greco-Gothic ideal comes with the church of Notre-Dame du Raincy, commissioned in 1922 as a memorial to those who were killed in the battle of the Ourcq in the First World War (figs. 5.15, 5.16). With this church, Perret arrived at the essentials of the free plan *avant la lettre,* inasmuch as the building comprised a network of 28 cylindrical concrete columns standing free within a hermetic, non-load-bearing envelope. The columns in question, each 37 feet high, with a longitudinal spacing of 33 feet, tapered upward from a 17-inch base to a 14-inch diameter at the crown. These columns may be read in both ontological and representational terms; first, because of the evident presence of an unfaced concrete support, and second, because of the imprint of the half-round and triangular timber fillets from

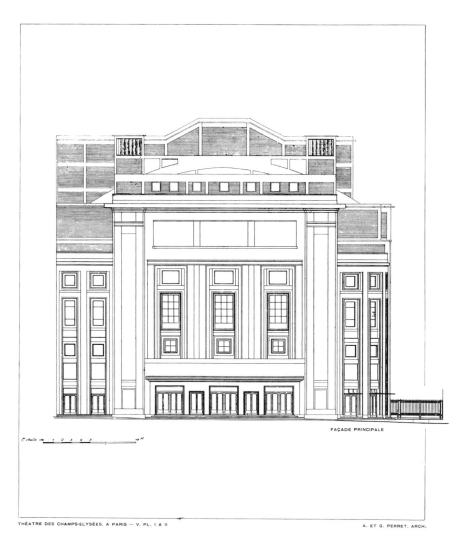

FAÇADE PRINCIPALE

THÉÂTRE DES CHAMPS-ELYSÉES, A PARIS ··· V. PL. I A II   A. ET G. PERRET, ARCH.

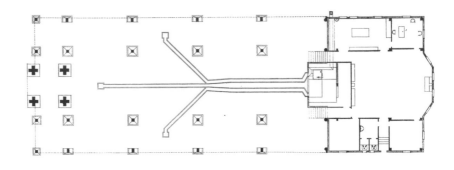

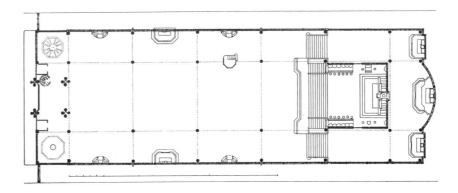

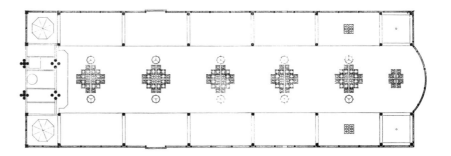

5.15
Auguste Perret, Church of Notre-Dame, Le Raincy, 1922–1924. Basement with heating ducts.

5.16
Auguste Perret, Church of Notre-Dame, Le Raincy, ground floor and reflected ceiling plan.

which the column formwork is constructed. These fillets bestow upon the column an ambiguous profile that may be interpreted as a conscious double reference, first to the tapering flutes of the Doric order and second to the clustering cylindrical forms of a typical Gothic pier. Apart from the Greco-Gothic implications of this double allusion, the freestanding columns within the *Hallenkirche* volume serve to engender that sublime, forest effect so much admired by Cordemoy and Laugier as the crowning attributes of the Gothic cathedral. As Perret himself put it in a letter written to *The American Architect* in 1924:

Ordinarily the exterior row of columns would have been buried in the enclosing walls and each of them indicated by a slight projection. In this building we have entirely isolated these columns from the wall, permitting the walls to pass freely outside of them. By exposing all of the columns free-standing there are four rows of columns seen instead of the usual two rows. This greater number of columns in sight tends greatly to increase the apparent size of the church with a sense of spaciousness and vastness. The small size of the columns, their greater height and lack of distracting detail aid materially in producing this effect.[7]

132

Perret's aims were patently the same, in this regard, as those displayed by J. N. L. Durand in his economic critique of Soufflot's Ste.-Geneviève, and this, if nothing else, is further evidence of a conceptual link between Notre-Dame du Raincy and Ste.-Geneviève. Vittorio Gregotti has identified this continuity of the Greco-Gothic ideal as a form of classicizing naturalism that permeates French culture from the Enlightenment onward, manifesting itself "as a secular religion of progress and reason and a quest for an unattainable natural objectivity."[8] The continuity with Ste.-Geneviève is further substantiated by the vaulting of Notre-Dame du Raincy, which takes the form of shallow concrete barrel vaults running transversely across the nave and longitudinally down the aisles (fig. 5.17). More-over, as in Ste.-Geneviève, there is an outer roof that serves to protect the two-inch-thick shell vaults spanning across the aisles and the nave (fig. 5.18). This second membrane consists of a lightweight, tiled, concrete vault system com-prised of flat inverted U-sections in the longitudinal section. Surprising as it may seem, this roof section appears to have been capable of spanning clear across the entire width of the church.

The Gothic overtones of Le Raincy were subtly incorporated into the 183-foot-long perimeter curtain wall, assembled out of 2-foot-square precast panels, each one framing rectangular, triangular, or circular apertures filled with clear or colored glass. These concrete panels or *claustra* were laid up as symmetrical ge-ometric grids, arranged in such a way as to produce a large cruciform pattern in the center of each bay. The "pointilliste" colored glass infill of the *claustra,* chro-matically varying from one bay to the next in accordance with the natural spec-trum, was the work of the symbolist artist Maurice Denis. The *claustra* had first been devised by Perret when he was working for his father on the construction of the cathedral of Oran, begun in 1902 to the designs of Albert Ballu (fig. 5.19). In Le Raincy Perret assures the rhythmic articulation of the curtain wall by treat-ing it as a relief construction in which a number of vertical and horizontal ribs are more pronounced than those produced by the normal jointing between the

5.17
Auguste Perret, Church of Notre-Dame, Le Raincy, sections.

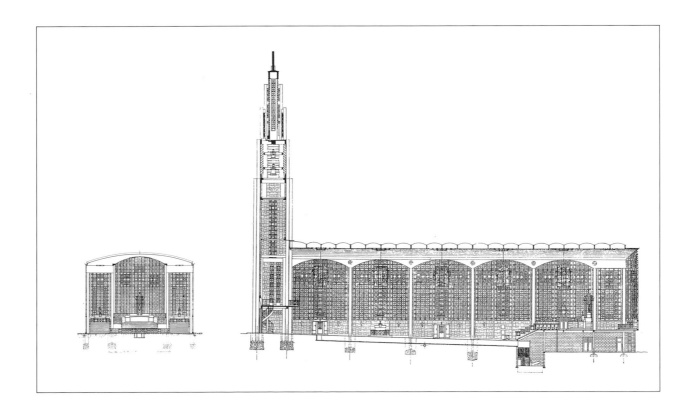

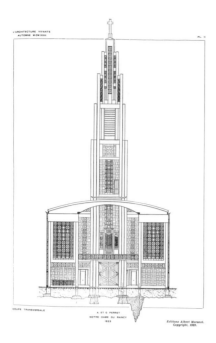

5.18
Auguste Perret, Church of Notre-Dame, Le Raincy, transverse section.

5.19
Auguste Perret and Albert Ballu, Oran cathedral, 1902–1908. Detail of claustra.

5.20
Auguste Perret, Church of Notre-Dame, Le Raincy, details of steeple.

claustra. This hierarchic emphasis served not only to stiffen the membrane but also to establish the border of each cruciform figure. By the permutation of only five different prefabricated *claustra* patterns, set within a bounding square (a cross, a circle, a diamond, a half-square, and a quarter square), Perret was able to avoid the monotony of a regularly reticulated curtain wall, while giving a certain scale to an otherwise uninflected, columnless exterior.

Equally Gothic, of course, was the square-planned, 145-foot-high spire and belfry, comprising, at grade, four cluster piers, each consisting of four 17-inch-diameter columns (fig. 5.20). These composite piers stepped back in three stages as the square plan progressively diminished to the pinnacle. While this arrangement maintained the same proportion and geometry as the rest of the church and served to integrate the hollow volume of the spire and organ loft with the space of the nave, it was somewhat less successful as an external profile. The conformity of the profile with the silhouette of a typical Gothic spire seems somewhat forced, while the stepped, set-back composition suggests by virtue of its apparent weight a stereotomic piling-up rather than a frame. In both Ste.-Geneviève and Le Raincy, the confusion between tectonic and stereotomic form arose out of a similar cause; namely, the presence of hidden reinforcement, which enabled the assembly to perform in a manner that was at variance with its essential nature. This disjunction was accompanied by a repression of the joint as such, which produced the curious telescopic appearance of the pseudo-spire of Le Raincy. It is significant that Perret's syntactical command of the concrete frame fails him exactly at the point where the aim is no longer the tectonic expression of the frame but the simulation of a nostalgic image, that is to say, the point at which the structure becomes pseudo-Gothic rather than a modernized version of the Greco-Gothic.

In two temporary works, designed in 1924 and 1925 respectively, Perret will return to a more straightforward level of tectonic articulation: the Palais de Bois erected in the Bois de Boulogne in 1924 (fig. 5.21), and the Théâtre des Arts Décoratifs, erected for the Exposition des Arts Décoratifs of 1925 (figs. 5.22, 5.23, 5.24).

The former was a tour de force in timber construction, employing standard mill sections in such a way as to construct a hierarchy of *load-bearing* and *load-borne* elements (compare Schopenhauer's *Stütze und Last*). Thus, an exposed boarded roof spans onto standard rafters that in turn take their support from purlins that then rest on deep timber beams, with corbeled brackets and plated timber columns. Light percolating into the structure along the perimeter between the purlins and the rafters imparts a radiance to the work that here and there is augmented by clerestory lights and the occasional top light, let into the roof. It seems in retrospect as though Perret was orchestrating the framework in a consciously "oriental" manner, for it is difficult to look at a photographic record of this work today without being reminded of traditional Japanese construction.

The Théâtre des Arts Décoratifs was a more didactic and ambitious undertaking. In this work Perret tried to transform the syntax of his evolving Greco-Gothic language into the articulate precepts of his later classical rationalism, thereby advancing his nationalistic ambition of evolving a new French order. Seating 900 people, Perret's temporary theater was as much a refinement of a new auditorium type as his Notre-Dame du Raincy had been a reinterpretation

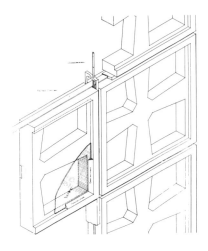

of the traditional *Hallenkirche*. It was in fact based on the shallow tripartite stage as this had been embodied in Henri Van de Velde's Werkbund Theater of 1914 and which had previously appeared in Max Kruger's *Stilbühne* dating from 1912. Directly influenced by the timber tectonic of the Palais de Bois, the syncopated orthogonal order of the theater broke down into an elongated Palladian system. Perret would expand and manipulate the a/ABABA/a peristylar foyer of the Champs-Elysées theater in such a way as it would come to embrace the entire volume of the Théâtre des Arts Décoratifs. Thus, 38 freestanding columns articulating the 180-by-40-foot enclosure would be so arranged as to produce internal columnar rhythms of a/AABAA/a in length and a/ABA/a in width (fig. 5.25). Thus the body of the building was divided into three parts in both directions, with the center being slightly larger in each instance. Disturbed by the lack of structural modulation on the exterior of Notre-Dame du Raincy, Perret arranged for 14 redundant columns to appear as representative orders on the blank exterior of the theater, including two columns set off from each corner in order to terminate the system. (Compare the corner details employed in the steel framing of the various buildings that Mies van der Rohe designed for IIT in Chicago.) Due to the temporary nature of the structure, Perret had to simulate reinforced concrete frame construction. Thus the columns were built up out of square timber

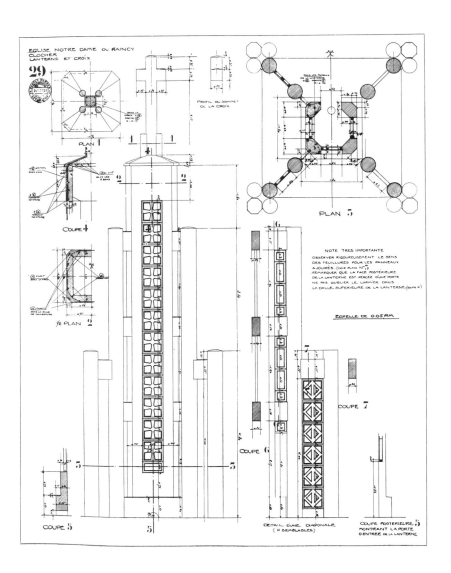

stanchions faced by four fluted quadrants, while the main beams were made out of reinforced, lightweight, clinker concrete. Perret exploited the temporary nature of the building as an occasion for realizing a prismatic crystalline aesthetic having its own intrinsic character. Thus, the entire auditorium was permanently lit during the day through 150 white linen screens that filled the squares of the latticework ceiling and its adjoining celestory lights (fig. 5.26). The weightless vaults covering the reading room of Labrouste's Bibliothèque Nationale may well have been the inspiration for this *velarium,* in that Perret's translucent grid was supported by a light steel armature spanning across the auditorium. The general iridescent effect was amplified through the color scheme of the interior, with side walls finished in matte aluminum paint, prominent features highlighted in shiny aluminum leaf, and seats upholstered in brown-gray fabric. The aura of this dematerialized interior as it responded to different light conditions was surely the opposite to the artificially illuminated interior of Perret's Ecole Normale de Musique of 1929, lined throughout in acoustical plywood panels (figs. 5.27, 5.28). The thin plywood surface of the latter, built out from the walls on timber battens, led the satisfied client, Alfred Corot, to remark, "He told us that he would make us a violin, but he made us a Stradivarius."[9] In both the theater and the concert chamber, Perret sought to establish an introspective tactile interior in which one would feel as though one had entered a world apart.

Two further tectonic attributes need to be noted as evidence of the complexity of the Théâtre des Arts Décoratifs. First, there is the fact that despite the simula-

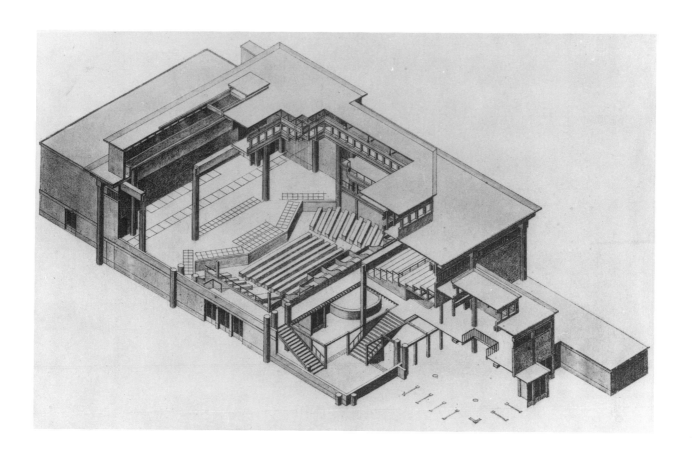

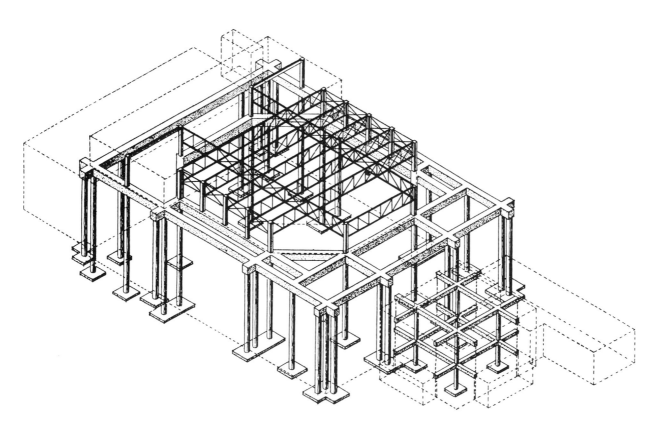

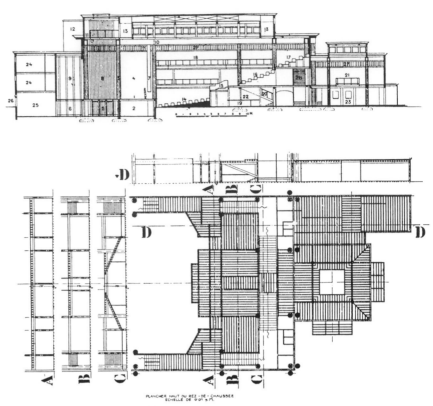

PLANCHER HAUT DU REZ-DE-CHAUSSÉE.

tion of concrete, the interior volume is formed through a highly articulate structure in which, as in the Palais de Bois, the play of the load-bearing against the load-borne evokes the Orient in a double sense, suggesting the culture of Japan by the orthogonal articulation of the structure and recalling one of the key features in Islamic space-making by the pendentive corners of the main auditorium (fig. 5.29). Second, as we have already noted, the building becomes a vehicle for evolving what Perret would regard as a new French classical-rational order. This surely accounts for the regular "fluting" of the columns, and for the ventilation frieze of alternating, half-round pipes running around the perimeter of the building as a vestigial entablature (fig. 5.30). A similar metaphorical frieze, composed of adjustable louvers, would be employed by Perret in the Ecole Normale de Musique.

Like the immediate generations that succeeded him, like Mies, Le Corbusier, and Louis Kahn, Perret sought to establish a systematic and inflected approach

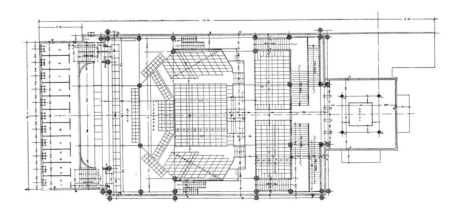

to architecture; one that would allow for different institutions to be given a hierarchically distinct expression. From a normative standpoint, Perret's method and syntax crystallized into a general system in two major works: his own apartment building completed in the rue Raynouard, Paris, in 1932 (figs. 5.31, 5.32), and the Musée des Travaux Publics started in Paris in 1936.

Notwithstanding Perret's perennial emphasis on the *charpente,* his work had already begun to assume a graduated expression depending on its institutional status. Typologically speaking, the expressive range ran from the trabeated frame of the public institution to load-bearing masonry in the private house. Within this representational spectrum lay the syntactical frame and infill of his upper-class villas, the Maison Nabar Bey built at Garches in 1931 being typical in this regard (fig. 5.33). By a similar token, Perret's small domestic works were largely built of unframed, load-bearing masonary, the Palladian Maison Cassandre at Versailles of 1926 being typical (fig. 5.34). At the same time, his apartment buildings implied a higher order of collective expression and hence were invariably framed throughout. Unlike Le Corbusier's general application of *pilotis* (the classic anticlassical trope set in conscious opposition to Perret's classical rationalism), Perret will only allow himself to use a peristyle in an honorific work, such as a public building or a set of monumental sequences like the entrances of the perimeter blocks that make up the inner residential fabric in his rebuilding of Le Havre.

While the plan of rue Raynouard is interesting in itself, what concerns us here is the way in which its status is reflected in the concatenation and refinement of its constructional elements. Here the concrete finish is differentiated in order to distinguish between frame and infill. As Peter Collins writes:

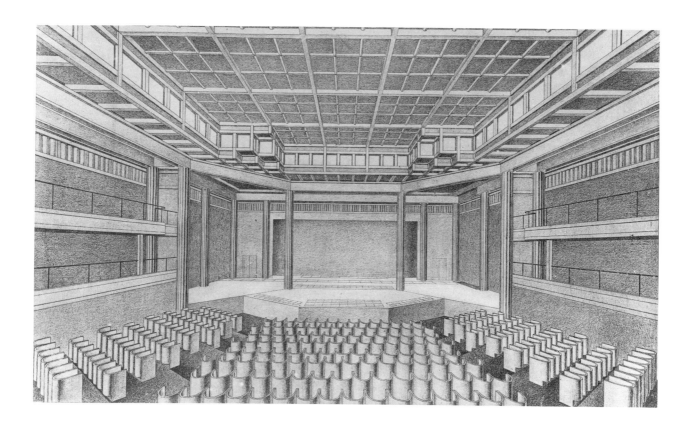

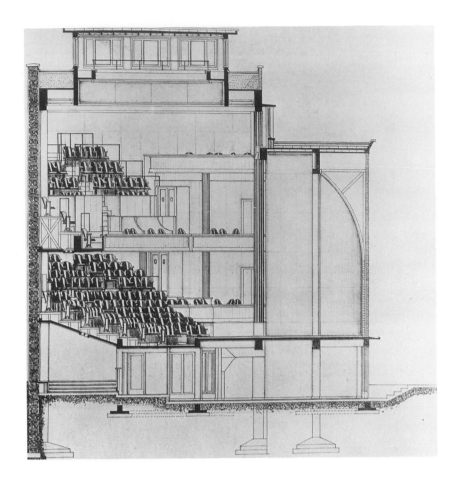

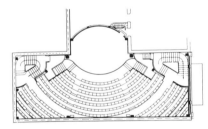

5.27
Auguste Perret, Ecole Normale de Musique,
Paris, 1929. Section.

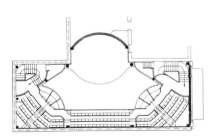

5.28
Auguste Perret, Ecole Normale de Musique,
orchestra and balcony-level plans.

*The general principle of this system, once stated, seems so self-evident that its
ingenuity may not be apparent, but it is important to appreciate that until this
date, it is doubtful if any architect had seriously considered combining in situ
and pre-cast concrete systematically in the same design, except to make the latter constitute permanent form-work for the former. By suggesting that the structural members should be cast in situ as a monolithic frame, and that all non-
load-bearing elements should be pre-cast to specific designs on the site itself,
rather than in a factory, Perret completely revolutionized one aspect of reinforced concrete building technique at a time when pre-casting was usually
thought of as essentially a means of commercial mass-production, and justifiable
if carried out by an independent firm which would advertise and distribute each
element ready-made.*[10]

Perret was an advocate of rational rather than optimized production, and for him
each repeatable piece was a tectonic unit designed as a particular component
for a specific job; in this instance, the on-site precasting molds would be discarded once the job was finished. In the rue Raynouard and in subsequent public works, at the scale of the frame the *modénature* of the facade and hence of
the body of the building as a whole would derive, in large part, from the hierarchical order built into the sequence of assembly. A sequential modulation was
set up between the fixing of the precast concrete window frames and the solid
precast infill panels that spanned between the window surround and the in situ

5.29
Auguste Perret, Théâtre de l'Exposition des Arts Décoratifs, interior.

5.30
Auguste Perret, Théâtre de l'Exposition des Arts Décoratifs, general view.

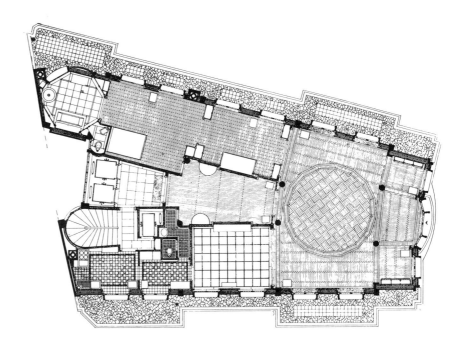

142

5.31
Auguste Perret, apartment building, 51 rue Raynouard, Paris, 1929–1932. Elevation. Note plate glass fenestration for Perret's professional offices.

5.32
Auguste Perret, apartment building, 51 rue Raynouard, plan of the penthouse.

5.33
Auguste Perret, Maison Nabar Bey, Garches, 1931. Elevation.

skeleton. Modulation in depth was similarly determined by the necessity for rebating joints and providing moldings for weathering purposes. In the case of the window frames themselves, the depth of the unit was determined by the need to accommodate the standard Parisian folding metal shutter (fig. 5.35). The overall rhythm of the surface, once again, reminds one of the modeling of François Mansart, particularly as the French windows, heavily framed in their precast concrete surrounds, were to extend fully between one floor and the next in a manner reminiscent of the so-called "wedged" windows characteristic of seventeenth-century French classicism. At the same time, the distinction that Perret consistently drew between in situ and precast concrete was reminiscent of the play between cast and wrought iron in the work of Viollet-le-Duc.

Perret's move away from *béton brut* toward the bush-hammering of concrete enabled him to discriminate between the exposed aggregate of the in situ skeleton and the latex smoothness of the precast elements. To achieve these effects, he relied on technical processes that had been developed and perfected during the preceding decade, the first consisting of vibrating the concrete for the purpose of achieving maximum consolidation, the second consisting of removing the superficial cement film in order to reveal the stone aggregate beneath. As Collins remarks:

[Perret pioneered] . . . a technique for removing the cement film known as bouchardage *or bush hammering. It matters little whether he was the first architect to apply to rough concrete surfaces this masonry technique for cleaning roughly quarried stone. What matters is that for Perret, the visual expression of the structural material was as important as the visual expression of the constructional system. Far from "lacking a sense of detail" he becomes obsessed with the desire to achieve it in profiling and coloration. He obtained the former by modulations in the timber framework. He attained the latter by using aggregates of varying size and color.*[11]

The development of the rue Raynouard apartment building compelled Perret to reassert the canonical status of the traditional French window as opposed to the *fenêtre en longueur* of Le Corbusier. However, Perret was by no means averse to using large areas of undivided plate glass where the particular program demanded unusually high levels of natural light, as in the case of his own drafting studio in rue Raynouard (fig. 5.31). Otherwise he saw the French window as being suffused with a particular cultural significance. As he put it, "la fenêtre en hauteur c'est le cadre de l'homme." For Perret, *la porte-fenêtre,* the French window, with its hinged double doors opening inward, was indicative of the presence of man. Here, a received tectonic element assumes symbolic anthropomorphic dimensions. For Perret the implications of the *porte-fenêtre* went even further, for it not only established the decorum of the bourgeois interior, its rhythm, space, and graduation of light, but it also induced the cadence of human movement within the room. This is particularly evident in 25 bis rue Franklin, where the *porte-fenêtre* serves as an essential punctuation in what is otherwise an *en suite* space. It provides a certain decorum for each action setting and engages in a dialogical play with the opaque subdividing double doors of the interior that serve to interconnect the five-room sequence of smoking, dining, salon, bedroom, and boudoir; the whole providing, as Henri Bresler has observed, a faceted parallel of the civic exterior.[12]

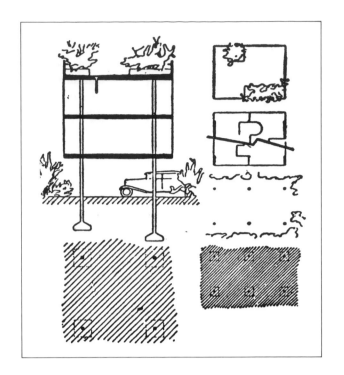

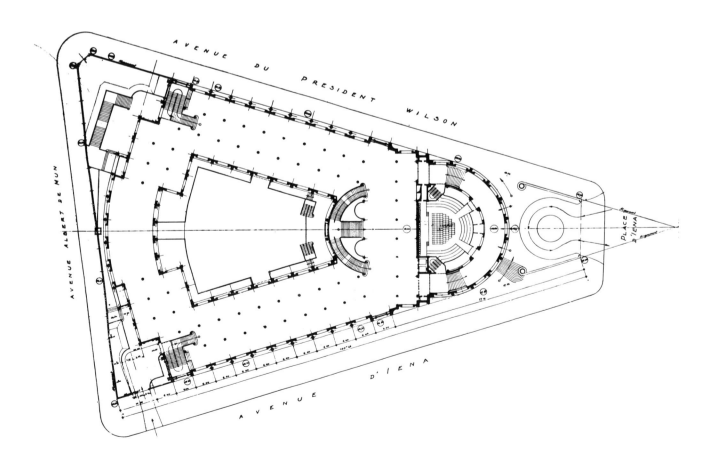

5.36
Le Corbusier, "Five Points of a New Architecture," plate from *La Maison de l'homme*, 1926.

5.37
Auguste Perret, Musée des Travaux Publics, Paris, 1936–1937. Elevation.

5.38
Auguste Perret, Musée des Travaux Publics, ground floor.

5.39
Auguste Perret, Musée des Travaux Publics, facade sections.
A, waterproof membrane
B, volcanic cement
C, cement
D, porous cement
E, F, hollow bricks
G, reinforced concrete
H, plywood
I, reinforced concrete infill
J, cork
K, granite floor
L, cement
M, plywood ceiling
N, air duct
O, cement panels
P, heating unit
Q, fan
R, heating tubes
S, hollow bricks

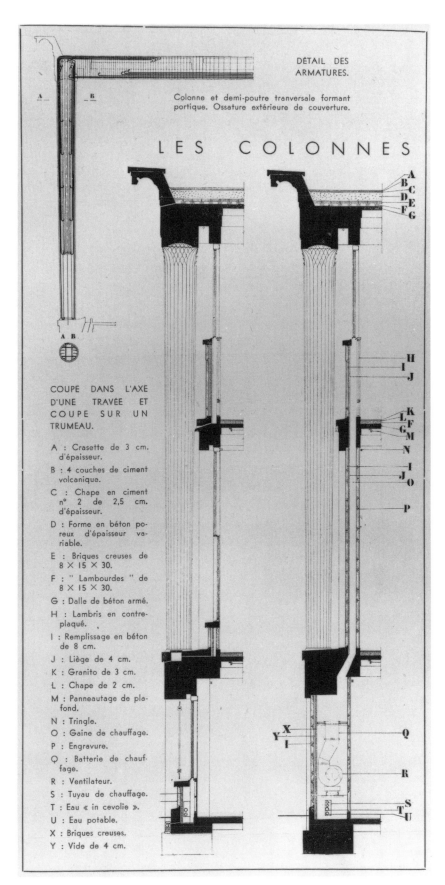

DÉTAIL DES ARMATURES.

Colonne et demi-poutre tranversale formant portique. Ossature extérieure de couverture.

LES COLONNES

COUPE DANS L'AXE D'UNE TRAVÉE ET COUPE SUR UN TRUMEAU.

A : Crasette de 3 cm. d'épaisseur.

B : 4 couches de ciment volcanique.

C : Chape en ciment n° 2 de 2,5 cm. d'épaisseur.

D : Forme en béton poreux d'épaisseur variable.

E : Briques creuses de 8 × 15 × 30.

F : " Lambourdes " de 8 × 15 × 30.

G : Dalle de béton armé.

H : Lambris en contreplaqué.

I : Remplissage en béton de 8 cm.

J : Liège de 4 cm.

K : Granito de 3 cm.

L : Chape de 2 cm.

M : Panneautage de plafond.

N : Tringle.

O : Gaine de chauffage.

P : Engravure.

Q : Batterie de chauffage.

R : Ventilateur.

S : Tuyau de chauffage.

T : Eau « in cevolie ».

U : Eau potable.

X : Briques creuses.

Y : Vide de 4 cm.

was nonetheless a geometrically precise transition, composed out of a set of larger intersecting planes (fig. 5.41). Here the points of all the triangles terminate above an arris of the faceted column, employing a generic method that will serve equally well irrespective of the number of faces in the formwork of the shaft, so that "the architect's task is limited to deciding dimensions, as it always was in the past."[16]

In the Musée des Travaux Publics, Perret brought his concrete syntax to a remarkable level of precision, striking the columns straight from the formwork but bush-hammering all other concrete surfaces in such a way as to expose the aggregate and stress both arrises and seams. This linear accent, running over every surface, created an unexpected atectonic effect, imparting to the aggregate surfaces the paradoxical suggestion that they may not be of a monolithic character (fig. 5.42). At the same time, large unbroken areas of steel-framed plate glass running behind the exterior peristyle interrupted the continuity established by the load-bearing concrete undercroft. This spatial elision helped to express the format of a "building within the building" that was, in fact, the leitmotiv of the entire structure (figs. 5.43, 5.44). At the same time, Perret overcame the redundancy of having to double up the columns around the perimeter of the work as he had been obliged to do in his Théâtre des Arts Décoratifs. In this regard, the museum culminates a dialectical evolution that passes from the thesis of Le Raincy, to the counterthesis of the Théâtre des Arts Décoratifs, and finally to the synthesis of the Musée des Travaux Publics. In terms of the articulation of the

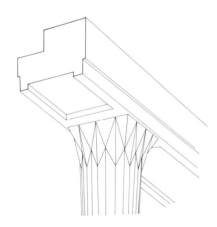

5.40
Auguste Perret, Musée des Travaux Publics,
interior.

5.41
Auguste Perret, City Hall, Le Havre, 1949. Detail of capital.

5.42
Auguste Perret, Musée des Travaux Publics,
perimeter detail.

5.43
Auguste Perret, Musée des Travaux Publics,
axonometric.

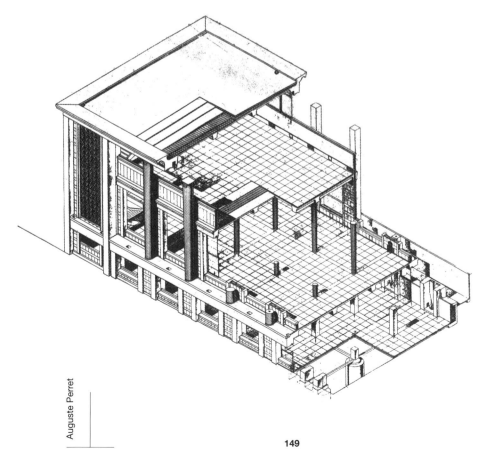

Auguste Perret

writings of Mies van der Rohe. Perret's credo took the form of a series of aphorisms like Mosaic tablets, classically arranged on the page and composed entirely of capital letters as though each sentence was destined to be carved in stone. At the same time, these aphorisms were arranged so as to succeed each other like the logical steps of an argument, although each one is an independent statement in itself. There are, in effect, sixteen separate statements. Some of them are accompanied by short glosses drawn from other writers. Perret begins:

Technique, permanent homage to nature, essential food for the imagination, authentic source of inspiration, the prayer of everything that is most efficacious, maternal language of every creator, technique, spoken poetically leads us to architecture.

This is followed by a statement that is almost a direct paraphrase of Viollet-le-Duc's own aphorism about structure that appears at the head of his *Dictionnaire raisonné de l'architecture française.* Perret writes, "Architecture is the art of organizing space. It is through construction that it expresses itself." He then goes on to distinguish between fixed and ephemeral form.

Mobile or immobile, all that occupies space belongs to the domain of architecture. Architecture constitutes itself out of space, limits it, closes it, encircles it. It has this privilege of creating magical places, total works of the spirit [l'esprit]. Architecture is of all the artistic expressions the one most subject to material condi-

5.48
Auguste Perret, Musée des Travaux Publics, interior of auditorium.

5.49
Auguste Perret, Musée des Travaux Publics, main staircase.

tions. The permanent conditions are imposed by nature, the transitory conditions are imposed by man. The climate with its temperature changes, the materials and their properties, stability and the laws of statics, optical deformities, the eternal and universal direction of lines and forms, impose conditions that are permanent. He the architect is the one who by virtue of a combination of scientific thought and intuition conceives of a vessel, a portico, a sovereign shelter capable of accommodating within its unity the diversity of organs arising out of functional need.

This passage is an implicit critique of our misguided aspirations for achieving a perfect fit of form and function that can only be of relevance in the most extreme survival situations. Moreover, it also suggests that our modern obsession with comfort is a self-indulgence that, over the last half-century, has only furthered the commodification of architecture. Instead, Perret accords primacy to the space of "human appearance" as this first appeared in the Greek polis, the subject citizen literally emerging from the peristyle much as Hegel had imagined him. Here Perret contrasts the permanence of the civic monument, even as a ruin, to the impermanence of the tangible everyday object. His position, in this regard, is also close to Le Corbusier's observation that the more intimate our relations are to an object, the more it will reflect our anthropomorphic figure; conversely, the more distant, the more it will tend toward abstraction.

Perret then turns his discourse toward the poetic primacy of construction.

Construction is the mother tongue of the architect. The architect is a poet who thinks and speaks in terms of construction. The large buildings of our time presuppose a framework, a framework rendered in steel or reinforced concrete. The framework is to a building what a skeleton is to an animal. Just as the skeleton of an animal is rhythmic, balanced and symmetrical, and contains and supports the most diverse and diversely situated organs, so the framework of a building must be composed, rhythmic, balanced and very symmetrical. It must be able to contain the most diverse and diversely situated organs and services demanded by function and appointment.

Perret places by the side of this aphorism a gloss taken from the writings of Charles Blanc, who was librarian at the Ecole des Beaux-Arts and author of the highly influential *Grammaire des arts de dessin* published in 1867. This gloss reads, "The profound study of ancient monuments reveals this luminous truth, that architecture at its highest level is not so much a construction that is decorated as a decoration that is constructed."

Perret's theoretical position implies a number of other ramifications that require comment here. The first is that he was to remain categorically opposed to the idea of decorative art throughout his life, even though he participated in the 1925 Exposition des Arts Décoratifs. Perret thought that this exhibition represented a regression from the cultural level attained even in the Paris exhibition of 1900. In an interview with Marie Dormoy at the time he states: "Decorative art should be forbidden. I would like to know who stuck these words together: art and decorative. It is a monstrosity. Where there is true art, there is no need for decoration."[20] The second point turns on Perret's opposition to the simulation of tectonic form and structure. There is an interesting footnote in Denis Honegger's "Auguste Perret: doctrine de l'architecture" that touches on this issue. Perret is supposed to have said to him on one occasion:

153

We no longer know the language of stone. Everything that we make in this material today is only a lie and a trick. We no longer know how to raise a vault and we anchor our stones with iron cramps. The visible lintels are backed up by iron or reinforced concrete beams. I challenge any contemporary architect, no matter who, to reconstruct the nave of Bourges with the same conscience and feeling for material. In our day we are content to make it of reinforced concrete, plaster it over, and paint the joints.[21]

Against such kitsch simulation, Perret continues to assert, like Semper, the primacy of the frame. He extends the anthropological legitimacy that Semper accords to the frame into a natural philosophy of construction. Thus, in his *Contribution à une théorie* he remarks with ethical overtones that remind one of Adolf Loos's polemical essay "Ornament and Crime" of 1908: "He who hides any part of the framework not only deprives architecture of its sole legitimacy but also strips from it its most beautiful ornament. He who hides a column makes a blunder, he who makes a false column commits a crime."[22]

In his aphoristic formulations, Perret will follow both Paul Valéry and Henri Bergson in stressing the fundamental importance of the durability of the framework, that is to say, its fundamental capacity to stand against time.[23] Thus he writes:

It is the framework that furnishes the building with elements and forms imposed by permanent conditions and that, subject to nature, attached to the past, establishes the durability [la durée] *of the work. Having satisfied the transitory and permanent conditions, the building, now subject to man and nature, will acquire character; it will have style, it will be harmonious. Character, style, harmony, these are the milestones that lead via truth to beauty.*[24]

In his introduction to his play *Histoire d'Amphion,* Valéry would go so far as to equate memory in literate culture with fundamental construction in architecture: "Even in the slightest comparison one must think of duration, that is *memory,* which is to say form, just as the builder of steeples and towers must think of *structure.*"[25]

It is difficult to overestimate the seminal role played by Valéry in the evolution of Perret's thought. Valéry seems first to have met Perret around 1909, some three years before the realization of the Théâtre des Champs-Elysées. Valéry was an *afficionado* of the theater, and apart from his contact with Perret he was on intimate terms with the entire circle that brought the theater into being, including Maurice Denis and Antoine Bourdelle, whose decor and sculptural relief, respectively, graced its interior, and Gabriel Thomas who was the main administrator. Valéry's attitude to architecture as set forth in *Eupalinos ou l'architecte* (1922) is polemically tectonic to the point of being retardataire, since for him true architecture is contingent upon it being made out of hewn stone. In this regard, Valéry makes a precise distinction between (1) simple *bearing* constructions, assembled out of cut stone, (2) *reticulated* construction usually framed out of wood, and (3) *consolidated* constructions cast in reinforced concrete. This differentiation may be seen both as a response to and as a critique of Perret's architectural endeavor in which he sought to combine the tectonic/paratactic configuration of classical architecture and the monolithic organic configuration of reinforced concrete. While Perret made a heroic effort to realize the tectonic potential of the concrete frame, his work was by definition removed from the deeper roots of the tectonic as Valéry had received them from Greek culture.[26]

Valéry would expand upon the purity of this etymological base in a typical Mediterranean fashion by distinguishing between Eupalinos the constructor in stone, who is heir to tradition and in charge of creating a hierarchic human world, and Tridon the builder of ships in wood, who works against and with the unknown to conquer the sea. Here *homo faber* appears in two aspects, the one turned toward the culture and the other toward nature; the first face is that of a world creator, while the second is that of an instrumentalizer.[27]

Perret's use of the terms character and style often seems to be synonymous; it is clear, however, that he associated style with some fundamentally significant inner order, whereas character was merely the outward manifestation of a particular instant. Thus he remarked to Marcel Mayer: "A locomotive merely has character; the Parthenon has both character and style. In a few years, the most beautiful locomotive of today will be merely a mass of scrap metal; the Parthenon will sing forever." "Style," Perret was fond of saying, after Viollet-le-Duc, "is a word that has no plural."[28] Perret's *Contribution à une théorie* closes with an aphorism that is almost a direct paraphrase of Mies's citation from St. Augustine, "Beauty is the splendor of truth," and he goes on to add, paralleling the thesis advanced at the same time in Le Corbusier's *Modulor,* that the enrichment of a structure through proportion is a reflection of man himself.[29] With this last observation, he ends his testament.

The Greco-Gothic ideal was to permeate the work of Perret at every level, and while his use of neo-Platonic form and his particular vision of human destiny were to remain unequivocally Greek, his attitude toward production and his feeling for construction were to be drawn from medieval culture. This double influence brought him to regard the Renaissance with considerable contempt.

The Renaissance was in my opinion a retrospective movement; it was not a "rebirth" but decadence, and one may say that even though, after the end of the Middle Ages, certain men of genius produced monuments that were masterpieces, such as the Val-de-Grâce, the Dome des Invalides and the Palace of Versailles, these edifices are merely magnificent stage decorations. . . . Versailles is badly constructed, and when Time will have exerted its mastery over this palace, we shall not be left with a ruin, but with a mass of unidentifiable rubble. This is not Architecture; Architecture is what makes beautiful ruins.[30]

Inasmuch as he had total control over the means of production, Perret was uniquely privileged to proclaim throughout his career that he was a "constructor" rather than an architect. This eminently tectonic assertion was backed up by a situation in which A & G Perret Constructeurs, the title of his architectural practice up to 1945, were always complemented by the building firm of Perret Frères that was invariably charged with the execution of the work. It was surely this symbiotic conjunction that enabled them to bring their work to such precise levels of resolution, including such delicate adjustments as correcting the "optical" deflection of beam spans. Of this procedure Peter Collins has written:

Whereas in Greek architecture such refinements . . . were the laborious result of sculptural dexterity, in Perret's architecture they derived solely from the natural resilience of wood. The formwork of every beam was planed flat and true by the workmen, and it was only when it was being set in place that these refinements were effected by means of graduated blocks (or scamilli impares *as Vitruvius would have called them) wedged underneath to give the upward curvature desired.*[31]

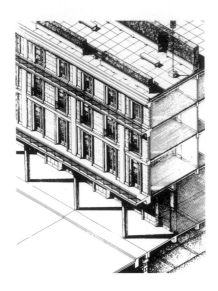

5.50
Auguste Perret, typical apartment blocks for Le Havre, 1949.

5.51
Antonin Raymond and Ladislav Rado, Reader's Digest Building, Tokyo, 1951. Detail section.

This capacity to achieve classic refinements with modern constructional means surely contributed to Perret's reputation as an evolutionary realist. However, it was the tectonic dimension of his work that would account for his resignation from the editorial board of *L'Architecture Vivante,* a journal that he had founded in order to further the cause of a modern architecture. Perret's departure from the masthead arose out of a confrontation with the editor, Jean Badovici, turning on the latter's decision to publish Mondrian's polemic "L'Architecture future de néo-plasticisme" in the autumn 1925 issue of the magazine. Perret had founded *L'Architecture Vivante* as an anti-Beaux-Arts publication, but his anti-academicism did not mean that he was willing to abandon the unfolding tradition of tectonic culture. The subsequent distance that he took from the modernist avant-garde and its various ideologies would lead not only to his alienation from the next generation but also to the scant treatment of his work in the received accounts of twentieth-century architecture.

We may say that the particular tectonic line pursued in Perret's work consistently displayed the following attributes: (1) the expression of the structural skeleton as an indispensable ordering principle, (2) the emphasis placed on the joint as a techno-poetic fulcrum, (3) the reinterpretation of traditional features so that they may still express a certain cultural continuity, (4) the resulting emphasis on certain key components, such as the cornice, the French window, and the helicoidal stair, seen as the apotheosis of a tectonic civilization, and (5) an adherence to the rational as a transferable method, dedicated to the continuation and development of a normative culture. This last is surely related to his appraisal of

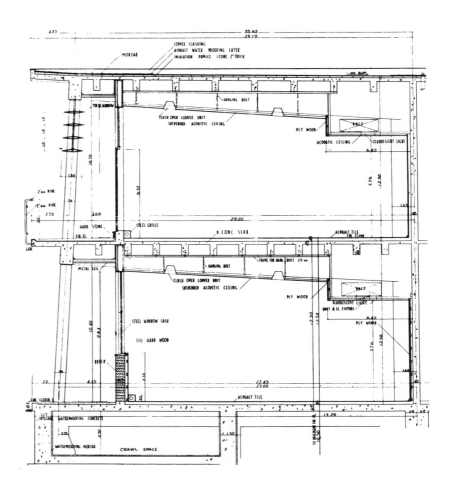

the banal as this appears in his 1945 plan for the reconstruction of Le Havre. In his 1933 address to the Institut d'Art et Architecture, Perret stated:

A country is only old by its monuments, for nature is eternally young. He who, without betraying the modern conditions of a programme, or the use of modern materials, produces a work which seems to have always existed, which, in a word, is banal, can rest satisfied. Astonishment and excitement are shocks which do not endure, they are but contingent and anecdotic sentiments. The true aim of Art is to lead us dialectically from satisfaction to satisfaction, until it surpasses mere admiration to reach delight in its purest form.[32]

Perret's significance today resides in the way in which his work maintained a line of development that, while distanced from the expressivity of the avant-garde, nonetheless avoided the two primary pitfalls of the second half of the twentieth century, pastiche historicism on the one hand and reductive functionalism on the other. Transcending this double bind, his legacy points toward a future in which tectonic and stereotomic elements may be dialectically combined. The potential for transferring his method to other structural materials is perhaps best indicated in his temporary constructions, above all his Palais de Bois and Théâtre des Arts Décoratifs. These works suggest a richer and freer articulation than that embodied in the "state style" of his late career. Thus both the limitation and promise of his legacy are reflected in the dichotomous nature of his influence. On the one hand then we have his rather academic followers, including Pierre Lambert and Jacques Poirrer, who directly assisted him in the reconstruction of Le Havre (fig. 5.50), and Denis Honegger, whose University of Fribourg, realized in 1939, was already an all too exemplary exercise in the Perret manner veering toward the decorative. On the other, there were his own more modernist pupils such as Erno Goldfinger, Paul Nelson, and Oscar Nitschke, and elsewhere distant followers like the Czech-American Antonin Raymond, whose Tokyo Golf Club of 1930[33] was an adaptation of Perret's structural classicism to Japanese conditions, and even Karl Moser, whose St. Anton's Church, Basel, completed in 1931, may be seen as a transposition of Perret's concrete syntax. Perhaps the very last work to internalize Perret's method, as opposed to his style, was Antonin Raymond and Ladislav Rado's Reader's Digest Building completed in Tokyo in 1951.[34] Everything in this diminutive but sublime piece—from the articulation of structure to the precision of its cast concrete—recalls the tectonic rigor of Perret at his best but without attempting to simulate the idiosyncratic *modénature* of his style.

6 Mies van der Rohe:
Avant-Garde and Continuity

All of Mies's constructions . . . are means by which to resist and to proceed. . . . So they are always capable of conferring meaning, or reorienting the context—always stubborn efforts to imagine existence as true life, always the never-betrayed possibility of an image of salvation.

This is what makes Mies's work solitary in the age of the project, in the age of total forgetfulness of the sense of the polis *(and of the decay of even the sense of the* civitas*), in the age of the formalistic autonomy of beauty, in the age of the complete oblivion of the sense of* kalón. *It is a solitude that is (absolutely) unknown, because it enters into controversy with, and is antagonistic to, individualism. Paradoxically, this solitude affirms the complete meaninglessness of the individual.*
Massimo Cacciari, "Mies's Classics,"*1988*

The career of Ludwig Mies van der Rohe (1886–1969) may be regarded as a constant struggle between three divergent factors: the technological capacity of the epoch, the aesthetics of avant-gardism, and the tectonic legacy of classical romanticism. Mies's lifelong effort to resolve these vectors is revealing in itself, since it enlightens us as to the nature of the avant-garde and indicates the relative incompatibility of abstract space and tectonic form. With this in mind Mies's career may be divided into the following phases: the Schinkelesque period (1911–1915), the G group period (1919–1925), the European transcendental phase (1925–1938), the IIT period (1938–1950), and finally his monumental technocratic practice lasting from 1950 to his death.

During the first stage of his career, ending in 1915, Mies van der Rohe remained immersed in the values of the Berlin *Schinkelschule,* and his most dramatic design of this period, namely, the Kröller-Müller House, projected in 1912 for Otterloo, near Arnheim, was evidently a modernized version of Schinkel's Italianate manner, close to the spirit of Peter Behrens's Wiegand House built in Berlin-Dahlem in the same year. In his second period, 1919–1925, Mies's work is directly affected by avant-gardist art, above all by Expressionism, Neoplasticism, and to some extent Suprematism. When he finally starts to build, however, in 1925, he turns, to the stereotomics of brick construction and then in 1927 to the direct tectonic potential of glass and steel.[1] This middle period is perhaps the most complex of his entire career, since here the conflict between avant-gardism and tradition attains its greatest intensity. After Mies's migration to the States in 1938, he seems to turn back toward normative building, that is to say to *Baukunst* rather than architecture, as we may judge from his earliest projects for the IIT campus in Chicago. As he was to put it in an interview with Christian Norberg-Schulz in 1958: "We do not like the word 'Design.' It means everything and nothing. Many believe they can do everything from designing a comb to planning a railway station—the result is nothing is good. We are only interested in building. We would rather that architects use the word 'building' and the best results would belong to the 'art of building.' "[2]

Mies's work begins to express the full range of this hypothetical hierarchy around 1945 with his monumentalization of the standard steel frame in the Alumni Memorial Hall, and this line of approach increases its hold over his output with the Farnsworth House, Fox River, Plano, Illinois, of 1946 and 860 Lake

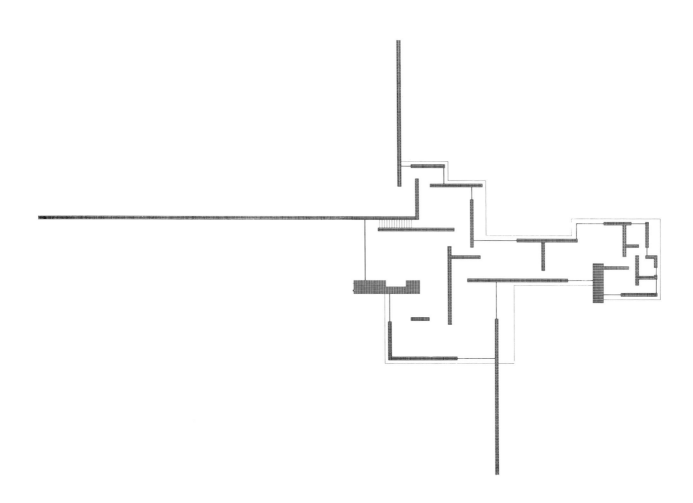

6.3
Mies van der Rohe, Brick Country House, project, 1923. Perspective.

6.4
Mies van der Rohe, Brick Country House, plan. This drawing, by Werner Blaser, is a reconstruction of the brickwork bonding of the walls of the country house.

6.5
Mies van der Rohe, Concrete Country House, project, 1924. Model.

6.6
Mies van der Rohe, Monument to Karl Liebknecht and Rosa Luxemburg, Berlin, 1926. Note the header courses in the atectonic position on the underside of the projecting forms.

wheeling nature of the bonding itself and through the unifying role played by projecting roof slabs. A similar contrast between stereotomic form and planar spatiality appears a few years later in the Berlin monument to Karl Liebknecht and Rosa Luxemburg of 1926 (fig. 6.6) and to some extent in the Wolf House, built in Guben in the same year (fig. 6.7). Particularly significant in this regard is the thoroughly *atectonic* placement of the brick header courses in the Luxemburg-Liebknecht memorial, which are deliberately situated underneath the lowest stretcher course of the projecting planes. The plan of the Wolf House, however, points in another direction, for while the main mass is asymmetrical, an inflection that is stressed through the oversailing concrete roof, rendered in white plaster, the plan is more traditional. It is by no means a free plan in the Neoplasticist sense, however (fig. 6.8), for, like the Hermann Lange and Esters houses, realized in Krefeld in 1928 and 1930 (figs. 6.9, 6.10), the principal rooms of the Wolf House interconnect with each other along a diagonal line. In the Esters House this visual continuity, which cuts across the ground floor of the dwelling, is punctuated by steel-framed, plate glass double doors that separate the smoking, living, and dining rooms (fig. 6.11). At the same time, as Werner Blaser demonstrates in his reconstruction of the masonry bonding for the Brick Country House, the tectonic means adopted in each instance were identical, namely double-sided, fair-faced brickwork, with all the dimensions and proportions worked out on a brick module (fig. 6.12).[6]

It is interesting to note the subtle variations that occur in the detailing of these houses. The Wolf House employs Flemish as opposed to the English bonding

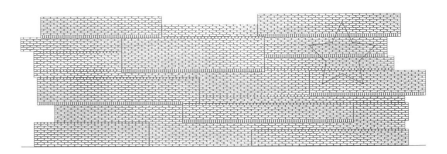

6.7
Mies van der Rohe, Wolf House, Guben,
1926.

6.8
Mies van der Rohe, Wolf House, floor plan.

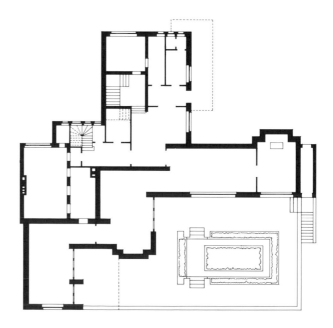

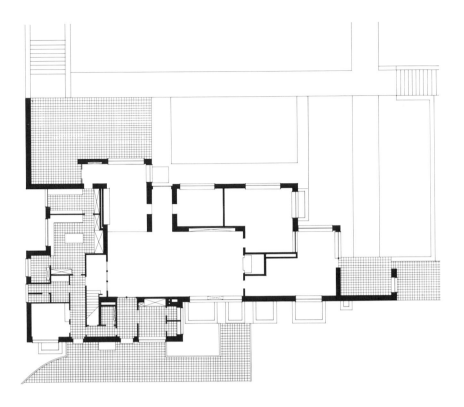

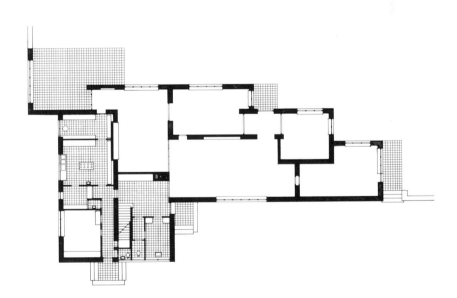

6.9
Mies van der Rohe, Hermann Lange House,
Krefeld, 1928. Floor plan.

6.10
Mies van der Rohe, Josef Esters House, Krefeld, 1930. Floor plan.

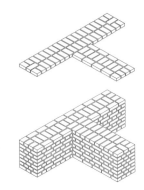

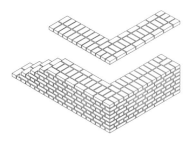

6.11
Mies van der Rohe, Josef Esters House, view through children's room and dining room to entrance.

6.12
Typical brick coursing by Mies (reconstruction by Werner Blaser for the Brick Country House of 1923).

6.13
Mies van der Rohe, Wolf House: reconstruction of original working drawing showing the precision with which the brick coursing was worked out.

that is used in the other two houses (fig. 6.13); header courses are used to cap the upstand walls of the Wolf House, while in the Lange and Esters houses the upstands are crisply terminated with metal copings (fig. 6.14). Moreover, the load-bearing walls of the Wolf House inhibit the incipient spatial dynamism of its plan, in comparison with the later Esters and Lange houses. At the same time, structural logic is variously compromised in all three works, since the steel lintels used in each case to span various horizontal openings remain totally unexpressed. In each instance, joists or trusses are concealed behind brick stretcher courses (fig. 6.15). This was not in any way a minor departure from standard practice, as we may judge from the complex structural devices used to support the masonry in the Lange House (fig. 6.16). Mies's engineer, Ernst Walther, complained at length about the economic and technical problems involved in achieving such large spans in brick openings. In a letter to Mies, he complained of his liberal use of Reiner beams and other elaborate structural devices.[7] However, such spans enabled Mies to provide large picture windows in both the Esters and Lange residences, the latter being equipped with retractable plate glass windows that could be lowered mechanically into the basement. These houses, together with the second Ulrich Lange and Hubbe houses projected in the thirties (figs. 6.17, 6.18), are particularly relevant to our understanding of Mies, since they were as formed by traditional constructional methods as they were influenced by avant-gardist spatial concepts. This possibly accounts for Mies's wistful remark that he would have liked to use more glass in these houses.

While Mies's free plan will finally manifest itself in the Barcelona Pavilion and the Tugendhat House, the only hint of spatial freedom in these early works resides in the ingenuity of the *en suite* planning, in which the living spaces are united with each other by a series of full-height, steel-framed double doors filled with glass (see fig. 6.11). As a result, the walls start to function as screens, producing a discernible contrast between a closed outer volume and a more open interior. This contrast is even more pronounced in the second Ulrich Lange and Hubbe houses projected in 1935 and in the Lemke courtyard house realized in Berlin in 1932 (figs. 6.19, 6.20). In each case, the dynamic space form is contained by bounding courtyard walls, which serve to stabilize the composition. This contrast between avant-gardist space and traditional envelope attains its ultimate articulation in the Tugendhat House, where the main living volume is an open, freely planned spatial continuum and the bedrooms are closed, traditional volumes, illuminated by pierced windows. The capacity of the retractable plate glass wall to transform the living room into an open air belvedere only serves to heighten this contrast.

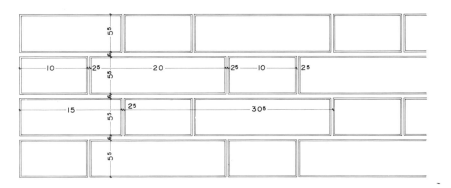

6.21
Mies van der Rohe, Glass Room, Werkbund
Exhibition, Stuttgart, 1927. View toward Lehm-
bruck sculpture.

6.22
Mies van der Rohe, Glass Room, Werkbund
Exhibition, Stuttgart, 1927.

tion, the translucent nature of both materials (fig. 6.24). The close conjunction of all these exhibits suggests Mies's affinity for German industry at the time and the way in which he aspired to inherit the mantle of Peter Behrens as the normative form-giver of the German industrial state. This aspiration is even implied in his use of the so-called *Skeletschrift* typeface; a lean, mechanical-looking type had been expressly devised for the occasion by Mies's assistant, Sergius Ruegenberg. Aside from his concern for the normative, Mies saw glass as embodying a new challenge, as it were, to the fundamental tectonic elements of the wall, the floor, and the ceiling. He was to state as much in his contribution to a prospectus written for the Union of German Plate Glass Manufacturers in 1933 wherein he stressed the symbiotic impact of glass on modern form.

What would concrete be, what steel without plate glass? The ability of both to transform space would be limited, even lost altogether, it would remain only a vague promise. Only a glass skin and glass walls can reveal the simple structural form of the skeletal frame and ensure its architectonic possibilities. And this is true not only of large utilitarian buildings. To be sure, it was with them that a line of development based on function (Zweck) and necessity began that needs no further justification; it will not end there, however, but will find its fulfillment in the realm of residential building. Only here, in a field offering greater freedom, one not so bound by narrower objectives, can the architectural potential of these technical methods be fully realized. These are truly architectural elements forming the basis for a new art of building. They permit us a degree of freedom in the creation of space that we will no longer deny ourselves. Only now can we give shape to space, open it, and link it to the landscape. It now becomes clear once more just what walls and openings are, and floors and ceilings. Simplicity of construction, clarity of tectonic means, and purity of materials have about them the glow of pristine beauty.[17]

Such a programmatic view of modern transparency was surely already evident in the Barcelona Pavilion of 1929, where tectonic value is unequivocally asserted in the eight freestanding cruciform columns, and where the space field is framed by the freestanding planes that bypass these supports (fig. 6.25). Aside from this patent opposition between columnar and planar form, it is possible to break down the Barcelona Pavilion into a series of polarities; tectonic versus stereotomic, still versus agitated, open versus closed, and above all, perhaps, traditional material versus space endlessness. The first dyad is tectonically self-evident, the second and third are related to the surfaces and the contents of the open and enclosed pools, while the last is evident in the opposition between the marble-faced pinwheeling planes and the symmetrical placement of the eight columns in relation to the roof. This pinwheel organization may also be read as a planimetric allusion to the Arts and Crafts asymmetrical plan form and hence to *building,* while the columnar peristyle recalls classical *architecture.* This last, reinforced by the particular treatment of the column casings, is further evidence of Mies's capacity to integrate tectonic meaning with abstract form.

Mies's Barcelona column is a dematerialized cruciform point support, and yet at the same time it is altogether more planar than the half-round cruciform column casings employed in the later Tugendhat House. The planar character of the Barcelona column derives from the orthogonal profile adopted by the bent, chromium-plated, sheet steel case covering the built-up steel core (fig. 6.26). Like Le Corbusier's *pilotis* in his Purist *plan libre,* this column has neither base

176

6.23
Mies van der Rohe in collaboration with Lilly Reich, silk exhibition, Exposition de la Mode, Berlin, 1927. Materials and colors: black, orange, and red velvet; gold, silver, black, and lemon-yellow silk.

6.24
Mies van der Rohe in collaboration with Lilly Reich, silk exhibition, German section, International Exposition, Barcelona, 1929.

6.25
Mies van der Rohe, German Pavilion, International Exposition, Barcelona, 1929. View toward small pool.

6.26
Mies van der Rohe, German Pavilion, International Exposition, Barcelona, plan of column.

nor capital. Both column types are, in fact, abstractions of the idea of support, since, due to the fact that no beams are expressed in either instance, a somewhat insubstantial act of bearing is conveyed by the form. In both instances the ceiling is treated as a flat, continuous plane. Here we see how modern, beamless construction favors the suppression of the frame; that is to say, it eliminates the very trabeation that for Perret was a prerequisite of tectonic culture. In this regard, both the Villa Savoye and the Barcelona Pavilion may be seen as atectonic, although they are by no means as extreme in this regard as Josef Hoffmann's Stoclet House of 1911. In drawing our attention to Hoffmann's atectonic propensity, Eduard Sekler will stress the dematerializing effect that the edge cable molding would exert on the facades of Hoffmann's building, and a similar judgment may also be applied to the treatment of its internal structure.[18] While columnar support is patently a key element in the structuring of the Barcelona Pavilion both technically and phenomenologically, the ontological interaction between support and burden (Schopenhauer's *Stütze* and *Last*) is patently absent. One may argue that this absence is more categoric than in the Villa Savoye, since in the latter the monolithic appearance of the reinforced concrete structure permits the perception of a certain fixity between column and soffit, particularly since both are monolithically expressed by being plastered and painted white throughout. In Barcelona, on the other hand, the riveted steel frame supports a faired-out, plastered soffit that appears to float independently of the chromium columns. This illusion of levitation is strengthened by the uninterrupted planar continuity of the ceiling and the floor, white plaster above and travertine below; an effect that is partially countered by the free assembly of pinwheeling planes and screens rendered in heavier material, in *vert antique* marble, in onyx, and in various kinds of glass of a translucent or transparent nature, set in chromium-plated frames (fig. 6.27). These last also tend to make any sense of fixity uncertain due to their proliferation of highlights and reflections. No one has perhaps written more perceptively of the illusory, empty character of this spatial field than the Catalan critic José Quetglas.[19]

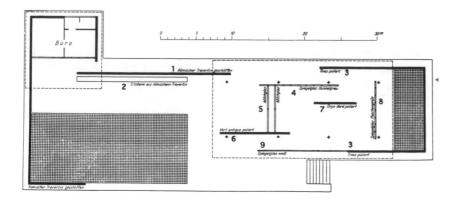

6.27

Mies van der Rohe, German Pavilion, International Exposition, Barcelona: plan published in 1929 indicating wall materials. Different and very subtle kinds of glass were used in the original Barcelona Pavilion, and this is one of the nuances that has not been followed in the recent reconstruction.

1. polished Roman travertine
2. bench of Roman travertine
3. polished Tinian marble
4. dark gray mirror glass
5. frosted glass
6. polished green antique marble
7. polished gold onyx
8. green bottle-mirror glass
9. white mirror glass

All of these vertiginous effects are emphasized, as Robin Evans would later observe, by the vertical mirroring of the volume about a horizon that happens to coincide not only with eye height but also with the central horizontal seam in the onyx plane, thereby suggesting a potential inversion of floor and ceiling that is paradoxically heightened rather than diminished by the differences in finish. As Evans remarks, since the floor reflects light and the ceiling receives it, the perceptual differences in the planar tone would have been greater had they been of the same material. Thus Mies would use "material asymmetry to create optical symmetry, rebounding the natural light to make the ceiling more sky-like and the ambience more expansive."[20] Traces of traditional value still remain, however, above all in the jointing of the travertine which tends not only to stress the tactility of the stone, as paving, but also to assert the presence of a *stereotomic* earthwork. Some vestige of the tectonic also remains in the columns, first, because the eight-column grid is perceivable as a peristyle, despite the asymmetrical freestanding planes, and second, because the reiterated highlights on the profiles of the casings effect a reference to classical fluting. Thus while the essential quality of chromium is its modernity, the form that it assumes in this instance also evokes a subtle traditional resonance.

The hallucinatory character of this synthesis is mediated in the Tugendhat House in Brno (Brünn) of the following year, where the bedrooms are excluded from the free plan and where the cruciform chromium-plated column casings are rounded (fig. 6.28). Here, with the single exception of the frosted glass in the entrance hall, the glazing is transparent and restricted to the perimeter of a simple rectangular envelope. This rather pragmatic attitude will inform the various row and courtyard houses that Mies designed between 1930 and 1935, beginning with the Gericke House projected for Wannsee in 1930 (fig. 6.29) and the Lemke House built in Berlin two years later, and continuing with such projects as the courtyard house with garage of 1934 and the Hubbe House and the first and second versions of the Ulrich Lange House projected for Krefeld of 1935. Despite this sobriety, the Tugendhat House (fig. 6.30) is in some respects more complex than the Barcelona Pavilion, for in addition to the opposites expressed in the pavilion, values of a more explicitly mythic and metaphorical nature find themselves incorporated into the Brno villa. Thus, the narrow winter garden, flanking the shorter side of the living volume, may be read as a third term between the petrified nature of the freestanding onyx plane subdividing the internal space and the living nature of the garden beyond. Here, as in the later Farnsworth House, the decorative manifests itself as an oscillating play between verdure as it is and verdure transformed either by reflection or by petrification. As in Adolf Loos's ironic use of heavily veined and matched marble, organic ornament appears here either as an intrinsic part of the material finish or as an optical effect, rather than through formal invention. At another level entirely, one may argue that the onyx dorée plane, separating the living room from the library, asserts, through its honorific character, the worldly cerebral status of the spaces on either side (fig. 6.31), while by a similar token the macassar ebony veneer to the semicircular dining alcove evokes through its material warmth the domestic, corporeal ritual of dining.

As in the large fenestration of the Lange House, the tectonic attains its most direct expression here in the *detailing* of the 80-foot-long plate glass window that, when withdrawn into the basement, converts the living space into a belvedere. Much as in the Krefeld houses, this intricate window section incorporates a retractable sun blind and a surface-mounted curtain track, plus a chromium balustrade and a series of chromium-plated heating tubes poised just above the floor. Once again, as in the Barcelona Pavilion, the suppression of the tectonic in the planar space-endlessness of the interior finds its countervailing reification

6.28

Mies van der Rohe, Tugendhat House, Brno, 1928–1930. Plans, section, and details. The entire plate glass wall of the living room may be slid into the basement in good weather.

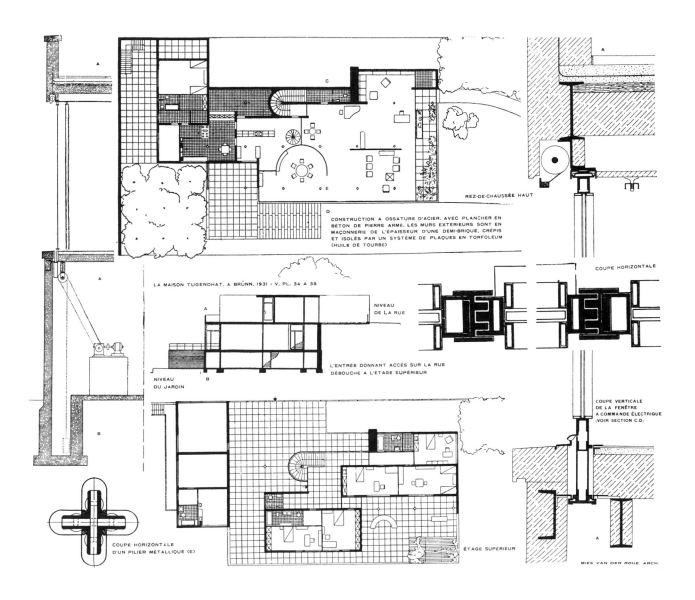

through the careful placement of material and the precision of small-scale detail (fig. 6.30). Again Lilly Reich enabled Mies to engage in an all but suprematist palette through the dissonant but rich furnishings employed throughout: the use of full-height curtains in black raw silk and black velvet on the winter garden wall and beige raw silk on the south wall, and the upholstery of the Tugendhat and Bruno chairs in emerald green leather and in ruby-red velvet and white vellum. All of this radiated out across a white linoleum floor, against separate sheets of retractable plate glass each some fifteen feet in length. That Mies intended a transcendental Baudelairean sense of *luxus* is borne out by Walter Riezler's contemporary appraisal of the house:

No one can deny the impression . . . of a particular spirituality of high degree dominating these spaces, a spirituality, to be sure, of a quite new kind. It is very much "tied to the present," and is therefore utterly different from the spirit dominating spaces of any earlier epoch. It is already the "spirit of technology"—not in the sense of that narrow-minded practicality that is so frequently deplored, but in the sense of a new freedom in living. . . . This is not to say that precisely this present project, namely the creation of a single residence for a high-spirited personality, is the very project that can best demonstrate the new spiritual ideas. Possibly, on the contrary, this project has been still somewhat determined by the sense of the epoch now approaching its end. But that is less important than the proof it provides that it is indeed possible to elevate oneself above the purely rational and functional thinking that has characterized modern architecture heretofore and into the realm of the spiritual.[21]

6.29
Mies van der Rohe, Gericke House, Wannsee, Berlin, 1930. Model.

6.30
Mies van der Rohe, Tugendhat House, view from dining room toward living room. The belvedere living room with a section of the glass wall removed. Here the tectonic quality of the work depends exclusively on the detailing, mostly carried out in polished chromium steel.

6.31
Mies van der Rohe, Tugendhat House, view toward library and living room.

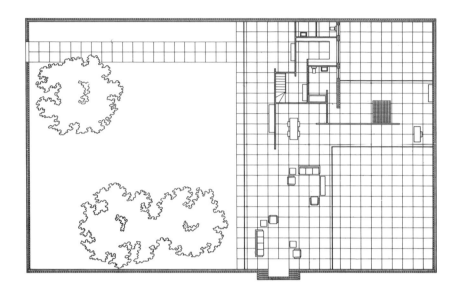

6.32
Mies van der Rohe, House with Three Courts,
project, 1934. Elevation.

6.33
Mies van der Rohe, House with Three Courts,
plan. Note the way the glass line does *not* coincide with the modular grid of the paving.

The unrealized House with Three Courts project of 1934 is in many respects the
most generic of Mies's courtyard houses (figs. 6.32, 6.33). The delimiting boundary of this house is a brick perimeter wall that is interrupted three times; first for
the entrance, then for the service core, and finally for the chimney. The floor of
the courtyard itself is divided into two planes, the one being paved in square
slabs of travertine and the other being lawn. The paved area is treated as a continuous domestic domain which in turn contains two subcourts, one for sleeping, one for living. The positioning of the plate glass enclosure outside the
modular grid suggests that these courts are to be read as outdoor rooms. At the
same time, the paving grid establishes the centers of the eight cruciform columns supporting the roof; a six-by-six modular spacing, as per the paving pattern. Within this overall frame the house breaks down into two elements: a
stereotomic domain comprising the bounding wall together with the travertine
paving, and a dematerialized *tectonic* domain, that is, the plate glass enclosure
with its marble-veneered walls and chromium-plated columns (fig. 6.34).

The two successive projects for the Ulrich Lange House and the Hubbe House,
all of 1935, elaborate a series of permutations derived from this three-court formula. Some of these variations depart from the generic type, such as the totally
enclosed volumes of the first Ulrich Lange House (fig. 6.35), the subdivided
double court of the second Ulrich Lange House, or the freestanding brick planes
at the center of the Hubbe House, projected for Magdeburg (see fig. 6.18). As in
the Barcelona Pavilion, the sublime interplay between natural form and sculpture evokes the spirit of romantic classicism. The picturesque lakeside vista,
punctuated by trees and projected beyond the interior of the Hubbe House, is
equally romantic, as are the wisteria-bedecked elevations of the first Ulrich
Lange House (fig. 6.36). This is the picturesque as we find it in Schinkel, al-

though the way in which these vistas are framed depends upon the presence of abstract space.

As Fritz Neumeyer has shown in his 1986 study *Das kunstlose Wort* (The Artless Word), Mies belonged to that generation of German intellectuals who were traumatized by the apocalypse of modernization that Germany had undergone throughout the second half of the nineteenth century. Like the Jesuit philosopher and theologian Romano Guardini by whom, as we now know, he was strongly influenced, Mies felt that the human intellect and spirit had no choice but to accept the radical transformations of the technological millennium as a fate that cannot be escaped. As Guardini put it in his 1927 *Briefe vom Comer See:*

We belong to the future. We must put ourselves into it, each one at his station. We must not plant ourselves against the new and attempt to retain a beautiful world, one that must perish. Nor must we try to build, with creative fantasy, a new one that claims to be immune to the ravages of becoming. We have to formulate the nascent. But that we can only do if we honestly say yes to it; yet with incorruptible heart we have to retain our awareness of all that is destructive and inhuman in it. Our time is given to us as a soil on which we stand, as a task that we have to master.[22]

Mies would respond quickly and directly to this challenge three years later in an essay entitled "Die neue Zeit" (The New Era):

Let us not give undue importance to mechanization and standardization. Let us accept changed economic and social conditions as a fact. All these take their blind and fateful course.

One thing will be decisive: the way we assert ourselves in the face of circumstance. Here the problem of the spirit begins. The important question to ask is not "what" but "how." What goods we produce or what tools we use are not questions of spiritual value.

How the question of skyscrapers versus low buildings is settled, whether we build of steel and glass are unimportant questions from the point of view of the spirit. . . .

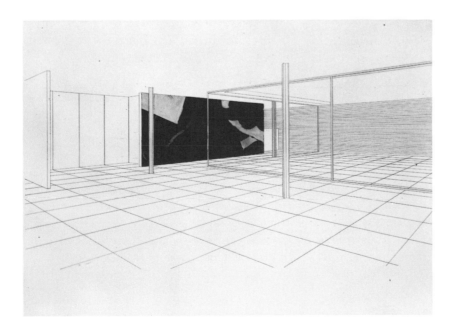

6.34
Mies van der Rohe, House with Three Courts, collage with composition by Georges Braque.

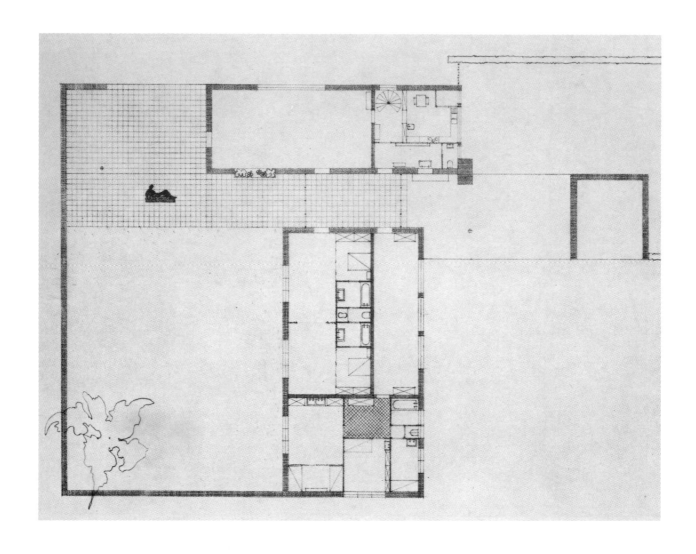

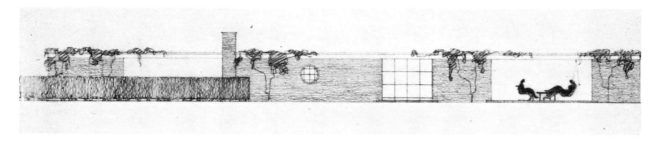

6.35
Mies van der Rohe, Ulrich Lange House (first version), Krefeld, 1935. Plan.

6.36
Mies van der Rohe, Ulrich Lange House (first version), elevations.

Yet it is just the question of value that is decisive. We must set up new values, fix our ultimate goals so that we may establish standards. For what is right and significant for any era—including the new era—is this: to give the spirit the opportunity for existence.[23]

This spirit of resignation and resistance was hardly new to Mies, for he had long since been preoccupied with the demise of craft culture and the positive potential of rationalized machine production. As he wrote in an essay entitled "Baukunst und Zeitwille" (Building Art and the Will of the Epoch) of 1924:

As I was born into an old family of stone masons, I am very familiar with hand craftsmanship, and not only as an aesthetic onlooker. My receptiveness to the beauty of handwork does not prevent me from recognizing that handicrafts as a form of economic production are lost. The few real craftsmen still alive in Germany are rarities whose work can be acquired only by very rich people. What really matters is something totally different. Our needs have assumed such proportions that they can no longer be met with methods of craftsmanship. . . . The need for even a single machine abolishes handicraft as an economic form. . . . Since we stand only in the beginning phase of industrial development, we cannot compare the initial imperfections and hesitancies to a highly mature culture of craftsmanship. . . . Old contents and forms, old means and work methods have for us only historical value. Life confronts us daily with new challenges: they are more important than the entire historical rubbish. . . . Each task represents a new challenge and leads to new results. We do not solve formal problems, but building problems, and the form is not the goal but the result of our work. That is the essence of our striving; and this viewpoint still separates us from many. Even from most of the modern building masters. But it unites us with all the disciplines of modern life. Much as the concept of building is, for you, not tied to old contents and forms, so it is also not connected to specific materials. We are very familiar with the charm of stones and bricks. But that does not prevent us nowadays from taking glass and concrete, glass and metal, into consideration as fully equivalent materials. In many cases, these materials correspond best to present day purposes.[24]

Fourteen years later, in his inaugural address at IIT, he would elaborate further on the same theme: "Thus, each material has its specific characteristics which we must understand if we want to use it. This is no less true of steel and concrete. We must remember that everything depends on how we use the material, not on the material itself."[25]

According to Werner Blaser, Mies regarded the perennial invention of arbitrary form as both trivial and absurd. He saw the discipline of construction as the sole guarantee of quality in architecture.[26] In 1961, in an issue of *Architectural Design* devoted to Mies, Peter Carter records him as saying:

Berlage was a man of great seriousness who would not accept anything that was fake and it was he who had said that nothing should be built that is not clearly constructed. And Berlage did exactly that. And he did it to such an extent that his famous building in Amsterdam, the Beurs, had a mediaeval character without being mediaeval. He used brick in the way the mediaeval people did. The idea of a clear construction came to me there, as one of the fundamentals we should accept. We can talk about that easily but to do it is not easy. It is very difficult to stick to this fundamental construction, and then to elevate to a structure. I must make it clear that in the English language you call everything structure. In Europe we don't. We call a shack, a shack, and not a structure. By structure, we have a philosophical idea. The structure is the whole, from top to bottom, to the last detail—with the same ideas. That is what we call structure.[27]

This passage is remarkable not only for its evocation of structural rationalism but also for its indirect allusion to medieval scholasticism. And yet, at the same time, Mies's preoccupation with progressive form remained as technological as it was aesthetic. This we may glean from a 1950 IIT address:

Technology is far more than a method. It is a world in itself. As a method it is superior in almost every respect. But only where it is left to itself, as in gigantic structures of engineering, there technology reveals its true nature. There it is evident that it is not only a useful means but that it is something that has a meaning and a powerful form—so powerful in fact, that it is not easy to name it. . . . Where technology reaches its real fulfillment it transcends into architecture.[28]

On the other hand, he seems to have been fully aware of the split in his work between the conservative nature of his tectonic structure and the radical stance of his spatial aesthetics. Thus, in an essay on the IIT curriculum, he wrote:

It is radical and conservative at once. It is radical in accepting the scientific and technological driving and sustaining forces of our time. It has a scientific character, but it is not science. It uses technological means but it is not technology. It is conservative as it is not only concerned with a purpose but also with a meaning, as it is not only concerned with a function but also with an expression. It is conservative as it is based on the eternal laws of architecture: Order, Space, Proportion.[29]

It would be hard to imagine something more overtly classical than this last triad, and yet Mies continues to differentiate between *Bauen* and *Baukunst,* between building and architecture, particularly after his Reichsbank competition entry of 1933. Indeed, this project implied a declension from a higher to a lower tectonic status *within* a single structure. This is evident in the differentiation between the gridded industrial glazing of the typical floor and the double-height, representative plate glass facade of the bank at street level (fig. 6.37). While the free plan is still in evidence, inasmuch as the curtain wall is projected in front of the column line throughout, Mies's previous preoccupation with the avant-gardist space form is relaxed somewhat, presumably because the public status of the institution demanded a more normative and symmetrical approach. At the same time the *sachlich* curtain wall of the repetitive floors is rendered even more normative, for as Ludwig Glaeser has remarked, Mies's model for the brick and glass banded perimeter of the Reichsbank was derived from the German industrial vernacular of *Fachwerkbauten* in which exposed steel framing was combined with brick and glass infill. This building system derived in its turn from traditional, timber-framed *Fachwerkbauten,* and by the second half of the nineteenth century this modified "steel frame" vernacular was already a common model for inexpensive factory sheds, to which countless industrial buildings erected throughout Europe adequately testify.[30] Despite this vernacular presence, Mies's Reichsbank, like his initial scheme for the Illinois Institute of Technology of 1939, features a continuous curtain wall rather than a frame and infill system, and it is this sense of dematerialized continuity that will be decisive in the formation of his American career.

6.37
Mies van der Rohe, Reichsbank, Berlin, 1933.
The Reichsbank as *Fachbauwerk*.

6.38
Mies van der Rohe, Promontory Apartments,
Chicago, 1949.

6.39
Mies van der Rohe, Promontory Apartments,
partial section and plan. Note the articulation
of the reinforced concrete structure both in
plan and in section.

188

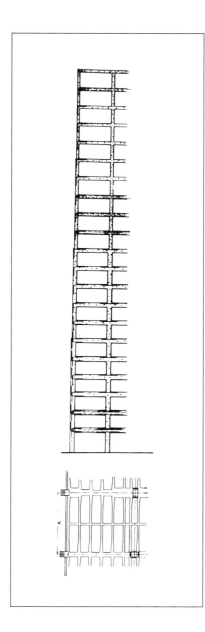

Despite their varying status, the very first building projected for the IIT campus, the Minerals and Metals Research Building of 1943, should be construed as an example of *Baukunst* rather than *Architektur,* and a similar objective restraint can be sensed in the Promontory Apartments built in Chicago between 1946 and 1949 (figs. 6.38, 6.39). The stepped rectangular reinforced concrete column employed in this last—the cross section of which diminishes as it rises due to a reduction in compressive load—may be regarded as a structurally rationalist element. A similar feature will be deployed by Mies in his IIT faculty apartments of 1951 (fig. 6.40), and a comparable level of constructional directness, indicative again of building rather than architecture, will appear in the infill panels of the Promontory Apartments (figs. 6.41, 6.42). An even more laconic version of the same infill comprising brick spandrels and standard steel sash will govern the character of the IIT apartments.

While the Resor House projected for Wyoming in 1938 still employs the cruci-form column, Mies will shortly abandon this element, along with the free plan. From now on, the tectonic focus shifts to the exposed steel frame with brick and glass infill. No one has written more cogently of the spatial consequences of this tectonic metamorphosis than Colin Rowe.

Mies's characteristic German column was circular or cruciform; but his new col-umn became H-shaped, became that I-beam which is now almost a personal sig-nature. Typically, his German column had been clearly distinguished from walls and windows, isolated from them in space; and typically, his new column be-came an element integral with the envelope of the building where it came to func-tion as a kind of mullion or residue of wall. Thus the column section was not without some drastic effects on the entire space of the building. The circular or cruciform section had tended to push partitions away from the column. The new tectonic tended to drag them towards it. The old column had offered a minimum of obstruction to a horizontal movement of space; but the new column presents a distinctly more substantial stop. The old column had tended to cause space to gyrate around it, had been central to a rather tentatively defined volume; but the new column instead acts as the enclosure or the external definition of a major volume of space. The spatial functions of the two are thus completely differenti-ated. . . . As an International Style element, the column put in its last appearance in the museum project of 1942; while in the Library and Administration Building project of 1944, the effects of the H-shaped column are already apparent and are clearly exhibited in the published drawings of its plans. From these drawings it is evident that the column is no longer to be allowed to float ambiguously beneath a slab. It is now—apparently for the first time—tied to a network of beams, and these beams have appointed definite positions for the screens, and for the most part the screens have already leapt into these positions—in fact only the extra-thick walls around the lavatories seem to have been able to resist the new attraction.[31]

As Rowe indicates, this change is of an epistemic nature, not only because the integration of frame and partition transforms the character of the space, but also because the revelation of the joint between column and beam represents a shift back toward the tectonic tradition, first manifest at IIT in the Minerals and Metals Building. Mies's general focus now begins to shift away from universal modernist space to the primacy of the frame and its joint. This change is funda-mental, for it means that the opposition between modernity and tradition will

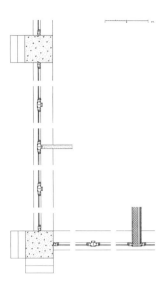

now no longer be mediated by an elision between columnar support and the system of spatial enclosure. At the same time, the suspended ceiling will be retained as a normative element, irrespective of the program, dispersing the tectonic energy of Mies's later work toward the perimeter of the space. The moment of this transition is already evident in the earliest buildings for the IIT campus, where the steel frame was only partially fireproofed, as in the project for the Library and Administration Building (figs. 6.43, 6.44) and in the Minerals and Metals Research Building (fig. 6.45). In the library project an exposed H-section is the main tectonic element (fig. 6.46), while in the research building an elongated version of an H-section appears at the reentrant corner columns. This is complemented by a normative composite column comprising two reversed channel sections, welded together to form a square box. This box column is set flush with the fair-faced infill brickwork on both sides (fig. 6.47). In each case, we are justified in speaking of a tectonic that is partially ontological and partially representational, although in the Minerals and Metals Building the deep steel sections facing the concrete downstand beams, as permanent formwork, are evidently a representation of the fireproofed steelwork within the concrete (fig. 6.48). In the library, the steel roof beams are shown partially concealed by a suspended ceiling (fig. 6.43). This "cutaway" solution was adopted in order to facilitate the servicing of the interstitial space while revealing the tectonic probity of the structural frame.[32] This expression is in strong contrast to the Minerals and Metals Building, where the steel roof beams are directly expressed on the interior. This difference in attitude toward the ceiling may perhaps be explained by the differ-

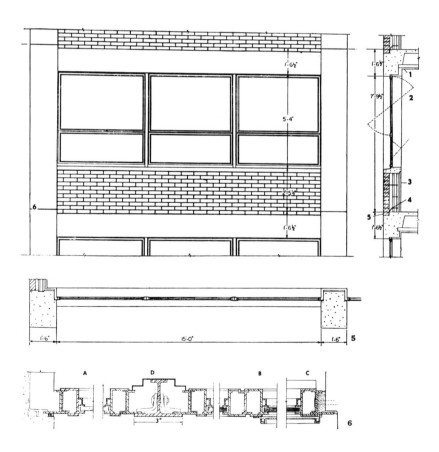

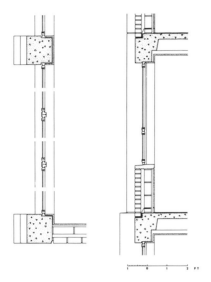

6.40
Mies van der Rohe, Carman Hall, Illinois Institute of Technology, Chicago, 1953. Horizontal detail.

6.41
Mies van der Rohe, Promontory Apartments, plan, section, elevation, and detail of brick and aluminum window infill.

6.42
Mies van der Rohe, Promontory Apartments, plan and section of infill, showing decreasing column section.

ent status of the works involved; for where in the first instance the building is a public institution, in the second it merely accommodates a utilitarian volume.

With the IIT Alumni Memorial Hall of 1945, Mies's expression becomes more monumental, in part because the steel frame had to be fireproofed throughout and in part because this was the most honorific building erected on the campus to date. Here, the primary tectonic elements break down into the *Kuntsform* of the representative steel profiles and the *Kernform* of the fireproofed steel within (fig. 6.49). The H-columns, encased in square concrete piers, are now set behind the skin, thereby permitting a more symmetrical treatment of the reentrant corners. These corners were compounded in part out of steel facing and angles, representing the column, and in part out of I-sections that formed the receiving frame for the 9-inch-brick solid infill walls spanning between the uprights of the framework. This corner treatment recalls the neoclassical corner favored by Schinkel, particularly in his Altes Museum and Schauspielhaus.

Three works projected in the mid-forties are seminal to Mies's subsequent career. These are the Farnsworth House, initially designed in 1946, the unrealized Hi-Way Restaurant of the same year, and the twin apartment towers known as 860 Lake Shore Drive, Chicago, designed in 1948.

The Farnsworth House returns us to the avant-gardist spatial paradigm but now in the form of a virtual volume suspended between the pure planar surfaces of a floor and a ceiling (figs. 6.50, 6.51). Where on the one hand Farnsworth asserts itself as a skeleton frame, on the other it amounts to an asymmetrical assembly comprising a prism and a platform, the one sliding past the other in a manner that is reminiscent of Schinkel's Italianate compositions. To some extent this house may be analyzed in terms of Semper's *Four Elements,* particularly with regard to its separation into stereotomic and tectonic elements; the former being embodied in the travertine paving of the twin platforms, while the latter assumed the form of the steel skeleton and its infill. The structural details are reduced to a minimal expression, from the open-jointed paving, laid absolutely flat, on top of the gravel-filled drain pans made of welded steel, to the eight face-mounted, full-height H-section columns carrying the steel-framed floor and roof (figs. 6.52, 6.53). The architectonic purity of this welded steel frame is heightened by grinding the welds flat and by finishing the steel in white paint. Here, once again, we seem to encounter a passing reference to Malevich's famous white-on-white paintings of the period 1917–1920. At the same time, the elision between the terrace and the house is reinforced by an overlap between the eight full-height columns of the house and the four stub columns of the terrace.

From a tectonic standpoint, there is an affinity between 860 Lake Shore Drive (1948–1951) (fig. 6.54) and the IIT Alumni Memorial Hall. In both instances, the steel frame is totally fireproofed in concrete and the columns and beams are represented by plated steel surfaces implanted on the outside of the fireproofed structure (fig. 6.55). In 860 the secondary framing system of the mullions, carrying the fenestration, is mounted on these steel plates, thereby rendering the overall assembly as a continuous curtain wall (fig. 6.56). It is important to note that the assembly of this wall depended upon the welding of these mullions, together with the steel spandrels and column plates, into a continuous floor-height frame, and on the lowering of this prefabricated bay into its final position from a tower crane mounted on the roof. The syncopated rhythms obtaining between the structural frame, the mullions, the face plates, and the glazing has been perceptively analyzed by Peter Carter in the following terms:

Mies's introduction of projecting steel mullions at the quarter points of each bay and on the column surfaces engenders a new and unexpected quality from the separate identities of the elements involved. The structural frame and its glass infill become architecturally fused, each losing a part of its particular identity in establishing the new architectural reality. The mullion has acted as a kind of catalyst for this change.

The columns and mullions determine window width. The two central windows are, therefore, wider than those adjacent to the column. These variants produce visual cadences of expanding and contracting intervals: column—narrow window—wide window, *then reversing,* wide window—narrow window—column, *and so on, of an extraordinarily subtle richness. And to this is added the alternating opacity of the steel and reflectivity of the glass caused by the blinker quality of the mullions* en masse. . . . *Before Mies's "860" solution, there were two clear basic possibilities for the enclosure of skeleton frame buildings. Either the skin acted as an infill between the structure or hung in front of it. . . . While acceptable on their own pragmatic terms, these solutions have, with the exception of the Seagram Building, rarely been touched by the magic of great architecture. At*

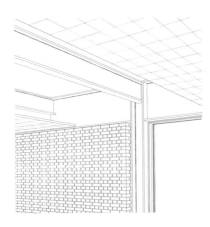

6.43
Mies van der Rohe, Library and Administration Building, Illinois Institute of Technology, Chicago, 1944.

6.44
Mies van der Rohe, Library and Administration Building, corner detail.

6.45
Mies van der Rohe, Minerals and Metals Research Building, Illinois Institute of Technology, Chicago, 1943. Laboratory.

6.46
Mies van der Rohe, Library and Administration Building, vertical and horizontal details.

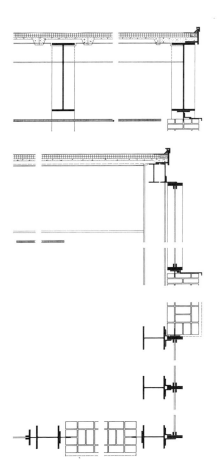

"860" the solution has come directly out of the problem of finding a single architectural expression which would embrace both skin and structure. At "860" the structure and the skin retain much of their individual identities but the application of the mullion has caused a philosophical transformation from pluralistic to a monotheistic character.[33]

Mies's neo-Suprematist sensibility assumes a perceptually dynamic character in the foreshortening of the mullioned facades of 860 Lake Shore Drive, where the mutual positioning of the two slabs is such as to engender a constantly changing three-quarters view of either the one or the other facade (fig. 6.57). As one moves around this rotational composition, the projecting mullions either open out to reveal the full extent of the infill glazing or close up to present the illusion of being a twenty-six-story relief construction in opaque steel. Viewed from a distance, the building appears as an assembly of virtual volumes and planes in space, whereas when approached frontally each slab and structural bay assumes the format of a symmetrical composition.

This generic curtain wall changes markedly in its tectonic attributes as Mies passes from one high rise building to the next. No two treatments are perhaps more contrasting in this regard than 860 Lake Shore Drive and the Seagram Building. In 860, the concrete fireproofed structural floors and columns are covered in steel plates onto which the mullions are face-welded, whereas in the Seagram the fireproofed frame is set back from the curtain wall, with the result that the floors are suppressed behind a continuous skin of brown-tinted glass, with the mullions running uninterruptedly across glazed spandrel panels (fig. 6.58). Equally hybrid, given the perceptual fusion of bronze anodized fenestration with brown glass, are the reentrant corners of the service shaft to the rear of the Seagram Building, where very dark green marble sheeting is used to give the im-

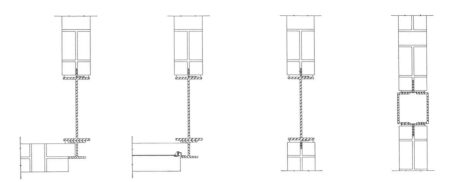

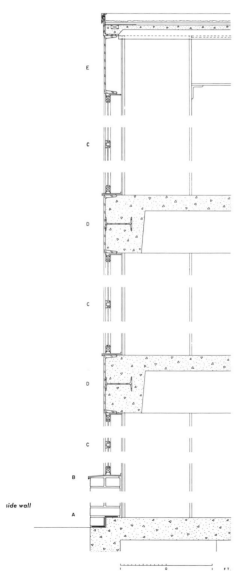

6.47
Mies van der Rohe, Minerals and Metals Research Building, horizontal details.

6.48
Mies van der Rohe, Minerals and Metals Research Building, vertical exterior details.

side wall

pression of a vertically striated, monolithic metal box. From this point of view we may claim that Seagram is the more membranous of the two works, substituting the steel-plated representation of the structural frame in 860 Lake Shore Drive with a plate glass curtain wall that does no more than represent its own tectonic autonomy.

The unrealized Hi-Way drive-in restaurant, designed for Joseph Cantor of Indianapolis in 1946, introduces the long-span trussed structure that Mies will explore, in various ways, during the remainder of his career. The roof of the Hi-Way Restaurant was to have been hung from the underside of two exposed lattice trusses, each spanning 150 feet. This format appears in two subsequent works, first in the Mannheim Theater proposal of 1952 (figs. 6.59, 6.60) and then in Crown Hall, built at IIT in 1956 (fig. 6.61). In the first instance, 15-foot-deep exposed lattice trusses are projected across 266 feet, while in the second, two-foot-deep stiffened steel beams span 150 feet. Within the glass cage of the former, Mies intended to suspend two theaters, set back to back and surrounded by a continuous foyer. Of these three works, Crown Hall is perhaps the most canonical, not only because it was the only one to be realized, but also because it combined the sectional schema of the Farnsworth House with the mullion-framing system of 860 Lake Shore Drive (figs. 6.62, 6.63). At the same time, in being analogously structured about a *corps de logis,* Crown Hall makes a distant allusion to Schinkel's Altes Museum, however much this axial order is mediated by the general diffusion of space throughout its interior. As Colin Rowe has written:

Like the characteristic Palladian composition, Crown Hall is a symmetrical and, probably, a mathematically regulated volume. But, unlike the characteristic Palladian composition, it is not an hierarchically ordered organization which projects its centralized theme vertically in the form of a pyramidal roof or dome. Unlike the Villa Rotonda, but like so many of the compositions of the twenties, Crown Hall is provided with no effective central area within which the observer can stand and comprehend the whole. The observer may understand a good deal of the interior while he is external to it (although even this Mies is disposed to disallow by planting a screen of trees across the front); but, once inside, rather than any spatial climax, the building offers a central solid, not energetically stated it is true, but still an insulated core around which the space travels laterally with the enclosing windows. Also, the flat slab of the roof induces a certain outward pull; and for this reason, in spite of the centralizing activity of the entrance vestibule, the space still remains, though in very much simplified form, the rotary peripheric organization of the twenties, rather than the predominantly centralized composition of the true Palladian or classical plan.[34]

The other long-span type favored by Mies comprised a two-way, space frame roof carried on perimeter point supports, set in from the corners. This type was first broached in his Fifty by Fifty House, projected in 1950, the name deriving from the fact that the house was roofed by a 50-by-50-foot space frame carried on four central columns, each being set at the midpoint of one side (figs. 6.64, 6.65). Mies was to project a similar cantilevered space frame roof on four subsequent occasions. The first of these was his 1953 project for a convention hall for Chicago, accommodating 79,000 people and measuring 720 feet along each of its sides. There followed three more modest variations on the same theme: the Bacardi Office Building, Santiago, Cuba, of 1957 (figs. 6.66, 6.67), the Georg Schäfer Museum proposal of 1960, and finally, the Neue Nationalgalerie in Berlin dating from 1962.

Like Viollet-le-Duc, Mies saw the "great space" as the ultimate proof of the stature of a civilization; a proof that in this century was more likely to be found in civil engineering than in architecture. Two projects from Mies's American career testify to the symbolic import that he would attach to the achievement of such a span and volume, and it is significant that he would employ the ultramodernist technique of photomontage in the representation of both of them. While the first of these is a project for an auditorium dating from 1942 (fig. 6.68), the second is

6.49
Mies van der Rohe, Alumni Memorial Hall, Illinois Institute of Technology, Chicago, 1945. Horizontal and vertical details.

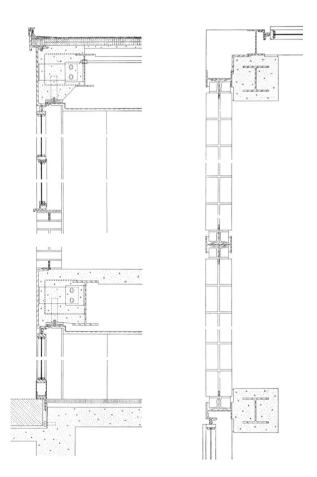

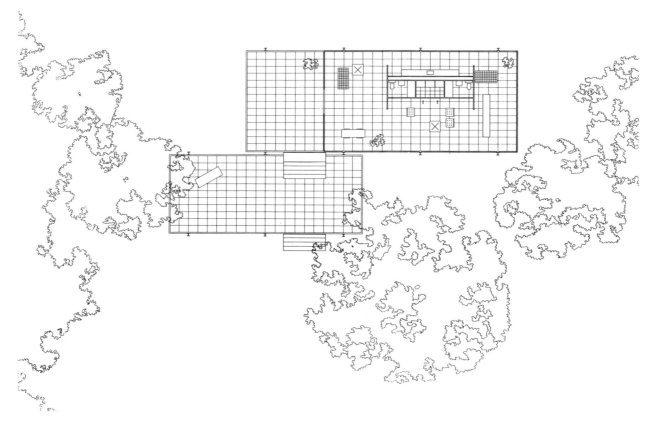

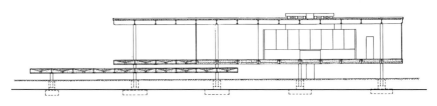

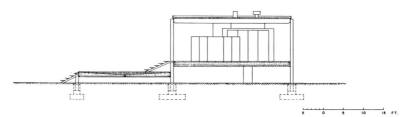

6.50
Mies van der Rohe, Farnsworth House, Plano,
Illinois, 1950. Plan.

6.51
Mies van der Rohe, Farnsworth House, longitudinal and transverse sections.

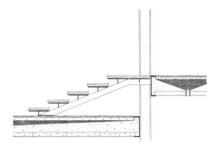

6.52
Mies van der Rohe, Farnsworth House, exterior stair detail.

6.53
Mies van der Rohe, Farnsworth House, exterior horizontal details.

the convention hall projected for Chicago in 1953 (figs. 6.69, 6.70). Where the former is rendered as a wood veneer and metal collage laid over a photograph of one of Albert Kahn's aircraft factories, the latter uses marbled paper to represent the stone-clad walls of a vast column-free hall. The structural roof of this 720-foot-square, steel space frame was projected as 30 feet deep, while the overall height of the structure would have risen to 110 feet. The sides of the hall would have been carried on two 60-foot corner cantilevers and five 120-foot-wide structural bays. The roof was projected as resting on lattice supports that in their turn took their bearing off hinge joints mounted on stub columns (fig. 6.71).

The last realized work of his life, the Neue Nationalgalerie in Berlin (fig. 6.72), was a homecoming for Mies in more ways than one, since in this final work he was able to reconcile the conflicting poles about which his work had been divided: namely, the infinite continuum of avant-gardist space and the constructional logic of tectonic form. These values were never more at variance with each other than in the main volume of Crown Hall, where the uninterrupted ceiling plane obscures the tectonic articulation of the peripheral structure. Despite their precise termination in a steel cornice that caps the roof line, the mullions at Crown Hall, when seen from the inside, appear to be totally unintegrated, since they extend beyond the suspended ceiling into a slot running around the perimeter of the loft space (fig. 6.73).

This aporia of the suspended ceiling, which occurs in various forms throughout Mies's late career, first approaches resolution in the concrete space frame of the Bacardi Building, which he projected in 1957. The ceiling plane is now the lower chord of a space frame supported on eight columns set in from the corners of a square plan (see fig. 6.66). This paradigm, translated into steel for the Georg Schäfer Museum, will become the parti for the square pavilion of the Neue Nationalgalerie. Although the space frame appears here as an infinite plane in space, it nonetheless establishes its tectonic presence through the intersecting grid of its rolled-steel chords (fig. 6.74). This egg crate grid, divided into sixteen square modules in both directions, receives columnar support four modules in from its extremities, on each of its sides. Furthermore, the chords of the space frame are spaced so as to coincide with the column heads of the eight supports.

With this reinterpretation of the Suprematist space field as a space frame structure carried on cruciform supports, Mies returns to the neoclassical resonance that is detectable throughout his work, even in his freely planned houses of the

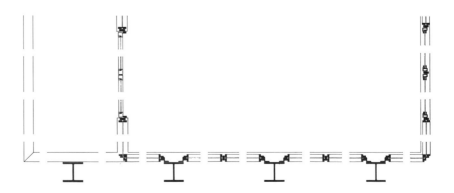

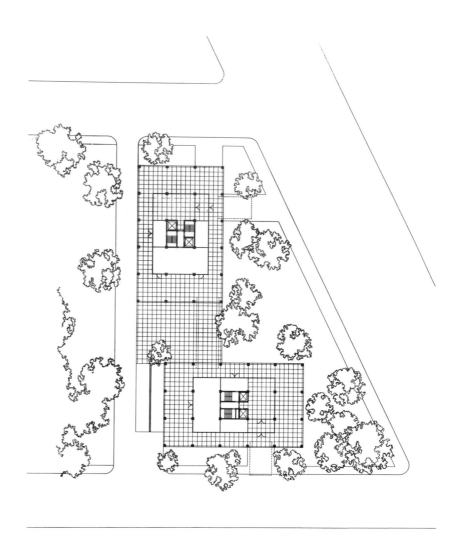

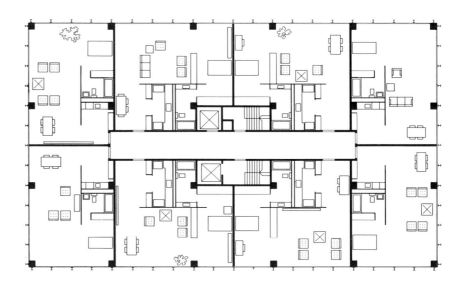

6.54
Mies van der Rohe, 860 and 880 Lake Shore
Drive Apartments, Chicago, 1951. Typical
floor plan as proposed by Mies; site plan.

6.55
Mies van der Rohe, 860 and 880 Lake Shore
Drive Apartments, vertical details.

6.56
Mies van der Rohe, 860 and 880 Lake Shore
Drive Apartments, horizontal details.

thirties. While these welded steel cruciforms, like their freestanding predecessors, serve as metaphors for the classical order of the antique world, they are, at the same time, removed both from classical precedent and from the dematerialized chromium plate supports of Mies's middle period. For now, the chromium-plated allusion to classical fluting has been replaced by the four T-sections welded into a cruciform about a central point (fig. 6.75). Thus the column of the Neue Nationalgalerie is capable of asserting its own structural and mythical character within the context of structural rationalism. In this instance its ontological authority is reinforced by the hinged column head, which, as a metaphorical capital, inverts the position and significance of the steel hinged joint as this had appeared in Peter Behrens's turbine factory of 1909. The hinge now appears as part of a surrogate entablature rather than the echinus of a stylobate. In their mode of support, the column and its hinge reinterpret the tectonic tradition of the Occident, while the egg crate roof, painted dark gray bordering on matte black, depends for its reading on the play of planes, situated at different spatial depths, so that the intersecting lower flanges of the space frame seem to hover as a slightly lighter grid below the dark inner soffit of the roof. Here Mies's black-on-black aesthetic, recalling Ad Reinhardt's minimalism,[35] becomes legible through the play of reflected light. By virtue of variations in luminosity it alludes through the uncertain depth of the space frame to the tradition of the avant-garde, and thus we pass in his last work from a highly accomplished tectonic solution to an intangible, almost mystical assertion of the sublime in the form of a universal plane suspended in space.

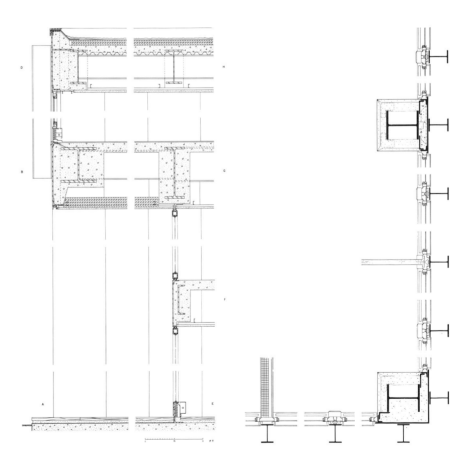

Mies van der Rohe

6.57
Mies van der Rohe, 860 and 880 Lake Shore Drive Apartments.

6.58
Mies van der Rohe, 860 and 880 Lake Shore Drive Apartments and Seagram Building, New York, 1958: curtain wall details.

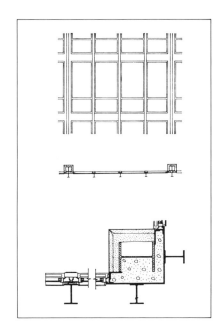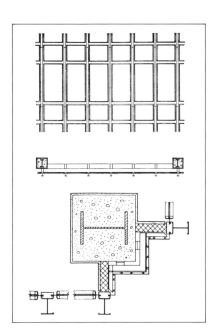

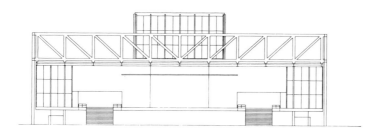

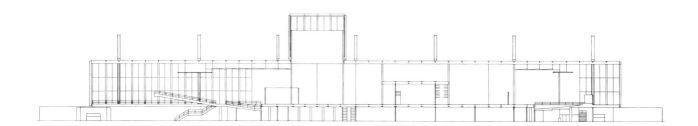

6.59
Mies van der Rohe, National Theater, Mann-heim, 1952. Section.

6.60
Mies van der Rohe, National Theater, Mann-heim, transverse section.

6.61
Mies van der Rohe, Crown Hall, Illinois Insti-tute of Technology, 1956. Elevation and plan.

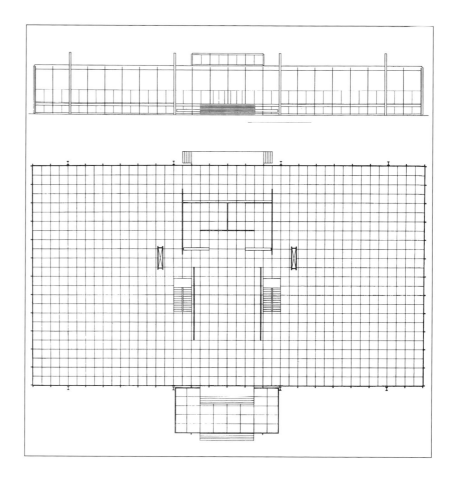

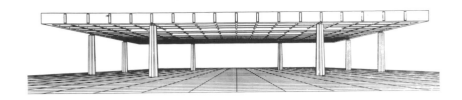

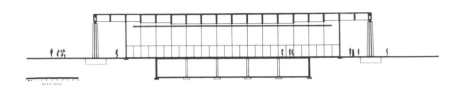

6.66
Mies van der Rohe, Bacardi Office Building,
Santiago de Cuba, 1957. Note how the concrete space frame structure progressively increases in depth from the perimeter cornice
as it moves to the center of the long span.

6.67
Mies van der Rohe, Bacardi Office Building,
section.

6.68
Mies van der Rohe, Concert Hall, project,
1942. A collage made over a photo of the interior of Albert Kahn's Glen L. Martin factory,
Baltimore.

sis was facilitated by the precise articulation of the components out of which his work was made. A similar elementarism is detectable in the work of Mies, and he was to acknowledge his debt to Schinkel in this regard when he remarked in 1959: "In the Altes Museum he [Schinkel] *separated* the elements, the columns and the walls and the ceiling, and I think that this is still visible in my later buildings."[38] This principle of *separation* seems to have enabled Mies to articulate quite different components whose conjunction would otherwise have been impacted.

With the exception of his furniture and his large-span structures, Mies tended to underemphasize the connectivity of the joint and its fabrication; a technical silence that attains its apotheosis perhaps in the flat welds of the Farnsworth House. Thus despite his appreciation of Viollet-le-Duc, Mies did not fully embrace the structurally rationalist principle of revealing the transmission of load or the Kahnian penchant for maintaining the marks of the assembly process as a form of ornament. Hence his recourse to welded steelwork in order to render the junctions as invisible as possible, and hence, also, the "separating" role played by his suspended ceilings that were an anathema to architects of a more structurally rationalist persuasion, such as Perret, Kahn, and Utzon.

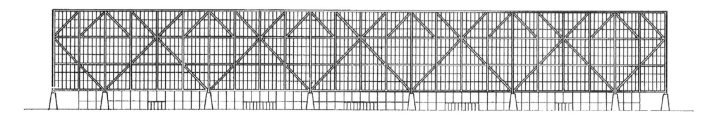

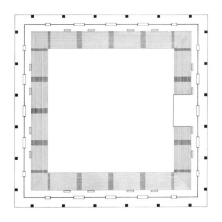

6.69
Mies van der Rohe, Convention Hall, project, Chicago, 1953. Elevation and plan.

6.70
Mies van der Rohe, Convention Hall project, interior perspective.

6.71
Mies van der Rohe, Convention Hall project: alternate structural systems with concrete (left) and steel (right) piers.

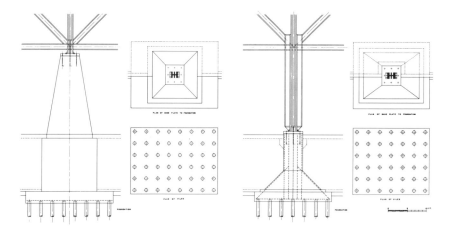

Mies attempted to express the technoscientific civilization of his time as a factual given, as though this "almost nothing" was the only authentic form that civilization could now attain. In assuming this Hegelian stance he came to regard modern technology as the manifestation of transcendental reason, comparable in its objectivity to the anonymity of building culture in the Middle Ages. And while tectonic value is constantly evident in his work, this is displaced at times by an autonomous drive toward dematerialization that is at variance with his

6.72
Mies van der Rohe, Neue Nationalgalerie, Berlin, 1968. Elevation and plan.

6.73
Mies van der Rohe, Neue Nationalgalerie, interior.

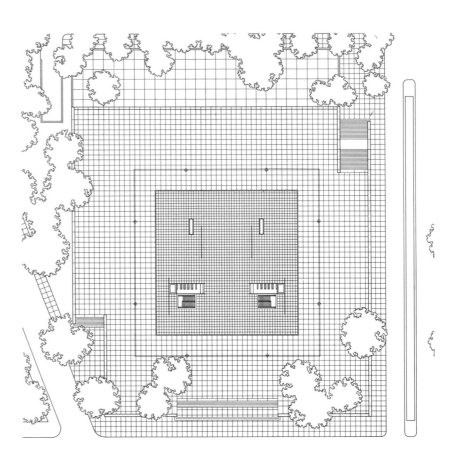

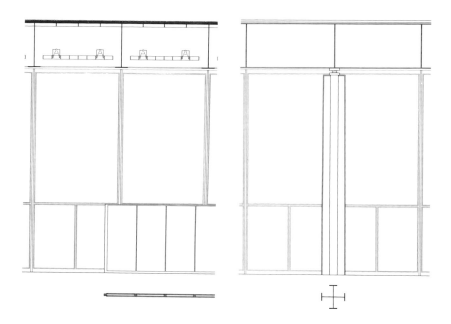

6.74
Mies van der Rohe, Neue Nationalgalerie, typical section.

6.75
Mies van der Rohe, Neue Nationalgalerie, column elevation and plan.

6.76
Mies van der Rohe, Museum for a Small City, project, 1943.

concern for cultural continuity and the permanence of material. The continuous travertine floor in the Farnsworth House is a case in point, for while it covers the entire floor, including the bathroom, it is countered in its materiality by the abstract immateriality of the suspended ceiling. At the same time Mies, like Louis Kahn, was drawn to the sublime, not only in terms of light and space but also in a temporal sense, so that, after the *Schinkelschule* by which he was influenced, his works aspired to a state of eventual ruination. This romantic prospect already finds reflection in the habitual planting of ivy against the pristine elevations of his buildings. Thus his concern for the precision of tectonic form was always tempered, not only by the infinite space field of the avant-garde and the dematerialized membrane but also by the ever-changing fateful forces of technology and time. By accepting the triumph of universal technology and by concentrating as a result on the "how" of technique rather than the "what" of institutional form, Mies strove to liberate the subject from the pathos of its insignificance when set against the flood tide of modernization. Like others of his generation, like Max Weber, Ernst Jünger, and Martin Heidegger and above all like the church architect Rudolf Schwarz, by whom he was directly influenced, Mies recognized modern technology as a dichotomous destiny that was at once both destroyer and provider. He saw it as the apocalyptic demiurge of the new era and as the inescapable matrix of the modern world. It was this that prompted him to shift the focus of architecture toward technique and away from type and space form, always assuming that the latter would be spontaneously fulfilled, either through the limitless freedom of the open plan or through the changing subdivision of cellular space. Within these parameters, the art of building for Mies meant the embodiment of the spirit in the banality of the real; the spiritualization of technique through tectonic form.

form. Kahn approached the issue of monumentality in an unusual way, emphasizing the character of the tectonic element above all other considerations.

Neither the finest material nor the most advanced technology need enter a work of monumental character for the same reason that the finest ink was not required to draw up the Magna-Carta. . . . In Greek architecture engineering concerned itself fundamentally with materials in compression. Each stone or part forming the structural members was made to bear with accuracy on each other to avoid the tensile action which stone is incapable of enduring. The great cathedral builders regarded the members of the structural skeleton with the same love of perfection and search for clarity of purpose. Out of periods of inexperience and fear when they erected over-massive, core-filled veneered walls, grew a courageous theory of a stone over stone vault skeleton producing a downward and outward thrust, which forces were conducted to a column or a wall provided with the added characteristic of the buttress. . . . The buttress allowed lighter walls between the thrust points and these curtain walls were logically developed for the use of large glass windows. This structural concept, derived from earlier and cruder theories, gave birth to magnificent variations in the attempts to attain loftier heights and greater spans creating a spiritually emotional environment unsurpassed.

The influence of the Roman vault, the dome, the arch, has etched itself in deep furrows across the pages of architectural history. Through Romanesque, Gothic, Renaissance and today, its basic forms and structural ideas have been felt. They will continue to reappear but with added powers made possible by our technology and engineering skill.[3]

This passage is revealing, for reading between the lines, it is possible to discern not only the specific nature of Kahn's formation, as a student at the University of Pennsylvania under the Beaux-Arts tutelage of Paul Cret, but also the terms in which he was to conceive his own architectural agenda. It says something for his French education that his own point of departure was to recall the long debate surrounding the evolution of the Greco-Gothic idea. This may explain why he would adopt a totally different attitude toward the steel frame than that assumed by Mies van der Rohe, for where Mies readily accepted the rolled steel joist as the structural norm of twentieth-century architecture, Kahn began his thesis on monumentality with an elaborate critique of this universal building element.

The I-beam is an engineering accomplishment deriving its shape from an analysis of the stresses involved in its use. It is designed so that the greater proportion of the area of cross-section is concentrated as far as possible from the center of gravity. The shape adapted itself to ease of rolling and under test it was found that even the fillets, an aid in the rolling process, helped convey the stresses from one section to another in continuity. Safety factors were adopted to cover possible inconsistencies in the composition of the material of manufacture. Large scale machinery and equipment needed in its fabrication lead to standardization.

The combination of safety factors (ignorance factor as one engineer termed it) and standardization narrowed the practice of engineering to the selection of members from handbooks, recommending sections much heavier than calculations would require and further limited the field of engineering expression stifling the creation of the more graceful forms which the stress diagrams indicated.[4]

Section Thru Beauvais
after Auguste Choisy

7.1

Louis I. Kahn, esquisse for a modern cathedral in welded tubular steel, 1944. The accompanying section through Beauvais cathedral is taken from Auguste Choisy's *Histoire de l'architecture*.

Kahn would follow this critique of standard engineering practice with a rather general advocacy of welded tubular steel construction.

Joint construction in common practice treats every joint as a hinge which makes connections to columns and other members complex and ugly. To attain greater strength with economy, a finer expression in the structural solution of the principle of concentrating the area of cross-section away from the center of gravity is the tubular form, since the greater the moment of inertia, the greater the strength. A bar of a certain area of cross-section rolled into a tube of the same area of cross-section (consequently of a larger diameter) would possess a strength enormously greater than the bar.

The tubular member is not new, but its wide use has been retarded by technological limitations in the construction of joints. Up until very recently, welding has been outlawed by the building codes. In some cases, where it was permitted, it was required to make loading tests for every joint.[5]

The above passages surely testify to the underlying influence of Viollet-le-Duc; above all, the reference to oversectioned members that do not reflect the stress variations to which they are subject and the double allusion to both graceless joints and a failure to consider the frame as a total system. Kahn is critical of the inorganic trabeated rigidity of the standard steel frame and so favors the more organic, one may even say neo-Gothic, potential of welded tubular steel. Kahn was to clarify his position with a number of sketches that illustrate the essay. The first of these is an esquisse for a modern cathedral in welded tubular construction (fig. 7.1). This is directly related, as the drawing indicates, to Auguste Choisy's axonometric of the structure of Beauvais cathedral as this appears in his *Histoire de l'architecture* of 1899. Of this, Kahn wrote:

Beauvais cathedral needed the steel we have. It needed the knowledge we have. Glass would have revealed the sky and become a part of the enclosed space framed by an interplay of exposed tubular ribs, plates and columns of a stainless metal formed true and faired into a continuous flow of lines expressive of their stress patterns. Each member would have been welded to the next to create a

211

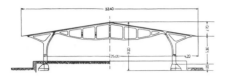

7.2
Robert Maillart, storage shed for S. A. Magazzini Generali, Chiasso, 1924. Section and partial elevation.

7.3
Louis I. Kahn, proposal for a welded tubular steel structure projected for Philadelphia, 1944.

continuous structural unity worthy of being exposed because its engineering gives no resistance to the laws of beauty having its own aesthetic life.[6]

The structural rationalist nature of this argument is self-evident, as is its relation to the production and statical limits of the materials involved. It is easy to see, for example, that Kahn's hopes for the future of welded tubular steel are not unlike those that he will later entertain toward reinforced concrete, and this, in turn, will be close to the attitude assumed by Auguste Perret with respect to the same material. It was patently evident to Kahn and Perret alike that reinforced concrete structural members could be easily modified in section in order to accommodate and reflect variations in stress. In this regard, the organic potential of the material had already been amply demonstrated by Eugène Freyssinet in his bowstring factory roofs and by Robert Maillart in the storage shed that he erected in Chiasso in 1924 (fig. 7.2).[7] One should also mention Pier Luigi Nervi in this connection, to whom Anne Tyng showed the City Tower project that she had designed with Kahn in 1953.[8]

That Kahn did not immediately fix on reinforced concrete as the material of the new monumentality testifies to Kahn's regard for the structural elegance of metal construction. He advocated welded tubular steel largely because of its lightweight modern industrial nature and the apparent ease with which it could be fabricated. In comparison to welded steel, reinforced concrete displayed a number of disadvantages. In the first place, there was the inelegance of having to build one structure in order to cast another; in the second, it possessed a tectonically ambiguous nature inasmuch as it was a "conglomerate": while it appeared to be compressive, it invariably concealed a tensile component. Welded tubular steel came close to Kahn's ideal building material, of which he spoke in later life to the effect that "I dream of space full of wonder. Spaces that rise and envelop flowingly without beginning, without end, of a jointless material white and gold. When I place the first line on paper to capture the dream, the dream becomes less (fig. 7.3).[9]

Although the oriental tone of this vision should not go unnoticed, it is clear that the paradigm evoked has much in common with the Gothic cathedral. The great

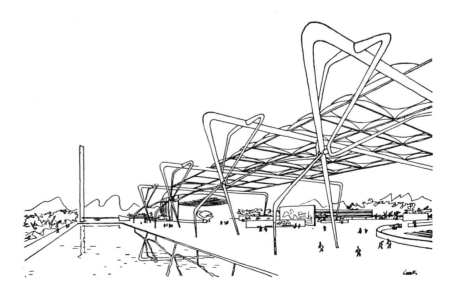

advantage of welded tubular steel lay in its potential for achieving an ontological tectonic comparable in its expressive substance to the self-evident continuity of Gothic stonework. What Kahn had in mind was the continuous flow of force that seemingly passes from vault to rib to pier in one and the same material. While this modulated continuity could be achieved in reinforced concrete, as Perret had already demonstrated, concrete lacked for Kahn the intrinsic lightness and clarity of welded tubular steel and was in this sense less modern. Furthermore, it could not be erected as a constructional continuity, since the process of construction did not allow its respective components, above all the steel rods, to *appear* in their final and appointed place.[10] The fact that it was a casting operation rather than an assembly made it categorically inimical to the precepts of structural rationalism.

The shortcomings of reinforced concrete from a tectonic standpoint had long been perceived by Viollet-le-Duc's prime pupil Anatole de Baudot, above all in his church St.-Jean de Montmartre, under construction in Paris from 1894 to 1904. As we have already seen, de Baudot, educated by both Henri Labrouste and Viollet-le-Duc, carried the legacy of structural rationalism into the twentieth century. St.-Jean de Montmartre (figs. 2.27, 2.28), completed when de Baudot was seventy, was the most significant work of his life. No two works, ostensibly both deriving from the precepts of Viollet-le-Duc, could be more opposed than Perret's 25 bis rue Franklin apartments and de Baudot's church in Montmartre. Where the one embraced the Hennebique system, the other categorically rejected it, not only because, unlike Gothic architecture, it failed to reveal the patterns of stress induced in its structural members, but also because it was incapable of generating an architectonic syntax arising out of the constructional process. As we have seen, it was for this reason that de Baudot's church was built out of a unique system of reinforced brick and concrete construction, developed in collaboration with the engineer Paul Cottancin and proposed under the name of *ciment armé,* in order to distinguish it from Hennebique's *béton armé.* To this end, de Baudot and Cottancin deployed cement-reinforced, perforated-brick arches, walls, and piers. These lean components were held in place by reinforcing wires that were painstakingly inserted into the perforated masonry; the interstices were thereafter charged with cement (fig. 7.4). Here Semper's textile revetment became transposed, as it were, into the substance of the building rather than its cladding. De Baudot employed a building system that resulted in a monolithic but articulate assembly, compounded of structurally taut and expressive elements comparable to those of Gothic architecture. These elements could be perceived as being determined to an equal degree by both gravity and the act of construction.

While Kahn never alluded to de Baudot, it is almost certain that he would have been aware of his work through his teacher, Paul Cret. Cret gave his own public assessment of de Baudot in his famous and influential essay "The Architect as Collaborator of the Engineer," published in 1927, three years after Kahn's graduation.[11] Although Cret takes pains in this essay to distance himself from de Baudot and to reassert the primacy of imitative form, structural rationalism nonetheless remained an important and seminal reference for him, and from this standpoint de Baudot may be adduced as a possible influence on Kahn. The case is further strengthened by the space-framed, vaulted roof structure in *ciment armé* that de Baudot projected during the last decade of his life. Kahn's tubular-steel-framed exhibition pavilion, with which he illustrated his 1944 essay on monumentality (fig. 7.3), is indicative of his structural naivete in that, unlike cast-iron tubing, it is impossible to extrude steel tubing with a continuously diminishing diameter. Nevertheless, the didactic intent of the proposal is obvious. The tapered components recall the tapered cast-iron members of Viollet-le-Duc's great hall featured in the *Entretiens,* where similar hypothetical variations in stress were to find reflection in the comparable varying diameter of the cast-iron tubular cross section.[12] Moreover, Kahn's account of space frame construction leaves one in no doubt as to his feeling for the difference between the *stereotomics* of the earthwork and the *tectonics* of the frame. More importantly, perhaps, this essay, dedicated to monumentality, concludes with an inventory of modern materials that reads, paradoxically enough, as though it had been compiled by a prewar functionalist.[13]

7.4
Anatole de Baudot, St.-Jean de Montmartre, Paris, 1894–1904. Construction details. This drawing shows the positioning of the reinforcing rods passing through the reinforced brickwork.

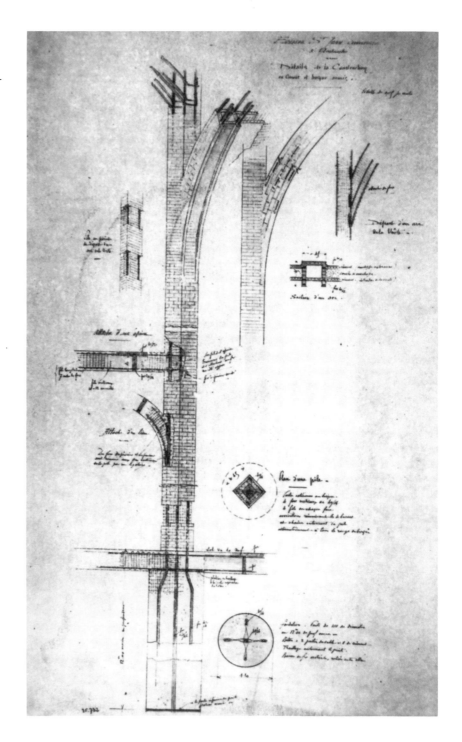

Steel, the lighter metals, concrete, glass, laminated woods, asbestos, rubber, and plastics, are emerging as the prime building materials of today. Riveting is being replaced by welding, reinforced concrete is emerging from infancy with pre-stressed reinforced concrete, vibration and controlled mixing, promising to aid in its ultimate refinement. Laminated wood is rapidly replacing lumber and is equally friendly to the eye, and plastics are so vast in their potentialities that already numerous journals and periodicals devoted solely to their many outlets are read with interest and hope. The untested characteristics of these materials are being analyzed, old formulas are being discarded. New alloys of steel, shatter proof and thermal glass and synthetics of innumerable types, together with the materials already mentioned, make up the new palette of the designer. . . . Standardization, pre-fabrication, controlled experiments . . . are not monsters to be avoided by the delicate sensitiveness of the artist. They are merely the modern means of controlling vast potentialities of materials for living, by chemistry, physics, engineering, production and assembly, which lead to the necessary knowledge the artist must have to expel fear in their use, broaden his creative instinct, give him new courage and thereby lead him to the adventures of unexplored places. His work will then be part of his age and will afford delight and service for his contemporaries.[14]

It is remarkable that Kahn's first theoretical statement would turn on a hypothetical synthesis between structural form and modern material technique, although he was to insist in conclusion that he did not wish to imply that monumentality could be attained scientifically or that it could be simply derived from the application of engineering methods. Viollet-le-Duc was nonetheless an influence on the remarkable space frame tower structure that Kahn and Anne Tyng were to project for Philadelphia in a number of different versions between 1952 and 1957 (figs. 7.5, 7.6, 7.7). The architects would describe the first version of their proposal in terms that the French master of structural rationalism would have appreciated.

In Gothic times, architects built in solid stones. Now we can build with hollow stones. The spaces defined by the members of a structure are as important as the members. These spaces range in scale from the voids of an insulation panel, voids for air, lighting and heat to circulate, to spaces big enough to walk through or live in. The desire to express voids positively in the design of structure is evidenced by the growing interest and work in the development of space frames. The forms being experimented with come from a closer knowledge of nature and the outgrowth of the constant search for order. Design habits leading to the concealment of structure have no place in this implied order. . . . I believe that in architecture, as in all art, the artist instinctively keep the marks which reveal how a thing was done. . . . Structures should be devised which can harbor the mechanical needs of rooms and spaces. . . . It would follow that the pasting over of the construction, of lighting and acoustical material, the burying of tortured, unwanted ducts, conduits, and pipe lines, would become intolerable. The desire to express how it is done would filter through the entire society of building, to architect, engineer, builder and craftsman.[15]

The influence of structural rationalism is revealed by the first sentence, while the degree of Kahn's involvement with modernization is indicated by his unprecedented attitude toward mechanical services. He becomes preoccupied at this juncture with the idea that services should be accorded the same tectonic sta-

215

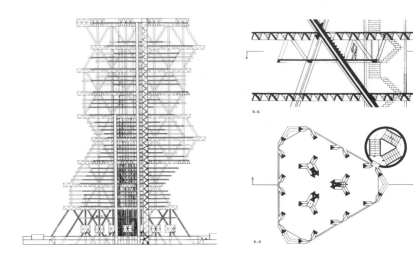

7.5
Louis I. Kahn, City Tower project ("Tomorrow's City Hall"), Philadelphia, 1957. Section through tower. Kahn's caption reads: "The concrete struts forming the triangulated frame come to a point every 66′ with 9 of these sections occurring in a total height of 616′. The column capitals at these intersections, 11′ deep, are spaces for service needs."

7.6
Louis I. Kahn, City Tower, detail plan and section.

tus as structural form. It is hard to overestimate the radical nature of this concern, for prior to Kahn's formulation of the theoretical opposition of "servant and served," contemporary architecture had failed to address the problems posed by the increase in the amount of services being installed in buildings in the second half of the twentieth century. Centralized air-conditioning imposed a quantum leap in this regard, but, unlike Mies, Kahn could not accept the suspended ceiling as a normative method for the accommodation of ducts in the servicing of open floor space, largely because a false ceiling inevitably conceals the basic floor structure. As far as Kahn was concerned, the fundamental structure of a building had to be made manifest both inside and out.

A transcendental strain is detectable in Kahn's thought at this juncture, a mode of beholding in which he appears to have become preoccupied with the latent order of nature as this had been revealed through scientific research. This is partly what he has in mind when he writes in 1944 of the purity of engineering form which has "no resistance to the laws of beauty having its own aesthetic life," [16] or in 1952 of forms that "come from a closer knowledge of nature."

Tyng (who first worked with Kahn in 1945, in the office of Stonorov and Kahn, and then, after 1947, in Kahn's own practice) clearly exercised a major influence on Kahn's development, introducing him to D'Arcy Thompson's *On Growth and Form* in 1952. Between 1951 and 1953, Tyng designed two independent works employing octatetrahedron geometry, a prototypical school and a house for her parents realized on the eastern Maryland shore in 1953. This triangulated space frame building, left open for habitation, was of the same order as Kahn's Yale University Art Gallery design of virtually the same date, although by now Kahn was also familiar with the work of Richard Buckminster Fuller, whom he had met while teaching in the architectural school at Yale. While Tyng played a major role in initiating the City Tower project, both Kahn and Tyng were influenced by the then recent realization that certain molecular structures were ordered according to tetrahedral geometry and by Fuller's development of the Octet (octahedron/tetrahedron) truss principle, a demonstration version of which was erected in 1959.[17] The tripartite tetrahedral ordering principle of the final version of the tower was thus imagined by Kahn and Tyng as a Transcendental construction, all but identical in its form with natural crystalline structure. Kahn would first employ this geometry in combination with the interstitial mechanical services in his Yale Art Gallery, under construction in New Haven between 1951 and 1953. In the final version of the City Tower, the term "servant space" would apply not only to the volume within the triagrid floors and the tetrahedral capitals, used for the accommodation of lavatories, but also to the provision of catwalks for the purpose of maintenance and for the horizontal transfer of ducts and pipes (fig. 7.6). At this point, the structuralist principle of giving primacy to the joint and the transmission of stress is no longer solely a matter of careful detailing but is further amplified through geometry to include the provision of hierarchic space as well. In this way a clear separation was maintained between the secondary "servant" spaces, such as the elevators, service cores, lavatories, etc., and primary "served" volumes. As Kahn put it later, with regard to his penchant for interstitial servicing elements, "I do not like ducts; I do not like pipes. I hate them really thoroughly, but because I hate them so thoroughly, I feel they have to be given their place. If I just hated them and took no care, I think they would invade the building and completely destroy it."[18]

Unlike either Perret or Viollet-le-Duc, Kahn will repudiate any direct relation to historical form, be it Classic or Gothic. And yet while he will distance himself from historicism he will nonetheless gravitate toward a transhistorical evocation that is modern without being utopian and referential without becoming eclectic. Thus certain analogical allusions abound in Kahn's work, evoking Roman, Romanesque, neoclassical, and above all Gothic paradigms, particularly with his advocacy of "keeping the marks which reveal how the thing was done." Equally Gothic in the City Tower proposal are the 11-foot-deep tetrahedral capitals or nodes provided not only to absorb the shear stress but also to accommodate services, lavatories, etc. This light yet monumental tetrahedral frame is conceptually dematerialized in contrast to the heavy treatment of its podium and masonry undercroft, with its massive cylindrical light wells and circular ramps. The Roman allusions in this instance are obvious, and yet Kahn's description of the sun control system projected for the surface of its crystalline curtain wall makes his commitment to modern technology equally evident.

7.7
Louis I. Kahn, City Tower, plaza-level plan.

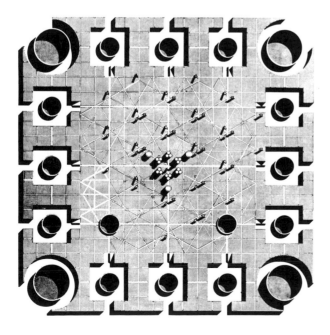

To shade the building from the sun and to hold its panels of glass, a permanent scaffolding of aluminum is planned to cover the entire exterior. From a distance windows per se, would not be apparent. A lacey network of metal reflecting the color of the light and its complementary color of shadow would be seen by the passer-by.[19]

Inasmuch as this project established an opposition between the tectonic of the skeleton frame and its skin and the stereotomic base of the earthwork, it may be seen as exemplifying Semper's *Four Elements of Architecture* of 1851. Close to a feeling for the Gothic, as this was embodied in Bruno Taut's concept of the city crown in his book *Die Stadtkrone* of 1919, we may interpret Kahn's City Tower as a dematerialized crystal set above an all-material base.[20]

Although tubular steel gave way to concrete in all of the versions of the City Tower and indeed in all of his work thereafter, the precept of a hollow structural form would remain a perennial theme throughout his career. This, plus the tactile presence of subordinate components such as the generic arch, window, and door would become irreducible elements for Kahn, because he saw them as deriving from the geometrical essences of archetypal, universal forms. For him they would stand as the ultimate morphemes of building culture without which one cannot create anything. And yet Kahn's overall notion of tectonic authenticity went beyond this necessary articulation and inflection of components to consider the experiential impact of the work on the subject. This much is implied in a statement that he made about the tactility of the Yale Art Gallery. He clearly saw the pseudo-Brutalist interior of this work as embodying a kind of psycho-ethical challenge. Thus he wrote: "One might feel that only persons who are in flight from themselves, who need plaster and wallpaper for their emotional security, can be uncomfortable in this building."[21] Despite this rather patronizing, all but trivial attitude, Kahn is nonetheless close in this work to the principles embodied in Perret's plaster-free Musée des Travaux Publics and to Perret's equally tectonic concern for the integration of services into the hollow interstitial structure of the building.

The way in which Kahn comes to terms with orthogonal geometry in the Yale Art Gallery will be decisive for the rest of his development (fig. 7.8), as will the manner in which its reinforced concrete skeleton is both revealed and concealed by the continuity and discontinuity of its cladding. The solution adopted recalls the tectonic/stereotomic interplay in Kahn's City Tower proposal, for here, in contrast to the homogeneity of the principal street elevation in brick, the return curtain wall in glass is subdivided so as to read as a tessellated, translucent skin. In order to express the common hermetic nature of both, Kahn alternates the manner of the structural expression between the northern and southern faces, so that where the curtain-walled facade, on the northwest and northeast elevations, serves to conceal the concrete floor and to reveal the columns, the converse applies on the main Chapel Street front, where the columns are suppressed except at the returns and where the floors read continuously throughout. These last are represented by horizontal stringcourses in stone, which are made of the same depth as the concrete ribs projecting from the tetrahedral floors. These stringcourses are of a similar tectonic order as the metal facing plates that cover and represent the floors in the fully glazed facades.

Within this play, the triagrid floor functions both as a structural network and as a distributive membrane, with tubular air ducts and electrical raceways running

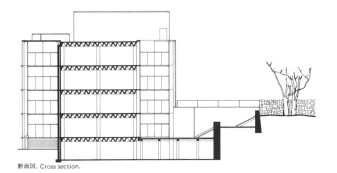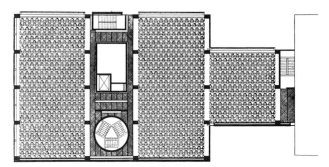

断面図. Cross section.

7.8
Louis I. Kahn, Yale University Art Gallery, New
Haven, 1951–1953. Cross section and re-
flected ceiling plan.

in the interstitial space of the monolithic but hollow concrete tetrahedrons that
make up the three-foot floor depth (figs. 7.9, 7.10). The fact that these triagrid
floors had, in the end, to be calculated as inclined structural beams, due to the
kind of calculations required by the city building code, hardly discredits the inventiveness and inherent probity of the design. One needs to note in this regard
that each octahedron space within the tetrahedron network is four times greater
in volume than the space of the tetrahedron itself. The ontological character of
this geometry no doubt accounts for the autocritical sketch that Kahn made
after the completion of the museum. As in the space frame proposed for the
floor and roof of the Adath Jeshurun Synagogue projected for Elkins Park,
Pennsylvania, in 1954–1955, this post-facto sketch proposes to support the
tetrahedral floors of the gallery on a number of inclined tetrahedral pylons (fig.
7.11). This hypothetical idealized gallery appears in two versions, first as a
square and then as an octagonal plan, fed in each instance by freestanding cylindrical services cores. Against this sketch, Kahn would append the note, "a
tetrahedral concrete floor asks for a column of the same structure."[22] This may
be read as a direct indication of the way in which his tectonic preconceptions
would be at variance, at times, with the spatial and structural requirements of
the work in hand.

Kahn's sketch of an alternative tetrahedral structure for the Yale Art Gallery may
derive from the fact that the floor as built was about 60 percent heavier than
what would have been required for a normal 40-foot span, and while the finished ceiling possessed all the ethical and aesthetic attributes that Kahn desired, the revealed structure was not, as we have noted, designed as initially
envisaged. The tetrahedral unit, as designed by Kahn and the engineer H. A.
Pfisterer, was to have been a two-foot-high pyramid having 3½-inch-thick sides,
cast integrally with a 4-inch concrete floor. While this made for a heavy floor, the
overall ingenuity of the concept lay in the integration of the mechanical services
running within the depth of the tetrahedrons.

Kahn's "servant versus served" theme is further articulated particularly where
the floor of the middle servant bay is distinguished from the honorific volumes it
serves by being made of flat concrete plank construction rather than being cast
in the form of the triagrid floors. This narrower structural bay accommodates
at the next level of detail three servant elements: a cylindrical tripartite stair, an
elevator/bathroom core, and a standard dogleg escape stair. Of these, the first
is the main public stair, and this accounts for its honorific format comprising an
equilateral triangular stair housed in a cylinder, as previously employed by Kahn

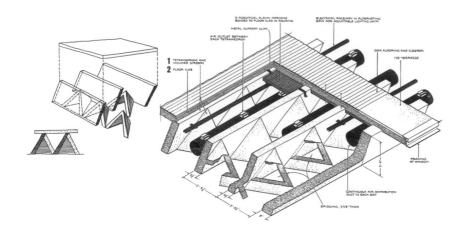

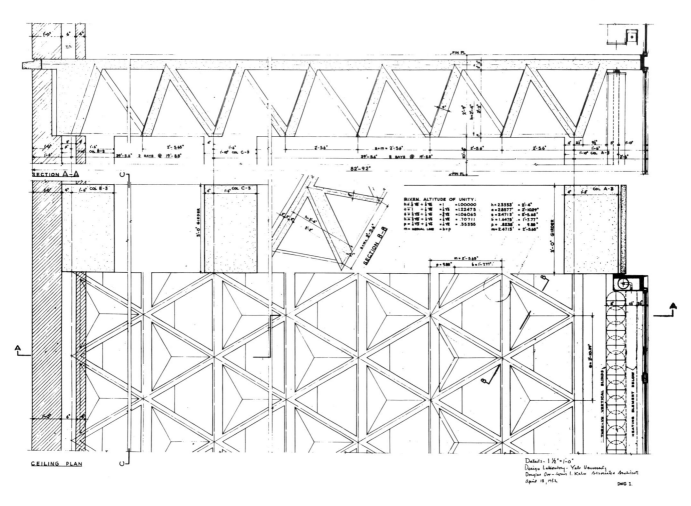

SECTION A-A

CEILING PLAN

SECTION B-B

Details- 1½"=1'-0"
Design Laboratory- Yale University
Douglas Orr- Louis I. Kahn Associated Architects
April 18, 1952

DWG 1.

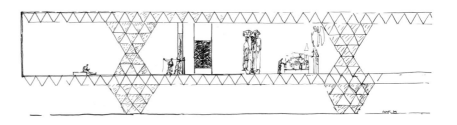

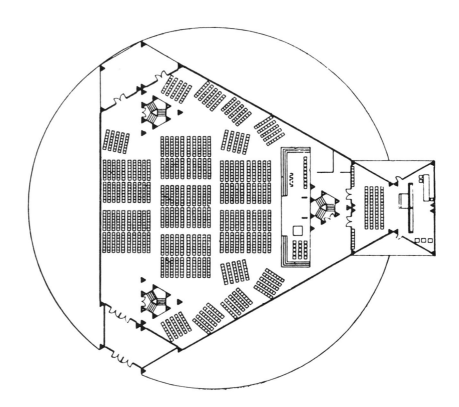

7.9

opposite, top

Louis I. Kahn, Yale University Art Gallery, isometric drawing showing integration of structural and air distribution systems.

7.10

opposite, center

Louis I. Kahn, Yale University Art Gallery, detail plan and section of floor structure.

7.11

opposite, bottom

Louis I. Kahn, Yale University Art Gallery, section sketch made after completion of the building (1954). Appended caption reads: "A tetrahedral concrete floor asks for a column of the same structure."

7.12

Louis I. Kahn, project for Adath Jeshurun Synagogue, Elkins Park, Pennsylvania, 1954. Second-floor plan.

in the City Tower design. The same honorific stair will appear in the plan for the Adath Jeshurun Synagogue projected for Elkins Park in 1954 (fig. 7.12). Meanwhile at Yale a second servant bay, accommodating another escape stair adjacent to the existing neo-Gothic Weir Hall, will also be simply rendered in concrete plank construction.

That Kahn was always concerned with the specific appearance of the constructional elements employed is evident from the care with which the Yale Art Gallery was detailed. This is confirmed by William Huff's memoir dealing with the construction of the gallery, particularly in the light of Kahn's concern for the quality of microtectonic elements.

In addition to his innovative handling of the basic concrete structural system, into which he deftly integrated the mechanical systems, and to the concrete's consequent exposure as one of the primary architectural finishes at the Yale Gallery addition, other major materials, such as the gallery floors and special concrete block, both of which played against the rugged concrete, evidenced his innate urge for the sensual. Other architects were using polished brick pavers or rubber tile or something like that for their floors. But in his free-searching survey of an inventory of imaginable, albeit viable, products, Lou stumbled upon the gymnasium floor, made up of carefully matched end-grain maple-strips—a wonderfully rich, as well as wonderfully comfortable and durable, material. And, saying that nothing looked more like a concrete block than the common 8 × 16 block, he had special 4 × 5 blocks manufactured, whose dimensions and proportions gave the walls wonderful scale and texture.[23]

Elsewhere, in the same memoir, Huff remarks on the recessed shadow joint adopted in the paneling of all of Kahn's interior cabinetwork: "Lou's detailing of doors and wood wall panels was strictly out of the Elizabethan age; but he had his own profiles. It allows the breathing of the wood so that the wood doesn't crack or check. Lou's panel doors were uniquely his 'look', but they acknowledged and incorporated the basic principles."[24]

Kahn's consciously archaic but critical and radical approach finds reflection in his intense awareness of the ontological distinction between column and wall, his Albertian preference for the primordial separation of the two, by virtue of light penetrating into the opaque impassivity of wall and thereby liberating the freestanding column from within its mass. This poetic intuition linked Kahn to the principle of structural articulation in Mies but at the same time distanced him from the Miesian free plan. In a 1957 interview given to the *Architectural Forum* he said: "You should never invade the space between columns with partition walls. It is like sleeping with your head in one room and feet in another. That I will never do."[25]

This tension between modernization and monumentality will assume a particularly dramatic form in Kahn's speculations about future urban development, and above all in the various plans that he projected for Philadelphia between 1952 and 1962. Kahn was to remain preoccupied with the myth and reality of Philadelphia throughout his life. For him, it could not be entered via the high-speed osmosis of the airport and the freeway; that is to say, by the experiential alienation picturesquely justified as a necessary, universal condition in the 1963 study *View from the Road* by Donald Appleyard, Kevin Lynch, and Jack Myer.[26] As far as Kahn was concerned, Philadelphia had to be approached through that which had graced all cities since time immemorial, an honorific gateway, which in the case of Philadelphia was the monumental Beaux-Arts peristyle of 30th Street Station. Something of Kahn's sense for the institutional and political continuity that is to be found in urban foundations may be gleaned from a text he wrote in the early sixties (fig. 7.13):

The city, from a simple settlement, became the place of the assembled institutions. Before, the institution was the natural agreement—the sense of commonality. . . . The measure of greatness of a place to live must come from the

7.13
Louis I. Kahn, "The City from a simple settlement . . . ," 1971.

*character of its institutions, sanctioned through how sensitive they are to re-
newed agreement and desire for new agreement, not through need, because it
comes from what already is.*[27]

By this date, twenty years after his initial essay on monumentality, the manifest
destiny of monumental form had become amplified, that is to say it had evolved
from an initial focus on the tectonic expressivity of built form to include within its
scope the seminal character of the civic institution. Kahn was well aware that all
traditional institutions were threatened by the processal aspects of late metropolitan development. Thus, his concern for the continuity of the city as an assembly of institutions is paralleled by his efforts to accommodate and overcome the
contrary demands being made upon the traditional city by the ever-changing dynamics of modern locomotion. This much is clear from the way he was to conceive of the automobile in relation to the city. Thus, we find him writing in 1961:

*The circumstantial demands of the car, of parking and so forth, will eat away all
the spaces that exist now and pretty soon you have no identifying traces of what
I call loyalties—the landmarks. Remember, when you think of your city, you think
immediately of certain places which identify the city, as you enter it. If they're
gone, your feeling for the city is lost and gone. . . . If because of the demands of
the motorcar, we stiffen and harden the city—omitting water, omitting the green
world—the city will be destroyed. Therefore the car, because of its destructive
value, must start us rethinking the city in terms of the green world, in terms of
the world of water, and of air, and of locomotion.*[28]

From the scale of the tectonic element to the scale of mega-urban form, Kahn
constantly attempted to introduce into the fundamental structure both the essential services and the character of the served place-form in order to neutralize the
destructive aspects of twentieth-century technology. Thus, his efforts to interpret modern space frame construction in the light of principles derived from
structural rationalism were to be paralleled by attempts to transform the elevated freeway into a new form of civic architecture. This preoccupation lay behind Kahn's paradoxical aphorism that "the street wants to become a building"
and his later projection of what he disingenuously referred to as "viaduct architecture."[29] This was also the primary impulse behind his 1957 plan for midtown
Philadelphia (fig. 7.14), above all his so-called Civic Center Forum, surrounded
by parking silos, of which he wrote:

*This strategic positioning around the city center would present a logical image
of protection against the destruction of the city by the motor car. In a sense the
problem of the car and the city is war, and the planning for the new growth of
cities is not a complacent act but an act of emergency. The distinction between
the two architectures, the architecture of the viaduct and the architecture of the
acts of man's activities, could bring about a logic of growth and a sound positioning of enterprise.*[30]

The ambivalent tension in Kahn's work between modernization and monumentality is perhaps never more evident than in the evolution of the cylindrical parking
towers by which the city center was to have been surrounded (fig. 7.15). In his
first version of these "wound-up streets" it is clear that Kahn cannot quite decide as to whether they should be treated as monuments or utilitarian semiotic
elements. Thus, we find him writing in 1953:

Louis Kahn

223

room *in se*. For him, the quality of light made manifest through its interaction with a specific structural volume was the essential determinant of its character (fig. 7.18). Hence, he would write:

Architecture comes from the Making of a Room. . . . The Room is the place of the mind. In a small room one does not say what one would in a large room. In a room with only one other person . . . the vectors of each meet. A room is not a room without natural light. Natural light gives the time of day and [allows] the mood of the seasons to enter.[34]

In a similar vein, Kahn wrote of the penetration of light into the multilevel free-way viaducts that he proposed for midtown Philadelphia in the early 1960s in terms of allowing a sliver of light to enter into the darkest room; to penetrate even into a cinema in order to reveal how dark it is.[35] The windowless, climate-controlled box was a total anathema to Kahn, as was the indifferently assembled, underdetailed modern building so often found in commercial architecture. Thus, as far as he was concerned, the joint, as revealed by light, was the tangible proof of the constructional probity of the work in much the same way as it had been the touchstone of tectonic form in the writings of Viollet-le-Duc and Semper.

Kahn's emphasis on the joint naturally leads to a comparison with Mies van der Rohe and to the drawing of certain parallels between their respective achievements. This is particularly true of their mature work, and above all of their comparable essays in reinforced concrete construction. Thus, one may compare

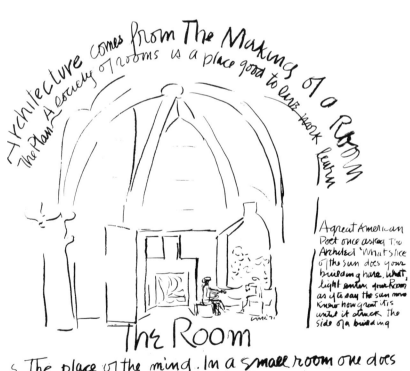

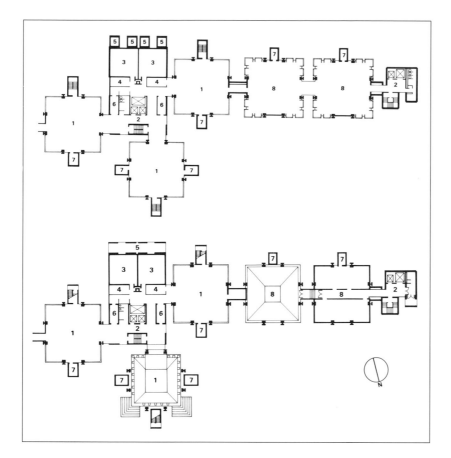

7.17
Louis I. Kahn, sketch of St. Cécile cathedral, Albi, France, 1959. Note the representing of the cylindrical elements as "wind-up" forms.

7.18
Louis I. Kahn, "Architecture comes from the Making of a Room . . . ," 1971.

7.19
Louis I. Kahn, Richards Medical Research Laboratories, University of Pennsylvania, Philadelphia, 1957–1961. Typical floor plan (above) and first-floor plan (below):
1. studio towers
2. elevators and stairways
3. animal quarters
4. animal service rooms
5. fresh air intake stacks
6. air distribution shafts
7. fume and exhaust stacks
8. biology building towers

Mies's Promontory Apartments of 1949 to Kahn's cylindrical parking/office silos, first published in 1953 as part of the midtown Philadelphia plan. An exposed trabeated reinforced concrete frame is the primary expressive element in each instance. Moreover, the structural frame is similarly articulated in each case; that is to say, the perimeter concrete columns, carrying the spandrels, diminish in section as they rise upward due to a decrease in compressive stress. Aside from this singular case, however, their preferred generic columns could hardly have been more different, with Mies favoring a standard rolled steel stanchion and Kahn preferring a hollow or solid concrete pier.

Kahn's preoccupation with hollow structure reaches its apotheosis with the Richards Medical Laboratories realized for the University of Pennsylvania between 1957 and 1961 (fig. 7.19). As others have remarked, this building synthesizes for the first time the multifarious aspects of his tectonic approach: the use of hollow structure at every conceivable scale, the articulation of servant and served spaces, the full integration of mechanical services, and not least the dialogical "gravitational/levitational" expression of static weight and gaseous exhaust. From this point onward, Kahn treats the structure as the potential generator of space, that is, as a hollow diaphragm from which the volume itself emerges by extension. At the same time, the articulation of the joint assumes an organic character; thus he was to write:

A building is like a human. An architect has the opportunity of creating life. It's like a human body—like your hand. The way the knuckles and joints come to-

Louis Kahn

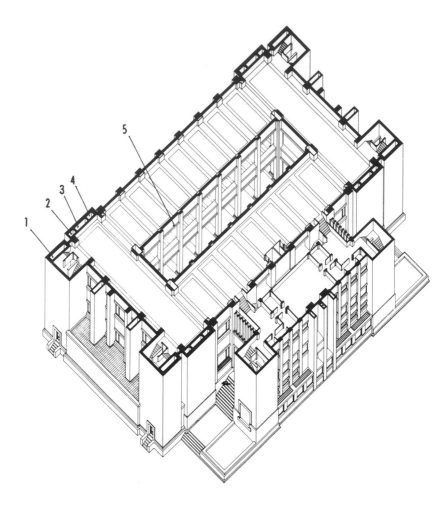

gether make each hand interesting and beautiful. In a building these details
should not be put in a mitten and hidden. You should make the most of them.
Space is architectural when the evidence of how it is made is seen and
comprehended.[36]

This anthropomorphic conception of the joint is to be given a more tectonic rendering in his homage to Carlo Scarpa, made shortly before his own death:

Design consults Nature
to give presence to the elements.
A work of art makes manifest the wholeness of 'Form',
the symphony of the selected shapes of the elements.
In the elements
the joint inspires ornament, its celebration.
The detail is the adoration of nature.[37]

This feeling for the organic surely derives in large measure from Frank Lloyd
Wright. Wright is, in any event, still an insufficiently acknowledged influence on
Kahn, not only in the Richards Medical Laboratories but throughout his career.
And while many earlier twentieth-century architects were inspired by Wright's do-
mestic architecture, including, of course, Hendrik Petrus Berlage and Ludwig
Mies van der Rohe, few if any were able to develop the introspective concatena-
tions of hierarchic form that characterized Wright's public buildings. In a round-
about way, this legacy fell to Kahn. The totally blank exterior of the hollow

7.20
Frank Lloyd Wright, Larkin Building, Buffalo,
1904. Axonometric at third-floor level. Note
the service ducts built into the walls of the
stair shafts. Numbers indicate built-in services according to the following key:
1. fresh air intake
2. utilities
3. foul air exhaust
4. miscellaneous ducts and services
5. tempered air outlets under balcony fronts
and ceiling beams

7.21
Louis I. Kahn, Richards Medical Research
Laboratories, perspective sketch from the
southwest, 1957 version showing cantilevered and ribbed exhaust stacks.

7.22
Louis I. Kahn, Richards Medical Research
Laboratories, early plan.

service towers in the Richards Laboratories and the division of the parti into servant and served spaces are all surely incipient in Wright's Larkin Building, Buffalo, of 1904 (fig. 7.20), and a similar relationship clearly obtains between the Richards Laboratories and the S. C. Johnson Administration complex built at Racine, Wisconsin, in 1937. It is significant that Wright's own 1945 description of the S. C. Johnson Building has much about it that could have been from the hand of Kahn:

Laid out upon a horizontal unit system twenty feet on centers both ways, rising into the air on a vertical unity system of three and half inches: one especially large brick course. Glass was not used as bricks in this structure. Bricks were bricks. The building itself became—by way of long glass tubing—crystal where crystal either transparent or translucent was felt to be most appropriate. In order to make the structure monolithic, the exterior enclosing wall material appeared inside wherever it was sensible.[38]

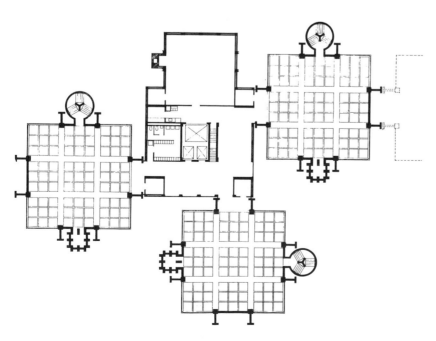

7.23
Louis I. Kahn, Richards Medical Research
Laboratories, plan and elevation sketches of
service towers, 1957 version.

In much the same spirit Kahn wrote of his laboratories as being "conceived in recognition of the realization that science laboratories are studios and that the air to breathe should be away from the air to throw away."[39] Here once again the hollow column comes into play, particularly in the initial sketches for the exhaust and air intake towers (figs. 7.21, 7.22, 7.23) against which Kahn would jot down the following notes: "The air supply gets smaller as it rises . . . the air return gets larger as it returns. The fumehood exhaust accumulates on its ascent. The column gets smaller as it rises. From this comes the design of the area around the column."[40] These ventilation manifolds, built out of corbeled masonry and dialectically conceived as opposing the ascent of gas to the descent

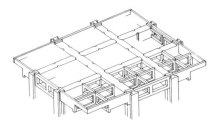

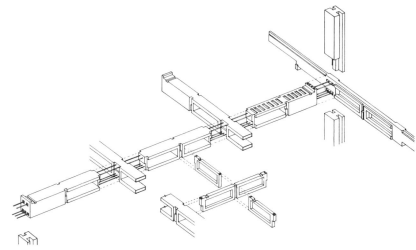

7.24
Louis I. Kahn, Richards Medical Research Laboratories, isometric drawing of precast concrete floor system.

7.25
Louis I. Kahn, project for Washington University Library, St. Louis, 1956.

of gravitational force, had eventually to be abandoned in favor of simpler boxlike sections for the process of air intake and foul exhaust. Nevertheless, as in the original sketches, a clear division was maintained between the stereotomics of the ventilation system built in brick and the tectonics of the columnar structure cast in concrete. As in the Yale Art Gallery, Kahn was able to integrate the horizontal distribution of services within the post-tensioned diagrid, two-way cantilevering floors of the laboratories, the structural depth being reduced toward the corners as the bending stress diminished. It is to the great credit of Kahn's engineer August Kommendant, with whom he would work continuously from 1956 to the end of his career, that this cantilevered Vierendeel was executed entirely of prefabricated concrete (fig. 7.24). Unlike the dialectic between ascendant air and descendant gravity, this horizontal interweaving of the services into the "space frame" of the flow structure was maintained throughout.

In one design after another, Kahn constantly strove to reveal the structural skeleton, together with its cross-sectional reduction in area as the load diminished. However, Kahn's project for the Washington University Library of 1956 (fig. 7.25) was his last didactically tectonic essay in this regard, for thereafter masonry would play a more decisive role in his work, either rendered as a screen wall or treated as a kind of stressed-skin construction, as in the calculated load-bearing concrete blockwork of the Tribune Review newspaper building erected in Greensburg, Pennsylvania, in 1961 (fig. 7.26). Where the masonry was not structural it was handled as though it were a representative shell or "ruin," that is to say, as though it were a screen running outside the structural and institu-

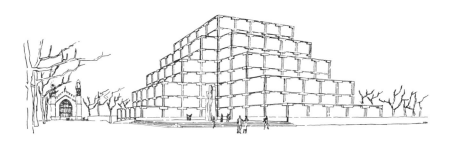

tional substance of the building (cf. Schinkel's Friedrich Werder Church, Berlin, of 1830). The interior face of this screen was invariably treated as a "space between," wherein the play of light could reveal the difference between the inner substance of a building and the outer surface of its appearance. This masonry encasement is first unequivocally adopted by Kahn in his project for a U.S. Consulate in Luanda, Angola, dating from 1959, wherein the outer envelope of the structure is partially covered by screens for the purpose of sun control (fig. 7.27). Of this provision Kahn would write:

I came to the realization that every window should have a free wall to face. This wall receiving the light of day would have a bold opening to the sky. The glare is modified by the lighted wall and the view is not shut off. In this way the contrast made by separated patterns of glare, which skylight grilles close to the window make, is avoided. Another realization came from the effectiveness of the use of breeze for insulation by the making of a loose sun roof independently supported and separated from the rainroof by a head room of 6 feet. Notice also that the piers that hold the main girders for the sun roof are completely independent of the rain roof. The rain roof is never pierced.[41]

This tectonic response to extreme climatic conditions had, however, its representational aspect, for both the cut-out frontal screen and the tessellated sun canopy on the roof evidently served to represent the honorific status of the building. Kahn was fully aware of this fact: "Considering the type of building it is, one should have the feeling of entrance and reception *not* by way of a sign but by its very character."[42] Kahn seems to have posited the idea of structure at two interlocking levels, first a general spatial structuring to be effected by the octatetrahedral system that, like Buckminster Fuller, he identified with the basic molecular order of the universe, and second a detailed structural order that employed the time-honored tropes of building culture: the cantilever, the catenary, the arch, the vault, the buttress, and the bridge. On occasion these primary and secondary levels—the spatial and the structural—would be conflated into one, as in the towers of the Richards Laboratories or the pseudo-vaults of the Kimbell Art Museum or the octagonal staggered cellular units initially envisaged for the structure of Eleanor Donnelly Erdman Hall at Bryn Mawr College in 1960. In all these instances, the resulting cellular space demonstrated his belated rediscovery that "a bay system is a room system," as he wrote in his notebook of 1955, in a passing reference to the Palladian plan.[43] This short pronouncement about the spatial implications of the generic structural bay was the main way in which Kahn distanced himself from the free plan or *plan libre* of the prewar European avant-garde. Influenced by Rudolf Wittkower's 1949 reappraisal of Palladianism, in which rooms were to be designated by their proportion and not according to their use, Kahn invariably projected clearly defined spaces, open to varying modes of appropriation. As we have already noted, he would eventually impose over structure and space a third corporeal order that we may identify as

7.26
Louis I. Kahn, Tribune Review Building, Greensburg, Pennsylvania, 1958–1961.

7.27
Louis I. Kahn, project for U.S. Consulate, Luanda, Angola, 1959–1961. Detail section, elevation, and isometric.

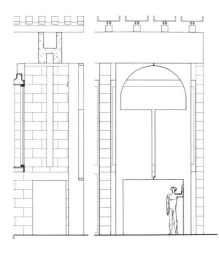

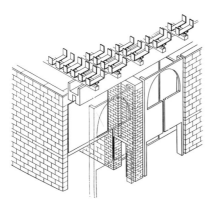

encasement, after the masonry-encased metal armatures to be found in the work of Labrouste and Viollet-le-Duc. While this third order was first justified by Kahn as a means of shielding the core of the building from glare, in his late monumental works such as the posthumously realized Bangladesh Parliament, the Sher-e-Bangla Nagar completed in Dacca in 1982, these three levels of structuring—the cellular, the structural, and the encasement—become fused, in certain sequences, into a single in situ concrete fabric engendering an all but infinite concatenation of interstitial space. In this instance it is significant, from a Semperian standpoint, that Kahn would elect to represent the concrete case of the building as a woven screen, the concrete being subdivided vertically by inlaid bands of stone. Within his entire oeuvre, Exeter Library (1967–1972) appears as the sole work in which the three levels of structuring become so compounded as to cancel each other out. Thus the brick piers sustaining the perimeter carrel wall running around all four sides of the library are totally at variance with the reinforced concrete column system holding up the book stacks. At the same time this overstructuring of the building has nothing whatever to do with the masklike facade that exploits its stepped-back brick piers, diminishing toward the top, to make a nostalgic allusion to the warehouse and mill vernacular of the eighteenth and nineteenth centuries, while the structure within has little to do with this tectonic tradition. Nothing could be further, one might note, from the tectonic fidelity of Schinkel's Bauakademie in this regard.

Kahn felt that the processes of modernization had a debilitating effect on received architectural forms, and even more importantly on the sociocultural essence of the institutions they once housed. As a result, he felt that modern institutions could no longer be predicated on historically derived types. For Kahn, these forms had either to be assembled piece by piece out of structurally articulate components, developed from the interaction of construction, gravity, ventilation, services, and light, or they had to be evoked as institutions, through employing geometrically determined forms or Platonic solids, that is to say, through the use of absolute plan forms derived from circles, triangles, squares, or other regular polygons. Kahn's intuition in this regard linked him to the rational Cartesian doubt that had dominated French thought since the end of the seventeenth century. As Marcello Angrisani has shown in his 1965 essay "Louis Kahn and History,"[44] Kahn welcomed the reappearance of the arbitrary architectural paradigms of the French Enlightenment, the massive, largely blank cubes, spheres, and pyramids and their various intersecting permutations that make up the visionary repertoire of Claude-Nicolas Ledoux and Étienne Boullée. At the end of the eighteenth century these architects were already to suggest a way for accommodating and representing the utopian (not to say apocalyptic) institutions of the unprecedented bourgeois, industrial world. In this regard Emil Kaufman's *Three Revolutionary Architects: Boullée, Ledoux and Lequeu,* published in Philadelphia in 1952, had a certain influence on Kahn, as is suggested by the Yale Art Gallery, the Trenton Bath House (fig. 7.28), and the Elkins Park synagogue, all dating from this period. Unlike Boulée and Ledoux, however, Kahn rarely used the primary forms in isolation, but always as the elemental parts of more complex assemblies.

In the Rochester Unitarian Church of 1959, Kahn will make his first didactic demonstration in this vein, that is to say the representation of the *what* of the institution, as opposed to the articulation of the *how* of its structure. As in the equilateral triangular plan adopted for the Elkins Park synagogue but never fully

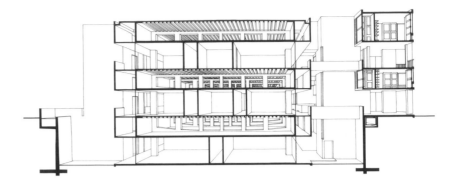

7.36
Louis I. Kahn, Salk Institute Laboratories, section through laboratory wing, final version as built.

than a garden court and thus suggesting that it should be left without any planting whatsoever. Kahn's account of the way this decision was made reveals a great deal about the spirit in which the entire work was achieved.

I asked Barragan to come to La Jolla and help me in the choice of the planting for the garden to the studies of the Salk Laboratory. When he entered the space he went to the concrete walls and touched them and expressed his love for them, and then said as he looked across the space and towards the sea, "I would not put a tree or blade of grass in this space. This should be a plaza of stone, not a garden." I looked at Dr. Salk and he at me and we both felt this was deeply right. Feeling our approval, he added joyously, "If you make this a plaza, you will gain a facade—a facade to the sky." [47]

Aside from the overall Mozarabic character of this provision, the specific nature of its detailing is Kahnian throughout. This much is evident from the way in which the watercourse is handled as a reciprocally symbolic system, with fountainhead and gargoyle rendered as the alpha and the omega of a self-contained microcosmos. The fountain is contained within an upstand cube, faced in travertine, in which three slots, set around three sides of a square basin, discharge their flow across shallow weirs, thereby forming a perfectly mitered, three-part trajectory of water cascading into the channel beneath. The symbolic and geometrical counterform to this source is the equally cubic gargoyle that, faced in the same travertine, discharges its flow into a monumental stone cistern set below the surface of the podium, in front of the sea. Since the rate of discharge requires a certain hydraulic pressure, the flow from the source is allowed to accumulate in two holding tanks, each one paralleled by a stone bench, before finally discharging into the cistern below. This entire assembly, court, water, and cistern, is held conjointly in a state of suspension before the undulating contours of a clifftop panorama, while the whole is preceded by an irregular grove of eucalyptus trees that deftly screen the court and the view of the ocean from the landward side. [48]

These primordial elements, as offset by the interplay between tectonic form and changing light, were to be integrated in an equally sublime way in the Kimbell Art Museum at Fort Worth, Texas, first projected by Kahn in 1966 and finally completed in 1972, two years before his death (fig. 7.37). The Kimbell may be seen as the apotheosis of his career, above all for the way in which one dominant tectonic element, namely a barrel vault, determines the overall character of the piece. The other determining factor is once again a stereotomic earthwork, here the manifest integration of the building into its site. And where the former, the split and articulated structure of a pseudo-vault, is the provider of light, the

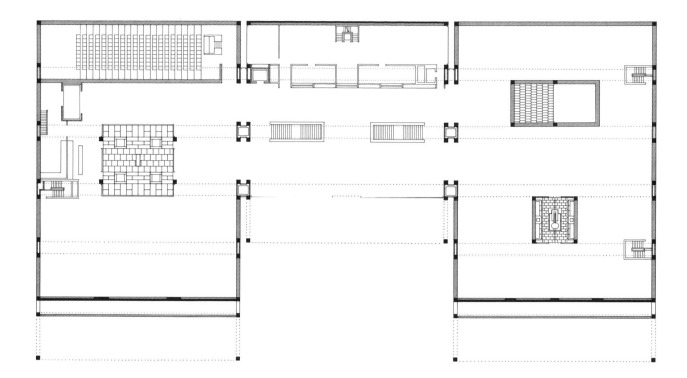

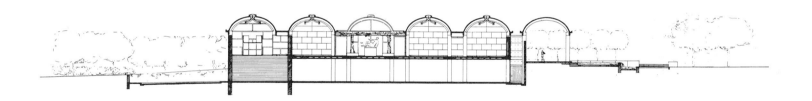

7.37

Louis I. Kahn, Kimbell Art Museum, Fort Worth, 1966–1972. Upper-floor plan and cross section.

latter is to evoke the presence of nature in a more telluric aspect. Thus while light is the ubiquitous natural element par excellence, Kahn was to inscribe the Kimbell into its site in such a way as to establish a categoric "clearing" and to endow the resultant precinct with a particular presence. In this respect, the Kimbell seems to demonstrate the importance that Martin Heidegger would attach to the boundary in his seminal essay "Building, Dwelling, Thinking" of 1954: "A boundary (*peras*) is not that at which something stops but, as the Greeks recognized, the boundary is that from which something begins its presenting."[49] Thus the implantation of the Kimbell amounted to the establishment of an earthwork in every conceivable sense, from the travertine revetment of its elevated podium to the acoustics of its graveled forecourt, from the solemnity of the Yaupon holly grove that crowns the entrance from the park to the more distant, low-slung deciduous planting of the park itself (fig. 7.38).

In the laconic remarks that accompany the presentation of the Kimbell, Kahn reveals, as nowhere else, the cosmological intent of his entire approach. Thus, of light he was to write: "We were born of light. The seasons are felt through light. We only know the world as it is evoked by light. To me, natural light is the only light because it has mood—it provides a ground of common agreement for

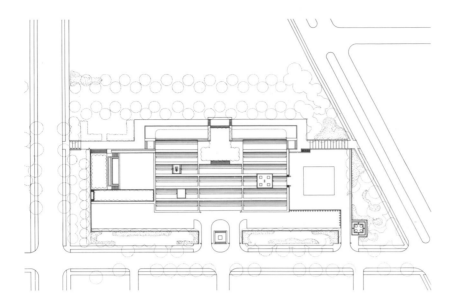

7.38
Louis I. Kahn, Kimbell Art Museum, site plan.

7.39
Louis I. Kahn, Kimbell Art Museum, section sketch (1967). "Of course there are some spaces that should be completely flexible, but there are also some that should be completely inflexible. They should be just sheer inspiration. . . ."

7.40
Louis I. Kahn, Kimbell Art Museum, sketch of gallery.

man—it puts us in touch with the eternal."[50] Elsewhere of the vaulted, top-lit galleries (figs. 7.39, 7.40) he wrote:

By the nature of the vault-like structure, you have the play of loft rooms with a space between each vault which has a ceiling at the level of the spring of the vault . . . the dimension of its light from above is manifest without partitions because the vaults defy division. Even when partitioned, the room remains a room. You might say that the nature of a room is that it always has the character of completeness.[51]

While Kahn goes on to speak about the paradoxical flexibility of these galleries, he also refers to those place-forms within the overall matrix that do not change, the three open courts that are let into the continuous vaulted roof. He will write of these incidental elements in terms that evoke the Mediterraneanism of Le Corbusier.

Added to the skylight from the slit over the exhibit rooms, I cut across the vaults, at a right angle, a counterpoint of courts, open to the sky, of calculated dimensions and character, marking them Green Court, Yellow Court, Blue Court, named for the kind of light that I anticipate their proportions, their foliation, or their sky reflections on surfaces or on water will give.[52]

Kahn causes us to focus on the precise nature of the joint at Kimbell and to discriminate, as Perret or Labrouste had done before him, between ornament and decoration. "I put the glass between the structure members and the members which are not of structure because the joint is the beginning of ornament. And

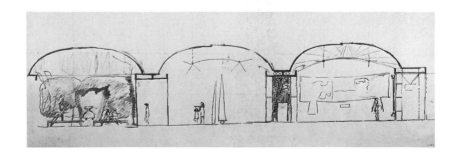

that must be distinguished from decoration which is simply applied. Ornament is the adoration of the joint."[53]

Kahn's habit of emphasizing the aggregate yet cast character of concrete, as opposed to the archaic, fossilized and glyptic character of travertine, made itself manifest at the Kimbell in a particular juxtaposition of these two materials. Of this particular aspect of Kahn's tectonic syntax, William Huff has written:

The only trouble with concrete, he told us, was that it looks awful when it's wet. Otherwise, it's a fantastic material. One way to counteract that, is to have in-sets of travertine or other marbles to take your eye off the concrete when the water streaks it. Lou knew how to do that. He knew how to integrate a travertine hand-rail with a concrete stair—the cool blue concrete against the warm yellow travertine; the porous rough concrete and the porous polished travertine trim.[54]

Of this paradoxical sameness and difference between concrete and travertine, Kahn wrote, with particular reference to the Kimbell:

Concrete does the work of structure, of holding things up. The columns are apart from each other. The space between must be filled. Therefore the travertine. . . . Travertine and concrete belong beautifully together because concrete must be taken for whatever irregularities or accidents in the pointing reveal themselves. Travertine is very much like concrete—its character is such that they look like the same material. That makes the whole building again monolithic and it doesn't separate things.[55]

Of Kahn's capacity to transform the quality of in situ concrete by virtue of its precision formwork, Huff goes on to remark:

Retrievable metal screw-ties are used both to hold in place and to separate at the specified distances two parallel sheets of plywood, between which concrete is poured to form a wall. Holes, carefully patterned, were left in the poured wall by wood plugs which are located at both ends of the ties. Instead of being "buttered in", as is common practice, these holes were plugged with lead, held ¼" back from the surface. Furthermore, where two sheets of plywood, in the same

plane, but, there is invariably bleeding of the concrete at the junctures. Here, vertical and horizontal projecting vee joints were formed by controlled tolerances, which allowed the bleeding to be molded into relief elements. The central vertical joint is an indented, poured joint, also plugged with lead.[56]

At the Kimbell, as in the Salk Laboratories, Kahn introduced a certain amount of volcanic ash or *pozzolana* into the concrete mix in order to give the concrete when cast and cured a brownish hue. As it happens, the *pozzolana* had the effect of reducing the expansion of the concrete in casting, although it produced dust and made a high finish more difficult to obtain. As at Salk, the tie cones for the formwork at the Kimbell were plugged with lead after the removal of the molds, and the gaps between the panels produced thin upstand seams on the surface of the finished concrete.[57]

Mention must be made of the way in which services are integrated into the galleries at Kimbell, not only the reflecting light baffles and lighting consoles below the crown of the vault, but also the service channels that run between the downstand beams under the springing (fig. 7.41). These metal service boxes, together with the moving partitions that are bracketed off longitudinal tracks let into their form, enabled Kahn to orient the space of the museum into two countervailing and ideologically distinct directions; on the one hand, the traditional gallery as a discrete room, running in the same direction as the vault, on the other, the lateral expanse of space running across the vault, capable of providing a flexible, open floor area appropriate to a wide range of exhibition formats.

The Kimbell Art Museum is a work that has been subjected to a great deal of controversy on both tectonic and technical grounds, not the least of which has been the character of the 104-foot-by-23-foot "false" vaults by which the building is covered. The roof of the museum reiterates in many ways the dilemma and the aspirations of the Greco-Gothic ideal, for in its evolution two conflicting impulses can be identified. On the one hand, there is the folded-plate, factory-like, concrete roof that Kahn projected in his spring 1967 design for the mu-

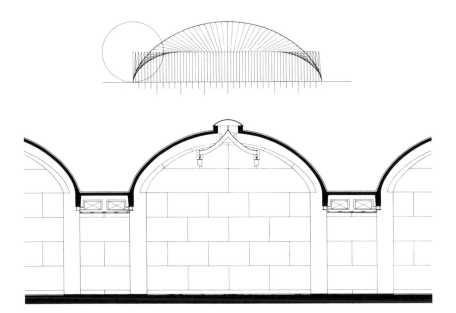

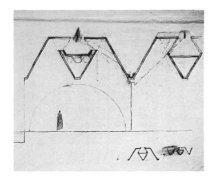

7.41
Louis I. Kahn, Kimbell Art Museum, section of cycloid, final version.

7.42
Louis I. Kahn, Kimbell Art Museum, early sketch of folded-plate roof structure.

seum (fig. 7.42), a design that clearly anticipated the folded-plate structure to be used in the final work. On the other hand, there are the semicircular, purely vaulted galleries projected by Kahn and his assistant Marshall Meyers in autumn of 1967, when Kahn proposed vaults having a 12-foot radius, set on top of a 12-foot-high beam line supported by columns at 24-foot centers. Nothing surely could have been more Platonic and monumental than this double-square gallery section, and this seems to have been why it was rejected by the client, namely, for being too magisterial, since the director Richard Brown wanted a villa for his museum rather than a palace. This pertinent critique was answered, so to speak, by the cycloid vault section that Meyers happened upon in Fred Anger-er's book *Surface Structures in Architecture* (1961). The introduction of the cycloid and the decision to pierce its apex with a continuous light slot brought the structure back to its original folded plate form, even if lateral ties were introduced across the slot, in order to permit the structure to act in both directions. The root of *vault* in the Latin verb *volvere*—meaning literally to revolve across— is particularly apt in the case of the cycloid vault, since the profile arises out of the rotation of a point on the circumference of a circle rolling along a line. There is a further incidental analogy between the roll of the vault and the curvature of the fountain flow that parallels the vaulted porticoes on either side of the main entry. To this cycloid section August Kommendant imparted certain engineering refinements: the deepening of the upstand beams around the slot, the thickening of the cycloid wall toward its base, in order to facilitate pouring, the casting of the cycloid as a second pour above the downstand beams, and finally the post-tensioning of the cycloids in the long direction in order to attain a clear span of 104 feet (figs. 7.43, 7.44). This hidden catenary cable network gave an uplift to the cycloid beams so as to counteract their inevitable deflection. Kommandant needed a diaphragm of a certain depth at the return ends of the vaults, and this led to a circumferential light slot of varying depth, let into the end wall of the section (fig. 7.45). In the final development of this form one might say that Kahn was neo-Gothic to the degree that he followed the precepts of Viollet-le-Duc and Greco-Gothic to the degree that he strove for the purity of the form, once the empirical engineering requirements were satisfied.

Doug Suisman's critical appraisal of the Kimbell highlights once again Kahn's familiar ambivalence toward the automobile, for by the time Kahn turned to the Kimbell he had already been struggling to integrate the automobile into his work for well over two decades (fig. 7.46). By this date we may say that the fundamental dilemma posed by the car had defeated him, and in this of course he was by no means alone. The fundamental hostility of the automobile to architecture and to urban civilization as a whole is surely a treatise that is waiting to be written. In any event, there is no doubt whatsoever that the conception of the Kimbell is basically antithetical to the car, or to put it conversely, the ideal way to enter this museum is hardly from its parking lot. Thus, as Suisman writes:

The first impression of the Kimbell parking lot facade is its blankness—no recognizable windows, unbroken panels of concrete and travertine, a dark horizontal gash for an entryway. . . . Passing into the recess of the entry your eyes have no time to adjust before entering the lobby, so your initial impression of the interior is a gloomy one indeed.

The ideal entrance is by way of the pedestrian approach from the park, but this is relatively unused:

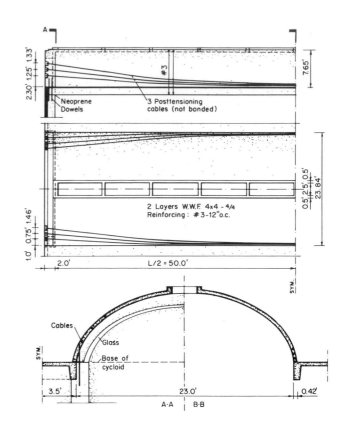

A

#3

7.65'

Neoprene Dowels

3 Posttensioning cables (not bonded)

2 Layers W.W.F. 4x4 - 4/4
Reinforcing: #3-12"o.c.

2.30' 1.25' 1.33'

0.75' 1.46'

1.0'

2.0'

0.5' 2.5' 0.5'

23.84'

L/2 = 50.0'

SYM.

Cables

Glass

Base of cycloid

SYM.

3.5'

23.0'

0.42'

A-A | B-B

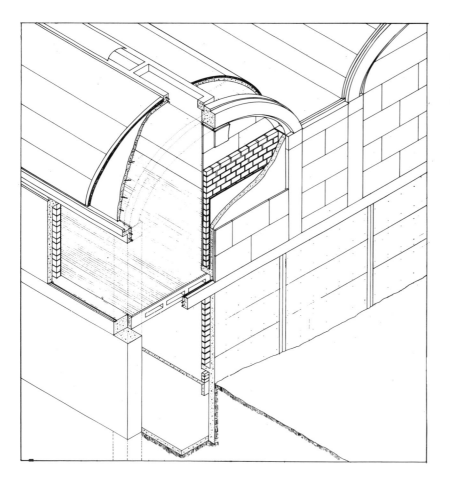

7.43
Louis I. Kahn, Kimbell Art Museum: side elevation of shells with post-tensioning cables; plan, post-tensioning cables, and skylight; cross section of shell-end arch, with glass separation between end arch and walls.

7.44
Louis I. Kahn, Kimbell Art Museum, isometric drawing of the elements of construction.

7.45
Kahn in the Kimbell auditorium.

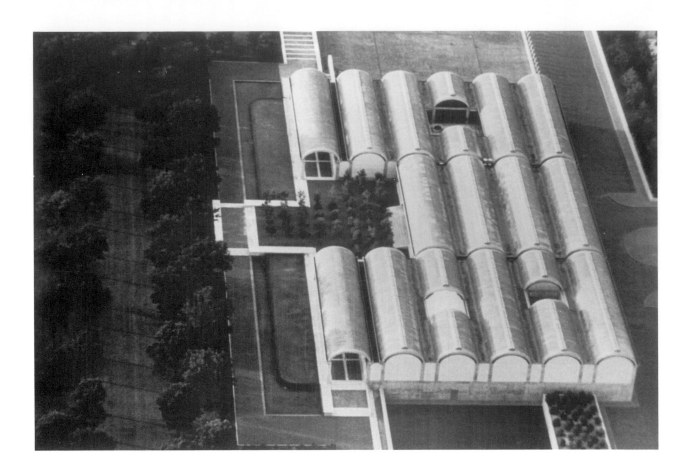

7.46
Louis I. Kahn, Kimbell Art Museum, view of entrance.

It's only later that you learn that a mere 15 per cent of all museum visitors actually enter through this so-called entrance where Kahn expected them; the other 85 per cent arrive by car, park in the lot, and enter through the basement. Could Kahn's reported failure to obtain a driver's license possibly explain this flagrant miscalculation of suburban habits?[58]

It is nonetheless clear that the traditional occidental monument, together with the institution it embodies, demands that one should arrive on foot and enter via a threshold in order to undergo an appropriate rite of passage between the representational portico of the monument and its internal space of public appearance, the very transition that is compromised everywhere today by the universal aporia of the automobile. For Kahn this was particularly distressing inasmuch as he had striven throughout his life for the full integration of modern technology with the substance of institutional form. As we have remarked, this rite of passage is ideally achieved at Kimbell in the approach from the park, where, passing under the foreground canopy of trees, one crosses a stepped threshold between the cascading fountains before entering the museum proper via a graveled forecourt and a grove of diminutive trees. Once upon this axis, one finds oneself in a green labyrinth, where the gravel underfoot is destabilizing and where the corresponding sound of one's footfall is overlaid by the continual rush of the water. In such a setting, perhaps more fitting for a temple than a museum, we find ourselves returned to the tactility of the tectonic in all its aspects; to a meeting between the essence of things and the existence of beings, to that pre-Socratic moment, lying outside time, that is at once both modern and antique.

pact on his work and thought (fig. 8.10). Here, amid the stepped pyramid forms of the Yucatán jungle, he was to experience a different view of the horizon that would remind him not only of the sea but also of seasonal changes in the Scandinavian climate. In "Platforms and Plateaus" he wrote:

By introducing the platform with its level at the same height as the jungle top, these people had suddenly obtained a new dimension of life, worthy of their devotion to their gods. On these high platforms—many of them as long as 100 meters—they built their temples. They had from here the sky, the clouds and the breeze, and suddenly the jungle roof had been converted into a great open plain. By this architectural trick they had completely changed the landscape and supplied their visual life with a greatness corresponding to the greatness of their gods.

Today you can still experience this wonderful variation of feeling from the closeness in the jungle to the vast openness of the platform top. It is parallel to the relief you feel here in Scandinavia when after weeks of rain, clouds and darkness, you suddenly come through all this, out into the sunshine again.[20]

On his return to Denmark, Utzon projected his audacious, neo-Wrightian Langelinie Pavilion (1953) and then went on to enter a number of Swedish competitions in collaboration with the Swedish architects Erik and Henny Anderson. This was the period during which he also associated with the Norwegian architects Arne Kosmo and Sverre Fehn. Out of the Anderson-Utzon collaboration came one realized work, the Svaneke Seamark watertower built on Bornholm Island in the Baltic in 1955, together with a remarkable high-rise housing complex and town center projected for Elineberg, Hälsingborg, Sweden, in 1954 (fig. 8.11). This last, a neighborhood unit comprising a school, a shopping center, and high-rise bachelor housing, was, in effect, a more sophisticated version of the housing that Utzon had previously projected for Morocco. The Elineberg scheme is seminal at a number of levels; first, because of the way in which six fourteen-story cluster towers are united as a single form by a podium containing parking; second, because these towers are made up of combinations of the same megaron unit; and third, because the upper floors of the smaller units step down in section from back to front, that is to say from their northern core walls down to their south-facing window walls (fig. 8.12). Of this ingenious inflection Utzon wrote:

The section shows clearly an attempt to see more than the grey Nordic sky from the flats. . . . The grey Nordic sky is namely what you see when you have the normal windowsill and balcony balustrade. Here the floors are terraced—the higher, the steeper the steps—so you can stand on the 14th floor and see the beautiful ocean 2 kilometers away. The windowsill and the balcony balustrade are at the same level as your feet. The facade with balconies in these concrete (slip-form) houses, with their rather closed northern, eastern and western fronts, is constructed of vibrated concrete elements, like sticks woven together, as seen on the elevation. . . . The dizzy feeling on the top floor has been reduced by protecting vertical elements and greenery will grow on them.[21]

Since these trellises increase their density across the facade the higher they go, thereby compensating for their distance from the ground by a greater sense of enclosure, the overall tower section may be seen as pursuing a similar notion of incremental form to what we will find in Louis Kahn's initial proposal for the Richards Laboratories (1959). In both instances, the aerial elements increase their

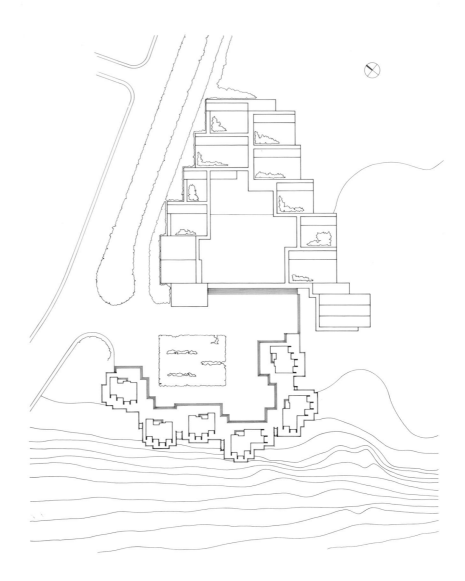

8.11
Jørn Utzon, housing complex and town center, Elineberg, Hälsingborg, Sweden, 1954. Site plan. Housing towers are stacked on a parking podium; a shopping center is located to the northeast of the housing cluster.

8.12
Jørn Utzon, Elineberg, section, plan, and elevation of housing tower. The sectional displacement of the floors increases on the upper levels of the building.

density as they rise upward—trellises in Elineberg and ventilating shafts in Philadelphia—while conversely the telluric elements increase their density as they descend, the exterior terraces and cross walls in Elineberg and cantilevering beam sections in Philadelphia. Of equal import, however, is Utzon's proposition to grow vines on the trellises so as to transform the cluster towers into cliffs of cascading greenery; a provision that would tend, as in much of Utzon's work, to attenuate the boundary separating culture from nature. One may even see this incremental trelliswork as an effort to compensate for the disappearance of ornament; to make up for that lack remarked on by Adolf Loos in "Ornament und Verbrechen" (Ornament and Crime) in 1908:

What makes our period so important is that it is incapable of producing new ornament. We have outgrown ornament and struggled through to a state without ornament. . . . The lack of ornament is a sign of intellectual power. Modern man uses the ornament of past and foreign cultures at his discretion. His own inventions are concentrated on other things.[22]

Loos capped this conclusion two years later by the following observation about the cultural disinheritance of the modern world.

256

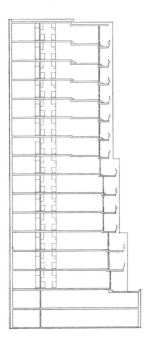

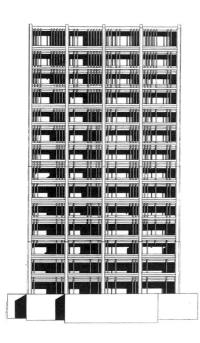

Mankind's history has not yet had to record a period without culture. The creation of such a period was reserved for the urban dweller during the second half of the nineteenth century. Until then the development of our culture has remained in a state of flux. One obeyed the commands of the hour and did not look forwards or backwards.[23]

Loos's own use of natural form as a surrogate ornament is most evident in his internal application of thin marble revetment. Loos used the stone as a thin screen, however, as a mask that he referred to ironically as inexpensive wallpaper; and this proto-Dadaist stance could hardly be further removed from the benevolent organicism underlying Utzon's work.

Utzon's involvement with China dates from 1959, when he went to the Far East to study traditional Chinese building methods. There he came across the twelfth-century Chinese building manual *Yingzao fashi,*[24] a document that prior to the twentieth century had served as the basic Chinese building code. Utzon found this text exemplary, largely because it demonstrated how a timber syntax, compiled out of interlocking standard components, could be used to create an extremely varied range of building types (fig. 8.13). What intrigued him about the system was the way in which the typical roof truss was not triangulated as it is in the West, but made up of stacked beams stepping up toward the apex. This trabeated additive structure, comprising straight beams plus elaborate cantilevered brackets, assured the expressive flexibility of the system (fig. 8.14). Without such a stepped approach the characteristic curve of the Chinese roof could never have been achieved (fig. 8.15). This additive method had a great impact on Utzon, but of even greater consequence was the fact that the same kit of parts could be used to assemble quite different roof forms, the type being modified according to local climatic conditions throughout China. Moreover, the system had inherent antiseismic properties inasmuch as the weight of the roof and the friction points between the joints had the capacity to dampen and absorb the shock waves. According to the Australian architect Peter Myers, Utzon kept a copy of the *Yingzao fashi* in his Sydney office and used it as his *vade mecum,* applying its fundamental principles to the development of the Sydney Opera House, which had been won in competition in 1957.[25] On his way back from China Utzon visited Japan, where he encountered a different and more delicate inflection of the original Chinese architecture as this appeared in the traditional Japanese architectural syntax of standard partitions, shutters, and modular floor panels, respectively the *shoji, amado,* and *tatami* of the Japanese house (see figs. 1.20, 1.21). In the following year, Utzon widened his experience of the Orient by visiting India, Nepal, and Tibet.

Utzon's Langelinie tower restaurant proposal of 1953 is effectively a reinterpreted pagoda form that owes a great deal to Wright's Johnson Wax research tower, built in Racine, Wisconsin, in 1947 (figs. 8.16, 8.17). In Langelinie, as in Racine, the basic structure comprises a cylindrical hollow service core, from which cantilevered platforms extend to embody the floors of the building (fig. 8.18). Where the floors in Wright's tower are of constant width and merely alternate between square and circular plan shapes, Utzon's circular platforms not only alternate between large and small but also progressively diminish in diameter as they rise toward the top, in a manner that simulates the traditional pagoda profile. The hollow concrete structure of the platforms, the use of voids within the structural diaphragm as air-conditioning ducts, the gently stepped section of

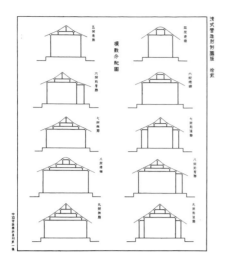

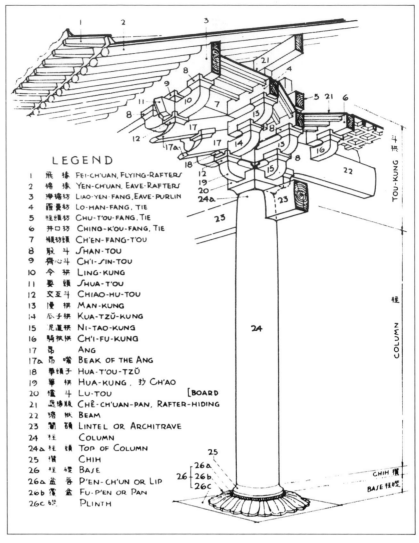

LEGEND

1	飛 椽	FEI-CH'UAN, FLYING-RAFTERS
2	檐 椽	YEN-CH'UAN, EAVE-RAFTERS
3	撩檐枋	LIAO-YEN-FANG, EAVE-PURLIN
4	羅漢枋	LO-HAN-FANG, TIE
5	柱頭枋	CHU-T'OU-FANG, TIE
6	井口枋	CHING-K'OU-FANG, TIE
7	順枋頭	CH'EN-FANG-T'OU
8	散 斗	SHAN-TOU
9	齊心斗	CH'I-SIN-TOU
10	令 拱	LING-KUNG
11	要 頭	SHUA-T'OU
12	交互斗	CHIAO-HU-TOU
13	慢 拱	MAN-KUNG
14	瓜子拱	KUA-TZŬ-KUNG
15	泥道拱	NI-TAO-KUNG
16	騎根拱	CH'I-FU-KUNG
17	昂	ANG
17a	昂 嘴	BEAK OF THE ANG
18	華頭子	HUA-T'OU-TZŬ
19	華 拱	HUA-KUNG, 抄 CH'AO
20	櫨 斗	LU-TOU
21	遮椽版	CHÊ-CH'UAN-PAN, RAFTER-HIDING [BOARD
22	搭梁	BEAM
23	闌 額	LINTEL OR ARCHITRAVE
24	柱	COLUMN
24a	柱 頭	TOP OF COLUMN
25	礩	CHIH
26	柱 礎	BASE
26a	盆 唇	P'EN-CH'UN OR LIP
26b	覆 盆	FU-P'EN OR PAN
26c	础	PLINTH

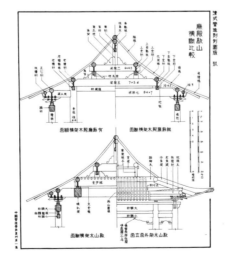

8.13
Plate from a Chinese building manual of the Ch'ing dynasty (1644–1911).

8.14
Chinese bracketing: the *tou kung* system.

8.15
Plate from a Chinese building manual of the Ch'ing dynasty.

8.16
Jørn Utzon, Langelinie Pavilion project, Copenhagen, 1953.

8.17
Frank Lloyd Wright, S. C. Johnson and Son Research Center, Racine, Wisconsin, 1947. Section.

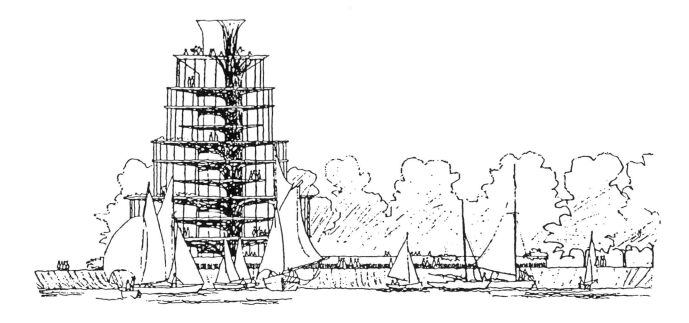

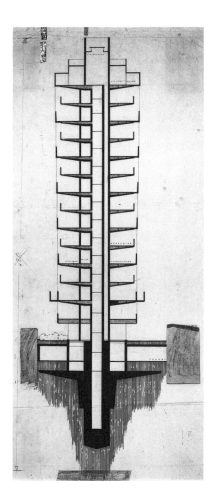

the dining levels, inflected so as to afford panoramic views to every table, the integrated structural core comprising lavatories, dumb-waiters, and elevators, the stepped tiers of the suspended glazing, all of these features testify to the power of Utzon's tectonic imagination and to his capacity to adapt a Wrightian paradigm to a different program.

It is hard to overestimate the influence of Wright on Utzon, for while there is nothing that is stylistically Wrightian about Utzon's work, Wright's tectonic concerns are evident in one form or another throughout the Danish architect's career. This influence is at its most explicit perhaps in the Langelinie Pavilion and in the Silkeborg Museum, designed in 1962 as a sculptural gallery for the Norwegian artist Asger Jørn, who had been a founder of the international Cobra group. The fact that the Cobra movement was equally non-Eurocentric in its cultural affinities is surely significant, given Utzon's own disposition.[26]

The parti of Silkeborg derived from Utzon's personal experience in China, stemming directly from his visit to the Tatung caves where he saw a collection of Buddhist sculptures cradled in the fissures of the earth. Utzon's radical transformation of this image into an underground museum was peculiarly appropriate to the *art brut* primitivism of the Cobra circle. Not withstanding this, the concentrically ramped galleries of the Silkeborg scheme (fig. 8.19) also came from a transposition of Wright's Guggenheim Museum (fig. 8.20), which had in its turn been derived from the inversion of an Assyrian ziggurat. In this development, Wright's first ziggurat project, the upward-spiraling Gordon Strong Automobile Objective and Planetarium of 1924 (fig. 8.21), becomes the inverted, hollowed-out, downward-spiraling Guggenheim Museum.[27] Typologically speaking, we pass via the Guggenheim, from the monumental but dematerializing thrust of the Gordon Strong spiral to the bowel-like, earthbound materiality of Utzon's Silkeborg. In this trajectory it was the inspiration of the oriental form that was a constant for both Wright and Utzon.

8.18

Jørn Utzon, Langelinie Pavilion, detail plan
and section.

8.19

Jørn Utzon, Silkeborg Museum, 1962. Gallery
floor plan and section.

8.20

Frank Lloyd Wright, Solomon R. Guggenheim
Museum, New York, 1946–1959. Section.

8.21

Frank Lloyd Wright, Automobile Objective
and Planetarium for Gordon Strong, Sugarloaf
Mountain, Maryland, 1924.

Shaped like two large intersecting double cisterns and equipped with interlocking circuits of circular ramps and an ingenious system of gridded roof lights,
Silkeborg has to be counted among the more unique of Utzon's early inventions,
and surely if one had the choice of realizing only one of his unbuilt works, this
would be a preference. An earthwork by definition, Silkeborg can be seen as the
categoric antithesis to the Langelinie Pavilion; the cavernous *mundus*[28] versus
the aerial pagoda. However, we need to note two other important aspects of the
work; first, the way in which Wright's metaphorical transposition of the generic
car ramp in the Guggenheim Museum (transposed from the Gordon Strong proposal) reappears in the swirling concentric trajectories of the passerelles con-
ducting visitors down into the bowels of Utzon's museum (fig. 8.22), and
second, the way in which the concentric organic geometry of the galleries is in-
geniously offset by translucent roof lights having a corrugated structural section,
capable of spanning the lower volumes at ground level (cf. Sverre Fehn's Nordic
Pavilion for the Venice Biennale of 1967). A similarly ribbed and striated structure reappears in the inverted vaults supporting the floor of the mezzanines situated between the ground and the subterranean cisterns.

As I have already remarked, Utzon's architecture may be read in terms of the
Semperian formula of the earthwork versus the roofwork. This countervailing but
complementary opposition generally appears in his work through the spectrum
of three different type forms of increasing hierarchical complexity, each type being largely determined by a variation in the roof. Thus we advance from the

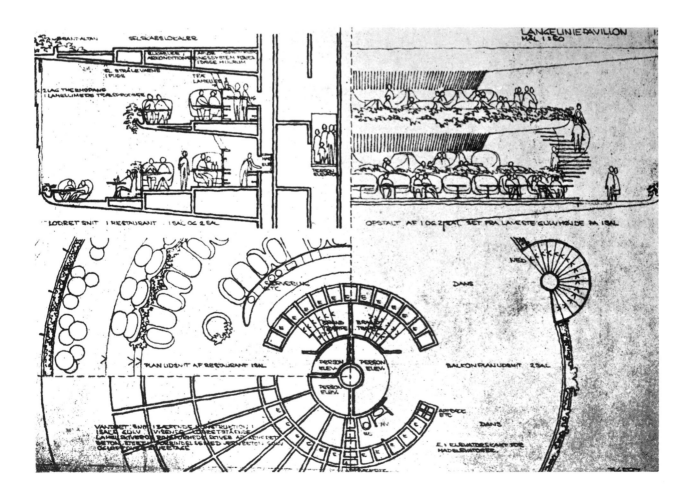

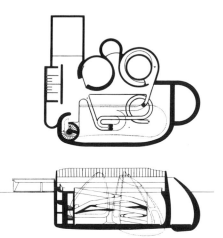

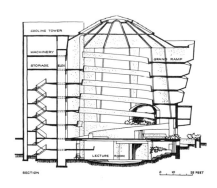

monopitch roof of Utzon's domestic atrium, to the folded slab roof of his typical concourse space, to his use of the shell-pagoda form for a larger assembly space. In each instance, significant differences occur in the nature of the wall spanning between earthwork and roofwork. In the first type, the main wall element is a load-bearing boundary that encloses both house and atrium, although this is paralleled by a lightweight screen wall running around the interior of the court. In this type the podium is reduced to a shallow platform accommodating the slope. In the second type the roofwork consists of a folded concrete slab suspended above the elevated earthwork, while in the third type the roofwork is a shell form set above a stepped podium. While these last two types are invariably bounded by screen walls, the Silkeborg Museum is something of an exception since it comprises an earthwork that is sunken into the ground and roofed by a mixture of folded-slab and shell form construction.

The first of these types, the atrium, appears in two related housing schemes realized early in Utzon's career, the Kingo and Fredensborg residential settlements of 1958 and 1963 respectively. The same typology also appears in a project for a new quarter designed for the town of Odense in 1963. The second paradigm, the folded slab roof, manifests itself in two different versions, the domestic and the civic. In the first instance, it shows up in Utzon's own house projected for Bayview, Sydney, between 1964 and 1965; in the second it crowns the parti for both the Helsingør school and the Zurich Opera House projects of 1963. Meanwhile the third type, the shell-pagoda suspended above the podium, recurs repeatedly throughout the first fifteen years of Utzon's practice, attaining its fullest expression in the Sydney Opera House.

If some kind of pagoda is a recurrent theme in Utzon's civic architecture, its domestic complement is the atrium house, with its potential to accommodate itself to any kind of topography. This is a primordial dwelling in which the roofwork

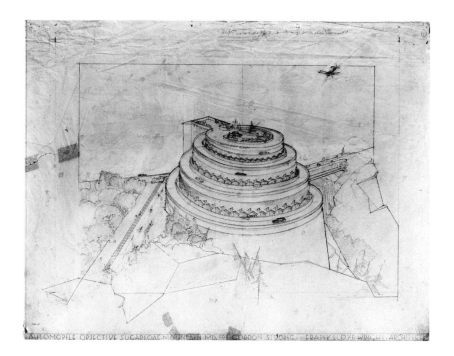

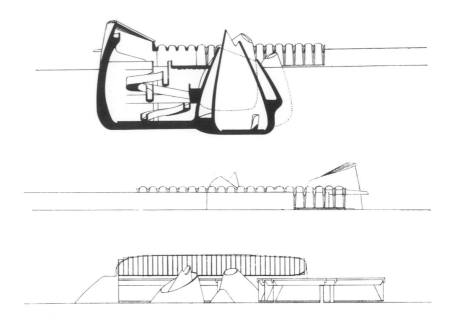

8.22
Jørn Utzon, Silkeborg Museum, section, west elevation, and north elevation. To be constructed out of prefabricated and reinforced concrete construction.

8.23
Jørn Utzon, Kingo housing, near Helsingør, Denmark, 1956. Site plan. Housing laid out on a modified Radburn principle.

8.24
Jørn Utzon, housing at Fredensborg, 1962–1963. Site plan.

and the earthwork are linked by a perimeter wall that gives shape to the morphology of the settlement. With the exception of its latent presence in his own house in Hellebaek, this wall first appears in his expandable *skånske hustyper* designed for towns in Skåne, southern Sweden, in 1953.[29] The same concept will be returned to in his Kingo housing scheme of 1956 in Helsingør (Elsinore), comprising some 63 single-story, square atrium houses, arranged in eleven contiguous clusters of varying size on a rather irregular site (fig. 8.23). All the courtyards face south, southwest, or southeast, while the walled-in northern elevations serve to link the garages and entries that line the perimeter of the development. This neo-Radburn approach to the site plan allows the residents to wander at liberty over an inner greensward that is loosely defined by the perimeter and by two fingers of patio housing that break up the inner domain.

Unlike his later Fredensborg settlement of 1962–1963 (fig. 8.24), Kingo comprises a much looser house form, in which the first line of demarcation is the courtyard itself. Utzon projected a number of alternative plans for Kingo and even suggested that, as in the Skåne type, the units may grow across time within the confines of the bounding wall (figs. 8.25, 8.26, 8.27). The different plans proposed by Utzon amount to a series of permutations on a standard three-bedroom L-shaped unit. At times the continuity of the L-form is only carried by the roof, with the living volume breaking down into a separate study or a semidetached room for an elderly person. In all the different versions, the carport is variously accommodated beneath the roof and the garden is treated in a variety of ways. In one instance the house is equipped with a conservatory, in another with a playroom, in yet another with a boatyard. As I have already noted, Wright's Usonian house is unquestionably an influence on the Utzon atrium dwelling as this appears in both Kingo and Fredensborg, the debt being acknowledged, as it were, by the use of the Wrightian cherokee red as a finish for the timber fenestration of Fredensborg. However, the Usonian house is not the only model to which these housing schemes are indebted. Thus, we find the use of tile-capped Chinese walls in both schemes and chimneys profiled after

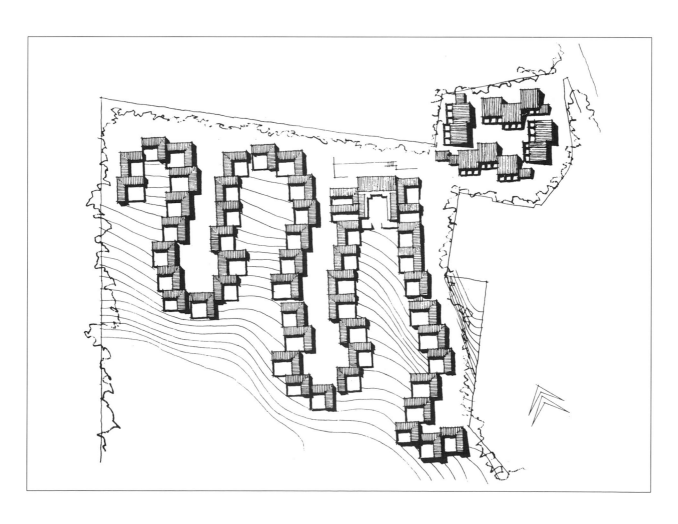

the shape of Middle Eastern ventilation shafts, a reference surely to the wind towers of Iran reinterpreted in Danish brickwork (cf. the Bad-Ghir of Yazd) (figs. 8.28, 8.29). Iberian culture is also evoked through the use of Spanish tiles and in the timber-battened grillwork to the pierced window openings. In his retrospective essay on the Fredensborg settlement Tobias Faber also cites a particular type of courtyard farm complex to be found in the Vaucluse area of southern France, and mentions the general influence of the Austrian architect Roland Rainer on Utzon.[30] Japanese rock gardens and Scandinavian dolmens are also surely evoked by Utzon's random placement of rocks in the surrounding greensward.

In the plan for Odense, Utzon assembles his carpet housing paradigm into a larger urban whole (fig. 8.30). In this instance, some two hundred patio dwellings are shown radiating out, Radburn style, from a "city crown," thereby positing a categorical opposition between the private fabric of the patio and the public realm of the city hall, roofed by a concrete shell. Utzon orchestrated this assembly in such a way as to resemble a traditional Islamic city, where each individual courtyard house is bonded to the next as part of a continuous fabric. This modular/morphological approach is present in all of Utzon's urban studies, irrespective of whether the basic unit is an atrium or a cross-walled megaron, as in the Elineberg or Birkehøj town plans respectively, dating from 1945 and 1960. In

8.25
Jørn Utzon, Kingo housing, alternative rectangular and square prototypes, allowing for growth.

8.26
Jørn Utzon, Kingo housing, house plan, one variation.

8.27
Jørn Utzon, southern Swedish house types competition, 1950, First Prize. Axonometric. This type will be reworked in the Kingo housing scheme of 1956.

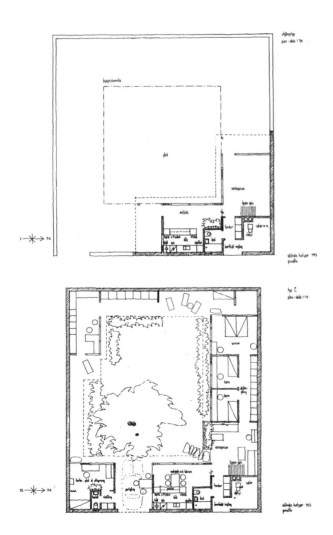

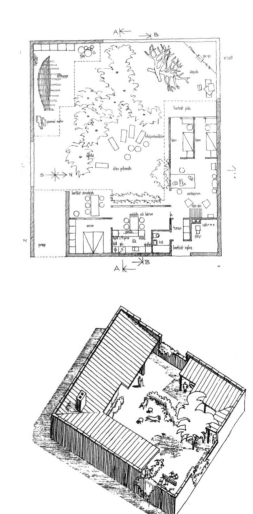

these plans, tripartite clusters of towers and terrace houses are respectively employed as the basic units from which the urban fabric is compounded (fig. 8.31). Inspired by Aalto's Kauttua housing (1937) (fig. 8.32), and by his radical terrace housing for Sunila (1936) (fig. 8.33), Utzon's terraced Birkehøj dwelling units fan out across the contours in groups of three, reminiscent of the adobe housing of the American Southwest. Of this arrangement he wrote:

The small square on top of the hill surrounded by houses with small flats for old people will create an environment with a peaceful protected atmosphere in a relatively open landscape, not unlike the feeling in small Italian villages. Great care has been taken to follow the landscape and to utilize its values. The standardized building elements will be combined in such a way . . . in the flats and in the single houses themselves to get a combination without the awful stiffness wellknown from many modern housing schemes. There are many ways to arrange the same books in a book-shelf. I can hardly see any reason for repetition of the

8.28
Jørn Utzon, Fredensborg housing, sections.

8.29
Jørn Utzon, Fredensborg housing.

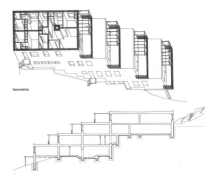

8.33
Alvar Aalto, housing at Sunila, Finland, 1936.
Isometric and section.

8.34
Jørn Utzon, competition scheme for World Exhibition, Copenhagen, 1959. Section.

denced by the Sydney Opera House, but also his folded-slab roofs projected as post-tensioned long-span structures in reinforced concrete. This particular form, rarely employed outside the engineering work of Eugène Freyssinet and Pier Luigi Nervi, first appears in the wide-span folded-plate roofs that Utzon proposed for his World Exhibition Center designed for Copenhagen in 1960 (fig. 8.34). Here we find both cantilevered and clear spans in folded-slab construction, varying from 80 feet in the first instance to 240 feet in the second. These audacious spans were being projected at a time when among the largest folded-plate structures in concrete was the 164-foot span employed by Nervi for the lecture hall that he built in 1956 for the UNESCO headquarters in Paris, as designed by Marcel Breuer and Bernard Zehrfuss (fig. 8.35).

A more moderate application of an all-encompassing folded-plate roof appears in Utzon's main entry for the Højstrup High School, projected for the Danish Trades Union as a college for further education to be built at Helsingør in 1958 (fig. 8.36).[32] Although no basement plans have been published for this work, one may assume that the undercroft was allocated to parking while its upper surface was terraced in such a way as to evoke a city in miniature, recalling in its orthogonal geometry and rhythmic scale those classic Maya sites that Utzon had visited nine years before (fig. 8.37). Instead of temples, the podium projected for Helsingør supported a series of classrooms arranged around a central sunken court or "agora." We may think of these classrooms, roofed by folded slabs, as surrogate city fabric and of the shell-roofed assembly hall as the civic center, the equivalent of a church or a city hall. This combination of shell form with folded-plate structure is offset here by a high-rise residential tower, modeled on the fourteen-story Elineberg tower of 1954 (fig. 8.38). However disjunctive this last may seem in the context of a low-rise school, it patently serves to reinforce a reading of the complex as a mini-city. A similar use of folded plates appears in Utzon's design for a shopping center projected at virtually the same time. In this instance the V-shaped concrete roof sections span 120 feet over the principal shopping hall with cantilevered end spans of 40 feet each (fig. 8.39).

The folded-plate concept will reappear at a totally different scale in Utzon's designs for his own house at Bayview, Sydney, worked on intermittently between 1961 and 1965. Designed for a sloping site overlooking Pittwater, this house went through four separate versions before it was finally accepted by the local authorities. Conceptually related to the Silkeborg Museum, the Bayview project clearly breaks down, once again, into an earthwork and a roofwork. Like many of Wright's houses, the house establishes the character of the site by extending its domain horizontally through outriding boundary walls (figs. 8.40, 8.41). This

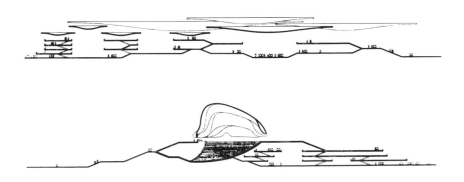

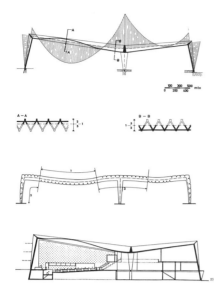

8.35
Pier Luigi Nervi, Marcel Breuer, and Bernard Zehrfuss, UNESCO Headquarters, Paris, 1953–1956. Structural diagrams (moment, tension, compression, and deflection) and building section of lecture hall.

8.36
Jørn Utzon, Højstrup Danish Trades Union High School for Further Education, Helsingør, Denmark, 1958. Roof plan.

not only increases the apparent size of the house but also establishes the territory of the dwelling within the topography rather than merely meeting the required area in a freestanding object. Like the Silkeborg Museum, the Bayview house is rendered as a kind of mirage on the horizon that announces itself largely through the skyline profile of its folded roof. It is significant that Utzon first projected this roof as a leaflike skeleton spanning some 50 feet across an earthwork compounded of terraced levels and stepped walls (fig. 8.42). An early sketch of this proposal carries the caption:

The roof can be hanging above, it can be spanning across or jumping over you in one big leap or in many small ones. The problem is to master the water-proofing, the structural requirements and the heat insulation in one mass-produced element, which in combination with itself can give various roof-forms, a nice problem to be solved. This platform courtyard-house shows a vivid roof-grouping formed by such an element-composition. [33]

Unlike his previous folded roofs, the Bayview roof structure is made out of U-shaped, hot-pressed plywood sections that are stacked side by side, and capped by a narrower plywood piece in the form of an inverted U, made water-proof through a bonded aluminum skin. These plywood sections span onto hollow-cored, concrete plank walls, the planks and roof being tied back to the in situ concrete footings by wire cables. The unity of the earthwork is assured through employing the same precast concrete planks for both the walls and the ground floor. Needless to say the plywood roofwork and the concrete earthwork were intended to be self-finishing forms inside and out, and Utzon would pursue this constructional ethic subsequently in his own Can Lis house, built in Porto Petro, Majorca, in 1974. Comprised of three separate units from the outset—main house, guest house, and studio—the fourth and final version of the Bayview house eliminates the freestanding guest wing and breaks up the main house into separate living and sleeping units cranked across the contours of

8.37
Jørn Utzon, Højstrup School, plan. The school is conceived as a *res publica* with classrooms grouped around a public courtyard and parking beneath.

8.38
Jørn Utzon, Højstrup School, section.

8.39
Jørn Utzon, scheme for a shopping center, 1959. Section.

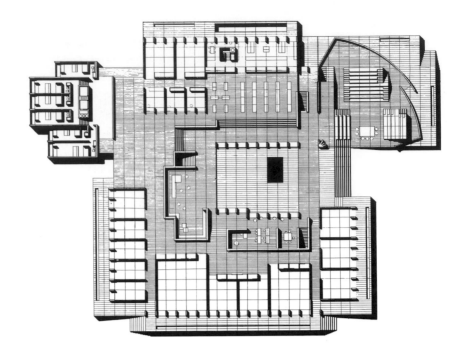

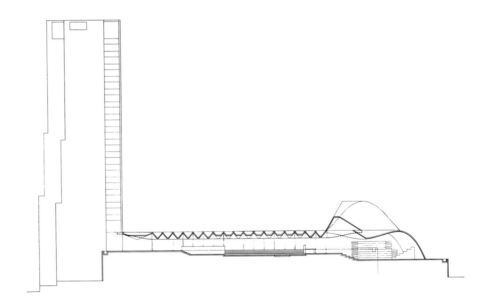

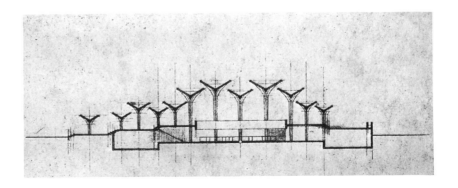

the site; a form that anticipates the parti of Porto Petro. While shallow concrete vaults will substitute for the plywood roof units devised for Sydney, Can Lis will realize many of the themes first broached by Utzon at Bayview (figs. 8.43, 8.44, 8.45, 8.46, 8.47).

Folded-slab construction plays an equally seminal role in Utzon's winning design for the Zurich Opera House of 1964 (figs. 8.48, 8.49). In this work the folded-plate roof covers not only the main auditorium but also the side and back stages, together with such ancillary facilities as a restaurant, a bar, foyers, etc. In this work Utzon will combine the undulating canoe-shaped vault developed for the Helsingør school with a subtle shift in the point of columnar support, which is now positioned either at midspan or at the prow of the vault. Similar support variations occur under the folded roof surrounding the forecourt, where the folded roof cantilevers out toward the open space. In the Zurich opera, as in the Helsingør school, this undulating roof is combined with the podium in such a way as to evoke a city in miniature, recalling here such equally microcosmic works as the Palais Royale, Paris, of 1785 or Wright's Midway Gardens, Chicago, of 1914. The discreet, introspective quality of the Zurich proposal stems from the fact that it is a theatrical precinct rather than a monumental, freestanding institution (figs. 8.50, 8.51). This typological referent is echoed inside the principal volume, where the main auditorium assumes an amphitheatral form instead of the classical proscenium stage.

Double walls occur throughout this project, and the resultant interstitial spaces, of varying thickness, function as "servant" spaces accommodating a wide range of subsidiary elements, including air-conditioning ducts, heating chambers,

8.40
Jørn Utzon, house for his family, Bayview, Sydney, Australia, 1961–1965. Northeast (top) and northwest (bottom) elevations. Bent plywood units laid over cross walls.

8.41
Jørn Utzon, house in Bayview, plan.

8.42
Jørn Utzon, house in Bayview, conceptual drawing: earthwork and roofwork.

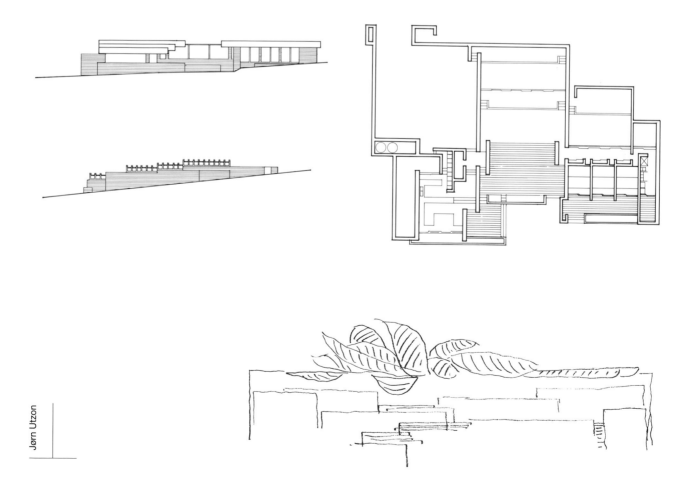

8.43
Jørn Utzon, house in Bayview, scheme four
(June 1965), roof plan.

8.44
Jørn Utzon, house in Bayview, scheme four,
plan of living and bedroom wings:
1. living room
2. terrace
3. court
4. dining
5. kitchen
6. storage
7. entry
8. WC
9. hall
10. enclosed link
11. garden court
12. drying court
13. bedrooms
14. bathrooms
15. laundry

8.45
Jørn Utzon, house for his family, Porto Petro,
Majorca, 1974. Plan:
1. entrance
2. covered outdoor area
3. atrium court
4. pantry
5. kitchen
6. dining area
7. living room
8. bedroom
9. bath

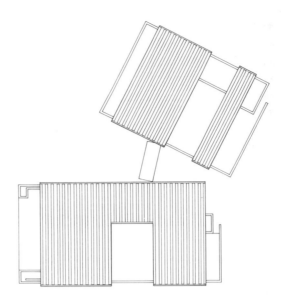

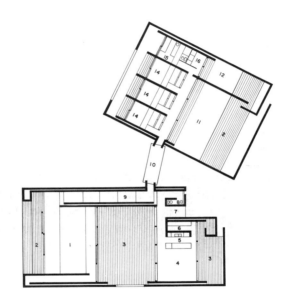

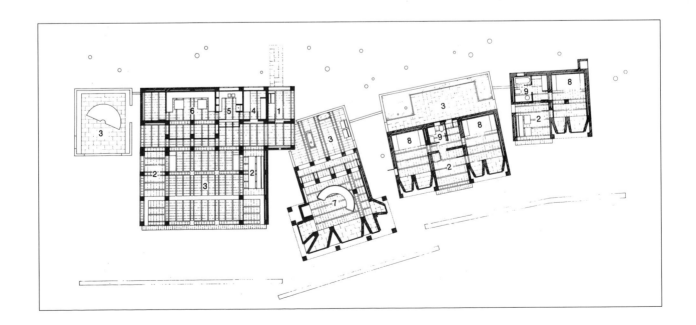

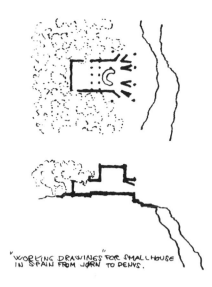

8.46
Jørn Utzon, Porto Petro house, conceptual sketches.

8.47
Jørn Utzon, Porto Petro house, section.

bars, kitchens, control rooms, lavatories, serveries, etc. A plate glass wall serves to separate the auditorium foyer from the exterior, and within this volume the audience would have had equally free access to the 1,200-seat amphitheater and the adjacent 400-seat experimental stage. Part Greek, part pre-Columbian, the main arena is let into the podium, while elsewhere, on the perimeter, the earthwork serves to house support services and an underground car park that is fed from a *porte-cochère* entry situated to one side (fig. 8.52). Utzon's Zurich proposal was sensitively related to the urban fabric, and the decision not to realize this work was surely a loss for both the city and the culture of this century.[34]

Throughout Utzon's work, shell roofs appear as public, symbolic elements that are readily distinguished from their attendant folded-plate roofs or from the podia upon which they are raised. The most complete realization of this last type is surely the Sydney Opera House, first projected by Utzon in 1957 as an entry to an international competition. It was eventually completed, without his supervision, sixteen years later in 1973 (figs. 8.53, 8.54). Of the twin forms from which Sydney is composed the earthwork/podium was the easiest to resolve (fig. 8.55). Indeed, its form changed little from the competition entry to the realized design. The shell roofs, on the other hand, were to prove intractable both conceptually and statically, let alone the technical difficulties that attended their erection. As initially projected, the shells were gestural rather than generational in character, and Utzon would be occupied with their unresolved geometrical structure for almost four years before he finally happened on a solution that would allow him to produce arched segments of varying curvature from the same range of precast modular units (fig. 8.56). The concrete shells of Sydney were finally generated by cutting a three-sided segment out of a sphere and by deriving regularly modulated curved surfaces from this solid (fig. 8.57). Utzon's Sydney proves the point that a tectonic concept and a structurally rational work may not necessarily coincide; a disfunction that recalls Damisch's critique of Viollet-le-Duc, that there is always some inescapable gap between the constructional means and the architectonic result (see chapter 2).

Within the history of European building, there are two moments when this aporia seems to arrive at the threshold of almost total closure. The first of these occurs during the high Gothic period, while the second arises in the second half of the nineteenth century with the perfection of ferro-vitreous construction. Even in these instances, however, discrepancies are to be found between the statical logic of the structure and the formal or constructional logic of its physical form. We know that the Gothic cathedral was largely built on an intuitive structural

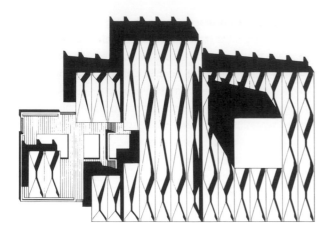

8.48
Jørn Utzon, Zurich Opera House, 1964. Roof
plan.

8.49
Jørn Utzon, Zurich Opera House, plans and
sections. Lower floor:
  1. garage exit
  2. garage entrance
  3. entry court
  4. upper-level entry
  5. box office
  6. foyer
  7. stairs to cloakroom and WCs
  8. office
  9. staff entrance
  10. stage manager
  11. wood shop
  12. gallery
  13. side stage
  14. main stage
  15. rear stage
  16. scene painting
  17. storage
  18. experimental theater
Upper floor:
  1. *Kunsthaus*
  2. entry court
  3. foyer
  4. buffet
  5. service space
  6. canteen
  7. office
  8. library and archive
  9. caretaker's dwelling
  10. wood shop
  11. gallery
  12. side stage
  13. main stage
  14. rear stage
  15. scene painting
  16. storage
  17. experimental stage
  18. auditorium

8.50
Jørn Utzon, Zurich Opera House, model.

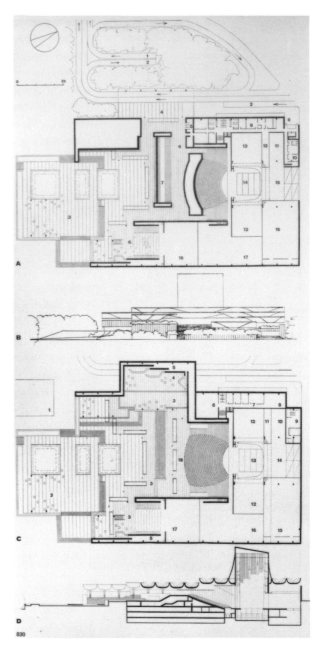

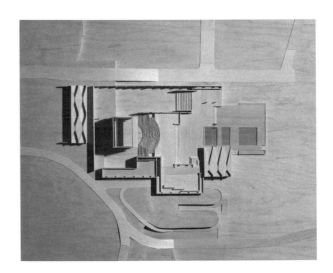

basis backed by generations of experience and that, as Pol Abraham demonstrated in 1933, certain ribs in a typical cross vault are structurally redundant.[35] They exist partly to assist in the erection of the vault and partly to complete its symmetrical order. In ferro-vitreous construction such discrepancies are less in evidence, although even in the Crystal Palace of 1851 we may find certain discrepancies between the varying loads carried by the hollow iron columns and the need to maintain a standard column diameter in order to facilitate assembly. In the genesis of the Sydney Opera House a comparable split occurs between the stresses set up at the springing of the arcuated vaults and the nature of their constructional form. This noncorrespondence was compounded by the magnitude of the dimensions involved, the main hall rising for some 179 feet above the podium to top out 29 feet higher than the roadbed of Sydney Harbour Bridge. At the same time, the shells had to span over large areas; the main hall being 400 feet long and 176 feet wide while the small hall was 352 feet long and 128 feet in width.

Utzon's idea of "building the site" at Bennelong Point was a direct response to a number of contextual features, including the city, the harbor, and the profile and size of the Sydney Harbour Bridge, with its twin masonry towers and its 1,650-foot riveted steel bowstring span. Utzon responded to this challenge with a profound sense of what was required to both *form* the building and *transform* its site and to combine the two adjacent megastructures into a panoramic unity. However, he would justify the particular character of the shells in terms of the ambient light.

Sydney is a dark harbour. The colours of the waterfront are dull and the homes are of red brick. There is no white to take away the sun and make it dazzle the eyes—not like in the Mediterranean countries or South America and other sunlit countries. So I had white in mind when I designed the opera house. And the roof, like sails, white in the strong day, the whole thing slowly coming to life as the sun shone from the east and lifted overhead. In the hot sun of the day it will be a beautiful, white, shimmering thing—as alive to the eyes as architecture can make anything, set in the blue-green waters of the harbour. At night the floodlit shells will be equally vibrant but in a softer more majestic way. . . . The final effect will at times resemble what we call Alpenglochen (Alpineglow)—*the colour you get on snowcapped mountains when the sun is setting—the beautiful pink and violet reflections from the combination of matt snow and shining ice. This*

8.51
Jørn Utzon, Zurich Opera House, model.

8.52
Jørn Utzon, Zurich Opera House, model.

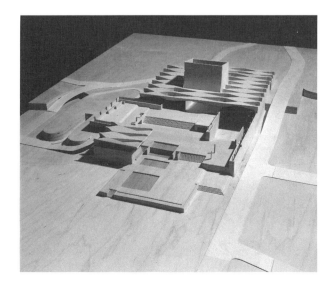

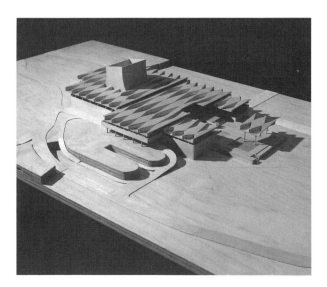

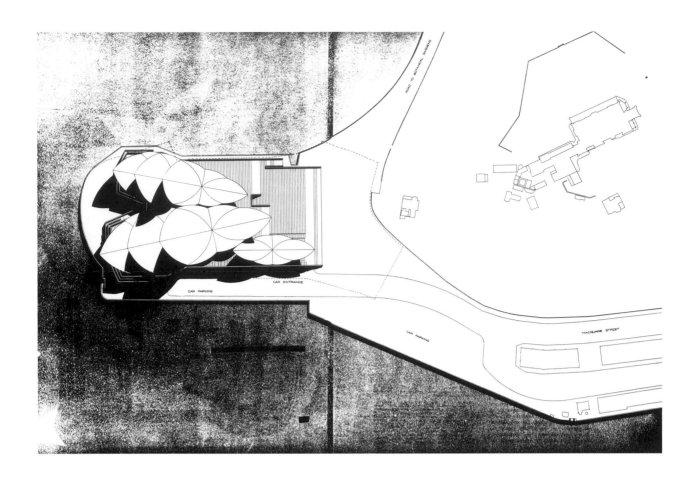

8.53
Jørn Utzon, Sydney Opera House, 1957–
1973. Site plan.

8.54
Jørn Utzon, Sydney Opera House, view from
the harbor with Sydney Harbour Bridge
beyond.

8.55
Jørn Utzon, Sydney Opera House, west
elevation.

8.56
Jørn Utzon, Sydney Opera House: west elevation of the major auditorium, indicating the final version of the structural arrangement all to
be covered, as shown, with precast concrete
lids faced with Höganäs tiles.

roof will be very sensitive. Unlike a building which has only light and shade, it will be a very live sort of thing, changing all day long.[36]

The London-based Danish engineer Ove Arup was fully appreciative of this vision when he wrote in 1965 of the difficulties of realizing Sydney, arguing that these problems stemmed as much from the unfortunate narrowness of Bennelong Point as from the boldness of Utzon's conception.[37] By placing the twin auditoria side by side and by having the audience enter from behind the stage, Utzon was able to reconcile the countervailing vectors of the site; that is to say, the waterfront of the city on the one hand and the promontory and harbor on the other (fig. 8.58). At the same time, he was able to combine the belvedere panorama of the prominent foyer/restaurant spaces with the necessary upward thrust of the auditorium roof as a striking sculptural form with which to respond to the parabolic arch of the adjacent bridge. Utzon's overriding sculptural intent in Sydney reminds one of the affinity he felt for the French sculptor Henri Laurens, and more specifically perhaps of a tomb for an aviator that Laurens had designed for the cemetery of Montparnasse in 1924 (fig. 8.59).

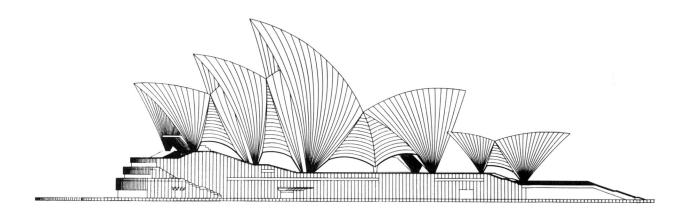

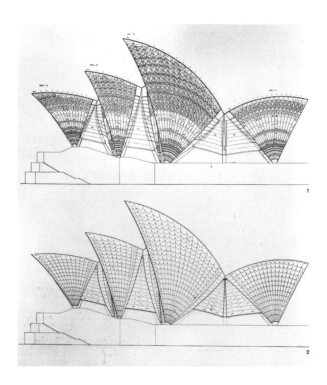

8.57
Jørn Utzon, Sydney Opera House, spherical model from which all shells are derived.

Aside from that of reconciling the sculptural and structural logic of the shell roofs spanning the auditoria, the overall arrangement brought with it other difficulties. In the first instance the unavoidable elimination of side stages, due to the mode of access and the narrowness of the site, necessitated the introduction of hydraulic stages within the basement of the podium; in the second, the structural-cum-sculptural profile of the shell roofs proved to be unstable from a statical point of view and neither architect nor engineer was able to reconcile the rib cage form of the shell with the statical instability of its overall shape. Statically speaking each shell needed four feet to stand on rather than two, and this shortcoming was compounded by Utzon's determination to build the shells out of precast concrete modular segments. These segments may be seen as the precast concrete equivalent of the cast-iron components of the Crystal Palace writ large, only this time in accordance with totally different technical and tectonic constraints. Utzon's preference for a building realized as an additive structure, comparable to Jensen-Klint's Grundtvig Church, did more than delay the resolution of the forms, for as Arup was to suggest, it would have made more statical sense to have conceived the shells as hybrid structures, combining a parabolic steel substructure with a precast concrete eggshell skin. It is worth quoting from Arup at length since one can hardly improve on the clarity of his exposition:

Utzon's design for the roof of each of the halls consisted of four pairs of triangular shells supported on one point of the triangle and each of the two symmetrical shells in a pair leaning against each other, like a pair of hands or fans. The shape of the gothic arch formed between the two supports in each pair did thus not follow the line of thrust—it should not have been pointed at the top—so that the deadload would induce heavy moments. If we counted on the shells being fixed at the supports we were up against the fact that just where the greatest strength is needed, the width of the shell is reduced to a minimum. Moreover, each pair of shells is not balanced longitudinally, but transmits a force to the next pair of shells. Longitudinal stability can therefore only be obtained by considering the whole system of four pairs of shells as one. These shell-pairs are connected by eight side-shells spanning like vaults between the sides of two adjoining pairs of shells, and by louvre walls, which are cross-walls closing the opening between the two shells of a pair—in a rather unsatisfactory fashion, structurally.

It soon became clear that any alteration to the cross-section which would eliminate some of the heavy moments induced by self-weight would completely destroy the architectural character, the crispness and the soaring sail-like quality of the structure. To replace the sails with rabbit-ears would be disastrous. And to make a domelike structure over the whole of each hall or both halls, which would probably have been easier, was of course out. So in the end Utzon and I decided that the scheme had to go forward as designed by Utzon, more or less. It is one of those not infrequent cases where the best architectural form and the best structural form are not the same.

If we had known at that time what we let ourselves in for, we might well have hesitated. We underestimated the effect of the scale of the structure. The trouble is that the thing escalates—the moments require more material, more material induces more moments, and so on. As you all know, one has to be very careful about transferring a statical system from one scale to another. We knew that, of course—but we realized that there would be a hidden strength in the longitudi-

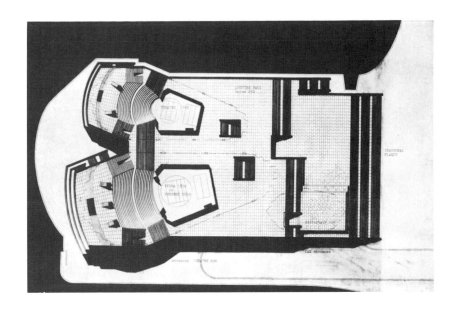

nal continuity and that we could utilize the louvre walls and perhaps combine stage towers and roof in some ways. And we had to say to the clients whether the scheme was feasible, and if we had hesitated on that score, it would probably have given the opponents of the scheme the upper hand. And we liked the scheme and the architect and the clients, and we knew we could do it somehow—so we went ahead. . . . Some time during 1961 it was clear that a slight inclination of the shells—which until then had risen vertically from their supports, would be very desirable and also the louvre walls assumed a much greater importance for the stability. And to reduce the weight we were also veering towards a solution with structural steel ribs, with concrete slabs inside and outside—required by the acoustical experts anyway—but this was heartily disliked by Utzon and I did not really like the idea either. I now almost think that it might have been easier, if not better.[38]

Utzon's shells began to assume their final shape in 1961 when he realized that one could derive all the shells from a single 246-foot-diameter sphere. This meant that all the ribs were identical, although compounded of different lengths

8.58
Jørn Utzon, Sydney Opera House, plan.

8.59
Henri Laurens, Aviator's Tomb projected for Montparnasse Cemetery, Paris, 1924.

and set at different angles to the axis of each shell. Inspired by the Chinese ceramic tradition, Utzon decided to face the shells in off-white, Swedish Höganäs tiles, employing a gloss finish for the main surface and matte for the seams. Utzon realized that the only way to get this textile cover perfectly in place would be to integrate the tiles with the precast concrete segments. In the event, the tiles were cast into precast concrete lids that were subsequently bonded onto the ribbed superstructure of the shells. Over one million Höganäs tiles were laid up in this way (fig. 8.60). The rationale behind this two-stage roofing process has been well accounted for by Utzon's top assistant on the site, the Australian architect Bill Wheatland.

Jørn had some tests made to see whether the tile cladding he was already visualizing could be efficiently laid by tilers working up in the air on scaffolding on the sides of the roof. Jørn decided that there was no chance of getting workmanship to the standard he wanted if the workmen had to climb hundreds of feet into the air and lay tiles while they clung to planks. Also, there was the risk of getting poor workmanship from tile-layer with a hangover or a headache who said: 'The hell with it today—I'll slap this lot on anyhow.' Jørn decided we must adopt the European technique wherein tiles are laid on panels on the ground. So the Opera House tiles were laid on the ground on big concrete trays (we call them lids) and the lids were hoisted to their places on the roof ribs, where they were attached with brackets and bolts. Jørn always says that the human eye is so keen that it can detect flaws in repetitive workmanship even on walls high up in the air and apart from any question of cheapness or speed, he looked on prefabricated building as a way to obtain first-grade workmanship. [39]

Getting all the heavy rib components into position, some 200 feet above the ground, was no mean feat, as Arup makes clear (figs. 8.61, 8.62):

When a unit weighing ten tons is placed a hundred feet up in the air and has to be supported temporarily on an adjustable steel erection arch and the last completed rib, which is not yet firmly attached to the rest of the shell, then all sorts of complicated things happen. The arch gives, the rib moves, the temporary prestress causes strains, temperature variations make their contribution—and we must know what happens. The whole structure acts as a mechanism with sliding joints and adjustable bolts and what not. [40]

8.60
Jørn Utzon, Sydney Opera House, details of arch ribs and precast lid elements. The drawing shows the system of tile revetment in relation to the precast concrete ribs that make up the shell. The dark "feathering" lines on the shell elevation indicate the differentiation between the matte tiles of the seams and the shiny tiles covering the main surface.

8.61
Jørn Utzon, Sydney Opera House, construction photograph.

8.62
Jørn Utzon, Sydney Opera House, axonometric showing the tower crane system of structural assembly.

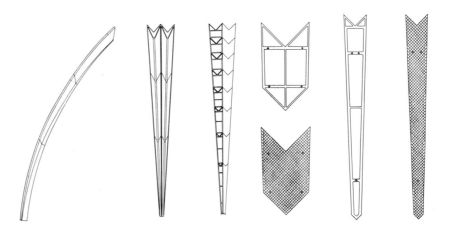

Utzon's penchant for folded-slab construction reemerged in Sydney in the design of the podium, where Utzon and Arup jointly decided to use such a section to achieve the 164-foot clear span of the podium deck.[41] This section ran across the site for almost the full width of Bennelong Point, some 280 feet (figs. 8.63, 8.64). Utzon insisted that this vast podium *porte-cochère* be kept column-free, not only to liberate the turning circles of buses and cars that would enter the opera undercroft at this point but also to create a monumental entry volume. As in Helsingør and Zurich the roof over this space would assume the form of a concrete folded slab, cast in situ, with the bulk of the structural concrete section

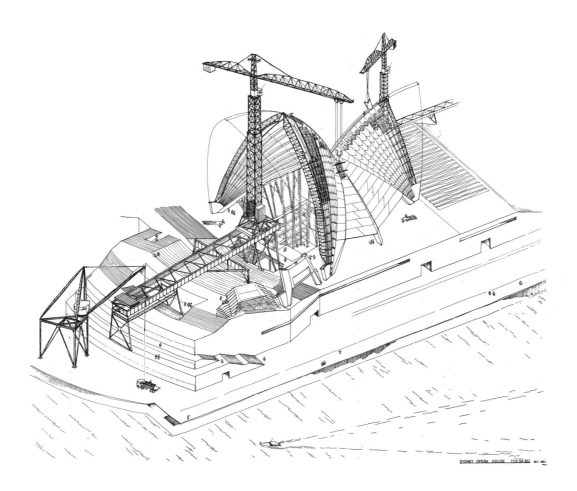

SYDNEY OPERA HOUSE   1112-SK.922 OCT 1963

8.63
Jørn Utzon, Sydney Opera House, longitudinal section through Minor Hall with roof plan
and floor plan.

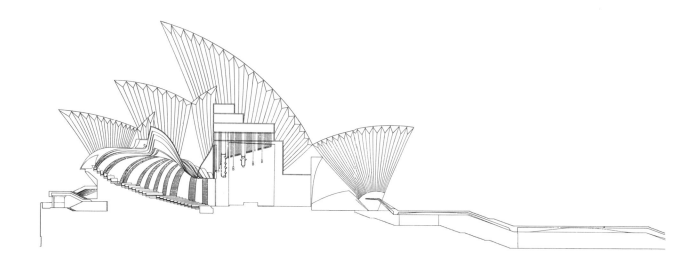

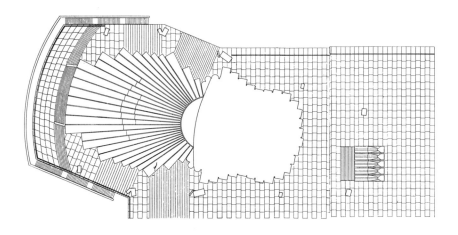

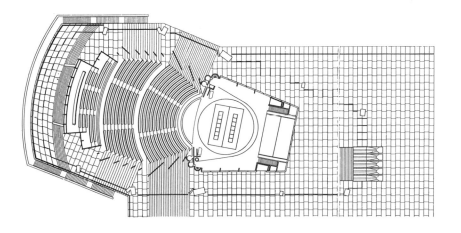

shifting from the bottom to the top as the effective bending moment shifted from positive to negative (fig. 8.62). Serving as a cranked profile for the concourse steps, this slab also acted partially as an arch.

Utzon's insistence on constructing the shells out of modular precast concrete elements is ultimately neo-Gothic in feeling, so it is hardly surprising to find him justifying the overall form in Gothic terms.

If you think of a Gothic church, you are close to what I have been aiming at. Looking at a Gothic church, you will never get tired. You will never finish looking at it. When you pass around it, or see it against the sky, it is as if something new goes on all the time. This is important—with the sun, the light and the clouds, it makes a living thing.[42]

While Utzon's Sydney breaks down all too readily into a Semperian earthwork and roofwork, it also has a Semperian screen wall spanning between the earthwork of the podium and the roofwork of the shells (fig. 8.65). Utzon would be prevented from bringing this element to its ultimate resolution largely because the political furor surrounding the opera house brought him to resign the commission before all the profiles and details of this curtain wall could be resolved. Prior to his resignation, however, he had already determined the basic principle of this membrane.[43] Attached to the leading edges of the shell roofs, the vertical hangers supporting the glass were to have been assembled out of segments of varying length and section so that the three-dimensional profile of the curtain wall could vary progressively from one deep mullion to the next. Glass would have been affixed to these hangers like the planar scales of a fish, while the hangers themselves were to have been formed of hot-pressed plywood, reinforced by an aluminum core and externally faced in bronze. It is difficult to imagine the full-faceted effect of this imbricated screen had it been realized. The greenhouse glazing built in its stead is obviously a much more economical version of Utzon's original concept. As far as Utzon was concerned, the coordinating role of this screen was to relate the podium paving grid to the three-dimensional curvature of the shells. At the same time he wanted to avoid vertical panes of glass, since such surfaces have the tendency to make glass read as a load-bearing element (fig. 8.66). Some measure of the complexity of this whole concept may be gleamed from Bartholomew's description of the final resolution.

In Utzon's final solution each basic mullion component is comprised of three molded plywood 'U' shaped pieces. These form the basic hollow structural system with a skin of hot-bonded bronze laminated to the exterior surface. These 'U' shaped channel pieces are produced in three sizes corresponding to the three planes of inclination in the wall created by the sweep of the mullion.

Vertically, the surface was built up to a sweep by varying inclinations. This tendency was most pronounced in the southern glass walls of the two foyers due to the delivering axes of the shells and the plane of the mullions governed by the four foot paving module of the podium (the mullions carry the four foot building grid vertically through to the shells). In the southern walls the glass is staggered horizontally in plan in response to the relationship between the mullion plan and the shell axis, and the vertical projection from the shell rib of each consecutive glass band. In the northern walls the mullions and shell axes are instead, parallel.

8.64
Jørn Utzon, Sydney Opera House, variable sections of the folded-slab roof that make up the deck of the podium.

283

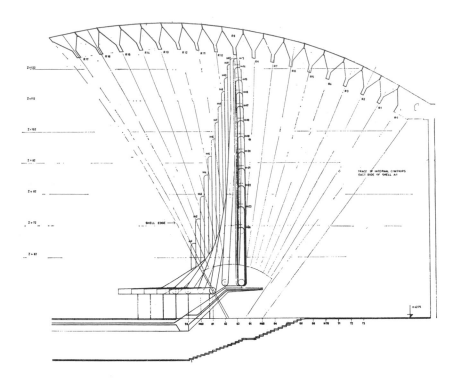

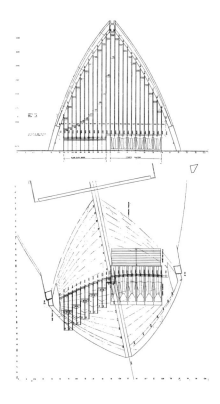

Tremendous flexibility was accommodated in the assembly of the elements. The mullion case was built up of five basic fins in 1/2 inch plywood, with two extra layers being added each time there was a bend. This sandwich system of fins could slip past each other to accommodate large variations in folds, staggering of glass panels and other adjustment tolerances. To these basic center layers were added 'U' shaped channel pieces each with sides of different lengths so that each adjacent mullion in the built wall could overlap allowing the glass to be fitted between this overlap, always having its top and bottom edges parallel to the cross grid of the podium paving geometry.[44]

In many respects this unrealized screen wall is a condensation of the tectonic vision permeating the entire building (fig. 8.67). Profoundly influenced by Wright, Utzon attempted to develop the opera house design in such a way as to extend the scope of Wright's organic architecture. Structural repetition was a key to everything that Utzon attempted at Sydney, and in this respect the curtain wall projected for the opera harked back to the suspended glazing proposed for the Langelinie Pavilion and thus to the textile-like, tubular glass fenestration employed by Wright in his Johnson Wax Administration Building of 1936 (fig. 4.29).

Apart from Sydney, Bagsvaerd Church, completed in a suburb of Copenhagen in 1977, represents the built apotheosis of Utzon's tectonic vision to date. As such it stands at the convergence of many different strands. On the one hand it may be seen as an extension of the Nordic Gothic Revival, that is to say, of the line that came to fruition in Jensen-Klint's masterly Grundtvig Church; on the other, the building patently derives in section from Utzon's preoccupation with the pagoda form. Interwoven with this fusion of occidental and oriental paradigms we find, once again, the perennial inspiration of Wright, recalling, in this instance, the parti of Wright's Unity Temple of 1904 (fig. 8.68). Thus, as if by happenstance, the bipartite, longitudinal plan of Bagsvaerd Church seems to paral-

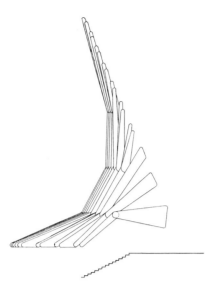

8.65
Jørn Utzon, Sydney Opera House, section showing system of plywood hangers carrying the curtain wall.

8.66
Jørn Utzon, Sydney Opera House. Top: elevation showing system of plywood hangars carrying the curtain wall. Bottom: plan showing geometrical intersection between entrance canopy and curtain wall hangars.

8.67
Jørn Utzon, Sydney Opera House, plywood mullions to the shells, showing varying curvature.

Jørn Utzon

lel only too nicely the plan form of Unity Temple. Aside from certain liturgical similarities, deriving no doubt from a common Protestant base (Unitarianism in one instance and a rather free interpretation of Lutheranism in the other), both buildings were to combine sacred and secular spaces within one continuous corpus. Both architects also chose to accommodate their ecclesiastical space in a squarish centralized volume. Moreover both buildings depend for their intrinsic organization on tartan-like systems of spatial subdivision and on thick-wall perimeter volumes that serve in both instances as vestigial aisles. In Unity Temple these shallow spatial bands provide for access stairs and also serve to accommodate shallow balconies, whereas in Bagsvaerd, aside from housing the organ loft, they double in the main as both light slots and corridors (fig. 8.69). However, in alignment, width, and general disposition Utzon's narrow aisles are closer perhaps to traditional church aisles than to the "thick wall" device used by Wright. Aside from these similarities and differences, the form of each work is inflected by an alien culture; by the evocation of Mesoamerica in the case of Wright and by Chinese culture in the case of Utzon. Tectonically speaking, Bagsvaerd is the more articulate work; a judgment that Wright would perhaps have been willing to endorse, given his ambivalence about the nature of reinforced concrete as a material having an unfortunate conglomerate nature. In this regard the rational-constructive logic of Bagsvaerd is closer to Wright's textile block work of the 1920s than to the ethos of his earlier Prairie period.

Like the traditional Nordic timber stave church to which it is related, Bagsvaerd is a framed structure despite the fact that it makes extensive use of monolithic, reinforced concrete. In this particular regard Bagsvaerd recalls Auguste Perret's transposition of trabeated timber construction into a reinforced concrete framework. In different ways both Perret and Utzon recall Semper's *Stoffwechseltheorie,* wherein a given material and structural method preserve their original tectonic character in a different constitutional format. Since Bagsvaerd is only partially framed, the level of tectonic transposition from one material to another varies, and by virtue of this variation the structural articulation of the church acquires its symbolic character. I have in mind, in this respect, the point at which the skeleton frame of the concrete structure gives way to shell vaulting while being cast of the same monolithic material throughout. Bagsvaerd is framed from the outside in as it were, so that the four parallel lines of 30-centimeter-square reinforced concrete columns change their character and function as they pass, on each flank, from the external to the internal column line. In each instance the external columns are articulated as vertical framing members throughout their height while the internal columns merge above the gallery level into a concrete diaphragm, cast integrally with the columns. This change from articulate frame to monolithic diaphragm provides the necessary abutment and support for the reinforced concrete shell vaults covering the 18-meter span over the nave. The shells or vaults at Bagsvaerd were built by spraying special concrete onto wire mesh reinforcement, the whole being sustained during casting by rough-boarded formwork, the imprint of which is clearly visible on the finished shell vaults. Given that, as in the case of Sydney, this span might have been achieved more economically in metal trusswork, this transition, depending on the continuity of the material, seems to derive from a particular symbolic intent; namely to represent the passage from the semisecular status of the aisles to the sacred character of the nave.

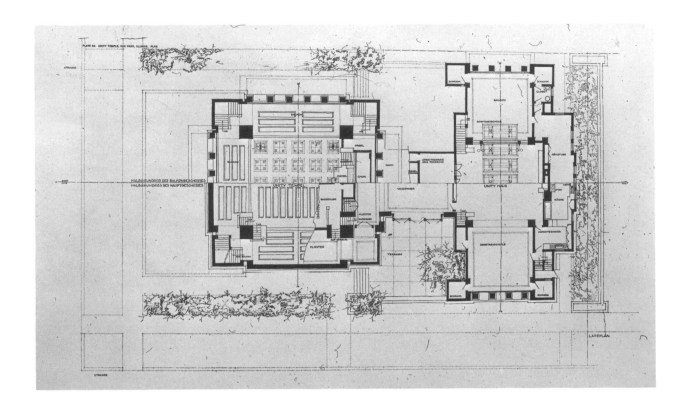

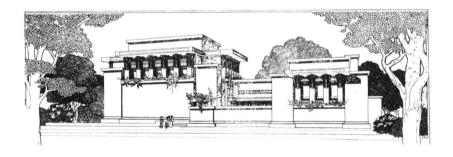

8.68
Frank Lloyd Wright, Unity Temple, Oak Park,
Illinois, 1906. Plan and perspective.

Aside from this differentiation, we can have little doubt as to the symbolism of
the shell form; the fact that it makes the traditional allusion to the celestial vault
and thereby to all the innumerable vaulted spaces of the Christian tradition. The
two preliminary sketches that Utzon issued with respect to Bagsvaerd confirm
this intention, for the first of these depicts a Cartesian view of the earth lying flat
beneath undulating cumulus (fig. 8.70). This perspectival, rationalistic flatness
lies in absolute contrast to the evanescent, light-giving arch of the heavens.
Both are implicated in the infinite, but where the one is a regular, man-made order, the other is an amorphous arching expanse of indeterminate form and immeasurable depth; the vault of the heavens versus the rationalized horizon of
the mortal earth. In this we seem to encounter an unconscious reference to the
Heideggerian *Geviert* or "foursome"; to the Earth, the Sky, Divinities, and Mortals.[45] In the second sketch these two planes are shown as encompassing the
house of God (fig. 8.71). The clouds have been transformed into longitudinal
vaults running across the perspectival axis of the nave, while on the foreshortening plane beneath, people are shown spontaneously gathering themselves into

an assembly. The very idea of the church as a social condenser shines through this rendering and gives resonance to the etymology of the Greek word *ecclesia,* meaning "house of assembly." The superimposed cross that emerges like a mirage on the surface of the second sketch aligns its horizontal bar with the span of the vault and its vertical axis with the central perspectival axis. The fact that this duality assumes a more complex and obscure form in the church as built is due to a number of factors, not the least of which is the transcultural character of Utzon's pagoda-vault that extends the idea of the sacred beyond any narrow Eurocentric focus on Christendom alone.

Thus the longitudinal cut through the multiple shell sections that span the nave at Bagsvaerd assumes the profile of a pseudo-pagoda, and while this all but imperceptible profile is hardly a direct reference to the Orient, it nonetheless endows the space with an atmosphere and a quality of light that seems extraneous to the Christian tradition. This transcultural trace, so to speak, seems to be echoed in the stepped longitudinal elevations, since such an eaves profile is as much Chinese as it is Hanseatic, as we may judge from the stepped gabled architecture of the Anhui, Zhejiang, and Jiangsu provinces.[46] Like the *fin-de-siècle* fascination with the East, the deeper impulses lying behind such hidden, possibly unconscious references are as elusive as they are complex. One thinks of Louis Sullivan's recourse to Saracenic form and ornament or of Wright's deep admiration for Japanese culture; one thinks of Bruno Taut's preoccupation with China or of Hans Poelzig's affinity for the tectonic iterations of Islamic architecture. This constantly recurring oriental tendency in modern architecture leads by extension to the non-Eurocentric, anthropological references underlying the structuralist work of Aldo van Eyck and Herman Hertzberger, architects who are close to Utzon's generation in terms of their age and cultural affinity. A Spenglerian awareness of spiritual decline is surely the common reflex lying behind many of these manifestations, and this impulse acquires a greater cogency

8.69
Jørn Utzon, Bagsvaerd Church, Copenhagen, 1976. Section and plan. Plan key:
1. entrance
2. church
3. sacristy
4. waiting room
5. office
6. candidate's room
7. parish hall
8. meeting rooms
9. kitchen
10. atrium garden
11. chapel

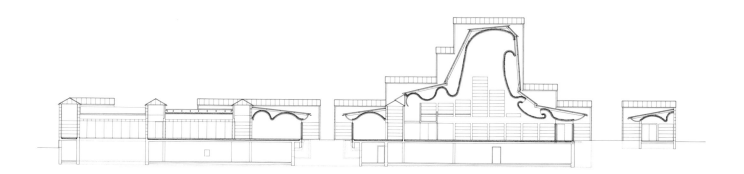

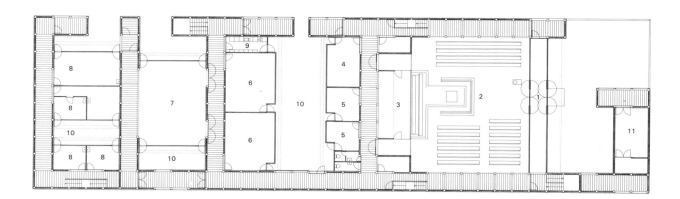

when the commission under consideration is a church. The nature of this dilemma is diachronic rather than synchronic, and the context within which this church has been realized is rather decisive in this respect. Thus, where Jensen-Klint could depend on the spiritual conviction of the Christian Socialist group of which he was a member, Utzon has had to build against the more skeptical ethos of our largely secular, consumerist society.

Reminiscent of a pagoda but tectonically removed from traditional Chinese roof construction, the vaults at Bagsvaerd have a Baroque aura about them, particularly with regard to the way in which they modulate light. As in Le Corbusier's Ronchamp chapel, light diffuses across the *béton brut* surface of the vaults in a constantly changing manner, producing luminous, chiaroscuro effects within the nave, depending on the time of day, the condition of the weather, and the season of the year. Equally Baroque is the fact that, for various reasons, the vaults are not allowed to register their presence on the exterior (fig. 8.72). Nevertheless the sectional organization is implied on the exterior through the pattern of the precast concrete elements, which introduce a stepped seam that approximates to the undulating vault as the cladding changes from plank to block units within the external infill wall. In order to differentiate front from back, this undulating rectilinear seam varies very slightly in its profile as one passes from the northern to the southern elevation.

As in Perret's Notre-Dame du Raincy of 1923, to which it may be compared, the main volume at Bagsvaerd is roofed by a double shell, in the first instance by the vaults themselves and in the second by a lightweight, waterproof, inclined shed form constructed out of corrugated asbestos siding. However, unlike Baroque outer domes that usually echo the volume within, this outer membrane conceals, as in Perret's church, the dynamic shape of the vaults spanning the interior. Thus the shed at Bagsvaerd is far from decorated. Indeed its extremely utilitarian form suggests an ordinary agricultural building rather than a semisacred, public structure. This reading is almost guaranteed by the use of asbestos

8.70
Jørn Utzon, Bagsvaerd Church, conceptual sketch.

8.71
Jørn Utzon, Bagsvaerd Church, conceptual sketch.

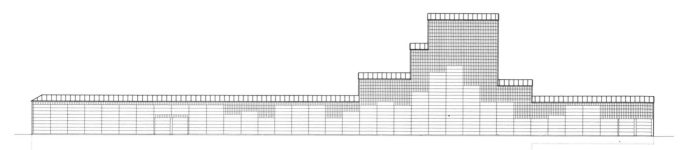

cement sheathing and the deployment of standard greenhouse glazing. Aside from providing economical roofing, the expressive motives lying behind this use of agricultural elements would appear to be threefold: first, to make an indirect allusion to the sacred barn that is encoded, so to speak, in the traditional barn-like form of the stave church (fig. 8.73); second, to represent an archetypal religious institution without resorting to the kitsch of pseudo-Gothic form; and third, to confront a suburban community with the authenticity of its preindustrial past; that is, to evoke a more ecologically stable moment in history when agriculture was the dominant mode of production and when the value crisis brought about by industrialization and the demise of faith had yet to occur.

This cryptic agrarian metaphor is reinforced by a subtle modification of the surrounding landscape. As in Fredensborg, rock forms have been randomly disposed about the surrounding greensward[47] in order to extend the building into the landscape, while birch saplings have been planted so as to frame the overall mass of the church and to provide enclosing cover for two adjacent parking lots (fig. 8.74). The fact that these stands of saplings have been planted with a view to their eventual maturity testifies to Utzon's faith in the durability of architectural form.[48] Thus Bagsvaerd does not yet fully exist and indeed will not come into its own until the surrounding trees have grown to their full height. This feeling for the long *durée* is quintessentially Nordic and close to both the elegiac sensibility of Gunnar Asplund's Woodland Cemetery Chapel (1923) and the civic deportment of Alvar Aalto's Säynätsalo City Hall (1949).[49] Thus Utzon would confirm in an interview with Per Jensen: "Well, we are not . . . really interested in how things will be in 25 years, whatever we build. Actually, what we are interested in is that if in 2000 years some people dig down, they will find something from a period with a certain strength and purity belonging to that period."[50]

Lit almost exclusively from above, Bagsvaerd Church, like Unity Temple, maintains an all but totally hermetic facade, despite the articulate distinction between frame and infill. The coursework of this last, together with its undulating seam representing the vaults within, imparts a textile character to this plaited, screenlike envelope. At the same time it assures that a simple "agrarian" mode of construction will be the dominant character of the work. This laconic principle of systematic assembly is reinforced by the asbestos cement sheeting and by the application of standard glazing to the light slots over the aisles. An ethic of constructional economy and precision prevails throughout, from the timber grills that enclose the entrance foyer to the built-in, bleached timber furnishings of the interior. And yet despite the consistent use of precast concrete elements

8.72
Jørn Utzon, Bagsvaerd Church, north elevation. Note the way in which the change in the size of the infill elements suggests the profile of the shell vault within.

8.73
Norwegian stave church, section.

inside and out, there seems to be nothing that is unduly utilitarian about Bagsvaerd. The subtle change in tone, as one enters, derives in part from the bleached purity of the woodwork and in part from the varying levels of luminosity emanating from the vaults over the nave and from the lanterns above the aisles. The fusion of light with structure is as crucial here as it is in the work of Louis Kahn.

One is tempted at this juncture to draw a number of parallels between Utzon, Kahn, and Perret. In all three there is the same insistence on the ontological probity of tectonic form. In Bagsvaerd as in Kahn's Tribune Newspaper Building of 1959, an equally meticulous distinction is maintained between the in situ concrete frame and the precast concrete infill; a distinction depending as much on surface quality as on a tectonic differentiation between tessellated and monolithic construction. The delicate contrast obtaining between concrete and travertine in Kahn's Kimbell Art Museum finds its parallel in Bagsvaerd in an equally subtle differentiation between the whitened, latex surface of the precast concrete and the white light that emanates from the bleached joinery, further offset by the open, earthenware altar screen, built in a triangular pattern out of Flensborg bricks set edgewise and painted white. This paradoxical play between sameness and difference sustains the homogeneity of the work while articulating its parts. We are close here to Jensen-Klint, to a building made of one material inside and out. The interior of Bagsvaerd is open to as many readings as its exterior. Thus while the precast concrete and the wooden furnishings of the interior attain a high level of precision and refinement, consciously recalling perhaps the purity of Shaker or even Shinto building, there remains, at the same time, a certain theatricality. This manifests itself in the perforated screen backing the altar, reminiscent of Perret not only for its cellular patterning but also for its evocation of the tripartite stage (fig. 8.75). This closeness to Perret is reinforced by the fact that Bagsvaerd eschews the uses of plaster, just as Perret tended to eliminate rendering from his public interiors.

Other devices strengthen the character of the church as a liturgical space, ranging from the theatrical lighting battens that flank the aisles on either side of the nave to the church raiments designed by Lin Utzon, the dominant color of which is rotated according to the season of the year. No less ritualistic and tectonic in

8.74
Jørn Utzon, Bagsvaerd Church, site plan showing the containment of the church by a screen of trees.

8.75
Jørn Utzon, Bagsvaerd Church, altar screen.

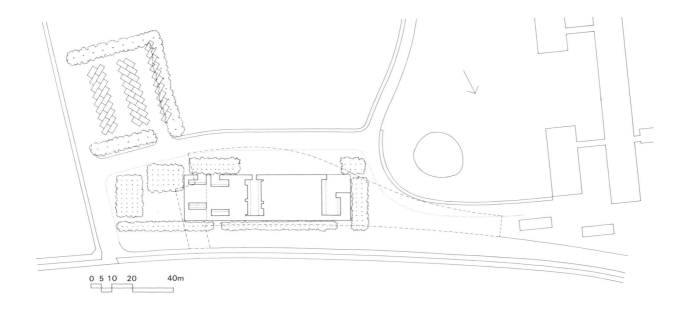

0 5 10 20 40m

their associations are the exposed white-metal organ pipes, together with their timber encasement (fig. 8.76). This muted, decorative enrichment has no doubt proved essential to the popular acceptance of the church as a religious space. Nonetheless Utzon's allegiance to a Klintian tectonic rigor prevails throughout, above all in the joinery, where even nail heads are allowed to protrude ever so slightly above the surface of the wood.

Like all of Utzon's civic work Bagsvaerd lends itself to being analyzed in Semperian terms, for, despite the absence of a podium as such, the body of the building breaks down into the quadripartite form of earthwork, hearth (altar), roofwork, and infill wall. Although the main floor is virtually at grade, Utzon has explicitly rendered it as an earthwork: first by building it out of precast concrete planks set on top of the reinforced concrete basement and second by assembling the dais and pulpit out of precast hollow concrete slabs similar to the planking used for the floor. The problematic Semperian screen wall, as was encountered in Sydney and Zurich, is resolved in Bagsvaerd through the continuity of the framework with the monolithic diaphragm of the shell. Since the frame is present as a rhythmic continuity throughout, the screen wall is readily integrated with both the roof and the frame. Elsewhere, as in the symbolic west front, gridded wooden fenestration runs continuously beneath the outriding eaves of the lowest horizontal vault. These transverse screen walls impart a further oriental inflection to the church in that the density of the mullions together with the wood-to-glass ratio and the counterpoint of the transoms seem to be derived from

Chinese prototypes, as does the ribbed precast guttering above the protruding vaults. The circular geometry governing the sectional profile of these last is related to the cross-sectioning of the sphere employed in generating the shells of the Sydney Opera House. In each instance a rhythmic, generative geometry is used to modulate the overall composition through its structure (fig. 8.77).

Bagsvaerd Church is the last realized public work over which Utzon has been able to exercise total control. Thus the structure not only represents a maturation of his thought but also the literal homecoming of his transcultural vision. Utzon's insistence on rational economic construction permeates every part of its fabric, displaying a mastery over prefabrication in which he is able to exploit a modular productive system as a source of inspiration rather than as a limitation. Like Wright, Utzon believes that the poetics of built form must derive in large measure from the totality of its tectonic presence and that it is this, plus an essential critical reflection on the status of the work in hand, that constitutes the mainspring of architectural form. Moreover, despite the Danish dimensions that are detectable in his work—the affinity for the Gothic, the strong feeling for craftsmanship, and a particular responsiveness to both climate and context—Utzon remains committed to the ideal of an emerging world culture that, while springing from local conditions, transcends them at the same time, thereby reintegrating and revitalizing different traditions through a kind of cultural transmigration.[51]

8.76
Jørn Utzon, Bagsvaerd Church, interior.

8.77
Jørn Utzon, Bagsvaerd Church, geometrical section.

8.78
Jørn Utzon, Farum Town Center, Farum, Denmark, 1966. First stage. Covered street formed out of standard precast concrete elements. The plan drawings on the right illustrate various forms of flexible combinations.

8.79
Jørn Utzon, Jeddah Stadium, 1969. Section, elevation, and plans of the precast structural system for the large stadium with combined football pitch.

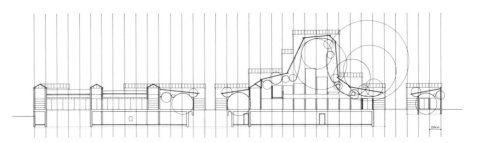

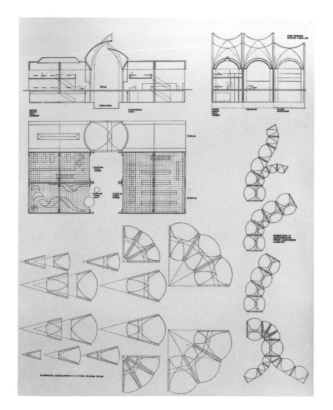

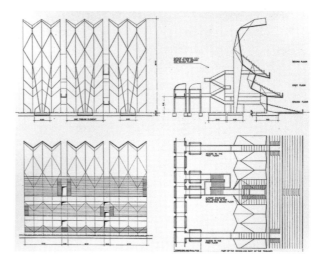

Utzon's preoccupation with the idea of an additive architecture dates from his design for Farum Town Center in 1966, where an extensive urban matrix was projected on the basis of the repetition of a single spatial unit derived from a series of precast concrete modules (fig. 8.78). Two different transcultural paradigms seem to be brought together in this work: the Middle Eastern bazaar as a homogeneous and introspective city-in-miniature and the Chinese tradition in which built form is assembled out of a limited number of parts. Utzon's synthesis of these rather different concepts within a repetitive precast system risks the reiteration of units at an inappropriate scale, for it is one thing to employ the standard brick or block as a basic module and quite another to select a full-height space cell as the primary repetitive unit. Nonetheless the fertility of this proposition is evident from Utzon's account of the additive principle, as set forth in the Danish magazine *Arkitektur* in 1970.

A consistent utilization of industrially produced building components can only be achieved if these components can be added to the buildings without having to be cut to measure or be adapted in any way.

Such a purely additive principle results in a new architectural form with the same expression . . . [by] adding more trees to a forest, more deer to a herd, more stones to a beach, more wagons to a marshalling yard; it all depends on how many different components are added in this game. Like a glove fits a hand, this game matches the demands of our age for more freedom in the design of buildings and a strong desire for getting away from the box-type house. . . .

When working with the additive principle, one is able—without difficulty—to respect and honour all the demands made on design and layout, as well as all the

Jørn Utzon

293

requirements for extensions and modifications. This is just because the architecture or perhaps rather the character of the building is that of the sum total of the components and not that of composition or that dictated by the facades. . . . The drawings are not a thing in se *with meaningless and dimension-less module lines; the module lines represent wall thicknesses and the lines on paper form the contours of the finished thing. The projects show the degree of freedom that can be achieved with the additive principle. . . . They also demonstrate the vital problems associated with the design of units or components, and provide some indication (e.g. in the stadium project) of the advantages in respect of production control, costs and erection time that can be achieved in comparison with a group of buildings constructed in a purely artisan fashion.*[52]

While much of this argument cites the familiar and, in some measure, proven advantages of rationalized, quasi-industrial production, it also implies the tectonic character that should be incorporated into the components and their interconnection from the beginning. That Utzon's joints are intrinsically morphological serves to distinguish them from such mechanical assemblies as Paxton's Crystal Palace or Max Bill's Swiss Landesausstellung exhibition building of 1963. Utzon's aim is to exploit the productive logic of the construction for tectonic ends rather than to celebrate the purely processal and economic elegance of a technological system.

That the repetitive, domed, cross-wall module of the traditional oriental bazaar should become the canonical prototype of Utzon's additive architecture is hardly an accident. We have already dwelt on Utzon's lifelong involvement with non-Eurocentric form, and to this we may add his Gothic preference for the vaulted cell as a volumetric unit, comparable as a building block to the role played by the atrium in his earlier housing schemes. Thus we should not be surprised if the more convincing applications of his additive principle should be encountered in projects destined for the Middle East: the Jeddah Stadium project of 1969 and above all his parliament building realized for the State of Kuwait in 1982. In his Jeddah proposal, Utzon was to combine, in different permutations, five generic structural units, each one being conceived in terms of its connective and constitutive role. These include a two-story bazaar module, a cylindrical roof element, a cylindrical vault suitable for covering restaurants, changing rooms, etc., and a stadium grandstand component, provided as a series of bents. In addition to its supporting function this unit also provides for a faceted

8.80
Jørn Utzon, National Assembly Building, Kuwait. 1982. Cross and longitudinal sections.

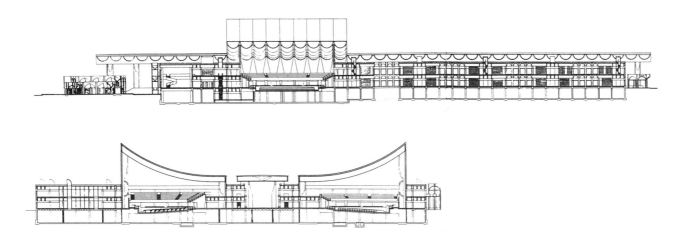

294

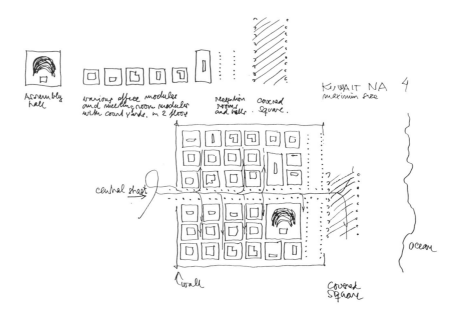

brise-soleil (fig. 8.79). A variation on this last element (structural unit no. 5) is intended to roof over long-span sports facilities. It is interesting to note that the folded-slab structural principle is present in almost all of these elements.

In the Kuwait parliament building Utzon combines the prefabricated additive principle with monolithic construction, the one complementing the other (figs. 8.80, 8.81). Where Farum Town Center was a small city core treated as though it were a medieval labyrinth, the Kuwait Parliament is a major state institution treated as a city-in-miniature, the *souk* being the common Middle Eastern paradigm in both instances. Thus we will find Utzon writing of his parliament building in the following terms.

The construction of the National Assembly also reflects the purity of Islamic construction. The building is a prefabricated concrete structure in which all elements are structurally designed to express the load they are carrying, the space they are covering—there are different elements for different spaces. They are all meant to be left visible—contrary to the constructions of the "cardboard architecture" of most modern office and administration buildings where hidden structures, lowered ceilings and gypsum walls give you an impression of being in a cardboard box.

In the National Assembly complex you see very clearly, what is carrying and what is being carried. You get the secure feeling of something built—not just designed.

The demand for very busy intercommunication between the various departments has led to the decision to arrange the complex as a two-storey building. This provides an easy orientation inside the building in contrast to the abrupt disorientated feeling you may experience in buildings with many floors with intercommunication depending on elevators.

When you enter the central street, you can see all the entrances to the various departments. The orientation is as simple as the orientation you get when you open a book on the first page with its table of contents presenting the headings of all the chapters. The central street leads toward the ocean into a great open

295

hall which gives shade to a big open square, where the people can meet their ruler. In Arab countries there is a tradition for very direct and close contact between the ruler and his people.

The dangerously strong sunshine in Kuwait makes it necessary to protect yourself in the shade—the shade is vital for your existence—and this hall which provides shade for the public meetings could perhaps be considered symbolic for the protection a ruler extends to his people. There is an Arab saying: "When a ruler dies, his shadow is lost."

This big open hall, the covered square, between the compact closed building and the sea, has grown out of this very special situation in quite a natural way— caused by the building's position directly on the beach. This big open hall connects the complex completely to the site and creates a feeling that the building is an inseparable part of the landscape, a feeling that it has always been there. The hall is just as much part of the openness of the ocean as it is part of the compact building and its structure. The hall seems born by the meeting between the ocean and the building in the same natural way as the surf is born by the meeting of the ocean and the beach—an inseparable part of both.[53]

Unlike Farum and Jeddah, the additive order of Kuwait is unified by the two monumental shell roofs respectively covering the open ocean square and the assembly itself (figs. 8.82, 8.83, 8.84).[54] Kuwait and Jeddah prove as it were the strength and weakness of the additive principle, for without such unifying vaulted forms there is a tendency for the aggregation to become a scaleless iteration of small units rather than the manifestation of a hierarchical order.

When one looks back on Utzon's achievement one is struck by the key role played by the Sydney Opera House, not only in regard to his own career but also with respect to the representation and accommodation of Australian cultural life. Whatever the travails suffered in the realization of this work, and however much it may fall short of Utzon's initial vision, the opera house has nonetheless become what he imagined it would be, a "door" through which a young continent would be able to realize its full potential, would be able to create, to quote Utzon, "an individual face for Australia in the world of art."

8.82
Jørn Utzon, National Assembly Building, preliminary plan; the mosque by the main entrance and one of the two meeting halls were later eliminated.

8.83
Jørn Utzon, National Assembly Building, model.

8.84
Jørn Utzon, National Assembly Building.

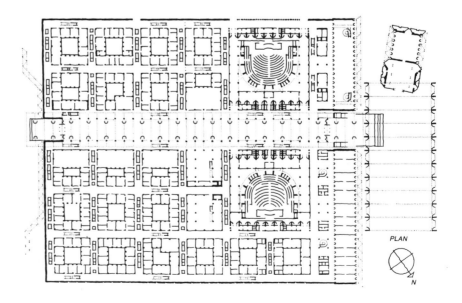

PLAN

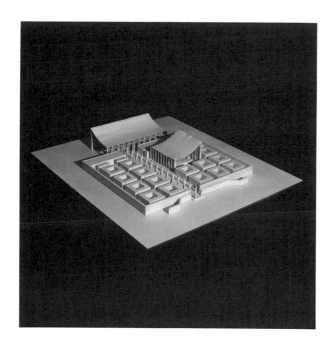

But the consequence of its achievement as a tectonic work goes even deeper, for with this remarkable pagoda form Utzon not only realized a specific site but also created an image for the nation. Thus just as the Eiffel Tower became a symbol of France, so has the Sydney Opera House become the icon of the Australian continent. While there may be many reasons for this, among them we must count the strong topographic relationship obtaining between the building and its site; like Kronborg Castle in Helsingør or, more to the point, Santa Maria della Salute in Venice, the opera house is a city crown poised on a promontory in the midst of a busy harbor, and the strength of its image stems from the ever-changing dynamism of its relationship to the surrounding panorama. Thus while it is firmly rooted on its podium, the double metaphor of the shell clusters is readily decipherable: on the one hand, the allusion to the spinnaker of a yacht under full sail; on the other, a city crown, radiant in the ever-changing Sydney light, that adds its essential rhythm to the historical accretion of the site, the islands, the lighthouse, the harbor and the bridge and all the vessels that ply their way in the archipelago.

9 Carlo Scarpa
and the Adoration of the Joint

These are only some of the thoughts evoked by bringing together philosophy and architecture under the sign of interpretation, and I realize that they are only hints, sparse suggestions. It may be necessary to take something else into account: namely, that edification has two principal meanings—to build and to be morally uplifting. Both are quite closely tied in today's rather vertiginous coming and going between architecture and philosophy, insofar as one can individuate even remote similarities between the two. That is, edification must be ethical, entailing communication of value choices. In the present situation of thought on the one hand and architectonic experience on the other (we shall consider this a provisional and limited conclusion), the only possibility of edifying in the sense of building is to edify in the sense of "rendering ethical," that is, to encourage an ethical life: to work with the recollection of traditions, with the traces of the past, with the expectations of meaning for the future, since there can no longer be absolute rational deductions. There follows then edification as a fostering of emotions, of ethical presentability, which can probably serve as the basis for an architecture which is determined not by the whole but by the parts.
Gianni Vattimo, 1987

The work of Carlo Scarpa (1906–1978) may be seen as a watershed in the evolution of twentieth-century architecture, not only for the emphasis that he placed upon the joint but also for his particular use of montage as a strategy for integrating heterogeneous elements. Throughout his work, the joint is treated as a kind of tectonic condensation; as an intersection embodying the whole in the part, irrespective of whether the connection in question is an articulation or a bearing or even an altogether larger linking component such as a stair or a bridge. All of this is immediately apparent in Scarpa's first work of consequence, the renovation and reorganization of the Fondazione Querini Stampalia in Venice, completed in 1963. In this instance, a stereotomic earthwork, laid into the undercroft of a sixteenth-century palace, is accessed by a lightweight bridge that acts as a kind of fixed hinge between the terra firma of the campo and the transformed shell of the palazzo (fig. 9.1).

In contrast to this lightweight, flat arch resting on stone abutments, Scarpa renders the earthwork as a monolithic concrete tray (fig. 9.2). Separated from the existing walls, this tray serves not only to contain but also to represent the seasonal flooding of the city. This shallow concrete walkway, paved with tiles, embodies the traditions of Venice in more ways than one, first by containing the *acqua alta* and second by affording direct gondola access through the existing *portego*.[1] The ceremonial nature of this last is implied by a winding stair descending to the canal and by openwork ornamental gates, dressed in metal, that fill the twin-arched openings of the portico (fig. 9.3). In this way, Scarpa arranges for two complementary entries: an everyday passage from the campo via a delicately articulated bridge, and a more honorific approach from the water; an approach that in its symbolic obsolescence is an elaborate reminder of the original mode of entering the palace. As Maria Antonietta Crippa has remarked, the whole of this sequence is treated as a kind of three-dimensional inlay.

The small entrance hall—its mosaic floor reminiscent of a design by Joseph Albers that Scarpa had originally intended to reproduce—gives onto a marble-dressed staircase leading to the library and also onto a gangway above the

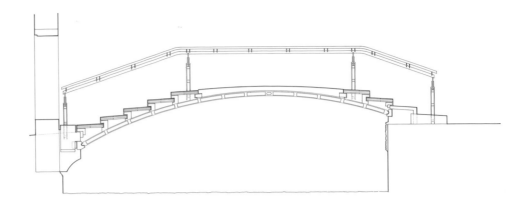

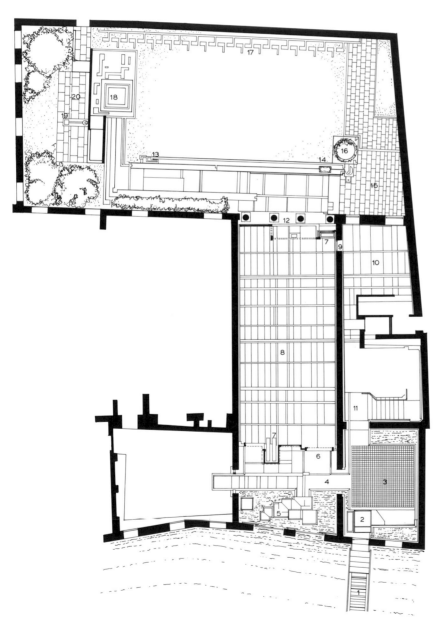

9.1
Carlo Scarpa, Fondazione Querini Stampalia,
Venice, 1963. Bridge.

9.2
Carlo Scarpa, Fondazione Querini Stampalia,
ground-floor plan:
  1. wooden bridge
  2. entry
  3. foyer
  4. concrete causeway
  5. steps down to canal entry
  6. gallery entrance
  7. radiators
  8. main gallery
  9. secret door
10. small gallery
11. stair to library
12. garden portico
13. fountain
14. stone lion
15. sump
16. old well
17. stepping stones
18. lily pond
19. outflow
20. porter's court
21. garden court

9.3
Carlo Scarpa, Fondazione Querini Stampalia,
ornamental gates.

9.4
Carlo Scarpa, Fondazione Querini Stampalia,
main exhibit hall.

entrance area that leads into the great hall on the ground floor opposite the portego. The stone gangway crossing the portego is almost like a bridge overlooking the lagoon; from it one can see the ebb and flow of water playing into the cisterns placed on various levels. A sheet of glass separates this gangway from the great hall. The radiators in the great hall are concealed within a parallelepiped with golden lines and glass panels fitting into each other, which has a geometric similarity to the mosaic in the entrance hall. Seventeenth century mouldings and remnants of walls, clearly distinct from modern additions, are visible throughout.[2]

Scarpa's characteristic use of revetment makes itself evident here in the travertine lining to the walls of the great hall, where, apart from the traditional use of stone cladding, there is the suggestion of a metonymic exchange between wood and masonry; between wood as it is employed in the deck and handrail of the bridge and travertine as it is laid up against the walls of the exhibition space (fig. 9.4). Stone thus appears in two aspects; in the first simply as cladding and in the second as a kind of "wood," where it is incised, inlaid, and hinged as

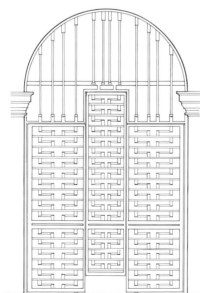

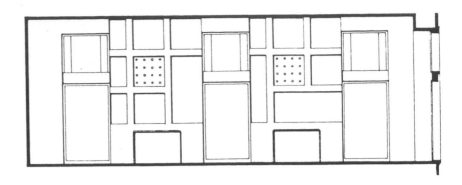

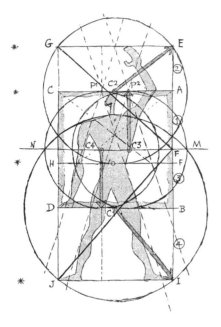

9.5
Theo van Doesburg, Café Aubette, Strasbourg, 1926–1928. Elevation of cabaret wall.

9.6
Le Corbusier, Modulor system, 1946.

though it were petrified cabinetwork. Such a reading is implied by a slotted brass rail, let into the stone cladding to form a horizontal groove at eye height, for the purposes of hanging pictures. This material interplay is enhanced by 10-centimeter-wide, ground-glass panels set flush with the travertine revetment. As translucent covers to neon tubes, these luminous accents run across the wall like a descant, echoing a similar modulation in the concrete floor that is subdivided by strips of Istrian stone of the same width. These translucent cover plates constitute a series of vertical accents that double up in pairs as they run down the depth of the space. Scarpa may have derived this syncopated arrangement in part from the Neoplasticist wall relief that Theo van Doesburg designed for the Café Aubette in 1926 (fig. 9.5) and in part from Le Corbusier's proportional system, as published in his book *Le Modulor* twenty years later (fig. 9.6).

Stone treated as cabinetwork is also evident in the hinged door to the side gallery, made out of a single sheet of travertine, that is cut out on its front and carved on its retroface (fig. 9.7). Throughout, brass is the key for this metonymic transposition between stone and wood, since the inlaid picture rail, running around the gallery, recalls a similar use of brass connectors in the bridge handrail. Such accoutrements allude both to marine detailing and to the kind of fittings found in eighteenth-century gentleman's furniture (fig. 9.8).

Like all of Scarpa's bridges, the Querini Stampalia *passerelle* is structured about the themes of bearing and transition, which may explain one of the least-noticed features of this bridge, namely its contrived asymmetry, particularly since the datum on either side is almost the same (see fig. 9.1).[3] It seems that this asymmetry arose out of the need to meet two different conditions: on one hand the bridge had to be high enough to permit gondolas to pass close to the campo; on the other hand it had to come down lower and more gradually in order to clear the lintel of the building entry. All of this is effected by displacing the bearings of the layered superstructure so that the point of the hinged support is 70 centimeters higher on the landward side. Thus, one steps up from abutments in Istrian stone before crossing two oak treads onto the curved oak deck of the bridge itself. The descent, on the other hand, is effected by five similar treads, the last of which lies flush with the stone threshold to the palace. Of the seven wooden treads, three are set flush with the surfaces to which they give access. This redundancy, together with the subdivision of the oak decking, makes the distinction between threshold and span ambiguous. The deck functions as a kind of tectonic elision that simultaneously both extends and curtails one's experience of crossing. This inflection finds its correspondence in the balustrading,

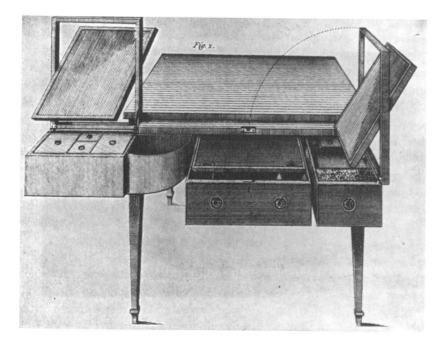

9.7
Carlo Scarpa, Fondazione Querini Stampalia, door to gallery annex.

9.8
Reflecting dressing table or Rudd's table, 1788.

which is shortened on the landward side and extended toward the building. The unequal spacing of uprights that results from this asymmetry necessitates a twin-rail balustrade, since an unbraced handrail would be insufficient for the long span. In this combination, a lower structural rail in tubular steel and an upper handrail in teak, we find that synthesis of structural economy and ergonomic form that is so characteristic of Scarpa's work.

The highest point of the *acqua alta,* indicated by the height of the concrete upstand in the entry, finds reflection in the surface treatment of the main exhibition space, where the travertine stops short at the same datum and the exposed aggregate concrete floor is taken up to meet it. The strips of Istrian stone subdividing this relatively inexpressive floor amount to a kind of basketwork that bonds the concrete tanking into a unity. These bands are irregularly modulated, thereby echoing but not following the syncopation of the wall revetment (see fig. 9.2). In addition to this modulation, these courses seem to be subtly aligned so as to correspond with an existing splay in the plan form of the building. Thus, while the first three transverse Istrian strips on entering the gallery are set at right angles to the walls of the exhibition space, the remaining strips, nine in all (five singles and two doubles), appear to be normal to the walls of the stair hall.[4] This subtle adjustment in alignment is accompanied by a diagonal inflection through

9.9
Carlo Scarpa, Fondazione Querini Stampalia, glass doors to garden.

9.10
Carlo Scarpa, Fondazione Querini Stampalia, water basins in garden.

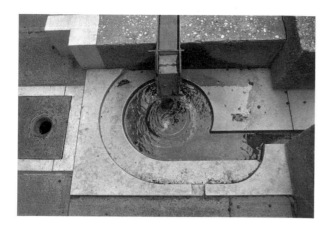 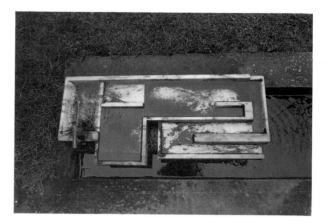

the space that passes from left to right toward the garden court. This movement is underlined by the placement of iron radiators; a vertical, encased stack at the entry and a single, freestanding horizontal radiator bracketed off the floor to one side of the glazed opening to the garden. The concrete stanchions supporting the armored plate glass garden doors are also treated as elements in a Neoplasticist composition, so that where the axis of one lies parallel to the cross axis of the hall the other is rotated ninety degrees; each being inscribed with a gilded bar on its face (fig. 9.9). This rotation is subtly reflected in the treatment of the glass itself, so that a 10-centimeter, ground-glass light panel planted on one of the stanchions is balanced by two 5-centimeter safety strips etched into the plate glass. A similar asymmetrical translucent light panel and safety strip are also incorporated into the glazed screen wall separating the exhibition hall from the initial foyer.

A parallel play with asymmetrical elements appears in the water channel running across the garden court, in which two different spirals, a rectilinear fountain in Apuan marble and a circular concrete drain, are the beginning and the end of a flow running from east to west, passing beneath a Venetian stone lion by which the channel is surmounted (fig. 9.10). This Islamic reference seems doubly significant in that the flow from the east not only serves to evoke the dependency of Venice on the Orient but also Scarpa's own genealogy; his self-characterization as "a man of Byzantium, who came to Venice by way of Greece." At the same time this fountain may be read as a metaphor for the life cycle. As Giuseppe Zambonini has written:

Water is used as a counterpoint to the treatment of the ground floor of the Palazzo. Its source is a small labyrinth carved in marble which suggests the pain of its forced birth. It is then channeled through a long trough, parallel to the Rio (Santa Maria Formosa) which extends almost the entire length of the garden. It then passes beneath a stone lion that faces the source and finally disappears into the drain which is magnificently expressive of the idea of vortex.[5]

The influence of China in Scarpa's work can hardly be overestimated, particularly when it comes to the walled gardens of both the Querini Stampalia and the Brion Cemetery in San Vito d'Altivole.[6] In both instances a frieze of enameled tiles, as an artificial horizon, is inlaid into certain sections of the perimeter walls. In Venice this is matched by the tiled lining of a lily pond laid out to the designs

of the painter Mario de Luigi (fig. 9.11). As Albertini and Bagnoli have suggested, these tiled ornaments in Murano glass initiate and enrich the promenade through the court.

The garden forms a rectangle roughly corresponding to two squares, each 12 m per side, cut by a concrete dividing wall. It is largely laid out with lawn and shrubs. A square copper container for papyrus plants is inset in a larger pond riveted with mosaic tesserae; here water collects before rechanneling. Isolated from this, a small basin (75 × 33.5 × 4.5–6 cm), formed of Apuan marble of a purplish hue, collects the water dripping into it from a small pipe and channels it into a miniature maze, where it fills a series of shallow concavities before flowing into a long, deep water course in which water lilies flourish. At the end opposite the small basin, serving as a bird bath for the winged inhabitants of the garden, a low cascade lends impetus to the flow of water, carrying it into proximity with an ancient and now dry wellhead. A short path with a number of steps completes the garden layout, branching off from the glazed wall of the portico to lead the visitor either toward the papyrus pool or in the direction of the wellhead.[7]

In Scarpa's work everything turns on the joint to such an extent that, to paraphrase Le Corbusier, the joint is the generator rather than the plan, not only in respect of the whole but also with regard to alternative solutions lying latent, as it were, within any particular part (fig. 9.12). These alternatives arise spontaneously from Scarpa's method, his habit of drawing in relief, wherein an initial charcoal sketch on card, one of his famous *cartoni,* becomes progressively elaborated and overlaid by traces, washes, and even white-out to be followed by further delineations, entering into a cyclical process of erasure and redesign respect of a given junction, without ever fully abandoning the first incarnation of the solution. In this way, as Marco Frascari has remarked, Scarpa's *cartoni* serve as an archaeology of the project: "In Scarpa's architectural production relationships between the whole and the parts, and the relationship between craftsmanship and draftsmanship, allow a direct substantiation *in corpore vili* of the identity of the process of perception and production, that is, the union of the construction with the construing."[8]

This observation stresses two essential aspects of Scarpa's method, first the gestural impulse passing almost without a break from the act of drafting to the act of making, and second a reciprocity obtaining between what Frascari characterizes as the *techne of logos* and the *logos of techne;* that is to say, between construing a particular form and constructing its realization (and then, later in the cycle, the moment in which the user construes the significance of the construction). We are close here to Giambattista Vico's anti-Cartesian idea of corporeal imagination. Scarpa would directly acknowledge this affinity on succeeding to the deanship of the Istituto Universitario di Architettura di Venezia by superimposing the Viconian motto *Verum Ipsum Factum* on the school's diploma and, later, by inscribing the same legend into his design for the school portal, thereby literally dedicating architects to the Viconian pursuit of "truth through making."

While Scarpa may have become familiar with Vico's thought by reading Benedetto Croce's *Aesthetica* of 1909, another source would have been the eighteenth-century Venetian architect Carlo Lodoli who was a contemporary and a promoter of Vico's ideas.[9] Vico's *Verum Ipsum Factum* would have been

9.11
Carlo Scarpa, Fondazione Querini Stampalia, lily pond.

9.12
Carlo Scarpa, Brion tomb, San Vito d'Altivole, 1969. Map of details.

important for Scarpa at two levels; first in confirming the cognitive aspect of his own activity and second in providing a philosophy of education. According to Vico, knowledge was to be acquired not through passive acceptance but through its active formulation—for only then can the subject take possession of it. For Scarpa, as for other architects, the first intervention in this process was the delineation of the thing to be constructed, while the second was the on-site process of its realization. As Hubert Damisch has remarked,

The essential goal therefore lies in the purpose of verification, if not actually experimentation, which Scarpa assigns to the drawing, which has to embody all necessary misgivings. For instance, a perspective image of a staircase does not allow sufficient accuracy in identifying the number of steps and their height, let alone the details of their jointing—jointing being a link-up with Cézanne's doubt.

A critical position of this kind acquires special significance at a time like the present, characterized by an attempt to reduce architectural thought to the single dimension of an image, to the detriment of its symbolical and real dimensions. In this there is no paradox; the man who revealed the full potential of museum architecture also uttered the most stringent criticisms of the ever-recurring error of confusing architecture with its image or any kind of scenography.[10]

A more precise analysis of the various levels involved in Scarpa's delineatory method has been provided by Sergio Los, who distinguishes between three kinds of drawings. The first is the *cartone,* Scarpa's initial drawing on stiff ochre card that would then be overlaid with variants of the same detail on tracing paper; if found to be sufficiently stable, these versions would be incorporated into the basic drawing on card. In this way the specific outline of the work would be developed, with incidental markings in pencil and in dilute black and red India ink. This evolutionary manner, so to speak, assured an indestructible record of the design process with regard to the initial schema. This procedure would be sustained, as we have seen, by detailed drawings on tracing paper in pencil, with colored crayon being employed to identify different layers and levels in both plan and section. In the end, of course, the final whole was traced over at the very last minute to produce a reliable construction document.[11]

Scarpa had such respect for craftsmanship that on occasion he would detail in such a way as to suit its procedural needs. This much is evident from his habit of forming L-shaped brackets out of steel plate, cut in such a way as to facilitate the meeting of two cuts at right angles to each other. Scarpa drilled a small hole at the crossing point so that the saw would change tone when it hit the intersection and thus produce a clean cut with no overrun. To finish this produc-

9.13
Carlo Scarpa, design for layout and display of Roman relics, Feltre, 1975–1978. Section.

9.14
Carlo Scarpa, Museo di Castelvecchio, Verona, 1953–1965. Section through entrance room.

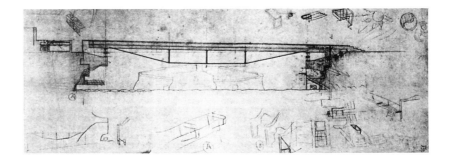

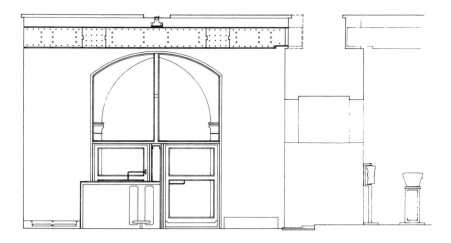

tive detail, Scarpa inserted a small brass washer at the point of the intersection.[12]

Scarpa's affinity for the archaic made itself manifest not only in the sculptural simplicity of his form but also in the hieratic elaboration of his joints. As we have already seen, rather than simply juxtapose the support and the load (*Stütze und Last*), Scarpa would "postpone" the final moment of support, as is evident from his 1975 project for a bridge over the archaeological remains at Feltre (fig. 9.13) or in the various capitals he would invent in his later years. A similar protraction is evident in the ground floor of the Museo di Castelvecchio in Verona, where intersecting concrete floor beams are carried at midpoint by built-up, riveted steel beams (fig. 9.14). the postponement of the bearing in this instance derived, as Scarpa himself would reveal, from the spatial continuity of the ground-floor enfilade subdivided into five cubic volumes. In each cube a transverse steel beam was introduced running along the east-west axis of the sequence and thereby unifying it. As he put it:

I wanted to preserve the originality of each room, but I didn't want to use the earlier beams of the restoration. Since the rooms were square, I set a paired steel beam to support the point where the two reinforced concrete beams crossed, so indicating the main lines of the building's formal structure. Where they crossed the importance of that square was emphasized because the crossing of the two beams in the centre implies the pillar which helps define the whole space. This is the visual logic I wanted to use as a frame of reference. The way the beams are made also brings out the visual logic but only in the details. I could have used the steel profiles already on the market.[13]

By establishing the point of the absent column, the cylindrical hinged joint between the concrete and steel, ostensibly introduced in order to allow for differential movement, was as crucial to the articulation of the space as the built-up character of the steel joist. This obsession with the elaboration of bearing would also be remarked on by Albertini and Bagnoli in their description of the attic colonnade in the Banca Popolare di Verona of 1978 (fig. 9.15).

A quite complex architectural system is applied to the top story of the Banca Popolare di Verona—almost a modern interpretation of an ancient order: supports

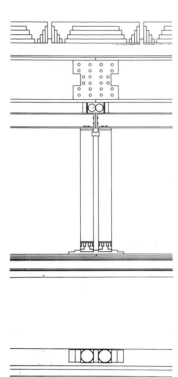

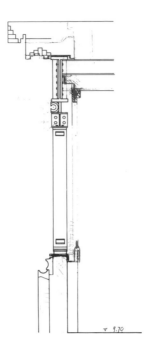

9.15
Carlo Scarpa, Banca Popolare di Verona,
1973–1981. Colonnade.

and architrave in metal, frieze in colored mosaic, and cornice in white Botticino stone. The long ribbon of the architrave, formed of two plate girders of differing dimensions (the larger 600 mm high, the smaller 180 mm high) joined by riveting plates, is supported at regular intervals by pairs of coupled colonettes in tubular iron (166 mm in diameter), replacing the metal sections of an earlier version.

The colonettes are fitted with muntzmetal collars, acting as linking elements to the architrave above and the base beneath. This is formed of deep flats, cut and milled, riveted to a flat (22 mm deep) laid on the masonry. The tall columns on the court front have a more elaborate muntzmetal link at the base: a motif frequently used by Scarpa and typical of Indian architecture, by means of which a square plan becomes, by successive divisions, first octagonal, then a sixteen-sided polygonal figure, ending up as a circle. A small block of muntzmetal, recessed to form the symbol of two intersecting rings, gleams against the dark iron above each pair of colonettes. Connectors of the same metal are used as the head and base of the columns to create a single support: these are small elements, distancers, screwed to the tubular shafts, articulating the proportions of the whole.[14]

Scarpa's excessively articulated joints may be read as a critical commentary on the economic expediency of our utilitarian age or, alternatively, as a heroic attempt to compensate for our inability to equal the poetic authority of classical form. Of this last he wrote:

Modern language should have its own words and grammar just as this happened in the case of classical forms. Modern shapes and structures should be used following a classical order. . . . I should like that a critic could discover in my works certain intentions that I have always had, namely an enormous desire to stay within tradition but without building capitals and columns, because these can no longer be built. Not even a God today could invent an Attic base, which is the only beautiful one; all the others are only slags. From this point of view even those designed by Palladio are awful. As regards columns and entablatures only the Greeks were able to reach the apex of pride. Only in the Parthenon do the shapes live like music.[15]

With the *factum* of Venetian craft at his side,[16] Scarpa steered an uneasy course between the legacy of Art Nouveau—one thinks of Hermann Obrist's Egyptoid column (fig. 9.16), or Perret's new concrete capital devised for the Musée des Travaux Publics (fig. 5.42)—and a more objective elaboration of the hinged joint in steel construction as this appears, say, in Peter Behrens's turbine factory of 1909 (fig. 9.17) or in Mies van der Rohe's Neue Nationalgalerie of 1968 (fig. 9.18). Scarpa evolved his joints not only as functional connections but also as fetishized celebrations of craft as an end in itself. This sense of "nearness," to evoke Heidegger's term, was not only expressed through Scarpa's elaboration of the joint but also through the patina and color of delicate surface finishes, demanding highly specialized techniques. I am alluding in particular to Scarpa's revival of *stucco lucido,* that traditional rendering technique in which colored pigment and marble dust are combined with lime plaster and other materials to yield highly polished surfaces reminiscent of dressed stone or lacquer.[17] Like the tempera technique in painting, the color in polished plaster appears to emanate from the interior of the rendering. A similar synthesis of luminosity and texture crops up in other aspects of Scarpa's palette, from the use of Murano glass tes-

9.16
Hermann Obrist, *Monument to the Pillar,* 1898.

9.17
Peter Behrens, AEG turbine factory, Berlin, 1909. Detail.

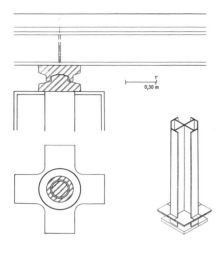

serae for the floor of his Olivetti store on the Piazza San Marco of 1966, to the constant interplay among tile, marble, metal, and wood that is so evident in the multiple finishes in which his work abounds.

Apart from the canonical joint and its attendant membrane, Scarpa often consolidated his work about iconic foci; about pivotal sculptural pieces such as Alberto Viani's abstract metal sculpture, poised above a sheet of black water, that plays such a prominent role in the spatial organization of the Piazza San Marco store (figs. 9.19, 9.20) or the fulcrum provided by the Cangrande statue in the Museo di Castelvecchio (fig. 9.21)[18] or the ubiquitous double circle motif that occurs at different scales throughout his work. While Scarpa's obsession with this motif has been attributed to many different sources, one of the more likely origins is the mystical ideogram known as *vesica piscis* (from *vesica,* bladder, and *piscis,* fish).[19] While the interlocking version of this icon is reminiscent of the oriental yin-yang symbol, it also represents the opposition between solar universality and lunar empiricism (fig. 9.22). Even if, as legend has it, Scarpa first encountered this symbol on a packet of Chinese cigarettes, he would surely have become aware of its place in the European tradition and of its latent cosmic attributes. He later became cognizant of the role played by this figure in the generation of certain church plans, such as Bernini's Sant'Andrea al Quirinale in Rome (fig. 9.23),[20] and from this he would also have known how such a construction may be used to proliferate a whole series of equilateral triangles deriving from a single side (fig. 9.24).

Whatever its attributes, it is somehow fitting that Scarpa would employ this figure as a definitive symbol in his last work, which, as it happened, would also be his own resting place: the Brion Cemetery, completed posthumously in 1979. Irrespective of the ultimate dialogical attributes of the *vesica piscis,* whether sun/

9.18
Mies van der Rohe, Neue Nationalgalerie, Berlin, 1968. Column details.

9.19
Carlo Scarpa, Olivetti shop, Piazza San Marco, Venice, 1957–1958. Ground-floor plan.

9.20
Carlo Scarpa, Olivetti shop, Piazza San Marco, section.

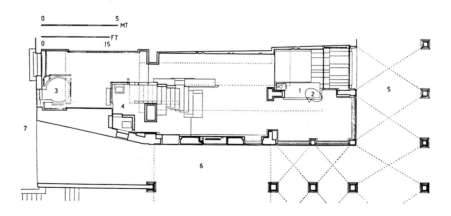

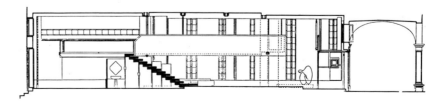

moon, male/female, Eros/Thantos, its three-dimensional rendering in pink and blue tiles may also have alluded to more modern sources, to the cosmological values of the primary colors in Dutch Neoplasticism or to the red and blue proportional series of Le Corbusier's *Modulor.*[21] However, the fact that Scarpa once employed the figure of the squared circle suggests a deeper familiarity with hermetic lore (fig. 9.25). I have in mind the "oculi" that he incorporated into the upper level of the Olivetti store, each one bisected by sliding teak and palisander screens that, reminiscent of Japanese *shoji,* serve metaphorically to open and close each eye (fig. 9.26).[22] In one form or another the *vesica piscis* will manifest itself in much of Scarpa's architecture as a kind of tectonic icon, from its first use in the Gavina shopfront realized in Bologna in 1963 (fig. 9.27) to its last in the Banca Popolare di Verona, completed after Scarpa's death, where it appears at different scales (fig. 9.28).

While Scarpa seems to have made little use of the root-three rectangle contained within the *vesica,* he nonetheless used an 11-centimeter module whenever possible, and this figure may be related to the inherent duality of the *vesica,* particularly when its multiple use yields the double numbers 22, 33, 44, and even 5.5 centimeters as a half-module. Of Scarpa's obsession with this double number pattern and its roots in traditional measure Frascari has written:

In China eleven is the number of the Tao, but it is not often taken in the quantitative sense of ten plus one; it signifies the unity of the decade in its wholeness.

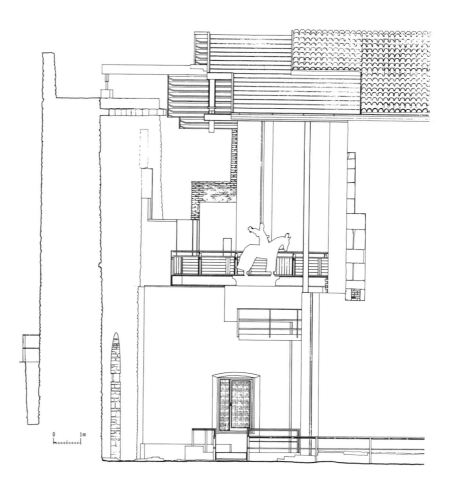

9.21
Carlo Scarpa, Museo di Castelvecchio, partial section, looking north through Cangrande space.

0   1m

to echo their figurative rhythm in the modulated shape of their base (fig. 9.39). However, as Sergio Los has observed, Scarpa's concern for the setting of a *topic* into a suitable *topos* went well beyond its appropriate mounting, to embrace its sequential and reciprocal placement within the overall narration of the space. In this way he tried to accord the uprooted fragment something of its lost aura. This surely accounts for the mounting of certain paintings on easels, so as to remind the viewer of their craft origin, as opposed to presenting such works always as fetishized, wall-hung images (fig. 9.40). One may possibly regard these stratagems as subtle ways of achieving a *Verfremdung* effect, that is to say, as a means for overcoming our habitually distracted way of beholding art. Nothing surely could be more tectonic than this return to "thingness" that, in Scarpa's case, is as evident in the framing of an object as in the fabric of the building in which it is housed. Here as elsewhere in his architecture, it is the working of the material itself that carries the semantic charge. We are presented with a tactile syntax that is grounded in difference, turning, that is, on evident transitions from rough to smooth, from polished to matte, from worked to unworked (fig. 9.41). Hence the differential reciprocity set up between the exposed concrete cross beams spanning over the ground-floor gallery—supported at midpoint by composite steel beams—and the in situ concrete slabs used to pave the gallery floor (figs. 9.42, 9.43). In the first instance we are confronted with an undressed *béton brut* finish that may be read as the petrification of the timber formwork, whereas in the second the tamped finish of the concrete floor—a technique traditionally reserved for the laying of *pastellone veneziano*—imparts to the top surface of the in situ slab a striation reminiscent of the grain to be found in stone. This association is reinforced by subdividing the concrete pours with bands of Istrian stone. What is intended in both instances, of course, is an allusion to another material rather than a simulation. This same

9.37
Carlo Scarpa, Museo di Castelvecchio, plan:
1. parallel hedges
2. lawn: great courtyard
3. entrance to Sala Boggian
4. entrance room
5. library
6. northeast tower
7. sculpture galleries
8. Cangrande space and statue

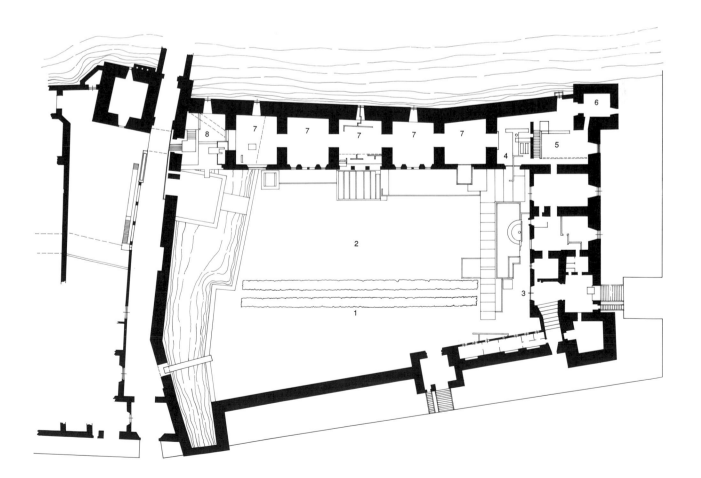

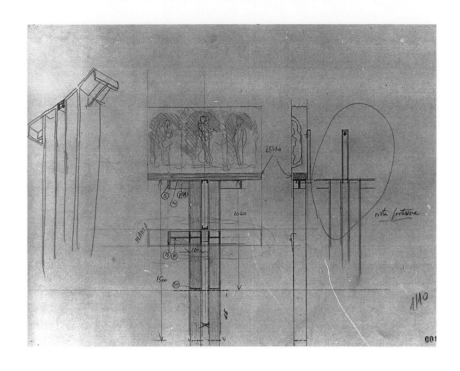

9.38
Carlo Scarpa, Museo di Castelvecchio, sculpture stand.

9.39
Carlo Scarpa, Museo di Castelvecchio, sculpture bracket.

concrete flooring is separated from the rough-plastered *spaca di cava* walls of the perimeter by a shallow recess that serves to establish the floor as a raised datum. We are returned here, as in Querini Stampalia, to a traditional Venetian earthwork complete with a perimeter channel in which to accommodate the surplus water of the *acqua alta.* At the same time, as Franco Fonatti has remarked, the subdivision of the concrete ground floor recalls the paving of the Piazza San Marco.[37]

Scarpa's penchant for the rhetorical joint reaches its apotheosis in the Banca Popolare di Verona, the penultimate work of his life, started in 1973 and posthumously completed by his assistant, Arrigo Rudi, three years after his death, in 1981 (figs. 9.44, 9.45). Within this complex and compact organization, Scarpa's denticulate molding is applied as a device by which to determine both the cornice of the loggia that crowns the building and the upper limits of its rusticated base. Within this earthwork the castellated profile reveals the massivity of the stone window surrounds and the stereotomic order of their joints (fig. 9.46). Elsewhere, it functions as a means to elevate and modulate the proportion of the facade. In this regard, the measure of its rhythm is inseparable from the syncopated order of the overall composition, as Albertini and Bagnoli have attempted to show.

The first axis of symmetry is picked up in the center line of the first span of the loggia, coinciding with the center line of the inverted molding on the cornice, an alignment that, as the eye travels down, takes in the center lines of the two stiffeners of the wing of the big girder, the round window and its dripstone, tying into the left-hand molding of the rectangular window beneath. The second axis starts in the next span, runs down through the center line of the small balcony to coincide with those of the projecting window and the window beneath. The third, instead, is that of the third base of the colonettes, which falls between two stones of the cornice, coincides with the axis of the girder riveting plate, that of the gilded-spheres motif, and ties in once more with that of the round window, its dripstone, and the rectangular window.

Moving to the right, the fifth span mirrors the situation of the first. In direct succession, the axis of the next pair of colonettes states itself forcefully between the two bay windows.

9.40
Carlo Scarpa, Museo di Castelvecchio, picture support and frame.

9.41
Carlo Scarpa, Museo di Castelvecchio, detail of the Sacello exterior, of local Prun stone.

325

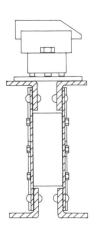

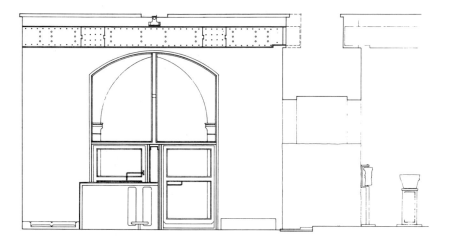

9.42
Carlo Scarpa, Museo di Castelvecchio, details of concrete and steel cross beam at
ground-floor gallery.

9.43
Carlo Scarpa, Museo di Castelvecchio,
ground-floor slab showing perimeter channel
and the relation to the rendered wall.

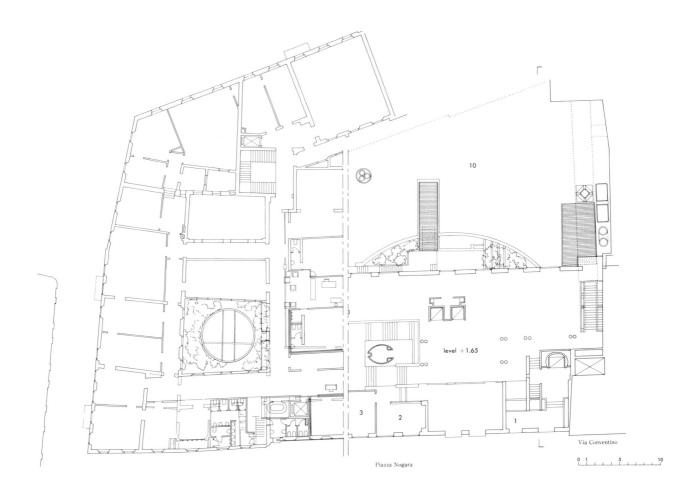

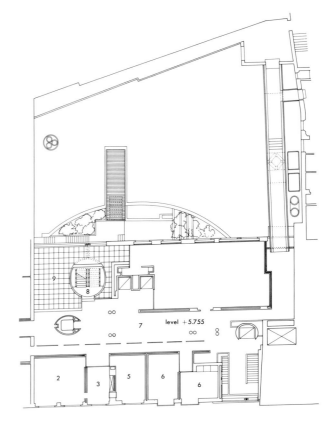

9.44

Carlo Scarpa, Banca Popolare di Verona,
ground-floor plan and second-floor plan:

1. entrance from Via Conventino
2. director
3. secretary
4. exchange
5. vice-director
6. reception
7. central corridor
8. staircase
9. terrace
10. courtyard

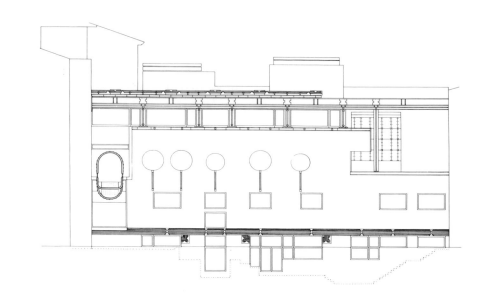

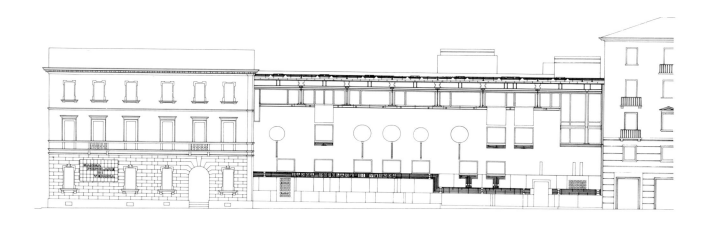

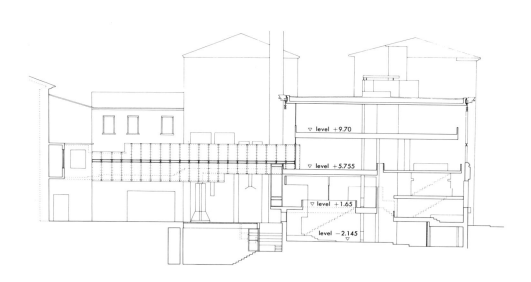

▽ level +9.70

▽ level +5.755

▽ level +1.65

level −2.145
▽

. . . Here, because of its greater breadth, the axis determines a duplication of the cornice stone molded on its lower extremity, and of the girder stiffeners. It subsequently runs between the two narrow balconies and the quadrangular windows beneath, of which the left-hand one is aligned exactly with the right-hand one below.[38]

The principal facade of the Banca Popolare (fig. 9.47) appears to be articulated according to Semper's four elements, so that we are presented with an earthwork in stone, a screen wall in plaster, and a steel framed loggia at the top of the building. The ziggurat molding serves to divide up the body of the building into these specific elements. Thus, the three dematerialized plate glass windows are countered by the contrasting weight of the ziggurat corbels arranged in T-formation beneath. A very similar figure is used to stress the massivity of the marble surround to the staff entrance on the Piazza Nogara. The powerful sculptural presence of this last is due in large measure to the revealed thickness of the marble, to the rupture of its surround by horizontal rustication, and last but not least to the presence of a single chamfered gun slit above the lintel (fig. 9.48). Once again one is reminded of Brancusi; this time perhaps of *The Gate of the Kiss* erected at Targu-Jiu in Romania in 1937. The phenomenological intensity of this facade is also due to the contrast between the rough finish of the *cocciopesto* plastered wall and the dressed surface of the Botticino marble.

This difference not only separates the rendering from the rustication but also distinguishes between the plaster and the polished stone surrounds of the seemingly circular window openings, assembled out of five separate pieces. Situated on axis beneath these surrounds are thin vertical grooves of red Veronese marble receiving the downpipes of the rainwater gulleys that drain the inner leaf of the double-layered facade. These lines not only accommodate the weathering of the facade but also emphasize the watermark from the very beginning, thereby anticipating the inevitable transformation of the building over time (figs. 9.49, 9.50). To the rear of this frontal screen, square wooden window frames are let into the inner leaf of the wall, thereby establishing an oriental interplay be-

9.45
Carlo Scarpa, Banca Popolare di Verona, courtyard elevation, front elevation, and section.

9.46
Carlo Scarpa, Banca Popolare di Verona, constructional details of cornice and axonometric of denticulate cornice.

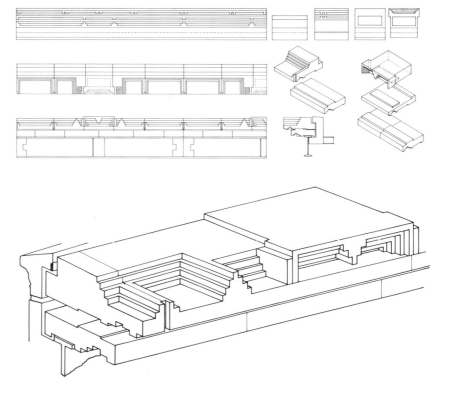

9.47
Carlo Scarpa, Banca Popolare di Verona,
front facade.

9.48
Carlo Scarpa, Banca Popolare di Verona,
entrance on Piazza Nogara.

9.49
Carlo Scarpa, Banca Popolare di Verona,
window details.

9.50
Carlo Scarpa, Banca Popolare di Verona, ana-
lytique of ornamental system.

tween the orthogonal timber fenestration and the circular oculi of the surface aperture (fig. 9.51).[39]

Aside from a characteristically rich spectrum of finishes, ranging from various tones of *stucco lucido* to panels of translucent onyx, the most striking aspect of the banking halls from a tectonic standpoint is the way in which a suspended ceiling is provided without compromising the probity of the structure, since the soffits of the concrete beams and their concrete columnar supports are left exposed, as cast from faceted formwork, except for a 1.5-meter-high sheath in steel that surrounds the base of each column (fig. 9.52). The suspended nature of the plaster ceiling is made manifest through its subdivision into fairly large areas by seams that not only impart scale to the expanse of the overall soffit, but also return the eye to the salient points at which the concrete column heads come through the plaster to lie flush with the ceiling.[40]

Excessively enriched, the tops of the twin columns are ornamented by incised gold bands set some 27.5 centimeters below the ceiling; close to the point of bearing itself, we again encounter a diminutive, gilded version of the *vesica piscis,* cast into a Muntz metal fitting that is wedged between the column heads (fig. 9.53). As in the Castelvecchio, the giant tatami-like panels of the suspended ceiling are rhythmically modulated so as to achieve an effect that is reminiscent of neoplasticism. This seems to induce a pinwheeling dynamic that is focused about certain elements, such as the onyx stair hall, the red elevator shaft, and a glazed cylindrical, metal-framed stair that rises to the top of the building (fig. 9.54). As Pier Luigi Nicolin has remarked, all of this elaboration was made with little regard for the conventional status of the building.

In his relation to institutional space, Scarpa's attitude is one of conscious indifference. As far as the bank is concerned, he limits himself to celebrating its wealth in the luxury of the materials used in the furnishings. There is no sign of rhetorically emphasizing the institution in the Louis Kahn manner, no indulgence in the requirement to interpret company philosophy in a "corporate image"; nor does this sophisticated and complex building seem to want to underpin the complex patterns of human interaction in the manner of Van Eyck.

The spatial complexity of the building, frequently underscored, is developed with a sort of private language and pleasure which hovers enjoyably about the web

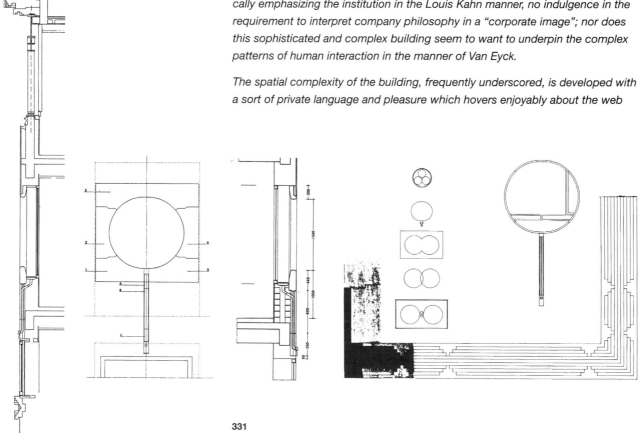

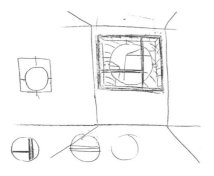

9.51
Carlo Scarpa, Banca Popolare di Verona, sketch of circular window.

9.52
Carlo Scarpa, Banca Popolare di Verona, second-floor hall.

9.53
Carlo Scarpa, Banca Popolare di Verona, column-ceiling joint.

9.54
Carlo Scarpa, Banca Popolare di Verona, exterior staircase.

of its functions, as if lingering over the effort made to render them feasible. This achieved freedom can only express itself in a space of "transparencies" in which materials, mechanisms, links, finishings, all share in this virtuosity of execution: its felicity troubled only by melancholy over the unrepeatability of the achievement.[41]

Scarpa's concern for the expressive probity of a building's basic structure would parallel that of Louis Kahn, as is evident from another late work, the Fondazione Masieri on the Grand Canal in Venice where an exposed concrete floor evidently rests on an unpainted steel framework. Set flush with the soffit of the in situ *béton brut* floor, the steel joists are supported at intervals by twin cylindrical columns, also made of steel, the steelwork being clear-sealed throughout in order to retard oxidation.

It is difficult to write about Scarpa's work in a systematic manner, for in the last analysis his achievement can only be comprehended as a continuum. It is this, perhaps more than anything else, that served to set him apart from the mainstream, for in his case there was never the intention of an ideal whole in either a humanist or an organic sense. There was only the "nearness of things" and their unfolding progression from part to part and joint to joint. Spatial interpenetration is largely absent in his work. Place is there, but only as a momentary location that is constantly modified by movement and the fluctuation of light. It is above all a disquisition on time, on the paradoxical durability and fragility of things; an all but cinematic sensibility, permeated by an ineradicable melancholy. Beyond this, Scarpa's work serves not only as a demonstration of tectonic authenticity but also as a critique of the two main utopias of our time; the organic utopia of Wright and the technological utopia of modern functionalism. That this was so, despite Scarpa's lifelong attachment to Wright and his affinity for industrial design, says much for Scarpa's sense of limit and for his capacity to offset the assumption of any particular criteria with a discreet sense of irony. Antiutopian to the core, he always addressed the specific terms of the brief and the boundaries of the site; yet despite this responsiveness, he never allowed his imagination to be stifled by precedent.

Like Alvar Aalto, Scarpa knew that the poor man cannot be saved by architecture, let alone by all the well-meaning exertions of the welfare state. Instead, he offered an architecture of disjunctive narrative in which what is is always accompanied by what has been and what might have been. The development of local craft was a key element in this undertaking, even if he refused any a priori typological approach to the generation of form. Thus, while constantly exigent about craft and dimensional precision, he rarely yielded to the systematization of modular production. Influenced by the ethical impulse of the Viennese Krausian circle and above all by the writings of Karl Kraus and Adolf Loos, Scarpa strove against Loos's renunciation of ornament for an ornament that was a kind of impenetrable writing. In this way, he lay, on his own confession, closer to Loos's other, Josef Hoffmann. At once critical and celebratory, Scarpa saw such cryptic, microtectonic inscriptions as somehow capable of transcending the ruinations of time. In this regard we may think of his work as an enchanted disenchantment.

10 Postscriptum:
The Tectonic Trajectory,
1903–1994

Good architecture starts always with efficient construction. Without construction there is no architecture. Construction embodies material and its use according to its properties, that is to say, stone imposes a different method of construction from iron or concrete.

I believe we can create contemporary architecture with all materials—with any material as long as we use it correctly according to its properties. In areas where we can find nothing but stone, we shall build with that stone, that is the local stone. We shall create contemporary architecture as we would have done with any other material (iron, concrete, wood) which we would have found in another area, because the leading ideas are the spirit of construction and the flexibility of our outlook and not the constructional whim foreign to the site. . . . The finite location; the climate, the topography and the materials available in each area determine the constructional method, the functional disposition, and finally the form. Architecture cannot exist without landscape, climate, soil, and manners and customs. This is the reason why we sometimes see old buildings looking contemporary and for the same reason we build today contemporary buildings which could have been built in the past. Since man from time immemorial to this day has always lived, moved about and breathed in the same way, since in our way of life perhaps nothing has changed basically . . . I can build with the most modern materials (iron, concrete, and with the ARTIFICIAL materials of contemporary building construction) a building which will be related harmoniously with the character of the landscape. I shall do this frequently in order to challenge my architectural inventiveness, and this I must do in order to be able to prove that true architecture can be created in any place with any material. But I cannot ignore a sentimental factor, which we must reveal in our construction, otherwise we shall be stagnant and inhuman . . . , then we shall choose our material not only according to the standards of economy and pure science but with the spirit of emotional freedom and artistic imagination. Hence architecture finally stands beyond pure purpose; higher than the achievements of logic and cold calculation.

Aris Konstantinidis, Architecture, *1964*

Although, as Konstantinidis insists, the tectonic must by its nature transcend the logic of calculation, the fact remains that any account of modern building culture must acknowledge the crucial role played by structural engineering. This much is surely self-evident from the seminal contributions made across the century by such distinguished engineers as Othmar Ammann, Ove Arup, Santiago Calatrava, Felix Candela, Eladio Dieste, Eugène Freyssinet, François Hennebique, Albert Kahn, August Kommendant, Fritz Leonhardt, Robert Maillart, Christian Menn, Ricardo Morandi, Pier Luigi Nervi, Félix Samuely, Eduardo Torroja, and E. Owen Williams. This is obviously nothing more than a rather random listing of a number of prominent structural engineers who have either been primary form-makers in their own right, as in the case of say Calatrava and Candela (fig. 10.1), or, as in the instance of Arup, Kommendant, and Samuely, have conceived their finest work in collaboration with architects. Between these two alternative modes of practice lie such unique figures as Robert Le Ricolais, Frei Otto, and Vladimir Suchov, who have worked mainly in the field of network suspension structures, and a number of idiosyncratic craftsman-constructors such as Konrad Wachsmann, Richard Buckminster Fuller, and Jean Prouvé. Within this broad spectrum the career of Owen Williams has been particularly remarkable for the concept and realization of a number of exceptionally brilliant reinforced concrete works between 1930 and 1954. Certainly his structurally plastic inventions bear comparison to those of an architect like Auguste Perret, who worked in the same material over the same period. Of mushroom column, in situ con-

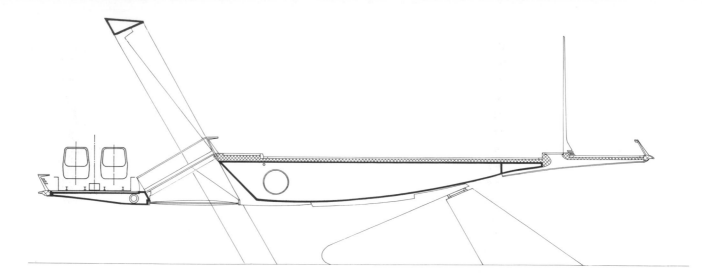

crete construction, Williams's Boots pharmaceutical plant, built in Nottingham
for Boots in 1932, remains, for all its indifference to the classical tradition, of
equal stature to the finest work of Perret (fig. 10.2).

Of all these engineers none perhaps has been more sensitive to the tectonic potential of structural form than Nervi, and it says much for Nervi's exceptional sensibility that he would regard the closely spaced columns of the Egyptian temple
as the consequence of a tectonic intention rather than as the outcome of a certain structural limitation. Moreover, no modern engineer has expressed himself
more lucidly as to the necessary relations that must obtain between structural
analysis and constructional form. As he was to put it toward the end of his career, in 1961:

*The experience acquired in almost fifty years of direct contact with activities in
various fields of design and construction have led me to an optimistic conclusion: the unlimited possibilities of design offered by scientific theories of construction, the executions made possible by new building materials and current
techniques, and the architectural themes growing ever greater and more complex as dictated by our social and economic developments, open horizons of unprecedented possibilities of construction as compared to what humanity has
achieved from prehistoric times to the present.*

*Nevertheless these marvelous possibilities cannot be fully developed if the three
fundamental factors of any construction—the architectural concept, the structural analysis . . . and the correct solution to the problems of execution—do not
proceed in close collaboration having as its aim the sole and unique goal of arriving at a proposed result combining functionality, solidity, and beauty.*[1]

Of the many omissions in this account of the evolution of tectonic culture none
is perhaps more glaring than that of the Dutch architect Hendrik Petrus Berlage,
who fell directly under Semper's influence by virtue of being an early graduate of
the Polytechnikum, now the ETH, the school that Semper founded in Zurich in
1855. This was not the only tectonic tradition to which Berlage was heir, however, for a major influence in the Netherlands in the 1880s was the structural
rationalist P. J. H. Cuypers, the designer of the Rijksmuseum (1885) and the Central Station in Amsterdam (1889). Cuypers was profoundly influenced by Viollet-
le-Duc, and this is the credo that he passed on to the younger generation, in-

cluding K. P. C. de Bazel, J. C. M. Lauweriks, and Berlage himself. As a result of this double formation Berlage can be seen as achieving a unique synthesis between the French and German traditions. This much is evinced by his masterwork, the Stock Exchange completed in Amsterdam in 1903 that was obviously a realization of one of the didactic illustrations to be found in Viollet-le-Duc's *Entretiens* of 1872. From the same source came his use of an overall proportional grid based on the isosceles triangle (the so-called Egyptian triangle) as a device for establishing the position and size of every element, no matter how small, not only in the Stock Exchange but in much of his subsequent work. Elsewhere, and above all in the interior of the main hall, patterned insets of multicolored brickwork and the hanging, castellated curtain relief of the enclosing walls, particularly in the upper reaches of the space, point to the influence of Semper's *Bekleidungstheorie* (fig. 10.3). That Berlage was fully aware of his indebtedness to Semper, not only for his theory of cladding but also for his broad socioanthropological and political views, is borne out in his writing.[2]

Like Louis Kahn after him, Berlage was to envision the walls of the environment as literally embodying the space of society; as being the matrix within which and by which the society is formed. In this regard his Stock Exchange building assumed the existence of a social community or *Gemeinschaft,* both within and without its volume. Thus the contingent street space around the structure is as

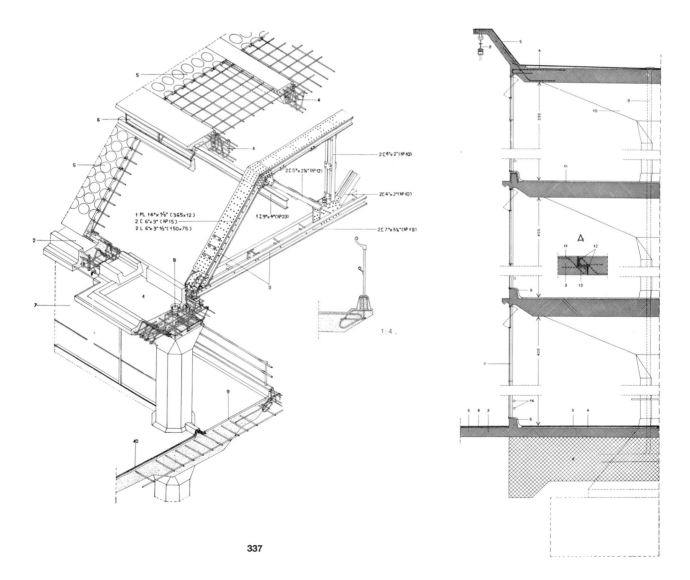

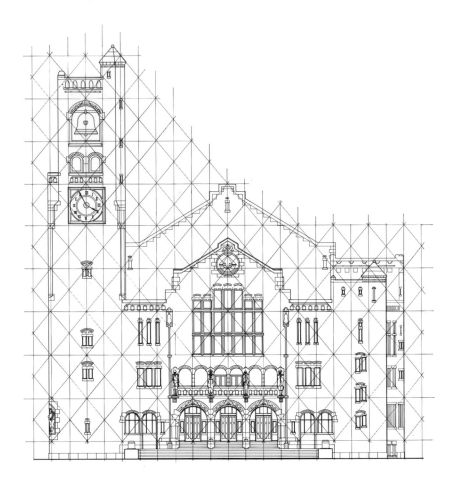

metrically modulated and defined by the building's face as its trading halls are influenced by the nature of their enclosing brick walls and glass roofs. Aside from displaying the hierarchical sequence of its construction, Berlage's masonry, stiffened and enriched by brick piers and by heavy stone dressings, seems to evoke the guild and burgher values that, even in the late nineteenth century, could still be experienced in the Netherlands as the continuation of a *modus vivendi* going back to the Middle Ages. For Berlage, both the art of diamond cutting and the intricate fair-faced brickwork of his Diamond Workers' Union Building of 1903 derived equally from a time-honored Dutch capacity for high-quality craftsmanship (fig. 10.4). For all that Berlage's socialism should appear to be a revolutionary daydream to his Marxist contemporaries, the fact that it should also be so eminently realizable (as opposed to the utopianism of William Morris) may have been due to the vestiges of a preindustrial culture that continued amid the industrialization of the Netherlands—to the persistence, that is, of rooted communal ideals that derived, in part, from the techno-agrarianism of the dike upon which the survival of the country depended. In terms of his tectonic development, Berlage came to adopt the technology of reinforced concrete only in the last decade of his career, beginning with the office building that he built in The Hague between 1920 and 1927 for the leading insurance company De Nederlanden van 1845. With its vaguely oriental syntax, corbeled-out in form but not in fact due to the homogeneity of the material, this work was almost the only occasion on which Berlage would employ fair-faced reinforced concrete (fig. 10.5). Similar to the late work of Perret, the concrete in this instance is of bush-hammered skeletonal construction, with brick and glass infill. Thus both architects attempted to treat concrete as though it were synthetic stone. With the single exception of a diminutive glass and concrete flower kiosk with inset lenses realized in The Hague in 1925 (fig. 10.6), Berlage would not attempt to use the material in its fair-faced form again. The assimilation and transformation of concrete in Berlage's work between 1925 and his death in 1934 is significant for the evolution of tectonic form in Dutch architecture, since the final work of his career, the Gemeentemuseum erected in The Hague between 1927 and 1935, is structured about a reinforced concrete frame that is faced on the outside in brick and on the inside is left fair-faced. Where the brick effectively covers the frame, tile appears in the interior as a form of infill cladding. Three particular inflections determine the tectonic character of this work. In the first instance, there is the frame itself, which, expressed as an armature throughout, is covered externally in a non-load-bearing brick skin. In the second, there are the internal partition walls, which are faced in ceramic tile so as to express their screenlike character. Finally there is the contrapuntal form of the brick skin, the bay windows, and the pitched-roof skylights that are alternately advanced and recessed in a fugal fashion, so as to express the changing spatial differential of the volumes within the gallery enfilade. As Chris Burrows has written:

For Berlage, the "clothing" is the obligatory brick. To overcome the material's traditional association as a load bearing element, . . . it is bonded in such a way as to suggest its role as a skin. Double courses of stretchers alternate with single courses of headers to convey a decidedly non-structural quality and even metaphorically to evoke the weave of Semper's space-defining mats. Furthermore,

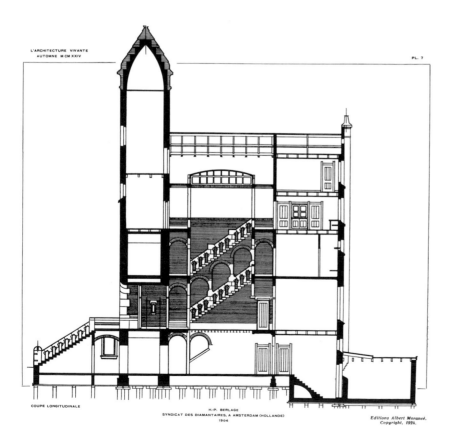

10.3
H. P. Berlage, Stock Exchange, Amsterdam, 1897–1903. South elevation with the system of proportions (1898 drawing).

10.4
H. P. Berlage, Diamond Workers' Union, Amsterdam, 1896–1903. Longitudinal section.

10.5
H. P. Berlage, office building for De Nederlanden van 1845, The Hague, 1920–1927.

10.6
H. P. Berlage, flower kiosk, The Hague, 1925.

structural elements characteristic of load-bearing masonry such as quoins are notably absent.

Internally, Berlage discovers the space-generating properties of the monolithic frame. Its orthogonal constituents imply the space which they delineate rather than positively enclosing it in the manner of the load-bearing wall. Adjacent spaces are individual at the same time as being part of one great space flowing through the entire building. This concept and use of space is in marked contrast to the distinct compartmentalization inherent in cellular masonry construction as illustrated by the spatial relationship in the Stock Exchange.[3]

This subtle tectonic differentiation will lie dormant in Dutch architecture for some thirty years before resurfacing in the work of Herman Hertzberger, where the interplay between the framework and volume will come to be simultaneously expressed both inside and out, in an equally rigorous manner.[4]

The other important architect largely omitted from this study is the Austrian Otto Wagner, although, unlike Berlage's, his architecture may be seen as a constant oscillation between the tectonic of the structure and the largely atectonic veil of the skin. This tension is immediately evident in his urban masterwork, the Postsparkassenamt, built in Vienna between 1904 and 1912 (fig. 10.7). While Semper's *Bekleidungstheorie* is again an influence, one may also detect the theoretical presence of Karl Bötticher, above all Bötticher's distinction between core form and art form that seems to manifest itself here as a constantly interpenetrating exchange between the underlying structural core and the outer membrane, this last making itself manifest in the Sterzing marble revetment, held in place by iron bolts covered with a sheet of lead and an aluminum cap. While these bolts are not the sole means of securing the masonry, they nonetheless perform the double function of both assisting the adhesion and representing the sheathing as a form of textile. In this regard they may be read as the links in a coat of chain mail or as knots in a knitted garment. Moreover, the fact that these studs are of metal makes them of the same order as the light metal, semistructural furnishings used elsewhere, from the horizontal metal balustrading of the *piano nobile* to the metal entry doors and ferro-vitreous canopy that together serve to articulate the entrance.

10.7
Otto Wagner, Postsparkassenamt, Vienna,
1904–1912.

10.8
Otto Wagner, St. Leopold, Steinhof, Vienna,
1907. Longitudinal section.

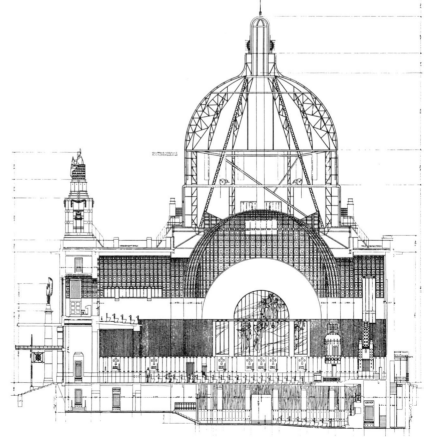

As in Mies van der Rohe's Seagram Building of 1958, there is a noticeable tendency to transfer the character of one material to the next. Thus we may compare the metalization of the glass in the Seagram Building, brought about by an elision between brown tinted glass and bronze anodized fenestration, to the metalization of stone in the case of Wagner's Postsparkassenamt or his St. Leopold Church at the Steinhof Sanatorium dating from 1907 (fig. 10.8). Both of these works convey the impression of being sheathed in metallic stone, an effect that achieves its greatest intensity in the interior of the church where the entire surface seems to consist of a stone membrane impregnated with metal. One recalls by way of contrast the tectonic work of Henri Labrouste, where the ferro-vitreous cage remains totally differentiated from its stone encasement. Here, on the contrary, the light steel trusswork supporting the dome is erected into position and then concealed. At the same time, small-scale, microstructural armatures are present as tectonic metaphors throughout the fabric, from the surrogate dome of the suspended baldachino to the various ornaments of the altar, the cross, and the candelabra (fig. 10.9). Paradoxical as it may seem, these devices reinforce the impression that the entire corpus is permeated by an interstitial metal network, not only by virtue of the repetitive stud pattern that covers the internal stone sheathing but also in terms of the railings, doors, reliefs, and light fittings that effectively articulate the space.

This synthetic contrast between the compressive crystalline nature of stone and the ductile character of metal is equally evident in Wagner's engineering work, above all in his *Stadtbahn* viaducts, where metal is used not only for the structural span but also for the wreaths that embellish the stone pylons on either side of the typical crossing, as in his Zeile Viaduct of 1898. In this case, dressed masonry confers its traditional status on the supporting pylons, which represent themselves as the supporting pillars of the benevolent state. Thus both metal and stone serve in this instance as symbolic elements. Elsewhere there is an explicit differentiation between *monument* and *instrument* as these two aspects play out their respective roles in Wagner's Nussdorf and Kaiserbad dams in the new Danube regulation works, under construction between 1894 and 1907 (figs. 10.10, 10.11). While the antithetical values of *Kunstform* and *Werkform* are

10.9
Otto Wagner, St. Leopold, Steinhof, altar detail.

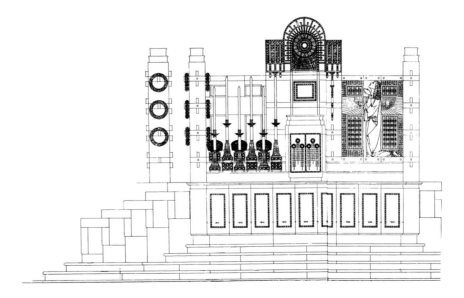

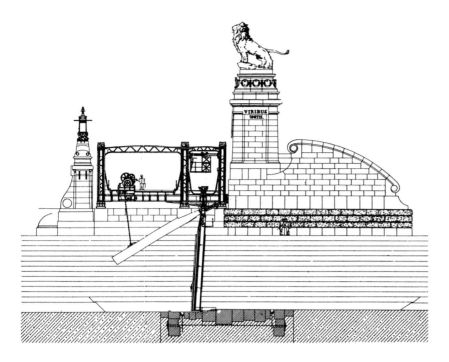

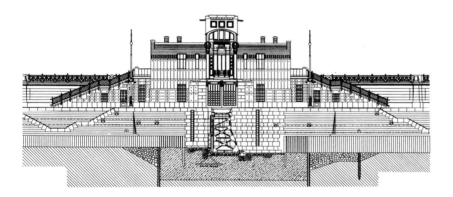

10.10
Otto Wagner, Nussdorf Dam, Vienna, 1894–
1898. Section showing one of the abutments.

10.11
Otto Wagner, Kaiserbad Dam, Vienna, 1904–
1907. Section of the sluice gate showing control building as seen from the canal.

clearly separated from each other in the Nussdorf dam, in the Kaiserbad installation a retractable sluice is housed in a sheet metal cabin. It is thereafter embellished with metal wreaths in such a way as to mediate between the instrumentality of the crane and the monumentality of its masonry emplacement.

In the history of twentieth-century architecture perhaps nothing is more unacknowledged than the emergence of tectonic form in the work of Le Corbusier. This is particularly evident after his atectonic Purist villas of the late twenties and his curtain-walled, machinist works of the next decade, which appear in retrospect to be technologically "productivist." While certain tectonic features are clearly expressed in the machinist works built between 1932 and 1935, the curtain wall facade of the Maison Clarté, Geneva, and the steel-framed, glass block front of the Porte Molitor apartments in Paris, constructional syntax will only begin to play a primary poetic role in Le Corbusier's work with his Maison Week-End of 1935 (fig. 10.12). This small house will be accompanied by the realization of three other works in which tectonic articulation will greatly determine the overall character of the architecture, the Mandrot House, near Toulon (1931), a

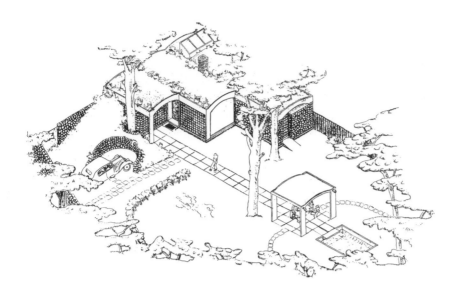

10.12
Le Corbusier, Maison Week-End, St.-Cloud,
near Paris, 1934–1935. Axonometric.

10.13
Le Corbusier, vacation house, Mathes, 1935.
West and east elevations.

10.14
Le Corbusier, reconstruction of the Hebrew
Temple, from *Vers une architecture,* 1923.

house at Mathes (1935) (fig. 10.13), and a seminal tented structure erected for the Paris World Exhibition in 1937.

Le Corbusier's Maison Week-End, built at St.-Cloud near Paris, announces a totally fresh departure, one that was to be as much at variance with the ideology of Purism as with the functionalism of the *Neue Sachlichkeit.* For while this house employed eminently modern techniques, such as reinforced concrete, steel-framed plate glass, glass lenses, plywood paneling, and industrial tiles, it also made abundant use of archaic building methods, evident in the rubble stone cross walls that carried the reinforced concrete vaults. It surely says something about the Mediterranean vernacular origin of the form that these roofs were of a rise and span that could easily have been achieved with Roussillon or Catalan vaulting. If the internal top-lit, ferro-vitreous banking hall of Wagner's Postsparkassenamt can be seen in retrospect as aspiring to a tectonic that will attain its apotheosis in the *Produktform* of the so-called High-Tech architects of the 1970s (one thinks of such architects as Norman Foster and Renzo Piano), then Le Corbusier's canonical weekend house may be seen as demonstrating the opposite thesis, namely a conscious move away from modernization and its faith in the inevitable benevolence of modern technology.

The Maison Week-End evokes a kind of eternal return in which neither the archaic nor the modern predominate. We may think of this house as a Nietzschean embodiment of vanquished historical states, as an aspiration for some transhistorical condition, removed from the nightmare of maximization and accelerating obsolescence. It is hardly an accident that this house, partially buried beneath the earth, should evoke a going-to-ground, as though it were a kind of archaeological manifestation, a troglodyte *objet trouvé* that while contaminated by modern technique remains irredeemably archaic. Le Corbusier's *Voyage d'Orient* (1912) and his later experiences in North Africa were both influential in this regard, for, as the shallow vaults of the house indicate, it may be seen as a piece of Cycladic fabric into which modern technology had been quite surreptitiously inserted.

Thus the Maison Week-End is a tectonic montage in which we pass from the white-washed, rubble-walled interior, with vaults lined in plywood sheet, to a full-height, plate-glass window, framed in steel, that, filling an entire bay, gives onto a freestanding concrete vault removed from the house. This last appears as an *al fresco* primitive hut, consisting of a thin-shell vault spanning onto equally thin concrete piers. This idealized tectonic form will be overwhelmed and absorbed by the coarse tectonic capacity of primitive building technique that, instead of allowing this vault to function as a unifying structural module, will render its effete piers redundant and thus replaceable by load-bearing rubble stone cross walls. Despite this conscious dissolution of an underlying structural grid, expressive detailing was to be of primary importance to the expressivity of the form. Thus as Le Corbusier wrote:

The designing of such a house demanded extreme care since the elements of construction were the only architectonic means. The architectural theme was established about a typical bay whose influence extended as far as the little pavilion in the garden. Here one was confronted by exposed stonework, natural on the outside, while on the interior, wood on the walls and ceiling and a chimney out of rough brickwork, with white ceramic tiles on the floor. Nevada glass block walls and a table of Cippolino marble.[5]

Where the Maison Week-End returned to the Mediterranean megaron, the Pavillon des Temps Nouveaux (1937) evoked the tent as the primordial nomadic form, the roof of which is simultaneously both cladding and structure since the stability of the whole depends upon the tensile surface of the fabric. This particular evocation of the eternal present had already been intimated by Le Corbusier in the pages of *Vers une architecture* (1923), above all in the reconstruction of the Hebrew temple in the wilderness that was depicted as a gridded temenos (fig. 10.14). The tectonic significance of the modular order in this instance resided in the fact that structure, cladding, and proportion were all integrated into

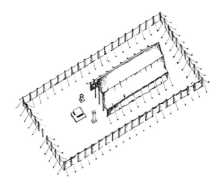

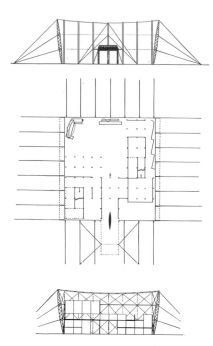

10.15
Le Corbusier, Pavillon des Temps Nouveaux, Paris, 1937. Main elevation, ground-floor plan, and cross section.

10.16
Le Corbusier, Pavillon des Temps Nouveaux, construction details.

a tensile membrane. Following this Judaic model, the modular order of the Pavillon des Temps Nouveaux coincides with the guy lines supporting its tented form.

Sustained by an "exoskeletonal" structure, the Pavillon des Temps Nouveaux was ordered about a grid that comprised six modules in one direction and seven in another (fig. 10.15). This adaptation of a nomadic paradigm entailed a typical Corbusian inversion in which the struts would be exterior to the tent and the tent itself would fall inward as a catenary rather than outward as a pitch. Like the Maison Week-End it was a synthesis of the archaic with the modern, the whole being stabilized by a system of wire cables and by steel latticework that jointly resembled the inverted superstructure of a dirigible (fig. 10.16). At the same time the Pavillon des Temps Nouveaux was an antithesis of the Maison Week-End, for where the one was permanent and heavy, the other was impermanent and light; where the one was roofed by rigid vaults, the other was covered by a pliable skin. Moreover, these different structural paradigms implied different institutional types, for where the house was an earthbound megaron, the tent, furnished with both altar and pulpit, rose up toward the light like an archetypal *templum.* This sacred tectonic/typological synthesis will be reinterpreted twenty years later in Le Corbusier's Ronchamp chapel (1956), where the tent/temple of the chapel will stand in opposition to the megaron form of the Maison du Gardien and the Maison des Pelerins, which will be built as attendant, load-bearing cross-wall structures comparable to the Maison Week-End (fig. 10.17).

The Philips Pavilion, built for the Brussels World's Fair of 1958 and designed in collaboration with the composer/architect Iannis Xenakis, may be regarded as the end of a tectonic trajectory in which Le Corbusier will finally reconcile both tent and vault into one complex hyperbolic, cable-stayed volume (fig. 10.18). The cladding of this folded volume in a chain mail of tesselated metal sheet takes us back, however inadvertently, to Wagner and Semper, and testifies to a tectonic continuity that passes from the saddleback section of the Pavillon des Temps Nouveaux through to the convoluted Möbius form of the Philips Pavilion, embracing en route not only Ronchamp but also the canopied exhibition stands that Le Corbusier projected for Liège and San Francisco in 1939 (fig. 10.19). In terms of built works, this trajectory will culminate for Le Corbusier in the yin/yang, steel plate roof structure of his Heide Weber Pavilion, posthumously completed in Zurich in 1967.

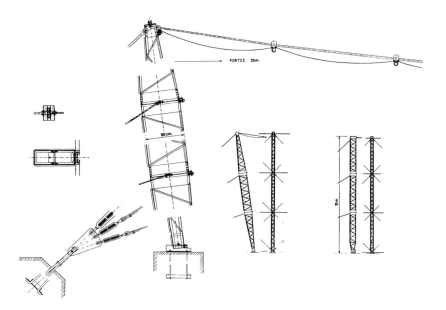

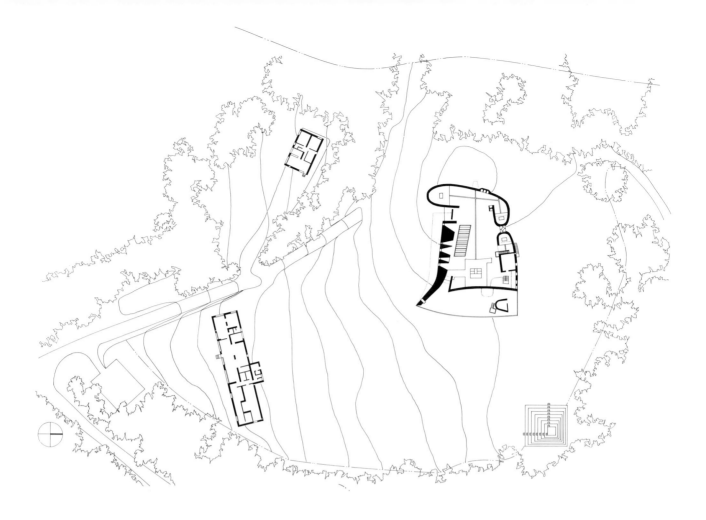

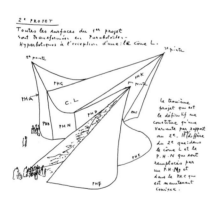

10.17
Le Corbusier, Chapel of Notre-Dame du Haut, Ronchamp, 1950–1956. Site plan.

10.18
Le Corbusier with Iannis Xenakis, Philips Pavilion, Brussels World's Fair, 1957–1958.

While the first fourteen years of Le Corbusier's Parisian career took him away from the tectonic, his return to expressive structure is perhaps not so surprising, particularly when one recalls that the Five Points of a New Architecture of 1925 amounted to a repudiation of the Greco-Gothic tradition. Inspired by the plasticity of reinforced concrete construction, Le Corbusier will progressively transpose the neoclassicism of his Purist period into a kind of archaism in which the purely cylindrical peristyle becomes the Egyptoid *pilotis*[6] and so on. This shift toward the primordial enabled him to transcend both the avant-gardism of the Purist line and the *idées reçues* of the Greco-Gothic.

To the extent that the tectonic in the second half of this century has been involved with the reiteration of vaulted spatial units, the Dutch architect Aldo van Eyck would also play a seminal role in the midcentury recovery of preclassical form, in the first place through his anthropological approach to the primitive building cultures of North Africa, and in the second through his didactic adaptation of these non-Eurocentric cultures to the orphanage that he built in Amsterdam in 1960. Deriving from his concept of "labyrinthine clarity," this residential school building depended upon the repetitive, hierarchical combination of two kinds of shallow concrete domes, each one springing from a square cell of different dimensions. While he initially eschewed van Eyck's domes, a similar although more pyramidal aggregational approach is evident in the early work of Louis Kahn; above all in his Trenton Bath House and Community Center projects dating from 1954.

347

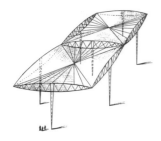

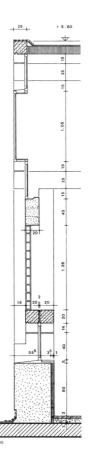

A more tectonic elaboration of van Eyck's space-making principle will wait upon the career of his most prolific pupil, the Dutch architect Herman Hertzberger, who will combine the anthropological insights of van Eyck with a structurally rationalist line inherited from the legacy of Berlage and Johannes Duiker. Hertzberger's first attempt at such a synthesis appears in the industrial laundry that he built in Amsterdam-Sloterdijk in 1964. The tectonic density of this work derives in part from the mutual articulation of its structure and fenestration (fig. 10.20) and in part from the successive, partially prefabricated assembly of its structural cells (fig. 10.21). In this regard it may be compared to the insurance company offices, De Nederlanden van 1845, that Berlage built in The Hague in 1927 (see fig. 10.5), since the exterior expression stems in each instance from the articulation of a concrete frame and from the concatenation of a number of discrete infill elements precisely articulated in respect of each other. Hertzberger's emphasis on microtectonic elements such as terraces, benches, sills, balustrades, and thresholds also owes much to Berlage, as we may judge from the *saku*[7] that plays such a prominent role in the main entry to the Montessori School that Hertzberger realized in Delft in 1966, for this feature seems to be a diminutive version of the monumental granite balustrade with which Berlage announced the entry to the Stock Exchange (fig. 10.22).

Hertzberger's original Montessori School is significant for the way in which it broadens the scope of his tectonic syntax, extending it into microspace and giving it an implicit sociocultural meaning. This is at once evident from the plan and section of the typical classroom (fig. 10.23), where the expressive structure of the building breaks down into a series of sequential components that both em-

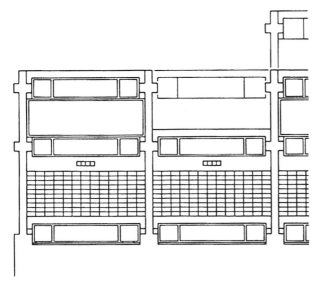

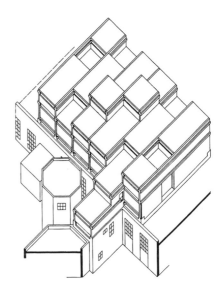

body and express the spatial progression; hence the orchestrated sequence of coat alcove, threshold, wet room, dry room, window, and terrace, together with the multiplicity of transitional, microspatial episodes, comprising sills, ledges, recesses, and shelves, with which each classroom abounds. As far as Hertzberger is concerned, tectonic elements become meaningful through being appropriated by the subject, so that in a limited sense the ultimate meaning of a work is contingent upon the uses to which it is put. This idea of a work being transformed through appropriation is made explicit in the sitting pit incorporated into a 1970 extension to the same school (fig. 10.24). Of the sixteen hollow wooden cubes packed flush into this square recess set in the floor of the principal foyer, Hertzberger would write:

10.19

opposite, top

Le Corbusier, project for an exhibition pavilion for Liège or San Francisco, 1939.

10.20

opposite, center and lower left

Herman Hertzberger, laundry addition, Amsterdam-Sloterdijk, 1962–1964. Detail elevation and detail section.

10.21

opposite, lower right

Herman Hertzberger, laundry addition, Amsterdam-Sloterdijk.

10.22

Herman Hertzberger, Montessori School, Delft, 1966, main entry.

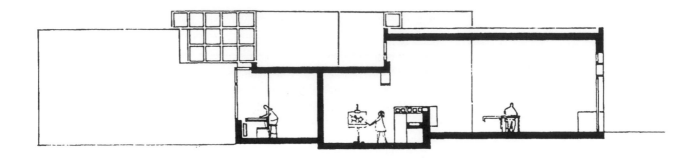

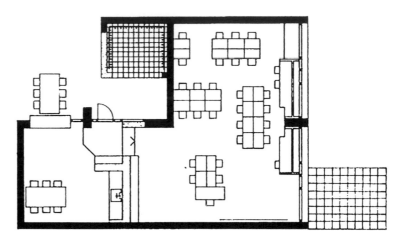

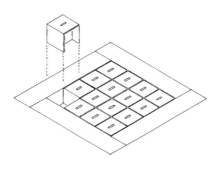

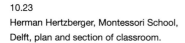

10.23
Herman Hertzberger, Montessori School,
Delft, plan and section of classroom.

10.24
Herman Hertzberger, Montessori School,
Delft, sunken sitting area.

When these are removed one has a square sunken sitting area. The scale of the hole is such that a whole class can fit into it to form a talking circle, or for story-telling. The hole is in many respects the negative form of the stone podium block [installed into the first phase of the school]. Where the block evokes images associated with mountain and viewpoint, the hole gives a feeling of protection, of a place one can retreat to, and evokes images connoting valley and hollow. The podium is an island in the sea, the hollow is a pond, which the children make into a swimming pool by adding a plank for walking over.[8]

Hertzberger's preoccupation with the corporeal appropriation of articulated structural form is first realized on a more public scale in his Centraal Beheer office building, completed in Apeldoorn in 1973. However inadvertently, this work may be seen as the synthesis of a number of different strands that lead from Semper and Viollet-le-Duc to culminate in a building that is as much indebted to Wright's Larkin Building of 1904 as it is to the tradition of Berlage. The fact that every precast beam, slab, upstand, concrete block, glass lens, and window bar has its rhythmic place within the orchestration of Centraal Beheer is immediately evident from the detailed sections (fig. 10.25). At the same time this complex structural assembly also establishes an explicit division between the earthwork of the parking, sustained by massive mushroom columns, and the framework of the offices above. The fact that the assembly system employed in Kahn's Richards Laboratories was partially repeated in the construction of this building testi-

350

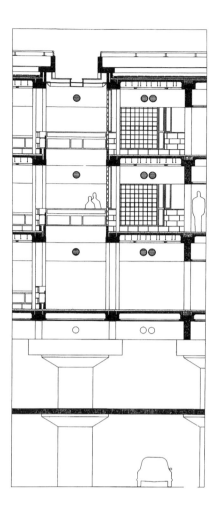

10.25
Herman Hertzberger, Centraal Beheer, Apeldoorn, 1970–1973. Section.

fies to the way in which all these works are part of the same tectonic tradition. As in Kahn's laboratories, the typical office platform, in the shape of a square, is carried on eight columns set in from the corners. The tartan circulation grid established by these structural coordinates serves to subdivide the basic square into four corner squares, which may then be variously arranged according to the changing requirements of the user (fig. 10.26). Of the appropriation of the resultant space Hertzberger writes:

The character of such an area will depend to a large extent on who determines the furnishing and decoration of the space, who is in charge, who takes care of it and who is or feels responsible for it. . . . The form of the space itself must have the competence to offer such opportunities, including the ability to accommodate basic fixtures, fittings, etc., and allow the users to fill in the spaces according to their personal needs and desires.[9]

The socio-anarchic nature of all this is obvious. What is less readily perceived, however, is the way in which this provision is integral to the overall woven character of the volume, together with the way in which this spatial warp and woof is a reworking of Wright's textile tectonic as this was already present in the Larkin Building. Kahn's Richards Laboratories are also a part of this legacy, not only because of their structural articulation but also because their internal subdivision breaks down into servant and served spaces, with the servant units carrying the mechanical services and stairs. A similar servant/served dyad articulates Centraal Beheer, and this affinity is paralleled by a system of modular assembly that assumes a comparable role in both works (fig. 10.27). Despite these Kahnian affinities, Dutch Structuralism remains a regional or even a national movement, not only in terms of its tectonic expressivity but also with regard to its sociocultural reception. Indeed, one may argue that despite his relative indifference to mass form, Hertzberger has remained inadvertently close to Berlage throughout his career; a proximity that has increased as he has become more concerned with the unifying boundary of the whole work, as in a school extension that he realized in Aerdenhout in 1990.

It is hard to imagine a building that is more removed from the Centraal Beheer than the three-story, glass-walled Willis Faber and Dumas insurance offices built at Ipswich, England, in 1974 to the designs of Foster Associates (fig. 10.28). In marked contrast to the Hertzberger building, the emphasis here is on the elegance and economy of the productive system; that is to say, on what the Swiss architect Max Bill once called the *Produktform.*[10] Foster indicated his affinity in this regard when he specifically acknowledged his debt to Bill's reinterpretation of the Crystal Palace in his Swiss National Exhibition Pavilion built in Lausanne in 1963 (fig. 10.29).[11] Unlike the Centraal Beheer, where the tectonic concept opens out toward a social appropriation of its volume, a typical Foster assembly invariably focuses on two equally dematerializing factors: in the first instance, on the spatially generative structure, be it a clear span or a repetitive framework, and in the second, on the production of a hermetic membrane that encases the structure in a gasketed or caulked skin. This combination has perhaps attained its most didactic synthesis to date in the Sainsbury Centre for the Visual Arts, built at the University of Norwich, England, in 1977 (fig. 10.30).[12] To the extent that the cross section of this structure divides into servant and served spaces, that is to say, into the thick but hollow lightweight servant wall, packed with me-

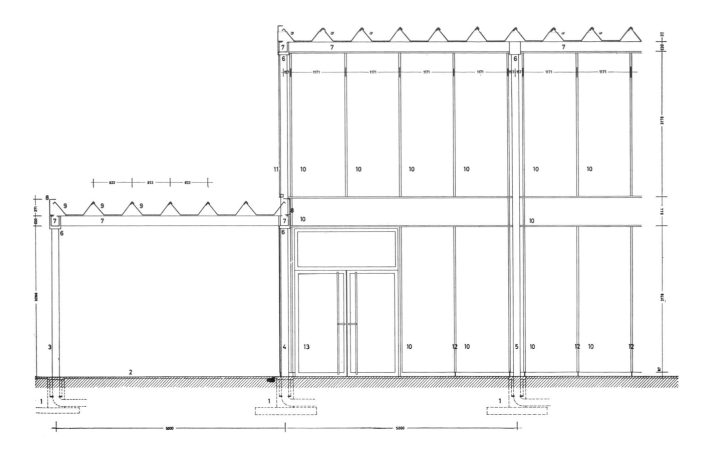

10.29

Max Bill, Swiss National Exhibition Pavilion,
Lausanne, 1963.

1. foundation
2. asphalt on gravel floor
3 and 5. tubular steel column with support-
    ing head
4. tubular steel column with two support-
    ing heads
6. supporting head
7. channel support
8. asbestos cement eaves element
9. asbestos cement roof element
10. wall element of white polyvinyl sheet
11. transparent polyester elements
12. chromium nickel section
13. double-winged door element

without; that is to say within the interstitial space, however it is constituted, rather than in an implicit interaction with the surrounding environment. Despite this similarity, the ideological base of each work could hardly be more divergent, for where Willis Faber reduces its exterior to the silence of a gasketed plate glass wall, hung like chain mail without mullions from the concealed cornice of its undulating perimeter, Centraal Beheer consolidates its mass form as a castellated pyramid, within which the repeated structural unit plays a reiteratively expressive role. Thus, where the one is a well-serviced package, symbolic of technological perfection, the other posits a concatenation of tactile form. In both, curiously enough, the main entrance can only be identified with difficulty, this perceptual shortcoming deriving in each instance from the uninflectable nature of the syntax employed.

This expressive inadequacy is already evident in the Crystal Palace of 1851, and a similar limitation will arise much later in the technocratic proposals of Fuller and Wachsmann, in which productive and geometrical means rather than institutional ends will be the prime movers of the form. Moreover while Carlo Scarpa and Konrad Wachsmann were equally preoccupied with the nature of the joint, Wachsmann could not have been further removed from Scarpa's cultural concerns, particularly when he described his prototypical aircraft hangar of 1959 (fig. 10.31) as a dematerialized structure and space "determined by the use of one type of connector, distributed and rhythmically repeated within a three-dimensional modular order."[13]

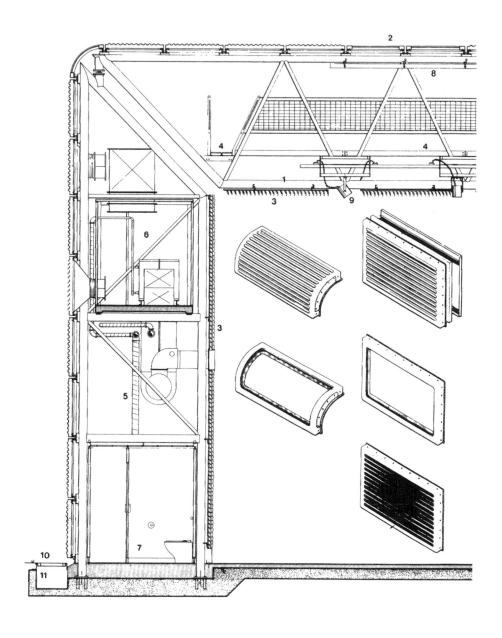

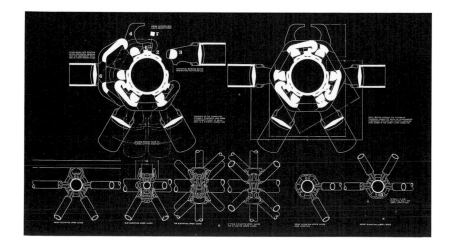

10.30
Foster Associates, Sainsbury Centre for the
Visual Arts, University of Norwich, England,
1977. Wall section.

10.31
Konrad Wachsmann, aircraft hangar, 1959.
Details.

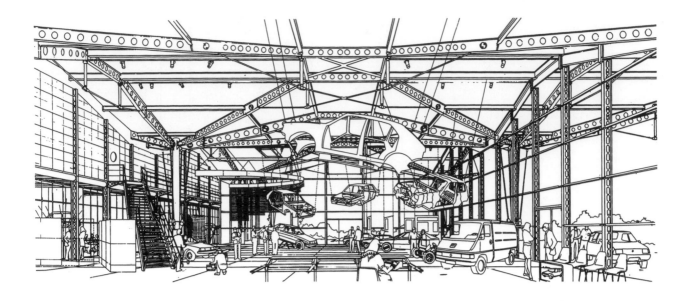

10.32
Foster Associates, Warehouse and Distribution Centre for Renault, Swindon, 1983. Perspective of showroom.

10.33
Foster Associates, Hong Kong and Shanghai Bank, Hong Kong, 1979–1985. Isometric drawing of the midlevel of the tower.

10.34
Herman Hertzberger, Ministry of Social Affairs, The Hague, 1979–1990.

In recent years both Foster and Hertzberger have tended to modify the exclusively productive character of their earlier work. Thus where Foster has abandoned the anonymity of the *undecorated* shed in favor of a series of buildings in which the basic structure plays a more expressive role, as in the Renault Centre, completed just outside Swindon in 1983 (fig. 10.32), or the Hong Kong and Shanghai Bank of 1985 (fig. 10.33), Hertzberger has increased the scale and spatiality of his modular units, as is evident, say, in his Ministry of Social Affairs completed in The Hague in 1990 (fig. 10.34). At the same time in his recent public work, such as the Ambonplein School, Amsterdam (1983–1986), he has employed a non-load-bearing perimeter wall held in front of the frame as a means of unifying the mass of the building.

While a more comprehensive study along these lines would include many other architects, I have elected to treat here only those works in which a *poetic of construction* is patently manifest or, as in the case of Le Corbusier, where the emergence of a tectonic expressivity constitutes a decisive moment within a more general development. Even with such exclusive criteria there remain many other architects whose work has been markedly affected by tectonic considerations. This is particularly true in Scandinavia, where two architects who have so far been absent from this account deserve particular mention, the Finnish master Alvar Aalto and the Norwegian Sverre Fehn. While tectonic form, as a consistently repetitive articulation, manifests itself rather sporadically in Aalto's architecture, it is only too present in his furniture and makes an equally decisive appearance in his all-wooden structures, such as the Finnish Pavilion built for the 1937 Paris Exhibition or the sports hall built at Otaniemi, Finland, in 1952 (fig. 10.35). Aalto would also exhibit marked tectonic sensibility in smaller utilitarian works, such as the warehouse that he built for the Karhula glass company in 1949 where composite timber roof trusses are bracketed off concrete pillars that divide the interior volume into three parallel bays (fig. 10.36). Here Aalto indulged in a particularly ingenious device as a means of inflecting the roof form in a particular direction. Thus while the trusses divide the space into three equal bays, the subsequent division of each truss into three segments would allow him to modulate the roof so as to yield one major and one minor monitor pitch.

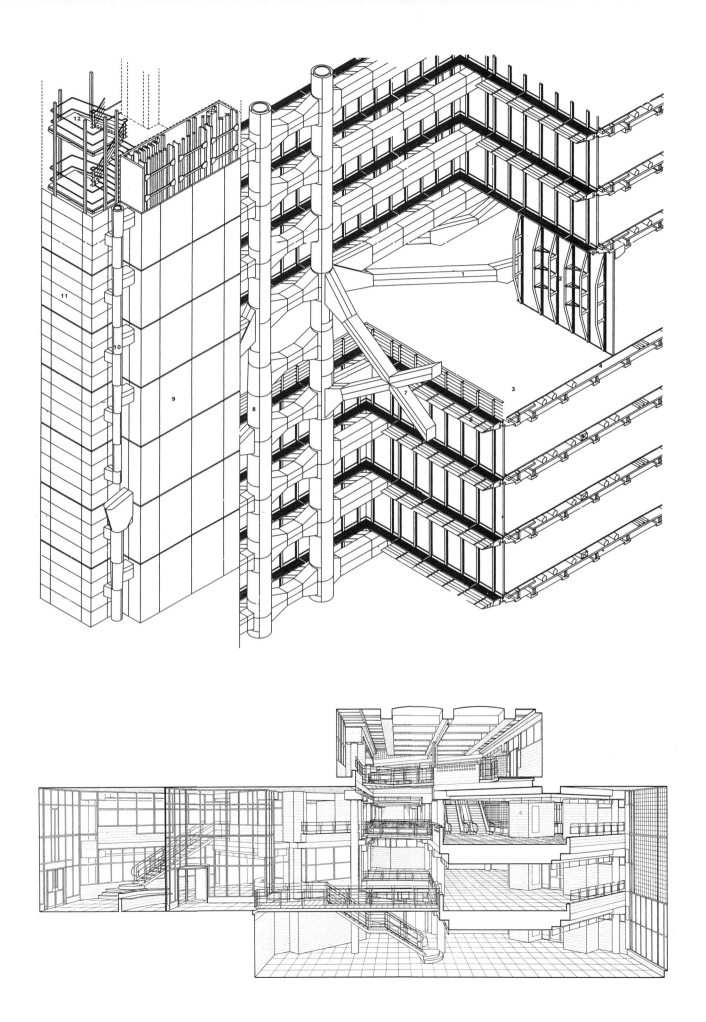

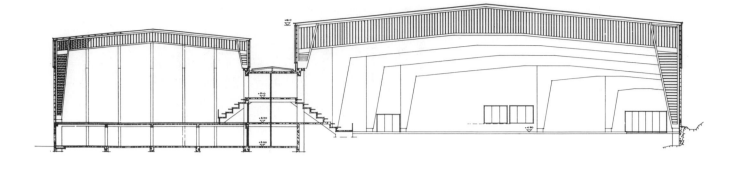

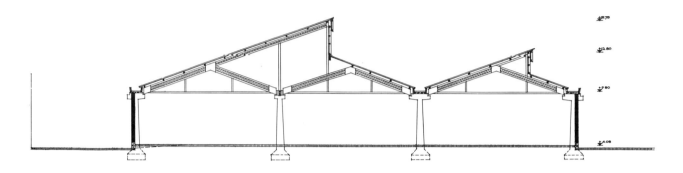

10.35
Alvar Aalto, gymnasium, Otaniemi, 1949–1952. Section. The construction is of nailed timber trusses assembled on the site and lifted into position.

10.36
Alvar Aalto, warehouse for Ahlström, Karhula, 1949.

A more plastic inflection of an equally directional character will be made at a much larger scale in the catenary roof of the large sports hall that he projected for Vienna in 1953. In general, Aalto displays a marked tendency to impart a topographic character to tectonic form. This impulse is evident in all of his work, so that the site is as much made by the building as the building is formed by the site. This last is the basis of the geological metaphor in Aalto's architecture; the tendency, that is, for the earthwork to appear as part of the building and for the roof to appear, at times, as though it were an extension of the landform. This phenomenon is particularly evident in his auditoria, where blank walls, in brick or in stone, rise from the ground in the form of escarpments.

Fehn, on the other hand, has often emphasized tectonic form as a large structural motif that encompasses the entire building, from his brilliant Nordic Pavilion built for the Venice Biennale in 1962 (fig. 10.37) to his municipal library projected for Trondheim in 1978 (fig. 10.38). He also seems to have felt an affinity for the joint as this appears in the work of Scarpa, as is particularly evident in his exhibition layouts for the Oslo Ethnographic Museum (1980). That construction has played a phenomenological role in all of Fehn's architecture is suggested by the theoretical position advanced in his book *The Thought of Construction,* written with Per Fjeld and published in 1983. In the title chapter we find the following reflection on the expressive range of constructional form:

The use of a given material should never happen by choice or calculation, but only through intuition and desire. The construction accords the material, in its opening towards light, a means of expressing its inherent color. However, a material is never a color without a construction. While stone has form, as a material it is defined by its shape, just as the keystone is defined by its precision. When stone is placed upon stone, its form resides in the joint.

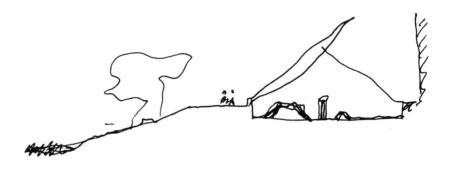

10.37
Sverre Fehn, Nordic Pavilion, Venice, built for the 1962 Biennale.

10.38
Sverre Fehn, National Library project, Trondheim, 1978, sketch.

. . . The calculated column expresses nothing more than a particular number. . . . No words are spoken and the alphabet remains unwritten. This is the world of silence. The calculated number celebrates the victory of the void, a fertile poverty. . . . In a world that is determined by calculation, material loses all capacity for the expression of constructive thought.

For the young architect each material is a measurement of strength. To apply the material to its ultimate capacity is natural for youth. The expression of this inherent force complements a natural vitality. The material's sensation carries its conviction and the energy of youth attains a structural perfection. With time certain architects will accept age as a tiredness which has a beauty of its own, allowing raw material a dimension of life and wisdom. The acquiescence of age is a recognition of maturity, a sign of personal growth. It is a generosity transcended through simplicity.[14]

This penetrating reflection alludes in part to his Venice pavilion, realized as a tectonic tour de force in long-span concrete construction when he was only 28. The structural *Gestalt* of this work consists of a single mega-beam spanning 25 meters that splits into two as it cantilevers out over a V-shaped column in order to avoid a large tree. This dynamic gesture is complemented by a double-layered concrete latticework roof, with a fiberglass gutter system suspended above. Spanning in one direction, this last is a translucent membrane that, in its suspended U-form in section, recalls the roof that Jørn Utzon proposed for his Sydney Bayview house at virtually the same time. Profoundly influenced by Scarpa's reading of Venice, this pavilion alludes to the lagoon on which the city has depended for its life.

The pavilion carries the ingredients of Venice. The city belongs to the water from which came its inspiration. The areas of green contrast with the water. The park with its landscape of grass and trees is very precious and scarce. Every existing tree grows unhindered inside the building, finding a total freedom through the roof. The main tree is honored, as the dominant structure gives room for its participation; this is the place where the unity between nature and building is at its maximum.

The transparent channels covering the roof pay homage to the rain. It is directed much like the water of the city and thereby provides sustenance for plants both inside and out, linking the pavilion with the cycle of the park. The leaves turn towards the sun and inflect the building according to the seasons. This honoring of sun and rain, framed in a place of the non-rational, is the beginning of a search for a higher order of architecture.[15]

There is a discernible if marginal return to tectonic values throughout the 1950s and 1960s, as one may judge not only from Fehn's Nordic Pavilion but also from the emergence of such architects as Amancio Williams in Argentina, Dolf Schnebli in Switzerland, and Sigurd Lewerentz in Sweden, as well as from the various strands of regionally inflected Italian modernism that became evident during this period. I am thinking in particular of the work of Ernesto Rogers, Angelo Mangiarotti, Franco Albini, and Gino Valle.[16] While the term "New Brutalism" was specifically coined by Alison and Peter Smithson, it became a convenient rubric by which to characterize much of this development, as we may judge from Reyner Banham's critical survey *The New Brutalism* of 1966. There will be a discernible return in these years to the expressive potential of structure, construction, and services, and in this regard we may cite not only the neo-Miesian Hunstanton School, built in Norfolk in 1954 to the designs of Alison and Peter Smithson, but also Williams's Maillart-like bridge house realized in Mar del Plata some nine years before.[17]

In a similar way a certain stereotomic expressivity may be seen as uniting works as diverse as Le Corbusier's Maison Jaoul, Paris (1956), Stirling and Gowan's Ham Common Housing, London (1958), Schnebli's Castioli House at Campione d'Italia (1960), and Lewerentz's St. Mark's Church completed near Stockholm in the same year.[18] In each of these works, load-bearing, fair-faced brickwork aspires to a common telluric sensibility; a testament to the existential authenticity of brick that in almost every instance is complemented by brick vaulting. Lewerentz's longstanding commitment to tectonic form warrants special comment, particularly for his load-bearing brick cemetery chapels completed in Malmö in 1945 (fig. 10.39). Lewerentz's entry into tectonic brickwork begins with these chapels and goes on to assume a more brutal, load-bearing form in his St. Mark's Church. This roughly coursed, warehouse aesthetic would be raised to a higher level in his St. Peter's Church, completed at Klippan in 1966. Here a varie-

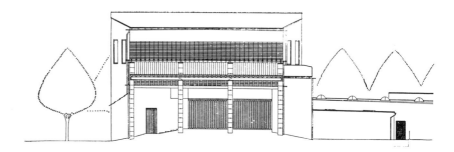

10.39
Sigurd Lewerentz, chapel at Malmö Cemetery, 1945.

gated, flat canopy of brick vaults, resting on a network of low-riding steel girders, encapsulates the entire church in a catacomb-like space, of which Colin St. John Wilson has written the following appraisal.

A square plan seems simple enough; but let the floor as it slopes down to the altar swell into a shallow mound and burst open to reveal a well for the baptismal shell; and let a raw steel column crowned with a cross-beam stand like a crucifix off-center of that space to vie with pulpit and altar as a center of focus, and a certain drama enters in.

The column itself is not what it at first appears to be: split in two from top to bottom, its twin cross-trees—which are not symmetrical—carry at their extremities yet further beams which are also split into pairs. Upon these beams stand steel struts to support the metal ribs that support the brick vaults at both springing and ridgelines alternately. Then again, these ribs to the vaults are neither horizontal nor do they run parallel but expand and contract as they run from wall to wall. Lewerentz speaks of the vaults as a recall of the ancient symbol of the heavens, but here his treatment of them is strangely moving and insinuates into the mind a closer analogy to the rhythm of breathing—the rise and fall, the interlocking of expansion and contraction. Lewerentz (who was qualified as an engineer) worked closely with the project engineer and himself proposed the use of smaller steel sections, paired, rather than larger single sections so that light could shine through the middle of the structural assembly. To what extent these shifts and discontinuities are brought about for visual reasons or in compensation for the difference in physical performance between steel section and brick vault I do not know; the fact is that a technical requirement is transformed into a mystery and how this transformation is brought about is unfathomable.[19]

Equally compelling but totally different constructional approaches are evident in Italy during this period, first in the intimate work of Scarpa, who will evolve his montage manner outside the mainstream, and second in the more structurally didactic work of Albini and Franca Helg, not to mention Rogers's Torre Velasca erected in Milan in 1958. Close to the microtectonics of Scarpa, particularly in an exhibition that he designed for the Palazzo Bianco in Genoa (1951), Albini will come to the fore at a more public and comprehensive scale in the department store that he designed with Helg and realized in Rome in 1961 (fig. 10.40). This structure returns us to the plaited discourse of Wagner's Postsparkassenamt, the skin being interwoven in this instance not only with the structure but also with the perimeter ductwork. Some idea of the complexity of the result may be gleaned from the following description.

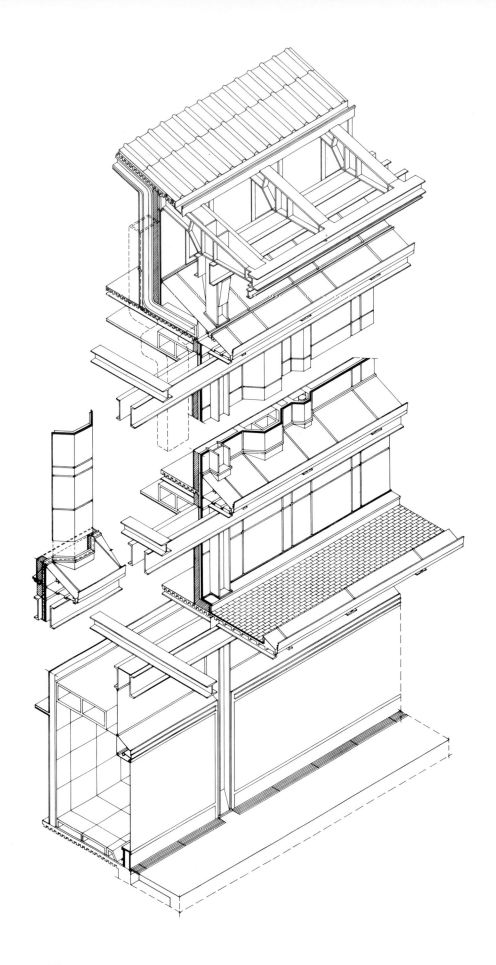

10.40
Franco Albini with Franca Helg, La Rinascente, Piazza Fiume, Rome, 1957–1961. Axonometric section.

10.41
Angelo Mangiarotti and B. Morasutti, Baranzate Church, Milan-Vialba, 1959.

*The structural composition of the La Rinascente building derives from the combi-
nation of formal and technological factors in its design. The building is marked
by certain bare decisions: locating the vertical service mains on the outside, mod-
ifying the shape of the curtain wall panels in line with the direction of the ducts;
leaving the external metal structure exposed and using the parametrical cornice
girders for the horizontal service mains, also leaving the heads of the secondary
girders exposed; using the rail on the top floor as a device for outlining the top of
the building, interrupting it at the corner with the Via Aniene. The corrugated design of the panels, although influenced by the technical needs of air-conditioning
pipes, complies with aesthetic criteria and has been used to recall surface features typical of Roman architecture. . . . [The contrast] between the main structure and the curtain walls lies in the use of color and plastic treatment. The
external wall was constructed of panels prefabricated from a crushed mix of cement, granite powder, and red marble; each panel is divided perpendicularly into
four parts, the third from the bottom being narrower and in a light ivory color.
The same contrast is to be found in the compositional method, since the panels,
which contain main ducts, bulge more or less as bow windows do to create a
surface that changes constantly according to the strength of the light.*[20]

Influenced by the spectacular concrete structures designed by Nervi and Morandi, certain Italian architects began to move toward precisely articulated structural assemblies in reinforced concrete. This tendency led at times to a kind of
tectonic minimalism, as is evident say in Mangiarotti and Morasutti's Baranzate
Church, realized near Milan in 1959 (fig. 10.41). Conceived as a *Hallenkirche* and

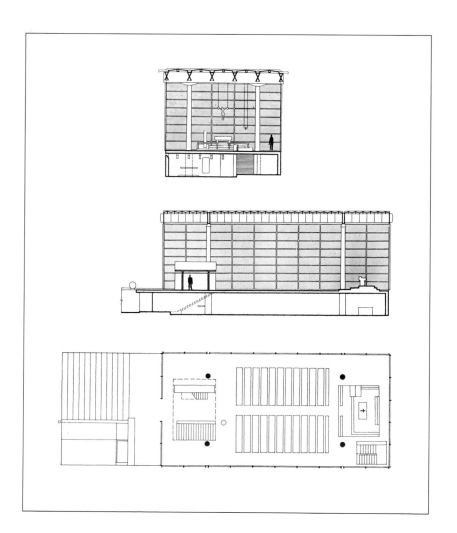

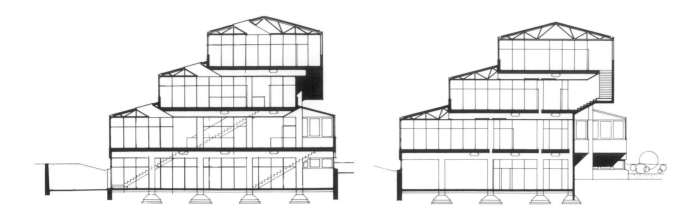

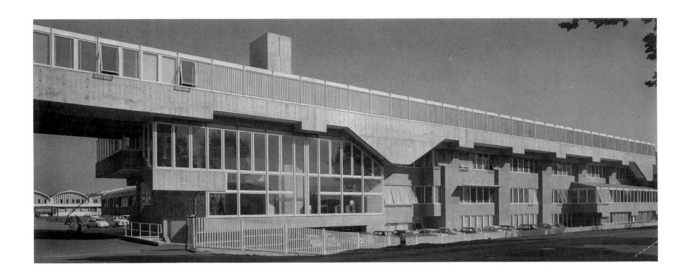

10.42
Gino Valle, factory for Zanussi Rex, Pordenone, 1961.

built entirely of concrete, the quadripartite structure of its nave comprises a diagrid roof carried on six longitudinal beams, two transverse girders, and four cylindrical columns. Clad throughout in a double-glazed, translucent envelope, this work may be seen as a midcentury interpretation of Perret's Notre-Dame du Raincy.

Gino and Nani Valle would pursue equally tectonic themes but with an inflection that was more evidently regional. This is particularly noticeable in their early work; in their bank at Latisana of 1956 and their Casa Quaglia built at Sutrio, near Udine, in 1953–1954. In structural terms both the bank and the house seem to be predicated on a Kahnian application of load-bearing brick piers, square in plan and eight in number, carrying a 15-by-23-meter lenticular metal roof in the case of the bank and a heavy traditional timber 15-by-15-meter truss system in the house (cf. Louis Kahn's Adler House project of 1954). In both instances, the main expression stems from a play between load-bearing and load borne, and this will persist as a theme in almost all of Valle's work, even if he will never again attain quite the same level of expressive simplicity. Valle's masterwork of this period is unquestionably his Zanussi Rex offices built at Pordenone in 1961 (fig. 10.42).[21] This work is particularly distinguished for its rhythmic use of a tiered and cantilevered concrete armature with concrete upstands, over which is suspended a stepped and pitched light trussed metal roofwork, clad in asbestos cement sheeting.

Among Italian architects of the past forty years who have made a consistent contribution to *Baukunst* in the Miesian sense, one must certainly include Vittorio Gregotti, who in both theory and practice has been consistent in his articulation of constructional form, most notably in his early housing built for Novara and Milan in 1962 and in his later institutional work executed for the universities of Palermo (1969) and Calabria (1973) and more recently, perhaps, in a number of stadia, including the main arena for the 1992 Barcelona Olympics (fig. 10.43). In all this work, recognition must also be accorded to the Japanese architect Hiromichi Matsui, who played a salient role in the office of Gregotti Associati in the second half of the 1960s and the early 1970s.

The British Brutalist movement will be brought to a close with the Economist Building completed in 1964 to designs of Alison and Peter Smithson (figs. 10.44, 10.45). This built fragment of the Smithsons' Berlin Hauptstadt proposal (1958) was a diminutive reinterpretation of American high-rise construction; one that attempted to reintegrate the romantic classicism of the *Schinkelschule* with its Gothic origins. However, where Mies will represent the fireproof steel frame through an application of steel facings (cf. 860 Lake Shore Drive), the Smithsons will face their concrete frame in roach-bed Portland stone, with gray aluminum trim running down the structural piers, along the sills, and up into the spandrels to form an aluminum-fenestrated curtain wall, anodized gray. The Gothicism of the resultant profile is emphasized through setting back the stone-faced structural mullions as they rise upward, a device evidently taken from Mies's Promontory Apartments. The Economist Building emerges today as that rare example of a modern building that has withstood the "flow of time," where the quality of the work has improved rather than the reverse.[22] In retrospect this structure would seem to come closest to Peter Smithson's archaeological ideal of a building that could, in some future time, be reconstructed from its ruined fragments. Close to the Semperian *Stoffwechseltheorie,* Smithson first advanced this thesis in 1966 in a remarkably insightful essay in which he compared the transformed timber

10.43
Gregotti Associates, main arena for 1992 Olympic Games, Barcelona, 1983.

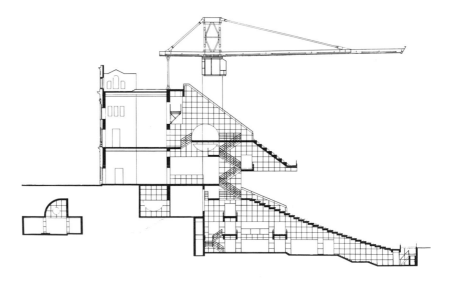

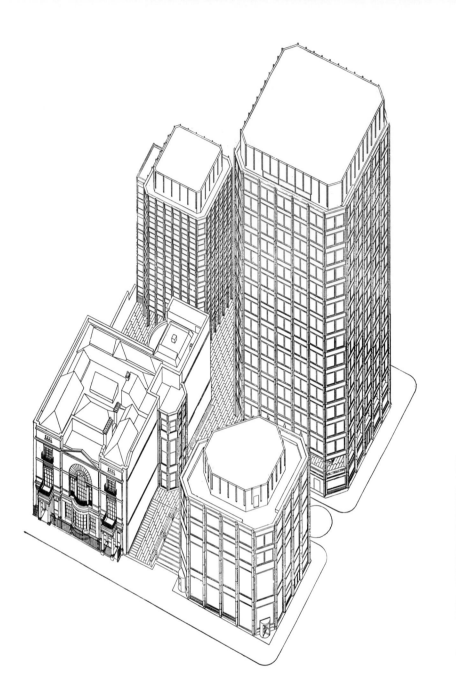

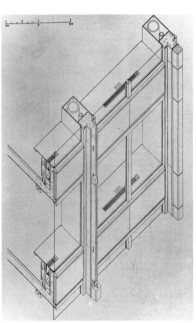

10.44
Peter and Alison Smithson, The Economist
Group, St. James Street, London, 1964.
Axonometric.

10.45
Peter and Alison Smithson, The Economist
Group, axonometric showing perimeter
construction.

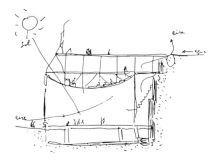

10.46

Alejandro de la Sota, Maravillas School gymnasium, Madrid, 1962.

character of the Greek classical Doric order to the comparable Japanese timber order of the Naiku and Geku sanctuaries at Ise.

The essence of the Doric is rectangularity of platform and an unusually densely formulated language. This "density" is not a question of internal consistency— but that it is capable of doing a lot of internal explaining, of telling us what to expect; for example, and most obviously (but withheld from me for 25 years) the angle of slope of the underside of the soffit of the cornice lets us know, without it being necessary for us to move away from the flank of the temple, the slope of the pediment. A wall with an incised line, or tiny projection tells us to expect a column around the corner. Even the pitching of the floor lets us sense where the outside is—for we know without thought that water most sensibly flows to the outside—the curvature is telling our feet, before our eyes, of the building's structuring. It is no exaggeration to say that one only needs a fragment of a temple to be put in touch with the building's whole form through eyes, feet, skin-sensation. Totally. And this is not a metaphysical nonsense, one is actually told about dimensions, angles, proportions of the whole in the fragment. That fragment is not an absolute part in the Renaissance sense, it is an explaining part in the primitive sense. This is what makes the parallel with the Ise shrines so extraordinary, for at Ise not only is one told of the whole by the fragment, by a stretch of fence for example, but one experiences the same sense of affront—of loss of meaning, of sacrilege almost, when the Order drifts away from its real structure explanatory-metaphor role. . . . It is tempting to generalize and say all architecture is metaphor of structure—that the Modern Architecture of the Heroic Period is a metaphor for a not-yet-existing, machine-built structure, that Romanesque and Gothic are metaphors for their actual structures, etc. . . . Kahn's Philadelphia Laboratory is such a metaphor. It is an architecture of pre-cast concrete.[23]

With the completion of the Economist Building, the British tectonic line passed to the so-called High-Tech architects, not only to Foster Associates, whose work has already been cited, but also to the Richard Rogers Partnership whose work would make an equally seminal contribution to the field, above all in their megastructural office complex, completed in London in 1984, as the new premises of Lloyds.

Spanish architectural practice has been one of the most tectonically consistent to be found anywhere in recent years. The most influential Spanish architect in this regard has been Alejandro de la Sota, whose laconic but flexible neoconstructivist approach dates from his Maravillas gymnasium, completed in the center of Madrid in 1962 (fig. 10.46). De la Sota took advantage of a natural cliff face to add to an existing school complex. Employing an exposed steel frame, a normative curtain wall, and a wire mesh fence enclosing a playground on the roof, and housing the whole beneath an inverted, suspended steel truss, de la Sota was able to create an expressive structure that was at once modular, well-detailed, and subtly inflected. It was an exemplary demonstration of an architecture that exploited both repetitive production and lightweight technology without compromising the tectonic expressivity of the work.

Among the many Spanish architects who have been partially influenced by de la Sota over the past thirty years, one thinks of Corrales and Molezun, whose Spanish Pavilion for the Brussels World's Fair of 1958 presaged the rebirth of Spanish architecture. Equally touched in various ways by de la Sota one may cite the work of Rafael Moneo, the Sevillian architects Cruz and Ortiz, and the Catalan architect Josep Llinas, with whom de la Sota has recently collaborated.[24] The Catalan architects Esteve Bonell and Francesc Rius have been able to continue the Iberian tectonic tradition in two remarkable stadia: a velodrome built in the Vall d'Hebron district of Barcelona in 1985 (fig. 10.47), and a basketball arena realized in 1991 in the nearby suburb of Badalona (figs. 10.48, 10.49, 10.50). In the case of the velodrome the architects strove to achieve a structure that in tectonic terms would be as laconic as possible.

A building having two scales, due to two [views], a distant one and a close one. On the other hand we wanted a building with a clear image, with a unitary architectural definition, one that would be capable of organizing the immediate environment . . . if we had to define the velodrome in a few words we would say that it possesses a certain classicism, [one that is] at the same time an elaborated modernism. Classicism because of the way in which it sets itself on the landscape and because of the rotundity of its conception. Modernism because of its pragmatic and realistic appearance, because of its simplicity and the way in which construction is coherent with the materials used.[25]

Reminiscent of the opposition between ideal and empirical form as we find this in the work of Le Corbusier, the elliptical, banked cycle track is enclosed by a circular ring that accommodates a variety of services around its perimeter, ranging from the main entrance to toilets, bars, and stairs. The monumental character of this work is assured by its scale and proportion and by the hierarchical interplay between the concrete undercroft containing services and the in situ concrete framed superstructure. This last is filled with bricks and the cement blocks set within the concrete blade walls that support the circular concrete canopy above. The feathering of this canopy on its inner and outer edges amounts to a kind of vestigial cornice that, together with the elegant artificial lighting masts in tubular steel, complete the skyline of the composition. Between the outer ring and the banked, elliptical seating surrounding the track lies a paved concourse for the accommodation of spectators during intermissions. The architects were to account for their constructive approach to the overall design in the following rather pragmatic terms:

Because of the short time available both for the design and its realization, which had to be carried out in ten months, materials and building techniques were chosen in order to avoid any particular difficulty. The structure of the external ring, the locker room's covering and the support of the seats are made of panels, pylons, pilasters or walls in reinforced concrete. The seat tiers, also in reinforced concrete, are the only pre-fabricated parts of the whole building.[26]

Like the Vall d'Hebron velodrome, the Badalona sports hall was also conceived as a modern variation on an ancient amphitheater, structured about the traditional format of the arena above with services below. In this case, however, the architects were to interpret the type as though it were a surrogate cathedral or "social condenser."[27] To this end the cigar-shaped mass form is set at an angle to the principal street so as to assert its independence from the surrounding urban fabric. The columnar structure of this 13,000-seat elliptical arena is extended above the last tier of seats in order to support a concrete ring beam from which a light-metal, sawtooth monitor roof is suspended. The cable-stayed trusses supporting these monitor lights are carried at midspan by a 2-meter-

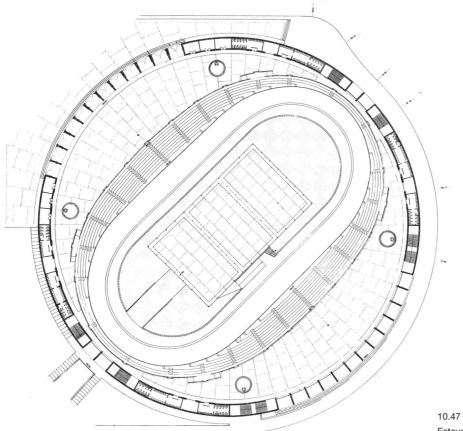

10.47
Esteve Bonell and Francesc Rius, velodrome,
Vall d'Hebron, Barcelona, 1985.

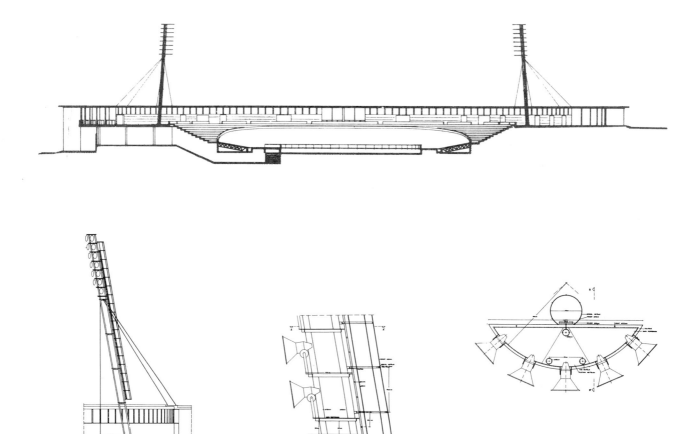

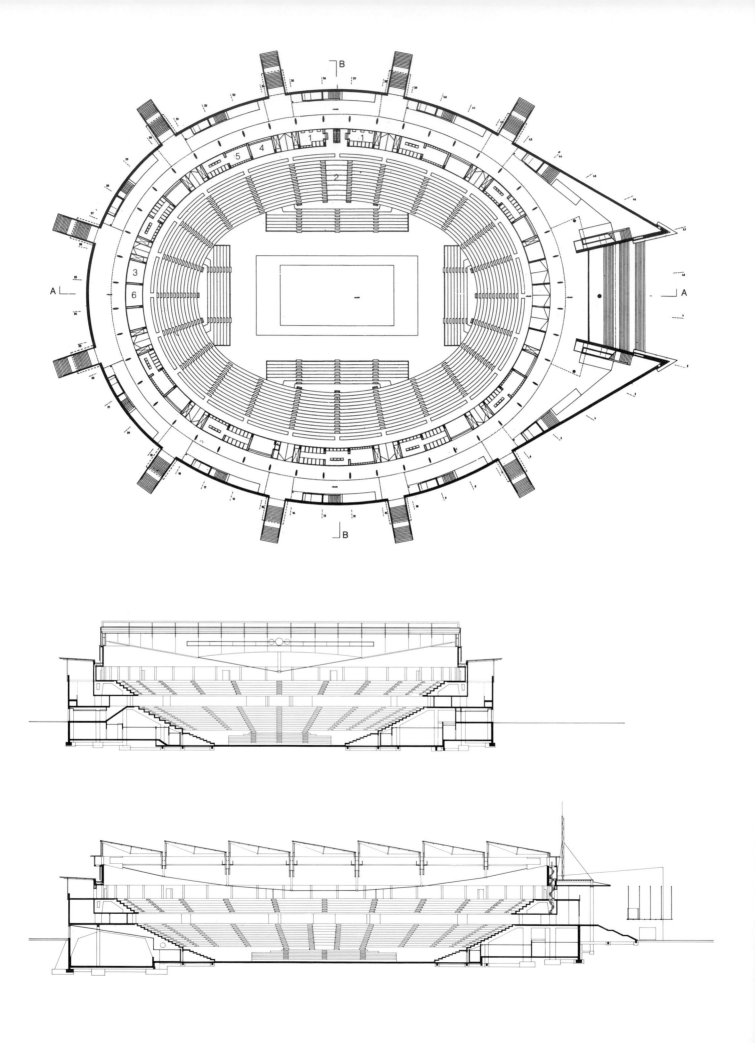

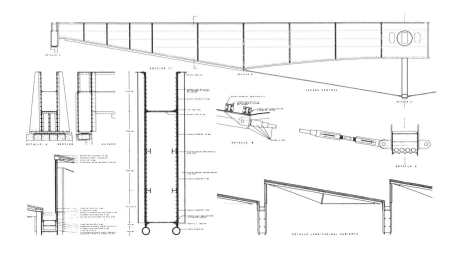

10.48
Esteve Bonell and Francesc Rius, sports hall,
Badalona, 1991. Plan and sections.

10.49
Bonell and Rius, sports hall, Badalona,
details.

10.50
Bonell and Rius, sports hall, Badalona,
interior.

diameter tubular beam, running down the central axis of the arena for its 120-meter span. The elegance of this steel-plated assembly, designed in collaboration with the engineers Robert Brufan and Agusti Obiol, recalls pioneer tubular steel construction of the previous century.[28]

Finally one should mention the Ticino school that has exhibited a strong feeling for the poetics of structure ever since Rino Tami's neo-Wrightian *autostrada* bridges of the early 1960s. I have in mind of course not only Mario Botta's earliest pieces in which he would display his prowess as a craftsman, but also his altogether more mannered Ransila offices built in Lugano in 1985; a work exemplary for its use of brick as an expressive cladding form (fig. 10.51). At a different end of the spectrum, and more comprehensively tectonic in its overall expression, one must acknowledge Livio Vacchini's early masterwork designed with Alberto Tibiletti, the so-called Macconi Building realized in Lugano a decade earlier. This is surely one of the finest exposed-steel-frame structures built in the last quarter of this century, rivaling the best of Mies's *Fachbauwerk* (fig. 10.52). Evocative as much of Otto Wagner as of Mies, however, this structure, filled with glass, glass brick, and blockwork and faced in dressed stone, also subtly recalls the trabeated *modénature* of Perret.

I would like to conclude this brief survey of the tectonic tradition in the second half of the twentieth century by returning to the gloss at the head of this chap-

10.51
Mario Botta, offices for Ransila, Lugano, 1981–1985. Details of exterior wall and windows.

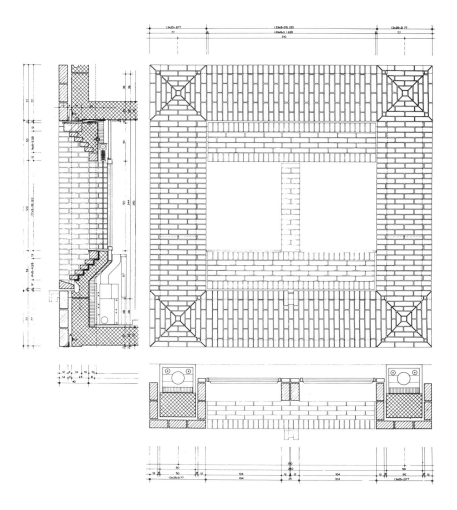

ter, for Aris Konstantinidis remains the only Greek of his generation besides Dimitris Pikionis who has been so singularly susceptible to the Greek landscape, and hence committed to the creation of a critical modern architecture that would remain appropriate to the time and place in which it is built. Just such an architecture is surely manifest in the small stone house with which he began his career in Eleusis in 1938, and in a similar but altogether more sophisticated house that he erected out of local stone in Sikia in 1951 (fig. 10.53). An equally compelling rapport at a topographic level is also achieved in the reinforced concrete hotel structure that he built near the mountains of Meteora, at Kalambaka, in 1959 (fig. 10.54).

Toward the end of his professional career, in 1975, Konstantinidis would publish an elegiac evocation of the Greek vernacular in which he was able to demonstrate its close ties to the landscape from which it stems and within which it remains embedded. Here in his *Elements for Self-Knowledge,* compounded of photographs, sketches, notes, and aphorisms, Konstantinidis sets forth the ontological limits of all architectural form. For Konstantinidis the vernacular lies forever beyond time because nobody can determine its age. Such a work may still be encountered, even now, in the rock walls of Andros or the terraces of Sifnos, both equally timeless in that they illustrate all too precisely the words of Fernand Léger: "Architecture is not art, it is a natural function. It grows out of the ground,

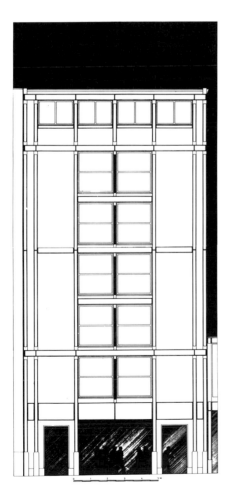

10.52
Livio Vacchini and Alberto Tibiletti, Macconi Building, Lugano, 1975.

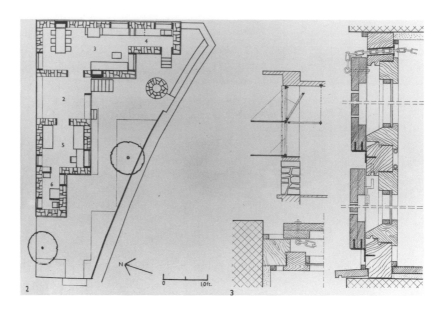

like animals and plants."[29] In contrast to this condition in which culture and life are not yet separated, Konstanidis writes of the spurious character of the new when it is pursued as an end in itself.

As for the efforts of a so-called "new" architecture to produce something unprecedented and advanced (admittedly, the modern age has discovered some "new" truths—in fact, it has discovered many, so many that Matisse once felt compelled to cry out: "No more new truths!"), let us accept once and for all that a truly unprecedented and advanced work is not that which uses superficial brilliance to make a temporary and sensational impact, or that which seeks to take one by surprise by means of ostentatious, acrobatic contortions, based on momentary "finds," but only that which is justified by a continuing, living tradition, that which endures because it is put to the test again and again, within each new context, so that it expresses afresh inner experiences, secretly nurtured disciplines, forms that have truly been handled over and over again. What we may accept as reality cannot possibly be what we see ready-made around us, but much more what we attempt to visualize in a dream, all of us together and each one of us separately, the dream of a new—truly new—life, shaped like a poem.[30]

10.53
Aris Konstantinidis, house, Sikia, 1951. Plan and details.

10.54
Aris Konstantinidis, hotel, Kalambaka, 1959.

10.55
Enric Miralles and Carme Pinós, Olympic archery training range, Barcelona, 1989–1990.

It is undeniable that over the course of this past century the tectonic has assumed many different forms, and it is equally clear that its significance has varied greatly from one situation to the next. Yet one thing persists throughout this entire trajectory, namely, that the presentation and representation of the built as a constructed thing has invariably proved essential to the phenomenological presence of an architectural work and its literal embodiment in form. It is this perhaps more than anything else that grounds architecture in a cultural tradition that is collective rather than individual; that anchors it, so to speak, in a way of building and place-making that is inseparable from our material history. The fact that this century has wantonly destroyed so much of its cultural and ecological heritage through the rapacity of industrial and postindustrial development in no way denies the validity of this profound truth. It is significant that the progressive loss of the vernacular throughout the last two centuries has largely stemmed directly from the elimination of the traditional agricultural base that gave rise to its form. A similar demise may now be observed in respect of the urban, industrial civilization of the nineteenth century with which our awareness of the tectonic value first came into being.

One may argue that the tectonic resists and has always resisted the fungibility of the world. Its tradition is such that it has constantly sought, at one and the same time, both to create the new and to reinterpret the old. Notwithstanding the idiosyncrasies of any particular architect, it is, in its essence, anti-individualistic, for unlike painting and sculpture it is not given to the subjective creation of images. In this sense the figurative is denied to architecture both subjectively and objectively; and while architecture inevitably possesses sculptural qualities, in and of itself it is not sculpture. It is exactly this that makes the architecture of Enric Miralles and Carme Pinós so ambiguous, since, as with much later modern work, it oscillates uneasily between the sculptural and the architectural. Thus it is at its best where the work is incised into the ground, as in their Olympic archery building or their cemetery at Igualada, both dating from 1992. Here the architecture both cuts into the earth and rises athletically above it, particularly in the archery structure where it counters the stereotomic form of the earthwork with the articulated counterpoint of propped folded plates in concrete, of which the shifting complexity of the shell roof is composed. As subject to tradition as to innovation, it returns us to the tectonic as Antoni Gaudí would have understood it, and thus via Gaudí to a line of thought that runs straight back to Viollet-le-Duc. By a similar token Igualada returns us to Louis Kahn's

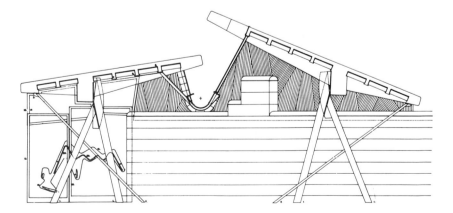

concept of "hollow stones." In this instance they assume the form of prefabricated concrete sarcophagi, from which the retaining walls of the necropolis are systematically constructed. Here they serve to transform a disused quarry by lining its sides with deep, hollow, prefabricated units keyed together in much the same way as prefabricated interlocking concrete plates are now used to stabilize autoroute embankments. The resulting tectonic is as much gravitational as it is engineered. However, once the work of Miralles and Pinos is no longer rendered as either a rampart or a cutting, the architecture tends to degenerate into structural exhibitionism as it flies only too free of the ground to aggregate into irreconcilable cacophonic figures, as in the civic center for Hostalets of 1992 or the sports hall for Huesca of 1994.

Here then as elsewhere, we are confronted with the time-honored challenge that Paul Ricoeur once formulated as "how to become modern and return to sources,"[31] or, to put it in other terms, how to maintain the tectonic trajectory in the face of a postindustrial civilization that seeks nothing less than the reduction of the entire world to one vast commodity.

The Owl of Minerva:
An Epilogue

It is indeed unfortunate that human society should encounter such burning problems just when it has become materially impossible to make heard the least objection to the language of commodity; just when power—quite rightly because it is shielded by the spectacle from any response to its piecemeal and delirious decisions and justifications—believes that it no longer needs to think; and indeed can no longer think.

It is sometimes said that science today is subservient to the imperatives of profit, but that is nothing new. What is new is the way the economy has now come to declare open war on humanity, attacking not only our possibilities for living, but our chances of survival. It is here that science—renouncing the opposition to slavery that formed a significant part of its own history—has chosen to put itself at the service of spectacular domination. . . .

What is false creates taste, and reinforces itself by knowingly eliminating any possible reference to the authentic. And what is genuine is reconstructed as quickly as possible, to resemble the false. . . .

Feuerbach's judgement on the fact that his time preferred "the sign of the thing to the thing signified, the copy to the original, fancy to reality," has been thoroughly vindicated by the century of spectacle, and in several spheres where the nineteenth century preferred to keep its distance from what was already its fundamental nature: industrial capitalism. Thus it was that the bourgeoisie had widely disseminated the rigorous mentality of the museum, the original object, precise historical criticism, the authentic document. Today, however, the tendency to replace the real with the artificial is ubiquitous. In this regard it is fortuitous that traffic pollution has necessitated the replacement of the Marly Horses in the Place de La Concorde, or the Roman Statues in the doorway of Saint-Trophime in Arles, by plastic replicas. Everything will be more beautiful than before, for the tourist's cameras."
Guy Debord, Commentaires sur la société du spectacle, 1988

For all of its marginality, tectonic culture still possesses a vestigially resistant core, particularly as this is manifest in its proclivity for the tactile. This dimension resists the maximizing thrust of capitalism, determined now, as never before, on the process of global commodification. In this context it is regrettable that the European Community should simultaneously both patronize architecture[1] and engender its demise, as is evident from its ruthless pursuit of a unified market, irrespective of the cultural cost. An unforeseen consequence of this economic impulse has been the recent attempts on the part of various member states to undermine the authority of the architect, and with it, one should note, the capacity of the profession to be effective in the design of civic form. In this regard, EC policy seems to be moving beyond the provisions of the U.S. antitrust laws of the seventies, when the American Institute of Architects lost its right to maintain a fixed scale of fees. This destabilization of the profession has been indirectly effected through EC pressure on its community members, which in their turn have introduced national legislation that seeks to deregulate the profession by challenging its legal status. To date this stratagem has emerged to varying degrees in Spain, Britain, and Austria.[2] One assumes that other EC countries will soon be pressured into following suit.

The impact of such a reductive strategy in Spain is particularly marked for a number of reasons; first, because Spain has produced a particularly high general level of architectural culture over the past twenty years; second, because Spanish architects have enjoyed a correspondingly higher social status than in any other European country; and third, because to date the Spanish profession has been better organized than any other comparable national body. As with other Spanish liberal professions, every major city has its own *collegio de arquitectos,* whose powers have now been summarily curtailed by legislation promulgated by the Spanish parliament in October 1992, in the name of opening the country to foreign architects under the terms of the EC agreement. The fact that there were other ways by which this policy could have been effected suggests that a broader economic strategy lies behind the form that this legislation has assumed. There can be little doubt that such measures will have a deleterious effect on the overall quality of Spanish architecture, since the *collegio* served as a local "guild" that not only maintained a standard of quality but also preserved a certain sense of regional identity. This it achieved mainly through its mandate over building permissions, since until recently all plans had to be approved not only by the municipality but also by the *collegio.* Moreover, since the *collegio* was the initial recipient of the fees on behalf of the architect, from which it deducted a small percentage for its services, it also acted to prevent any undercutting of the fee structure, while at the same time insuring the architect against exploitation by unscrupulous clients who might otherwise refuse to settle their final accounts. This fiscal power also enabled the *collegio* to function as an independent cultural institution, staging exhibitions, organizing lectures, and subsidizing magazines and other publications. Whether it will be possible to maintain such activities in the future remains to be seen.

As a further consequence of its federalist policies, the EC has been attempting to restructure and shorten European architectural education. And while this may be justified as nothing more than the necessary provision of a common European curriculum for the training of architects and thus as being of the same order as pursuing a common European policy with regard to human rights, this rationalization masks a subtly reductive approach to educational reform that, in my view, is also being unduly influenced by maximizing interests. I am not thinking so much of the understandable emphasis now being placed on computer-aided design (although this too has its reductive aspects) but rather of the move to discontinue more reflective, critical methods of instruction, plus the current tendency of studio teaching to oscillate between the simplistic application of technique and the generation of fashionable images. There is, at the same time, a tendency to privilege technology as though this were an essential but totally acultural discourse.[3] The ambivalent role played by the culture industry in late modern society also emerges here in that, as I have already intimated, architecture is no more immune to the impact of the media than any other field. Hence the stress placed on photographic representation in current practice; one that often includes within its purview, however unconsciously, an entirely photogenic preconception of architectural form. And yet unlike the other plastic arts, architecture cannot even be nominally represented by a single photographic image, although this is often the mode in which it is disseminated for professional and lay public alike. Seen in this light building appears to be imagistic and perspectival rather than tactile and spatial.

In July 1993, the Spanish architect Rafael de la Hoz made the following public assessment of the restructuring then being introduced into architectural education in Spain and other European countries, as part of an EC strategy for shortening the length of architectural education with the ostensible intent of improving its efficiency and reducing its cost, a draconian transformation being carried out with precious little regard for the time it takes a student to mature or for the most appropriate way in which the knowledge of the field should be conveyed.

Trapped in the impossible situation of adapting the syllabus to the now insufficient teaching time available, faculties today are divided between "humanists" and "technologists," with each group endeavoring to exclude the other. . . . "When I am to choose between A or B," Lyautey is supposed to have said, "I assuredly should choose A + B." In any event there is no such dilemma if the time allocated for correct instruction is sufficient. However, the situation, far from being resolved, is worsening, particularly after the arrival of that other powerful coterie, favoring, the "massification" of the profession; that is today, those technocrats who want to consider architecture as just another commodity. For them, it is imperative to reduce the duration of our studies even further in order to cause a demographic explosion and increase the number of architects beyond market capacity, thereby making supply exceed demand and reducing the price for architectural services. . . . For the first time in history generations of architects are coming out of European universities that are worse prepared than their forebears. . . . Paradoxically, by trying to create more competitive architects, only less competent ones are being produced.[4]

As de la Hoz suggests, much of this restructuring may be attributed to a global policy that favors monetarist economics and the increased privatization of the public sphere, not to mention the obvious interest of maximizing builder-developers in limiting the authority of the architect. At the same time, the consolidation of the construction industry favors ever larger units of production, and this plus the increased fluidity of international capital creates a climate that is generally inimical to the critical cultivation of architectural form. This has long since been evident in the practice of the "package deal," where architectural and engineering services are provided within the industry itself. However, it has to be admitted that this integration of design and production has, on occasion, been able to produce works of outstanding quality. This is particularly true in the case of Japan, where large contracting firms have been able to produce works of exceptional refinement.

Despite this corporatization of the industry, the independent architect still continues to practice, particularly at the small and intermediate scale, not only as a designer but also, at times, as a general contractor and project manager.[5] This is especially the case in Switzerland, where the architect has traditionally organized the building process into its respective stages and further controlled the operation not only through strict site supervision but also through the direct selection of subcontractors. In all this, the architect is dependent on the competence of specialized fabricators and above all on his own capacity for integrating the various trades and components. This skill has also been displayed by highly disciplined, so-called "high-tech" architectural practices, which have often gone outside the traditional building industry to find components of an otherwise unattainable finish and performance.[6]

These different procedures both professionally and productively seem to correspond to two rival tendencies in late modern economy: on the one hand, a vestigial Fordism[7] entailing guaranteed markets and rather large amounts of investment; on the other, a more hybrid approach to production fed by a more flexible accumulation of both capital and resources. In general, we may say that where the former tends to directly satisfy the market demand that arises "spontaneously," as it were, out of the convergence of consumerism with bureaucratic norms, the latter strives to transcend such limitations and in so doing to respond in a more articulated and reflective way to specific requirements and local conditions. Moreover, where the one seeks a relatively prompt return on the investment and hence is only marginally concerned about the durability of the product, the other displays the tendency to make a more fundamental commitment to the permanence of the work and to its appropriate maturation over time.[8] In other words, where the one optimizes commodification, the other tends to resist it.

One needs to set these alternatives in a larger historical context, one that recognizes not only the general parameters of the postmodern condition but also the way in which the generic building process has radically changed in the last century and a half. In so doing one has to acknowledge the extent to which the second half of this century has seen the erosion of almost every fundamental reference, even to the extent of eclipsing the utopian tradition of the "new." Not least among the consequences of this process has been the decline of the welfare state and the emergence of multinational capitalism. These transformations are perhaps only symptoms of a profounder value crisis, covering a wide range of experience. One recalls in this context such reactionary formations as the rise of fundamentalist religion and the proliferation of small regional conflicts having an arcane and brutal character. All of this transpires in a climate in which the idea of progress is by no means as assured as it was in the first quarter of the present century. The perpetual amelioration of the human condition is a vision that is difficult to sustain in a world in which the rate of technological change has escalated beyond our capacity to assimilate it. This is most evident, perhaps, from the way in which nature is being ravaged by technology to such an extent that, for the first time, the survival of the species is called into question. Thus while the escalating process of modernization continues unabated, the concept of modernity as an ideal has lost its conviction. Mallarmé's slogan "Il faut être absolument moderne" carries little assurance as a call to arms in an age in which the *novum* is no longer new in the same euphoric sense. Moreover, despite the advances of technoscience as these may be discretely applied for the benefit of human life, one remains apprehensive about the tendency of technology to become a new nature covering the entire globe. Against this tendency, the phenomenon of uneven development is a redeeming influence in that building, like agriculture, tends to be grounded in time-honored processes that are essentially anachronistic.

At the same time one has nonetheless to recognize the critical impact that countless technical innovations have had upon the character of the built environment; innovations that since the end of the eighteenth century have brought about the progressive dematerialization of built form, together with the all too literal mechanization and electrification of its fabric. This penetration of electromechanical technique into tectonic form has been accompanied by many now familiar improvements in the construction and equipment of buildings, ranging from devices as singular as the invention of the balloon frame in 1834 to a more comprehensive incorporation of electromechanical technique, including plumbing, central heating, electric lighting, air-conditioning, and of late a whole range of increasingly exotic communicational devices. As R. Gregory Turner indicates in his study *Construction Economics and Building Design: A Historical Approach,* these innovations together with the major changes wrought by the introduction of steel and reinforced concrete construction have had the effect of shifting the focus away from the relatively undifferentiated mass of traditional stereotomic construction to the articulation of built form into the Semperian categories of podium, "hearth," frame, and envelope. Turner shows that in the past thirty-five years each of these components has grown increasingly independent and has developed its own economic criteria. As he puts it: "Separate design professionals, consultants, craftsmen and code officials each focus on one component and are occasionally contracted with individually by clients. Design now consists of an architect devising an envelope and infill that will conceal the work of structural, mechanical, electrical, and plumbing engineers."[9]

Irrespective of Turner's indifference to the cultural consequences of this ever-proliferating division of labor, there is no denying that while load-bearing masonry was one of the main means of enclosing space from archaic times to the Baroque, it thereafter tended to become greatly reduced in thickness and eventually became transposed into a thin lightweight membrane that either enveloped or subdivided the basic volume. We already sense a recognition of this change in Paxton's characterization of the Crystal Palace as a table covered with a tablecloth, while Edward Ford has described this development as an abandonment of the monolithic in favor of a layered fabric, particularly during the last quarter of the nineteenth century and first two decades of the twentieth.[10]

This dematerialization of building has since been taken further by the development of gypsum, dry-wall construction, the introduction of glass-reinforced fiber products, and the advent of high-strength glues and sealants that facilitate the application of a wide variety of veneers, ranging from plywood to thin layers of machine-cut stone. Turner proceeds to show that while the cost of the earthwork/podium has remained relatively stable at about 12½ percent of the budget of a building, mechanical services have risen to consume some 35 percent since the late nineteenth century. At the same time with the transition from load-bearing wall to skeleton frame construction, the amount devoted to the basic structure has dropped from around 80 percent in former times to some 20 percent today. Conversely the amount allocated to lightweight partitioning has risen from 3 to 20 percent, thereby leaving around 12½ percent to be devoted to the building envelope. That we spend more today on building services than on any other single item is surely indicative of the importance we now attach to environmental control. This maximization of comfort, verging on gratuitous consumption, leads, as D. Andrew Vernooy has argued, to a phenomenological and cultural devaluation of the tectonic and to a state affairs in which *simulation* rather than *presentation* and *representation* becomes the main expressive mode.

The seminal achievements of heroic Modernism, which used the structural system as the syntactic basis of configuration, are now difficult to duplicate in the context of current ordinance and performance. . . . For the most part, the envelope has been relieved of the burden of structural clarity. . . . Faced with the need to reconsider the plastic responsibility of the exterior wall, one asks to what

What all of these works demonstrate in different ways is a mastery over the means of production and an ability to break down the construction of a building into its constituent parts and to use this articulation as a stratagem bestowing an appropriate character on the work in hand. This regionally inflected but universal approach highlights the crossroads at which the profession stands, for the fact is that either architects will maintain their control over the *métier* of building design, irrespective of the scale at which it occurs, or the profession as we know it will cease to exist. We may say that the profession will either rise to the occasion by coming to terms with the transformed techno-economic character of building or it will be overwhelmed by the thrust of development, by escalating rate of change, and by all the special interests, large and small, that these combined forces bring in their wake. Whether architects will be able to reposition themselves with sufficient pertinence and rigor as to be able to resist or mediate these forces remains to be seen. In any event, indicators suggest that they will only be able to do so in a sporadic and interstitial way since late capitalism displays an indifference toward tectonic culture at many different levels, from its disdain for the physical and historical continuity of civic form to its latent disregard for the wholesale entropy of the built environment as it presently exists. One thing seems certain, that except for relatively small or prestigious commissions, the architect will have little prospect of maintaining control over every single aspect of the fabric. As we have seen, this is in part due to the increased technological character of building that today has attained such a complexity that no single practitioner can master all the processes involved. Thus it will be increasingly incumbent upon the architect to direct the different sectors of the industry to design their respective components in support of an overriding tectonic paradigm, and then to refine the combined result through a process of careful coordination. Even now, this is the only means by which large constructions can be orchestrated in a responsible way. Through such methodical stratagems architects are enabled to reinstate their authority and to overcome, as it were, the redundancy of the somewhat circular working drawing–shop drawing procedure as it presently exists. Such operational refinements will increasingly depend on the coordinating capacity of the computer and on the ability of architects to understand the constraints and tolerances of the procedures involved. Surely no one has foreseen the cultural potential of this cybernetic approach with greater optimism than Piano's prime collaborator, the engineer Peter Rice, who wrote of his role in the design of the Centre Pompidou in the following way:

By using the castings as the main building joints, the shapes and form were liberated from the standard industrial language. The public could see the individual design preference. Modern computers and analysis techniques and modern testing methods made this possible. We were back to the freedom of our Victorian forefathers. The individual details were exploited to give a personal design philosophy full rein. The final design was of course the work of more than one person. Many architects, engineers and craftsmen at the foundry contributed to the actual shape of each piece. And each piece was subject to the rigors of detailed structural analysis to ensure that it was fit for its purpose in every way and this too influenced the shape and final configuration. But this does not matter. The pieces are indeed better for all the different expertise which went into their make-up. They are more logical, more self-evidently correct in their form. What matters is that they are free of the industrial tyranny. They require people to look and perceive so that they may understand. This brings to mind another myth about technology. The feeling that technological choice is always the result of a predetermined logic. The feeling that there is a correct solution to a technical question is very common. But a technical solution like any other decision is a moment in time. It is not definitive. The decision is the result of a complex process where a lot of information is analyzed and examined and choices made on the evidence. It is a moment in time and place where the people, their background and their talent is paramount. What is often missing is the evidence of human intervention, the black box syndrome. So by looking at new materials, or at old materials in a new way we change the rules. People become visible again.[17]

For all that Rice's tone is technocratic, he patently alludes to a poetic formal dimension that is capable of transcending instrumentality as an end in itself. He is thus concerned with the revelation of the human spirit, through the specific manner in which a work comes to be collectively developed and realized. As an engineer he understood only too well that a technological device is a cultural choice and not simply a matter of reductive logic. This surely is the stand of the critical intellect against the mindless optimizing process of our "spectacular" bureaucracies, against the current tendency to maximize any one single value irrespective of the costs involved, whether environmental or otherwise. Truth, as Le Corbusier wrote, does not now lie in extremes; it lies, as he put it with self-deprecating irony, in a constant struggle to maintain a state of equilibrium whatever one's metier. Hence the wider ideological implications of his beautiful metaphor of the architect as acrobat. "Nobody asked him to do this. Nobody owes him any thanks. He lives in the extraordinary world of the acrobat."[18]

But are we not all in the last analysis acrobats, that is to say, is not the species as a whole caught on its technological high wire from which if it finally falls it will be impossible to recover? In the meantime the culture of the tectonic still persists as a testament to the spirit: the poetics of construction. All the rest, including our much-vaunted manipulation of space, is mixed up with the lifeworld, and in this it belongs as much to society as to ourselves.

Caroline van Eck shows how Schinkel's concern for the reconciliation of intellectual freedom with natural law may be traced back to Schlegel's *Kunstlehre* of 1801–1802. See Bergdoll, *Karl Friedrich Schinkel,* p. 48, and Caroline van Eck, *Organicism in Nineteenth Century Architecture: An Inquiry into Its Theoretical and Philosophical Background* (Amsterdam: Architectura and Natura Press, 1994), pp. 114–124.

23
Kurt W. Forster, "Schinkel's Panoramic Planning of Central Berlin," p. 74.

24
In his *History of the Modern Styles of Architecture* of 1862, James Ferguson wrote of the Bauakademie: "The ornamentation depends wholly on the construction, consisting only of piers between the windows, string-cornices marking the floors, a slight cornice, and the dressings of the windows and doors. All of these are elegant, and so far nothing can be more truthful or appropriate, the whole being of brick, which is visible everywhere. Notwithstanding all this, the Bauschule cannot be considered as entirely successful, in consequence of its architect not taking sufficiently into consideration the nature of the material he was about to employ in deciding on its general characteristics. Its simple outline would have been admirably suited to a Florentine or Roman palace built of large blocks of stone, or to a granite edifice anywhere; but it was a mistake to adopt so severe an outline in an edifice to be constructed of such small materials as bricks. Had Schinkel brought forward the angles of his building and made them more solid in appearance, he would have improved it to a great extent."

25
Schinkel, while appreciative of Hirt's erudition, did not approve of his academicism, and this led to a widening gulf between them culminating in Hirt's pedantic criticism of the Altes Museum.

26
See Arthur Schopenhauer, *Die Welt als Wille und Vorstellung* (The World as Will and Idea, 1819), English translation in *The Works of Schopenhauer,* ed. Will Durant (New York: Ungar, 1955), pp. 131–133:

For just because each part bears just as much as it conveniently can, and each is supported just where it requires to be and just to the necessary extent, this opposition unfolds itself, this conflict between rigidity and gravity, which constitutes the life, the manifestation of will, in the stone, becomes completely visible, and these lowest grades of the objectivity of will reveal themselves distinctly. In the same way the form of each part must not be determined arbitrarily, but by its end, and its relation to the whole. The column is the simplest form of support, determined simply by its end. . . . All this proves that architecture does not affect us mathematically, but also dynamically, and that what speaks to us through it is not mere form and symmetry, but rather those fundamental forces of nature, those first Ideas, those lowest grades of the objectivity of will. The regularity of the building and its parts is partly produced by the direct adaptation of each member to the stability of the whole, partly it serves to facilitate the survey and comprehension of the whole, and finally, regular figures to some extent enhance the beauty because they reveal the constitution of space as such. But all this is of subordinate value and necessity, and by no means the chief concern; indeed symmetry is not invariably demanded, as ruins are still beautiful.

27
See Mitchell Schwarzer, "Ontology and Representation in Karl Bötticher's Theory of Tectonics," *Journal of the Society of Architectural Historians* 52 (September 1993), p. 276.

28
Wolfgang Herrmann, *Gottfried Semper: In Search of Architecture* (Cambridge, Mass.: MIT Press, 1984), p. 141. Herrmann is quoting from Karl Bötticher's *Die Tektonik der Hellenen,* 2 vols. (Potsdam, 1852), vol. 1, p. xv.

29
Herrmann, *Gottfried Semper,* p. 141.

30
There is a difference between the position adopted in *Die Tektonik der Hellenen* and the 1846 essay. In the former the fusion of Hellenic and Germanic styles is style solely as a matter of cultural synthesis; in the later text it is made dependent on the new material, iron.

31
Karl Bötticher, "The Principles of the Hellenic and Germanic Way of Building," trans. Wolfgang Herrmann in *In What Style Should We Build,* p. 158.

32
Ibid., p. 159.

33
Ibid., p. 163.

34
The issue of polychromy in antique Greek sculpture had first been raised by the publication of Quatremère de Quincy's text "Le Jupiter Olympien" in 1816. However, Quatremère resisted the idea of polychromy in architecture except insofar as it arose out of the natural color of the materials themselves. The possibility that the Greeks painted their temples was advanced again by Leo von Klenze's colored reconstruction of the temple at Aegina in Hittorf's *L'Architecture polychrome chez les Grecs* of 1827 and by Henri Labrouste's *envoi* from the French Academy in Rome in 1828 consisting of his reconstruction of the Greek temples at Paestum.

35
Harry Francis Mallgrave, "Gustave Klemm and Gottfried Semper," *Res* (Spring 1985), p. 76.

36
Rosemarie Haag Bletter, "On Martin Fröhlich's Gottfried Semper," *Oppositions* 4 (October 1974), p. 148.

37
In *De l'architecture égyptienne,* his 1803 rewriting of his 1785 entry to the competition of the Académie Royale des Inscriptions et Belles-Lettres, Quatremère de Quincy posited a triadic origin to all building: the tent, the cave, and the hut.

38
Joseph Rykwert, "Semper and the Conception of Style," in *Gottfried Semper und die Mitte des 19. Jahrhunderts* (Basel and Stuttgart: Birkhäuser, 1976), pp. 77–78.

39
Ibid., p. 72.

40
Ibid.

41
However, as for Ruskin and Pugin, the Crystal Palace was a traumatic form for Semper. He saw it as a vacuum enclosed by glass and thereafter thought it essential that the use of iron should be tempered by the deployment of masonry forms.

42
In his 1987 essay "Gottfried Semper, architetto e teorico," Benedetto Gravagnuolo cites those various fragmented passages in *Moderne Architektur* in which Wagner criticizes Semper for not having insisted sufficiently that architecture always derives from the principle of construction and that new constructional means must eventually produce new constructional forms: "In his way Otto Wagner is correct in maintaining that Semper didn't push himself to the extreme consequence of the modern project. His architecture remains arrested before the problematic threshold of the symbolic status of building. . . . In his discourse about building there was a kernel of inertia . . . that remained opposed to taking an integral and a critical view about the triumph of hegemonic modernization over the collective values of civilization and the ethnological culture to which it belongs. The modern theory that new form necessarily arises from new techniques is absent from his discourse. Style for Semper must not follow function but must represent through architecture the feeling of an epoch." See *Gottfried Semper: architettura, arte e scienza* (Naples, 1987), p. 34.

43
See James Duncan Berry, "The Legacy of Gottfried Semper: Studies in Späthistoricismus," Ph.D. dissertation, in the History of Art and Archi-

tecture, Brown University, 1989. I am totally indebted to Duncan Barry for his study of Georg Heuser.

44
See Otto Wagner, *Modern Architecture,* trans. Harry Mallgrave (Santa Monica: Getty Center for the History of Art and the Humanities, 1988), pp. 91–99. The text is from the 1902 edition, but for these passages the 1914 version is virtually the same.

45
I am indebted to Mitchell Schwarzer for drawing my attention to Bötticher's later use of the term *Werkform* to refer to technically innovative constructional form. Schwarzer, "Ontology and Representation," pp. 278–280.

46
Gottfried Semper, "Style in the Technical and Tectonic Arts or Practical Aesthetics," in Harry Mallgrave and Wolfgang Herrmann, eds., *Gottfried Semper: The Four Elements and Other Writings* (Cambridge: Cambridge University Press, 1989), pp. 257–258.

47
Fritz Neumeyer, "Iron and Stone: The Architecture of the Grossstadt," in Harry Mallgrave, ed., *Otto Wagner: Reflections on the Raiment of Modernity,* (Santa Monica: Getty Center for the History of Art and the Humanities, 1993), p. 135.

48
See Schwarzer, "Ontology and Representation," p. 280. Of the part played by *Einfühlung* implicitly in Wagner and by anticipation, so to speak, in the case of Bötticher, Schwarzer writes, with regard to Richard Streiter's critique of Bötticher's *Tektonik* in 1896: "Bötticher's theory represents an ideological bridge between the speculative aesthetics of Sulzer, Moritz and Schelling and the ideas of projective visuality and *Einfühlung* (empathy) that later appeared in the writings of Conrad Fiedler, Adolf Hildebrand and Theodor Lipps."

4   Frank Lloyd Wright and the Text-Tile Tectonic

Epigraph: Grant Carpenter Manson, *Frank Lloyd Wright to 1910: The First Golden Age* (New York: Reinhold, 1958), pp. 38–39.

1
Barry Bergdoll, "Primordial Fires: Frank Lloyd Wright, Gottfried Semper and the Chicago School" (paper delivered at Buell Center Symposium on Fallingwater, Columbia University, 8 November 1986), p. 4.

2
Roula Geraniotis, "Gottfried Semper and the Chicago School" (paper delivered at Buell Center Symposium on the German influence on American architects, Columbia University, 1988) p. 5.

3
Donald Hoffman, *The Architecture of John Wellborn Root* (Baltimore and London: Johns Hopkins University Press, 1973), p. 91. See also J. A. Chewing's entry on Root in *Macmillan Encyclopedia of Architects* (New York: Free Press, 1982), vol. 3, p. 606.

4
Geraniotis, "Gottfried Semper," p. 5.

5
Ibid., p. 11.

6
David Van Zanten, entry on Owen Jones in *Macmillan Encyclopedia of Architects,* vol. 2, p. 514.

7
Louis Sullivan, "Suggestions in Artistic Brickwork" (1910), reprint, *Prairie School Review* 4 (Second Quarter, 1967), p. 24.

8
Frank Lloyd Wright, "In the Cause of Architecture IV," *Architectural Record,* October 1927; reprinted in *In the Cause of Architecture: Essays by Frank Lloyd Wright for Architectural Record, 1908–1952,* ed. Frederick Gutheim (New York: McGraw-Hill, 1975), p. 146.

9
James F. O'Gorman, *The Architecture of Frank Furness* (Philadelphia: Philadelphia Museum of Art, 1973), pp. 33, 37.

10
Narciso Menocal, *Architecture as Nature: The Transcendentalist Idea of Louis Sullivan* (Madison: University of Wisconsin Press, 1981), pp. 7, 31.

11
Owen Jones, *The Grammar of Ornament* (1856; reprint, New York: Portland House, 1987), p. 154.

12
Ibid., p. 5.

13
Ibid., p. 95.

14
Ibid., p. 156.

15
Louis Sullivan, *A System of Architectural Ornament According with a Philosophy of Man's Power* (1924; reprint, New York: Eakins Press, 1966), text accompanying plate 3.

16
Gottfried Semper, *The Four Elements of Architecture and Other Writings,* trans. Harry Mallgrave and Wolfgang Herrmann (New York: Cambridge University Press, 1989). See in particular the prolegomena to "Style in the Technical and Tectonic Arts" (1860), p. 196.

17
Rudolf Gelpke, "Art and Sacred Drugs in the Orient," *World Cultures and Modern Art* (Munich: Bruckman, 1972), pp. 18–21. Gelpke argues after Georg Jacob and Henri Michaux that the culture of Islam has a mystical hallucinatory origin.

18
Claude Humbert, *Islamic Ornamental Design* (New York: Hastings House, 1980), pp. 13, 16, 17.

19
Frank Lloyd Wright, *Frank Lloyd Wright: Writings and Buildings,* ed. Edgar Kaufman and Ben Raeburn (New York: Horizon Press, 1960), pp. 57–58.

20
Ibid., pp. 65–66.

21
Sigfried Giedion, *Space, Time and Architecture,* 15th ed. (Cambridge, Mass.: Harvard University Press, 1967), pp. 353–354. See also p. 347 for an illustration of St. Mary's Church, Chicago, of 1833, the first all-balloon-frame building.

22
Romeo and Juliet was refaced in board and batten in 1939.

23
Kenneth Martin Kao, "Frank Lloyd Wright: Experiments in the Art of Building," *Modulus* 22 (University of Virginia, 1993), p. 77. Kao shows the wood-siding details for six successive houses, including the Gerts Double Cottage of 1902.

24
G. C. Manson, "Wright in the Nursery: The Influence of Froebel Education on the Work of Frank Lloyd Wright," *Architectural Review,* June 1953, pp. 349–351. Of the 20 Froebel "gifts," numbers 14, 15, and 17 are of particular importance since they directly involve the art of weaving. It is also interesting to note, with regard to the importance that Semper attached to music and dance, that the more advanced Froebel exercises also entail music and dance wherein the geometric-relationship "gifts" would be acted out three-dimensionally.

25
Frank Lloyd Wright, "On Building Unity Temple," in *Frank Lloyd Wright: Writings and Buildings,* p. 76.

26
Wright, *Frank Lloyd Wright: Writings and Buildings,* p. 225.

27

It is generally accepted that Wright's post facto dating of some of his early projects was not always reliable.

28

David A. Hanks, *The Decorative Designs of Frank Lloyd Wright* (New York: Dutton, 1979), p. 120. It is interesting to note that these blocks had green and red flushed glass laid into their perforations.

29

Wright was working on the Barnsdall House from 1916 to 1918 prior to the final establishment of the Olive Hill site. Subject to a tight budget, Wright elected to build the house out of brick and lath and plaster on concrete foundations. The finials, lintels, sills, and copings of the house were out of precast concrete, so-called "art-stone." See Kathryn Smith, *Frank Lloyd Wright: Hollyhock House and Olive Hill* (New York: Rizzoli, 1992), pp. 119–120.

30

It has come to light that the Millard House was not built with Wright's patent hollow-walled textile block system of 1923. In this pioneering work, the two leaves of the block were closely interlocked. See Robert L. Sweeney, *Wright in Hollywood* (Cambridge: MIT Press, 1994), pp. 20–21.

31

Wright, *Frank Lloyd Wright: Writings and Buildings,* pp. 215–216.

32

Frank Lloyd Wright, "In the Cause of Architecture. VIII. Sheet Metal and a Modern Instance," *Architectural Record,* October 1928; reprinted in *In the Cause of Architecture,* pp. 217–219.

33

M. F. Hearn, "A Japanese Inspiration for Frank Lloyd Wright's Rigid-Core High-Rise Structures," *Journal of the Society of Architectural Historians* (March 1991), p. 70.

34

Ibid. Reference to D. Seckel, *The Art of Buddhism* (New York: Crown, 1963), pp. 121–122.

35

Kathryn Smith, *Frank Lloyd Wright: Hollyhock House and Olive Hill,* relates this goal to the practice of using decorative grillage in Islamic architecture known by the term *mashrabiya.*

36

For details of these blocks, see Sweeney, *Frank Lloyd Wright in Hollywood,* pp. 189–191.

37

Frank Lloyd Wright, *An American Architecture* (New York: Horizon, 1955), p. 218.

38

See the entire issue dedicated to the work of Wright, *Architectural Forum,* January 1938, p. 79.

39

John Sergeant, *Frank Lloyd Wright's Usonian Houses* (New York: Whitney Library of Design, 1976), p. 19.

40

Jonathan Lipman, *Frank Lloyd Wright and the Johnson Wax Buildings* (New York: Rizzoli, 1986), pp. 8–12.

41

Frank Lloyd Wright, *An Autobiography* (London: Faber & Faber, 1945), p. 472.

5   Auguste Perret and Classical Rationalism

Epigraph: Leonardo Benevolo, *Storia dell'architettura moderna* (Cambridge, Mass.: MIT Press, 1971), pp. 327–331. English translation of a two-volume Italian history first published in 1960.

1

See Peter Collins, *Concrete: The Vision of a New Architecture* (London: Faber & Faber, 1959), pp. 174, 175. The otherwise impeccably consistent text is contradictory on this point. Collins insists on Claude-Marie Perret's antipathy to concrete, claiming that no works of the firm could be carried out in this material until after his death in 1905, and yet he knew only too well that 25 bis rue Franklin was executed in this material.

2

For Julien Guadet see Reyner Banham, *Theory and Design in the First Machine* (New York: Praeger, 1960).

3

See Banham, *Theory and Design in the First Machine Age,* p. 30. Of Choisy's influence on Perret, Banham writes of "Auguste Perret's transposition of wood-framing technique on to reinforced construction, [as] a procedure which he, apparently, held to be warranted by Choisy. . . . But Perret's structural methods owe a further debt than this to Choisy, and to his views on Gothic structure in particular. Gothic, as has been said, was one of Choisy's two preferred styles, because it constitutes in his eyes, the culmination of logical method in structure." Here Banham quotes Choisy to the effect that "the [Gothic] structure is the triumph of logic in art; the building becomes an organized being whose every part constitutes a living member, its form governed not by traditional models but by its function, and only its function." Later Banham continues, in the chapter dealing with the French protomodern academic succession: "The three pre-1914 buildings [25 bis rue Franklin, the rue Ponthieu garage, and the Théâtre des Champs-Elysées] depend, as Perret himself admitted, on a Choisyesque transposition of reinforced concrete into the forms and usages of wooden construction—a rectangular trabeated grid of posts and beams. This procedure which makes little use of the monolithic qualities and less of the plastic ones of the material, the assertions of Perret's followers notwithstanding, appears to have a complicated derivation" (p. 38).

4

Auguste Perret, *Contribution à une théorie de l'architecture* (Paris: Cercle d'études architecturales André Wahl, 1952), unpaginated. (First published in *Das Werk* 34–35 [February 1947]).

5

Collins, *Concrete,* p. 186.

6

For the most exhaustive recent treatment of the complex history behind the building of this theater see Dossiers du Musée d'Orsay no. 15, *1913 Le Théatre des Champs-Elysées* (Paris: Editions de la Réunion des Musées Nationaux, 1987), pp. 4–72. Particular attention should be given to Claude Loupiac's essay "Le Ballet des architectes" in which he shows how four architects were commissioned in succession: first Henri Fivax in 1906, then Roger Bouvard between 1908 and 1910, and then Henri Van de Velde and Bouvard together in 1911. Auguste Perret was asked to collaborate with Van de Velde in May of that year and shortly after was able to gain complete control over the work, following Van de Velde's resignation in July.

7

Ibid., p. 242.

8

Vittorio Gregotti, "Auguste Perret, 1874–1974: Classicism and Rationalism in Perret," *Domus,* no. 534 (May 1974), p. 19.

9

Collins, *Concrete,* p. 254.

10

Ibid., p. 217.

11

Peter Collins, "Perret, Auguste," *Macmillan Encyclopaedia of Architects* (New York: Free Press, 1982), vol. 3, p. 394.

12

Henri Bressler, "Windows on the Court," *Rassegna* 28 (1979).

13

See Bressler, "Windows on the Court." The English translation in this unpaginated appendix describes the dichotomous character of the interior space at 25 bis rue Franklin: in the following terms:

From the entrance hall the triptych doors give onto three main rooms like a miniature of the stage of the Teatro Olimpico. In the center, the room is lit by a large bow-window, which corresponds symmetrically to the entrance niche where a console stands and is (potentially) surmounted by a mirror. On the sides, the rooms split, offering oblique visual axes which reveal the apartment's largest perceptible dimensions. In the center of the main hall it appears as if there were only one large room which regresses to infinity thanks to the many mirrors laid out face to face on the small fireplaces of the dining and main rooms. In truth, here all elements are part of this spatial explosion: the diagonal position of the partitions, of doors and windows, the transparency and reflections of the double glass doors and the light channeled into the splay of the loggias which are reflected in the mirrors. Thus we stand, plunged into an almost magic, marvelous box, despite its limited size. . . . It is certainly true, however, that such a device able to multiply doors and double doors at will (there are seven double doors in the entrance gallery) turns out to be rather difficult to furnish. A few consoles, chests of drawers or clothes closets can be set against the remaining free wall spaces. . . . To ensure that this arrangement, which opens as an integral unit, might rediscover the virtues of a true apartment, Perret cut the walls back until they seem like panels, he redesigned the door springers and underscored the ensemble with the figures of the different rooms: stylobates, moldings, vegetation-motif frames; he manages to somehow reuse the entire catalogue of definitions of the traditional lodging. In short, he in no way attempted to violate the boundaries of lifestyles and their social codes of behavior: the apartment must lend itself fully to the reception ritual; it appears that even the Baroness of Staffe in person might be received in this apartment.

Once within the main hall, guests may cross through the double glass doors in proper order, with arms linked, and enter the dining room. After dinner, the gentlemen can retire to the fumoir, *while the ladies reach the "gynaeceum" of the lady-of-the-house, and, the most intimate among them, the boudoir. All present may then meet again in the main hall to delight in some sort of merry-making. The main rooms lend themselves to the reception device. All is offered to sight, multiplied by the effects of light and mirrors. Nothing keeps the guests from believing that the hall doors—access to facilities and bathrooms—do not lead to bedrooms.*

If you seek, instead, some place amenable to intimacy, suffice to close the doors and pull a curtain or two; each room, with the exception of the fumoir *(whose access runs oblique to the dining room), is completely autonomous.*

In my view this dichotomous arrangement, so precisely described by Bressler, anticipates the ambivalent but equally illusionistic devices that Louis Kahn will employ, seventy years later, in the Kimbell Art Museum at Fort Worth, Texas, when he will attempt to combine the traditional gallery of discrete rooms with open flexible loft space.

14
Bruno Reichlin, "The Pros and Cons of the Horizontal Window: The Perret-Le Corbusier Controversy," *Daidalos* 13 (September 1984), pp. 71–82.

15
Collins, *Concrete*, pp. 206–207.

16
Ibid., p. 208.

17
See Steen Eiler Rasmussen, *Experiencing Architecture* (Cambridge: MIT Press, 1964), chapter 10, "Hearing Architecture."

18
It is interesting to note that even in repetitive domestic work, as in the apartments designed for Le Havre, Perret attempted unsuccessfully to eliminate plasterwork and suspended ceilings. See Collins, *Concrete*, p. 275.

19
The following excerpts are from Perret, *Contribution à une théorie de l'architecture* (unpaginated).

20
Marie Dormoy, "Interview d'Auguste Perret sur l'Exposition internationale des arts décoratifs," *L'Amour de l'Art,* May 1925, p. 174.

21
Denis Honegger, "Auguste Perret: doctrine de l'architecture," *Techniques & Architecture* 9, nos. 1–2 (1949), p. 111.

22
Perret, *Contribution à une théorie de l'architecture.*

23
One is reminded in this of the German word for object, *Gegenstand,* meaning literally to "stand against."

24
Perret, *Contribution à une théorie de l'architecture.*

25
Paul Valéry, "The History of Amphion," in *The Collected Works of Paul Valéry,* ed. Jackson Mathews, vol. 3 (Princeton: Princeton University Press, 1960), p. 215. Valéry published *Eupalinos ou l'architecte* in 1921. In an unpublished analysis of this text (1985), Georgios I. Simeoforidis has written: "This is an important text that has not yet found its acknowledgement from and within architectural culture. Valéry's interest in architecture was a product of his own *durée* . . . architecture was Valéry's first love, an *amour* for the construction of both ships and building. Valéry was very interested in naval architecture following his other love, his *amour* for the sea, the Mediterranean sea. His philosophical . . . thought is a liaison between *construction* and *knowing,* a liaison that he finds in the architect, but also in the poet and the thinker. All are concerned with a process that has two moments: analysis and synthesis, repetition and composition. The poet is an architect of poems, the architect is a poet of buildings; both 'construct' through mental work. Valéry gives to construction a specific quality, as making and doing, *faire.* . . . It is ultimately this idea of *poiein, faire,* that could be extremely significant in architecture, especially if we understand the word construction, in the physical and mental range of its manifestation, as an act that has to have a form and a memory."

26
I am indebted for much of this to an unpublished essay on Paul Valéry by Georgios Simeoforidis, particularly for his reference to the work of the Greek architect and theoretician Panayiotis Michelis and his distinction between the tectonic/paratactic order of classicism and the monolithic/organic order of concrete. Clearly Michelis's *The Aesthetics of Concrete Architecture* deserves to be translated from the Greek and hence to be better known. Among Simeoforidis's sources it is worth mentioning *Paul Valéry Méditerranéen* by Gabriel Fauré (Paris: Les Horizons de France, 1954).

27
With the term *homo faber* (man the maker), I am alluding to the profound insights to be found in Hannah Arendt's *The Human Condition* (Chicago: University of Chicago Press, 1958), pp. 158–174. She writes: "If one permits the standards of *homo faber* to rule the finished world . . . then *homo faber* will eventually help himself to everything as though it belongs to the class of *chremata,* of use objects, so that to follow Plato's example, the wind will no longer be understood in its own right as a natural force but will be considered exclusively in accordance with human needs for warmth or refreshment—which, of course, means that the wind as something objectively given has been eliminated from human experience." Later she writes (p. 173): "If the *animal laborans* needs the help of *homo faber* to ease his labor and remove his pain and if mortals need his help to erect a home on earth, acting and speaking men need the help of *homo faber* in his highest capacity, that is, the help of the artist, of poets and historiographers, of monument-builders or writers, because without them, the only product of their activity, the story they enact and tell, would not survive at all."

28
Collins, *Concrete*, pp. 157, 158.

29
Perret, *Contribution à une théorie de l'architecture.*

30
Collins, *Concrete*, p. 163. It is ironic to say the least that this argument would come so close to paraphrasing the so called Law of Ruins promulgated by Albert Speer under the Third Reich. For Speer, however, it was reinforced concrete that was seen as the nemesis, since as far as he was concerned this material was incapable of producing sublime

38
Graeme Shankland, "Architect of the 'Clear and Reasonable': Mies van der Rohe," *The Listener,* 15 October 1959, pp. 620–622.

7   Louis Kahn: Modernization and the New Monumentality, 1944–1972

Epigraph: Maria Bottero, "Organic and Rational Morphology in the Architecture of Louis Kahn," *Zodiac* 17 (1967), pp. 244, 245.

1
Sigfried Giedion, José Luis Sert, and Fernand Léger, "Nine Points on Monumentality," in Sigfried Giedion, *Architecture, You and Me* (Cambridge: Harvard University Press, 1958), pp. 48–52.

2
See Paul Zucker, ed., *The New Architecture and City Planning* (New York: Philosophical Library, 1944).

3
Louis I. Kahn, "Monumentality," in Zucker, ed., *The New Architecture and City Planning,* pp. 578–579.

4
Ibid., pp. 579–580.

5
Ibid., p. 580.

6
Ibid., pp. 581–582. However, as Pol Abraham was to observe, the cross ribs of a Gothic vault are at times structurally redundant and are deployed for formal reasons and to facilitate assembly. See Pol Abraham, *Viollet-le-Duc et le rationalisme médiéval* (Paris: Vincent Fréal, 1934).

7
For details of this construction see David P. Billington, *Robert Maillart and the Art of Reinforced Concrete* (Cambridge, Mass.: Architectural History Foundation and MIT Press, 1990), pp. 28–29.

8
Information given by Anne Griswold Tyng to the author in February 1993. When Tyng was in Rome in the fall of 1953 she showed the City Tower project to Nervi, who regarded the proposed structure as a three-dimensional version of his two-dimensional "folded" and triangulated concrete structures.

9
Louis Kahn, "Form and Design," *Architectural Design* 31, no. 4 (April 1961), pp. 145–148. Kahn's distinction between form and design was to reverse in many respects the emphasis that Mies van der Rohe placed upon the "how" of architecture rather than the "what." That the "what" was of more importance to Kahn was largely due to his profound commitment to the institution, or what he called an "availability" in a civic and spiritual sense. In "Form and Design" he would write: "Form is 'what', Design is 'how'. Form is impersonal. Design belongs to the Designer. Design is a circumstantial act, how much money there is available, the site, the client, the extent of knowledge. Form has nothing to do with circumstantial conditions. In architecture it characterizes a harmony of spaces good for a certain activity of man."

To these distinctions Maria Bottero would add the following illuminating gloss in her essay "Organic and Rational Morphology in the Architecture of Louis Kahn": "The Psyche is the source of what a thing wants to be . . . he means that life (or the drive towards *being*) runs through us but does not belong to us individually, so that man finds himself curiously decentralized with respect to his own work: which as Kahn himself says, is an achievement all the greater, the less it pertains to *Design* (i.e. the contingent, measurable, and subjective) and the more it belongs to *Form* (i.e. the transcendental, immeasurable, and universal). Between *Form* and *Design,* the creative process takes place as an indefinitely repeated shuttling process, and by this the plot of the work is laboriously woven; a plot which is a strip stretched across the non-homogeneous, the non-continuous, or in the end—the unconscious."

10
Anne Tyng manifests that this expressive dilemma was overcome to some extent by the invention of post-tensioned, reinforced concrete in which the steel rods, inserted into tubes cast in situ, effectively articulated the tensile reinforcement in relation to the compressive concrete. In this instance the tectonically expressive potential depends on the necessity of leaving the restraining plates and tensioning bolts exposed during the course of construction.

11
For this essay see Theo. B. White, ed., *Paul Philippe Cret: Architect and Teacher* (Philadelphia: Art Alliance Press, 1973), pp. 61–65.

12
In fact there is no change in the compressive stress in Viollet-le-Duc's support, and the tapering in this instance has two functions; first to express the idea of the statical force, and second to facilitate constructional joints and bearing.

13
See Hannes Meyer's inaugural address as the director of the Bauhaus in 1928, given under the title "Bauen" (Building), in which he itemized a whole range of explicitly modern, nontraditional man-made materials such as ferro-concrete, wire, glass, aluminum, asbestos, plywood, ripolin, silicon steel, cold glue, casein, cork, rolled glass, and synthetic rubber, leather, resin, horn, and wood. See Claude Schnaidt, *Hannes Meyer: Buildings, Writings and Projects* (London: Tiranti, 1965), p. 95.

14
Kahn, "Monumentality," p. 587. Kahn's interest in pioneering new materials was to continue throughout his life. See in particular his use of "pewter finish" stainless steel cladding for the Yale Center for British Art, posthumously completed by Pellecchia & Meyers, Architects. This dull, variable surface is produced by omitting final baths in the fabricating process. That the revetment is a skin, a *Bekleidung* in the Semperian sense, is indicated by the weathering details employed throughout.

15
Louis Kahn, "Toward a Plan for Midtown Philadelphia," *Perspecta* 2 (1953), p. 23.

16
Kahn, "Monumentality," pp. 581–582.

17
As Konrad Wachsmann shows in his book *The Turning Point of Building* (New York: Reinhold, 1961), this form of tetrahedral spatial geometry had first been explored by Alexander Graham Bell in his trussed kites of the turn of the century (see pp. 29, 30) and in the 80-foot tetrahedral space frame tower erected on Bell's estate in Canada in 1907. According to Robert Mark and Fuller himself (see *The Dymaxion World of Buckminster Fuller* [New York: Anchor/Doubleday, 1973], p. 57), Fuller first load-tested a tetrahedron/octahedron truss at the University of Michigan in 1953. Fuller patented this combination as the Octet truss and a demonstration truss 100 feet long, 35 feet wide, and 4 feet deep was exhibited at the Museum of Modern Art, New York, in 1959. The exceptional structural efficiency of this device is borne out by the following description: "In Fuller's three-way-grid Octet Truss system, loads applied to any one point are distributed radially outward in six directions and are immediately frustrated by the finite hexagonal circles entirely enclosing the six-way distributed load." One should also note that this truss was composed of struts alone without any special hub joints.

Kahn's relationship to R. Buckminster Fuller was complex. Both men were teaching at Yale University in the early fifties. Despite Tyng's patent interest in Fuller at the time, Kahn justly wanted to distance himself from Fuller's position in retrospect, as he was to make clear in his 1972 interview with John Cook and Heinrich Klotz, when in referring to the Yale Art Gallery he pointed out that Fuller's structural concepts were incapable of producing a flat ceiling. See John W. Cook and Heinrich Klotz, *Conversations with Architects* (New York: Praeger, 1973), p. 212.

18
See Richard Saul Wurman and Eugene Feldman, *The Notebooks and Drawings of Louis I. Kahn* (Cambridge: MIT Press, 1973), unpaginated.

19
Louis Kahn, "Order in Architecture," *Perspecta* 4 (1957), p. 64. In a 1957 brochure, published by the Universal Atlas Cement Company, which was the sponsor of the main version of the City Tower proposal, we learn that the tower was projected as rising to a height of 616 feet, with principal floor levels at every 66 feet, and standing on a podium measuring 700 by 700 feet. This last comprised three levels, an elevated pedestrian plaza, a shopping concourse at grade, and a service/parking level beneath. The main tetrahedral floor slabs were 3 feet deep with spans up to 60 feet from one diagonal strut to the next. In a descriptive text Kahn and Tyng would write: "The skin of a tower is usually regarded as an enclosure playing no part in the structural concept of the building. . . . This is rationalized into an acceptance of the skin as only skin. . . . Instead this intermediary element between the building and the outside forces should be conceived as the beginning of a structural reaction against these forces. In this tower the many positioned sun louvres, related to the growth of the building, act an initial break-up of sun, wind and temperature change . . . out of this purposeful design comes a beautiful tracery texture with everchanging light and shade."

20
See Bruno Taut's *Die Stadtkrone* (Jena: Eugen Diederichs, 1919).

21
Kahn, "Order in Architecture," p. 69. The reference to "Brutalist" in the previous sentence refers of course to the British New Brutalist movement, to which the art gallery was related by such critics as Reyner Banham. See Banham, *The New Brutalism* (New York: Reinhold, 1966); also his "The New Brutalism," *The Architectural Review,* December 1955, pp. 355–362. Important not only for Banham's critique of Kahn but also for his neo-Palladian analysis of the work of Peter and Alison Smithson.

22
Kahn, "Order in Architecture," p. 67.

23
William Huff, "Louis Kahn: Sorted Reflections and Lapses in Familiarities," *Little Journal* (Society of Architectural Historians, New York Chapter) 5, no. 1 (September 1981), p. 15.

24
Ibid., p. 12.

25
See Walter McQuade, "Architect Louis Kahn and His Strong-Boned Structures," *Architectural Forum* 107, no. 4 (October 1957), pp. 134–143. William Huff comments on the typical Kahnian use of the term "invade" in this comment. Clearly Kahn had in mind the column and (screen) wall arrangements in Mies's Barcelona Pavilion. See Huff's memoir in the *Little Journal* above.

26
Donald Appleyard, Kevin Lynch, and John R. Myer, *The View from the Road* (Cambridge: MIT, 1964).

27
In Romaldo Giurgola and Jaimini Mehta, *Louis I. Kahn* (Boulder, Colorado: Westview Press, 1975), p. 224.

28
Louis Kahn, "The Animal World," *Canadian Art* 19, no. 1 (January/February 1962), p. 51.

29
Heinz Ronner, Sharad Jhaveri, and Alessandro Vasella, *Louis I. Kahn: Complete Works, 1935–74* (Boulder, Colorado: Westview Press, 1977), pp. 31, 29.

30
Ibid., p. 29.

31
Kahn, "Toward a Plan for Midtown Philadelphia," p. 17.

32
Kahn, "Order in Architecture," p. 61.

33
Alexandra Tyng, *Beginnings: Louis I. Kahn's Philosophy of Architecture* (New York: Wiley & Sons, 1984), p. 79.

34
Giurgola and Mehta, *Louis I. Kahn,* p. 187.

35
Nell E. Johnson, ed., *Light Is the Theme: Louis I. Kahn and the Kimbell Art Museum* (Fort Worth, Texas, 1975), p. 38.

36
Architectural Forum, October 1957, quoted in McQuade, "Architect Louis Kahn and His Strong-Boned Structures," p. 142.

37
Louis Kahn, foreword to *Carlo Scarpa architetto poeta* (London: Royal Institute of British Architects, Heinz Gallery, 1974).

38
Frank Lloyd Wright, *An Autobiography* (London: Faber & Faber, 1945), pp. 409–410.

39
Kahn, "Form and Design," p. 151.

40
Ronner, Jhaveri, and Vasella, *Louis I. Kahn: Complete Works,* p. 111.

41
Ibid., p. 140.

42
Louis Kahn, "Louis Kahn," *Perspecta* 7 (1961), p. 11.

43
It is likely that this entry was made after receiving from Colin Rowe Rudolf Wittkower's book *Architectural Principles in the Age of Humanism* (1949). See David De Long, "The Mind Opens to Realizations," in *Louis I. Kahn: In the Realm of Architecture* (Los Angeles: Museum of Contemporary Art; New York: Rizzoli, 1991), p. 59.

44
Marcello Angrisani, "Louis Kahn e la storia," *Edilizia Moderna,* no. 86 (1965), pp. 83–93.

45
Kahn, "Louis Kahn," p. 18.

46
See August E. Kommendant, *18 Years with Architect Louis I. Kahn* (Englewood, N.J.: Aloray, 1975), pp. 41–73. It would seem that Kommendant played a major role in the evolution of the first section for the Salk labs, devising the 100-foot-span, prefabricated, prestressed, box-truss girders carrying 50-foot-span prestressed folded plates over the laboratories in the other direction. These trusses were 9 feet deep, as was the upper floor.

47
Alexandra Tyng, *Beginnings,* p. 171.

48
This original relationship to the landscape has recently become compromised by a rather bulky addition to the campus.

49
Martin Heidegger, "Building, Dwelling, Thinking," in *Poetry, Language, Thought* (New York: Harper & Row, 1971), p. 154. For an exposition on the relation between Kahn's architecture and Heidegger's thought see Christian Norberg-Schulz, "Kahn, Heidegger and the Language of Architecture," *Oppositions* 18 (1979), pp. 29–47.

50
Ronner, Jhaveri, and Vasella, *Louis I. Kahn: Complete Works,* p. 345.

51
Johnson, ed., *Light Is the Theme,* p. 34.

52
Ibid., p. 22.

53
Ibid., p. 22.

54
Huff, "Louis Kahn," p. 16. Kahn was particularly sensitive to the weathering of wall surfaces in his work. Thus in defending the blank brick facade to the Yale Art Gallery, he was to tell Klotz and Cook, "A wall is a wall. I considered rain as important to the wall, so I introduced those ledges to the wall at intervals. I could have left the wall bare just for monumentality." See Cook and Klotz, *Conversations with Architects,* p. 179.

55
Johnson, ed., *Light Is the Theme,* p. 44.

56
Huff, "Louis Kahn," p. 29.

57
See Patricia Cummings Loud, *The Art Museums of Louis I. Kahn* (Durham: Duke University Press, 1989), pp. 135–150.

58
Doug Suisman, "The Design of the Kimbell: Variations on a Sublime Archetype," *Design Book Review,* Winter 1987, p. 38.

8 Jørn Utzon: Transcultural Form and the Tectonic Metaphor

Epigraph: Philip Drew, *The Third Generation: The Changing Meaning of Architecture* (New York: Praeger, 1972), pp. 44–46.

1
Jørn Utzon, "Platforms and Plateaus: The Ideas of a Danish Architect," *Zodiac* 10 (1962), p. 116. It is interesting to note in this regard the early influence of the Danish painter Carl Kylberg on Utzon and the fact that Kylberg was involved with Indian philosophy. See Henrik Sten Møller's "Jørn Utzon on Architecture," *Living Architecture* (Copenhagen) no. 8 (1989), ed. Per Nagel. This being a conversation between Sten Møller and the architect. In this interview Utzon also reveals his strong affinity for the architecture of Luis Barragán.

2
Utzon, "Platforms and Plateaus," p. 116.

3
Bruno Taut, *Die Stadtkrone* (Jena: Eugen Diederichs, 1919).

4
Steen Eiler Rasmussen, *Experiencing Architecture* (London: Chapman and Hall, 1959), p. 169. "Use few or no shaped bricks. Do not copy details, make them yourself from the material . . . the style is created by the material, the subject, the time and the man."

5
Sverre Fehn and Per Feld, *The Thought of Construction* (New York: Rizzoli, 1983), pp. 36–43.

6
See Lisbeth Balslev Jørgensen's entry on P. V. Jensen-Klint in *Macmillan Encyclopedia of Architects,* vol. 2 (New York: Free Press, 1982), p. 497.

7
Robert Bartholomew, "Jørn Utzon: His Work and Ideas" (unpublished thesis, University of New South Wales, Australia, 1981), p. 92. See also Jørn Utzon, Royal Gold Medal address, *RIBA Journal,* October 1978, p. 427.

8
Kjeld Helm-Petersen, "Jørn Utzon: A New Personality," *Zodiac* 5 (1959), pp. 70–105.

9
Bartholomew, "Jørn Utzon," p. 92: Michael Tomaszewski in an interview with Robert Bartholomew. See also the interview with Richard Le Plastrier in the same text, p. 93: "If you look at the beams in the Opera House over the concourse and see the change in section you start to understand that they are like the hulls of the boats."

10
Utzon was in Stockholm from 1942 to 1945, where he encountered Osvald Sirén's books on Chinese architecture. See Tobias Faber's essay in *Jørn Utzon: Houses in Fredensborg* (Berlin: Ernst & Sohn, 1991), p. 7.

11
Ibid. Faber cites two early housing schemes that he designed together with Utzon in 1945 and 1948 respectively; one for Bellahøj in Copenhagen and the other for Boras in Sweden.

12
Jørn Utzon and Tobias Faber, "Tendenze: Notidens Arkitektur," *Arkitekten* (Copenhagen, 1947), pp. 63–69.

13
Acceptera (Stockholm: Tidem, 1931; reprinted 1980). This was an anonymously authored polemical statement arising out of the 1930 Stockholm exhibition. Written by E. G. Asplund, Gregor Paulson, et al., it was in fact a series of militant position papers in relation to an emerging welfare state policy on architecture and design.

14
Utzon and Faber, "Tendenze."

15
D'Arcy Wentworth Thompson, *On Growth and Form,* ed. J. T. Bonner (Cambridge: Cambridge University Press, 1971). First published in 1917, the book was expanded and revised in 1942.

16
Bernard Rudolfsky, *Architecture without Architects* (New York: Museum of Modern Art, 1965).

17
See Margit Staber, "Hans Scharoun: ein Beitrag zum organischen Bauen," *Zodiac* 10 (1963). Scharoun was born and brought up in Bremen. While icebergs are not cited in this piece, Scharoun nonetheless refers to his Philharmonie in Berlin as his "Nordic" theater.

18
Bartholomew, "Jørn Utzon," p. 8.

19
Jørn Utzon, "Own Home at Hellebaek, Denmark," *Byggekunst* 5 (1952), p. 83. "When some clients of Mies objected to the doors continuing to the ceiling, on the grounds of their warping, Mies retorted, 'Then I won't build.' Here, an essential principle of the structure had been put into question and in such a case he wouldn't budge." Utzon, as cited in Bartholomew, "Jørn Utzon."

20
Utzon, "Platforms and Plateaus," p. 114.

21
Jørn Utzon, "Elineberg," *Zodiac* 5 (1959), p. 86.

22
Adolf Loos, "Ornament and Crime" (1908), in *The Architecture of Adolf Loos* (London: Arts Council of Great Britain, 1985), p. 100.

23
Adolf Loos, "Architecture" (1910), in *The Architecture of Adolf Loos.*

24
See Else Glahn, "Chinese Building Standards in the 12th Century," *Scientific American,* May 1981, pp. 162–173. See also by the same author, "Yingzao Fashi: Chinese Building Standards in the Song Dynasty," in Paula Behrens and Anthony Fisher, eds., *The Building of Architecture,* Via, no. 7 (Philadelphia: University of Pennsylvania; Cambridge: MIT Press, 1984), pp. 89–101.

25
Peter Meyers, in Bartholomew, "Jørn Utzon," p. 112. Utzon was introduced to the *Yingzao fashi* by Professor Liang, whom he met in the Danish Academy in Peking (Utzon, interview with Robert Bartholomew, ibid., p. 44).

26
Cobra, founded in 1948, saw itself as a continuation of the prewar international Surrealist movement. As such it rejected rational Western culture, which it associated with the nightmare of the Second World War. Led by Dutch and Danish artists, the movement drew participants from Belgium, France, England, Germany, and Sweden. While the

name Cobra was derived from the first letters of the capital cities in which its major members lived and worked, Copenhagen, Brussels, and Amsterdam, the acronym Cobra had other connotations, to wit the reference to a snake that was both deadly and holy. As Willemijn Stokvis has written in his 1987 study of Cobra, *An International Movement in Art after the Second World War*: "Wishing to reach the very source of human creativity, they took their examples from those forms of art which appeared not to have been tainted with the rules and conventions of the Western World: from, for example, primitive peoples with their totems and their magic signs, from Eastern calligraphy, from prehistoric art and from the art of the Middle Ages." Intimations of this interest and work can be found in the prewar work of the Danish sculptor Ejer Bille, such as his *Mask Fortegn* (Mask, Sign) of 1936. Aside from Jørn, the Danes Henry Heerup and Carl-Henning Pederson played major roles in this movement. A number of architects were, as it were, on the fringes, including Thone and Erik Ahlsen of Sweden and the Dutch architect Aldo van Eyck. See also *Cobra 1948–51*, ed. Christian Dotremont (Paris: Jean-Michel Place, 1980).

27

One of Wright's early sectional sketches for the Guggenheim Museum is inscribed with the title ziggurat. On one drawing, however, Wright will also employ the term Taruggiz, to indicate that the form had indeed been derived from an inversion of a ziggurat.

28

See Mircea Eliade's *The Sacred and the Profane* (New York: Harcourt, Brace & World, 1959). Eliade illustrates the concept of the *axis mundi* with the sacred pole of the Kwakiutl tribe of British Columbia, for whom the *axis mundi* is "the trunk of a cedar tree, thirty to thirty-five feet high, over half of which projects through the roof. This pillar plays a primary part in the ceremonies; it confers a cosmic structure on the house" (p. 36). Elsewhere he writes, "The historian of religion encounters other homologies that presuppose more developed symbolism . . . such, for example, is the assimilation of the belly on the womb to a cave, of the intestines to a labyrinth, of breathing to weaving, of veins and arteries to the sun and moon, of the backbone to the *axis mundi*" (p. 169). See also Joseph Rykwert, *The Idea of a Town* (Cambridge: MIT Press, 1988).

29

See Faber's essay in *Jørn Utzon: Houses in Fredensborg*, p. 6.

30

Ibid., p. 7.

31

Utzon, "Elineberg," p. 90.

32

One should note that the Danish engineer Pove Ahm of the Ove Arup Partnership served as the structural consultant on the Højstrup High School and also on the Bank Melli and to some extent even the Sydney Opera House. Ahm was also a close personal friend of Utzon.

33

Utzon, "Platforms and Plateaus," p. 131.

34

Utzon will return to his parti for the Zurich Opera House in his 1965 entry for the Wolfsburg Theater competition.

35

Pol Abraham, *Viollet-le-Duc et le rationalisme médiéval* (Paris: Vincent Fréal & Cie., 1934).

36

See Bartholomew, "Jørn Utzon," p. 168. See also Pat Westcott, *The Sydney Opera House* (Sydney: Ure Smith, 1968), p. 132.

37

Robin Boyd, "A Night at the Opera House," *Architecture Plus*, August 1973, pp. 49–54. This text, written just before Boyd's untimely death in 1972, reasserts the argument that the point was too narrow to place the two halls side by side.

38

Ove Arup, "Sydney Opera House," in *Architectural Design*, March 1965, p. 140. Between 1959 and 1965 the shell structure of the opera house went through ten different versions. See *Sydney Opera House* (Sydney: Sydney Opera House Trust, 1988), a reprint of the technical report by Ove Arup & Partners that first appeared in *The Structural Engineer* in March 1969.

39

John Yeomans, *The Other Taj Mahal* (London, 1968), p. 58. See also Shelly Indyk and Susan Rich, "The Sydney Opera House as Envisaged by Jørn Utzon," unpublished thesis.

40

Arup, "Sydney Opera House," p. 142.

41

Ove Arup & Partners clearly played a major role in the design and realization of the entire structure, not only Arup himself but also such serious engineers as Pove Ahm, Jack Zunz, and the then tyro engineer Peter Rice. In a letter to the author (October 3, 1990) Sir Jack Zunz of the Ove Arup partnership writes: "Utzon was a most inspiring man to work with. He was probably the most inspirational architect I have met. Walking down a street with him was like seeing the world anew. His visual perception and sensitivity is unique and astounding. He always joked about his shortcomings in the use of the English language, yet he used words to conjure up visual images in the most inventive and evocative ways. While my admiration for his gifts are unbounded, there are *buts*. . . . "

As far as Zunz is concerned, Utzon, contrary to his claims, never solved the problem of converting a 3,000-seat concert hall into a 2,000-seat opera house, and his overingenious unrealized curtain wall devised for the space beneath the shell vaults would remain for Zunz unbuildable. For a more generous assessment of Zunz's experience of working on Sydney, see his "Sydney Opera House Revisited," a lecture given at the Royal College of Art, London, in 1988.

42

Jørn Utzon, "The Sydney Opera House," *Zodiac* 14 (1965), p. 49.

43

It is important to note, as Alex Popov does in a letter to the author (May 25, 1992), that Utzon's "retreat" from Sydney was accompanied by an intensity of output in the tectonic sense not seen since Nervi. To prove his point Popov cites the Kuwait parliament, Farum Town Center, Bagsvaerd Church, the Zurich Opera, and the project for a theater in Beirut. He writes: "I think that after the opera house debacle an intensely feverish period of creative activity ensued which was to reveal that he really did have all the solutions to the opera house, contrary to commonly held opinion in Sydney that he did not know how to solve the acoustics or the glass or that he was naive in structure."

44

Bartholomew, "Jørn Utzon," p. 207.

45

For a detailed gloss of Heidegger's concept of the Fourfold see Vincent Vycinas, *Earth and Gods: An Introduction to the Philosophy of Martin Heidegger* (The Hague: Martinus Nijhoff, 1969), in particular pp. 224–237. Vycinas writes: "The foursome (Geviert) is the interplay of earth, sky, god and men as mortals. In this interplay the world as openness is stirred up in the sense of being opened. World is not something which is dynamic, but is dynamism itself. This dynamism is the coming-forward from concealment into revelation—it is an event of truth. Event, again, indicated not merely a taking place in time, but the becoming what one is, the entering into one's own self. In German 'eigen' is 'our' and 'Er-eignis' is not only an 'event' but also the 'entering-into-one's-own-self' by gathering oneself into unity of self-possession."

46

The author is indebted to Shun-Xun Nan of Beijing University for this information. In a letter to the author (February 10, 1993) he writes: "The stepped gable wall and pitched roof of the Bagsvaerd Church and its wall/opening relationship is reminiscent of those in South China. . . . These are popular in Anhui, Zhejiang and Jiangsu provinces. . . . The grand open shed of the National Assembly building in Kuwait reminds me of the open shed or pavilion type of open hall which is the center of the house in the South, where ancestral worship takes place and where the elders meet friends and the younger generation."

47

It is interesting to note in this context the mythical role played by boating in Viking society, reflected in the archaic stone ships staked out in rocks in various parts of Denmark, at Lindholm Hoje near Nørresundby, at Hojlyngen near Ehesbjerg, and at Glarendrup in North Funen. See P. V. Glob, *Denmark: An Archaeological History from the Stone Age to the Vikings* (Ithaca: Cornell University Press, 1971).

48

These saplings were in fact planted by Utzon himself at his own personal expense.

49

Mention should also be made in this regard of Sigurd Lewerentz's Malmö Cemetery chapel, completed in 1945. A very comparable, dryly constructed tectonic is evident in this work, with its tiled monopitched roofs and trabeated portico. See G. E. Kidder Smith's *Sweden Builds: Its Modern Architecture and Land Policy: Background, Development and Contribution* (New York: A. Bonnier, 1950), pp. 174–175, and Janne Ahlin's *Sigurd Lewerentz, Architect* (Cambridge: MIT Press, 1987).

50

See Bartholomew, "Jørn Utzon," p. 422. See also Svend Simonsen, *Bagsvaerd Church* (Bagsvaerd Parochial Church Council, 1978). This pamphlet, edited by the pastor of the church, carries an interview between Jørn Utzon and Per Jensen in which Utzon makes a number of revealing statements about his approach to the design, including the following: "We discussed back and forth whether to place our altar in the middle of the floor, but we got afraid of that—[of] people looking in each other's eyes, while centering their thoughts on, for example, a funeral. We gave that up. We chose a certain broad angle toward a place which is not so stagelike, but where what's going on happens lengthwise. That's why we ended up with a broad room."

This text also gives certain dimensions and technical details. The concrete frames vary in height from 4.5 to 7.56 meters while the aisles between them are 2.45 meters wide. The shell vaults, spanning 17.35 meters, are made of special concrete sprayed onto wire mesh yielding a thickness that varies from 80 to 100 millimeters. These rough-cast, timber-boarded shells are asphalted on the outside and covered with rock wool insulation. The earthwork and altar flagstones are of precast white concrete, while the altar screen is made of Flensborg bricks placed edgewise in a triangular pattern so as to symbolize the Trinity.

51

Of Utzon's direct influence mention needs to be made of Rafael Moneo, who assisted Utzon on the initial designs for the Sydney Opera House. Others of a slightly younger generation include Rick Le Plastrier, who aside from practicing on his own account now teaches at the University of Hobart in Tasmania, and Alex Popov, Utzon's direct pupil and one time son-in-law who now works for himself in Sydney. Popov worked on the detailing of Bagsvaerd when he was in Utzon's office. His most recent work, a house built in the Walter Burley Griffin suburb of Castlecrag, displays something of Utzon's influence. See *Vogue Living,* April 1990. For Le Plastier's work as a "tectonic" teacher see Rory Spence, "Constructive Education," *The Architectural Review,* July 1989, pp. 27–33.

52

Jørn Utzon, "Additive Arkitektur," *Arkitektur* (Copenhagen) 14, no. 1. (1970).

53

Jørn Utzon, "The Importance of Architects," in Denys Lasdun, *Architecture in an Age of Skepticism* (New York: Oxford University Press, 1984), p. 222.

54

There is an uncanny resemblance between the roof of the Kuwait National Assembly (1980) and Boris Podrecca's Kika supermarket built in Wiener Neustadt, Vienna, in 1985. See *Parametro,* March 1987, pp. 44–47.

9 Carlo Scarpa and the Adoration of the Joint

Epigraph: Gianni Vattimo, Turin Conference with Pietro di Rossi, c. 1987.

1

For the parameters of Scarpa's brief, given to him by Giuseppe Mazzariol who was then the director of the foundation, see Giuseppe Mazzariol, "A Work of Carlo Scarpa: The Restoration of an Ancient Venetian Palace," *Zodiac* 13 (1964), pp. 218–219. The relevant passage reads: "The ground floor of the seventeenth-century Querini Stampalia palace had been devastated in the last century by a vaguely neoclassic scenic arrangement with ornamental colonnades which completely spoiled the fundamental and original passages of the buildings. The first research work carried out by Scarpa aimed at discovering the location of the old foundations through tests, so as to restore to their original sites a few works which had been dug up and placed elsewhere for purely ornamental reasons. The result of this first and fundamental rearrangement was the shape of the 'portego' (portico). With the reconstruction of this central nucleus—the only one which could be recovered with some iconological legitimacy—there began the work of general rearrangement which, paying due attention to certain very precise functional needs, has been articulated into four fundamental themes: the bridge accessible by way of the small square; the entrance with the embankment against high tides; the 'portego' hall; and the garden. . . . [The *acqua alta*] ruined the practicability of the landzone of the palace, where a big public library, a famous gallery, and an important state institute were housed. The remedy to this limited access would be a direct entrance from the square, as a substitute for the entrance used since the end of the century, a doorway situated in a poorly lit and not easily accessible side lane. The client also commissioned two halls, for meetings and exhibits; one situated inside, the other outside, in the area of an abandoned and impracticable rear courtyard. The artist was then faced with two associated problems: 1) the elevation of the whole pavement area of the zone overlooking the canal to a level corresponding to the highest levels reached by the high tides in the last ten years, and 2) a system for lining ceilings and walls so as to offset the effects of humidity. In fact, the absorption of humidity very quickly corrodes any plaster or marble facing. To eliminate this serious drawback, Scarpa used panels fastened with wall clamps so as to ensure the complete and continuous ventilation of all the walling."

2

Maria Antonietta Crippa, *Carlo Scarpa* (Cambridge: MIT Press, 1986), p. 157.

3

Here as elsewhere I am indebted to the recent work of Richard Murphy, who points out that there is in fact a difference in level despite the fact that one of Scarpa's drawings suggests the two levels are virtually the same. See Richard Murphy's analytical essay in *Querini Stampalia Foundation/Carlo Scarpa,* Architecture in Detail Series (London: Phaidon, 1993).

4

A similar distortion occurs in the planning of the Banca Popolare di Verona, where a seemingly orthogonal plan is actually out of rectangular alignment by 1.5 degrees in order to conform to the inclination of the party walls in the adjacent buildings.

5

Giuseppe Zambonini, "Process and Theme in the Work of Carlo Scarpa," *Perspecta* 20 (1983), p. 31. One should note, after Richard Murphy (see note 3 above), that this water channel is stocked with fish and that Scarpa had apparently once remarked, "Let's have some trout here!"

6

A number of books on Chinese gardening were held in Scarpa's library including Osvald Sirén, *Gardens of China* (New York: Ronald Press, 1949), and Henry Inn, ed., *Chinese Houses and Gardens* (New York, 1940).

7

Bianca Albertini and Sandro Bagnoli, *Carlo Scarpa* (Cambridge: MIT Press, 1988), p. 221. It is interesting to note that, as Murphy points out, the papyrus basin had been previously used in Scarpa's Turin pavilion of 1961.

8

Marco Frascari, "The Tell-the-Tale Detail," in Paula Behrens and Anthony Fisher, eds., *The Building of Architecture,* Via, no. 7 (Philadelphia: University of Pennsylvania; Cambridge: MIT Press, 1984), p. 24. Frascari has written a whole series of insightful articles on the work of Scarpa including "A Heroic and Admirable Machine: The Theatre of the Architecture of Carlo Scarpa, Architetto Veneto," *Poetics Today* 10 (Spring 1989), pp. 103–124; and "Italian Facadism and Carlo Scarpa," *Daidalos* 6 (December 1982), pp. 37–46.

9

Lodoli entertained very similar anti-Cartesian views to Vico's. In his essay "Lodoli on Function and Representation," from his anthology *The Necessity of Artifice* (New York: Rizzoli, 1982), pp. 115–122, Joseph Rykwert writes that Lodoli was closely related to "Giambattista Vico, the Neapolitan philosopher, lawyer and rhetorician, to whom the *verum* and *factum* of Baconian experimental philosophy had an important corollary: that the touchstone of the verifiable or knowable was what we and our like had made. And that therefore historical and not geometrical knowledge could provide us with the only real certitude. . . . Moreover Lodoli taught his pupils the independence of Italic and Etruscan institutions of Greek precept—an idea to which Vico had given great force in his book *On the Ancient Wisdom of the Italians* and which he was to refine through the various editions of his major work, the *New Science.*"

10

See Hubert Damisch, "The Drawings of Carlo Scarpa," in Francesco Dal Co and Giuseppe Mazzariol, eds., *Carlo Scarpa: The Complete Works* (Milan: Electa; New York: Rizzoli, 1985), pp. 209, 212. Damisch writes: "Scarpa's approach was completely dominated by the problem of *realization*. From this viewpoint, it seems that the Venetian architect's attitude has curious similarity to Cézanne. Scarpa harbored the same doubt as Cézanne, if we believe what Merleau-Ponty tells us. And it is this doubt, clearly methodological, which gives his work, seemingly so modest, a historical incisiveness that some consider extraordinary. Now this doubt can be grasped best of all by examining his practice as a draftsman." Damisch is alluding here to Maurice Merleau-Ponty's essay "Le Doute de Cézanne," first published in 1945 and translated into English in *Sense and Non-sense* (Evanston: Northwestern University Press, 1964). Merleau-Ponty wrote that "the work itself completed and understood, is proof that there was *something* rather than *nothing* to be said" (p. 19).

In their essay dealing with the life of Carlo Scarpa in *Carlo Scarpa: The Complete Works,* Giuseppe Mazzariol and Giuseppe Barbieri note that for Scarpa the drafting materials were of the utmost importance; hence a given pencil, ink, and paper were recognized in every case as being capable only of certain tasks, just as the results produced with specific building materials differ one from another. They also quote Mamolio Brusatin to the effect that "every object manipulated and laid open by his draftsmanship is virtually a geological record, a convincing explanation that the objects and appurtenances of the city are not just remote reproductions of the present and of the things of today, but also tell us everything about their having really lived and having really died."

11

See Sergio Los, "The Design for the Central Pavilion of the Biennale," in Dal Co and Mazzariol, eds., *Carlo Scarpa: The Complete Works,* pp. 164, 165. See also Los's essay "Carlo Scarpa, Architect," in *Carlo Scarpa* (Cologne: Taschen, 1993), pp. 44, 48.

12

See Stephen Groak, *The Idea of Building* (London: Spon, 1992), pp. 151, 152.

13

Cited in Richard Murphy, *Carlo Scarpa and the Castelvecchio* (London: Butterworth, 1990), p. 56. Murphy's detailed analysis and documentation of the Castelvecchio is without parallel.

14

Albertini and Bagnoli, *Carlo Scarpa,* p. 205.

15

Sergio Los, *Carlo Scarpa: architetto poeta* (Venice: Edizioni Cluva, 1967). At the end of this text Los gives a brief account of his posthumous realization of Scarpa's gate for the school of architecture in Venice. A somewhat different version of the same text is given in the transcript of a lecture that Scarpa delivered in Madrid in 1978. See Carlo Scarpa, "A Thousand Cypresses" in Dal Co and Mazzariol, eds., *Carlo Scarpa: The Complete Works,* p. 287.

16

In his study of the Querini Stampalia, Richard Murphy records the names of leading members of Scarpa's regular production team who traveled with him, much as Frank Lloyd Wright had developed such a team for the realization of his Prairie Style. Murphy lists Servevio Anfodillo (joinery), Paolo Zanon (steel), Silvio Fassio (concrete), Eugenio de Luigi (stucco), as well as the engineer Maschietto and the draftsman Luciano Zinatto. We are close here to Ruskin's culture of craftsmen.

17

Scarpa was perhaps more familiar with the lore of Italian plaster finishes than any other Italian architect of his generation, and the revival and popularity of polished plaster is due in no small measure to his efforts. Some sense of the degree to which this technique has been elaborated in Italy may be gleaned from the fact that traditional Roman plastering comprises seven successive layers of plaster finish. Something of the scope of this technique with all its regional variations, may be gleaned from a study commissioned by the Comune di Verona. See Giorgio Forte, *Antiche ricette di pittura murale* (Venice: Noale, 1984). I am indebted to Sergio Los for providing me with this information.

18

As Licisco Magagnato has informed us, it took Scarpa five years to finally resolve the positioning of the Cangrande statue that was the ultimate symbolic "joint" of the museum.

See Licisco Magagnato, "The Castelvecchio Museum," in Dal Co and Mazzariol, eds., *Carlo Scarpa: The Complete Works,* p. 160.

19

See Robert Lawlor, *Sacred Geometry* (London: Thames and Hudson, 1982), p. 31.

20

See Guido Pietropoli, "L'invitation au voyage," *Spazio e Società,* June 1990, pp. 90–98. Pietropoli confirms that Scarpa was also well aware of the use of the *vesica piscis* figure by Borromini, but only after he had already built the intersecting circles at Brion. He writes: "It was obvious that he wasn't so much upset about the aesthetic effect of his design, but more because Borromini's geometric construction was more accurate, more true, from a strictly symbolic point of view. According to the strict law of analogy ruling the relationship and harmony between material form and spiritual significance, all possible harmonies within a symbolic theme must be highlighted. Borromini's design adds the so-called 'AURA' or 'MANDOLA' to the eros expressed by the two intersecting circles. The 'Mandola' consists of two facing equilateral triangles which, metaphorically, refer to King Soloman's seal. In my opinion this is one of the symbols of the 'Mandola' which can also be interpreted as the expression of balance acquired between lay and sacred love."

21

Le Corbusier, *The Modulor* (1950; first English edition 1954). It is interesting to note that Le Corbusier's choice of his standard height of 2.20 meters (the height of a man with his arms upraised) should correspond to Scarpa's modular system based on permutations of the number 11. Le Corbusier would also entertain the double-circular theme, particularly in the regulating lines used to control the composition of the enameled doors in Ronchamp. See Le Corbusier, *The Chapel at Ronchamp* (New York: Praeger, 1957), pp. 124–125. See note 23.

22

Japanese culture was as omnipresent in Scarpa's work as the art and architecture of China. What is less well known perhaps was the way in which his architecture was appreciated by contemporary Japanese practitioners. Typical in this regard is Fumihiko Maki's insightful comment about the *suki* aspect of Scarpa's work: "A generalization that might be made about superior architectural works whether past or present, East or West, is that they reveal at a stroke 'something' that many architects and non-architects of the time had unconsciously wanted to express. Architectural creation is not invention but discovery; it is not a pursuit of something beyond the imagination of an age. These few works of Scarpa are attractive in that they also respond in this sense to the latent desire we share. However, unlike Mies's Barcelona Pavilion or Le Corbusier's Savoye, they do not represent the prototypes of the 'age'. Although they belong to the impregnative world of the same period, Scarpa's works have been developed in the still imagination of a private world. Scarpa believed only in seeing and created so that the creation could be seen. The ability to choose and reconstruct, based on a superior power of appreciation and a still, private hedonism—this is truly the art of *suki,* and in this I sense the true value and limitations of the designs of Carlo Scarpa." Cited by Gianpiero Destro Bisol in "L'antimetodo di Carlo Scarpa," *Ricerca Progretto* (Bulletin of the Department of Architecture and Urbanism in the University of Rome), no. 15 (July 1991), pp. 6–12.

23
Marco Frascari, "A Deciphering of a Wonderful Cipher: Eleven in the Architecture of Carlo Scarpa," *Oz* 13 (1991). One may add to Frascari's list of somewhat arcane dimensions the equally odd fact that there are 22 books in the Old Testament, 22 generations from Adam to Jacob, and that God is supposed to have made 22 works. Frascari's account of this numerical obsession parallels almost to the letter that given by Scarpa himself in "A Thousand Cypresses," p. 286. In both instances, however, we are confronted with a description of a system that fails to account for its origin. The esoteric character of this obsession with the double numbers leads one to wonder whether Scarpa was familiar with René Schwaller de Lubicz's alchemical study *The Temple in Man* that first appeared in French in 1949. In a parallel text published in 1957, Schwaller de Lubicz writes: "In considering the esoteric meaning of Number, we must avoid the following mistake: Two is not One and One; it is not a *composite*. It is the multiplying *Work;* it is the notion of the plus in relation to the minus; it is a new *Unity;* it is sexuality; it is the origin of Nature, *Physis,* the *Neter* Two." See Robert Lawlor's introduction to the *The Temple in Man* (Rochester, Vermont, 1981), p. 10.

Other elements in Scarpa's work suggest familiarity with the writings of Schwaller de Lubicz. This is particularly true of chapter 4 in *The Temple in Man* where Schwaller de Lubicz describes the rebuilding of temples on preexisting foundations as symbolizing "water, that is to say the mud of the waters." He also remarks on the fact that the Egyptians (like Scarpa) were in the habit of introducing subtle distortions of the orthogonal into their plan forms, so that, as he puts it, "certain chambers apparently square or rectangular in plan will be slightly rhomboidal or trapezoidal. One need only examine, in their angles, the cut of the stones to establish that for this distortion, an exceptional effort was required to give these angles a few degrees more or less than a right angle" (*The Temple in Man,* pp. 69, 71).

24
It is more than likely that Scarpa was cognizant of the alchemical wheels of Ezekiel that resemble the *vesica pisci*. A similar duality also appears in the icon of the philosopher's egg from which a double-headed eagle is hatched wearing spiritual and temporal crowns. Moreover Scarpa's identification of himself as a man of Byzantium who came to Venice by way of Greece may be seen as an allusion to the two great alchemical traditions; the Pythagorean school of South Italy that sought to structure the world in terms of number and the Ionian school that sought the secret of reality in the analysis and synthesis of substances. See Jack Lindsay, *The Origins of Alchemy in Greco-Roman Egypt* (London: Muller, 1970). The dragon or snake biting its own tail is of alchemical and Gnostic origin. In some versions, it is shown as half light and half dark and in this respect resembles the Chinese yang-yin principle, depicting the continual transition of one value into its opposite. Assimilated to Mercury, the ouroboros is symbolic of self-fecundation, of the primitive idea of a self-sufficient nature that continually returns to its own beginning. See J. E. Cirlot, *A Dictionary of Symbols* (New York: 1962), p. 235.

25
Pietropoli, "L'invitation en voyage," p. 12. Of the latent Orphic mythology in the Brion assembly, Pietropoli writes (p. 12):

On the other side of the cemetery, permanently against the light except during the semi-darkness of dawn and dusk, there is a large pond of black water, the lake of our hearts. In order to reach the island we must turn right going through the tunnel/Orphic flute; our footsteps are noisy and heavy because the ground is hollow and water flows underneath; to enter we must use all our strength and body weight to lower a glass door; in doing this we have to bend over, like a kind of dive and a return to the fetal position. When we have passed through the opening, if we glance back we can see our image reflected in the glass pane as it swings upward. In front of us there is only a concrete wall with a line of mosaic tiles and a sign to turn left, once again toward the heart, and bowing our heads we can enter the water pavilion.

This is a strange rectangular building supported on four iron pillars placed in the form of a vortex. The upper part is made with fir-wood planks, which have turned silver-grey in the sun, arranged so as to give the impression of a pathway with a labyrinth-like perspective, evoking the idea of convolutions of the brain; coverings of green marine plywood patterned with copper nails stoop downward allowing us to see only the pond.

A series of hastily drawn designs, time had almost run out (we were about to leave for Sendai in Japan where Scarpa died on November 28, 1978), show four virtual areas, a sort of disassembling of the "lake of my heart" into atriums and ventricles: the poet (the pavilion), and the ancient fairy tales (the cross with the water jet and the hibiscus, the desert rose), the man (the pond with the bamboo canes) and, once again, the interlocking circles (the eros).

In the center of the pavilion a vertical crack with a deliberate viewpoint allows us to see only the "arco solio" with the tombs of the father and mother: this is the only link with society that, even in our self-conceit, we cannot deny.

26
This whole "alchemical" contraption recalls Marcel Duchamp's Large Glass or Bachelor Machine, *La Mariée mise à nu par ses célibataires mêmes.* It is thus a double metaphor; on the one hand, a heart, that is to say a pump; on the other, it appears to be the related act of coitus.

27
With a certain artistic license, Francesco Dal Co writes: "Significantly, the water flows towards the great basin, gushing out from the very spot where the 'arks' rest, under the protection of the 'arcosolium.' Springing out from the place of death, it flows around the 'isle of meditation' on which stands the pavilion that Scarpa designed while imagining it haunted by the full-bodied forms of youthful women." See Dal Co, "The Architecture of Carlo Scarpa," in Dal Co and Mazzariol, eds., *Carlo Scarpa: The Complete Works,* p. 68.

28
See Paolo Portoghesi, "The Brion Cemetery by Carlo Scarpa," *Global Architecture,* no. 50 (1979): *Carlo Scarpa Cemetery Brion-Vega, S. Vito, Treviso, Italy 1970–72.* Portoghesi writes first of Scarpa's alchemical understanding of Venice and then of the arcosolium that constitutes the fulcrum of the Brion Cemetery. Thus we read: "For Scarpa, then, Venice was a way of seeing and using, a way of connecting things in function of the values of light, texture, color, capable of being grasped only by an eye used to observing . . . water, glass, together with stones and bricks exposed to an inclement atmosphere which doesn't allow the material to hide its structure, but continually forces it to discover, by consuming itself, its most hidden qualities." Later of the double tomb we read: "It could be said that Scarpa reflected at length on the word *arca* (in Italian *arca* means both ark and sarcophagus) and its historical meanings, on the Latin origin which defines its sense, close to that of coffin or monumental sarcophagus, on the transformations undergone in the Christian world. . . . From the arch of the catacomb niches we pass to the Romanesque and Gothic tomb which in the Po area assumes the form of an architectural casket, a shrine in scale. . . . The tomb of the Brion family is thus contemporaneously 'arch', 'bridge', 'roof', 'overturned boat' . . . each of these connotations, these words, projects a symbolic value onto the place, symbols of death in that they are symbols of life, since death isn't given except dialectically, as life which bears within itself its negation and the negation of its negation."

29
Needless to say it also refers to Scarpa's obsession with the "double" throughout his work.

30
Sergio Los arrives at parallel Semperian interpretations of Scarpa's work through Konrad Fiedler's "Essay on Architecture," with which Scarpa was apparently familiar. See Sergio Los, "Carlo Scarpa Architect," p. 38.

31
Francesco Dal Co, "The Architecture of Carlo Scarpa," p. 63.

32
See A. K. Coomaraswamy, "Ornament" (1939), in *Selected Papers,* ed. R. Lipsey, vol. 1 (Princeton: Princeton University Press, 1977), pp. 32–33. For Coomaraswamy the articulation of order out of chaos requires the appearance of decoration as a way of both measuring and joining at the same time.

33
Heino Engel, *The Japanese House* (Rutland/Tokyo: Tuttle, 1964), p. 48. The importance of measure and the intimate relation between craft dimension and proportion has been commented on by P. H. Schofield in his study of proportional systems in architecture: "Architecture, much more than painting, pottery or sculpture, is a co-operative art, the work of many men. In order that men can co-operate in this art, in order, for instance, that the joiner can make a window frame to fill the opening left by the mason, and that both can work to the design of the architect, they need a language of size, a system of measures. Logically only one measure is required, such as a foot or a meter, used in conjunction with an effective system of numeration. This, however, presupposes the existence of simple methods of arithmetical calculation, and on the other hand of a reasonably high general level of mathematical education. To the Egyptian, burdened by a clumsy method of arithmetic and a low standard of mathematical literacy, outside the priestly class, such a method would be impracticable."

The earliest tendency would be to develop a system of many measures, each one with a name of its own. And, as Vitruvius points out, such a system was ready to hand in the measures of the human body. "Making a large number of not very widely separated measures commensurable would automatically lead to the repeated use of rather small whole numbers. It would in fact lead quite automatically to the establishment in some degree of a pattern of proportional relationships between the measures." See P. H. Schofield, *The Theory of Proportion in Architecture* (Cambridge: Cambridge University Press, 1958), pp. 27–28.

34
Dal Co, "The Architecture of Carlo Scarpa," p. 56.

35
Portoghesi, "The Brion Cemetery by Carlo Scarpa": "If decoration can be talked about with regard to Scarpa, it is still in the utopia of 'organic decoration', born from things instead of superimposing itself on them. The crystallographic decoration of the Brion cemetery seems to be a result of the 'natural' flaking of the crystalline blocks, of the revelation of a hypothetical structure of every prismatic block or of every slab, considered as products of successive crystalline layers sedimented around an ideal geometric matrix, a translation in 'mineral' terms of the system of growth through the concentric wind typical of the vegetal trunk."

36
Marco Frascari, "The Tell-the-Tale Detail," p. 24. Sergio Los employs the terms *hypotactic* and *paratatic* to distinguish between Scarpa's notion of an underlying whole as determined by the geometry or the "enfilade" and the *paratactic* type forms in which it was invariably broken down. Los, "Carlo Scarpa Architect," p. 46.

37
Franco Fonatti, *Elemente des Bauens bei Carlo Scarpa* (Vienna: Wiener Akademiereihe, 1988), p. 59.

38
Albertini and Bagnoli, *Carlo Scarpa,* pp. 21–22.

39
Scarpa was exceptionally sensitive to the size and deportment of any window and the light that must of necessity emanate from its form. Thus as Carlo Betelli has written: "The range of solutions explored, discarded, and finally adopted is one of the most exciting testimonies to Scarpa's approach to architectural design. They reveal, first of all, that no window is the same as any other not only because the orientation is different, but also because its age and the size and the shape of the room it illuminates vary. Second, the various systems of grilles and the asymmetrical combinations of vertical and horizontal elements are all ways of designing with light and turning it into an event." Carlo Betelli, "Light and Design," in Dal Co and Mazzariol, eds., *Carlo Scarpa: The Complete Works.*

40
A similar treatment of the suspending ceiling also occurs in the first-floor gallery sequence of the Castelvecchio, where the subdivision of its cobalt lacquered surface is played against a central gridded ventilation grill, framed out in wood, and set flush with the ceiling. The subdividing wooden strips between the panels assume a slightly different pattern in each gallery.

41
Pierluigi Nicolin, "La Banca di Carlo Scarpa a Verona," *Lotus* 28 (1981), p. 51.

10 Postscriptum: The Tectonic Trajectory, 1903–1994

Epigraph: Aris Konstantinidis, "Architecture," translated by Marina Adams, in *Architectural Design,* May 1964, p. 212.

1
See the statement by Pier Luigi Nervi published in *Nervi: Space and Structural Integrity,* exhibition catalog (San Francisco: Museum of Art May/June 1961).

2
See Pieter Singelenberg, *H. P. Berlage: Idea and Style* (Utrecht: Haentjens Dekker & Gumbert, 1972), p. 11. Singelenberg writes of Berlage: "In 1905, roughly half a century after Semper's London publication, he wrote similarly in *Gedanken über Stil* that one could not talk about the evolution of the arts without involving political and economic relations. He too thought in terms of a hopeless state of affairs, saw the cause of the situation in the rule of capital and found the reaction to this, social democracy, the greatest movement ever known to history. Like Semper he worried about human freedom, but in a socialist society the danger would no longer lie in capitalism, but in the misuse of possibilities."

Berlage upheld Semper's theory that the "technical arts" preceded architecture, and his *Over Stijl in Bouw en Meubelkunst* (On Style in Architectural and Furniture Design), published in 1904, is a Semperian argument for the unity of style emerging out of a long period of evolution.

3
Chris Burrows, "H. P. Berlage: Structure, Skin, Space" (unpublished PTGD4 Architecture thesis, Polytechnic of the South Bank, London, 1989), p. 80.

4
However, the case may, of course, be made that Johannes Duiker also developed this tradition of the expressive skeleton frame in Dutch architecture beginning with his Zonnestraal Sanatorium, Hilversum, of 1926.

5
Le Corbusier and P. Jeanneret, *Oeuvre Complète 1934–1938,* 6th ed. (Zurich: Girsberger, 1958), p. 125.

6
I am thinking in particular of the *pilotis* of the Unité d'Habitation, Marseilles, of 1952, which may be seen as Egyptoid on account of the battered profile, tapering upward.

7
The term *saku* is taken from Islamic architecture and refers to the recessed bench that establishes, as it were, the threshold of the typical Arabic urban dwelling.

8
Herman Hertzberger, in Arnulf Luchinger, ed., *Herman Hertzberger, Buildings and Projects 1959–1986* (The Hague: Arch-Edition, 1987), p. 62.

9
Ibid., p. 119.

10
Max Bill, *Form* (Basel: Karl Verner, 1952), p. 11.

11
See "Swiss National Exhibition, Lausanne," *Architectural Design,* November 1963, pp. 526–529.

12
See Andrew Peckham, "This Is the Modern World," *Architectural Design,* February 1979, pp. 2–26.

13
Konrad Wachsmann, *The Turning Point of Building: Structure and Design* (New York: Reinhold, 1961), p. 187.

14
Per Olaf Fjeld, *Sverre Fehn: The Thought of Construction* (New York: Rizzoli, 1983), pp. 46–47.

15
Ibid., p. 112.

16
While architects such as Ernesto Rogers sought a subtle reinterpretation of historical type form—even if only at the level of structure and silhouette, as in his twenty-nine-story Torre Velasca, built in Milan in 1957, a work that consciously attempted to echo the medieval fortress towers of Lombardy—others such as the Argentine Amancio Williams attempted to create an architecture in which structural invention was inseparable from spatial form and vice versa. In general, Italian work during this period tended toward a kind of "tectonic historicism," as in Franco Albini and Franca Helg's Treasury Museum of San Lorenzo, Genoa (1952–1956), or Ignazio Gardella's Zattere building completed in Venice between 1954 and 1958. Of the Torre Velasca, Manfredo Tafuri has written: "Rolled up in its materiality, the tower expanded toward the sky like an energized volcano, assuming the appearance of a medieval tower paradoxically magnified. It stands as a 'homage to Milan,' achieved through means that could not yet be accused of historicism. The Velasca took its place in the city, commenting lyrically on an urban corpus about to disappear. Once again, the expectation was that a catharsis would emerge from intentions hidden in the recesses of a single object." Elsewhere in the same passage he writes of Albini's "buried architecture" as possessing its own language. "Isolated from the external world, it elicits a dialogue between technical elegance—a further tool for achieving supreme detachment-forms." In a similar vein Tafuri would see Gardella's Zattere as a kind of coda to the Torre Velasca, one that was greeted at the time as indicative of a dangerously evasive historicist climate. See Tafuri, *History of Italian Architecture 1944–1985* (Cambridge: MIT Press, 1989), pp. 50–52.

While militant left-wing critics such as G. C. Argan would dub Gardella's Zattere the Ca'd'Oro of modern architecture, and others of more liberal Brutalist persuasion such as Reyner Banham would generally deplore the Italian "retreat" from the modern movement, the gap separating Italian contextualism of the 1950s from the ethical British Brutalist line hardly seems as great as it once was. Both positions were in any event equally committed to the tectonic.

17
Son of the Argentine composer Alberto Williams, Amancio Williams has been one of the most brilliant "theoretical" architects of this century, in the sense that very few of his works have been realized. In almost all of his work, including the house over a stream built for his parents in Mar del Plata in 1945, the fundamental structural idea of the work is inseparable from the tectonic and spatial concept. This is very evident in such works as the suspended office building (1946) or the canopied exhibition building erected in Palermo (1963). See Pablo and Claudio Williams et al., *Amancio Williams* (Buenos Aires, 1990), the complete works of Amancio Williams as published by Archivo Amancio Williams.

18
The fact that Lewerentz visited the site every day for two years during construction, from 1958 to 1960, surely testifies to his commitment to the actual act of construction. See Janne Ahlin's monograph *Sigurd Lewerentz Architect 1885–1975* (Stockholm: Bygförlaget, 1987), pp. 154–156.

19
See Colin St. John Wilson, "Sigurd Lewerentz and the Dilemma of the Classical," *Perspecta 24* (1988), pp. 72–73. Jon Hendrikson of Stockholm has suggested that a Greek architect, Michael Papadopoulos, who had previously worked with Dimitris Pikionis on the Philopapon Hill site adjacent to the Acropolis in Athens, also assisted Lewerentz at Klippan.

20
See Leonardo Fiori and Massimo Prizzon, eds., *La Rinascente: il progetto di architettura* (Milan: Abitare Segesta, 1982), pp. 39, 47.

21
Joseph Rykwert, "The Work of Gino Valle," *Architectural Design,* March 1964, p. 128.

22
See Eduard Sekler, "Architecture and the Flow of Time," *Tulane School of Architecture Review,* no. 9 (1990).

23
Peter Smithson, "A Parallel of the Orders," *Architectural Design,* November 1966, pp. 561–563.

24
Where they happen to be graduates of the school of Madrid, many of these architects have been equally influenced by both de la Sota and Javier Sáenz de Oiza, above all Moneo, who, after he returned from the Utzon atelier in Copenhagen, worked on Sáenz de Oiza's Torres Blancas apartments completed just outside Madrid in 1966. See Pauline Saliga and Martha Thorne, eds., *Building in a New Spain* (Barcelona: Gustavo Gili; Chicago: Art Institute of Chicago, 1992).

25
Esteve Bonell and Francesc Rius, source unknown.

26
Esteve Bonell and Francesc Rius, "Velodrome of Barcelona," *Casabella* 49 (December 1985), p. 62.

27
This scientistic term was coined by the Soviet avant-garde in the early 1920s in order to refer to the newly invented socialist workers' club as an institution that was hypothetically capable of unifying and transforming the society. Using a more industrial electrical metaphor, El Lissitzky characterized the workers' club as a *soziales Kraftwerk.* See Anatole Kopp, *Town and Revolution* (New York: Braziller, 1970), pp. 115–126.

28
The reappearance of Brunel's technology here would appear to relate to a passing remark made by the engineer Peter Rice in his 1991 RIBA Gold Medal address: "The Victorians succeeded where we do not. Industry and its power and capacity were new to them. Designers enjoyed the freedom to experiment, to enjoy themselves, to innovate, to explore the possibilities of this new power to manufacture and create."

29
See Aris Konstantinidis, *Elements for Self-Knowledge: Towards a True Architecture* (Athens, 1975), p. 290.

30
Ibid., p. 313.

31
Paul Ricoeur, "Universal Civilization and National Cultures," in *History and Truth* (Evanston: Northwestern University Press, 1965).

The Owl of Minerva: An Epilogue

Epigraph: see Guy Debord, *Comments on the Society of the Spectacle* (London: Verso, 1988), pp. 38, 39, 50, 51.

1

See *Mies van der Rohe Pavilion. Award for European Architecture, 1988–1992.* The Commission of the European Community, the European Parliament, and the Mies van der Rohe Pavilion, Barcelona, gave this award for the first time in 1988 to Alvaro Siza for the Borges & Irmão Bank built in Vilo do Conde, Portugal, in 1982.

2

For the British attempt in this regard see Bryan Appelyard, "Demolishing the Architect," *The Independent,* September 22, 1993.

3

The department of architecture in the Technical University of Delft has introduced the so-called "Case Study" pedagogical method borrowed from the medical school in Maastricht. As a result, lecturing, as a method of instruction, has been reduced to a minimum.

4

Rafael de la Hoz, "Delenda est Architectura," address given at the AIA/UIA Convention, Chicago, July 1993, and at the Biennale de Arquitectura held in Buenos Aires in September of the same year.

5

I am alluding to the emergence of the construction manager as a separate profession standing between the architect and the client.

6

In the design of his Sainsbury Centre for the Visual Arts in the University of Norwich, Norman Foster was to utilize components manufactured by the aerospace industry. On another occasion Richard Rogers & Partners would employ insulated paneling produced by refrigerated truck manufacturers.

7

Fordism is the term adopted by radical economists to characterize the period of 1950 to 1970, when Taylorized productive processes, facilitated by massive investment in machine tool production and by guaranteed markets, dominated industrial production in the West. Daniel Legorgne and Alain Lipietz have characterized the emerging period of so called "post-Fordism" in the following terms: "History is alive again. On the ruins of Fordism and Stalinism, humankind is at a crossroads. No technological determinism will light the way. The present industrial divide is first and foremost a political divide. The search for social compromise, around ecological constraints, macroeconomic consistency, gender and ethic quality, all mediated by the nature and degree of political mobilization will decide the outcome." See Michael Storper and Allen J. Scott, eds., *Pathways to Industrialization and Regional Development* (London: Routledge, 1992).

8

In an essay entitled "Architecture and the Flow of Time" (*Tulane School of Architecture Review,* no. 9 [1990]), Eduard Sekler writes of the relation between time and tradition:

Architecture and time are interwoven in many ways and subject to mutual influence. Time (chronos), according to the Orphic philosophers, has as its mate necessity (ananke). But forgetting is also time's mate, and in the fight against its all-devouring power, architecture is one of man's most faithful allies.

In the past, a work derived its authenticity not only from the personality of the creator but also from the fact that the work was in keeping with the highest social and spiritual aims of the culture in which it originated.

Today such unifying goals are less easily definable. Often they have been replaced by the much vaunted ideal of individual self-realization, an ideal that forces the artist to rely exclusively on his/her own spiritual resources of strength; authenticity then becomes something very personal, something at times even questionable.

9

R. Gregory Turner, *Construction Economics and Building Design: A Historical Approach* (New York: Van Nostrand Reinhold, 1986).

10

See Edward Ford, *The Details of Modern Architecture* (Cambridge: MIT Press, 1990), p. 352. Rather polemically he writes of layered construction: "The idea that walls in ancient or medieval architecture were monolithic was largely an illusion. Marbles have always been veneered, interiors have always been plastered, and even in a simple stone wall quality stone was always placed on the surface. . . . In the traditional monolithic wall, all functions—structure, insulation, waterproofing and finish—are performed by one or two materials. In the modern layered wall, there is a separate component for each function."

11

D. Andrew Vernooy, "Crisis of Figuration in Contemporary Architecture," in *The Final Decade: Architectural Issues for the 1990s and Beyond,* vol. 7 (New York: Rizzoli, 1992), pp. 94–96.

12

Gottfried Semper, *Wissenschaft, Industrie und Kunst* (Brauschweig, 1852). For the pertinent extract in English see Hans M. Wingler, *The Bauhaus* (Cambridge: MIT Press, 1969), p. 18.

13

Unlike the nineteenth-century rail or harbor facilities, twentieth-century airports are never finished; they are always in a state of construction and reconstruction. Leonardo da Vinci Airport in Rome, built in 1961 to handle six million passengers a year, is a case in point. By the beginning of this decade the annual throughput was over 17 million. It is estimated that by the year 2005 this figure will have climbed to 40 million and by 2030 to 60 million. The consequences of escalating tourism on this scale hardly bear contemplation, let alone the impact it will have on the environment in general.

Other institutional types have become just as fungible in less dramatic ways, even as a matter of state policy. I have in mind in particular the policy established in 1992 by the Dutch State Architect Professor Ir Kees Bijuboutt, who declared that henceforth law courts should be designed and built as though they were ordinary office buildings.

14

See Vittorio Gregotti, "Cultural Theatrics," *Casabella,* no. 606 (November 1993), pp. 2, 3, 71: "The most distressing consequence of these attitudes is the distance, the enormous gap, which has been created between saying and doing. The valid efforts of its theorists apart, it is certain that the translation of languages from one discipline to another presents significant obstacles; even if we acknowledge its legitimacy, the more indirect it is the more effective it becomes, insinuating itself into the material of design. . . . In substance the attempt to directly transfer the inventions of visual artists or theoretical conclusions of philosophers into architecture nearly always results in caricatures or disasters."

15

See France Vanlaethem, "Pour une architecture épurée et rigoureuse" (interview with Alvaro Siza), *ARQ* (Montreal), no. 14 (August 1983), p. 16.

16

See "Renzo Piano Building Workshop 1964/1991: In Search of a Balance," *Process Architecture* (Tokyo), no. 700 (1992), pp. 12, 14.

17

See the RIBA catalogue *The Work of Peter Rice* (London: RIBA Publications, 1992).

18

Le Corbusier, *My Work,* trans. James Palmes (London: Architectural Press, 1960), p. 197.

Bibliography

Abalos, Inaki, and Juan Herreros. *Técnica y arquitectura en la ciudad contemporanea, 1950–1990*. Madrid: Nevea, 1992.

Abraham, Pol. *Viollet-le-Duc et le rationalisme médiévale*. Paris: Vincent Fréal, 1934.

Agacinski, Sylvianne. "Shares of Invention." *D: Columbia Documents of Architecture and Theory* 1 (1992), 53–68.

Ahlin, Janne. *Sigurd Lewerentz, Architect*. Cambridge: MIT Press, 1987.

Albertini, Bianca, and Sandro Bagnoli. *Carlo Scarpa: Architecture in Details*. Cambridge: MIT Press, 1988.

Albini, Franco, and Franca Helg. "Department Store, Rome." *Architectural Design* 32 (June 1962), 286–289.

Allen, Edward. *Stone Shelters*. Cambridge: MIT Press, 1969.

Ambasz, Emilio. *The Architecture of Luis Barragán*. New York: New York Graphic Society, 1976.

Anderson, Stanford. "Modern Architecture and Industry: Peter Behrens, the AEG and Industrial Design." *Oppositions* 21 (Summer 1980).

Ando, Tadao. "Shintai and Space." In *Architecture and Body*. New York: Rizzoli, 1988.

Angeli, Marc. "The Construction of a Meta-Physical Structure: Truth and Utility in Nineteenth Century Architecture." *Modulus* 22 (Charlottesville, 1993), 26–39.

Angerer, Fred. *Surface Structures in Building: Structure and Form*. New York: Reinhold, 1961.

Angrisani, Marcello. "Louis Kahn e la storia." *Edilizia Moderna* 86 (1965), 83–93.

Antoniades, E. "Poems with Stones: The Enduring Spirit of Dimitrios Pikionis." *A + U* 72 (December 1976), 17–22.

Appia, Adolphe. *L'Oeuvre d'art vivant*. Geneva: Atar, 1921.

Appleyard, Donald, Kevin Lynch, and John R. Myer. *The View from the Road*. Cambridge: MIT Press, 1964.

Arendt, Hannah. *The Human Condition*. Chicago: University of Chicago Press, 1958.

Arkitektur 7 (1963). (Entire issue devoted to P. V. Jensen-Klint and Kaare Klint.)

Arup, Ove. "Sydney Opera House." *Architectural Design* 35 (March 1965).

Arup, Ove. *Sydney Opera House*. Sydney: Sydney Opera House Trust, 1988. (Reprint of the 1969 retrospective paper by the engineers.)

Asplund, E. G., Gregor Paulson, et al. *Acceptera*. Tidem, Stockholm, 1931 (reprinted 1980).

Bachelard, Gaston. *The Poetics of Space*. Boston: Beacon, 1969. Translation of *La Poétique de l'espace*, 1958.

Badovici, Jean. *L'Architecture Vivante* (journal), 1923–1933. Reprint, New York, 1975.

Badovici, Jean. *Grandes constructions: béton armé—acier—verre*. Paris: Albat Morance, 1925.

Banham, Reyner. *The Architecture of the Well-Tempered Environment*. London: Architectural Press, 1969.

Banham, Reyner. *The New Brutalism*. New York: Reinhold, 1966.

Banham, Reyner. "On Trial: Louis Kahn and the Buttery-Hatch Aesthetic." *Architectural Review* 131 (March 1962).

Banham, Reyner. *Theory and Design in the First Machine Age*. New York: Praeger, 1960.

Bartholomew, Robert. "Jørn Utzon: His Work and Ideas." Thesis, University of New South Wales, Australia, 1981.

Beaux, D. "Maisons d'Islande et Génie du Lieu." *Le Carré Bleu* (March 1984).

Beaver, Patrick. *The Crystal Palace 1851–1936: A Portrait of Victorian Enterprise*. London: Hugh Evelyn, 1970.

Benedikt, Michael. *For an Architecture of Reality*. New York: Lumen Books, 1987.

Benevolo, Leonardo. *History of Modern Architecture*. 2 vols. Cambridge: MIT Press, 1971. Translation of *Storia dell'architettura moderna*, 1960.

Bergdoll, Barry. "Gilly, Friedrich." In *Macmillan Encyclopedia of Architects*. New York: Free Press, 1982.

Bergdoll, Barry. *Karl Friedrich Schinkel: An Architecture for Prussia*. New York: Rizzoli, 1994.

Bergdoll, Barry. "Primordial Fires: Frank Lloyd Wright, Gottfried Semper, and the Chicago School." Paper delivered at the Buell Center, Columbia University, 1988.

Bergdoll, Barry. "Schinkel, Karl Friedrich." In *Macmillan Encyclopedia of Architects*. New York: Free Press, 1982.

Berlage, H. P. *Gedanken über Stil in der Baukunst*. Leipzig: Julius Zeitler, 1905.

Berry, James Duncan. "The Legacy of Gottfried Semper: Studies in *Späthistoricismus*." Ph.D. dissertation, Brown University, 1989.

Bettini, S. "L'architettura di Carlo Scarpa." *Zodiac* 6 (1960), 140–187.

Bill, Max. *Form*. Basel: Karl Verner, 1952.

Bill, Max. *Robert Maillart: Bridges and Constructions*. Zurich, 1949; rpt. New York: Praeger, 1969.

Bill, Max. "Swiss National Exhibition, Lausanne." *Architectural Design* 33 (November 1963), 526–529.

Billington, David P. *Robert Maillart and the Art of Reinforced Concrete*. Cambridge: MIT Press, 1989.

Billington, David P. *Robert Maillart's Bridges: The Art of Engineering*. Princeton: Princeton University Press, 1979.

Bindman, David, and Gottfried Riemann. *Karl Friedrich Schinkel, "The English Journey": Journal of a Visit to France and Britain in 1826*. New Haven: Yale University Press, 1993.

Bisol, Giampiero Destro. "L'antimetodo di Carlo Scarpa." *Ricerca Progetto* (Bulletin of the Department of Architecture and Urbanism in the University of Rome), 15 (July 1991), 6–12.

Bjerknes, Kristian, and Hans-Emil Liden. "The Stave Churches of Kaupanger." Oslo, 1975.

Blake, Peter. *The Master Builders*. New York: Knopf, 1960.

Blaser, Werner. *Mies van der Rohe: The Art of Structure*. New York: Praeger, 1965.

Bletter, Rosemarie Haag. "On Martin Frohlich's Gottfried Semper." *Oppositions* 4 (October 1974).

Bletter, Rosemarie Haag. "Semper, Gottfried." In *Macmillan Encyclopedia of Architects*. New York: Free Press, 1982.

Bonell, Esteve. "Civic Monuments." *Architectural Review* 188 (July 1990), 69–74.

Bonell, Esteve. "Velodromo a Barcelona." *Casabella* 519 (December 1985), 54–64.

Bonell, Esteve, and Francesc Rius. "Velodrome, Barcelona." *Architectural Review* 179 (May 1986), 88–91.

Borbein, Adolf Heinrich. "Tektonik: zur Geschichte eines Begriffs der Archäologie." *Archiv für Begriffsgeschichte* 26, no. 1 (1982).

Borradori, Giovanna. "Weak Thought and Postmodernism: The Italian Departure from Deconstruction." *Social Text* 18 (Winter 1987/88), 39–49.

Borsi, Franco, and Ezio Godoli. *Paris 1900*. New York: Rizzoli, 1978.

Bottero, Maria. "Carlo Scarpa il veneziano." *World Architecture/Two* (London, 1965).

Bottero, Maria. "Organic and Rational Morphology in the Architecture of Louis Kahn." *Zodiac* 17 (1967).

Bötticher, Karl. *Die Tektonik der Hellenen*. 2 vols. Potsdam, 1852.

Bourdieu, Pierre. "The Berber House or the World Reversed." *Social Science Information* 9 (April 1970), 151–170.

Bressler, Henri. "Windows on the Court." *Rassegna* 28 (1979).

Brownlee, David B., and David G. DeLong. *Louis I. Kahn: In the Realm of Architecture*. New York: Rizzoli, 1992.

Brusatin, Manlio. "Carlo Scarpa's Minimal Systems." *Carlo Scarpa; il progetto per Santa Caterina a Treviso*. Treviso: Ponzano, 1984.

Buddensieg, Tilman. *Industriekultur: Peter Behrens and the AEG*. 1979; rpt. Cambridge: MIT Press, 1984.

Buel, Albert W. *Reinforced Concrete*. New York: Engineering News Publishing Co., 1904.

Burrows, Chris. "H. P. Berlage: Structure, Skin, Space." Unpublished thesis, Polytechnic of the South Bank, London, 1989.

Burton, Joseph Arnold, and David van Zanten. "The Architectural Hieroglyphics of Louis I. Kahn: Architecture as Logos." Unpublished abstract.

Butler, E. M. *The Tyranny of Greece over Germany*. 1935; rpt. Boston: Beacon Press, 1958.

Cacciari, Massimo. *Architecture and Nihilism: On the Philosophy of Modern Architecture*. New Haven: Yale University Press, 1993.

Cacciari, Massimo. "Mies's Classics." *Res* 16 (Autumn 1988), 9–16.

Carter, Peter. "Mies van der Rohe: An Appreciation on the Occasion, This Month, of His 75th Birthday." *Architectural Design* 31 (March 1961).

Carter, Peter. *Mies van der Rohe at Work*. New York: Praeger, 1974.

Champigneulle, Bernard. *August Perret*. Paris: Arts et Métiers Graphiques, 1959.

Chermayeff, Serge, and Christopher Alexander. *Community and Privacy: Toward a New Architecture of Humanism*. Garden City: Doubleday, 1963.

Chewing, J. A. "Root, John Wellborn." In *Macmillan Encyclopedia of Architects*. New York: Free Press, 1982.

Choay, Françoise. *Das Unesco-Gebäude in Paris*. Teufen, Switzerland, 1958.

Choisy, Auguste. *Histoire de l'architecture*. 2 vols. Paris: E. Rouveyre, n.s., 1899.

Christie, Sigrid and Hakon. *Nord Kirker Akershus*. Oslo, 1969.

Cirlot, J. E. *A Dictionary of Symbols*. London: Routledge & Paul, 1962.

Clarke, Somers, and R. Engelbach. *Ancient Egyptian Construction and Architecture*. London: Oxford University Press, 1930; rpt. New York: Dover, 1990.

Clotet, Luis, and Ignacio Paricio, eds. *Construcciones*. Monografías de Arquitectura y Vivienda, no. 43. Madrid, 1993.

Coaldrake, William H. *The Way of the Carpenter: Tools and Japanese Architecture*. New York and Tokyo: Weatherhill, 1990.

Collins, George. "Antonio Gaudi: Structure and Form." *Perspecta* 8 (1963).

Collins, Peter. *Concrete: The Vision of a New Architecture*. London: Faber & Faber, 1959.

Collins, Peter. "Perret, Auguste." In *Macmillan Encyclopedia of Architects*. New York: Free Press, 1982.

Columbia University. *Architecture and Body*. New York: Rizzoli, 1988.

Conrads, Ulrich, and Bernhard Leitner. "Audible Space: Experiences and Conjectures." *Daidalos* 17 (1985), 28–45.

Cook, John W., and Heinrich Klotz. "Louis Kahn." In *Conversations with Architects*. New York: Praeger, 1973.

Cook, Peter. "Trees and Horizons: The Architecture of Sverre Fehn." *Architectural Review* 170 (August 1981), 102–106.

Coomaraswamy, A. K. *Selected Papers*. Ed. R. Lipsey. Princeton: Princeton University Press, 1977.

Correa, Charles. *The New Landscape—Bombay*. Bombay: Book Society of India, 1985.

Correa, Charles. "Regionalism and Architecture." Lecture at the Bienal, Buenos Aires, 1991.

Coulton, J. J. *Ancient Greek Architects at Work: Problems of Structure and Design*. Ithaca: Cornell University Press, 1977.

Crippa, Maria Antonietta. *Carlo Scarpa: Theory, Design, Projects*. Cambridge: MIT Press, 1986.

Dal Co, Francesco. *Figures of Architecture and Thought: German Architecture Culture, 1880–1920*. New York: Rizzoli, 1990.

Dal Co, Francesco, and Giuseppe Mazzariol. *Carlo Scarpa: The Complete Works*. Milan: Electa; New York: Rizzoli, 1985.

Damisch, Hubert. "The Space Between: A Structuralist Approach to the *Dictionnaire*." *Architectural Design* 50, nos. 3/4 (1980).

Debord, Guy. *Commentary on the Society of the Spectacle*. London: Verso, 1990. Translation of *Commentaires sur le société du spectacle*, 1988.

Denyer, Susan. *African Traditional Architecture*. London: Heinemann, 1978.

De Vere Allen, James, and Thomas H. Wilson. "Swahili Houses and Tombs of the Coast of Kenya." *Art and Archaeology Research Papers*, no. 16 (London, December 1979).

De Zurko, Edward R. *Origins of Functionalist Theory*. New York: Columbia University Press, 1957.

Dimitracopoulou, A. "Dimitris Pikionis." *AAQ* 2/3 (1982), 62.

Dini, Massimo. *Renzo Piano: Projects and Buildings, 1964–1983*. New York: Rizzoli, 1984.

Disosway, Mason Hollier, ed. "Craft and Architecture." *Modulus* 22 (Charlottesville, 1993).

Dormoy, Marie. "Interview d'Auguste Perret sur l'Exposition internationale des arts décoratifs." *L'Amour de l'Art* (May 1925).

Dotremont, Christian, ed. *Cobra 1948–51*. Paris: Jean-Michel Place, 1980.

Drew, Philip. *Leaves of Iron: Glenn Murcutt, Pioneer of an Australian Architectural Form*. Sydney: Law, 1985.

Drew, Philip. "The Petrification of the Tent: The Phenomenon of Tent Mimicry." *Architecture Australia* (June 1987), 18–22.

Drew, Philip. *Tensile Architecture*. Boulder: Westview Press, 1979.

Drew, Phillip. *The Third Generation: The Changing Meaning of Architecture*. New York: Praeger, 1972.

Drexler, Arthur. *The Architecture of Japan*. New York: Museum of Modern Art, 1955.

Drexler, Arthur, ed. *The Architecture of the Ecole des Beaux-Arts*. New York: Museum of Modern Art, 1977.

Duboy, Philippe, and Yukio Futagawa. "Banca Popolare di Verona Head Offices." *Global Architecture* 63 (Tokyo, 1983).

Durand, Jean-Nicolas-Louis. *Nouveau Précis des Leçons d'Architecture, donné à l'Ecole Impériale Polytechnique*. Paris, 1813.

Eastlake, Charles. *A History of the Gothic Revival*. 1872; rpt. New York: Humanities Press, 1970; 2d ed. 1978.

Eco, Umberto. "A Componential Analysis of the Architectural Sign/ Column/ ." *Semiotica* 5, no. 2 (1972). Translation by David Osmond-Smith.

Eliade, Mircea. *The Sacred and the Profane*. New York: Harcourt, Brace & World, 1959.

Elliot, Cecil D. *Technics and Architecture: The Development of Materials and Systems for Buildings*. Cambridge: MIT Press, 1992.

Engel, Heino. *The Japanese House*. Rutland, Vermont: Charles E. Tuttle, 1964.

Engel, Heino. *Measure and Construction of the Japanese House*. Rutland, Vermont: Charles E. Tuttle, 1985.

Evans, Robin. "Mies van der Rohe's Paradoxical Symmetries." *AA Files* 19 (Spring 1990).

Faber, Tobias. *Jørn Utzon, Houses in Fredensborg*. Berlin: Ernst & Sohn, 1991.

Fanelli, Giovanni. *Architettura moderna in Olanda 1900–1940*. Florence: Marchi & Bertolli, 1968. (English translation.)

Fanelli, Giovanni, and Roberto Gagliani. *Il principio del rivestimento: prolegomena a una storia dell'architettura contemporanea*. Rome: Laterza, 1994.

Fathy, Hassan. *Architecture for the Poor: An Experiment in Rural Egypt*. Chicago: University of Chicago Press, 1973.

Fehn, Sverre. "Archaic Modernism." *Architectural Review* 179 (February 1986), 57–60.

Fehn, Sverre. "Biennale di Venezia: 10 architetti per il nuovo palazzo del cinema al Lido." *Domus* 730 (September 1991), 54–56.

Fehn, Sverre. "Has a Doll Life." *Perspecta* 24 (1988).

Fehn, Sverre. *The Poetry of the Straight Line*. Helsinki: Museum of Finnish Architecture, 1992.

Fehn, Sverre. "Three Museums." *AA Files* 9 (Summer 1985), 10–15.

Fehn, Sverre. "The Tree and the Horizon." *Spazio e Società* 3 (1980).

Fichten, John. *Building Construction before Mechanization*. Cambridge: MIT Press, 1986.

Fichten, John. *The Construction of Gothic Cathedrals: A Study of Medieval Vault Erection*. Chicago: University of Chicago Press, 1961; 2d ed. 1981.

Fjeld, Per Olaf. *Sverre Fehn: The Thought of Construction*. New York: Rizzoli, 1983.

Fonatti, Franco. *Elemente des Bauens bei Carlo Scarpa*. Vienna: Wiener Akademiereihe, 1984.

Ford, Edward R. *The Details of Modern Architecture*. Cambridge: MIT Press, 1990.

Forster, Kurt W. "Schinkel's Panoramic Planning of Central Berlin." *Modulus* 16 (Charlottesville, 1983).

Forte, Giorgio. *Antiche ricette di pittura murale*. Venice: Noale, 1984.

Frampton, Kenneth. "Louis Kahn and the French Connection." *Oppositions* 22 (Fall 1980).

Frampton, Kenneth. *Modern Architecture: A Critical History*. London: Thames & Hudson, 1980.

Frampton, Kenneth, Anthony Webster, and Anthony Tischhauser. *Calatrava Bridges*. Zurich: Artemis, 1993.

Frascari, Marco. "The Body and Architecture in the Drawings of Carlo Scarpa." *Res* 14 (Autumn 1987), 123–142.

Frascari, Marco. "A Deciphering of a Wonderful Cipher: Eleven in the Architecture of Carlo Scarpa." *Oz* 13 (1991).

Frascari, Marco. "A Heroic and Admirable Machine: The Theatre of the Architecture of Carlo Scarpa, Architetto Veneto." *Poetics Today* 10 (Spring 1989), 103–124.

Frascari, Marco. "A 'Measure' in Architecture: A Medical-Architectural Theory by Simone Stratico, Architetto Veneto." *Res* 9 (Spring 1985).

Frascari, Marco. "A New Corporeality of Architecture." *Journal of Architectural Education* 40, no. 2 (1987).

Frascari, Marco. "The Tell-the-Tale Detail." In Paula Behrens and Anthony Fisher, eds., *The Building of Architecture*. Via no. 7. Philadelphia: University of Pennsylvania; Cambridge: MIT Press, 1984.

Frascari, Marco. "The True and the Appearance: Italian Facadism and Carlo Scarpa." *Daidalos* 6 (December 1982).

Frei, Hans. "Über Max Bill als Architect." In *Konkrete Architektur*. Baden: Verlag Lars Müller, 1991.

Fuerst, Walter René, and Samuel J. Hume. *Twentieth Century Stage Decoration*. 2 vols. New York: Alfred A. Knopf, 1929; rpt. New York: Dover, 1967.

Futagawa, Yukio, ed. *Frank Lloyd Wright Monograph*. Text by Bruce Breohs Pfeiffer. 12 vols. Tokyo, 1984–1988.

Gage, John, ed. *Goethe on Art*. Berkeley and Los Angeles: University of California Press, 1980.

Gans, Deborah, ed. *Bridging the Gap*. New York: Van Nostrand Reinhold, 1959.

Gehlen, Arnold. *Man in the Age of Technology*. New York: Columbia University Press, 1980.

Gehlen, Arnold. "Die Säkularisierung des Fortschritts." In Gehlen, *Einblicke*, ed. K. S. Rehberg, vol. 7. Frankfurt: Klochtermann, 1978.

Gelpke, Rudolf. "Art and Sacred Drugs in the Orient." *World Cultures and Modern Art*. Munich: Bruckman, 1972.

Geraniotis, Roula. "Gottfried Semper and the Chicago School." Paper delivered at Buell Center symposium on the German influence on American architects, Columbia University, 1988.

Ghermandi, Martino. "I moderni e gli antichi romani." *Costruire* 58 (June 1988), 90–93.

Giedion, Sigfried. *Architecture and the Phenomenon of Transition: Three Space Conceptions of Architecture*. Cambridge: Harvard University Press, 1971.

Giedion, Sigfried. *Architecture, You and Me*. Cambridge: Harvard University Press, 1958.

Giedion, Sigfried. *The Beginnings of Architecture*. Princeton: Princeton University Press, 1964.

Giedion, Sigfried. "Jørn Utzon and the Third Generation." *Zodiac* 14 (1965).

Giedion, Sigfried. *Mechanization Takes Command*. New York: Oxford University Press, 1948; 2d ed. 1955.

Giedion, Sigfried. *Space, Time and Architecture*. Cambridge: Harvard University Press, 1941; 3d ed. 1954.

Girsberger, H. *Alvar Aalto*. London, 1963.

Giurgola, Romaldo, and Jaimini Mehta. *Louis I. Kahn*. Boulder: Westview Press, 1975.

Glaeser, Ludwig. *Mies van der Rohe: Drawings in the Collection of the Museum of Modern Art*. New York, 1969.

Glaeser, Ludwig, and Yukio Futagawa. "Mies van der Rohe: Farnsworth House, Plano, Illinois 1945–1950." *Global Architecture* 27 (Tokyo, 1974).

Glahn, Else. "Chinese Building Standards in the 12th Century." *Scientific American* (May 1981), 162–173.

Glahn, Else. "*Yingzao Fashi*: Chinese Building Standards in the Sung Dynasty." In Paula Behrens and Anthony Fisher, eds., *The Building of Architecture*. Via no. 7. Philadelphia: University of Pennsylvania; Cambridge: MIT Press, 1984.

Glob, P. V. *Denmark: An Archaeological History from the Stone Age to the Vikings*. Ithaca: Cornell University Press, 1971.

Grassi, Giorgio. *L'architettura come mestiere*. Milan: Cluva, 1980.

Grassi, Giorgio. "Avant-Garde and Continuity." *Oppositions* 21 (Summer 1980).

Basic Data Underlying Clinical Decision Making in Vascular Surgery

JOHN M. PORTER, M.D.
LLOYD M. TAYLOR, JR., M.D.

Editors

Compiled from

ANNALS OF VASCULAR SURGERY

International Journal of Vascular Surgery

QUALITY MEDICAL PUBLISHING, INC

ST. LOUIS, MISSOURI
1994

Printed in the United States of America.

Quality Medical Publishing, Inc.
11970 Borman Drive, Ste. 222
St. Louis, Missouri 63146

This publication was supported in part by an educational grant
from W.L. Gore & Associates, Flagstaff, Arizona.

ISBN 0-942219-71-6

GW/WW/WW
5 4 3 2 1

Preface

From the first issue of *Annals of Vascular Surgery*, the section on Basic Data was entrusted to John Porter's editorship. Over the years this particular signature has been the object of uniform praise from our readers. It is a repository of data pertinent to clinical decision making and applicable to specific subsets of patients within each disease category. Over the last year John Porter has gradually transferred the editorship of this section to Lloyd Taylor, who is now in charge of it. This compendium includes those sections on Basic Data published from July, 1989 through May, 1994. We would be very pleased if it should become a tool that enhances scientific choice in clinical practice.

Our thanks to Drs. Porter and Taylor for their discriminating editorship and to Quality Medical Publishing for their collaboration in the publication of this book.

Ramon Berguer, *Detroit*   **Edouard Kieffer,** *Paris*

We continue to believe that the essence of the practice of vascular surgery, as well as the practice of medicine in general, is decision making based on incomplete and/or imperfect data. Such decision making can be made somewhat easier if the physician has available references providing timely data on the topic in question. The objective of the Basic Data section in *Annals of Vascular Surgery* is to provide the practicing physician with timely and relevant data concerning selected clinical topics. In so far as the series has succeeded, credit is due entirely to the contributing authors. With this edition of Basic Data, we are pleased to announce that the baton is passing from Dr. John M. Porter, who began the series, to Dr. Lloyd M. Taylor, Jr. We both hope the Basic Data section has been and will continue to be helpful to you in your practice. Please feel free to contact us with any suggestions you may have.

John Porter, *Portland*   **Lloyd M. Taylor, Jr.,** *Portland*

Contents

TRAUMA/INFECTION

AORTA AND VISCERAL BRANCHES

EXTREMITIES

CAROTID/VERTEBRAL ARTERIES

VEINS

Diagnosis

1

Noninvasive Vascular Testing

Gregory L. Moneta, MD, D. Eugene Strandness, Jr, MD, Seattle, Washington

The noninvasive vascular laboratory is becoming more and more important in the diagnosis and care of patients with peripheral vascular disease. Proper interpretation of results of any noninvasive test requires knowledge of the inherent limitations of each modality of testing as well as its ability to detect clinically relevant findings. The accuracy of a particular noninvasive vascular test is usually determined in comparison to arteriography. Unfortunately arteriography is not a perfect standard.[9,57] There is both significant inter- and intra-observer variability in the interpretation of arteriograms. Nevertheless, because arteriograms serve as the basis of many clinical decisions in vascular surgery, arteriography is considered the "gold standard" in the evaluation of noninvasive vascular testing.

Every noninvasive test should be evaluated in terms of its sensitivity, specificity, positive predictive value (PPV), and negative predictive value (NPV). This is done by constructing a 2 × 2 table for each clinically important variable with respect to the accepted "gold standard" (Fig. 1). Sensitivity refers to the ability of the test to detect the variable in question. Specificity is the ability of the test to accurately predict a variable not present. PPV refers to how often the variable in question is actually present when the test says it is. NPV refers to how often the variable is actually not present when the test indicates it is not present. When interpreting these values it is also important to understand the frequency of the disease in the sample population. For example, if the frequency of a particular finding is relatively

rare in a population, a test with a high sensitivity and positive predictive value is desirable. Specificity and negative predictive value will be high regardless of whether the test is accurate or not. However, if the frequency of the disease is high in a population, a test with a high specificity is necessary to distinguish the few normals from the large number of diseased.

The purpose of this report is to review the sensitivities, specificities, PPV, and NPV for the most commonly employed noninvasive vascular tests with respect to clinically important parameters. The percentages given in Tables I to IV represent calculations derived from pooled data of the individual references cited. Only studies in which the data could be analyzed in terms of sensitivities, specificities, PPV, and NPV are included.

From the Department of Surgery, Division of Vascular Surgery, University of Washington, Seattle, Wash.

"Test" "Standard"

	+	−
+	a	b
−	c	d

a = true positives   b = false positives
c = false negatives   d = true negatives

$$\text{Sensitivity} = \frac{a}{a + c} \qquad \text{Specificity} = \frac{d}{b + d}$$

$$\text{PPV} = \frac{a}{a + b} \qquad \text{NPV} = \frac{d}{c + d}$$

Fig. 1. 2 × 2 Table for determining sensitivity, specificity, positive predictive value (PPV) and negative predictive value (NPV).

1

Table I. Extracranial cerebrovascular disease (mode of testing versus arteriography)

Test	Variable	Sensitivity (%)	Specificity (%)	PPV (%)	NPV (%)	Ref.
Periorbital	>50% ICA stenosis	76	96	92	86	23,38,43,48
Doppler	ICA occlusion	NA*	NA	NA	NA	
OPG-Gee	>50% ICA stenosis	86	93	95	82	1,5,41
	ICA occlusion	NA	NA	NA	NA	
Continuous	50%-90% ICA stenosis	89	96	91	96	29,36,59,62
wave Doppler	ICA occlusion	91	98	84	99	7,29,59,62
Duplex scanning	50%-99% ICA stenosis	94	93	87	97	11,23,29,36,58
	ICA occlusion	83	99	95	97	7,11,23,28,29,36,58
B-mode imaging	50%-90% stenosis	73	77	63	85	51,62
	ICA occlusion	53	98	53	97	13,15,35,51,62
	Ulceration[†]	56	87	65	83	16,21,26,47,62

*Not applicable.
[†]Compared with pathology specimen.

Table II. Deep venous thrombosis (mode of testing versus arteriography)

Test	Thrombosis location	Sensitivity (%)	Specificity (%)	PPV (%)	NPV (%)	Ref.
Continuous wave Doppler ultrasound	Ilio/femoral/pop*	92	81	90	84	20,45,53,60
Phleborheography	Ilio/femoral/pop	89	92	87	93	10,12,14,19,24
Occlusive impedance plethysmography	Ilio/femoral/pop	90	93	83	96	17,27,32,33,39
Strain gauge plethysmography[†]	Ilio/femoral/pop	97	83	86	96	4,6,8,18
Duplex/B-mode ultrasound	Ilio/femoral/pop	95	96	98	92	20,31,49,55

*Iliac/femoral/popliteal arteries.
[†]Criteria for positivity vary from laboratory to laboratory.

Table III. Doppler ultrasound and renal evaluations

Variable	Diagnostic criteria	Confirmation	Sensitivity (%)	Specificity (%)	PPV (%)	NPV (%)	Ref.
Transplant rejection	$\dfrac{PSV - \text{lowest } DV}{PSV} \geq 0.8$	Biopsy or clinical course	69	86	74	82	52
	$\dfrac{PSV}{PDV} > 2$	Biopsy or clinical course	95	95	95	95	54
	"↓ diastolic flow"	Biopsy	96	100			44
Transplant artery stenosis	↑ PSV, ↑ spectral broadening	Arteriography	100	90	76	100	25,50
Native renal artery stenosis	PSV > 100 cm/sec	Arteriography (50%)	42	92	85	62	2
	Acceleration index >3.8	Arteriography	100	93	83	100	30
	$\dfrac{PSV \text{ renal artery}}{PSV \text{ aorta}} > 3.5$	Arteriography (>60%)	84	97	94	93	56

PSV = peak systolic velocity; DV = diastolic velocity; PDV = peak diastolic velocity; Acceleration index = systolic velocity after 1 s/transmitted ultrasound frequency.

Table IV. Duplex scanning and detection of high-grade peripheral arterial stenosis*[37]

Artery	Sensitivity (%)	Specificity (%)	PPV (%)	NPV (%)
Iliac	89	90	75	96
Common femoral	67	98	80	96
Superficial femoral	84	93	90	88
Profunda	67	81	53	88
Popliteal	75	97	86	93
All segments	82	92	80	93

*>50% stenosis.

REFERENCES

1. Abu Rahma AF, Diethrich EB. Comparison of various oculoplethysmography modalities. J Vasc Surg 1985;2:288-291.
2. Avasthi PS, Wyatt FV, Greene ER. Noninvasive diagnosis of renal artery stenosis by echo-Doppler velocimetry. Kidney Int 1984;25:824-829.
3. Bandyk DF, Thiele BL. Noninvasive assessment of carotid artery disease. West J Med 1983;139:486-501.
4. Barnes RW, Hokanson DE, Wu KK, et al. Detection of deep vein thrombosis with an automatic electrically calibrated strain gauge plethysmograph. Surgery 1977;82:219-223.
5. Belkin M, Bucknam CA, Giuca JE, et al. Combined oculopneumoplethysmography and duplex scan. Arch Surg 1985;120:809-811.
6. Boccalon H, Chikhany G, Lozes A, et al. Venous plethysmography applied in pathologic conditions. Angiology 1981;32:822-832.
7. Bornstein NM, Beloev ZG, Norris JW. The limitations of diagnosis of carotid occlusion by Doppler ultrasound. Ann Surg 1988;207:315-317.
8. Bounameaux H, Krahenbuhl B, Vukanovic S. Diagnosis of deep vein thrombosis by combination of Doppler ultrasound flow examination and strain gauge plethysmography: An alternative to venography only in particular conditions despite improved accuracy of the Doppler method. Thromb Haemost 1982;47:141-144.
9. Chikos PM, Fisher LD, Hirsch JH, et al. Observer variability in evaluating extracranial carotid artery stenosis. Stroke 1983;14:885-892.
10. Classen JN, Richardson JB, Koontz C. A three-year experience with phleoborheography: A noninvasive technique for the diagnosis of deep venous thrombosis. Ann Surg 1982;195:800-802.
11. Colhoun E, Macerlean D. Carotid artery imaging using duplex scanning and bidirectional arteriography: A comparison. Clin Radiol 1984;35:101-106.
12. Collins GJ, Rich NM, Anderson CA, et al. Phleborheographic diagnosis of venous obstruction. Ann Surg 1979;189:25-28.
13. Comerota AJ, Cranley JJ, Cook SE. Real-time B-mode carotid imaging in diagnosis of cerebrovascular disease. Surgery 1981;89:718-729.
14. Comerota AJ, Cranley JJ, Cook SE, et al. Phleborheography—results of a ten-year experience. Surgery 1982;91:573-581.
15. Comerota AJ, Cranley JJ, Katz ML, et al. Real-time B-mode carotid imaging: A three-year multicenter experience. J Vasc Surg 1984;1:84-95.
16. Comerota AJ, Katz ML, White JV. B-mode carotid imaging. In Kempczinski RF, Yao JST, eds. Practical Noninvasive Vascular Diagnosis, 2nd ed. Chicago: Yearbook Medical Publishers, 1987, 320-338.
17. Cooperman M, Martin EW, Satiani B, et al. Detection of deep venous thrombosis by impedance plethysmography. Am J Surg 1979;137:252-254.
18. Cramer M, Beach KW, Strandness DE Jr. The detection of proximal deep venous thrombosis by strain gauge plethysmography through the use of an outflow capacitance discriminant line. Bruit 1983;7:17-23.
19. Cranley JJ. Diagnosis of deep vein thrombosis by phleborheography. In Bernstein EF, ed. Noninvasive Diagnostic Techniques in Vascular Disease. St. Louis: CV Mosby, 1985;730-741.
20. Dauzat MM, Laroche J-P, Charms C, et al. Real-time B-mode ultrasonography for better specificity in the noninvasive diagnosis of deep venous thrombosis. J Ultrasound Med 1986;5:625-631.
21. Davenport KL, Sterpetti AV, Hunter WJ, et al. Real-time B-mode carotid imaging and plaque morphology. J Vasc Tech 1987;11:176-182.
22. Duke LJ, Slaymaker EE, Lamberth WC, et al. Results of ophthalmosonometry and supraorbital photoplethysmography in evaluating carotid arterial stenoses. Circulation 1979 (suppl 1);60:I-127–I-131.
23. Eikelboom BC, Ackerstaff RGA, Ludwig JW, et al. Digital video subtraction angiography and duplex scanning in assessment of carotid artery disease: Comparison with conventional angiography. Surgery 1983;94:821-825
24. Elliott JP, Hageman JH, Belanger AC, et al. Phleborheography: A correlative study with venography. Henry Ford Hosp Med J 1980;28:189-192.
25. Ferretti G, Salomone A, Malfi B, et al. Duplex scanning and the transplanted kidney. Lancet 1986;1:219.
26. Fischer GG, Anderson DC, Farber R, et al. Prediction of carotid disease by ultrasound and digital subtraction angiography. Arch Neurol 1985;42:224-227.
27. Fori ME, Gurewich V. Fibrin degradation products and impedance plethysmography measurements in the diagnosis of acute deep venous thrombosis. Arch Intern Med 1980;140:903-906.
28. Glover JL, Bendick PJ, Jackson VP, et al. Duplex ultrasonography, digital subtraction angiography and conventional angiography in assessing carotid atherosclerosis. Arch Surg 1984;119:664-669.
29. Hames TK, Humphries KN, Ratliff DA, et al. The validation of duplex scanning and continuous wave Doppler imaging: A comparison with conventional angiography. Ultrasound Med & Biol 1985;11:827-834.
30. Handa N, Ryuzo F, Etani H, et al. Efficacy of echo-Doppler examination for the evaluation of reno-vascular disease. Ultrasound Med Biol 1988;14:1-5.
31. Hannan LJ, Stedje KJ, Skorcz MJ, et al. Venous imaging of the extremities: Our first twenty five hundred cases. Bruit 1986;10:29-32.
32. Harris WH, Athanasoulis C, Waltman AC, et al. Cuff impedance phleobography and ^{125}I fibrinogen scanning versus roentgenographic phlebography for diagnosis of thrombophlebitis following hip surgery. J Bone Joint Surg 1976;58A:939-944.
33. Hull R, Vanaken WG, Hirsh J, et al. Impedance plethysmography using the occlusive cuff technique in the diagnosis of venous thrombosis. Circulation 1976;53:696-700.
34. Jacobs NM, Grant EG, Schellinger D, et al. Duplex carotid sonography: Criteria for stenosis accuracy and pitfalls. Radiology 1985;154:385-391.

35. James M, Ernest F, Forbes JS, et al. High resolution dynamic ultrasound imaging of the carotid bifurcation: A prospective evaluation. Radiology 1982;144:853-858.

36. Johnston KW, Baker WH, Burnham SJ, et al. Quantitative analysis of continuous wave Doppler spectral broadening for the diagnosis of carotid disease: Results of a multicenter study. J Vasc Surg 1986;4:493-504.

37. Kohler TR, Nance DR, Cramer MM, et al. Duplex scanning for diagnosis of aortoiliac and femoropopliteal disease: A prospective study. Circulation 1987;76:1074-1080.

38. Kohler TR, Zierler RE, Martin RL, et al. Noninvasive diagnosis of renal artery stenosis by ultrasonic duplex scanning. J Vasc Surg 1986;4:450-456.

39. Liapis CD, Satiani B, Kuhns M, et al. Value of impedance plethysmography in suspected venous disease of the lower extremity. Angiology 1980;31:522-525.

40. Lye CR, Sumner DS, Strandness DE Jr. The accuracy of the supraorbital Doppler examination in the diagnosis of hemodynamically significant carotid occlusive disease. Surgery 1976;79:42-45.

41. McDonald PT, Rich NM, Collins GJ, et al. Doppler cerebrovascular examination, oculoplethysmography and ocular pneumoplethysmography. Arch Surg 1978;113:1341-1347.

42. Moneta GL, Taylor DC, Strandness DE Jr. Noninvasive assessment of cerebrovascular disease. Ann Vasc Surg 1986;1:489-498.

43. Moore WS, Bean B, Burton R, et al. The use of ophthalmosonometry in the diagnosis of carotid artery stenosis. Surgery 1977;82:107-113.

44. Neumyer MM, Gifford RRM, Thiele BL. Identification of early rejection in renal allografts with duplex ultrasonography. J Vasc Tech 1988;12:19-23.

45. Nicholas GG, Miller FJ Jr, Demuth WE, et al. Clinical vascular laboratory diagnosis of deep venous thrombosis. Ann Surg 1977;186:213-216.

46. Nicholls SC, Strandness DE Jr. Noninvasive diagnosis of cerebrovascular insufficiency. Int Surg 1984;69:199-206.

47. O'Donnell TF Jr, Erdoes L, Mackey WC, et al. Correlation of B-mode ultrasound imaging and arteriography with pathologic findings at carotid endarterectomy. Arch Surg 1985;120:443-449.

48. Perler BA, Carr J, Williams GM. Oculoplethysmography and supraorbital Doppler evaluation of carotid disease: A reappraisal. Am Surg 1985;51:107-110.

49. Raghavendra BN, Horii SC, Hilton S, et al. Deep venous thrombosis: Detection by probe compression of veins. J Ultrasound Med 1986;5:89-95.

50. Reinitz ER, Goldman MH, Sais J, et al. Evaluation of transplant renal artery blood flow by Doppler sound-spectrum analysis. Arch Surg 1983;118:415-419.

51. Ricotta JJ, Bryan FA, Bond MG, et al. Multicenter validation study of real-time (B-mode) ultrasound arteriography, and pathologic examination. J Vasc Surg 1987;6:512-520.

52. Rifkin MD, Needleman L, Pasto ME, et al. Evaluation of renal transplant rejection by duplex Doppler examination: Value of the resistive index. AJR 1987;148:759-762.

53. Strandness DE Jr, Sumner DS. Ultrasonic velocity detector in the diagnosis of thrombophlebitis. Arch Surg 1972;104:180-183.

54. Steinberg HV, Nelson RC, Murphy FB, et al. Renal allograft rejection: Evaluation by Doppler US and MR imaging. Radiology 1987;162:337-342.

55. Sullivan ED, Peter DJ, Cranley JJ. Real-time B-mode venous ultrasound. J Vasc Surg 1984;1:465-471.

56. Taylor DC, Ketler MD, Moneta GL, et al. Duplex ultrasound in the diagnosis of renal artery stenosis: A prospective evaluation. J Vasc Surg 1988;7:363-369.

57. Thiele BL, Strandness DE Jr. Accuracy of angiographic quantification of peripheral atherosclerosis. Prog Cardiovasc Diseases 1983;26:223-236.

58. Thiele BL, Strandness DE Jr. Duplex scanning and ultrasonic arteriography in the detection of carotid disease. In Kempczinski RT, Yao JST, eds. Practical Noninvasive Vascular Diagnosis, 2nd ed, Chicago: Yearbook Medical Publishers, 1987;339-363.

59. Trockel U, Hennerici M, Aulich A, et al. The superiority of combined continuous wave Doppler examination over preorbital Doppler for the detection of extracranial carotid disease. J Neurol, Neurosurg and Psych 1984;47:43-50.

60. Yao JST, Henkin RE, Bergan JJ. Venous thromboembolic disease: Evaluation of new methodology in treatment. Arch Surg 1974;109:664-668.

61. Yap HK, Dietrich RB, Kangarloo H, et al. Acute renal allograft rejection, comparative value of ultrasound versus magnetic resonance imaging. Transplantation 1987;43:249-252.

62. Zwiebel WJ, Austin CW, Sackett JF, et al. Correlation of high resolution, B-mode and continuous wave Doppler sonography with arteriography in the diagnosis of carotid stenosis. Radiology 1983;149:523-532.

2

Cardiac Testing and Cardiac Risk Associated With Vascular Surgery

Richard A. Yeager, MD, Portland, Oregon

Exercise electrocardiography as well as various radionuclide cardiac tests provide information that is predictive for the arteriographic presence of coronary artery disease, adverse cardiac events, and patient survival. A condensed interpretation of these data is difficult due to variability with study methodologies and patient populations. Nevertheless, some practical information can be derived from available data which may prove useful to the vascular surgeon who frequently faces a difficult surgical decision in patients with associated coronary artery disease.

The various tests should be viewed as complementary rather than competitive, since they frequently reflect different parameters of myocardial function. Dipyridamole–assisted thallium-201 imaging is used to assess segmental myocardial hypoperfusion, whereas electrocardiographic ab-

From the Division of Vascular Surgery, Department of Surgery, Oregon Health Sciences University, and Portland Veterans Administration Medical Center, Portland, Ore.

normalities associated with exercise may be related to metabolic changes caused by regional myocardial hypoxia and ion flux.[1] Radionuclide arteriography can provide important prognostic information by measuring ventricular function at rest and with exercise.

The vascular surgeon is keenly interested in the ability of these tests to predict perioperative cardiac complications, including myocardial infarction (MI) and cardiac death. Variability of study end-points and end-point definitions is a confounding factor that adversely affects meaningful interpretation of these data. The incidence of perioperative MI in these studies greatly depends on the authors' method of identification and criteria for defining MI. Although no perfect test exists for the prediction of perioperative cardiac complications following vascular surgery, the three tests analyzed (exercise ECG, thallium-201 imaging, and radionuclide arteriography) have proved useful for preoperatively assessing cardiac risk.

Table I. Incidence of perioperative MI with vascular surgery

Procedure	Overall MI incidence (%)	Fatal MI incidence (%)	Ref.
Carotid endarterectomy	2.0	0.8	2-9
Abdominal aortic aneurysm repair	6.4	2.2	10-17
Ischemic lower extremity revascularization	6.0	2.3	18-22
Mixture of general vascular surgery	5.5	2.9	23-30

MI = myocardial infarction.

Table II. Incidence of perioperative MI following vascular surgery according to method of study and criteria for MI

Method and MI criteria	MI incidence (%)	Ref.
Retrospective	3.0	2-4,6,7,9,14, 15,19,22-26
Prospective using ECG changes and cardiac enzyme elevation	9.7	8,16,17,27-29
Prospective using MB isoenzyme elevation as only criterion	14.7	13,20

Table III. Ability of test to predict presence of arteriographically significant coronary artery disease

Test (criterion for positive test)	Sensitivity (%)	Specificity (%)	Ref.
Exercise electrocardiography (ST depression)	60-75	75-85	1,31-33
Stress–thallium scan (exercise defect)	80-90	80-90	1,34,35
Intravenous dipyridamole thallium imaging (transient or persistent defect)	93	80	36
Radionuclide arteriography (resting EF <50% or wall motion abnormality)	48	88	37
Radionuclide arteriography (resting or exercise abnormality)	85	59	38
Radionuclide arteriography (new exercise–induced wall motion abnormality)	76	95	39,40

EF = ejection fraction.

Table IV. Prediction of perioperative MI or cardiac death associated with vascular surgery*

Test with criterion for positivity	Sensitivity (%)	Specificity (%)	Positive predictive value (%)	Ref.
Dipyridamole thallium imaging (redistribution)	92	66	22	27,30,41-43
Exercise ECG (ischemic ST-T segment depression)	50	79	21	21,27,44
Radionuclide arteriography (EF ≤35%)	44	94	52	13,17,20

*Cardiac complications other than MI or cardiac death are excluded.

Table V. Prediction of perioperative cardiac complications* associated with vascular surgery

Test with criterion for positivity	Sensitivity (%)	Specificity (%)	Positive predictive value (%)	Ref.
Dipyridamole thallium imaging (redistribution)	89	69	38	27,[†]29,30, 41-43[†]
Exercise ECG (ischemic ST-T segment depression)	49	78	39	21,27,[†]28, 29,45
Radionuclide arteriography (EF ≤35%)	41	94	50	8,13,[†]17,[†] 20[†]

*Cardiac death, MI, pulmonary edema, ventricular arrhythmia, cardiac ischemia.
[†]Included only MI or cardiac death.

Table VI. Prediction of perioperative MI or cardiac death associated with elective aortic surgery

Method of risk assessment with criterion for positivity	Sensitivity (%)	Specificity (%)	Positive predictive value (%)	Ref.
Goldman classification (class 2 & 3)	64	59	16	12*
Dipyridamole thallium imaging (two or more areas of redistribution)	100	72	26	46
Radionuclide arteriography (EF ≤35%)	46	91	40	13,17

*Included cardiac death, MI, pulmonary edema, and ventricular tachycardia as endpoints.

Table VII. Survival data based on resting radionuclide arteriography ejection fraction

Patient population	Results	Survival (%) 1 yr	2 yr	Ref.
Patients with known or suspected coronary artery disease	EF <30%	75-80	55-65	47
Patients after MI with preadmission New York Heart Association Functional Classes II-IV	EF <40%, ventricular ectopy ≥ 10 depolarizations/hr, pulmonary rales upper lung fields		40	48
Patients after MI with preadmission New York Heart Association Functional Class I	EF ≥40%, ventricular ectopy < 10 depolarizations/hr, no pulmonary rales in upper lung fields		97	48
Patients after MI	EF ≥51%		95	49
	0.41 ≤ EF <0.51		88	
	EF ≤0.40		79	
Patients after MI with clinical ventricular failure	EF ≥51%		93	49
	0.41 ≤ EG <0.51		81	
	EF ≤0.40		74	

Table VIII. Prediction of future cardiac events

Patient population	Test	Results	Positive predictive value (%) Death, or MI by 19 mo	Death, MI, or new onset severe angina by 36 mo	Cardiac death, MI, or coronary bypass by 60 mo	Ref.
Patients after MI	Resting radio-nuclide arte-riography	EF <35%	36			50
	Intravenous dipyridamole thallium scan	Redistribution defects	33			50
	Exercise thal-lium scan	Multiple defects with exercise, redistribution, increased thallium lung activity		86		51
Patients with known or suspected coronary artery disease	Exercise thal-lium scan	Normal scan			5	52
		Abnormal myo-cardial thallium scan but normal thallium activity in the lungs			25	52
		Increased thal-lium uptake by the lungs			67	52

Table IX. Survival data based on various types of stress testing

| Patient population | Test | Results | Survival (%) | | | Ref. |
			1 yr	3 yr	4 yr	
Chest pain patients	Exercise thallium scan	Normal	99			53,54
Patients with arteriographically significant coronary artery disease	Exercise ECG	Negative Positive			90 77	55
Patients with arteriographically significant coronary artery disease and resting radionuclide EF >20% and <55%	Exercise radionuclide arteriography	Normal response Abnormal response		93 73		56
Patients with arteriographically significant three-vessel coronary disease	Exercise radionuclide arteriography and ECG	ST segment depression ≥ 1 mm and decreased radionuclide EF with exercise			71	57

REFERENCES

1. Berger BC, Brest AN. Exercise electrocardiography and stress thallium-201 imaging in coronary artery disease. Cardiovasc Clin 1983;13:253-277.
2. Sundt TM Jr, Sandok BA, Whisnant JP. Carotid endarterectomy: Complications and preoperative assessment of risk. Mayo Clin Proc 1975;50:301-306.
3. Ennix CL Jr, Lawrie GM, Morris GC Jr, et al. Improved results of carotid endarterectomy in patients with symptomatic coronary disease: an analysis of 1546 consecutive carotid operations. Stroke 1979;10:122-125.
4. Riles TS, Kopelman I, Imparato AM. Myocardial infarction following carotid endarterectomy: A review of 683 operations. Surgery 1979;85:249-252.
5. Hertzer NR, Lees CD. Fatal myocardial infarction following carotid endarterectomy: Three hundred thirty-five patients followed 6-11 years after operation. Ann Surg 1981;194:212-218.
6. O'Donnell TF Jr, Callow AD, Willet C, et al. The impact of coronary artery disease on carotid endarterectomy. Ann Surg 1983;198:705-712.
7. Till JS, Toole JF, Howard VJ, et al. Declining morbidity and mortality of carotid endarterectomy: The Wake Forest University Medical Center experience. Stroke 1987;18:823-829.
8. Kazmers A, Cerqueira MD, Zierler RE. The role of preoperative radionuclide left ventricular ejection fraction for risk assessment in carotid surgery. Arch Surg 1988;123:416-419.
9. Yeager RA, Moneta GL, McConnell DB, et al. Analysis of risk factors for myocardial infarction following carotid endarterectomy. Arch Surg 1989;124:1142-1145.
10. Hertzer NR. Fatal myocardial infarction following abdominal aortic aneurysm resection: Three hundred forty-three patients followed 6-11 years postoperatively. Ann Surg 1980;192:667-673.
11. Brown OW, Hollier LH, Pairolero PC, et al. Abdominal aortic aneurysm and coronary artery disease: A reassessment. Arch Surg 1981;116:1484-1488.
12. Jeffery CC, Kunsman J, Cullen DJ, et al. A prospective evaluation of cardiac risk index. Anesthesiology 1983;58:462-464.
13. Pasternack PF, Imparato AM, Bear G, et al. The value of radionuclide angiography as a predictor of perioperative myocardial infarction in patients undergoing abdominal aortic aneurysm resection. J Vasc Surg 1984;1:320-325.
14. Ruby ST, Whittemore AD, Couch NP, et al. Coronary artery disease in patients requiring abdominal aortic aneurysm repair: Selective use of a combined operation. Ann Surg 1985;201:758-764.
15. Yeager RA, Weigel RM, Murphy ES, et al. Application of clinically valid cardiac risk factors to aortic aneurysm surgery. Arch Surg 1986;121:278-281.
16. Blombery PA, Ferguson IA, Rosengarten DS, et al. The role of coronary artery disease in complications of abdominal aortic aneurysm surgery. Surgery 1987;101:150-155.
17. Kazmers A, Cerqueira MD, Zierler RE. The role of preoperative radionuclide ejection fraction in direct abdominal aortic aneurysm repair. J Vasc Surg 1988;8:128-136.
18. Hertzer NR. Fatal myocardial infarction following lower extremity revascularization: Two hundred seventy-three patients followed six to eleven postoperative years. Ann Surg 1981;193:492-498.
19. Kallero KS, Bergqvist D, Cederholm C, et al. Arteriosclerosis in popliteal artery trifurcation as a predictor for myocardial infarction after arterial reconstructive operation. Surg Gynecol Obstet 1984;159:133-138.
20. Pasternack PF, Imparato AM, Riles TS, et al. The value of the radionuclide angiogram in the prediction of perioperative myocardial infarction in patients undergoing lower extremity revascularization procedures. Circulation 1985;72(Suppl.II):II-13–II-17.
21. Von Knorring J, Lepantalo M. Prediction of perioperative cardiac complications by electrocardiographic monitoring during treadmill exercise testing before peripheral vascular surgery. Surgery 1986;99:610-613.

22. Taylor LM Jr, Edwards JM, Phinney ES, et al. Reversed vein bypass to infrapopliteal arteries: Modern results are superior to or equivalent to in-situ bypass for patency and for vein utilization. Ann Surg 1987;205:90-97.

23. Cooperman M, Pflug B, Martin EW Jr, Evans WE. Cardiovascular risk factors in patients with peripheral vascular disease. Surgery 1978;84:505-509.

24. Jamieson WRE, Janusz MT, Miyagishima RT, et al. Influence of ischemic heart disease on early and late mortality after surgery for peripheral occlusive vascular disease. Circulation 1982;66(Suppl.I):I-92–I-97.

25. Diehl JT, Cali RF, Hertzer NR, et al. Complications of abdominal aortic reconstruction: An analysis of perioperative risk factors in 557 patients. Ann Surg 1983;197:49-56.

26. McPhail N, Menkis A, Shariatmadar A, et al. Statistical prediction of cardiac risk in patients who undergo vascular surgery. Can J Surg 1985;28:404-406.

27. Leppo J, Plaja J, Gionet M, et al. Noninvasive evaluation of cardiac risk before elective vascular surgery. J Am Coll Cardiol 1987;9:269-276.

28. McPhail NV, Calvin JE, Shariatmadar A, et al. The use of preoperative exercise testing to predict cardiac complications after arterial reconstruction. J Vasc Surg 1988;7:60-68.

29. McPhail NV, Ruddy TD, Calvin JE, et al. A comparison of dipyridamole-thallium imaging and exercise testing in the prediction of postoperative cardiac complications in patients requiring arterial reconstruction. J Vasc Surg 1989;10:51-56.

30. Eagle KA, Coley CM, Newell JB, et al. Combining clinical and thallium data optimizes preoperative assessment of cardiac risk before major vascular surgery. Ann Intern Med 1989;110:859-866.

31. Hlatky MA, Pryor OB, Harrell FE Jr, et al. Factors affecting sensitivity and specificity of exercise electrocardiography. Multivariable analysis. Am J Med 1984;77:64-71.

32. Goldschlager N. Use of treadmill test in the diagnosis of coronary artery disease in patients with chest pain. Ann Intern Med 1982;97:383-388.

33. Gianrossi R, Detrano R, Mulvihill D, et al. Exercise-induced ST depression in the diagnosis of coronary artery disease: A meta-analysis. Circulation 1989;80:87-98.

34. Beller GA, Gibson RS. Sensitivity, specificity, and prognostic significance of noninvasive testing for occult or known coronary disease. Prog Cardiovasc Dis 1987;29:241-270.

35. Detrano R, Janosi A, Lyons KP, et al. Factors affecting sensitivity and specificity of a diagnostic test: The exercise thallium scintigram. Am J Med 1988;84:699-710.

36. Leppo J, Boucher CA, Okada RD, et al. Serial thallium-201 myocardial imaging after dipyridamole infusion: diagnostic utility in detecting coronary stenoses and relationship to regional wall motion. Circulation 1982;66:649-657.

37. Jones RH, McEwan P, Newman GE, et al. Accuracy of diagnosis of coronary artery disease by radionuclide measurement of left ventricular function during rest and exercise. Circulation 1981;64:586-601.

38. Campos CT, Chu HW, D'Agostino HJ Jr, et al. Comparison of rest and exercise radionuclide angiocardiography and exercise treadmill testing for diagnosis of anatomically extensive coronary artery disease. Circulation 1983;67:1204-1210.

39. Beller GA, Gibson RS, Watson DD. Radionuclide methods of identifying patients who may require coronary artery bypass surgery. Circulation 1985;72(Suppl. V):V-9–V-22.

40. Gibson RS, Beller GA. Should exercise ECG testing be replaced by radioisotope methods? In Brest A, ed. Controversies in Cardiology: Cardiovascular Clinics. Philadelphia: FA Davis 1982, pp 1-31.

41. Boucher CA, Brewster DC, Darling RC, et al. Determination of cardiac risk by dipyridamole-thallium imaging before peripheral vascular surgery. N Engl J Med 1985;312:389-394.

42. Sachs RN, Tellier P, Larmignat P, et al. Assessment by dipyridamole-thallium-201 myocardial scintigraphy of coronary risk before peripheral vascular surgery. Surgery 1988;103:584-587.

43. Fletcher JP, Antico VF, Gruenewald S, et al. Dipyridamole-thallium scan for screening of coronary artery disease prior to vascular surgery. J Cardiovasc Surg 1988;29:666-669.

44. Arous EJ, Baum PL, Outler BS. The ischemic exercise test in patients with peripheral vascular disease. Arch Surg 1984;119:780-783.

45. Cutler BS, Wheeler HB, Paraskos JA, et al. Applicability and interpretation of electrocardiographic stress testing in patients with peripheral vascular disease. Am J Surg 1981;141:501-506.

46. Cutler BS, Leppo JA. Dipyridamole thallium 201 scintigraphy to detect coronary artery disease before abdominal aortic surgery. J Vasc Surg 1987;5:91-100.

47. Borer JS, Bacharach SL, Green MV, et al. Assessment of ventricular function by radionuclide angiography: Applications and results. Cardiology 1984;71:136-161.

48. The Multicenter Postinfarction Research Group. Risk stratification and survival after myocardial infarction. N Engl J Med 1983;309:331-336.

49. Nicod P, Gilpin E, Dittrich H, et al. Influence on prognosis and morbidity of left ventricular ejection fraction with and without signs of left ventricular failure after acute myocardial infarction. Am J Cardiol 1988;61:1165-1171.

50. Leppo JA, O'Brien J, Rothendler JA, et al. Dipyridamole-thallium-201 scintigraphy in the prediction of future cardiac events after acute myocardial infarction. N Engl J Med 1984;310:1014-1018.

51. Gibson RS, Watson DD, Craddock GB, et al. Prediction of cardiac events after uncomplicated myocardial infarction: A prospective study comparing predischarge exercise thallium-201 scintigraphy and coronary angiography. Circulation 1983;68:321-336.

52. Gill JB, Ruddy TD, Newell JB, et al. Prognostic importance of thallium uptake by the lungs during exercise in coronary artery disease. N Engl J Med 1987;317:1485-1489.

53. Pamelia FX, Gibson RS, Watson DD, et al. Prognosis with chest pain and normal thallium-201 exercise scintigrams. Am J Cardiol 1985;55:920-926.

54. Wackers FJT, Russo OJ, Russo D, et al. Prognostic significance of normal quantitative planar thallium-201 stress scintigraphy in patients with chest pain. J Am Coll Cardiol 1985;6:27-30.

55. McNeer JF, Margolis JR, Lee KL, et al. The role of the exercise test in the evaluation of patients for ischemic heart disease. Circulation 1978;57:64-70.

56. Jones RH, Floyd RD, Austin EH, et al. The role of radionuclide angiocardiography in the preoperative prediction of pain relief and prolonged survival following coronary artery bypass grafting. Ann Surg 1983;197:743-753.

57. Bonow RD, Kent KM, Rosing DR, et al. Exercise-induced ischemia in mildly symptomatic patients with coronary-artery disease and preserved left ventricular function: Identification of subgroups at risk of death during medical therapy. N Engl J Med 1984;311:1339-1345.

Diagnosis

3

Lower Extremity Venous Hemodynamics

G. Belcaro, D. Christopoulos, A. N. Nicolaides, London, United Kingdom

Chronic venous insufficiency may result from outflow obstruction, reflux, or a combination of both. The first question the physician asks is whether obstruction or reflux are present. The second question is where they are located anatomically, if present. The third is how much obstruction or reflux exists (Table I). This last question can be answered in terms of hemodynamics. The tables below list the normal and abnormal hemodynamic values for different anatomically defined conditions.

Ambulatory venous pressure (Table II) is defined as the lowest pressure during a ten-tiptoe exercise. It is the oldest diagnostic quantitative test. Ambulatory venous pressure will be high in the presence of popliteal reflux (Table III). For ambulatory venous pressure from 40 to 80 mm Hg there is a linear relationship with the incidence of ulceration irrespective of what (obstruction or reflux) and where it is (superficial or deep) (Table IV). Ambulatory venous pressure reflects the net effect of all abnormalities that affect hemodynamics.

Photoplethysmographic (PPG) refilling time is similar to ambulatory venous pressure–refilling time. It can identify normal limbs and limbs with superficial and deep venous disease (Table V). However, it is a poor measure of the severity of deep venous disease. Ambulatory venous pressure may be in the range of 45 to 90 mm Hg, whereas the PPG-refilling time is very short (< 10 sec). In this situation a reduction in ambulatory venous pressure (for example, as a result of valve transplantation) will have little effect, if any, on refilling time.

Air-plethysmography provides quantitative information about the various components of the calf muscle pump (Table VI): the amount of blood in the reservoir (venous volume), the stroke volume of single step (ejected volume), the ejection fraction (EF), the amount of reflux in ml/sec (VFI), and finally the residual volume (RV) as a result of ten-tiptoe movement. The residual volume fraction is linearly related to the ambulatory venous pressure and provides an indirect method to measure ambulatory venous pressure noninvasively.

Tables VII through IX show the relationship between the air-plethysmographic parameters and the incidence of chronic swelling, skin changes, and ulceration.

The arm/foot pressure differential (ΔP) with needles in arm and foot veins when the patient is horizontal is the most direct method of assessing

Table I. Grades of reflux in the deep veins on descending venography[1,2]

Grade 0	No reflux below the confluence of the superficial and profunda femoris veins, i.e., the uppermost valve of the superficial femoral vein is competent
Grade 1	Reflux beyond the uppermost valve of the superficial femoral vein but not below the middle of the thigh
Grade 2	Reflux into the superficial femoral vein to the level of the knee; popliteal valves competent
Grade 3	Reflux to a level just below the knee; incompetent popliteal valves but competent valves in the axial calf veins
Grade 4	Reflux through the axial veins (femoral, popliteal, and calf veins) to the level of the ankle

From the Irvine Laboratory for Cardiovascular Investigation and Research, Academic Surgical Unit, St. Mary's Hospital Medical School, London, U.K.

the severity of outflow obstruction (Table X). The maximum venous outflow (MVO) using strain gauge plethysmography and one-second outflow fraction (OF) using air-plethysmography are non-invasive methods of assessing obstruction (Table XI). The relationship between the arm/foot pressure differential (ΔP) and the OF is shown in Table XII.

The immediate and long-term effects of elastic compression on venous hemodynamics are shown in Tables XIII and XIV. It appears that graduated elastic compression reduces ambulatory venous pressure by decreasing reflux and increasing the ejection fraction, resulting in a reduced residual volume fraction. The latter is the amount of blood in the calf and determines the ambulatory venous pressure. The improved hemodynamics persist when the compression is removed and the limb is retested 4 weeks later.

Venous hypertensive microangiopathy is the result of chronic venous hypertension. It consists of an increased skin blood flow and a reduction in the venoarteriolar reflex. The latter is a physiologic vasoconstrictory response to standing. It prevents high pressure and flow in the capillary bed. In the presence of hypertensive microangiopathy, the high flow is associated with an increased capillary permeability and rate of ankle swelling on standing. Transcutaneous PO_2 measurements are related to the number of nutrient capillary loops open and not to overall blood flow (fibrosis and edema tend to obliterate them). However, because of the high diffusion rate of CO_2, transcutaneous PCO_2 measurements are related to overall skin blood flow. Therapeutic methods that improve venous hemodynamics and venous hypertension also improve the microcirculation. The measurements shown in Table XV provide a means of studying and understanding the microcirculation and associated skin changes in the gaiter area of the leg.

Table II. Ambulatory venous pressure and refilling time measured with cannulation of the foot vein[*][3]

Type of limb	AVP (mm Hg)		RT$_{90}$ (sec)	
	No ankle cuff	Ankle cuff	No ankle cuff	Ankle cuff
Normal	15-30	15-30	18-40	18-40
Primary varicose veins with competent perforating veins	25-40	15-30	10-18	18-35
Primary varicose veins with incompetent perforating veins	40-70	25-60[†]	5-15	8-30[†]
Deep venous reflux (incompetent popliteal valves)	55-85	50-80	3-15	5-15
Popliteal reflux and proximal occlusion	60-110	60-120	—	—
Proximal occlusion and competent popliteal valves	25-60	10-60	—	—

AVP = ambulatory venous pressure; RT$_{90}$ = refilling time.
*Standard exercise: ten tiptoe movements.
†In one third of these limbs AVP remained more than 40 mm Hg and RT$_{90}$ less than 15 seconds despite the application of the ankle cuff.

Table III. Relationship among venographic grades of reflux in the deep veins, ambulatory venous pressure, and refilling time[4]

	AVP (mm Hg)		RT$_{90}$ (sec)	
	No ankle cuff	Ankle cuff	No ankle cuff	Ankle cuff
Grades 0-2	30-70	10-45	2-15	13-45
Grades 3-4	50-95	40-90	1-8	2-14

Table IV. The incidence of active or healed ulceration in relation to ambulatory venous pressure in 251 limbs[5]

II	P (mm Hg)	Incidence of ulceration (%)
34	<30	0
44	31-40	12
51	41-50	20
45	51-60	38
34	61-70	57
28	71-80	68
15	>80	73

Table V. PPG refilling time without and with an ankle cuff to occlude the superficial veins[6]

	Standing		Sitting	
	No ankle cuff	Ankle cuff	No ankle cuff	Ankle cuff
Normal	18-80*	18-80	26-100	26-100
SVI	5-18	18-50	2-25	18-50
DVI	3-12	6-18†	2-28	2-30

SVI = superficial venous insufficiency; DVI = deep venous insufficiency.
*RT_{90} > 18 sec without cuff identifies normal limbs.
†RT_{90} < 18 sec with cuff identifies limbs with deep venous disease.

Table VI. Air-plethysmography[7-12]

	Units	Coefficient of variation (%)	Normal limbs	Primary varicose vein	DVD
Direct measurements					
Functional venous volume (VV) (the increase in leg volume on standing)	ml	10.8-12.5	100-150	100-350	70-320
Venous filling time (time taken to reach 90% of VV)	sec	8.0-11.5	70-170	5-70	5-20
Ejected volume (decrease in leg volume as a result of one tiptoe maneuver)	ml	6.7-9.4	60-150	50-180	8-140
Residual volume (volume of blood left in the veins after ten tiptoe maneuvers)	ml	6.2-12	2-45	50-150	60-200
Desired movements					
Venous filling index (average filling rate: 90% VV/VFT 90)	ml/sec	5.3-8	0.5-1.7	2-25	7-30
Ejection fraction = (EV/VV) × 100	%	2.9-9.5	60-90	25-70	20-50
Residual volume fraction = (RV/VV) × 100	%	4.3-8.2	2-35	25-80	30-100

DVD = deep venous disease; VFT 90 = venous filling time; EV = ejected volume; RV = residual volume.

Table VII. Incidence of the sequelae of venous disease in relation to the venous filling index[7-12]

VFI (ml/sec)	Chronic swelling (%)	Ulceration (%)	Skin changes with/without ulcers (%)
<3	0	0	0
3-5	12	0	0
5-10	46	46	61
>10	76	58	76

VFI = venous filling index.

Table VIII. Incidence of ulceration in relation to the residual volume fraction of the calf muscle pump in 175 limbs with venous disease[11]

Residual volume fraction (%)	Number	Incidence of ulceration (%)
<30	20	0
31-40	24	8
41-50	48	27
51-60	43	42
61-80	32	72
>80	8	87

Table IX. Incidence of ulceration in 175 limbs with venous disease in relation to ejection fraction and venous filling index[11]

	EF >40%		EF <40%	
	No.	Incidence of ulceration (%)	No.	Incidence of ulceration (%)
VFI <5	41	2	19	32
VFI 5-10	37	30	19	63
VFI >10	32	41	27	70

EF = ejection fraction.

Table X. Arm/foot pressure differential in limbs with outflow obstruction[13]

Grade	ΔP* at rest	Pressure increment during hyperemia
I. Fully compensated	<4	<6
II. Partially compensated	<4	>6
III. Partially decompensated	>4	>6 (often 10-15)
IV. Fully decompensated	>>>4 (often 15-20)	No further increase

*Arm/foot pressure differential.

Table XI. Maximum venous outflow (MVO)[14,15]

Obstruction	Normal	Moderate	Severe
MVO strain gauge (1 sec) (ml/100ml/mm)	>45	45-30	<30
One-second outflow fraction using air-plethysmography (percent of varicose vein)	>40	40-30	<30

Table XII. Relationship between arm/foot pressure differential and outflow fraction using air-plethysmography[15]

	Arm/foot pressure differential (ΔP)	
	>5 mm Hg	<5 mm Hg
One-second outflow fraction using air-plethysmography	14%-33%	35%-60%

Table XIII. Effect of applying graduated elastic compression on venous hemodynamics*[16]

	Mean percentage change	
	Limbs with SVI (n = 22)	Limbs with DVD (n = 9)
Venous pressure		
Ambulatory venous pressure	$-48^{\dagger}$	$-18\%^{\dagger}$
Refilling time	$+114^{\dagger}$	$+56\%$ NS
Air-plethysmography		
Venous volume (ml)	$-9^{\S}$	$+3$
Venous filling time	$+24$	$+57^{\dagger}$
Venous filling index	$-25^{\dagger}$	$-28^{\dagger}$
Ejected volume	$+7$ NS	$+49^{\S}$
Ejection fraction	$+19^{\dagger}$	$+49^{\dagger}$
Residual volume	$-29^{\dagger}$	-10 NS
Residual volume fraction	$-22^{\dagger}$	$-14^{\dagger}$

*Medium compression (18 mm Hg) at ankle for superficial venous incompetence (SVI) and high compression (27 mm Hg) at ankle for deep venous disease (DVD); Kendall Research Center, Barrington, Ill.
†$P < 0.01$ Wilcoxon test for paired samples.
§$P < 0.05$.

Table XIV. Effect of graduated elastic compression for 4 weeks on venous hemodynamics in 20 limbs with superficial venous incompetence (primary varicose veins)*[17]

Venous pressure	Mean percentage change
Ambulatory venous pressure (mm Hg)	$-16^{\dagger}$
Air-plethsmography	
Venous volume (ml)	$-5.5^{\dagger}$
Venous filling index (ml/sec)	$-15^{\dagger}$
Ejected volume (ml)	-3
Ejection fraction (%)	$+21^{\dagger}$
Residual volume (ml)	$-30^{\dagger}$
Residual volume fraction (%)	$-27^{\dagger}$

*Limbs tested without elastic stockings: graduated medium compression thigh length stockings with 30 mm Hg ankle compression, manufactured by Kendall Futuro, Cincinnati, Ohio, were worn for 4 weeks.
†$P < 0.01$ Wilcoxon test for paired samples.

Table XV. Effects of venous hypertension on microcirculation of perimalleolar skin and graduated elastic compression (25 mm Hg at the ankle) for 3 weeks[18-24]

	Normal	Primary varicose vein		DVD	
		Before GEC	After GEC	Before GEC	After GEC
Number	15	32	32	31	31
Ambulatory venous pressure (mm Hg) range	>30	39-57	39-57	43-79	43-79
Laser Doppler					
Resting flow (red cell flux)					
Mean	0.65	0.93	0.72	1.12	0.83
SD	(0.6)	(0.11)	(0.1)	(0.8)	(0.9)
Percent reduction resting flow on standing caused by venoarteriolar reflux	37	19	26	3	16
PO$_2$ (mm Hg)					
Mean	74	65	69	52	66
SD	(8)	(8)	(7)	(9)	(7)
PCO$_2$ (mm Hg)					
Mean	28	33	30	38	32
SD	(6)	(5)	(6)	(7)	(5)
Strain gauge plethysmography					
Rate of ankle swelling (ml/100ml/min)					
Mean	1.01	1.54	1.34	1.95	1.44
SD	(0.008)	(0.01)	(0.012)	(0.01)	(0.011)

GEC = graduated elastic compression.

REFERENCES

1. Herman RJ, Neiman HL, Yao JST. Descending venography: A method of evaluating lower extremity valvular function. Radiology 1980;137:63-69.
2. Kistner RL. Surgical repair of the incompetent femoral valve. Arch Surg 1975;110:1336-1342.
3. Nicolaides AN, Zukowski AJ. The value of dynamic venous pressure measurements. World J Surg 1986;10:919-924.
4. Nicolaides AN. Diagnostic evaluation of patients with chronic venous insufficiency. In Rutherford RB, ed. Vascular Surgery. Philadelphia: WB Saunders, 1989, pp 1583-1602.
5. Nicolaides AN, Sumner D. The investigation of patients with DVT and chronic venous insufficiency. London and Nicosia: Med-Orion Publishing Co., 1991.
6. Nicolaides AN, Miles C. Photoplethysmography in the assessment of venous insufficiency. J Vasc Surg 1987;5:405-412.
7. Christopoulos DG, Nicolaides AN, Szeniro G, et al. Air plethysmography and the effect of elastic compression on venous hemodynamics of the leg. J Vasc Surg 1987;5:148-159.
8. Christopoulos D, Nicolaides AN, Szendro G. Venous reflux: Quantification and correlation with the clinical severity of chronic venous disease. Br J Surg 1988;75:352-356.
9. Christopoulos D, Nicolaides AN. Noninvasive diagnosis and quantitation of popliteal reflux in the swollen and ulcerated leg. J Cardiovasc Surg 1988;29:535-539.
10. Christopoulos D, Nicolaides AN, Galloway JMD, et al. Objective noninvasive evaluation of venous surgical results. J Vasc Surg 1988;8:683-687.
11. Christopoulos D, Nicolaides AN, Irvine A, et al. Pathogenesis of venous ulceration in relation to the calf muscle pump function. Surgery 1989;106:829-835..
12. Christopoulos D. Non-invasive evaluation of calf muscle pump function in venous disease. PhD Thesis. London University, 1989.
13. Raju S. New approaches to the diagnosis and treatment of venous obstruction. J Vasc Surg 1986;4:42.
14. Fernandes E, Fernandes J, Horner J, et al. Ambulatory calf volume plethysmography in the assessment of venous insufficiency. Br J Surg 1979;66:327-330.
15. Christopoulos D, Nicolaides AN, Duffy P, et al. Noninvasive diagnosis and quantitation of outflow obstruction in venous disease. J Cardiovasc Surg 1989;30:72.
16. Christopoulos D, Nicolaides AN, Belcaro G, et al. The effect of elastic compression on the calf muscle pump function. Phlebology 1990;5:13-19.
17. Christopoulos D, Nicolaides AN, Belcaro G. The long term effect of elastic compression on the venous haemodynamics of the leg. Phlebology 1991;6:85-93.
18. Belcaro G, Grigg M, Nicolaides AN. Laser-doppler evaluation of skin flow in the perimalleolar region in relation to posture in venous hypertension. Ann Vasc Surg 1989;3:5-7.
19. Belcaro G. Microvascular evaluation by laser-doppler flowmetry of the effects of centellase in the treatment of severe venous hypertension and leg ulcers. Phlebology 1986;2: 61-65.
20. Belcaro G, Rulo A, Williams MA, et al. Combined evaluation of postphlebitic limbs by laser-doppler flowmetry and transcutaneous PO_2/PCO_2 measurements. VASA 1988;17-4:259-261.
21. Belcaro G. The role of transcutaneous PCO_2 in association with laser-doppler flowmetry in venous hypertension. Phlebology 1988;3:189-190.
22. Belcaro G. Alteration of the laser-doppler flow versus skin temperature curve in patients with chronic venous hypertension and skin ulcerations. In Negus D, Jantet G, eds. Phlebology 85. London, J. Libbey & Co, 1986, pp 549-550.
23. Belcaro G, Rulo A, Grigg M, et al. Evaluation of the effects of elastic compression by laser-doppler flowmetry. Phlebology 1988;41-4:797-802.
24. Belcaro G, Rulo A. A study of capillary permeability in patients with venous hypertension by a new system: The vacuum suction chamber (VSC) device—a preliminary report. Phlebology 1988;3:255-260.
25. Belcaro G, Christopoulos D, Nicolaides AN. Skin flow and swelling in postphlebitic limbs. VASA 1989;18-2:136-139

4

Diagnostic Imaging in Peripheral Vascular Disease

Blaine E. Kozak, MD, Portland, Oregon

Diagnostic imaging for peripheral vascular disease includes multiple modalities. Computed tomography (CT), ultrasound, digital subtraction arteriography, special arteriographic techniques, and magnetic resonance imaging (MRI) now supplement clinical examinations and standard arteriography and, in selected cases, may replace them.

Any evaluation and objective comparison of imaging modalities is made more difficult by interobserver variation, operator dependency, and the varying abilities of the physicians interpreting the studies. Further problems arise due to lack of standard diagnostic criteria, categories of disease, and methods of measurement. In ultrasound studies, for example, some authors require precisely equivalent matching of categories of stenosis when calculating the sensitivity and specificity of their examinations. Others accept variation of one stenosis category above or below the measurement made by arteriography as being equivalent.

Complications of imaging studies are difficult to compare because of the inherent subjectivity of both detection and severity assessment of adverse reactions and outcomes. Hematoma formation at

From the Department of Diagnostic Radiology, Emanuel Hospital and Health Center, Portland, Ore.

an arterial puncture site is a typical example. No standard is recognized as being significant or reportable as a complication. This is clearly reflected in the reported numbers of local arteriographic complications, most of which are hematomas. Similarly, contrast media reactions are detected, described, and grouped differently in various studies.

The adequacy of imaging techniques, such as arteriography, relies not only on the radiologist's skill in performing and interpreting the examination, but also on their detailed knowledge of the operative procedures that may be performed subsequently, including detailed familiarity with the arteriographic information essential for planning surgery. Lack of the information required rather than the lack of available imaging techniques, appears to be the major obstacle to providing better preoperative arteriography.

Major controversies exist concerning the use of nonionic and lower osmolar contrast agents even though their benefits in many risk categories, particularly a history of previous contrast agent reaction or significant asthma, have been clearly established.

This review summarizes data relevant to clinical decision making regarding imaging studies, including their risks, benefits, and complications in patients with peripheral vascular disease.

Table I. Carotid artery imaging with ultrasound

Detected lesion	Imaging modality	Comparison	Sensitivity (%)	Specificity (%)	Accuracy (%)	Ref.
Stenosis 50% +	Duplex	Arteriography	92-98	92-93	92-95	1*,2[†]
by diameter	Color duplex	Arteriography	90	79	87	3[‡]
Occlusion	Ultrasound only	Arteriography	78	96		4
	Duplex	Arteriography	93-100	96-100		1,2,4,5
	Color duplex	Arteriography	100	93		5
Plaque with	Ultrasound only	Endarterectomy	91	65	82	6
hemorrhage	Ultrasound only	Endarterectomy	93	84	87	4
	Duplex	Endarterectomy	94	88	90	7
Plaque with	Real-time	Arteriography	8			2
ulceration	B-mode	Endarterectomy	39-89	72-87	60-87	4[§],8
	Duplex	Endarterectomy	64		92	1,9
Accuracy of	Duplex	Arteriography			83-92	5,10[‖]
measurement	Color duplex	Duplex			91-98	5,11[#]
% stenosis	Color duplex	Arteriography			71-96	5,12**
Inadequate	Duplex	3-8[††]				7,10
studies	Color duplex	11-13[‡‡]				5,12

*Diagnostic criteria not given.

[†]150 cm/sec peak systolic velocity internal carotid artery.

[‡]125 cm/sec peak systolic velocity internal carotid artery.

[§]Arteriography sensitivity: 59%; specificity: 73% in same series.

[‖]Study in reference 10 had accuracy 87%; additional 10% differed by one stenosis group; accuracy fell to 83% for stenosis greater than 50%.

[#]In reference 11 accuracy was 91%; additional 9% differed by one stenosis group.

**Used intraarterial digital subtraction arteriography.

[††]Reasons: calcifications, uncooperative.

[‡‡]Reasons: calcifications, body habitus, deep vessels, high bifurcation, unable to extend neck adequately.

Table II. Complications of carotid arteriography

Type of examination	No. of cases	Total all complications (%)	Death (%)	Non-CNS (%)	CNS Temporary (%)	CNS Permanent (%)	Ref.
Various*	5531	26.3	0.03	21.7[†]	4.5	0.6	13
Various[‡]	4748		0.7			0.48	14
Femoral[§]	5000	1.4	0.02	0.4	0.9	0.04	15
Non-teaching	4187	0.9	0.03	0.3	0.6		
Teaching	813	3.9	0.0	1.1	2.8		
Various[‖]	1328	12.5	0.2	6.3	5.4	0.6	16
Various[#]	603	2.3	0.0	0.5	1.0	0.0	17
Various**	1517	8.5	0.06	6.8	2.3	0.3	18

CNS = central nervous system.

*Femoral approach: 59.1%; direct carotid: 37.8%.

[†]Local hematoma accounted for 20.3%; without hematoma would reduce total complications to 6.2% and local complications to 1.6%.

[‡]Direct carotid puncture in 82% of patients.

[§]Femoral approach used except in rare instances; percent not stated.

[‖]Femoral approach: 66%; direct puncture: 23%; retrograde brachial: 12%.

[#]Femoral approach: 77%; axillary: 22%; direct puncture: 1.3%; 5 Fr catheters.

**Femoral approach: 96%; direct carotid: 2.4%; retrograde brachial: 4.6%; axillary: 0.13%; 5 Fr catheters.

Table III. Carotid artery digital subtraction arteriography (DSA)

| Type of injection | No. of patients | Complications (all non-CNS) | | % Adequacy | | | Compared with arteriography | | | Ref. |
		Mild	Severe	Both	One	None	Sensitivity	Specificity	Accuracy	
IV	130	3.1	1.5	26*	48[†]	8				19
IV	100	0	0	60[‡]	23[§]	17			73[‖]	20
							95	99	97[#]	
							54	70	64**	
								Overall:	70	
IV	78[††]			33-75[‡‡]	25	20[††]			73-96[§§]	21
IV	500			92.5[‖‖]	7.5		93	94	58-94[##]	22
IV	2488	1.5	0.24***							23
IA	59	3.4	0	93[†††]						24

*Both bifurcation seen in two views: most stringent standard.
[†]One bifurcation seen in two views: one in one view was 43.5%.
[‡]Both bifurcations seen in at least one view.
[§]One bifurcation seen in at least one view.
[‖]Accuracy for exact degree of stenosis match.
[#]Accuracy for being within one stenosis category match with good to excellent quality DSA.
**Within one stenosis category with poor quality DSA; 36% with exact match.
[††]Excluded unsatisfactory examinations from study, approximately 20%.
[‡‡]33% "optimal" in all views; 75% acceptable or optimal in all views.
[§§]If exact match: 73%; if within one stenosis category: 96%.
[‖‖]All bifurcations diagnostic or excellent in one view.
[##]Accuracy for stenoses greater than 60%; fell to 58% for all arteries.
***65% complications were contrast related.
[†††]Both carotid arteries seen in two views: most stringent standard.

Table IV. Complications of brachial arteriography

Catheter size	No. of patients	Selective/ nonselective	Pulse loss (%)	Hemorrhage (%)	Aneurysm (%)	Ref.
7 Fr 8 Fr sheath	1820	Selective	1.3-2.7			25,26
5 Fr	1000	Mixed	0.1		0.1	27
5 Fr	45	Nonselective	0.0	9	2	28
4 Fr	1317	Nonselective	0.5-2.5* 0.0-0.7[†]			24,29-32
4,5 Fr	72	Mixed	4	3		33
4 Fr	73	Selective	1.6*/0.2[†]	1.8		34[‡]

*Temporary pulse loss.
[†]Permanent pulse loss.
[‡]One patient each (0.2%) with brachial stenosis and brachial dissection.

Table V. Value of aortography in abdominal aneurysm resection[35-44]

| Arteriography studies | Renal arteries | | | | Visceral arteries | | Value* change in plan (%) |
	Involved (%)	Aberrant from aneurysm (%)	Stenosis/ occlusion (%)	Recon- structed (%)	Stenosis celiac SMA (%)	Recon- structed (%)	
980[†]	4-9	2-7	3-34 (average 20%)	2-43 (average 10%)	6-27 (average 15%)	0-7 (average 36%)	0-75

SMA = superior mesenteric artery.
*Five studies recommended preoperative arteriography in all patients; of these, three had a value (change in plan) 20%, 72%, and 75%; two were not stated; the other studies recommended arteriography only for specific indications.
[†]Three patients had major complications, including one death.[40,43]

Table VI. Accuracy of CT and aortography in patients with abdominal aortic aneurysms (AAA)[45]

Examination	Aneurysm detection (%)	Proximal extent (%)	Multiple renal arteries			Iliac extent (%)	Iliac aneurysm (%)	Diameter within 1 cm (%)	Psuedo-aneurysm detection (%)
			2 (%)	3 (%)	4 (%)				
CT*	100	94	98	29	0	76	33	100	100
Arteriography*	96	100	100	100	100	100	100	42	0

*50 patients were studied with both CT and arteriography; all had surgery as the standard for comparison.

Table VII. Accuracy of MRI and aortography in patients with AAA[46]

	No. of patients	MRI (%)	Arteriography (%)	Surgery
Accuracy of prediction aneurysm being supra- or infrarenal*	20	94[†]	100[‡]	Standard for comparison
Accuracy prediction aneurysm distal extent with respect to aortic bifurcation*		81	100	Standard for comparison
Accessory renal arteries identified		0 (0/5)	Standard for comparison	Not routinely determined
Stenotic or occluded celiac, mesenteric, and renal arteries identified		35 (8/23)	Standard for comparison	Not routinely determined
Retroaortic left renal vein		100	0 (0/2)	Standard for comparison
Aneurysm size within 1 cm		81	47	Standard for comparison

*For those patients in study who went to surgery.
[†]Three patients did not have complete MRI; two claustrophobic, one with significant motion.
[‡]One patient did not have arteriogram because of renal failure.

Table VIII. Lower limb arteriography and distal vessel visualization

Number of arteriograms	Adequacy of visualization of distal vessels		Subsequent operative arteriograms		Ref.
	Standard (%)	Special technique (%)	Performed (%)	Add information (%)	
200	82.5 (165/200)	71 (25.35)*	0.5 (1)[†]	0.5	47
52[‡]	75 (15/20)	100 (52/52)[§]			48
		66 (8/12)[‖]			
		95 (19/20)[#]			
100		87 (174/200 legs)**			49
45		89 (40/45)[††]			50
		100 (4/4)[‡‡]			
28	Not reported	36 (16/44)[§§]	64 (28/44)	0	51

*Selective catheter positioning, intraarterial tolazoline; there was better visualization in one patient, but an operative arteriogram was still needed; see footnote [†].
[†]One patient with occlusion of superficial femoral and popliteal arteries needed operative arteriogram before bypass; remaining patients had either no surgery or amputation.
[‡]Each patient had two arteriographic runs.
[§]60 cc contrast agent injected external iliac artery.
[‖]30 cc contrast agent injected external iliac artery.
[#]60 cc contrast agent injected external iliac artery with inflow occlusion; this method gave better vessel opacification than method in footnote [§], but no better diagnostic adequacy.
**Long injection time, large volume of injection, and late filming; 13% not seen on initial arteriogram because of timing errors.
[††]Occlusion balloon in external iliac artery to block inflow; four failures were caused by timing errors and one because of equipment malfunction.
[‡‡]DSA was used in 4 of the 5 initial failures in footnote [††].
[§§]DSA following standard arteriograms that detected no bypassable runoff vessels.

Table IX. Complications of arteriography: Overall complication rates

	Transfemoral	Transaxillary	Translumbar	Total	Ref.
		Entry site			
Number of cases	83,068	4590	4118	91,776	52
				11,402	55
Total complications	1441	151	119	1711	52
	(1.73%)	(3.29%)	(2.89%)	(1.86%)	
				413	55
				(3.6%)*	
Deaths	24	4	2	30	52
	(0.03%)	(0.09%)	(0.05%)	(0.03%)	
				7	55
				(0.06%)	

*Minor complications were 2.9%; local hematoma, contrast agent injection into vessel wall or perforation without sequelae; major complications were 0.7%.

Table X. Complications of arteriography: Puncture site complications

Type of complication	Transfemoral (%)	Transaxillary (%)	Translumbar (%)	Ref.
		Entry site		
Hematoma	0.26-0.9*	0.68-1.18	0.53	52-54
Thrombosis/occlusion	1.14	0.51-0.76	0	52-54
Pseudoaneurysm	0.05	0.17-0.22	0.05	52,54
Arteriovenous fistula	0.01	0.02	0	52
Limb loss	0.01	0.02	0	52
Delayed hemorrhage	1.2	0		53
Permanent neurologic deficit		0.17		54
Total	0.47-2.24	1.7-2.1	0.58	52-54

*Large or pronounced; moderate femoral hematoma was 3.1%, and moderate axillary hematoma 3.2%.[52]

Table XI. Complications of arteriography: Systemic complications[52]

	Trans-femoral (%)	Trans-axillary (%)	Trans-lumbar (%)
		Entry site	
Cardiac	0.29	0.26	0.36*
Cardiovascular collapse	0.03	0.04	0.07*
Neurologic	0.17	0.46	0.02[†]
Seizures	0.06	0.15	0.00[‡]

*Not statistically different.
[†]Statistically significant differences among techniques $p < 0.05$.
[‡]Statistically significant differences among techniques $p < 0.01$.

Table XII. Puncture of prosthetic vascular grafts

No. of graft punctures (no. of patients)	Graft complications (%)	Ref.
50 (41)	0	56
100	0	57
86 (58)	3.5*	58
50	2.0[†]	59
700	0.3	57

*Three patients had graft thrombosis.
[†]One catheter separation during removal.

Table XIII. Systemic heparinization during arteriography

Systemic heparin	No. of patients	Hematoma Small (%)	Large (%)	Late bleeding (%)	Pulse change or emboli (%)	Artery occlusion (%)	Entry site clot (%)	Ref.
No	93				8.6	2.0	53.7	60
No	173						44	61
No	200	5.5	1.0	1.5		1.0	6.5	62
Yes*	200	6.0	1.0	6.0		0.0	2.0	
No	25				3.4			63
Yes†	57				0.75			
Yes‡	525				0.2		2.5	64

*45 units/kg body weight; average 3250 units.
†Bolus 2000 units IV and 3000 units intraarterial infusion via sheath; bolus of 1000 units given after each hour of elapsed time.
‡45 units/kg body weight.

Table XIV. Patient radiation dosages during arteriography

Type of study	Skin (mrad)	Testes (mrad)	Ovaries (mrad)	Red marrow (mrad)	Thyroid (mrad)	Uterus (mrad)	Lens (mrad)	Ref.
Abdominal aorta cut-film	37,000	900	7000	2800	0-1	7000		65
Renal DSA*	23,000	500	1000	800	50	800		65
Cerebral cut-film	17,000 to 23,000	0-1	0-1	500 to 1150	4000 to 8700	0-1	320	65,66
Cerebral DSA	3700			55	740		15	66

1.0 mrad = 0.01 mGy.
*Renal DSA should closely approximate DSA examination of the abdominal aorta.

Table XV. Recommendations for use of lower osmolar contrast media

American College of Radiology Clinical Standards of Patient Care[67]
1. Patients with previous significant adverse reaction to contrast material, strongly allergic history, or asthma
2. Patients with cardiac dysfunction, severe arrhythmias, unstable angina pectoris, recent myocardial infarction, pulmonary hypertension, and congestive heart failure
3. Patients with generalized severe debilitation
4. Patients undergoing potentially painful examinations such as peripheral arteriography, external carotid arteriography, and lower limb phlebography
5. Patients undergoing examinations such as digital arteriography where motion must be minimized to optimize image quality

Table XVI. Complications of administration of contrast media

No. of examinations	Deaths	Mortality rate	ADRs with ionic contrast media			ADRs with nonionic contrast media			Ref.
			Total (%)	Severe (%)	Very severe (%)	Total (%)	Severe (%)	Very severe (%)	
11,546,000	99	1:117,000							68
912,300	15	1:61,000							69
318,500	8	1:40,000							70
33,000	1	1:33,000							71
112,003	11	1:10,000	4.95	0.1*					72
337,647	2	1:169,000	12.66	0.22[†]	0.04	3.13	0.04	0.004	73
109,546[‡]				0.09[‡]			0.02		74
13,176[§]			4.1	0.4[§]		0.69	0.0		75

ADR = adverse drug reaction.
*Severe ADRs required hospitalization.
[†]Severe ADRs included dyspnea, sudden drop in blood pressure, loss of consciousness, cardiac arrest, or a combination of these.
[‡]72% received ionic contrast media, 28% received nonionic; severe ADRs required urgent therapy and hospitalization.
[§]45.6% received ionic contrast media, 54.6% received nonionic; severe ADRs included cardiac arrest, shock, loss of consciousness, and symptomatic cardiac arrhythmias.

Table XVII. Risk of adverse reaction by history of prior contrast agent administration and prior reaction[73]

Prior contrast agent exposure	Prior ADR	ADR with ionic contrast media		ADR with nonionic contrast media	
		Total (%)	Severe (%)	Total (%)	Severe (%)
Yes	Yes	44.04	0.73	11.24	0.18
	No	9.02	0.13	2.21	0.03
No		13.71	0.26	3.03	0.04

Table XVIII. Risk of adverse reaction to contrast media with history of asthma[73]

ADR with ionic contrast media		ADR with nonionic contrast media	
Total ADR (%)	Severe (%)	Total ADR (%)	Severe (%)
19.68	1.88	7.75	0.23

Table XIX. Corticosteroid use to reduce reactions to contrast media[76]

Type of reaction	Percent change in ADRs with steroid pretreatment*		
	All patients	Low-risk patients	High-risk patients
All reactions 1-3[†]	−31	−29	−37
Type 1 reactions	−33	−43	−31
Type 2 reactions	−23	+1	−45
Type 3 reactions	−62	−86	−34
Reactions needing treatment	−42	−35	−37

Low-risk = no history of ADR or allergic history; high-risk = previous ADR or allergic history.
*All patients received ionic contrast material. Pretreatment consisted of a two-dose regimen of methylprednisolone 12 and 2 hours before contrast media administration.
[†]Type 1 = one episode nausea, vomiting, sneezing, or vertigo; Type 2 = hives, more than one episode vomiting, fever, and/or chills; Type 3 = shock, laryngospasm, laryngeal edema, bronchospasm, loss of consciousness, seizures, change in blood pressure, angina, arrhythmias, angioedema, or pulmonary edema.

REFERENCES

1. Moore WS, Ziomek S, Quiñones-Baldrich WJ, et al. Can clinical evaluation and noninvasive testing substitute for angiography in the evaluation of carotid artery disease? Ann Surg 1988;208:91-94.

2. Robinson ML, Sacks D, Perlmutter GS, et al. Diagnostic criteria for carotid duplex sonography. AJR 1988;151:1045-1049.

3. Polak JF, Dobkin GR, O'Leary DH, et al. Internal carotid artery stenosis: Accuracy and reproducibility of color Doppler-assisted duplex imaging. Radiology 1989;173:793-798.

4. O'Donnell TF Jr, Erdoes L, Mackey WC, et al. Correlation of B-mode ultrasound imaging and arteriography with pathologic findings at carotid endarterectomy. Arch Surg 1985;120:443-449.

5. Steinke W, Kloetzsch C, Hennerici M. Carotid artery disease assessed by color Doppler flow imaging: Correlation with standard Doppler sonography and angiography. AJNR 1990;11:259-266.

6. Reilly L, Lusby R, Hughes L, et al. Carotid plaque histology using real-time ultrasonography. Am J Surg 1983;146:188-193.

7. Bluth EI, Kay D, Merritt CRB, et al. Sonographic characterization of carotid plaque: Detection of hemorrhage. AJR 1986;146:1061-1065.

8. O'Leary DH, Holen J, Rocotta JJ, et al. Carotid bifurcation disease: Prediction of ulceration with B-mode ultrasound. Radiology 1987;162:523-525.

9. Goodson SF, Flanigan DP, Bishara RA, et al. Can carotid duplex scanning supplant arteriography in patients with focal carotid territory symptoms. J Vasc Surg 1987;5:551-557.

10. Jacobs NM, Grant EG, Schellinger D, et al. Duplex carotid sonography: Criteria for stenosis, accuracy and pitfalls. Radiology 1985;154:385-391.

11. Hallam MJ, Reid JM, Cooperberg PL. Color-flow Doppler and conventional duplex scanning of the carotid bifurcation: Prospective double-blind, correlative study. AJR 1989;152:1101-1105.

12. Erickson SJ, Mewissen MW, Foley WD, et al. Stenosis of the internal carotid artery: Assessment using color Doppler imaging compared with angiography. AJR 1989;152:1299-1305.

13. Olivecrona H. Complications of cerebral angiography. Neuroradiology 1977;14:175-181.

14. Hass WK, Fields WS, North RR, et al. Joint study of extracranial arterial occlusion. II. Arteriography, techniques, sites, and complications. JAMA 1968;203:159-166.

15. Mani RL, Eisenberg RL, Mc Donald EJ Jr, et al. Complications of catheter cerebral arteriography: Analysis of 5,000 procedures. I. Criteria and incidence. AJR 1978;131:861-865.

16. Swanson PD, Calanchi PR, Dyken ML, et al. A cooperative study of hospital frequency and character of transient ischemic attacks. II. Performance of angiography among six centers. JAMA 1977;237:2202-2206.

17. Kerber CW, Cromwell LD, Drayer BP, et al. Cerebral ischemia. I. Current angiographic techniques, complications, and safety. AJR 1977;130:1097-1103.

18. Earnest F IV, Forbes G, Sandok BA, et al. Complication of cerebral angiography: Prospective assessment of risk. AJR 1984;142:247-253.

19. Hoffman MG, Gomes AS, Pais SO. Limitations in the interpretation of intravenous carotid digital subtraction angiography. AJR 1984;142:261-264.

20. Chilcote WA, Modic MT, Pavlicek, et al. Digital subtraction angiography of the carotid arteries: A comparative study in 100 patients. Radiology 1981;139:287-295.

21. Earnest F IV, Houser OW, Forbes GS, et al. The limitations of intravenous digital subtraction angiography in the evaluation of atherosclerotic cerebrovascular disease: Angiographic and surgical correlation. Mayo Clin Proc 1983;58:735-746.

22. Wood GW, Lukin RR, Tomsick TA, et al. Digital subtraction angiography with intravenous injection: Assessment of 1,000 carotid bifurcations. AJR 1983;140:855-859.

23. Pinto RS, Manuell M, Kricheff II. Complications of digital intravenous angiography: Experience in 2488 cervicocranial examinations. AJR 1983;143:1295-1299.

24. McCreary JA, Schellhas KP, Brant-Zawadzki M, et al. Outpatient DSA in cerebrovascular disease using transbrachial arch injections. AJNR 1985;6:795-801.

25. Fergusson DJG, Kamada RD. Percutaneous entry of the brachial artery for left heart catheterization using a sheath: Further experience. Cath Cardiovasc Diag 1986;12:209-211.

26. Maouad J, Hebert JL, Fernandez F, et al. Percutaneous brachial approach using the femoral artery sheath for left heart catheterization and selective coronary angiography. Cath Cardiovasc Diag 1985;11:539-546.

27. Field JR, Lee L, McBurney RF. Complications of 1,000 brachial arteriograms. J Neurosurg 1972;36:324-332.

28. Gaines PA, Reidy JF. Percutaneous high brachial aortography: A safe alternative to the translumbar approach. Clin Radiol 1986;37:595-597.

29. Brant-Zawadzki M. Outpatient DSA using transbrachial approach. AJR 1986;146:649.

30. Becker GJ, Kicks ME, Holden RW, et al. Screening for occlusive vascular disease with intraarterial DSA: Preliminary experience with a high flow 4-F catheter. Radiology 1984;153:838.

31. Hicks ME, Kreipke DL, Becker GJ, et al. Cerebrovascular disease: Evaluation with transbrachial intraarterial digital subtraction angiography using a 4-F catheter. Radiology 1986;161:545-546.

32. Gritter KJ, Laidlaw WW, Peterson NT. Complications of outpatient transbrachial intraarterial digital subtraction angiography. Radiology 1987;162:125-127.

33. Grollman JH, Marcus R. Transbrachial arteriography: Techniques and complications. Cardiovasc Intervent Radiol 1988;11:32-35.

34. Barnett FJ, Lecky DM, Freiman DB, et al. Cerebrovascular disease: Outpatient evaluation with selective carotid DSA performed via a transbrachial approach. Radiology 1989;170:535-539.

35. Kahn PC, Callow AD. Catheter arteriography in the evaluation of abdominal aortic aneurysms. AJR 1966;98:879-887.

36. Brewster DC, Retana A, Waltman AC, et al. Angiography in the management of aneurysms of the abdominal aorta. N Engl J Med 1975;292:822-825.

37. Cyr R, Trudel J, Rabbat AG, et al. Angiography: An essential diagnostic aid in asymptomatic aortic aneurysm. Can J Surg 1977;20:57-59.

38. Kwann JH, Connolly JE, Molen RV, et al. The value of arteriography before abdominal aneurysmectomy. Am J Surg 1977;134:108-114.

39. Baur GM, Porter JM, Eidemuller LR, et al. The role of aortography in abdominal aortic aneurysm. Am J Surg 1978;136:184-189.

40. Alexander RH, Evans MT, Blikken WG. Angiography in patients with abdominal aortic aneurysm. South Med J 1981;74:669-672.

41. Bell DD, Gaspar MR. Routine aortography before abdominal aneurysmectomy. Am J Surg 1982;144:191-193.

42. Satiana B, Veazey CR, Smith RB, et al. Preoperative aortography before abdominal aortic aneurysmectomy. Am Surg 1978;44:650-654.

43. Numo IM, Collins GM, Bardin JA, et al. Should aortography be used routinely in the elective management of abdominal aortic aneurysm? Am J Surg 1982;144:53-57.

44. Couch NP, O'Mahony J, McIrvine A, et al. The place of abdominal aortography in abdominal aneurysm resection. Arch Surg 1983;118:1029-1034.

45. Papanicolaou N, Wittenberg J, Ferrucci JT Jr, et al. Preoperative evaluation of abdominal aortic aneurysms by computed tomography. AJR 1986;146:711-715.

46. Koslin DB, Kenney PJ, Keller FS, et al. Preoperative evaluation of abdominal aortic aneurysm by MR imaging with aortography correlation. Cardiovasc Intervent Radiol 1988;11: 329-335.

47. Kozak BE, Bedell JE, Rosch J. Small vessel leg angiography for distal vessel bypass grafts. J Vasc Surg 1988;8:711-715.

48. Smith TP, Cragg AH, Berbaum KS, et al. Techniques for lower-limb angiography: A comparative study. Radiology 1990;174:951-955.

49. Thomas ML, Tanqueray AB, Burnand KG. Visualization of the plantar arch by aortography: Technique and value. Br J Radiol 1988;61:469-472.

50. Cardella JF, Smith TP, Darcy MD, et al. Balloon occlusion femoral angiography prior to in-situ saphenous vein bypass. Cardiovasc Intervent Radiol 1987;10:181-187.

51. Crummy AB, Steighorst MF, Turski PA, et al. Digital subtraction angiography: Current status and use of intraarterial injection. Radiology 1982;145:303-307.

52. Hessel SJ, Adams DF, Abrams HL. Complications of angiography. Radiology 1981;138:273-281.

53. Sigstedt B, Lunderquist A. Complications of angiographic examinations. AJR 1978;130:455-460.

54. Molnar W, Paul DJ. Complications of axillary arteriotomies. Radiology 1972;104:269-276.

55. Lang EK. A survey of the complications of percutaneous retrograde arteriography. Radiology 1963;81:257-263.

56. Wade GL, Smith DC, Mohr LL. Follow-up of 50 consecutive angiograms: Obtained utilizing puncture of prosthetic vascular grafts. Radiology 1983;146:663-664.

57. Smith DC. Catheterization of prosthetic vascular grafts: Acceptable technique (editorial). AJR 1984;143:1117-1118.

58. Da Silva JR, Eckstein MR, Kelemouridis V, et al. Aortofemoral bypass grafts: Safety of percutaneous puncture. J Vasc Surg 1984;1:642-645.

59. Mani RL. Aortofemoral graft catheterization (letter). AJR 1977;129:759.

60. Formanek G, Frech RS, Amplatz K. Arterial thrombus formation during clinical percutaneous catheterization. Circulation 1990;41:833-839.

61. Siegelman SS, Caplan LH, Annes GP. Complications of catheter angiography: Study with oscillometry and "pullout" angiograms. Radiology 1968;91:251-253.

62. Antonovic R, Rosch J, Dotter CT. The value of systemic arterial heparinization in transfemoral angiography: A prospective study. AJR 1976;127:223-225.

63. Debrun GM, Vinuela FV, Fox AJ. Aspirin and systemic heparinization in diagnostic and interventional neuroradiology. AJR 1982;139:139-142.

64. Wallace S, Medellin H, DeJongh D, et al. Systemic heparinization for angiography. AJR 1972;116:204-209.

65. Judy PF, Zimmerman RE. Dose to critical organs. In McNeil BJ, Abrams HL, eds. Brigham and Women's Hospital Handbook of Diagnostic Imaging. Boston: Little Brown, 1986;318-324.

66. Pavlicek W, Weinstein MA, Modic MT, et al. Patient doses during digital subtraction angiography of the carotid arteries: Comparison with conventional angiography. Radiology 1982; 145:683-685.

67. American College of Radiology. ACR policies relating to clinical standards of patient care. 1989, p. I-S-1-3.

68. Pendergrass HP, Tondreau RL, Pendergrass EP, et al. Reactions associated with intravenous urography: Historical and statistical review. Radiology 1958;71:1-12.

69. Wolfromm R, Dehouve A, Degand F, et al. Les accidents graves par injection intraveineuse de substances iodees pour urographie. J Radiol Electrol 1966;47:346-357.

70. Ansell G. Adverse reactions to contrast agents: Scope of problem. Invest Radiol 1970;5:374-384.

71. Witten DM, Hirsch FD, Hartman GW. Acute reactions to urographic contrast medium: Incidence, clinical characteristics and relationship to history of hypersensitivity states. AJR 1973;119:832-840.

72. Shehadi WH. Adverse reactions to intravascularly administered contrast media: A comprehensive study based on a prospective survey. AJR 1975;124:125-152.

73. Katayama H, Yamaguchi K, Kozuka T, et al. Adverse reactions to ionic and nonionic contrast media. Radiology 1990; 175:621-628.

74. Palmer FJ. The RACR survey of intravenous contrast media reactions: Final report. Aust Radiol 1988;32:426-428.

75. Wolf GL, Arenson RL, Cross AP. A prospective trial of ionic vs nonionic contrast agents in routine clinical practice: Comparison of adverse effects. AJR 1989;152:939-944.

76. Lasser EC. Pretreatment with corticosteroids to prevent reactions to IV contrast material: Overview and implications. AJR 1988;150:257-259.

5

Lipid Abnormalities in Peripheral Vascular Disease

Joseph H. Rapp, MD, San Francisco, California

Reports from the Framingham Study found correlations between elevated plasma cholesterol and triglyceride levels and atherosclerosis in the peripheral circulation,[1] although the association did not appear to be as strong as for coronary artery disease (CAD).[2] With more sophisticated assays of plasma lipids, lipoprotein fractionations, and determination of apoprotein levels, a closer relationship between peripheral vascular disease (PVD) and abnormalities of lipid metabolism has been observed. Elevated plasma lipid values have been reported in one third to one half of patients with PVD.[3-7] Since hypertriglyceridemia is quite common and a reciprocal relationship exists between triglyceride levels and high-density lipoprotein (HDL), speculation has arisen that an important factor in these patients is HDL reduction. Low HDL cholesterol levels are associated with PVD,[2,8-12] and plasma HDL apoprotein concentrations have been used to separate patients with PVD both from controls[8,10,11,13] and from patients with CAD.[10]

NORMAL LIPID LEVELS

Table I lists the mean and the 95th percentile for total cholesterol and triglyceride levels and for low-density lipoprotein (LDL) cholesterol values in the United States population at 50 years of age. The fifth percentile is given for HDL cholesterol values.

Table II lists the plasma lipoproteins, their associated apoproteins, and their relative atherogenicity. There are several apoprotein levels and ratios that correlate with the presence of PVD. A-I and A-II levels have been found to have predictive value,[8,13] as have the A-I/B[10] and A-I/C-III ratios.[13] However, current lipid-lowering therapy is directed at reducing the levels of plasma cholesterol and triglycerides, not apoproteins. Therefore, apoprotein determinations primarily remain a research tool with little utility in current clinical practice.

A routine lipid profile is shown in Table III. We routinely measure total triglyceride, total cholesterol with LDL, and HDL cholesterol levels. If a patient has a normal triglyceride level, little is gained by ascertaining the triglyceride and cholesterol content of very low–density lipoprotein (VLDL). However, with elevated levels of triglycerides and cholesterol, examination of VLDL may reveal that a considerable portion of cholesterol is being carried in this fraction, suggesting a Type IIb or III phenotype or the presence of remnants of VLDL or chylomicron metabolism.

CURRENT THERAPY FOR HYPERLIPIDEMIA

Diet. There is considerable epidemiologic and experimental evidence linking the diet of the industrialized world, which is rich in saturated fat and cholesterol, to the high rate of atherosclerosis in North Americans and Europeans.[16-20] This diet may be atherogenic despite relatively normal fasting plasma lipid levels.[21,22] Therefore, we recommend some dietary modification along with smoking cessation counseling and hypertension management for all symptomatic patients.

In a hyperlipidemic patient aggressive dietary treatment can lower the plasma cholesterol level

From the Department of Surgery, San Francisco Veterans Administration Hospital, University of California, San Francisco, Calif.

This work has been supported in part by Grants from the Heart Lung and Blood Institute (HL 4L4104), the Veteran's Administration, and the Pacific Vascular Research Foundation.

by over 40%.[21] Maximum lowering occurs with a low saturated fat, 100 mg cholesterol diet. However, this diet severely restricts the amount of animal products one can eat. For example, there are 50 mg of cholesterol in a teaspoon of butter, approximately 30 mg in one ounce of beef, and 200 to 250 mg in one egg yolk. Attainable reductions are listed in Table IV, but they require a substantial change in dietary habits for most patients. Table V lists factors that affect the total plasma HDL cholesterol level.

Hypertriglyceridemia. Plasma triglycerides can reside in chylomicrons, VLDL, or their remnants. If chylomicrons are increased (Type 1 hyperlipidemia), the treatment is essentially dietary with restriction of dietary fat, although substitution of Omega-3 fatty acids (fish oil) in the diet may be of benefit.

Elevations of VLDL or remnant particles can be effectively treated with niacin or the fibric acid derivatives (see Table VI).[25] Several reviews exist on the subject.[25,26,27] Often, the added benefit of lowering the triglyceride level is a reciprocal reduction in the level of HDL cholesterol.

Hypercholesterolemia. Treatment should always begin with a reduction in dietary cholesterol. The goal for therapy (see Table VI) should be to bring the patient's cholesterol level into the normal range. A major advance in this field has been the use of HMG CoA reductase inhibitors.

Combined hypertriglyceridemia and hypercholesterolemia. The Type IIb and III hyperlipidemic patients fall into this category. The Type III patients particularly have severe PVD as well as coronary artery disease. Treatment of these individuals is essentially the same as for hypertriglyceridemia alone. It can be quite rewarding with documentation of improved flow after treatment.[28]

Low HDL cholesterol. There are multiple causes of reduced HDL, and several factors have been shown to increase HDL concentrations (Table V). As with other lipoproteins, there are subclasses of HDL, notably HDL_2 and HDL_3. HDL_2 cholesterol

Table I. Normal plasma lipid values[15]

	Total cholesterol	Total triglyceride	LDL cholesterol	HDL cholesterol
Men				
Mean	213	154	142	44
95th percentile	274	313	197	63
5th percentile				30
Women				
Mean	222	112	145	60
95th percentile	292	214	214	89
5th percentile				35

Both cholesterol and triglyceride levels increase with age; values listed are for white 50-year-old North American men and women.

Table III. Representative lipid profiles

	VLDL		LDL		HDL	
	Chol	TRG	Chol	TRG	Chol	TRG
Normal	15	80	120	10	50	5
Hypercholesterolemia (Type IIa)	25	80	>190	20	35	5
Hypertriglyceridemia (Type IV)	50	>200	120	30	25	10
Combined (Type IIb or III)	80	>200	>190	80	30	10

VLDL = very low-density lipoproteins; Chol = cholesterol; TRG = triglycerides.

Note: These are representative values; in practice, large variations occur.

Table II. Lipoprotein composition[14] and atherogenicity

	VLDL	Remnants	LDL	HDL
Density (gm/dl)	<1.006	<1.006-1.019	1.019-1.063	>1.21
Cholesterol (%)	4-7	Variable	5-8	3-5
Cholesterol esters	15-22	Variable	45-50	15-20
Triglyceride	45-65	Variable	3-9	2-7
Protein	6-10	Variable	18-22	45-55
Apoproteins				
Apo B	X	X	X	—
Apo A-I	X	?	—	X
Apo A-II	X	?	—	X
Apo E	X	X	X	X
Apo Cs	X	X	—	X
Atherogenicity	+ +	+ + + +	+ + + +	– – –

Note: Remnants are included with LDL; density 1.006 to 1.063 gm/dl in the standard lipid profile.

appears to have a more favorable impact on the atherosclerotic process. However, at the present time the lipoprotein subclass field is still evolving. Consequently, in this review factors effecting HDL levels are presented in terms of total HDL cholesterol levels.

DIABETES, LIPIDS, AND PERIPHERAL VASCULAR DISEASE

In the Framingham Study, the presence of diabetes had a unique effect on the incidence of coronary disease in women but had minimal, if any, effect in men.[29] When comparing diabetics with and without macrovascular disease, there are significant increases in the total triglyceride level[30,31] and in the levels of cholesterol,[30,32,33] VLDL cholesterol, triglycerides,[30,33] and LDL cholesterol,[33] and reduced levels of HDL.[33,34] Poor diabetic control can result in elevated plasma cholesterol

levels,[35-38] which respond to improved blood glucose levels.[39-43] In general, after improving diabetes control, hyperlipidemic diabetics are treated as outlined above.

EFFICACY OF LOWERING LIPID LEVELS

In experimental animals reduction of hypercholesterolemia can have dramatic results on lesion size.[44] Aggressive lipid lowering can also yield significant benefits in limiting lesion progression in both PVD[28,45,46] and the coronary circulation.[47-50] Also, hyperlipidemia is associated with recurrent stenosis after carotid endarterectomy[51-53] and it has a negative impact on the patency of aortocoronary saphenous vein bypass.[54-56]

Table IV. Plasma cholesterol lowering by diet*

	Cholesterol change (%)
Cholesterol reduction to <100 mg/day	5-20
Reduce total fat to 20% calories with P/S ratio >1.0	10-20

*Approximate numbers based on references 16,20,23,24.

Table V. Factors that effect total plasma HDL cholesterol levels

Decreases HDL	Increases HDL
Smoking [60-62]	Niacin[69-71]
Poorly controlled diabetes mellitus[57-59]	Fibric acid derivatives[79]
Testosterone[64]	Exercise[72-75]
Hypertriglyceridemia[63]	Estrogens[64]
Obesity[60,65]	Moderate alcohol intake[76-78]
Polyunsaturated fat[66-68]	

Table VI. Current lipid-lowering medications

Drug	Dosage	Action	Comments
Bile acid sequestants (cholestryamine and colestipol)	4-10 gm b.i.d.	Decrease LDL cholesterol by 5%-35%; increase VLDL production; binds cholesterol in gut	Poor compliance in high dosages; gastric distress, and constipation common; increased VLDL a contraindication to use
Nicotinic acid	1-5 gm q.i.d.	Reduces hepatic synthesis VLDL, LDL; decreases LDL by 15%-30%; decreases TRG by 20%-30%; increases HDL cholesterol by 15% or more	Cutaneous flushing common; abdominal pain, diarrhea, hepatitis rare; contraindicated in patients with liver disease
Fibric acid derivatives (clofibrate, gemfibrozil [Lopid])	Varies	Reduce hepatic synthetic VLDL; increase clearance VLDL and LDL; reduce LDL cholesterol by 10%-30%, TRG by 20%-30%, and increase HDL cholesterol by 10%-20%	Well tolerated; Ciprofibrate, Fenofibrate more effective but not available in USA
HMG CoA reductase inhibitors (lovastatin)	5-20 mg b.i.d.	Reduce synthetic cholesterol and increase clearance LDL; reduce LDL cholesterol by 25%-40%	Well tolerated; several other drugs soon to be released by Food and Drug Administration

TRG = triglycerides.
Combination therapy with a bile salt–binding resin, nicotinic acid, and recently with lovastatin have resulted in up to a 60% lowering of plasma cholesterol levels.[79]

REFERENCES

1. Gordon T, Kannel WB. Predisposition to atherosclerosis in the head, heart, and legs. JAMA 1972;221:661-666.
2. Gordon T, Kannel WB, Castelli WP, et al. Lipoproteins, cardiovascular disease and death: The Framingham Study. Arch Int Med 1981;141:1128-1131.
3. Sloan JM, McKay JS, Sheridan B. The incidence of plasma insulin, blood sugar and serum lipid abnormalities in patients with atherosclerotic disease. Diabetologia 1971;7:431-432.
4. Greenhalgh RM, Rosengarten DS, Mervart I, et al. Serum lipids and lipoproteins in peripheral vascular disease. Lancet 1971;2:947-950.
5. DaVignon J, Lussier-Cacan S, Ortin-George M. Plasma lipid and lipoprotein patterns in angiographically graded atherosclerosis of the legs and in coronary heart disease. Canad Med Assoc J 1977;116:1245-1250.
6. Granceschini G, Bondioli A, Mantero M, et al. Increased apoprotein B in VLDL of patients with peripheral vascular disease. Arteriosclerosis 1982;2:74-80.
7. Trayner IM, Mannarino E, Clyne CAC, et al. Serum lipids and high density lipoprotein cholesterol in peripheral vascular disease. Br J Surg 1980;67:497-499.
8. Bradby GVT, Valente AJ, Walton KW. Serum high density lipoproteins in peripheral vascular disease. Lancet 1978;2:1271-1274.
9. Reckless JPD, Betteridge DJ, Wu P, et al. High-density and low-density lipoproteins and prevalence of vascular disease in diabetes mellitus. Br Med J 1978;1:883-886.
10. Vergani C, Trovato G, Dioguardi N. Serum total lipids, apoproteins A and B in cardiovascular disease. Clin Chem Acta 1978;87:127-133.
11. Pilger E, Pristautz H, Pfeiffer KP, et al. Risk factors for peripheral atherosclerosis. Arteriosclerosis 1983;3:57-63.
12. Gordon T, Castelli WP, Hjortland ML, et al. Diabetes, blood lipids, and the role of obesity in coronary heart disease risk for women: The Framingham Study. Ann Int Med 1977;87:393-397.
13. McConathy WR, Greenhalgh RM, Alaupouic P, et al. Plasma lipid and apolipoprotein profiles of women with two types of peripheral arterial disease. Atherosclerosis 1984;50:295-306.
14. Herbert PN, Assman G, Gotto AM, et al. Familial lipoprotein deficiency: Abetalipoproteinemia, hypobetalipoproteinemia, and Tangier disease. In Stanbury JB, Wyngaarden JB, Fredrickson DS, Goldstein JL, Brown MS, eds. The Metabolic Basis of Inherited Disease. 5th ed. New York: McGraw Hill, 1966, pp 589-621.
15. The Lipid Research Clinics Population Studies Data Book. Vol 1, NIH Publication No. 80-1527. Bethesda, Md.: Department of Health and Human Services. 1980.
16. Ahrens EH, Hisch J, Insull W. The influence of dietary fats on serum lipid levels in man. Lancet 1957;1:943-951.
17. Keys A, Anderson JT, Grande F. Serum cholesterol responses of man to changes in fats in the diet. Lancet 1957;1:787-796.
18. Keys A, Anderson JT, Grande F. Prediction of serum cholesterol responses of man to changes in fats in the diet. Lancet 1957;2:957-959.
19. Connor WE, Connor SL. The key role of nutritional factors in the prevention of coronary heart disease. Prev Med 1972;1:49-66.
20. Connor WE, Stone DB, Hodges RE. The interrelated effects of dietary cholesterol and fat upon the human serum lipid levels. J Clin Invest 1964;43:1691-1699.
21. Connor WE, Connor SL. The dietary prevention and treatment of coronary heart disease. In Connor WE, Bistrow JD, eds. Coronary Heart Disease: Prevention, Complications and Treatment. Philadelphia: JB Lippincott, 1985, pp 43-64.
22. Zilversmit DG. Atherogenesis: A postprandial phenomenon. Circulation 1979;60:473-485.
23. Schonfeld G. Dietary treatment of hyperlipidemia. Clin Chem 1988;34:B111-B114.
24. Connor WE, Connor SL. Dietary treatment of familial hypercholesterolemia. Arteriosclerosis 1989;1-91–1-105.
25. Grundy SM, Vega GL. Fibric acids: The effects on lipids and lipoprotein metabolism. Am J Med 1987;83:9-20.
26. Avins AL, Haber RJ, Hulley SB. The status of hypertriglyceridemia as a risk factor for CAD. Clin Lab Med 1989;9:153-168.
27. Grundy SM. Hypertriglyceridemia: Mechanisms, clinical significance, and treatment. Med Clin N Am 1982;66:519-535.
28. Zelis R, Mason DT, Braunwald E, et al. Effects of hyperproteinemias and their treatment on the peripheral circulation. J Clin Invest 1970;49:1007-1015.
29. Kannel WB, McGee DL. Diabetes and cardiovascular disease: The Framingham study. JAMA 1979;241:2035-2038.
30. Laakso M, Pyorala K. Lipid and lipoprotein abnormalities in diabetic patients with peripheral vascular disease. Atherosclerosis 1988;75:55-63.
31. Zimmerman BR, Palumbo PJ, O'Fallon WM, et al. A prospective study of peripheral occlusive arterial disease in diabetes. III. Initial lipid and lipoprotein findings. Mayo Clin Proc 1981;56:233-242.
32. Janka HU, Standi E, Mehnert H. Peripheral vascular disease in diabetes mellitus and its relation to cardiovascular risk factors: Screening with the doppler ultrasonic technique. Diabetologia 1980;3:207-213.
33. Beach KW, Brunzell JD, Conquest LL, et al. The correlation of arteriosclerosis obliterans with lipoproteins in insulin-dependent and non-insulin dependent diabetes. Diabetes 1979;28:836-840.
34. Welborn TA, Knuiman M, McCann V, et al. Clinical macrovascular disease in Caucasoid diabetic subjects: Logistic regression analysis of risk variables. Diabetalogia 1984;27:568-573.
35. Sosenko JM, Breslow JL, Miettinen OS, et al. Hyperglycemia and plasma lipid levels: A prospective study of young insulin-dependent diabetic patients. N Engl J Med 1980;302:650-654.
36. Glasgow AM, August GP, Hung W. Relationship between control and serum lipids in juvenile-onset diabetes. Diabetes Care 1981;4:76-80.
37. Lopes-Virella MF, Wohltmann HJ, Loadholt CB, et al. Plasma lipids and lipoproteins in young insulin-dependent diabetic patients: Relationship with control. Diabetologia 1981;21:216-223.
38. Sosenko JM, Breslow J, Miettinen OS, et al. Hyperglycemia and plasma lipid levels: Covariations in insulin-dependent diabetes. Diabetes Care 1982;5:40-43.
39. Tamborlane WV, Sherwin RS, Genel M, et al. Restoration of normal lipid and amino acid metabolism in diabetic patients treated with a portable insulin-infusion pump. Lancet 1979;1:1258-1261.
40. Dunn FL, Pietri A, Raskin P. Plasma lipid and lipoprotein levels with continuous subcutaneous insulin infusion in Type I diabetes mellitus. Ann Intern Med 1981;95:426-431.
41. Agardh CD, Nilsson-Ehle P, Schersten V. Improvement of the plasma lipoprotein pattern after institution of insulin treatment in diabetes mellitus. Diabetes Care 1982;5:322-325.
42. Lopes-Virella MF, Wohltmann HJ, Mayfield RK, et al. Effect of metabolic control on lipid, lipoprotein, and apolipoprotein levels in 55 insulin-dependent diabetic patients. Diabetes 1983;32:20-25.
43. Pfeifer MA, Brunzell JD, Best JD, et al. The response of plasma triglyceride, cholesterol, and lipoprotein lipase to

treatment in non-insulin-dependent diabetic subjects without familial hypertriglyceridemia. Diabetes 1983;32:525-531.

44. Armstrong ML, Warner ED, Connor WE. Regression of coronary atheromatosis in rhesus monkeys. Circ Res 1970;27: 59-63.

45. Barndt R Jr, Blankehorn DH, Crawford DW, et al. Regression and progression of early femoral atherosclerosis in treated hyperlipoproteinemic patients. Ann Int Med 1977;86: 139-146.

46. Duffield RGM, Lewis B, Miller NE, et al. Treatment of hyperlipidemia retards progression of symptomatic femoral atherosclerosis: A randomized controlled trial. Lancet 1983; 2:639-642.

47. Kuo PT, Hayase K, Kostis JB, et al. Use of combined diet and colestipol in long-term (7-7½ years) treatment of patients with type II hyperlipoproteinemia. Circulation 1979;59: 199-211.

48. Blankehorn DH, Nessim SA, Johnson RL, et al. Beneficial effects of combined colestipol-niacin therapy on coronary atherosclerosis and coronary venous bypass grafts. JAMA 1987;257:3233-3240.

49. Frick MH, Elo O, Haapa K, et al. Helsinki heart study: Primary-prevention trial with gemfibrozil in middle-aged men with dyslipidemia: Safety of treatment, changes in risk factors, and incidence of coronary heart disease. N Engl J Med 1987;317:1237-1245.

50. Levy RI, Brensike JF, Epstein SE, et al. The influence of changes in lipid values induced by cholestyramine and diet on progression of coronary artery disease results of the NHLBI type II coronary intervention study. Circulation 1984; 69:325-337.

51. Rapp JH, Qvarfardt P, Krupski WC, et al. Hypercholesterolemia and early restenosis after carotid endarterectomy. Surgery 1987;101:277-282.

52. Colyvas N, Phillips N, Stoney RJ, et al. Lipoprotein profiles in patients with recurrent carotid stenosis. Surgical Forum 1989;40:281-283.

53. Das MB, Hertzer NR, Ratiff NB, et al. Recurrent carotid stenosis. Ann Surg 1985;202:28-35.

54. Campeau L, Enjalbert M, L'Esperance J, et al. The relationship of risk factors to the development of atherosclerosis in saphenous-vein bypass grafts and the progression of disease in the native circulation. N Engl J Med 1984;311:1329-1332.

55. Neitzel F, Barboriak JJ, Pintark, et al. Atherosclerosis in aortocoronary bypass grafts: Morphologic study and risk factor analysis 6-12 years after surgery. Atherosclerosis 1986; 6:594-600.

56. Lie JT, Lauorie GM, Morris GC. Aortocoronary bypass saphenous vein graft atherosclerosis. Am J Cardiol 1977;40: 906-914.

57. Lopes-Virella MFL, Stone PG, Colwell JA. Serum high-density lipoprotein in diabetic patients. Diabetologia 1977;13: 285-291.

58. Calvert GD, Graham JJ, Mannik T, et al. Effects of therapy on plasma high density lipoprotein cholesterol concentration in diabetes mellitus. Lancet 1978;2:66-68.

59. Kennedy AL, Lappin TR, Lavery TD, et al. Relation of high-density lipoprotein cholesterol concentration to type of diabetes and its control. B Med J 1978;2:1191-1194.

60. Shephard RJ, Cox M, West C. Some factors influencing serum lipid levels in a working population. Atherosclerosis 1980;35: 287-300.

61. Williams P, Robinson, Bailey A. High-density lipoprotein and coronary risk factors in normal men. Lancet 1979;1:72-75.

62. Criqui MH, Wallace RB, Heiss G, et al. Cigarette smoking and plasma high-density lipoprotein cholesterol: The lipid research clinics program prevalence study. Circulation 1980; 62(Suppl. IV):IV-70–IV-76.

63. Mjs OD, Rao SN, Bjru L, et al. A longitudinal study of the biological variability of plasma lipoproteins in healthy young adults. Atherosclerosis 1979;34:75-81.

64. Kraus RM. Regulation of high density lipoprotein levels. Med Clin N Am 1982;66:403-430.

65. Garrison RJ, Wilson PW, Castelli WP. Obesity and lipoprotein cholesterol in the Framingham offspring study. Metabolism 1980;29:1053-1060.

66. Nichaman MZ, Sweeley CC, Olson RE. Plasma fatty acids in normolipemic and hyperlipemic subjects during fasting and after linoleate feeding. Am J Clin Nutr 1967;20:1057-1069.

67. Shepherd J, Packard CJ, Patsch JR, et al. Effects of dietary polyunsaturated and saturated fat on the properties of high density lipoproteins and the metabolism of apolipoprotein A-1. J Clin Invest 1978;61:1582-1592.

68. Vessby B, Boberg J, Gustafsson IB, et al. Reduction of high-density lipoprotein cholesterol and apolipoprotein A-1 concentrations by a lipid-lowering diet. Atherosclerosis 1980; 35:21-27.

69. Blum CB, Levy RI, Eisenberg S, et al. High-density lipoprotein metabolism in man. J Clin Invest 1977;60:795-807.

70. Carlson LA, Olsson AG, Ballantyne D. On the rise in low density and high density lipoproteins in response to the treatment of hypertriglyceridaemia in type IV and type V hyperlipoproteinemias. Atherosclerosis 1977;26:603-609.

71. Shepherd J, Packard CJ, Patsch JR, et al. Effects of nicotinic acid therapy on plasma high-density lipoprotein subfraction distribution and composition and on apolipoprotein A metabolism. J Clin Invest 1979;63:858-867.

72. Huttunen JK, Lansimies E, Voutilainen E, et al. Effect of moderate physical exercise on serum lipoproteins. Circulation 1979;60:1220-1229.

73. Streja D, Mymin D. Moderate exercise and high density lipoprotein cholesterol. JAMA 1979;242:2190-2192.

74. Kiens B, Jorgensen I, Lewis S, et al. Increased plasma HDL-cholesterol and apo A-1 in sedentary middle-aged men after physical conditioning. Eur J Clin Invest 1980;10: 203-210.

75. Wood PD, Haskell WL, Blair SN, et al. Increased exercise level and plasma lipoprotein concentrations: a one-year, randomized, controlled study in sedentary, middle aged men. Metabolism 1983;32:31-39.

76. Johansson BG, Medhus A. Increase in plasma alpha-lipoproteins in chronic alcoholics after acute abuse. Acta Med Scand 1974;195:273-277.

77. Belfrage P, Berg B, Hagerstrand I, et al. Alterations of lipid metabolism in healthy volunteers during long-term ethanol intake. Eur J Clin Invest 1977;7:127-131.

78. Haskell WL, Camargo C Jr, Williams PT, et al. The effect of cessation and resumption of moderate alcohol intake and serum high-density-lipoprotein subfractions. A controlled study. N Engl J Med 1984;310:805-810.

79. Illingworth DR, Bacon S. Treatment of heterozygous familial hypercholesterolemia with lipid-lowering drugs. Arteriosclerosis 1989;9:I-121–I-134.

Atherosclerosis

Diabetes Mellitus and Vascular Surgery

D. Eugene Strandness, Jr., MD, Seattle, Washington

To accurately describe the role diabetes plays in the pathogenesis of arteriosclerosis and its relationship to clinical practice, one must not only compare diabetics to nondiabetics of similar age and sex but one must also identify those factors unique to diabetics. Of the approximately six million Americans with diabetes mellitus, 90% have type II (non–insulin-dependent) diabetes. The remaining 10%, the type I patients, must take insulin for survival. The profound differences between type I and type II diabetics have a direct bearing both on how we perceive the disease and how we approach its management.

Of all amputations done in America, half are done in diabetics for reasons other than trauma. This high incidence of limb loss has been attributed to a variety of factors, including extensive atherosclerosis, peripheral neuropathy, increased susceptibility to infection, Mönckeberg's medial sclerosis, and microvascular disease.

This section delineates the pertinent factors based on current information, keeping in mind that much more is unknown than known. The one myth that needs to be dispelled is that of the role of the microcirculation in the promotion of tissue ischemia and death. The commonly held idea about a specific diabetic microangiopathy pertains only to the eyes, the kidneys, and perhaps the heart. Evidence of microcirculatory lesions other than a thickening of the capillary basement membrane in the lower limbs of diabetic patients is unconvincing at present.

Diabetes is diagnosed and the type is determined on the basis of the clinical presentation and the results of the plasma glucose tolerance test after a 12-hour fast (Table I). The most frequently seen differences between the diabetic and nondiabetic population are reviewed in Table II. These differences reflect the patient population seen in a vascular clinic and do not represent the findings in an unselected population without known arterial disease. As noted in Table III, arteriosclerosis obliterans (ASO) is two to four times more prevalent in type II as compared with type I diabetics. This reflects the much younger age of type I diabetics. The prevalence of ASO in type II diabetics is 12 to 28 times greater than that observed in age- and sex-matched controls.

The higher levels of cholesterol and low density lipoprotein (LDL) and the lower levels of high density lipoprotein (HDL) in women may explain in part the higher incidence of ASO seen in type II diabetic women (Table IV). Hypertension is a well-known risk factor for ASO. Both systolic and diastolic blood pressures tend to be significantly higher in diabetic patients (Table V).

The progressive nature of ASO in type II diabetic patients is shown in Table VI. The factors related to progression are shown in Table VII. There is evidence that limb salvage can be accomplished by vein bypasses to the tibial arteries. Thus, it appears that the terminal branches of the tibial-peroneal arteries are both frequently patent in diabetics and are amenable to grafting (Table VIII).

Although the incidence of stroke is twice as common in diabetic patients, the explanation is uncertain.[15] One obviously suspected cause is an increased prevalence of high-grade carotid artery stenosis (Table IX). The relationship between the usual risk factors and the prevalence of a >50% diameter-reducing stenosis of the carotid bifurcation is shown in Tables X to XIII.

From the Department of Surgery, Section of Vascular Surgery, University of Washington School of Medicine, Seattle, Wash.

Table I. Subject classification method for establishing the diagnosis of diabetes mellitus[4]

Criterion	Sign or symptom
Type I	Rapid onset, requires insulin to remain ketosis-free
Type II	12-hour fasting plasma glucose > 140 mg dl
Elevated fasting* plasma glucose	> 115 but < 140 mg dl
Normal fasting plasma glucose	< 115 mg dl

*Classification used by National Diabetes Data Group; labelled as Impaired Glucose Tolerance.

Table II. Clinical characteristics of nondiabetic and type II diabetic patients with arterial disease

	Nondiabetics	Type II diabetics	Ref.
Location of occlusive lesions			2,5,6
Aortoiliac	Common (6.2%)	Uncommon (1.7%)	
Femoropopliteal	Common (43%)	Common (75%)	
Tibial-peroneal	Less common (57%)	Common (81%)	
Medial calcification	Not seen	Common	7,8
Neuropathy	Not seen	Common	2
Resistance to infection	Normal	Low?	

Table III. Prevalence of arteriosclerosis obliterans (ASO) defined as ankle/arm index < 0.90[9]

	No.	Mean age (yr)	Mean fasting glucose level	Smokers (%)	ASO (%)
Community controls	101	61.4	96	42	1
Friend controls*	43	57.3	99	58	2
Type I	141	34	219	52	6
Type II					
Diet	40	58	239	65	28[†]
Insulin	175	56	219	67	12[§]
Oral	94	56	184	68	22

*Friends of patients with diabetes mellitus who had similar lifestyles.
[†]Diet-treated smokers had significantly more ASO than those treated with oral hypoglycemic agents ($p < 0.043$).
[§]Insulin-treated type II smokers had significantly less ASO than all other type II smokers taken together ($p < 0.003$.)

Table IV. Lipoprotein patterns in type I and type II diabetic patients (median values in mg/dl)[10]

	Type II diet treated		Type II oral hypoglycemic agents		Type II insulin		Type I	
	M	F	M	F	M	F	M	F
Cholesterol	226	248*	221	219	208	230*	191	212*
HDL cholesterol	41	48[†]	40	46[†]	45	54	46	58
LDL cholesterol	144	152*	142	133	132	145	123	132*
Triglycerides	188*	148*	150*	154*	119*	112	93	98

M = males; F = females.

Study population. type II diet: males 47, females 43; type II oral agents: males 45, females 43; type II insulin: males 98, females 61; Type I: males 77, females 68.

Control population for comparison, Pacific Northwest Bell Telephone Company Health Survey. Each diabetic subject was assigned to corresponding percentile range for the subject's age and sex.

*Distributions are significantly higher than corresponding cohort from Bell population.

[†]Distributions are significantly lower than corresponding cohort from Bell population.

Table V. Blood pressures in type II diabetic patients as compared with controls[11,12]

	Systolic*	Diastolic[†]
Type II diabetic	142 ± 20	80 ± 10
Controls	131 ± 17	78 ± 10

*T = 5.82, $p < 0.001$.
[†]T = 2.22, $p < 0.03$.

Table VI. Prevalence of ASO and incidence of progression over 2-year period in type II diabetic patients and controls in age range of 50 to 70 years[13]

	Type II diabetics n = 252			Controls n = 158	
	Progression			Progression	
	Yes	No	BKA	Yes	No
No disease at baseline	28	169		5	149
Disease at baseline	45	7	3*	1	3

BKA = below-knee amputation.

*Three cases of bilateral BKA could not be evaluated for progression.

Fisher's exact test yielded $p < 0.000005$ for progression with and without disease at time of entry into the study for type II diabetics.

Table VII. Role of risk factors in prevalence and progression of peripheral arterial disease in type II diabetic patients[13]

Risk score	Prevalence (%)	Progression (%)
0	0	—
1	3	0
2	10	83
3	21	82
4	25	78
5	52	93
6	100	100

Risk score = smoking > 25 years plus; recent smoking and > 25 years plus; duration of diabetes > 10 years plus; HDL cholesterol < 40 mg/dl; systolic blood pressure > 145 mm Hg plus; obesity index < 2.83 g/cm².

Table VIII. Role of distal bypasses for the salvage of diabetic limbs in 96 patients (94% diabetic)*[14]

Category	Percent
Superimposed infection	42%
Conduit used	100% vein
Perioperative mortality	1.9%
Graft patency to 18 months	82%
Limb salvage to 18 months	87%
Patient survival to 18 months	80%

*97 bypasses done to distal tibial arteries.

Table IX. Carotid bifurcation stenosis* in control and type II diabetic patients over 50 years of age[11]

Carotid artery stenosis	Control	Type II[†]
Yes[§]	1 (0.7%)	26 (9.5%)
No	128	245
Total	129	271

*>50% diameter reduction by duplex scan.
[†]Also includes patients with elevated fasting plasma glucose levels.
[§]Fisher's exact test: $p = 0.0003$.

Table X. Prevalence of >50% carotid artery stenosis as a function of age in type II diabetic patients[11]

	Decades of life				
	40-49	50-59	60-69	70-79	80-89
Yes	0	5	9	9	3
No	25	97	124	53	8
Percent	0	5.2	7.3	17	38

Table XI. History of cigarette smoking and >50% carotid artery stenosis in type II diabetic patients over age 50[11]

	Carotid artery stenosis	
History of smoking	Yes*	No
Yes	22 (85%)	154 (63%)
No	4	91
Total	26	245

Fisher's exact test: $p = 0.02$.
*Population includes those with elevated fasting plasma glucose.

Table XII. Estimated prevalence of >50% carotid artery stenosis in smoking and nonsmoking type II diabetic patients[12]

	Prevalence of carotid artery stenosis	
	Male	Female
Smoker	0.084	0.039
Nonsmoker	0.027	0.012

Mean values chosen for this estimate: age = 61; systolic blood pressure/diastolic blood pressure = 1.78; cholesterol = 226 mg/dl.

Table XIII. Relative importance of various risk factors in an average type II diabetic patient[11]

Value varied	Prevalence of carotid artery stenosis >50%
None (baseline value)	0.041
Age = 67 (75th percentile)	0.065
Age = 56 (25th percentile)	0.028
SBP/DBP = 1.89 (75th percentile)	0.044
SBP/DBP = 1.63 (25th percentile)	0.038
Cholesterol = 253 (75th percentile)	0.056
Cholesterol = 190 (25th percentile)	0.027

Mean values used for this estimate: age = 61; systolic blood pressure (SBP)/diastolic blood pressure (DBP) = 1.78; cholesterol = 226 mg/dl.

REFERENCES

1. Diabetes in America. Diabetes data compiled in 1984. NIH publication No. 85 1468, August 1985.
2. Strandness DE Jr, Priest RE, Gibbons GE. A combined clinical and pathological study of diabetic and nondiabetic peripheral arterial disease. Diabetes 1964;13:366-372.
3. Vracko R, Strandness DE Jr. Basal lamina of abdominal and skeletal muscle capillaries in diabetics and nondiabetics. Circulation 1967;35:690-700.
4. National diabetes data group. Classification and diagnosis of diabetes mellitus and other categories of glucose metabolism. Diabetes 1979;28:1039-1057.
5. Gensler SW, Haimovici H, Hoffert P, et al. Study of vascular lesions in diabetic, nondiabetic patients. Arch Surg 1965;91:617-622.
6. Wheelock FC Jr. Transmetatarsal amputations and arterial surgery in diabetic patients. N Engl J Med 1961;264:316-320.
7. Lindbom A. Arteriosclerosis and arterial thrombosis in the lower limbs. Acta Radiol 1950;80(suppl):38-48.
8. Neubauer B. A quantitative study of peripheral arterial calcification and glucose tolerance in elderly diabetics and nondiabetics. Diabetologia 1971;7:409-413.
9. Beach KW, Brunzell JD, Strandness DE Jr. Prevalence of severe arteriosclerosis obliterans in patients with diabetes mellitus: Relation to smoking and form of therapy. Arteriosclerosis 1982;2:275-280.
10. Beach KW, Brunzell JD, Conquest L, et al. The correlation of arteriosclerosis obliterans with lipoproteins in insulin-dependent and non–insulin-dependent diabetes. Diabetes 1979;28:836-840.
11. Chan A, Beach KW, Martin DC, et al. Carotid artery disease in NIDDM diabetes. Diabetes Care 1983;6:562-569.
12. Beach KW, Strandness DE Jr. Diabetes and associated risk factors in insulin-dependent and non–insulin-dependent diabetes. Diabetes 1980;29:882-888.
13. Beach KW, Bedford GR, Bergelin RO, et al. Progression of lower extremity arterial occlusive disease in type II diabetes. Diabetes Care 1988;11:464-472.
14. Ponposelli FB Jr, Jepsen SJ, Gibbons GW, et al. Efficacy of the dorsal pedal bypass for limb salvage in diabetic patients: Short-term observations. J Vasc Surg 1990;11:745-751.
15. Garcia ML, McNamara PM, Gordon T, et al. Morbidity and mortality in diabetes in Framingham population: Sixteen year follow-up study. Diabetes 1974;23:105-111.

7

Regression of Atherosclerosis

William C. Krupski, MD, Denver, Colorado

Evaluation of interventions to induce regression of atherosclerosis has been a prominent component of atherosclerosis research. As early as 1924, Aschoff[1] suggested that fatty streaks might be reversible, observing that these lesions were less common in aortas studied at autopsy at the end of World War I. This viewpoint was reiterated by Cowdry,[2] Ophuls,[3] and Hueper.[4] Wilens[5] hypothesized that lesions might be likely to regress in chronic wasting diseases, a concept inferred from 1456 autopsies in malnourished individuals in Finland in World War II (1940-1946) compared with autopsies performed at an earlier era (1933-1938).[6] The reciprocal relationship of extent of atherosclerosis and poor nutritional status has been demonstrated in patients with carcinoma,[7] pulmonary tuberculosis,[8] and cachexia.[9] As Malinow[10] has cautioned, however, postmortem evidence is difficult to interpret. Differences in the extent of lesions may be related to arrest of *progression* rather than *regression,* absence of thrombotic complications, and patient selection (i.e., patients in the control group may have died from complications of atherosclerosis).

Reversibility of arterial lesions in animals was first demonstrated in 1933 by Anitschkow using a rabbit model of diet-induced atherosclerosis.[2] Horlick and Katz[11] conclusively demonstrated that cessation of cholesterol feeding of chicks induced regression of plaques. Bevans et al.[12] soon showed regression of atherosclerosis in a canine model, which was later confirmed by DePalma et al.[13] Since those seminal observations, numerous studies have verified plaque regression by various interventions such as discontinuation of atherogenic diets or pharmacologic regimens in birds, rodents, swine, rabbits, and nonhuman primates. A representative list of some of these

From the Section of Vascular Surgery, University of Colorado Health Sciences Center, Denver, Colo.

investigations is given in Table I.[14-40] The ability to bring about regression depends on the animal model used (including species studied and type of inciting agent used to produce atherosclerosis), the severity of the initial lesion and the plasma cholesterol concentration,[36] and certain nonlipid characteristics of plaque such as the extent of calcification and the composition of fibrous tissue, which adversely affect the rate of regression.[41,42]

Extrapolations from animal experiments to human atherosclerosis are treacherous. There are differences between animals and humans in the role of dietary cholesterol and saturated fats, the anatomy and composition of lesions, the interval required for plaque development, and the levels of plasma lipoproteins attained during the intervention period.[10] Nonetheless, regression of atherosclerosis in animals led to the hypothesis that similar outcomes could be achieved in humans, prompting many clinical epidemiologic trials of lipid-lowering interventions. In appraising such trials, awareness of methodologic shortcomings is essential (Table II).[43-53] During the past three decades, nineteen randomized, controlled clinical trials involving either primary or secondary prevention of coronary heart disease (CHD) have been performed. Seven trials concerned primary prevention: two evaluated diet[54,55] and five assessed a drug (Table III).[56-63] Twelve trials concerned secondary prevention: five evaluated diet,[64-69] six assessed a drug,[70-76] and one appraised surgery (Table IV).[77]

Using the available results, a recent meta-analysis of these trials concluded that the prevention or regression of CHD by lipid-lowering interventions is not substantiated because there is only a nonsignificant tendency for a decreased incidence of fatal CHD, a reduction that has no effect on death from all causes (Table V).[78]

Text continued on p. 43.

Table I. Atherosclerosis in animal models in which regression of disease produced by various interventions has been objectively documented

Animal	Intervention	Ref.
Chickens	Cessation of atherogenic diet	11
Chickens	Estrogen	14
Pigeons	Intestinal bypass	15
Rats	Estrogen	16
Mice	Genetic manipulation to increase ApoA-1 (the major protein component of high-density lipoprotein)	17
Canines	Cessation of atherogenic diet	12,13
Swine	Cessation of atherogenic diet	18,19
Swine	Clofibrate	20
Swine	Pyridinocarbamate	21
Rabbits	Cessation of atherogenic diet	22
Rabbits	Calcium antagonists (diltiazem, verapamil)	23,29
Rabbits	Antihypertensives (propranolol, prazosin)	24
Rabbits	Free radical scavengers-antioxidants (probucol, butylated hydroxytoluene)	25,30
Rabbits	Fat-free specially modified total parenteral nutrition solution	26
Rabbits	Inhibition of cholesterol synthesis (HMG-CoA reductase inhibitor [Lovastatin])	27,31
Rabbits	Fish oil	29
Rhesus monkeys	Cessation of atherogenic diet	32,34,36
Cynomolgus monkeys	Cessation of atherogenic diet	33,38
Cynomolgus monkeys	Alfalfa meal	35
Pigtail macaques	Ethanol	37
Rhesus monkeys	Free radical scavenger-antioxidant (probucol)	39
Rhesus monkeys	Exercise (increasing HDL)	40

Table II. Flaws in epidemiologic data regarding prevention of atherosclerosis trials that diminish broad applicability

	Ref.
1. National mortality rates from coronary heart disease (CHD) are inaccurate because of misdiagnosis, coding changes, and variable physician awareness.	43,44
2. CHD is not a specific disease entity, but an imprecise clinical diagnosis with no finite end point. Coronary arteries are normal in 20% to 30% of patients with chest pain.	43,45,46
3. The lipid hypothesis is a theory not of atherogenesis but of lipid accumulation in the vessel wall.	47
4. Hypercholesterolemia is a metabolic storage disorder; it is a misconception that hypercholesterolemia in animals or familial hypercholesterolemia induces conventional atherosclerosis.	48,49
5. Clinical trials are mostly composed of individuals <60 years old, whereas 80% of CHD victims are >60 years old.	50,51
6. Most clinical trials before 1984 were flawed by poor study design, inadequate sample size, nonuniform exposure to risk, absence of double-blind protocol, failure to achieve comparable groups, inadequate cholesterol reduction, inconclusive results, and poor statistical analysis.	52
7. Reliance on mean cholesterol for a group is misleading because it is unknown whether clinical end points occur more commonly with the higher or lower serum levels within the group.	52,53

Table III. Primary epidemiologic prevention of atherosclerosis trials*

Study (yr)	Ref.	Mean duration (yr)	No. of patients (T/C)	Subjects	Interventions	Mean age (yr)	% Men	Cholesterol (mmol/L): Entry/change
Diet								
Los Angeles Veterans Administration (1968)	54	3.6	424/422	Age >55: No diabetes, alcohol abuse, serious diseases	Cholesterol-lowering diet	63	100	6.05/0.77 (13%)
Minnesota Coronary Survey (1975)	55	1	4541/4516	Men and women residents of mental hospitals: No cholesterol restrictions	Cholesterol-lowering diet	48	50	5.35/0.72 (13%)
Upjohn Study (1978)	56	2.1	1149/1129	Men and women: Cholesterol >6.5 mmol/L; no serious diseases	Colestipol vs. placebo	54	48	7.78/1.01 (13%)
WHO Clofibrate Study (1978)	57,58	5.3	5331/5296	Age 30-59: Cholesterol in top third of screening; no CHD, diabetes, hypertension	Clofibrate vs. placebo	46	100	6.41/0.66 (10%)
Drugs								
Lipid Research Clinics Primary Prevention Trial (1984)	59	7.4	1906/1900	Age 35-59: LDL cholesterol >4.5 mmol/L + clinical CHD; no diabetes, hypertension	Cholestyramine + diet vs. placebo + diet	48	100	7.55/0.98 (13%)
Helsinki Heart Study (1987)	60,61	5.0	2051/2030	Age 40-55: Cholesterol >5.2 mmol/L + clinical CHD; no type I diabetes	Gemfibrozil + diet vs. placebo + diet	47	100	7.47/0.67 (9%)
EXCEL: Expanded clinical evaluation of lovastatin (1991)	62,63	0.9	6582/1663	Age 28-70: Cholesterol >6.21 and <7.76 mmol/L; no diabetes or serious diseases	Lovastatin (4 groups) + diet vs. placebo + diet	56	59	6.67/2.17 (32%)

T/C = treated group/control group; LDL = low-density lipoprotein; CHD = coronary heart disease.
*From Cucherat M, Boissel JP. Meta-analysis of results from clinical trials on prevention of coronary artery disease by lipid-lowering interventions. Clin Trials Meta-Analysis 1993;28:109-129.

Table IV. Secondary epidemiologic prevention of atherosclerosis trials*

Study (yr)	Ref.	Mean duration (yr)	No. of patients (T/C)	Major entry criteria	Interventions	Mean age (yr)	% Men	Cholesterol (mmol/L): Entry/change
Diet								
MRC low-fat diet (1965)	64	3.0	123/129	Age <65: History of MI; no CHF, hypertension, serious illness; no cholesterol restrictions	Low fat vs. ordinary diet	NS	100	6.80/0.39 (6%)
Rose et al. (1965)	65	1.2	28/26	Age <70: History of MI or angina; no CHF or serious diseases	Corn oil + low fat vs. ordinary diet	55	100	6.70/0.79 (12%)
Oslo Diet Heart Study (1966)	66,67	5.0	206/206	Age 30-60: MI between 1956-1958 & alive in 1958; no serious diseases	Low saturated fat & cholesterol vs. ordinary diet	56	100	7.65/0.62 (8%)
MRC soya bean oil (1968)	68	3.5	199/194	Age <60: History of MI; no hypertension, obesity, oral anticoagulants	Soya bean oil + low fat vs. ordinary diet	NS	100	7.03/0.93 (13%)
Woodhill et al. (1978)	69	NS	221/237	Age 30-59: History of MI or angina	Low saturated fat & high polyunsaturated fat vs. ordinary diet	49	100	7.27/0.28 (4%)
Drugs								
Scottish Society of Physicians (1971)	70	3.4	350/367	Age 40-69: History of MI or angina; no CHF or diabetes; no cholesterol restrictions	Clofibrate vs. placebo	52	79	7.01/1.01 (14%)
Newcastle-Upon-Tyne (1971)	71	3.7	244/253	Age <65: History of MI or angina; no CHF, hypertension, serious diseases; no cholesterol restrictions	Clofibrate vs. placebo	52	80	6.34/0.80 (13%)
Coronary Drug Project (clofibrate) (1975)	72	6.2	1103/2789	Age 30-64: History of MI; no class 3 or 4 NYHA function; no cholesterol restrictions	Clofibrate vs. placebo	NS	100	6.46/0.44 (7%)

T/C = treated group/control group; MRC = Medical Research Council; NS = not stated; MI = myocardial infarction; CHF = congestive heart failure; NYHA = New York Heart Association; CAD = coronary artery disease; LDL = low-density lipoprotein.

*From Cucharat M, Boissel JP. Meta-analysis of results from clinical trials on prevention of coronary artery disease by lipid-lowering interventions. Clin Trials Meta-Analysis 1993;28:109-129.

Continued.

Table IV. Secondary epidemiologic prevention of atherosclerosis trials — cont'd

Study (yr)	Ref.	Mean duration (yr)	No. of patients (T/C)	Major entry criteria	Interventions	Mean age (yr)	% Men	Cholesterol (mmol/L): Entry/change
Drugs–cont'd								
Coronary Drug Project (niacin) (1977)	73	6.2	1119/2789	Age 30-64: History of MI; no class 3 or 4 NYHA function; no cholesterol restrictions	Niacin vs. placebo	NS	100	6.46/0.78 (12%)
Carlson et al. (1977)	74	<3	279/279	Age <70; History of MI; no CHF, type I diabetes, serious disease; no cholesterol restrictions	Clofibrate + niacin vs. placebo	59	79	6.44/0.93 (14%)
NHLBI Type II Coronary Intervention Study (1984)	75,76	5.0	71/72	Age 21-55: Arteriographic CAD and 10th percentile for LDL cholesterol; no severe angina	Cholestyramine + low-fat diet vs. placebo + low-fat diet	46	81	7.65/0.41 (5%)
Surgery								
Surgical Control of Hyperlipidemias (POSCH) (1990)	77	9.7	421/417	Age 30-64: History of MI; total cholesterol >5.69 mmol/L or LDL >3.62 mmol/L; no other risks	Ileal bypass + low-fat diet vs. no surgery + diet	51	91	6.49/1.45 (22%)

Table V. Meta-analysis of atherosclerosis prevention trials*

Variable	No. of trials/No. patients	Odds ratio (95% CI)[†]
Total mortality	16/47005	0.99 (0.92-1.06)
Primary prevention	7/38940	1.07 (0.96-1.19)
Secondary prevention	9/8065	0.93 (0.85-1.03)
Nonfatal myocardial infarction	14/30370	0.75 (0.69-0.83)
Primary prevention	5/21638	0.74 (0.65-0.86)
Secondary prevention	9/8732	0.76 (0.68-0.86)
All heart disease	16/39427	0.79 (0.74-0.84)
Primary prevention	6/30695	0.82 (0.74-0.92)
Secondary prevention	10/8732	0.76 (0.70-0.83)
Fatal heart disease	15/39175	0.88 (0.80-0.96)
Primary prevention	6/30695	0.90 (0.75-1.09)
Secondary prevention	9/8480	0.87 (0.78-0.96)
Deaths due to cancer	11/37495	1.23 (0.99-1.54)
Primary prevention	6/30695	1.35 (1.04-1.75)
Secondary prevention	5/6800	1.00 (0.67-1.49)
Deaths not related to illness	10/28438	1.36 (0.95-1.97)
Primary prevention	6/21638	1.52 (0.93-2.47)
Secondary prevention	4/6800	1.19 (0.68-2.06)

*From Cucharat M, Boissel JP. Meta-analysis of results from clinical trials on prevention of coronary artery disease by lipid-lowering interventions. Clin Trials Meta-Analysis 1993;28:109-129.

[†]Odds ratio indicates the number of treated patients with the outcome variable in proportion to untreated (control) patients with the outcome variable. Thus a low number indicates a "positive (desired) effect," and a high number indicates a "negative (undesired) effect." If outcome rates are equal, the odds ratio is 1.

Table VI. Limitations of trials purported to show regression of atherosclerosis by serial arteriography

	Ref.
1. When a trial yields a positive result, one cannot assume that this translates into a clinical benefit (e.g., in the INTACT study, nifedipine decreased new coronary lesions but mortality was higher than for placebo treatment).	98,99
2. Visual assessment of arteriographic changes is inaccurate.	100-103
3. Arteriography frequently underestimates the severity of lesions or misses them entirely.	104-106
4. Endothelial dysfunction precedes arteriographic demonstration of atherosclerosis, and hypercholesterolemia impairs vasomotor tone.	107-109
5. Compensatory enlargement of vessels may be misinterpreted as regression.	110-112
6. "Relative" percent diameter stenosis measurements (a) do not reflect functional significance; (b) rely on arbitrary determinations of adjacent "normal" arteries for the denominator; (c) do not account for diffuse disease; and (d) permit fallacious *pseudoregression* determinations (see Fig. 1).	97,113-120
7. Although no measurement is ideal, absolute measurements such as minimum diameter (not applied in any large clinical trial) has many advantages, including good reproducibility.	93,97
8. In arteriographic studies there was a change from occlusion to stenosis in over 50% of subjects, suggesting that variance was due to lysis of thrombus not regression of atherosclerotic plaque.	121,122
9. Commonly, one lesion may worsen while another appears to improve in the same patient; whereas *lesion*- vs. *patient*-based analysis is more powerful, statistical assessment is very complex.	97,103
10. In contrast to ultrasound studies of peripheral vessels, arteriographic trials cannot be applied to the general population, and there is a high dropout rate.	123
11. If lesions progress episodically rather than linearly, serial arteriography will not detect changes.	123,124
12. More severe stenoses (which do not necessarily produce more clinical events) tend to progress or regress more than mild lesions, and different arteries (e.g., right vs. left coronary) behave differently.	125,126
13. Many biases are present in available studies related to timing of arteriograms (e.g., the week after myocardial infarctions when lipid levels fall 10% to 30%), selection of control patients, medication differences between groups, measurement of HDL and other cholesterol-carrying lipoproteins, technologic limits of precisely defining degree of stenoses, and others.	127-134

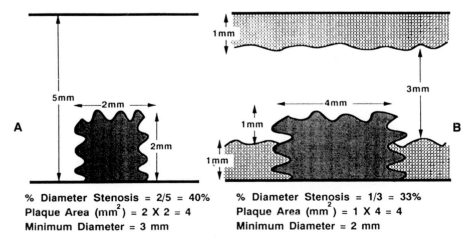

% Diameter Stenosis = 2/5 = 40%
Plaque Area (mm²) = 2 X 2 = 4
Minimum Diameter = 3 mm

% Diameter Stenosis = 1/3 = 33%
Plaque Area (mm²) = 1 X 4 = 4
Minimum Diameter = 2 mm

Fig. 1. Pseudoregression of atherosclerosis. Measurement of the lesion in **A** indicates a diameter stenosis of 40%. Whereas total amount of the major lesion and the overall extent of atherosclerosis has increased in **B**, measurement of diameter stenosis is calculated to be only 33% and plaque volume is found to be unchanged. Determination that a lesion has decreased when in fact it has remained stable or actually increased is termed *pseudoregression*.

Table VII. Arteriographic trials on regression of coronary artery atherosclerosis

Study (yr)	Ref.	Location	Mean duration (yr)	No. of patients (T/C)	Mean age[1] (yr)	% Men
Cohn et al. (1975)	83	San Francisco, Calif.	1	16/24	48	NS
Kuo et al. (1979)	135	Piscataway, N.J.	3-4	25/0	38-65	60
Rafflenbeul et al. (1979)	125	Birmingham, Ala.	1.3	25/0	NS	NS
Nash et al. (1982)	136	Syracuse, N.Y.	2	25/17	54	88
Nikkila et al. (1984)	137	Helsinki, Finland	7	28/20	44	93
Campeau et al. (1984)	138	Montreal, Canada	5	82/0	58	83
NHLBI Type II (1984)	75,76	Multicenter, U.S.A.	5	71/72	46	81
Leiden (1985)	139	Leiden, Netherlands	2	39/0	49	90
CLAS-I (1987)	87	Los Angeles, Calif.	2	80/82	54	100
Chesbro et al. (1989)	140	Rochester, Minn.	4.6	283 Total[2]	NS	NS
Waters et al. (1990)	99	Montreal, Canada	2	168/167	51	83
POSCH (1990)	77	Multicenter, U.S.A.	9.7	417/421[3]	51	91
Lifestyle Heart Trial (1990)	141	San Francisco, Calif.	1.25	22/19	58	88
INTACT (1990)	142	Multicenter, international	3	173/175	53	NS
FATS (1990)	143	Seattle, Wash.	2.5	74/46	47	100
CLAS-II (1990)	144	Los Angeles, Calif.	4	75/63	54	100
UCSF (1990)	145	San Francisco, Calif.	2.1	32/40	42	56
STARS (1992)	146	London, U.K.	3.25	50/24	50	100

T/C = Treated group/control group; NHLBI = National Heart, Lung, and Blood Institute type II hyperlipoproteinemia; CLAS = Cholesterol-Lowering Atherosclerosis Study; POSCH = Program on the Surgical Control of the Hyperlipidemias; INTACT = International Nifedipine Trial on Antiatherosclerotic Therapy; FATS = Familial Atherosclerosis Treatment Study; UCSF = University of California, San Francisco; STARS = St. Thomas Atherosclerosis Regression Study; NS = not stated; CABG = coronary artery bypass; MI = myocardial infarction.

[1] Age at entry into trial averaged between groups.
[2] Reportedly evenly divided between treatment and control groups, but numbers not stated in abstract.
[3] Follow-up coronary arteriograms in 84.7% of treatment group and 80.7% of controls.
[4] Regression defined as 20% decrease in diameter stenosis.
[5] Lipids measured 10 years after coronary bypass surgery.

Random?	Major entry criteria	Interventions	Cholesterol (mmol/L): Entry/change	Regression (No.)
Yes	Proven CAD: Most had operative therapy	Clofibrate vs. placebo	6.73/0.22 (3%)	None
No	Age 38-65: Type II hyperlipoproteinemia	Diet + colestipol (no control)	10.67/3.68 (34%)	None
No	Unstable angina: ICU care; re-arterio after 1 yr	"Optimal medical therapy"	NS	5/25 (25%)[4]
No	Symptomatic CAD: >50% stenosis; cholesterol >6.4 mmol/L	Diet + colestipol vs. diet + placebo	7.23/1.51 (20%)	None
No	Age <57: 2-3 vessel CAD; cholesterol >7.2 mmol/L	Diet + clofibrate ± nicotinic acid vs. diet	7.70/1.39 (18%)	None
No	Previous CABG: 10 yr postop	No special care	7.12/NS[5]	None
Yes	Age 21-55: CAD; tenth percentile for LDL cholesterol	Cholestyramine + diet vs. placebo + diet	7.65/0.41 (5%)	3/116 (2.6%)[6]
No	Age <60: 1 or more >50% CAD stenoses	Diet	6.90/0.7 (10%)	None
Yes	Age 40-59: Previous CABG; cholesterol 4.8-9.1 mmol/L	Colestipol + niacin + diet vs. placebo + diet	6.35/1.70 (26%)	13/80 (16%)[7]
Yes	Low risk: Medically treated CAD	Aspirin + dipyridamole vs. placebo	NS	(4%)
Yes	Age <65: 5%-75% stenoses in 4 coronary arteries	Nicardipine vs. placebo	6.87/0 (0%)	140/2323 (6%)[8]
Yes	Survived 1st MI; cholesterol >5.69 mmol/L	Partial ileal bypass vs. control	6.48/1.43 (22%)	27/187 (14%)[9]
Yes	Age 35-75: 1-3 vessel CAD; no recent MI or lipid drugs	Diet, exercise, no stress or smoking vs. control	5.88/1.43 (24%)	18/22 (82)[10]
Yes	Age <65: CAD but most vessels normal; ≥1 risk factor	Nifedipine vs. placebo	6.65/−0.05 (0%)	18/598 (3%)[11]
Yes	Age <62: Positive family history of CAD; high apolipoprotein B levels	(A) Lovastatin + colestipol (B) Niacin + colestipol vs. (C) Placebo	(A) 7.12/3.41 (48%) (B) 6.99/1.58 (22%) (C) 6.79/0.24 (4%)	(A) 12/38 (32%) (B) 14/36 (39%) (C) 5/46 (11%)
Yes	Same as CLAS-I: 2 additional yr	Same as CLAS-I: 2 Additional yr	6.37/1.60 (25%)	10/56 (18%)
Yes	Age 19-72: Familial hypercholesterolemia (LDL >5.18)	Colestipol + niacin ± lovastatin vs. diet ± resin	9.79/3.04 (31%)	13/40 (32%)[12]
Yes	Age <66: Cholesterol >6.0; angina pectoris or known CAD; no lipid drugs	(A) Usual care (B) Diet (C) Diet + cholestyramine	(A) 7.07/0.14 (2%) (B) 7.19/1.02 (14%) (C) 7.44/1.88 (25%)	(A) 1/24 (4%) (B) 13/26 (38%) (C) 8/24 (33%)

[6]"Definite" regression: no difference between treatment and control groups.

[7]Regression in 2.4% of lesions in control group.

[8]Regression defined as 10% improvement in diameter stenosis; no intergroup difference.

[9]Vs. 6.3% in controls in arteriograms obtained at 7 years; no difference in overall mortality between groups.

[10]"Average lesion change scores (% diameter stenosis after intervention minus before intervention) in . . . the direction of regression"; average percentage diameter stenosis reduced from 40.0% to 37.8%.

[11]Analysis by lesions in nifedipine group. Patient analysis showed 42/175 (24%) had some lesions regress; there were no intergroup differences.

[12]Of 457 lesions measured, within-patient change in % stenosis was +0.80 in controls and −1.53 in treated group.

Table VIII. Arteriographic trials on regression of femoral artery atherosclerosis

Study (yr)	Ref.	Location	Mean duration (yr)	No. of patients (T/C)	Mean age[1] (yr)	% Men
Ost & Stenson (1967)	147	Stockholm, Sweden	3.5	31/0	NS	NS
Barndt et al. (1977); Blankenhorn et al. (1978)	148,149	Los Angeles, Calif.	1	25/0	22-65	76
Brooks et al. (1980); Blankenhorn & Brooks (1981)	150,151	Los Angeles, Calif.	1.3	54/0[2]	47	100
Duffield et al. (1983)	152	London, U.K.	1.6	12/12	55	88
Olsson et al. (1990)	153	Uppsala, Sweden	1	20/25	52	100
CLAS (1991)	154	Los Angeles, Calif.	2	77/76	54	100
PQRST (1993)	155,156	Multicenter, Sweden	3	152/152	NS	NS

T/C = treated group/control group; NS = not stated; CLAS = Cholesterol-Lowering Atherosclerosis Study; PQRST = Probucol Quantitative Regression Swedish Trial.

[1] Age at entry into trial averaged between groups.

[2] Although the report states that patients were "randomized" to "high level" or "low level" interventions (regarding diet and exercise), results are not reported in terms of this "randomization."

[3] Change in lesions "in a negative direction" at several levels of the femoral artery; no patient-specific analysis reported.

[4] Total arterial segments studied; no patient-specific data reported.

[5] A total of 5/17 (29%) patients showed regression in at least one segment in the treatment group compared with 0/25 (0%) patients in the control group.

[6] A total of 35/77 (45%) of treatment group regressed vs. 26/76 (28%) of controls ($p = 0.02$).

Table IX. Pilot ultrasound studies of carotid artery atherosclerosis regression

Study (yr)	Ref.	Location	Mean duration (yr)	No. of patients (T/C)	No. of subjects	Interventions	Regression (No.)
Hennerici et al. (1991)	157	Dusseldorf, Germany	1.5	7/0	4 flat and 17 soft carotid artery plaques studied in 7 men with hypercholesterolemia	Heparin-induced extracorporeal LDL precipitation from plasma	7/7 (100%)*
CLAS (1993)	158	Los Angeles, Calif.	4	24/22	See Tables VII and VIII	See Tables VII and VIII	−0.05 mm[†]

T/C = treated group/control group; CLAS = Cholesterol-Lowering Atherosclosis Study.

*Whereas all patients had some regression, 2/4 (50%) flat lesions regressed and 6/17 (35%) soft lesions regressed; overall, 8/21 (38%) lesions showed some regression.

[†] Mean intima-media thickness decrease after 4 years of treatment vs. +0.07 mm increase in wall thickness in control group.

Random?	Major entry criteria	Interventions	Cholesterol (mmol/L): Entry/change	Regression (No.)
No	Claudication and abnormal serum lipids	Nicotinic acid	NS	3/31 (10%)
No	Age 22-65: Type IV or II hyperlipoproteinemia	Diet ± clofibrate ± neomycin ± tibric acid	8.48/1.26 (15%)	9/25 (36%)
No	Age 40-49: Survived myocardial infarction	Diet + exercise	5.90/0.27 (5%)	35%-48%[3]
Yes	Stable claudication: Cholesterol >6.5 mmol/L; no major illness	Diet + cholestyramine or clofibrate ± nicotinic acid vs. diet	8.05/1.99 (25%)	71/300 (24%)[4]
No	Asymptomatic: Cholesterol >9.5 mmol/L	Nicotinic acid + fenofibrate vs. placebo	9.68/3.31 (34%)	5/42 (12%)[5]
Yes	Age 40-59: Previous CABG; cholesterol 4.8-9.1 mmol/L	Colestipol + niacin + diet vs. placebo + diet	6.35/1.70 (26%)	56/153 (37%)[6]
Yes	Age <71: Hypercholesterolemia, with or without peripheral vascular disease	Probucol vs. placebo	Completed in December 1992	Completed in December 1992

Ten additional trials were not included in the meta-analysis because the authors believed that treatment was not randomly allocated,[79-81] there was no control group,[82-84] patients were not representative,[85-87] or no outcome data were reported.[88] Two other oft-cited studies warrant mention: The Finnish Mental Hospital Study[89] and the Multiple Risk Factor Intervention Trial (MRFIT).[90] The Finnish trial had a unique crossover design in which patients in two mental hospitals "switched" from cholesterol-lowering to regular diets or vice versa after 6 years; although it was concluded that the therapeutic diet was associated with a reduction in the incidence of CHD, the study suffers from many of the problems listed in Table II. The large, prospective, and expensive MRFIT screened 361,662 men and enrolled 12,866 for special intervention to reduce risk factors or usual care; there were *no* statistical differences in mortality from CHD or total mortality between groups.

Because of the deficiencies in clinical end-point studies for determining the natural history of atherosclerotic vascular disease and the effect of therapy on it, arterial imaging studies employing arteriography or ultrasonography have been proposed as an alternative. This strategy permits trials that require only 100 to 200 patients to demonstrate a treatment benefit instead of the several thousand needed to show clinical efficacy in epidemiologic studies.[91-93] However, the link between progressing atherosclerosis and clinical complications remains unclear. Are subjects with rapid progression more likely to suffer adverse clinical events than those with regression? Of note, most stenoses that occlude and produce myocardial infarctions are <70% and often are <50% in diameter, and in only one third of patients is infarction caused by the most severe coronary artery stenosis.[94,95] Ideal patients for an arteriographic trial have coronary artery disease but mild symptoms to maximize the probability of finishing the study without needing invasive intervention. Therefore lesions causing <50% stenoses are ideal because they do not cause symptoms but are at risk for progression.[96]

Although quantification of arterial occlusive disease using computer-assisted analysis is a major advance compared with either epidemiologic studies or visual assessment of arteriograms, the interpretation of computed measurements is not indisputable and may lead to erroneous conclusions.[97] The use of quantitative coronary arteriography to measure progression or regression of atherosclerosis is based on the assumption that a change of volume of the atherosclerotic plaque will affect the size and shape of the contrast-filled lumen. However, there are many reasons why arteriograms may be misleading (Table VI).[98-134] Fig. 1 illustrates *pseudoregression,* suggesting no progression of disease when the lesion has actually increased.

Table VII summarizes the characteristics and outcomes of 17 arteriographic studies of the effects of intervention on the status of coronary artery atherosclerosis.* Methodologic difficulties listed in Table VI were ubiquitous. Overall, while rate of progression was slightly retarded by treatment, actual regression of lesions was relatively uncommon. Similar findings have been reported in eight serial arteriographic studies of femoral arteries[147-156] (Table VIII) and two serial ultrasound studies of carotid arteries[157,158] (Table IX). Several clinical trials using B-mode ultrasonography of progression or regression of carotid or femoral artery atherosclerosis are currently in progress, including Atherosclerosis Risk in Communities (ARIC),[159] Cardiovascular Health Study (CHS),[160] Kuopio Ischaemic Heart Disease Risk Factor Study (KIHD),[161] Multicenter Isradipine Diuretic Atherosclerosis Study (MIDAS),[162] Pravastain, Lipids, and Atherosclerosis in the Carotids (PLAC-2),[163] and Asymptomatic Carotid Artery Plaque Study (ACAPS).[163] In view of methodologic limitations of these trials, valid assessment of the severity of atherosclerosis in vivo requires considerably improved technology.

---

*References 75-77, 83, 87, 99, 125, 135-146.

REFERENCES

1. Aschoff L. Atherosclerosis. In Lectures in Pathology (delivered in the United States, 1924). New York: PB Hoeber, chap 6, p 131.
2. Cowdry EV. Arteriosclerosis. New York: Macmillan, 1933.
3. Ophuls W. The pathogenesis of arteriosclerosis. In Cowdry EV, ed. Arteriosclerosis. New York: Macmillan, 1933, pp 249-270.
4. Hueper WC. Arteriosclerosis. Arch Pathol 1945;38:162-350.
5. Wilens SL. The absorption of arterial atheromatous deposits in wasting disease. Am J Pathol 1947;23:793-804.
6. Vartiainen T, Kanerva K. Arteriosclerosis and war-time. Ann Med Intern Fenniae 1947;36:748-758.
7. Wanscher O, Blemmesen J, Nielson A. Negative correlation between atherosclerosis and carcinoma. Br J Cancer 1951; 5:172-180.
8. Eilersen P, Faber M. The human aorta. VI. The regression of atherosclerosis in pulmonary tuberculosis. Arch Pathol 1960;70:103-109.
9. Wilens SL, Dische MR, Henderson D. The low incidence of terminal myocardial infarction and the reversibility of cardiac hypertrophy in cachexia. Am J Med Sci 1967;253:651-660.
10. Malinow MR. Regression of atherosclerosis in humans: Fact or myth? Circulation 1981;64:1-3.
11. Horlick L, Katz LN. Retrogression of atherosclerotic lesions on cessation of cholesterol feeding in the chick. J Lab Clin Med 1949;34:1427-1442.
12. Bevans M, Davidson JD, Kendall FE. Regression of lesions in canine arteriosclerosis. Arch Pathol 1951;51:288-292.
13. DePalma RG, Hubay CA, Insull W, et al. Progression and regression of experimental atherosclerosis. Surg Gynecol Obstet 1970;131:633-647.
14. Pick R, Stamler J, Rodbard S, et al. Estrogen induced regression of coronary atherosclerosis in cholesterol-fed chicks. Circulation 1952;6:858-865.
15. Subbiah MTR, Dicke BA, Kottke BA, et al. Regression of naturally occurring atherosclerotic lesions in pigeon aorta by intestinal bypass surgery. Early changes in arterial cholesterol ester metabolism. Atherosclerosis 1978;31:117-123.
16. Moskowitz MS, Moskowitz AA, Bradford WL, et al. Changes in serum lipids and coronary arteries of rat in response to estrogens. AMA Arch Pathol 1956;61:245-255.
17. Rubin EM, Krauss RM, Spangler EA, et al. Inhibition of early atherogenesis in transgenic mice by human apolipoprotein AI. Nature 1991;353:265-267.
18. Daoud AS, Jarmolych J, Augustyn JM, et al. Regression of advanced atherosclerosis in swine. Arch Pathol Lab Med 1976;100:372-379.
19. Fritz KE, Augustyn JM, Jarmolych J, et al. Regression of advanced atherosclerosis in swine: Chemical studies. Arch Pathol Lab Med 1976;100:380-395.
20. Jarmolych J, Daoud AS, Fritz KE, et al. Mophological effects of moderate diet and clofibrate on swine atherosclerosis. Arch Pathol Lab Med 1978;102:289-292.
21. Lee WM, Lee KT, Thomas WA. Partial suppression by pyridinocarbamate of growth and necrosis of atherosclerotic lesions in swine subjected to an atherogenic regimen that produces advanced lesions. Exp Mol Pathol 1979;30:85-90.
22. Weber G, Fabbrini E, Capaccioli E, et al. Repair of early cholesterol-induced aortic lesions in rabbits after withdrawal from short-term atherogenic diet. Scanning electron-microscopic (SEM) and transmission electron-microscopic (TEM) observations. Atherosclerosis 1975;22:565-571.
23. Sugsno M, Nakashima Y, Matsushuma T, et al. Suppression of atherosclerosis in cholesterol-fed rabbits by diltiazem injection. Arteriosclerosis 1986;6:237-245.
24. Blau A, Neusy AJ, Lowenstein T. The effects of propranolol and prazosin on plasma lipids and aortic atherosclerosis in cholesterol-fed rabbits. J Hypertension 1986;4(Suppl):S485-S490.
25. Kita T, Nagano Y, Tokode M, et al. Probucol prevents the progression of atherosclerosis in Watanabe heritable hyperlipidemic rabbit, an animal model for familial hypercholesterolemia. Proc Natl Acad Sci USA 1987;84:5928-5932.
26. Dudrick SJ. Regression of atherosclerosis by the intravenous infusion of specific biochemical nutrient substrates in animals and humans. Ann Surg 1987;206:296-314.
27. LaVille AE, Seddon AM, Shaikh M, et al. Primary prevention of atherosclerosis by lovastatin in a genetically hyperlipidaemic rabbit strain. Atherosclerosis 1989;78:205-210.
28. Badimon JJ, Badimon L, Fuster V. Regression of atherosclerotic lesions by high density lipoprotein plasma fraction in the cholesterol-fed rabbit. J Clin Invest 1990;85:1234-1241.
29. Zhu BQ, Sievers RE, Isenberg WM, et al. Regression of atherosclerosis in cholesterol-fed rabbits: Effects of fish oil and verapamil. J Am Coll Cardiol 1990;15:231-237.
30. Bjorkhem I, Henriksson-Freyschuss A, Breuer O, et al. The antioxidant butylated hydroxytoluene protects against atherosclerosis. Arterioscler Thromb 1991;11:15-22.

31. Zho BQ, Sievers RE, Sun YP, et al. Effect of lovastatin on suppression and regression of atherosclerosis in lipid-fed rabbits. J Cardiovasc Pharmacol 1992;19:246-255.

32. Eggen DA, Strong JP, Newman WP II, et al. Regression of diet-induced fatty streaks in rhesus monkeys. Lab Invest 1974;31:294-301.

33. Armstrong ML, Megan MB. Arterial fibrous proteins in cynomolgus monkeys after artherogenic and regression diets. Circ Res 1975;36:256-261.

34. Vesselinovitch D, Wissler RW, Hughes R, et al. Reversal of advanced atherosclerosis in rhesus monkeys. Part 1. Light-microscopic studies. Atherosclerosis 1976;23:155-176.

35. Malinow MR, McLaughlin P, Naito HK, et al. Effect of alfalfa meal on shrinkage (regression) of atherosclerotic plaques during cholesterol feeding in monkeys. Atherosclerosis 1978;30:27-35.

36. Clarkson TB, Bond MG, Bullock BC, et al. A study of atherosclerosis regression in *Macaca mulatta*. IV. Changes in coronary arteries from animals with atherosclerosis induced for 19 months and then regressed for 24 to 48 months at plasma cholesterol concentrations of 300 or 200 mg/dl. Exp Mol Pathol 1981;34:345-368.

37. Rudel LL, Leathers CW, Bond MG, et al. Dietary ethanol-induced modifications in hyperlipoproteinemia and atherosclerosis in nonhuman primates *(Macaca nemestrina)*. Arteriosclerosis 1981;1:144-152.

38. Armstrong ML, Heistad DD, Marcus ML, et al. Hemodynamic sequelae of regression of experimental atherosclerosis. J Clin Invest 1983;71:104-110.

39. Wissler RW, Vesselinovitch D. Combined effects of cholestyramine and probucol on regression of atherosclerosis in rhesus monkey aortas. Appl Pathol 1983;1:89-96.

40. Kramsch DM, Aspen AJ, Abramowitz BM, et al. Reduction of coronary atherosclerosis by moderate conditioning exercise in monkeys on an atherogenic diet. N Engl J Med 1981;305:1483-1489.

41. Van Winkle M, Levy L. Further studies on the reversibility of serum sickness cholesterol-induced atherosclerosis. J Exp Med 1970;132:345-368.

42. Wagner WD, Clarkson TB, Foster J. Contrasting effects of ethane-1-hydroxy-1, 1-diphosphonate (EHDP) on the regression of two types of dietary-induced atherosclerosis. Atherosclerosis 1977;27:419-435.

43. Stehbens WE. An appraisal of the epidemic rise of coronary heart disease and its decline. Lancet 1987;1:606-611.

44. Stehbens WE. Review of the validity of national coronary heart disease mortality rates. Angiology 1990;41:85-94.

45. Gazes PC. Angina pectoris: Classification and diagnosis. Part 2. Mod Concepts Cardiovasc Dis 1988;57:25-27.

46. Mukerji V, Alpert MA, Hewett JE, et al. Can patients with chest pain and normal coronary arteries be discriminated from those with coronary artery disease prior to coronary angiography? Angiography 1989;40:276-282.

47. Stehbens WE. The role of hemodynamics in the proliferative lesions of atherosclerosis. In Yoshida Y, Yamaguchi T, Caro CG, et al., eds. Role of Blood Flow in Atherogenesis. Berlin: Springer Verlag, 1988, pp. 47-53.

48. Stehbens WE. Vascular complications in experimental atherosclerosis. Prog Cardiovasc Dis 1986;29:221-237.

49. Stehbens WE, Wierzbicki E. The relationship of hypercholesterolemia to atherosclerosis with particular emphasis on familial hypercholesterolemia, diabetes mellitus, obstructive jaundice, myxedema, and the nephrotic syndrome. Prog Cardiovasc Dis 1988;30:289-306.

50. World Health Statistics Annual 1986. Geneva: World Health Organization, 1987.

51. Stehbens WE. Diet and atherogenesis. Nutr Rev 1989;47:1-12.

52. Stehbens WE. Reduction of serum cholesterol levels and regression of atherosclerosis. Pathology 1991;23:45-53.

53. Rifkind B. Clinical trials of cholesterol lowering. Atheroscler Rev 1988;18:59-70.

54. Dayton S, Pearce ML, Hashimoto S, et al. A controlled clinical trial of a diet high in unsaturated fat in preventing complications of atherosclerosis. Circulation 1969;40(Suppl II):II-1-II-63.

55. Franz ID, Dawson EA, Ashman PL, et al. Test of effect of lipid lowering by dict on cardiovascular risk. The Minnesota Coronary Survey. Arteriosclerosis 1989;9:129-135.

56. Dorr AE, Gundersen K, Scheiner JC, et al. Colestipol hydrochloride in hypercholesterolemic patients—effect on serum cholesterol and mortality. J Chron Dis 1978;31:5-14.

57. Report from the Committee of Principal Investigators. A co-operative trial in the primary prevention of ischaemic heart disease using clofibrate. Br Heart J 1978;40:1069-1118.

58. Report of the Committee of Principal Investigators. WHO cooperative trial on primary prevention of ischaemic heart disease with clofibrate to lower cholesterol: Final mortality follow-up. Lancet 1984;2:600-604.

59. Lipid Research Clinics Program. The Lipid Research Clinics Coronary Primary Prevention Trial results. I. Reduction in incidence of coronary heart disease. II The relationship of reduction in incidence of coronary heart disease to cholesterol lowering. JAMA 1984;251:351-374.

60. Frick MH, Elo O, Haapa K, et al. Helsinki Heart Study: Primary-prevention trial with gemfibrozil in middle-aged men with dyslipidemia. Safety of treatment, changes in risk factors, and incidence of coronary heart disease. N Engl J Med 1987;317:1237-1245.

61. Manninen V, Elo MO, Frick MH, et al. Lipid alterations and decline in the incidence of coronary heart disease in the Helsinki Heart Study. JAMA 1988;260:641-651.

62. Bradford RH, Shear CL, Chrenos AN, et al. Expanded clinical evaluation of lovastatin (EXCEL) study results. Arch Int Med 1991;151:43-49.

63. Bradford RH, Shear CL, Chrenos AN, et al. Expanded clinical evaluation of lovastatin (EXCEL) study: Design and patient characteristics of a double-blind, placebo controlled study in patients with moderate hypercholesterolemia. Am J Cardiol 1990;66:44B-55B.

64. A Research Committee. Low-fat diet in myocardial infarction. Lancet 1965;2:501-504.

65. Rose GA, Thomson WB, Williams RT. Corn oil in treatment of ischaemic heart disease. Br J Med 1965;1:1531-1533.

66. Leren P. The effect of plasma cholesterol lowering diet in male survivors of myocardial infarction. Acta Med Scand [Suppl] 1966;466:12-87.

67. Leren P. The Oslo Diet Heart Study. Eleven-year report. Circulation 1970;42:935-942.

68. Report of a Research Committee of the Medical Research Council. Controlled trial of soya bean oil in myocardial infarction. Lancet 1968;2:693-699.

69. Woodhill JM, Palmer AJ, Leelarthaepin B, McGilchrist C, et al. Low fat, low cholesterol diet in secondary prevention of coronary heart disease. Adv Exp Med Biol 1978;109:317-330.

70. Report by a Research Committee of the Scottish Society of Physicians. Ischemic heart disease. A secondary prevention trial using clofibrate. Br Med J 1971;4:775-784.

71. Group of Physicians of Newcastle-Upon-Tyne Region. Trial of clofibrate in the treatment of ischaemic heart disease: Five-year study by a group of physicians of the Newcastle Upon Tyne region. Br Med J 1971;4:767-775.

72. The Coronary Drug Project Research Group. Clofibrate and niacin in coronary heart disease. JAMA 1975;231:360-381.

73. Canner PL, Berge KG, Wenger NK, et al. Fifteen-year mortality in coronary drug project patients: Long-term benefit with niacin. J Coll Cardiol 1986;8:1245-1255.

74. Carlson LA, Danielson M, Exberg I, et al. Reduction of myocardial reinfarction by the combined treatment with clofibrate and nicotinic acid. Atherosclerosis 1977;28:81-86.

75. Brensike JF, Levy RI, Kelsey SF, et al. Effects of therapy with cholestyramine on progression of coronary arteriosclerosis: Results of the NHLBI Type II Coronary Intervention Study. Circulation 1984;69:313-324.

76. Levy RI, Brensike JF, Epstein SE, et al. The influence of changes in lipid values induced by cholestyramine and diet on progression of coronary artery disease: Results of the NHLBI Type II Coronary Intervention Study. Circulation 1984;69:325-337.

77. Buchwald H, Varco RL, Matts JP, et al. Effect of partial ileal bypass surgery on mortality and morbidity from coronary heart disease in patients with hypercholesterolemia: Report of the Program on the Surgical Control of the Hyperlipidemias (POSCH). N Engl J Med 1990;323:946-955.

78. Cucherat M, Boissel JP. Meta-analysis of results from clinical trials on prevention of coronary heart disease by lipid-lowering interventions. Clin Trials Meta-Analysis 1993;28:109-129.

79. Morrison LM. Diet in coronary atherosclerosis. JAMA 1960;173:884-888.

80. Hood B, Sanne H, Orndahl G, et al. Long-term prognosis in essential hypercholesterolemia: The effect of strict diet. Acta Med Scand 1965;178:161-173.

81. Bierenbaum ML, Green DP, Florin A, et al. Modified-fat dietary management of the young male with coronary disease. JAMA 1967;202:119-123.

82. Krasno LR, Kidera GJ. Clofibrate in coronary heart disease. Effect on morbidity and mortality. JAMA 1972;219:845-851.

83. Cohn K, Sakai FJ, Langston MF. Effect of clofibrate on progression of coronary disease: A prospective angiographic study in man. Am Heart J 1975;89:591-598.

84. Manninen V, Mälkönen M, Eisalo A, et al. Gemfibrozil in the treatment of dyslipidaemia: A 5-year follow-up. Acta Med Scand 1982(Suppl);668:82-87.

85. Christakis G, Rinzler SH, Archer M, et al. Effect of the Anti-Coronary Club Program on coronary heart disease risk-factor status. JAMA 1966;198:129-136.

86. Acheson J, Hutchinson EC. Controlled trial of clofibrate in cerebral vascular disease. Atherosclerosis 1972;15:177-183.

87. Blankenhorn DH, Nessim SA, Johnson RL, et al. Beneficial effects of combined colestipol-niacin therapy on coronary atherosclerosis and coronary venous bypass grafts. JAMA 1987;257:3233-3240.

88. Detre KM, Shaw L. Long-term changes of serum cholesterol with cholesterol-altering drugs in patients with coronary heart disease. Veterans Administration drug-lipid cooperative study. Circulation 1971;50:998-1004.

89. Turpeinen O, Karvonen MJ, Pekkarinen M, et al. Dietary prevention of coronary heart disease: The Finnish Mental Hospital Study. Int J Epidemiol 1979;8:99-118.

90. Multiple Risk Factor Intervention Trial Research Group. Multiple risk factor intervention trial: Risk factor changes and mortality results. JAMA 1982;248:1465-1977.

91. Reiber JHC, Serruys PW, Kooijman CJ, et al. Assessment of short-, medium-, and long-term variations in arterial dimensions from computer-assisted quantitation or coronary cineangiograms. Circulation 1985;71:280-288.

92. Furberg CD. Can we measure and predict atherosclerotic progression? Circulation 1993;87(Suppl II):II-82.

93. Brown BG, Hillger LA, Lewis C, et al. A maximum confidence approach for measuring progression and regression of coronary artery disease in clinical trials. Circulation 1993;87(Suppl II):II-66–II-73.

94. Ambrose JA, Tannenbaum MA, Alexopoulos D, et al. Angiographic progression of coronary artery disease and the development of myocardial infarction. J Am Coll Cardiol 1988;12:56-62.

95. Little WC, Constantinescu M, Applegate RJ, et al. Can coronary angiography predict the site of a subsequent myocardial infarction in patients with mild-to-moderate coronary artery disease? Circulation 1988;78:1157-1166.

96. Moise A, Theroux P, Taeymans Y, et al. Clinical and angiographic factors associated with progression of coronary artery disease. J Am Coll Cardiol 1984;3:659-667.

97. De Feyter PJ, Serruys PW, Davies MJ, et al. Quantitative coronary angiography to measure progression and regression of coronary atherosclerosis. Value, limitations, and implications for clinical trials. Circulation 1991;84:412-423.

98. Echt DS, Liebson PR, Mitchell LB, et al. Mortality and morbidity in patients receiving encainide, flecainide, or placebo. The Cardiac Arrhythmia Suppression Trial. N Engl J Med 1991;324:781-788.

99. Waters D, Lesperance J, Francetich M, et al. A controlled clinical trial to assess the effect of a calcium channel blocker on the progression of coronary atherosclerosis. Circulation 1990;82:1940-1953.

100. Sanmarco ME, Brooks SH, Blankenhorn DH. Reproducibility of a consensus panel in the interpretation of coronary angiograms. Am Heart J 1978;96:430-437.

101. Beauman GJ, Vogel RA. Accuracy of individual and panel visual interpretations of coronary arteriograms: Implications for clinical decisions. J Am Coll Cardiol 1990;16:108-113.

102. Azen SP, Cashin-Hemphill L, Pogoda J, et al. Evaluation of human panelists in assessing coronary atherosclerosis. Arterioscler Thromb 1991;11:385-394.

103. Waters K, Lesperance J, Craven TE, et al. Advantages and limitations of serial coronary arteriography for the assessment of progression and regression of coronary atherosclerosis. Implications for clinical trials. Circulation 1993;87(Suppl II):II-38–II-47.

104. Grondin CM, Dyrda I, Pasternac A, et al. Discrepancies between cineangiographic and postmortem findings in patients with coronary artery disease and recent myocardial infarction. Circulation 1974;49:703-708.

105. Arnett EN, Isner JM, Redwood DR, et al. Coronary artery narrowing in coronary heart disease: Comparison of cineangiographic and necropsy findings. Ann Int Med 1979;91:350-356.

106. Thomas AC, Davies MJ, Dilly S, et al. Potential errors in the estimation of coronary arterial stenosis from clinical arteriography with reference to the shape of the coronary arterial lumen. Br Heart J 1986;55:129-139.

107. Bossaller C, Habib GB, Yamamoto H, et al. Impaired muscarinic endothelium-dependent relaxation and cyclic guanosine 5'-monophosphate formation in atherosclerotic human coronary arteries. J Clin Invest 1987;79:170-174.

108. Vita JA, Treasure CB, Nabel EG, et al. Coronary vasomotor response to acetylcholine relates to risk factors for coronary artery disease. Circulation 1990;81:491-497.

109. Zeiher AM, Drexler H, Wollschlager H, et al. Modulation of coronary vasomotor tone in humans: Progressive endothelial dysfunction with different early stages of coronary atherosclerosis. Circulation 1991;83:391-401.

110. Glagov S, Weisenberg E, Zarins CK, et al. Compensatory enlargement of human atherosclerotic coronary arteries. N Engl J Med 1987;316:1371-1375.

111. Zarins CK, Weisenberg E, Kolettis G, et al. Differential enlargement of artery segments in response to enlarging atherosclerotic plaques. J Vasc Surg 1988:7:386-394.

112. Stiel GM, Stiel LSG, Schofer J, et al. Impact of compensatory enlargement of atherosclerotic coronary arteries on angiographic assessment of coronary heart disease. Circulation 1989;80:1603-1609.

113. White CW, Wright CB, Doty DB, et al. Does visual interpretation of the coronary angiogram predict the physiologic importance of a coronary stenosis? N Engl J Med 1984;310: 819-824.

114. Marcus ML, Armstrong ML, Heistad DD, et al. Comparison of three methods of evaluating coronary obstructive lesions: Postmortem arteriography, pathologic examination, and measurement of regional myocardial perfusion during maximal vasodilation. Am J Cardiol 1982;49:1699-1706.

115. Harrison DG, White CW, Hiratzka LF, et al. The value of lesion cross-sectional area determined by quantitative coronary angiography in assessing the physiologic significance of proximal left anterior descending coronary arterial stenoses. Circulation 1984;69:1111-1119.

116. Zijlstra F, van Ommeren J, Reiber JHC, et al. Does quantitative assessment of coronary artery dimensions predict the physiological significance of coronary stenosis? Circulation 1987;75:1154-1161.

117. Kirkeeide RL, Gould KL, Parsel L. Assessment of coronary stenoses by myocardial perfusion imaging during pharmacologic coronary vasodilation: VII. Validation of coronary flow reserve as a single integrated functional measure of stenosis severity reflecting all its geometric dimensions. J Am Coll Cardiol 1986;7:103-113.

118. Roberts CS, Roberts WC. Cross-sectional area of the proximal portions of the three major epicardial coronary arteries in 98 necropsy patients with different coronary events: Relationship to heart weight, age and sex. Circulation 1980; 6:953-959.

119. Stone PH, Gibson M, Pasternak PC, et al. Natural history of coronary atherosclerosis using quantitative angiography in men, and implications for clinical trials of coronary regression. Am J Cardiol 1993;71:766-772.

120. Schwartz CJ, Valente AJ, Sprague EA, et al. Atherosclerosis. Potential targets for stabilization and regression. Circulation 1992;86(Suppl III):III-117–III-123.

121. Bruschke AVG, Kramer JR, Bal ET, et al. The dynamics of progression of coronary atherosclerosis studied in 168 medically treated patients who underwent coronary arteriography three times. Am Heart J 1989;117:296-305.

122. Stary HC. What is the nature of the coronary atherosclerotic lesions that have been shown to regress in experiments with nonhuman primates and by angiography in man. Vasa 1984;13:298-305.

123. Margitec SE, Bond G, Crouse JR, et al. Progression and regression of carotid atherosclerosis in clinical trials. Arterioscler Thromb 1991;11:443-451.

124. Roederer GO, Langlois YE, Lusiani L, et al. Natural history of carotid artery disease on the side contralateral to endarterectomy. J Vasc Surg 1984;1:62-72.

125. Rafflenbeul W, Smith LR, Rogers WL, et al. Quantitative coronary arteriography: Coronary anatomy of patients with unstable angina pectoris reexamined 1 year after optimal medical therapy. Am J Cardiol 1979;43:699-707.

126. Rafflenbeul W, Urthaler F, Lichtlen P, et al. Quantitative difference in "critical" stenosis between right and left coronary artery in man. Circulation 1980;62:1188-1196.

127. Sharrett AR. Invasive versus noninvasive studies of risk factors and atherosclerosis. Circulation 1993;87(Suppl II): II-48–II-53.

128. Gore JM, Goldberg RJ, Matsumoto AS, et al. Validity of serum cholesterol within 24 hours of acute myocardial infarction. Am J Cardiol 1984;54:722-725.

129. Al-Muhtaseb N, Hayat N, Al-Khafaji M. Lipoproteins and apolipoproteins in young male survivors of myocardial infarction. Atherosclerosis 1989;77:131-138.

130. Ahnve S, Angelin B, Edhag O, et al. Early determination of serum lipids and apolipoproteins in acute myocardial infarction: Possibility for immediate intervention. J Intern Med 1989;226:297-301.

131. Chambers J, Bass C. Chest pain with normal coronary anatomy: A review of natural history and possible etiologic factors. Prog Cardiovasc Dis 1990;33:161-184.

132. Rohlfing JJ, Brunzell JD. The effects of diuretics and adrenergic-blocking agents on plasma lipids. West J Med 1986;145:210-218.

133. Miller NE, Hammett F, Saltissi S, et al. Relation of angiographically defined coronary artery disease to plasma lipoprotein subfractions and apolipoproteins. Br Med J 1981; 282:1741-1744.

134. Paulin S. Assessing the severity of coronary lesions with angiography. N Engl J Med 1987;316:1405-1407.

135. Kuo PT, Hayase K, Kostis JB, et al. Use of combined diet and colestipol in long-term (7-7.5 years) treatment of patients with type II hyperlipoproteinemia. Circulation 1979;59:199-211.

136. Nash DT, Gensini G, Esente. Effect of lipid-lowering therapy on the progression of coronary atherosclerosis assessed by scheduled repetitive coronary arteriography. Int J Cardiol 1982;2:43-55.

137. Nikkila EA, Viikinkoski P, Valle M, et al. Prevention of progression of coronary atherosclerosis by treatment of hyperlipidaemia: A seven year prospective angiographic study. Br Med J 1984;289:220-223.

138. Campeau L, Enjalbert M, Lesperance J, et al. The relation of risk factors to the development of atherosclerosis in saphenous-vein bypass grafts and the progression of disease in the native circulation: A study 10 years after aortocoronary bypass surgery. N Engl J Med 1984;311:1329-1332.

139. Arntzenius AC, Kromhout D, Barth JD, et al. Diet, lipoproteins, and the progression of coronary atherosclerosis: The Leiden Intervention Trial. N Engl J Med 1985;312:805-811.

140. Chesbro JH, Webster MWI, Smith HC, et al. Antiplatelet therapy in coronary disease progression: Reduced infarction and new lesion formation [abst]. Circulation 1989;89(Suppl II):II-266.

141. Ornish D, Brown SE, Scherwitz LW, et al. Can lifestyle changes reverse coronary heart disease? The Lifestyle Heart Trial. Lancet 1990;336:129-133.

142. Lichtlen PR, Hugenholtz PG, Rafflenbeul W, et al. Retardation of angiographic progression of coronary artery disease by nifedipine. Results of the International Nifedipine Trial on Antiatherosclerotic Therapy (INTACT). Lancet 1990;335: 1109-1113.

143. Brown G, Albers JJ, Fisher LD, et al. Regression of coronary artery disease as a result of intensive lipid-lowering therapy in men with high levels of apolipoprotein B. N Engl J Med 1990;323:1289-1298.

144. Cashin-Hemphill L, Mack WJ, Pogada JM, et al. Beneficial effects of colestipol-niacin on coronary atherosclerosis: A 4-year follow-up. JAMA 1990;264:3013-3017.

145. Kane JP, Malloy MJ, Ports TA, et al. Regression of coronary atherosclerosis during treatment of familial hypercholesterolemia with combined drug regimens. JAMA 1990;264:3007-3012.

146. Watts GF, Lewis B, Brunt JNH, et al. Effects on coronary artery disease of lipid-lowering diet, or diet plus cholestyramine, in the St Thomas' Atherosclerosis Regression Study (STARS). Lancet 1992;339:563-569.

147. Ost CR, Stenson S. Regression of peripheral atherosclerosis during therapy with high doses of nicotinic acid. Scand J Clin Lab Invest 1967;93(Suppl):241-245.

148. Barndt R, Blankenhorn DH, Crawford DW, et al. Regression and progression of early femoral atherosclerosis in treated hyperlipoproteinemic patients. Ann Int Med 1977;86:139-146.

149. Blankenhorn DH, Brooks SH, Selzer RH, et al. The rate of atherosclerosis change during treatment of hyperlipoproteinemia. Circulation 1978;57:355-361.

150. Brooks SH, Blankenhorn DH, Chin HP, et al. Design of human atherosclerosis studies by serial angiography. J Chron Dis 1980;33:347-357.

151. Blankenhorn DH, Brooks SH. Angiographic trials of lipid-lowering therapy. Arteriosclerosis 1981;1:242-249.

152. Duffield RGM, Miller NE, Brunt JNH, et al. Treatment of hyperlipidaemia retards progression of symptomatic femoral atherosclerosis: A randomized controlled trial. Lancet 1983;2:639-642.

153. Olsson AG, Ruhn G, Erikson U. The effect of serum lipid regulation on the development of femoral atherosclerosis in hyperlipidaemia: A non-randomized study. J Int Med 1990;227:381-390.

154. Blankenhorn KH, Azen SP, Crawford DW, et al. Effects of colestipol-niacin therapy on human femoral atherosclerosis. Circulation 1991;83:438-447.

155. Holme I, Malmaeus I, Olsson AG, et al. Repeated measurements over time: Statistical analysis of the angiographic outcomes in the Probucol Quantitative Regression Swedish Trial (PQRST). Clin Trials Meta-Analysis 1993;28:95-108.

156. Walldius G, Regnstrom J, Nilsson J, et al. The role of lipids and antioxidative factors for development of atherosclerosis: The Probucol Quantitative Regression Swedish Trial (PQRST). Am J Cardiol 1993;71:15B-19B.

157. Hennerici M, Kleophas W, Gries FA. Regression of carotid plaques during low density lipoprotein cholesterol elimination. Stroke 1991;22:989-992.

158. Blankenhorn DH, Selzer RH, Crawford DW, et al. Beneficial effects of colestipol-niacin therapy on the common carotid artery: Two- and four-year reduction of intima-media thickness measured by ultrasound. Circulation 1993;88:20-28.

159. Probstfield JL, Byington RP, Egan DA, et al. Methodological issues facing studies of atherosclerotic change. Circulation 1993;87(Suppl II):II-74 — II-81.

160. Fried LP, Borhani NO, Enright P, et al. The Cardiovascular Health Study: Design and rationale. Ann Epidemiol 1991;1:263-276.

161. Salonen JT, Salonen R. Ultrasound B-mode imaging in observational studies of atherosclerotic progression. Circulation 1993;87(Suppl II):II-56–II-65.

162. MIDAS Research Group: Furberg CD, Byington RP, Borhani NA. Multicenter Isradipine Diuretic Atherosclerosis Study (MIDAS). Am J Med 1989;86(Suppl 4A):37-39.

163. Margitic SE, Bond MG, Crouse JR, et al. Progression and regression of carotid atherosclerosis in clinical trials. Arterioscler Thromb 1991;11:443-451.sclerosis has increased in

Associated Coronary Disease in Peripheral Vascular Patients

Norman R. Hertzer, MD, Cleveland, Ohio

The complications of associated coronary artery disease (myocardial infarction, arrhythmia, or congestive heart failure) always have been the leading causes of early mortality and late death among patients who require peripheral vascular reconstruction. For a number of reasons, however, it is only relatively recently that this critical issue has received the attention that it clearly deserves. First, the technical aspects of vascular surgery have become sufficiently standardized that greater attention has been devoted to other refinements, such as the preoperative evaluation and perioperative monitoring of patients with additional risk factors. Moreover, the conventional history and standard electrocardiogram now may be supplemented by objective information obtained with either stress or dipyridamole testing, radionuclide myocardial imaging, or angiocardiography to document left ventricular performance. Finally, both cardiac catheterization and aortocoronary bypass are safer and more widely available than ever before.

The management of incidental coronary disease is highly controversial. How prevalent is it? What is the impact of a positive cardiac history or abnormal findings of noninvasive studies on operative risk? On late survival? Do the recognition and treatment of coexistent coronary disease really make any difference? Few indisputable answers are available for these compelling questions, largely because coronary anatomy has rarely been documented in noncardiac patients. Those at greatest risk for double- or triple-vessel lesions represent a discrete subset (double- or triple-vessel lesions) within a larger cohort (associated coronary involvement). These subsets lie within the overall group of patients needing treatment for peripheral vascular disease, and very little is known about them on the basis of traditional clinical reports. Nevertheless, the following tables and illustrations summarize the collective experience presently available.

From the Department of Vascular Surgery, The Cleveland Clinic Foundation, Cleveland, Ohio.

Table V. Coronary arteriographic findings according to the clinical cardiac status in a series of 1000 patients presenting with peripheral vascular disease[11]

Coronary arteriographic classification	Clinical coronary disease			
	None		Suspected	
	No	%	No	%
Normal coronary arteries	64	14	21	4
Mild to moderate CAD*	218	49	99	18
Advanced compensated CAD	97	22	192	34
Severe, correctable CAD	63	14	188	34
Severe, inoperable CAD	4	1	54	10

*CAD = Coronary artery disease.

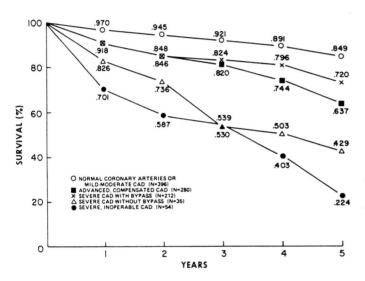

Fig. 1. Cumulative 5-year survival rate for the prospective series of patients described in Table V. The survival rate for the coronary bypass subset was statistically superior ($p = 0.001$) to that for patients with severe, uncorrected coronary artery disease (CAD).[12]

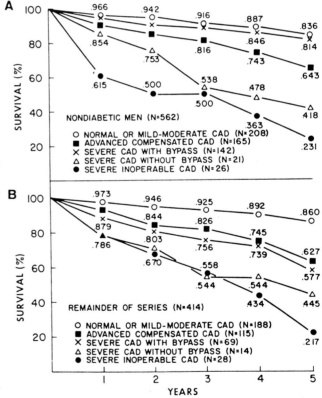

Fig. 2. Cumulative 5-year survival rate in the same series for the following cohorts: **A,** nondiabetic men; **B,** all other patients. Survival rate after coronary bypass in nondiabetic men was statistically superior ($p = 0.0002$) to that for similar patients with uncorrected or inoperable coronary artery disease (CAD), as well as the bypass survival rate in women or people with diabetes ($p = 0.003$).[46]

REFERENCES

1. Blombery PA, Ferguson IA, Rosengarten DS, et al. The role of coronary artery disease in complications of abdominal aortic aneurysm surgery. Surgery 1986;101:150-155.

2. Bouchard JP, Fabia J, Simard D, et al. Carotid endarterectomy: Survival rates of 227 patients. Can Med Ass J 1975; 113:949-951.

3. Brown OW, Hollier LH, Pairolero PC, et al. Abdominal aortic aneurysm and coronary artery disease: A reassessment. Arch Surg 1981;116:1484-1488.

4. Cooperman M, Pflug B, Martin EW Jr, et al. Cardiovascular risk factors in patients with peripheral vascular disease. Surgery 1978;84:505-509.

5. Crawford ES, Bomberger RA, Glaeser DH, et al. Aortoiliac occlusive disease: Factors influencing survival and function following reconstructive operation over a twenty-five-year period. Surgery 1981;90:1055-1066.

6. Crawford ES, Saleh SA, Babb JW III, et al. Infrarenal abdominal aortic aneurysm: Factors influencing survival after operation performed over a 25-year period. Ann Surg 1981;193: 699-709.

7. Diehl JT, Cali RF, Hertzer NR, et al. Complications of abdominal aortic reconstruction: An analysis of perioperative risk factors in 557 patients. Ann Surg 1983;197:49-56.

8. Hertzer NR. Fatal myocardial infarction following abdominal aortic aneurysm resection: Three hundred forty-three patients followed 6-11 years postoperatively. Ann Surg 1980; 192:667-673.

9. Hertzer NR. Fatal myocardial infarction following lower extremity revascularization: Two hundred seventy-three patients followed six to eleven postoperative years. Ann Surg 1981;193:492-498.

10. Hertzer NR, Arison R. Cumulative stroke and survival ten years after carotid endarterectomy. J Vasc Surg 1985;2:661-668.

11. Hertzer NR, Beven EG, Young JR, et al. Coronary artery disease in peripheral vascular patients: A classification of 1000 coronary angiograms and results of surgical management. Ann Surg 1984;199:223-233.

12. Hertzer NR, Young JR, Beven EG, et al. Late results of coronary bypass in patients with peripheral vascular disease. I. Five-year survival according to age and clinical cardiac status. Clev Clin Q 1986;53:133-143.

13. Hollier LH, Plate G, O'Brien PC, et al. Late survival after abdominal aortic aneurysm repair: Influence of coronary artery disease. J Vasc Surg 1984;1:290-298.

14. Jamieson WRE, Janusz MT, Miyagishima RT, et al. Influence of ischemic heart disease on early and late mortality after surgery for peripheral occlusive vascular disease. Circulation 1982;66:1-92-1-97.

15. Kallero KS, Bergqvist D, Cederholm C, et al. Arteriosclerosis in popliteal artery trifurcation as a predictor for myocardial infarction after arterial reconstructive operation. Surg Gynecol Obstet 1984;159:133-138.

16. Kallero KS, Bergqvist D, Cederholm C, et al. Late mortality and morbidity after arterial reconstruction: The influence of arteriosclerosis in popliteal artery trifurcation. J Vasc Surg 1985;2:541-546.

17. Lord RSA. Late survival after carotid endarterectomy for transient ischemic attacks. J Vasc Surg 1984;1:512-519.

18. Malone JM, Moore WS, Goldstone J. Life expectancy following aortofemoral arterial grafting. Surgery 1977;81:551-555.

19. Martinez BD, Hertzer NR, Beven EG. Influence of distal arterial occlusive disease on prognosis following aortobifemoral bypass. Surgery 1980;88:795-805.

20. Pasternack PF, Imparato AM, Bear G, et al. The value of radionuclide angiography as a predictor of perioperative myocardial infarction in patients undergoing abdominal aortic aneurysm resection. J Vasc Surg 1984;1:320-324.

21. Reigel MM, Hollier LH, Kazmier FJ, et al. Late survival in abdominal aortic aneurysm patients: The role of selective myocardial revascularization on the basis of clinical symptoms. J Vasc Surg 1987;5:222-227.

22. Ruby ST, Whittemore AD, Couch NP, et al. Coronary artery disease in patients requiring abdominal aortic aneurysm repair: Selective use of a combined operation. Ann Surg 1985;201:758-764.

23. Soreide O, Lillesltol J, Christensen O, et al. Abdominal aortic aneurysms: Survival analysis of four hundred thirty-four patients. Surgery 1982;91:188-193.

24. Thompson JE, Austin DJ, Patman RD. Carotid endarterectomy for cerebrovascular insufficiency: Long-term results in 592 patients followed up to thirteen years. Ann Surg 1970; 172:663-679.

25. Tomatis LS, Fireens EE, Verbrugge GP. Evaluation of surgical risk in peripheral vascular disease by coronary arteriography: A series of 100 cases. Surgery 1972;71:429-435.

26. Whittemore AD, Clowes AW, Hechtman HB, et al. Aortic aneurysm repair: Reduced operative mortality associated with maintenance of optimal cardiac performance. Ann Surg 1980;192:414-421.

27. DeWeese JA, Rob CG. Autogenous venous bypass grafts five years later. Ann Surg 1971;174:346-356.

28. DeWeese JA, Rob CG, Satran R, et al. Results of carotid endarterectomies for transient ischemic attacks — five years later. Ann Surg 1973;178:258-264.

29. Hicks GL, Eastland MW, DeWeese JA, et al. Survival improvement following aortic aneurysm resection. Ann Surg 1975; 181:863-869.

30. Szilagyi DE, Hagemann JH, Smith RF, et al. Autogenous vein grafting in femoropopliteal atherosclerosis: The limits of its effectiveness. Surgery 1979;86:836-851.

31. Yeager RA, Weigel RM, Murphy ES, et al. Application of clinically valid cardiac risk factors to aortic aneurysm surgery. Arch Surg 1986;121:278-281.

32. Arous EG, Baum PL. The ischemic exercise test in patients with peripheral vascular disease: Implications for management. Arch Surg 1984;119:780-783.

33. Boucher CA, Brewster DC, Darling RC, et al. Determination of cardiac risk by dipyridamole thallium imaging before peripheral vascular surgery. N Engl J Med 1985;312:389-394.

34. Cutler BS, Leppo JA. Dipyridamole thallium 201 scintigraphy to detect coronary artery disease before abdominal aortic surgery. J Vasc Surg 1987;5:91-100.

35. Dipasquale G, Andreoli A, Pinelli G, et al. Cerebral ischemia and asymptomatic coronary artery disease: A prospective study of 83 patients. Stroke 1986;17:1098-1101.

36. Von Knorring J, Lepantalo M. Prediction of perioperative cardiac complications by electrocardiographic monitoring during treadmill exercise testing before peripheral vascular surgery. Surgery 1986;99:610-613.

37. Rokey R, Rolak LS, Harati Y, et al. Coronary artery study. Ann Neurol 1984;16:50-53.

38. Hertzer NR, Young JR, Beven EG, et al. Late results of coronary bypass in patients presenting with infrarenal aortic aneurysms: The Cleveland Clinic Study. Ann Surg 1987;205: 360-367.

39. Hertzer NR, Young JR, Beven EG, et al. Late results of coronary bypass in patients presenting with lower extremity ischemia: The Cleveland Clinic Study. Ann Vasc Surg 1986; 1:411-420.

Table III. Arterial involvement in Takayasu's arteritis[5,16-27]

Site	Incidence (%)	Bilateral involvement (%)
Subclavian artery	85	47
Descending aorta	58	
Renal artery	62-75	29
Carotid artery	44	19
Mesenteric arteries SMA (14%-19% >celiac >IMA)	24-43	
Ascending aorta	30	
Abdominal aorta	20	
Coronary ostia	17 case reports	

SMA = superior mesenteric artery; IMA = inferior mesenteric artery.

Table IV. Clinical signs in Takayasu's arteritis[2-5,7,28-35]

Findings	Incidence (%)	Manifestations
Large vessel stenosis	>0-94	Bruit over carotids, aorta; pulse discrepancy
Ocular signs	25-37	Blurred vision, diplopia, amaurosis fugax
Hypertension	50-60	HBP, CHF
Joint symptoms	55	Synovitis
Stroke	5-14	CVA
Aortic valve incompetence	10	CHF

HBP = high blood pressure; CHF = congestive heart failure; CVA = cerebrovascular accident.

Table V. Laboratory findings in Takayasu's arteritis[3-5,36]

Findings	Incidence (%)
Elevated ESR (>50 mm/1 h)	80 (70-100)
Anemia	25
Leukocytosis	10
Tuberculin sensitivity	10-100

ESR = erythrocyte sedimentation rate.

Table VI. Character of lesions in Takayasu's arteritis[7,37]

Lesion type	Incidence (%)
Purely stenotic	85
Purely dilative	2
Mixed	13

Table VII. Temporal arteritis

	Epidemiologic data and characteristics	Ref.
Incidence	2.9 cases/100,000/yr 17.4 cases/100,000/yr over age 50 yr	38,39
Age at diagnosis	9.5% >50 yr Few cases in young adults and adolescents	39
Male:female	1:2	40
Size of artery involved	Medium-sized vessels 14% large artery involvement	41-45
Mortality	Same as general population	39,46

Table VIII. Clinical signs and symptoms in patients with temporal arteritis[21,39,46-53]

Symptoms	Incidence (%)
Headache	60-90
Fever	48
Polymyalgia rheumatica	47
Weight loss	45
Anorexia	36
Malaise	29
Depression	25
Localized arterial symptoms	
Tenderness	55
Absent pulse	51
Nodularity	35
Ocular involvement	
Visual impairment	36-58
Blindness	16
Amaurosis fugax	12
Diplopia	12-15
Bilateral visual loss (second eye affected 33% of the time; simultaneously or within 7 days)	5.5-31
Claudication	
Jaw	36-50
Extremity	8

Table IX. Laboratory findings in
temporal arteritis[54-56]

Normochromic, normocytic anemia
Elevated erythrocyte sedimentation rate
Normal sedimentation rate in 22.5% (*not* related to a
milder disease)

Table X. Temporal artery biopsy for diagnosis of
temporal arteritis[39,57-64]

Findings	Incidence (%)
Positive biopsy for clinical suspicion	13-36
False negative biopsy	5-44
Positive biopsy on first side sampled	86
Positive biopsy after several days of steroid treatment	60
Positive biopsy after 1 week of treatment	10
Second biopsy required for diagnosis	14
Skin lesions present	28

REFERENCES

1. Hall S, Barr W, Lie JT, et al. Takayasu arteritis: A study of 32 North American patients. Medicine 1985;64:89-99.
2. Warren AU, Anderson P, Hemmingsson A. Takayasu's arteritis: A hospital-region based study on occurrence, treatment and prognosis. Angiology 1983;34:311-320.
3. Nakao K, Ikeda M, Kimata S. Takayasu's arteritis: Clinical report of 84 cases and immunological studies of seven cases. Circulation 1967;35:1141-1155.
4. Van Der Heijden JTM, Krenning EP, Hennemann G. Takayasu's arteritis: Case report and review of the literature. Neth J Med 1984;27:74-79.
5. Lupi-Herrera E, Sanchez Torres G, Marcushamer J, et al. Takayasu's arteritis: Clinical study of 107 cases. Am Heart J 1977;93:94-103.
6. Fraga A, Mintz G, Valle L, et al. Takayasu's arteritis: Frequency of systemic manifestations (study of 22 patients) and favorable response to maintenance steroid therapy with adrenocorticosteroids (12 patients). Arthritis Rheum 1972;15:617-624.
7. Hall S, Buchbinder R. Takayasu's arteritis. Rheum Dis Clin N Am 1990;16:411-422.
8. Hall S, Nelson AM. Takayasu's arteritis and juvenile rheumatoid arthritis. J Rheumatol 1986;13:431-433.
9. Hachiya J. Current concepts of Takayasu's arteritis. Semin Roentgenol 1970;5:245-259.
10. Robbs JV, Human RR, Rajaruthnam P. Operative treatment of nonspecific aortoarteritis (Takayasu's arteritis). J Vasc Surg 1986;3:605-616.
11. Bloss RS, Duncan JM, Cooley DA, et al. Takayasu's arteritis. Surg Consid 1979;27:574-579.
12. Ueno A, Awane Y, Wakabayashi A, et al. Successfully operated obliterative brachiocephalic arteritis (Takayasu) associated with the elonged coarctation. Jpn Heart J 1978;8:538-544.
13. Lupi E, Sanchez GT, Horwitz S, et al. Pulmonary artery involvement in Takayasu's arteritis. Chest 1975;67:69-74.
14. Bardi K, Bouziri S, Jaafoura H, et al. Venous involvement in Takayasu's disease: Does it exist? Ann Vasc Surg 1988;2:232-234.
15. Sen KP. Obstructive disease of the aorta and its branches. Indian J Surg 1968;30:289-329.
16. Ogunbiyi OF, Falase AO. Aortic arch syndrome: Takayasu's arteritis in Nigeria. Afr J Med, Med Sci 1989;18:211-214.
17. Schrire V, Asherson R. Arteritis of the aorta and its major branches. Q J Med 1964;23:439-455.
18. Wiggelinkhuizen J, Cremin BJ. Takayasu's arteritis and renovascular hypertension in childhood. Paediatr 1978;62:209-217.
19. Giordano JM, Leavitt RY, Hoffman G, et al. Experience with surgical treatment of Takayasu's disease. Surgery 1991;109:252-258.
20. Kohrman MH, Huttenlocher PR. Takayasu's arteritis: A treatable cause of stroke in infancy. Ped Neurol 1986;2:154-158.
21. Cupps TR, Fauci A. The Vasculitides. Philadelphia: WB Saunders 1981; pp 99-115.
22. Tech PC, Tan LK, Chia BL, et al. Nonspecific aorto arteritis in Singapore with special reference to hypertension. Am Heart J 1978;95:683-695.
23. Nussaume O, Bouttier S, Duchatelle JP, et al. Mesenteric infarction in Takayasu's disease. Ann Vasc Surg 1990;4:117-121.
24. Lagneau P, Michel JB, Vuong PN. Surgical treatment of Takayasu's disease. Ann Surg 1987;205:157-168.
25. Kieffer E, Bahnini A, Bletry O, et al. Le lesions aortiques de la maladie de Takayasu. In Kieffer E ed. Chirurgie de l'aorte thoracique descendate et thoracoabdominal. Paris: L'Expansion Scientifique 1986, pp 179-200.
26. Pokrovsky AV, Sultananaliev TA, Spirdonov AA. Surgical treatment of vascorenal hypertension in nonspecific aortoarteritis (Takayasu's disease). J Cardiovasc Surg 1983;24:111-118.
27. Fiessinger JN, Tawfik-Taher S, Capron L, et al. Maladie de Takayasu: Criteres diagnostiques. Nouv Presse Med 1982;11:583-586.
28. Achar KN, Al-Nahib. Takayasu's arteritis and ulcerative colitis. Am J Gastroenterology 1986;81:1215-1217.
29. Braunwald E. Aortic arteritis syndrome. In Heart Disease, 2nd ed. Philadelphia: WB Saunders Co., 1984, pp 1558-1560.
30. Ischikawa K. Natural history and classification of occlusive thromboaortopathy (Takayasu's disease). Circulation 1978;57:27-35.
31. Wolfe SM. Takayasu's arteritis. JAMA 1989;89:90-94.
32. Lupi-Herrera E, Sanchez-Torres G, Castillo PU. Cutaneous reactivity to PPD and antigens of mycobacteria (*Kansasii, avium,* and *fortuitum*) in patients with unspecific arteritis. Arch Inst Cardiol Mex 1972;42:717-725.
33. Ducailar C, Thulmond A, Semler H, et al. Aortic valve replacement for Takayasu's disease. Ann Thorac Surg 1987;43:102-104.
34. Duborg O, Thomas D, Sirinell A, et al. Aortic regurgitation in Takayasu's disease: Three operated cases and a review of the literature. Arch Mal Coeur 1984;77:998-1005.
35. Altieri PI, Toro JM, Martinez J. Localized Takayasu's disease producing coronary ostial lesions. Bol Assoc Med PR 1984;76:168-169.
36. Paloheimo JA. Obstructive arteritis of Takayasu's type. Med Scand 1967;Suppl 468:7-45.
37. Liu YQ. Radiology of aorto-arteritis. Radiol Clin N Am 1985;23:671-688.

Heparin-associated thrombocytopenia (HAT) is observed in 4%–10% of patients receiving heparin and is more common with bovine heparin as compared with porcine heparin.[24] Although most patients with this syndrome have been treated with full dose intravenous heparin for 7-10 days, HAT has also been described with prophylactic subcutaneous heparin[25] and in patients with heparin-coated indwelling venous catheters.[27] Heparin-related intravascular thrombosis is relatively unusual, with an estimated frequency in prospective trials ranging from 0.4% to 1.6%. Thrombotic complications related to heparin are usually arterial, although venous thromboembolism may also be a component.[24]

Recently, several other conditions have been observed to be associated with an increased risk of vascular disease. Homocystinuria, a hereditary autosomal recessive disorder usually due to cystathione β-synthase deficiency, is characterized by mental retardation, ocular and skeletal malformations, and premature atherosclerosis and intravascular thrombosis.[27] Heterozygotes and possibly others with elevated blood homocyst(e)ine* levels (as might occur in vitamin B12 deficiency, for example) may also be at increased risk for thrombosis.[28] The mechanism of this effect is uncertain, although investigators have proposed that homocyst(e)ine may damage vascular endothelium[29] or may activate endogenous clotting factor V[30] and decrease protein C activation by the endothelial cell.[31] The association of hyperhomocyst(e)inemia and vascular disease is of particular interest in that levels of circulating homocyst(e)ine might be lowered by such low toxicity agents as pyridoxine, folate or vitamin B12.[28,32,33]

Lipoprotein(a) [Lp(a)] is a plasma lipoprotein of uncertain function that has recently been found to be an independent predictor of atherosclerosis.[34,35] The structure of Lp(a) closely resembles that of plasminogen, and it has been proposed that this unique lipoprotein may bind to fibrin(ogen) and thereby attenuate fibrin-mediated enhancement of the tissue plasminogen activator (tPA) effect on plasminogen.[35] Lp(a) has also been shown to increase plasminogen activator inhibitor-1 expression by cultured endothelial cells.[36] In addition to being a risk factor for coronary artery and cerebrovascular disease, elevated Lp(a) levels have also been noted to be associated with early vein graft stenosis following coronary artery bypass surgery.[37]

*Homocyst(e)ine as defined in this article includes the free and protein bound forms in plasma of homocysteine. The term encompasses homocysteine, as well as the disulfides, homocystine, and mixed disulfide (homocysteine-cysteine).

Table I. Conditions associated with hypercoagulability

Antithrombin III deficiency
Protein C deficiency
Protein S deficiency
Dysfibrinogenemia
Abnormalities of fibrinolysis
Antiphospholipid antibodies
Heparin-associated thrombocytopenia
Hyperhomocyst(e)inemia
Elevated lipoprotein (a)
Myeloproliferative syndromes
Paroxysmal nocturnal hemoglobinuria
Malignancy
Pregnancy

Table II. Frequency of hypercoagulable states in patients with venous thromboembolism

Author	No. of patients	ATIII No. (%)	Pro C	Pro S	Abnormal fibrinogen	Abnormal plasminogen	APLA
Felez[3,38]	578	20 (3.5)	15 (2.6)	20 (3.5)	2 (<1)	2 (<1)	11 (1.9)
Grossman[39]	99	8/62 (12.9)	10/79 (12.7)	13.75 (17.3)			
Gladson[40]	139	(3)	9 (7)	7 (5)	(1)	(1)	(2)
Briet[4]	113 (+FH)	5 (4.4)	13 (11.5)	15 (13.3)	2 (1.8)	4 (3.5)	
	90 (−FH)	1 (1.1)	1 (1.1)	1 (1.1)			
Ben-Tal[41]	107	8 (7.5)	7 (6.5)	3 (2.8)	1 (1)		4 (3.7)
Scharrer[42]	158	(5)	(9.4)	(6.3)	(0.6)	(1.2)	
Malm[43]	241	31 (1.2)	8 (3.3)	2 (<1)		2 (<1)	
Broekmans[44]	800		(4)	(4)			
Vikydal[45]	752	(3.6)					
Mannucci[46]	95	7 (7.5)	7 (7.5)	5 (5)	1 (1)	1 (1)	

ATIII = antithrombin III; Pro C = protein C; Pro S = protein S; APLA = antiphospholipid antibodies; +FH = positive family history of thromboembolism; −FH = negative family history of thromboembolism.

Table III. Frequency of hypercoagulable states in surgical patients

Author	No. of patients	Population	ATIII	Pro C	Pro S	Decreased plasminogen	APLA	HAT
Donaldson[47]	158	Vascular surgery patients	2/157 (1.3)	4/157 (7.5)	1/157 (<1)		5/142 (3.5)	4.156 (2.6)
Eldrup-Jorgensen[48]	20	Vascular surgery patients <51 yr prospective	3/20 (15)	4/20 (20)	2/20 (10)	3/20 (10)		
Eldrup-Jorgensen[23]	57	Vascular surgery patients 23-57 yr retrospective review	3 (5.3)	1 (1.7)	9 (15.8)			
Hallett[49]	51	Vascular surgery patients	2 (3.9)					
Flinn[50]	165	Vascular surgery patients	27 (16.4)					

HAT = heparin-associated thrombocytopenia.

Table IV. Antiphospholipid antibodies (APLA) in patients with vascular disease or arterial thrombosis

Author	Patients	Results
Eldrup-Jorgensen[23]	57 patients <51 yr with lower extremity arterial occlusive disease	9.57 (15.8%) had APLA, including 5 with LLA and 8 with ACLA
Ahn[22]	84 consecutive patients with APLA; retrospective review of surgical history (23/84 patients)	23 patients underwent 51 surgical procedures (18 vascular, 33 nonvascular); 9/18 vascular procedures and 3/7 vascular surgery patients with APLA had thrombotic complications
Gastineau[17]	219 patients with APLA	20 episodes of arterial thrombosis identified
Love[51]	Computer-assisted collection of published series of patients with APLA	25% incidence of thrombosis in patients with LLA; 28% incidence of thrombosis in patients with ACLA

LLA = lupus-like anticoagulant; ACLA = anticardiolipin antibody.

Table V. Prospective, randomized trials on the incidence of heparin-associated thrombocytopenia (HAT): Full-dose bovine versus porcine heparin

Author	Heparin	Incidence (%)
Bell[52]	Bovine	13/50 (26)
	Porcine	9/99 (9)
Ansell[53]	Bovine	5/54 (9.2)
	Porcine	5/50 (10)
Bailey[54]	Bovine	2/29 (6.8)
	Porcine	1/32 (3.1)
Green[55]	Bovine	2/45 (4.4)
	Bovine	13/45* (28.8)
	Porcine	0/44 (0)
	Porcine	7/44* (15.9)
Powers[56]	Bovine	5/65 (7.7)
	Porcine	0/60 (0)

*Drop in platelet count >50,000.

Table VI. Selected additional prospective studies on the incidence of HAT

Author	Heparin	Incidence	Comments
Kakkasseril[57]	Bovine	9/142 (6)	Total, vascular surgery patients
	Bovine	2/72 (3)	No prior heparin therapy
	Bovine	7/70 (10)	Prior heparin therapy
Bell[58]	Bovine	16/52	10 of 16 had elevated FDP, 5 of those had decreased fibrinogen
Malcolm[59]	Porcine	9/66 (<150K)	4/38 patients (<150K) on subcutaneous heparin (mean 9.9 days)
		2/66 (<100K)	0/38 patients (<100K) on subcutaneous heparin (mean 9.9 days)

FDP = fibrin/fibrinogen degradation product.

Table VII. Selected series of HAT patients with thromboembolic complications

Author	Patients	Comments
Makhoul[60]	25 patients with HAT and thrombosis	All 25 patients had positive in vitro evidence of platelet activation with bovine heparin; 16 patients had venous thrombosis* and 19 patients had arterial thrombosis*
Laster[61]	169 patients with HAT	30 patients (17.8%) had thromboembolic complications; included 6 PE, 15 iliofemoral or aortic thrombi, 5 venous thrombi and 6 others; 4 patients required lower extremity amputation
Ramirez-Lassepas[62]	137 stroke patients treated with heparin	21 patients (15.3%) had a drop in platelet count of ≥40%; this was associated with a statistically significant increase in the occurrence of new ischemic events and death
Stanton[63]	10 surgical patients with HAT and thrombosis	2/10 (20%) required major limb amputation; 5/10 (50%) overall mortality. Drawn from a total of 20,000 patients from vascular or general surgery service over 10 years. Approximately 3,000 of these patients received heparin; 10 (0.33%) developed "white clot syndrome"
Kappa[64]	16 patients who developed thrombocytopenia or new thrombosis on heparin	16 selected patients; all had positive in vitro evidence of platelet activation with heparin; 6 had thrombocytopenia alone; 7 had thrombocytopenia and thrombosis; 3 had thrombosis without thrombocytopenia. Mortality rate was 18.8%

*10 patients had arterial and venous events.
PE = pulmonary embolism.

Table VIII. Incidence of hyperhomocyst(e)inemia in patients with vascular disease

Author	Method	Patients	Age (yr)	Incidence (%)
Clarke[65]	Methionine loading	PVD	<55	7/25 (28)
		CVD	<55	16/38 (42)
Boers[66]	Methionine loading	PVD	<50	7/25 (28)
		CVD	<50	7/25 (28)
Brattstrom[32]	Methionine loading and basal level	PVD (37) and CVD (35)	<55	30/72 (42)
Malinow[67]	Basal level	PVD + CVD		22/47 (47)

PVD = peripheral vascular disease; CVD = cerebrovascular disease.

Table IX. Selected additional studies demonstrating an association between homocyst(e)ine levels and vascular disease

Author	Method	No. of patients	Results
Coull[68]	Basal	CVD (31)	H(e) level > control, $p < 0.2$
		Acute stroke (41)	H(e) level > control, $p < .0009$
		Acute TIA (27)	H(e) level > control, $p < .05$
Araki[69]	Basal	CVD[1] (45)	H(e) level > control, $p < .05$
		CVD[2] (20)	H(e) level > control, $p < .05$
Brattstrom[70]	Methionine loading	CVD (19)	MDS level > control, $p < .05$

H(e) = Homocyst(e)ine; TIA = transient ischemic attack.

Table X. Lipoprotein (a) levels in patients with vascular disease

Author	Patients	Results
Murai[71]	Coronary artery disease	29/47 (61.7%) had elevated Lp(a)
	Cerebral infarction	72/156 (46.2%) had elevated Lp(a)
Zenker[72]	46 patients with cerebrovascular disease (age 40-65)	Mean Lp(a) levels higher than 37 controls
Koltringer[73]	79 patients with cerebrovascular disease (age >40)	Mean Lp(a) levels significantly higher than in 21 controls
Wiseman[74]	157 patients with a history of femoropopliteal bypass (113 patients, 44 occluded)	Mean Lp(a) levels significantly higher in patients with occluded grafts
Hoff[37]	167 patients with a history of saphenous vein–coronary artery bypass graft	135 patients with graft stenosis had mean Lp(a) level double that seen in 32 patients without stenosis

REFERENCES

1. Schafer AI. The hypercoagulable states. Ann Int Med 1985; 102:814-828.
2. Mannucci PM, Tripodi A. Laboratory screening in inherited thrombotic syndromes. Thromb Haemost 1987;57:247-251.
3. Felez J. Biochemical aspects of the pathogenesis of venous thrombosis. Acta Chir Scand Suppl 1990;556:9-17.
4. Briet E, Engesser L, Brommer EJP, et al. Thrombophilia: Its causes and a rough estimate of its prevalence. Thromb Haemost 1987;58:39(abstr).
5. Bauer KE, Rosenberg R. Role of antithrombin III as a regulator of in vivo coagulation. Semin Hematol 1991;28:10-18.
6. Clause LH, Comp PC. The regulation of hemostasis: The protein C system. N Engl J Med 1986;314:1298-1304.
7. Coller BS, Owen J, Jesty J, et al. Deficiency of plasma protein S, protein C, or antithrombin III and arterial thrombosis. Arteriosclerosis 1987;7:456-462.
8. Israels SJ, Seshia SS. Childhood stroke associated with protein C or S deficiency. J Pediatr 1987;111:562-564.
9. Comp PC, Debault LE, Esmon NL, et al. Human thrombomodulin is inhibited by IgG from two patients with non-specific anticoagulants. Blood 1983;62:229A(Abstr).
10. Marciniak E, Romond EH. Impaired catalytic function of activated protein C: A new in vitro manifestation of lupus anticoagulant. Blood 1989;74:2426-2432.
11. Ruiz-Arguelles GJ, Ruiz-Arguelles A, Alarcon Segoria D, et al. Natural anticoagulants in systemic lupus erythematosus: Deficiency of protein S bound to C4bp associates with recent history of venous thromboses, antiphospholipid antibodies, and the antiphospholipid syndrome. J Rheumatol 1991;18:552-558.
12. Vigano-D'Angelo S, D'Angelo A, et al. Protein S deficiency occurs in the nephrotic syndrome. Ann Int Med 1987;107:42-47.
13. Roerger LM, Morris PC, Thurnau CR, et al. Oral contraceptives and gender affect protein S status. Blood 1987;69:692-694.
14. Carrell N, Ganriel DA, Blott PM. Hereditary dysfibrinogenemia in a patient with thrombotic disease. Blood 1983;62:439.
15. Towne JB, Baudyk DF, Husscy CV, Tollack VT. Abnormal plasminogen: A genetically determined cause of hypercoagulability. J Vasc Surg 1984;1:896-902.
16. Jorgensen M, Bonnevie-Nielsen V. Increased concentration of the fast-acting plasminogen activator inhibitor in plasma associated with familial venous thrombosis. Br J Haematol 1987;65:175-180.
17. Gastineau DA, Kazmier JF, Nichols WL, et al. Lupus anticoagulant: An analysis of the clinical and laboratory features of 219 cases. Am J Hematol 1985;19:265-275.
18. Elias M, Eldor A. Thromboembolism in patients with the "lupus" type circulating anticoagulant. Arch Int Med 1984;144:510-515.
19. Carrera LO, Machin SJ, Deman R, et al. Arterial thrombosis, intrauterine death and "lupus" anticoagulant: Detection of immunoglobulin interfering with prostacyclin formation. Lancet 1981;1:244-246.
20. Angles-Cano E, Claurel JP, Sultany Y. Predisposing factors to thrombosis in systemic lupus erythematosus: possible relation to endothelial cell damage. J Lab Clin Med 1979;94:312-323.
21. Sanfelippo MJ, Drayna CJ. Prekallikrein inhibition associated with the lupus anticoagulant: A mechanism of thrombosis. Am J Clin Pathol 1988;77:275-279.
22. Ahn SS, Kalunian K, Rosove M, et al. Postoperative thrombotic complications in patients with the lupus anticoagulant: Increased risk after vascular procedures. J Vasc Surg 1988;7:749-756.
23. Eldrup-Jorgensen J, Brace L, et al. Lupus-like anticoagulants and lower extremity arterial occlusive disease. Circulation 1989;80(suppl III):III54–III58.
24. Warkentin TE, Kelton JG. Heparin-induced thrombocytopenia. Progress in Hemostasis and Thrombosis, Vol. 10:1-34.
25. Hrushesky W. Thrombocytopenia induced by low-dose subcutaneous heparin. Lancet 1977;ii:1286.
26. Laster J, Silver D. Heparin-coated catheters and heparin-induced thrombocytopenia. J Vasc Surg 1988;7:667-672.
27. Mudd SH, Levy HL, Skovby F. Disorders of transsulfuration. The Metabolic Basis of Inherited Disease, 6th ed. New York: McGraw-Hill, 1989, pp 693-734.
28. Malinow MR. Hyperhomocyst(e)inemia: A common and easily reversible risk factor for occlusive atherosclerosis. Circulation 1990;81:2004-2006.
29. Harker LA, Ross R, Slichter SJ, et al. Homocystine-induced arteriosclerosis: The role of endothelial cell injury and platelet response in its genesis. J Clin Invest 1976;58:731-741.
30. Rodgers GM, Kane WH. Activation of endogenous factor V, by a homocysteine-induced vascular endothelial cell activator. J Clin Invest 1986;77:1909-1916.
31. Rodgers GM, Conn MT. Homocysteine, an atherogenic stimulus, reduces protein C activation by arterial and venous endothelial cells. Blood 1990;75:895-901.
32. Brattstrom L, Israelsson B, Norring B, et al. Impaired homocysteine metabolism in early-onset cerebral and peripheral

occlusive arterial disease: Effects of pyridoxine and folic acid treatment. Atherosclerosis 1990;81:51-60.

33. Brattstrom C, Israelsson B, Lindgarde F, et al. Higher total plasma homocysteine in vitamin B12 deficiency than in heterozygosity for homocystinuria due to cystathionine β-synthetase deficiency. Metabolism 1988;37:175-178.

34. Scanu AM, Lawn RM, Berg K. Lipoprotein(a) and atherosclerosis. Ann Int Med 1991;115:209-218.

35. Loscalzo J. Lipoprotein(a): A unique risk factor for atherothrombotic disease. Arteriosclerosis 1990;10:672-679.

36. Etingin OR, Hajjar DP, Hajjar KA, et al. Lipoprotein(a) regulates plasminogen activator inhibitor-1 expression in endothelial cells: A potential mechanism in thrombogenesis. J Biol Chem 1991;266:2459-2465.

37. Hoff HF, Beck GJ, Skibinski CI, et al. Serum Lp(a) levels as a predictor of vein graft stenosis after coronary artery bypass surgery in patients. Circulation 1988;77:1238-1244.

38. Felez J, Rodriguez-Pinto C, Velasco F, et al. High incidence of congenital hemostatic disorders among 578 patients with primary and secondary thrombosis. Blood 1987;70:372A (abstr).

39. Grossman B, Duncan A. Prevalence of primary coagulation deficiencies in patients with deep venous thrombosis. Thromb Haemost 1987;58:72(abstr).

40. Gladson CL, Griffin JH, Hack V, et al. The incidence of protein C and protein S deficiency in 139 young thrombotic patients. Blood 1985;66:350A(abstr).

41. Ben-Tal O, Zivelin A, Seligsohn U. The relative frequency of hereditary thrombotic disorders among 107 patients with thrombophilia in Israel. Thromb Haemost 1989;61:50-54.

42. Scharrer I, Hack-Wunderle V, Heyland H, et al. Incidence of defective T-PA release in 158 unrelated young patients with venous thrombosis in comparison to Pc-, PS-, ATIII-, fibrinogen- and plasminogen deficiency. Thromb Haemost 1987;58:72(abstr).

43. Malm J, Laurell M, Nillson IM, et al. Protein C, protein S, and the fibrinolytic system in patients with a history of thrombosis. Thromb Haemost 1987;58:229(abstr).

44. Broekmans AW, Van Der Linder IK, Jansen-Koeter Y, et al. Prevalence of protein C, and protein S deficiency in patients with thrombotic disease. Thromb Res 1986;42:135(abstr).

45. Vikydal R, Dorninger C, Kyrle PA, et al. The prevalence of hereditary antithrombin-III deficiency in patients with a history of venous thromboembolism. Thromb Haemost 1985;54:744-745.

46. Mannucci PM, Tripodi A. Diagnostic screening of congenital thrombotic syndromes. Thromb Haemost 1987;57:247(abstr).

47. Donaldson MC, Weinberg DS, Belkin M, et al. Screening for hypercoagulable states in vascular surgical practice: a preliminary study. J Vasc Surg 1990;11:825-831.

48. Eldrup-Jorgensen J, Flanigan DP, Brace L, et al. Hypercoagulable states and lower limb ischemia in young adults. J Vasc Surg 1989;9:334-341.

49. Hallett JW Jr, Greenwood LH, Robison JG. Lower extremity arterial disease in young adults. Ann Surg 1985;11:647-652.

50. Flinn WR, McDaniel MD, Yao JST, et al. Antithrombin III deficiency as a reflection of dynamic protein metabolism in patients undergoing vascular reconstruction. J Vasc Surg 1984;1:888-895.

51. Love PE, Santoro SA. Antiphospholipid antibodies: Anticardiolipin and the lupus anticoagulant in systemic lupus erythematosus (SLE) and in non-SLE disorders. Ann Int Med 1990;112:682-698.

52. Bell WR, Royall RM. Heparin-associated thrombocytopenia: A comparison of three heparin preparations. N Engl J Med 1980;303:902-907.

53. Ansell JE, Price JM, Shah S, et al. Heparin-induced thrombocytopenia: What is its real frequency? Chest 1985;88:878-882.

54. Bailey RT, Ursick JA, Heim KL, et al. Heparin-associated thrombocytopenia: A prospective comparison of bovine lung heparin, manufactured by a new process, and porcine intestinal heparin. Drug Intell Clin Pharmacol 1986;20:374-378.

55. Green D, Martin GJ, Shoichet SH, et al. Thrombocytopenia in a prospective, randomized, double-blind trial of bovine and porcine heparin. Am J Med Sci 1984;288:60-64.

56. Powers PJ, Kelton JG, Carter CJ. Studies on the frequency of heparin-associated thrombocytopenia. Thromb Res 1984;33:439-443.

57. Kakkasseril JS, Cranley JJ, Panke T, et al. Heparin-induced thrombocytopenia: A prospective study of 142 patients. J Vasc Surg 1985;2:382-384.

58. Bell WR, Romasulo PA, Alving BM, et al. Thrombocytopenia occurring during the administration of heparin: A prospective study in 52 patients. Ann Int Med 1976;85:155-160.

59. Malcolm ID, Wigmore TA, Steinbrecher VP. Heparin-associated thrombocytopenia: Low frequency in 104 patients treated with heparin of intestinal mucosal origin. Can Med Assoc J 1979;120:1086-1088.

60. Makhoul RG, Greenberg CS, McCann RL. Heparin-associated thrombocytopenia and thrombosis: A serious clinical problem and potential solution. J Vasc Surg 1986;4:522-528.

61. Laster J, Cikrit D, Walker N, et al. The heparin-induced thrombocytopenia syndrome: An update. Surgery 1987;102:763-770.

62. Ramirez-Lassepas M, Cipolle RJ, Rodvold KA, et al. Heparin-induced thrombocytopenia in patients with cerebrovascular ischemic disease. Neurology 1984;34:736-740.

63. Stanton PE, Evans JR, Lefemine AA, et al. White clot syndrome. South Med J 1988;81:616-620.

64. Kappa JR, Fisher CA, Berkowitz HD, et al. Heparin-induced platelet activation in sixteen surgical patients: Diagnosis and management. J Vasc Surg 1987;5:101-109.

65. Clarke R, Daly L, Robinson K, et al. Hyperhomocysteinemia: An independent risk factor for vascular disease. N Engl J Med 324:1149-1155.

66. Boers GHJ, Smals AGH, Trijbels FJM, et al. Heterozygosity for homocystinuria in premature peripheral and cerebrovascular occlusive arterial disease. N Engl J Med 1985;313:709-715.

67. Malinow MR, Kang SS, Taylor LM, et al. Prevalence of hyperhomocyst(e)inemia in patients with peripheral arterial occlusive disease. Circulation 1989;79:1180-1188.

68. Coull BM, Malinow R, Beamer N, et al. Elevated plasma homocyst(e)ine concentration as a possible independent risk factor for stroke. Stroke 1990;21:572-576.

69. Araki A, Sako Y, Fukushima Y, et al. Plasma sulfhydryl-containing amino acids in patients with cerebral infarction and in hypertensive subjects. Atherosclerosis 1989;79:139-146.

70. Brattstrom LE, Hardebo JE, Hultberg BL. Moderate homocysteinemia—a possible risk factor for arteriosclerotic cerebrovascular disease. Stroke 1984;15:1012-1026.

71. Murai A, Miyahara T, Fujimoto N, et al. Lp(a) lipoprotein as a risk factor for coronary heart disease and cerebral infarction. Atherosclerosis 1986;59:199-204.

72. Zenker G, Koltringer P, Bone G, et al. Lipoprotein(a) as a strong indicator for cerebrovascular disease. Stroke 1986;17:942-945.

73. Koltringer P, Jurgens G. A dominant role of lipoprotein(a) in the investigation and evaluation of parameters indicating the development of cervical atherosclerosis. Atherosclerosis 1985;58:187-198.

74. Wiseman S, Kenchington G, Dain R, et al. Influence of smoking and plasma factors on patency of femoropopliteal vein grafts. Br Med J 1989;299:643-647.

11

Nonatherosclerotic Causes of Lower Extremity Claudication

Thomas C. Park, MD, Daniel W. Hamre, MD, John M. Porter, MD, Portland, Oregon

Clinicians dealing with patients with claudication have appropriately focused on atherosclerosis, as it is the cause of symptoms in 90%–95% of claudicants. A small percentage of patients, however, experience claudication unrelated to atherosclerosis or its attendant complications. One may assume that practitioners of various specialties of internal medicine, such as neurology, immunology, or medical genetics should be the primary physicians involved in the diagnosis and treatment of such patients. Unfortunately, such is not usually the case. In most medical communities, vascular surgeons must assume the primary responsibility, using various internists as consultants. Thus, the fully trained vascular surgeon must be familiar with the nonatherosclerotic causes of lower extremity ischemia.

The primary causes of nonatherosclerotic claudication and limb ischemia are listed below, with the details of these conditions presented in the following tables. Buerger's disease is not discussed herein, as it is the subject of a separate Basic Data section.[1]

  I. Congenital-metabolic
    A. Ehlers-Danlos syndrome
    B. Pseudoxanthoma elasticum
 II. Congenital-anatomic
    A. Popliteal artery entrapment syndrome
    B. Persistent sciatic artery
    C. Abdominal aortic coarctation
    D. Cystic adventitial disease
III. Arteritis-Behçet's disease
IV. Radiation arteritis
 V. Ergot intoxication
VI. Neurogenic claudication

From the Division of Vascular Surgery, Oregon Health Sciences University, Portland, Ore.

Table I. Ehlers-Danlos syndrome

		Ref.
Etiology	Nine types of Ehlers-Danlos known, various biochemical defects leading to disorder of collagen synthesis and processing	12,16
	Type IV: arterial ecchymotic type (deficiency of type III collagen)	
Incidence	Unknown, but 4% of Ehlers-Danlos patients are type IV	3-5,12
Age	Mean 26, ±12 yr	3
Vessels involved	Aorta, visceral, subclavian-axillary, carotid-vertebral, iliac, femoral, popliteal trifurcation, brachial-radial, coronary arteries	3-5,12
Vascular symptoms	Spontaneous rupture of arteries with ecchymosis in lower extremity	2,3,8,10,12
	50% spontaneous hemorrhage (popliteal trifurcation > femoral = aorta > iliac)	
	42% aneurysm or dissection (visceral > carotid > brachial-radial > aorta)	
Other symptoms	Hyperplastic skin, hypermobile joint, and fragile skin	
Diagnosis	Duplex and CT scan preferred	3,5
	Avoid arteriogram: 67% morbidity and 17% mortality	
Treatment	Conservative with compression and transfusion in lower extremity	5,7,9
	Standard repair frequently unsuccessful, extremely friable arteries	
	Surgical repair with buttressed sutures or ligation of the involved artery	
Outcome	44% die before intervention; 29% operative mortality; 64%-76% overall mortality; 51% die before age of 40	3,9

Table II. Pseudoxanthoma elasticum

		Ref.
Etiology	Inherited disorder of elastic fibers	13-24
	Precise biochemical abnormality unknown	
Incidence	1:160,000	13,15,16,19,20,23
Male/female	1:1	16
Age	2nd-4th decade	13,21-24
Vessels involved	Stenosis or occlusion of peripheral, cerebral, or coronary arteries	22
Pathology	Fragmentation and clumping of the elastic tissue and medial calcification of muscular arteries and endocardium	13-24
Vascular symptoms	18% intermittent claudication	13-24
Nonvascular symptoms	Gastrointestinal hemorrhage, visual impairment, hypertension, angina	13-24
Diagnosis	85% with angioid streaks of fundus	13-24
	Skin biopsy: fragmented, calcified elastin	
	Xanthomatous papular rash	
	Advanced, marked arterial calcification	
Treatment	Standard vascular repair works satisfactorily but requires suturing to highly calcified arteries	17,20-22
Outcome	Progressive disease with slightly decreased life expectancy	15,21-24
	Revascularization outcome not affected	

Table III. Popliteal artery entrapment

		Ref.
Etiology	Congenital anatomic variants in popliteal fossa, resulting in popliteal artery compression or occlusion (at least 20 different anatomic variants) Popliteal artery medial to medial head of gastrocnemius in 60%-74% Popliteus and soleus muscle may be involved	25-33,35, 37-39
Incidence	Unknown ≈300 cases reported 3/86 in autopsy study	25,27,29, 34,36,38
Male/female	7-10:1	26-29,32,33
Age	60% <30 yr	25,27,29, 34,36,38
Symptoms	90% claudication 10% acute ischemia	26-29,32,33
Bilateral	20%-36%	27,30,32-34
Diagnosis	Duplex: popliteal artery attenuation with duplex scan in both neutral and plantar/dorsiflexion, but not specific as seen in 30%-50% of normals also Arteriogram: medial deviation of popliteal artery, segmental occlusion, and post-stenotic dilatation CT scan/MRI: may reveal detailed anatomic relations	25,33,35-37
Treatment	Early operation to avoid occlusion, embolization Complete exposure of popliteal artery (posterior approach) Divide entrapping structure Interposition vein graft if arterial damage (avoid patching)	25-33,36,37
Outcome	94% patency if early myotomy only 58%-80% with revascularization	26,28,33

Table IV. Persistent sciatic artery

		Ref.
Etiology	Persistence of embryonic sciatic artery (branch of hypergastric artery) with hypoplasia or atresia of iliofemoral artery	40,43-45,47
Incidence	0.01%-0.06% of arteriograms 63%-79% with complete sciatic artery; 7%-8% with incomplete sciatic artery; 26% are bilateral	43,45,48,49
Age	6 mo-84 yr	43,45
Associated condition	44% develop aneurysms in sciatic artery; 12% of aneurysms are bilateral AV malformation, lymphatic anomaly, and neurofibromatosis have been reported	41-43,45,46
Symptoms	31% buttock pain/mass (aneurysm); 25% claudication; 11% gangrene; 12% hemihypertrophy of limb	43-45
Diagnosis	Absent femoral pulse with palpable popliteal pulse (rare) Arteriogram with selective catheterization of internal iliac arteries	43-48

Treatment and outcome	Occluded sciatic artery: standard leg bypass, usually to popliteal artery
	Aneurysm:
	  80% success with resection and primary anastomosis
	  86% success with proximal-distal ligation and vein bypass (avoids injury to sciatic nerve)
	Arteriographic occlusion with bypass reported
		40,45-48

Table V. Abdominal aortic coarctation

		Ref.
Etiology	Probable congenital development defect	50,51,53,54,57,60
Incidence	2% of all aortic coarctations	52-55,60
	1:62,500 in an autopsy study	
Age	2nd-3rd decade	50,54,56,58,60
Signs and symptoms	Hypertension either asymptomatic or with headache and fatigue	50-60
	Claudication, cardiac failure, diminished lower extremity pulses, abdominal bruit	
Vessels involved	80% renal artery stenosis (bilateral); 22% splanchnic artery stenosis; 70% multiple renal arteries	54,56-60
Diagnosis	Aortography with detailed study of splanchnic and renal arteries	50-60
Medical Tx	By 4th decade; death due to cerebral hemorrhage and cardiac failure associated with untreated hypertension	50,54-60
Surgical treatment	Thoracoabdominal aortic bypass with renal revascularization	50,54-58,60
	0%-8% operative mortality	
Surgical outcome	89%-100% are normotensive or attain easily controlled hypertension	50,54-58,60
	Normal growth, development, and life span	
	Excellent long-term graft patency reported	

Table VI. Cystic adventitial disease

		Ref.
Etiology	Intramural cyst between media and adventitia	61,66,71
	Microtrauma, exotopic ganglion, and synovial rest inclusions are possible causes	
Incidence	1/1,200 claudication	61,63,67
	1/1,000 arteriograms	
Age	11-70 yr; Mean, 42 yr	61,63,67
Male/female	4.6:1	61
Location	Popliteal > femoral > iliac > radial > ulnar	61,64,65,68
Symptoms	Sudden onset of calf cramps followed by intermittent claudication exacerbated by flexion of knee	61,62
Diagnosis	Arteriogram: smooth hourglass narrowing or curvilinear stenosis (scimitar sign)	61,62
	1/3 complete occlusion	
Treatment	Cyst evacuation with patent artery effective, but cyst may recur	61,66,68,71
	Local patch angioplasty less successful	
	Resection and bypass (vein) for occlusion	

Outcome[61]					
Nonresection (56 patients)			Resection (42 patients)		
Method	Success (%)	Follow-up	Method	Success (%)	Follow-up
Aspiration (2)	100	24 mo	Vein graft (30)	95	38 mo
Open evacuation (41)	90	23 mo	Synthetic graft (7)	86	30 mo
Evacuation/vein patch (9)	78	18 mo	Homograft (2)	100	15 mo
Evacuation/synthetic patch (4)	75	N/A (mean)	End-to-end (3)	100	12 mo (mean)

Table VII. Behçet's disease

		Ref.
Etiology	Unknown: immune mechanism suspected	72,81
	Nonspecific panarteritis linked to HLA B5	
Incidence	0.005% of U.S. population (more prevalent in Turkey, Greece, and Japan)	72,75,77,
	2.2%-7.7% have arterial complications	80,81
	6%-50% have venous thrombosis	
Male/female	9:1	72
Age	20-56 yr (mean = 30 yr)	72
Pathology	Fragmentation and splitting of elastic fibers, degeneration of vasa vasorum with perivascular round cell infiltrate	72,79
Vascular symptoms	Claudication or mass in lower extremity	72,79
	Aneurysm (58%-65%); occlusion (33%-35%); both (9%)	
Nonvascular symptoms	Orogenital aphthous ulcers, uveitis, erythema nodosum–like lesions, and mesenteric vasculitis	72-81
Location	Aneurysm: aorta 28%; pulmonary 23%; popliteal 7%; iliac 6%; carotid 4%	72,79
	Occlusion: pulmonary 20%; subclavian 14%; popliteal 9%; iliac 7%; femoral 5%; aorta 2%	
Diagnosis	CT scan/arteriogram	72-81
	Pseudoaneurysms develop at arterial puncture site	
Treatment	Chlorambucil and azathioprine have been used	74,76
	Resection with bypass for aneurysm	
Outcome	20% mortality in patients with arterial involvement	72,74,75,80
	Vessels are fragile, leading to high recurrence of pseudoaneurysm at anastomosis	
	Frequent thromboses of vascular grafts	

Table VIII. Radiation disease

		Ref.
Etiology	Radiation lower abdomen and pelvis for CA of cervix, ovary, bladder, prostate, testicle, and lymphoma	82,83,86
Pathology	Acute: injury to endothelium with increased permeability to lipids, platelet + fibrin deposition	82,83,86
	Weeks: fibrosis and hemolytic necrosis of media and adventitia	
	Months: thickening of intima, adventitial and periadventitial fibrosis with variable incidence of large artery occlusion or aortoiliac arteries	
Incidence	Unknown	82-87
Dosage	4125-7500 rads	82-87
Age	9.5-75 yr (mean = 65 yr)	82,83
Interval	2-24 yr (mean = 9 yr)	82-87
Location	Iliac > femoral > aorta	82-87
Symptoms	Claudication	82,83
	Rest pain	
Diagnosis	Arteriogram: segmental occlusion with diffuse involvement	82-87
Treatment	Standard revascularization technique with extraanatomic bypass to avoid radiated field	82-87
	Avoid thromboendarterectomy	
	Successful early PTCA reported (2 cases) but no follow-up available	

58. Stanley JC, Graham LM, Whitehouse WM Jr, et al. Developmental occlusive disease of the abdominal aorta and the splanchnic and renal arteries. Am J Surg 1981;142:190-196.

59. Roques X, Bourdeaud'hui A, Choussat A, et al. Coarctation of the abdominal aorta. Ann Vasc Surg 1988;2:138-144.

60. DeBakey ME, Garrett HE, Howell JF, et al. Coarctation of the abdominal aorta with renal arterial stenosis: Surgical considerations. Ann Surg 1967;165:830-843.

61. Flanigan DP, Burnahm SJ, Goodreau JJ, et al. Summary of cases of adventitial cystic disease of the popliteal artery. Ann Surg 1979;189:165-175.

62. Owen ER, Speechly-Dick EM, Kour NW, et al. Cystic adventitial disease of the popliteal artery: A case of spontaneous resolution. Eur J Vasc Surg 1990;4:319-321.

63. Bunker SR, Lauten GS, Hutton JE. Cystic adventitial disease of the popliteal artery. AJR 1981;136:1209-1212.

64. Durham JR, McIntyre KE. Adventitial cystic disease of the radial artery. J Cardiovasc Surg 1989;30:517-520.

65. Velasquez G, Zollikofer C, Nath HP, et al. Cystic arterial adventitial degeneration. Radiology 1980;134:19-21.

66. Hildreth DG. Cystic adventitial disease of the common femoral artery. Am J Surg 1975;130:92-96.

67. Roth JA, Kearney P, Wittman CJ. Cystic adventitial degeneration of the common femoral artery. Arch Surg 1977;112:210-212.

68. Marzo L, Peetz DJ, Bewtra C, et al. Cystic adventitial degeneration of the femoral artery: Is evacuation and cyst excision worthwhile as a definitive therapy? Surgery 1987;101:587-593.

69. Fox RL, Kahn M, Adler J, et al. Adventitial cystic disease of the popliteal artery: Failure of percutaneous transluminal angioplasty as a therapeutic modality. J Vasc Surg 1985;2:464-467.

70. Samson RH, Willis PD. Popliteal artery occlusion caused by cystic adventitial disease: Successful treatment by urokinase followed by nonresectional cystotomy. J Vasc Surg 1980;12:591-593.

71. Jay GD, Ross FL, Mason RA, et al. Clinical and chemical characterization of an adventitial popliteal cyst. J Vasc Surg 1989;9:448-451.

72. Hamza M. Large artery involvement in Behçet's disease. J Rheumatol 1987;14:554-559.

73. International Study Group for Behçet's Disease. Criteria for diagnosis of Behçet's disease. Lancet 1990;335:1078-1080.

74. Bartlett ST, McCarthy WJ III, Palmer AS, et al. Multiple aneurysms in Behçet's disease. Arch Surg 1988;123:1004-1008.

75. Little AG, Zarins CK. Abdominal aortic aneurysms and Behçet's disease. Surgery 1982;91:359-362.

76. Yazici H, Pazarli H, Barnes CG, et al. A controlled trial of azathioprine in Behçet's syndrome. N Engl J Med 1990;322:281-285.

77. Ozer ZG, Cetin M, Kahraman C. Thrombophlebitis in Behçet's disease. VASA 1985;14:379-382.

78. Dhobb M, Ammar F, Bensaid Y, et al. Arterial manifestations in Behçet's disease: Four new cases. Ann Vasc Surg 1986;1:249-252.

79. Park JH, Han MC, Bettmann MA. Arterial manifestation of Behçet's disease. AJR 1984;143:821-825.

80. Jenkins AM, MacPherson AIS, Nolan B, et al. Peripheral aneurysms in Behçet's disease. Br J Surg 1976;63:199-202.

81. O'Duffy JD. Behçet's syndrome. N Engl J Med 1990;322:326-328.

82. Rosenfeld JC, Savarese RP, DeLaurentis DA. Management of extremity ischemia secondary to radiation therapy. J Cardiovasc Surg 1987;28:266-269.

83. McCready RA, Hyde GL, Bivins BA, et al. Radiation-induced arterial injuries. Surgery 1983;93:306-312.

84. Benson EP. Radiation injury to large arteries. Radiology 1973;106:195-197.

85. Gunthaner DR, Schmitz L. Percutaneous transluminal angioplasty of radiation-induced arterial stenoses. Radiology 1982;144:77-78.

86. Savlov ED, Nahhas WA, May AG. Iliac and femoral arteriosclerosis following pelvic irradiation for carcinoma of the ovary. Obstet Gynecol 1969;34:345-351.

87. Lee DH, Sapire D, Markowitz R, et al. Radiation injury to abdominal aorta and iliac artery sustained in infancy. S Afr Med J 1976;50:658-660.

88. Wells KE, Steed DL, Zajko AB, et al. Recognition and treatment of arterial insufficiency from Cafergot. J Vasc Surg 1986;4:8-15.

89. Baader W, Herman C, Johansen K. St. Anthony's fire: Successful reversal of ergotamine-induced peripheral vasospasm by hydrostatic dilatation. Ann Vasc Surg 1990;4:597-599.

90. Tanner JR. St. Anthony's fire, then and now: A case report and historical review. Can J Surg 1987;30:291-293.

91. Weaver R, Phillips M, Vacek JL. St. Anthony's fire: A medieval disease in modern times: Case history. Angiology 1989;40:929-932.

92. Tarnower A, Alquire P. Ergotism masquerading as arteritis. Postgrad Med 1989;85:103-108.

93. Kemerer VF, Dagher FJ, Osher Pais S. Successful treatment of ergotism with nifedipine. AJR 1984;143:333-334.

94. Shackford SR, Davis JW. Refractory vasospasm occurring in a trauma patient receiving dihydroergotamine and heparin. Crit Care Med 1988;16:909-910.

95. Cunningham M, Torrente A, Ekow JM, et al. Vascular spasm and gangrene during heparin-dihydroergotamine prophylaxis. Br J Surg 1984;71:829-831.

96. Dagher FJ, Pais SO, Richards W, et al. Severe unilateral ischemia of the lower extremity caused by ergotamine: Treatment with nifedipine. Surgery 1985;97:369-373.

97. Harats N, Worth R, Benson MD. Spinal claudication in systemic amyloidosis. J Rheumatol 1989;16:1003-1006.

98. Kondo M, Matsuda H, Kureya S, et al. Electrophysiological studies of intermittent claudication in lumbar stenosis. Spine 1989;14:862-866.

99. Moreland LW, Lopez-Mendez A, Alarcon G. Spinal stenosis: A comprehensive review of the literature. Sem Arth Rheum 1989;19:127-149.

100. Madsen JR, Heros RC. Spinal arteriovenous malformation and neurogenic claudication: Report of two cases. J Neurosurg 1988;68:793-797.

101. Dodge LD, Bohlman HH, Rhodes RS. Concurrent lumbar spinal stenosis and peripheral vascular disease. A report of nine patients. Clin Ortho Rel Res 1988;230:141-148.

102. Schnebel B, Kingston S, Watkins R, et al. Comparison of MRI to contrast CT in the diagnosis of spinal stenosis. Spine 1989;14:332-337.

103. Stanton PE Jr, Rosenthal D, Clark M, et al. Differentiation of vascular and neurogenic claudication. Am Surg 1987;53:71-76.

104. Ciric I, Mikheal MA. Lumbar spinal-lateral recess stenosis. Neurol Clinics 1985;3:417-423.

105. Goodreau JJ, Creasy JK, Flanigan DP, et al. Rational approach to the differentiation of vascular and neurogenic claudication. Surgery 1978;84:749-757.

106. Karayannacos PE, Yashon D, Vasko JS. Narrow lumbar spinal canal with "vascular" syndromes. Arch Surg 1976;111:803-806.

107. Verbiest H. Neurogenic Intermittent Claudication. New York: American Elsevier, 1976.

12

Genetic and Metabolic Causes of Arterial Disease

James I. Fann, MD, Ronald L. Dalman, MD, and E. John Harris, Jr., MD, Stanford, California

Heritable disorders of the arterial wall constitute a substantial minority of arterial diseases of importance to the vascular surgeon. The pathophysiologic basis of these entities is compromised mural integrity caused by the altered architecture and tensile strength of collagen, elastin, or the extracellular matrix stabilizing these fibers. Included in this category of arterial diseases are Marfan syndrome, Ehlers-Danlos syndrome, pseudoxanthoma elasticum, some of the mucopolysaccharidoses, homocystinuria, and a newly described variant, hyperhomocyst(e)inemia. Although distinct yet often subtle phenotypic features may be present at birth, the majority of

From the Department of Cardiothoracic Surgery and the Division of Vascular Surgery, Department of Surgery, Stanford University School of Medicine, Stanford, Calif.

patients escape diagnosis until some catastrophic event occurs, which is often vascular in origin. The term "cystic medial necrosis" has been abandoned because it represents a descriptive term for a nonspecific pathologic process affecting the tunica media and does not characterize a separate disease entity. Elastin and collagen fragmentation, fibrosis, and subsequent medial necrosis are common morphologic features of aging associated with aortic injury and repair. In the genetic and metabolic diseases discussed herein, this process of mural injury is accelerated, and each disorder has some unique characteristic in this process. The following tables reflect the condensation of relevant information concerning these genetic and metabolic disorders, including recent developments in their diagnosis and treatment. Interestingly, advances in molecular biology have provided new insight into the specific genetic defects responsible for the disorders with the promise of focused molecular biologic therapies in the near future.

Table III. Pseudoxanthoma elasticum

		References
History	Gronblad (1929) noted skin and ocular changes; vascular abnormalities recognized (1940s)	51-53
Etiology	Exact defect unknown; at least four (possibly five) distinct forms; type I autosomal dominant form produces cutaneous changes and vascular complications (angina, coronary artery disease, and peripheral vascular disease); type II autosomal dominant variant produces minimal vascular symptoms and few cutaneous changes; the recessive types I and II are associated with milder vascular and retinal changes and increased cutaneous laxity; the fifth type (autosomal recessive) associated with severe ophthalmologic lesions	52, 54-58
Incidence	1/70,000 to 1/160,000	59, 60
Male/female ratio	Women greater than men	61,62
Age at presentation	Childhood, young adult; characteristically symptomatic arterial occlusive disease in third or fourth decade, although disease may be recognized as early as age 9	55-58, 60, 61, 63-66
Pathology	Medial elastic degeneration, followed by calcification, fragmentation, and secondary intimal proliferation causing luminal narrowing; cardiac pathology includes fibroelastic endocardial thickening	55, 63, 67
Vessels involved	Degenerative arteriosclerosis involving medium-sized arteries, sparing aorta; tortuosity, narrowing, and angiomatoid malformation of visceral and peripheral arteries	55, 63
Clinical presentation		
Cardiovascular	Account for life-threatening complications; diminished pulses and chronic occlusive arterial disease in 24% to 80%; premature arteriosclerosis, intermittent claudication, periodic abdominal pain, angina, and myocardial infarction; renovascular hypertension; degenerative vascular changes result in hypertension (up to one fourth of patients); mitral valve prolapse	52, 54-59, 61, 63-68
Nonvascular	Loose skin with multiple creases; small yellow-orange cutaneous papules in intertriginous areas; chorioretinal abnormalities	52, 54-57, 59, 63, 67
Diagnosis	Confirmed by histopathology (cutaneous elastic fiber mineralization); radiograph shows extensive arterial calcification in young patients without other risk factors for arteriosclerosis	54, 56, 62, 66, 69, 70
Treatment		
Medical	Hypertensive management; control risk factors for atherogenesis	55, 57
Surgical	Same indication as for patients with arteriosclerotic occlusive disease; conventional techniques (autogenous vein bypass grafting and endarterectomy) have been employed	18, 19, 65, 71, 72
Long-term prognosis	Life expectancy is reduced; patients may lead normal lives until their fifth or sixth decade; silent cardiovascular disease can develop at early age and close follow-up is important	56, 63

Table IVA. Mucopolysaccharidoses—General

		References
Etiology	Inherited disorders of proteoglycan metabolism and degradation; currently seven variants, characterized by storage and urinary excretion of abnormal quantities of mucopolysaccharides	18, 73, 74
Incidence	Overall incidence approximately 5/100,000	73, 74
Pathology	Aorta and pulmonary artery show intimal lesions of mucopolysaccharide deposition or pseudoatheromas; endocardial thickening and fibroelastosis occur	73, 75, 76
Vessels involved	Coronary and pulmonary arteries; aorta	18, 75, 76
Clinical presentation		
Cardiovascular	Mitral valve disease most common; mild to moderate aortic regurgitation occurs; tricuspid and pulmonic valvular disease is less common; coronary artery disease seen, although myocardial infarction has not been reported; systemic hypertension contributes to myocardial insufficiency	73, 75-78
Nonvascular	Phenotypic characteristics (see Table IVC)	
Diagnosis	Abnormal urinary excretion of proteoglycan (see Table IVB) and characteristic phenotype (see Table IVC)	
Treatment	Directed at clinical symptomatology (see Table IVC)	
Prognosis	Patients typically succumb at young age; deaths are of cardiopulmonary origin, a combination of hypoxia and compromised left ventricular function; narrowing of coronary arteries do not necessarily imply symptomatic coronary ischemia since there has been no reported cases of myocardial infarction	73, 76

Table IVB. Mucopolysaccharidoses—Specific

Eponym	Type	Deficient enzyme	Stored mucopolysaccharide	Incidence	Inheritance	References
Hurler	MPS-I-H	α-L-iduronidase	DS, HS	1/100,000	Autosomal recessive	73-76, 79
Scheie	MPS-I-S	α-L-iduronidase	DS, HS	1/500,000	Autosomal recessive	73-76, 78, 80
Hunter	MPS-II	Iduronate sulfatase	DS, HS	1 to 2/150,000	X-linked recessive	73-76, 81
Sanfilippo A	MPS-III-A	Heparan N- sulfatase	HS	Rare	Autosomal recessive	73-76
Sanfilippo B	MPS-III-B	N-acetyl-α-D-glucosaminidase	HS	Rare	Autosomal recessive	73-76
Sanfilippo C	MPS-III-C	Lysosomal N-acetylase	HS	Rare	Autosomal recessive	73-76
Sanfilippo D	MPS-III-D	N-acetyl-α-D-glucosaminide-β-sulfatase	HS	Rare	Autosomal recessive	73-76
Morquio A	MPS-IV-A	Galactose, N- acetyl galactosamine-6-sulfatase	KS	Very rare	Autosomal recessive	73-76
Morquio B	MPS-IV-B	β-galactosidase	KS	Very rare	Autosomal recessive	73-76
Maroteaux-Lamy	MPS-VI	Arylsulfatase B, N-acetylgalactosamine-4-sulfatase	DS	Very rare	Autosomal recessive	74, 76, 77, 82
Sly-Neufeld	MPS-VII	β-glucuronidase	DS, HS	Very rare	Autosomal recessive	74

DS = dermatan sulfate; HS = heparan sulfate; KS = keratan sulfate.

Table IVC. Mucopolysaccharidoses — Specific

Eponym	Clinical presentation	Cardiovascular	Diagnosis	Treatment	Prognosis	References
Hurler	Skeletal; ocular; neurologic, corneal clouding; mental retardation; gibbus deformity	Mucopolysaccharide deposition in coronary arteries, aorta, pulmonary arteries; diminished pulses; cool limbs	Urine DS, HS	None	Death before age 10 in most cases	73-76, 79
Scheie	Coarse facial features; diffuse corneal clouding; mild to moderate skeletal abnormalities; broad hands; short stubby feet; fixation of phalangeal joints	Aortic valve disease; aortic regurgitation; mitral valve disease; coronary artery disease	Urine DS, HS skin biopsy	Valve replacement	Normal intelligence, survival into adulthood	73-76, 78, 80
Hunter	Stiff joints; dwarfism; hepatosplenomegaly; progressive deafness; normal intelligence	Cardiomegaly; coronary artery disease; valvular insufficiency (mitral more than aortic); diminished pulses; cool limbs	Urine DS, HS	Valve replacement	Longer survival than Hurler syndrome	73-76, 81
Sanfilippo	Severe mental retardation; mild somatic stigmata; corneal clouding unusual; mild facial and skeletal abnormalities	No cardiovascular involvement	Urine HS	None	Death occurs in second decade	73-76
Morquio	Corneal clouding	Aortic valve disease	Urine KS	Valve replacement	Survive into adulthood	73-76
Maroteaux-Lamy	Dwarfism; coarse facial features; stiff joints; corneal opacity	Mitral and aortic stenosis and insufficiency	Urine and tissue DS	Valve replacement	Death in first decade	74, 76, 77, 82
Sly-Neufeld	Hepatosplenomegaly; dysostosis multiplex; white cell inclusions; mental retardation	Aortic valve disease	Urine DS	?	?	74

DS = dermatan sulfate; HS = heparan sulfate; KS = keratan sulfate.

Table V. Homocystinuria and hypermonocyst(e)inemia

		References
History	Field (1962) reported syndrome of elevated urinary ho-mocysteine associated with abnormalities in four organ systems: eye, skeleton, central nervous system, and vascular system; Mudd (1964) identified cystathionine β-synthase as enzymatic defect; Barber and Spaeth (1967) developed categorization of homocystinuria by responsiveness of plasma and urinary homocysteine to exogenous pyridoxine (vitamin B_6); Boers (1985) described association of heterozygous cystathionine β-synthase trait and premature arterial occlusive disease	83-86
Etiology	Homocystinuria (cystathionine β-synthase deficiency) is an inborn error of transsulfuration pathway; in homozygous form, cystathionine β-synthase deficiency is characterized by high levels of homocystine, methionine, and homo-cysteine-cysteine mixed disulfide in urine and plasma; a heterozygous form of cystathionine β-synthase deficiency can lead to impaired homocysteine metabolism with elevated plasma homocysteine levels; other causes of impaired homocysteine metabolism include deficiencies of vitamin B_6, vitamin B_{12}, and folate	87-91
Incidence		
Homozygous cystathionine β-synthase deficiency	1/335,000	
Heterozygous cystathionine β-synthase deficiency	1/70 to 200	86, 87
Male/female ratio		
Homozygous	1:1	92
Heterozygous	Not defined	
Age at presentation		
Homozygous	Childhood, 2 to 30 years old. Risk of thromboembolic disease increases with age: 25% by age 16, 50% by age 29	87, 92
Heterozygous	Adulthood; may identify risk for premature atherosclerosis; onset younger than 50 years old	86, 93, 94
Pathology	Thrombi and emboli reported in almost every major artery and vein; diffuse or patchy intimal thickening with fibrosis; fragmentation of medial muscle fibers with increased interstitial collagen; elastic tissue of large arteries may be fragmented; atherosclerotic aneurysmal degeneration of abdominal aorta has been described	87, 95-102
Vessels involved	Nearly every large or medium-sized artery; any major vein	87, 100, 101
Clinical presentation		
Vascular	Arterial occlusion can occur in any vessel at any age, leading to hemiparesis, seizures, cor pulmonale secondary to pulmonary artery occlusion, leg ischemia, or hypertension secondary to renal artery occlusion; also, high risk for venous thrombosis; heterozygous trait or hyper-homocyst(e)inemia may cause premature coronary artery disease, cerebrovascular disease, or peripheral arterial disease with myocardial infarction, transient ischemic attack, stroke, claudication, ischemic leg ulcers, and early failures of arterial reconstruction	88, 90-92, 94, 100-106

Table V. Homocystinuria and hypermonocyst(e)inemia—cont'd

		References
Nonvascular	Major nonvascular features of homozygous form include abnormalities of ocular (lenticular dislocation, usually downward, and associated myopia and quivering of iris), skeletal (osteoporosis, dolichostenomelia, or thinning and lengthening of long bones, pectus excavatum, pes cavus, and genu valgum), and central nervous systems (mental retardation with median IQ of 64, seizure disorders, psychiatric abnormalities)	87, 92, 107-109
Diagnosis	Based on typical clinical signs and biochemical abnormalities; the most consistent biochemical finding in homozygous state is homocystinuria, verified by urinary cyanide-nitroprusside reaction; direct enzyme assay for cystathionine β-synthase deficiency can be performed on liver biopsy specimens, cultured skin fibroblasts, or phytohemagglutinin-stimulated lymphocytes; hyperhomocyst(e)inemia in patients with symptomatic occlusive atherosclerosis defined by measurement of free and protein-bound forms of homocysteine, homocysteine disulfide, and mixed disulfide homocysteine-cystine by high-pressure liquid chromatography. Some advocate methionine loading test prior to evaluation of plasma homocyst(e)ine levels	92, 110-115
Treatment		
Medical	High-dose pyridoxine first used successfully in homocystinuric children; in most adult patients, small doses of folate are usually effective in reducing elevated levels of plasma homocyst(e)ine; for folate-resistant patients, small doses of pyridoxine, choline, cyanocobalamin, riboflavin, troxerutin, and betaine have been successful in reducing plasma homocyst(e)ine levels	113-116
Surgical	Standard endarterectomy and bypass techniques employed with success for arterial occlusive disease, although long-term results with hyperhomocyst(e)inemia may be inferior to those in patients with normal homocyst(e)ine levels; for homozygous patients undergoing any surgical procedure, deep venous thrombosis prophylaxis is recommended	105, 106, 113, 115
Prognosis	In homozygous patients, mortality by age 20 was less than 5% among those responsive to pyridoxine and 20% among those not responsive; thromboembolism was responsible for the large majority of deaths; role of nutritional modifications in hyperhomocyst(e)inemia remains incompletely defined	116

REFERENCES

1. McKusick VA. Heritable Disorders of Connective Tissue, 4th ed. St. Louis: CV Mosby, 1972, pp 61-201.
2. Achard C. Arachnodactylie. Bull Mem Soc Med Hop (Paris) 1902;19:834.
3. Boerger F. Ueber zwei Falle vin Archnodaktylie. Z Kinderheilk 1914;12:161.
4. Baer RW, Taussig HB, Oppenheimer EH. Congenital aneurysmal dilitation of the aorta associated with arachnodactyly. Bull Hopkins Hosp 1943;72:309.
5. Pyeritz RE, McKusick VA. The Marfan syndrome: Diagnosis and management. N Engl J Med 1979;300:772-777.
6. Roberts WC, Honig HS. The spectrum of cardiovascular disease in the Marfan syndrome: A clinicomorphologic study of 18 necropsy patients and comparison to 151 previously reported necropsy patients. Am Heart J 1982;104:115-135.
7. Francke U, Furthmayr H. Genes and gene products involved in Marfan syndrome. Semin Thorac Cardiovasc Surg 1993;5:3-10.
8. Spangler RD, Nora JJ, Lortscher RH, et al. Echocardiography in Marfan's syndrome. Chest 1976;69:72-78.

9. Brown OR, DeMots H, Kloster FE, et al. Aortic root dilatation and mitral valve prolapse in Marfan's syndrome. Circulation 1975;52:651-657.

10. Geva T, Hegosh J, Frand M. The clinical course and echocardiographic features for Marfan's syndrome in childhood. Am J Dis Child 1987;141:1179-1182.

11. Marsalese DL, Moodie DS, Vacante M, et al. Marfan's syndrome: Natural history and long-term follow-up of cardiovascular involvement. J Am Coll Cardiol 1989;14:422-428.

12. Hirata K, Triposkiadis F, Sparks E, et al. The Marfan syndrome: Cardiovascular physical findings and diagnostic correlates. Am Heart J 1992;123:743-752.

13. El Habbal MH. Cardiovascular manifestations of Marfan's syndrome in the young. Am Heart J 1992;123:752-757.

14. Lafferty K, McLean L, Salisbury J, et al. Ruptured abdominal aortic aneurysm in Marfan's syndrome. Postgrad Med J 1987;63:685-687.

15. Petrovic P, Avramov S, Pfau J, et al. Surgical management of extracranial carotid artery aneurysms. Ann Vasc Surg 1991;5:506-509.

16. Goyette EM, Palmes PW. Cardiovascular lesions in arachnodactyly. Circulation 1953;7:373-379.

17. Missri JC, Swett DD. The Marfan's syndrome: A review. Cardiovasc Rev Rep 1982;3:11.

18. Fann JI, Dalman RL. Heritable arteriopathy. Semin Vasc Surg 1993;6:46-55.

19. Porter JM, Taylor LM, Harris EJ. Nonatherosclerotic vascular disease. In Moore WS, ed. Vascular Surgery: A Comprehensive Review, 3rd ed. Philadelphia: WB Saunders, 1991, pp 97-130.

20. Gott VL, Pyeritz RE, Magovern GJ, et al. Surgical treatment of aneurysms of the ascending aorta in the Marfan syndrome. N Engl J Med 1986;314:1070-1074.

21. Pyeritz RE. Propranolol retards aortic root dilatation in the Marfan syndrome [abst]. Circulation 1983;68(Suppl III):III-365.

22. Fann JI, Glower DD, Miller DC, et al. Preservation of the aortic valve in patients with type A aortic dissection complicated by aortic valve regurgitation. J Thorac Cardiovasc Surg 1991;102:62-75.

23. van Meekeren JA. De dilatabilitate extraordinaria cutis. In Observations Medicochirugicae. Amsterdam: 1682.

24. Ehlers E. Cutis laxa Neigung zu haemorrhagien in der Haut, Lockerung mehrerer Artikulationen. Dermatol Ztschr 1901; 8:173-174.

25. Danlos M. Un cas de cutis laxa avec tumeurs par contusion chronique des condes et des genoux (xanthome juvenile pseudodiabetique de M.M. Hallopeault Mace de Lepinay). Bull Soc Fr Dermatol Syph 1908;19:70.

26. McKusick VA. Heritable Disorders of Connective Tissue, 4th ed. St. Louis: CV Mosby, 1972, pp 292-360.

27. Barabas AP. Heterogeneity of the Ehlers-Danlos syndrome. Description of three clinical types and a hypothesis to explain the basic defect(s). Br Med J 1967;2:612-613.

28. Sack G. Status dysvascularis: Ein Fall von besonderer Zerreisslichkeit des Blutgefasse. Dtsch Arch Kin Med 1936;178:663-671.

29. Hollister DW. Heritable disorders of connective tissue: Ehlers-Danlos syndrome. Pediatr Clin North Am 1978;25:575-591.

30. Cikrit DF, Miles JH, Silver D. Spontaneous arterial perforation: The Ehlers-Danlos spector. J Vasc Surg 1987;5:248-255.

31. Ruby ST, Kramer J, Cassidy SB, et al. Internal carotid artery aneurysm: A vascular manifestation of type IV Ehlers-Danlos syndrome. Conn Med 1989;53:142-144.

32. Tsipouras P, Byers PH, Schwartz RC, et al. Ehlers-Danlos syndrome type IV: Cosegregation of the phenotype to a COL3A1 allele of type III procollagen. Hum Genet 1986;74:41-46.

33. Bellenot F, Boisgard S, Kantelip B, et al. Type IV Ehlers-Danlos syndrome with isolated arterial involvement. Ann Vasc Surg 1990;4:15-19.

34. Beighton P, Horan FT. Surgical aspects of the Ehlers-Danlos syndrome. A survey of 100 cases. Br J Surg 1969;56:255.

35. Curley SA, Osler T, Demarest GB. Traumatic disruption of the subclavian artery and brachial plexus in a patient with Ehlers-Danlos syndrome. Ann Emerg Med 1988;17:850-852.

36. Valverde A, Tricot JF, deCrepy B, et al. Innominate artery involvement in type IV Ehlers-Danlos syndrome. Ann Vasc Surg 1991;5:41-45.

37. Hunter GC, Malone JM, Moore WS, et al. Vascular manifestations in patients with Ehlers-Danlos syndrome. Arch Surg 1982;117:495-498.

38. Lach B, Nair SG, Russell NA, et al. Spontaneous carotid-cavernous fistula and multiple arterial dissections in type IV Ehlers-Danlos syndrome. J Neurosurg 1987;66:462-467.

39. Pope FM, Martin GR, Lichtenstein JR, et al. Patients with Ehlers-Danlos syndrome type IV lack type III collagen. Proc Natl Acad Sci USA 1975;72:1314-1316.

40. Byers PH, Holbrook KA, McGillivray B, et al. Clinical and ultrastructural heterogeneity of type IV Ehlers-Danlos syndrome. Hum Genet 1979;47:141-150.

41. Stillman AE, Painter R, Hollister DW. Ehlers-Danlos syndrome type IV: Diagnosis and therapy of associated bowel perforation. Am J Gastroenterol 1991;86:360-362.

42. Prockop DJ, Kivirikko KI. Heritable disease of collagen. N Engl J Med 1984;34:376.

43. Weinbaum PJ, Cassidy SB, Campbell WA, et al. Pregnancy management and successful outcome of Ehlers-Danlos syndrome type IV. Am J Perinatol 1987;4:134-137.

44. Wright CB, Lamberth WC, Ponseti IV, et al. Successful management of popliteal arterial disruption in Ehlers-Danlos syndrome. Surgery 1979;85:708-712.

45. Soucy P, Eidus L, Keeley F. Perforation of the colon in a 15-year-old girl with Ehlers-Danlos syndrome type IV. J Pediatr Surg 1990;25:1180-1182.

46. Thomas JT, Frias JL. The cardiovascular manifestations of genetic disorders of collagen metabolism. Ann Clin Lab Sci 1987;7:377-382.

47. Pope FM, Narcisi P, Nicholls AC, et al. Clinical presentations of Ehlers-Danlos syndrome type IV. Arch Dis Child 1988;63:1016-1025.

48. Krog M, Almgren B, Eriksson I, et al. Vascular complications in the Ehlers-Danlos syndrome. Acta Chir Scand 1983;149:279-282.

49. Serry C, Agomuoh OS, Goldin MD. Review of Ehlers-Danlos syndrome: Successful repair of rupture and dissection of abdominal aorta. J Cardiovasc Surg 1988;29:530-534.

50. Burnett HF, Bledsoe JH, Char F. Abdominal aortic aneurysmectomy in a 17-year-old patient with Ehlers-Danlos syndrome: Case report and review of the literature. Surgery 1973;74:617.

51. Gronblad E. Angioid streaks—Pseudoxanthoma elasticum: Verlaufige Mittelung. Acta Ophthalmol (Copenh) 1929;7:329.

13

Buerger's Disease (Thromboangiitis Obliterans)

Joseph L. Mills, MD, John M. Porter, MD, Lackland AFB, Texas, and Portland, Oregon

Buerger's disease is a clinical syndrome characterized by segmental thrombotic occlusions of small and medium arteries in the lower and upper extremities. Affected patients are predominantly young male smokers who present with distal ischemia and, frequently, localized digital gangrene.[1,2] Although previously thought to occur almost exclusively in men, Buerger's disease definitely develops in women, in whom it seems to be appearing with increasing frequency. For reasons that are not clear, the incidence of Buerger's disease in North America has declined precipitously in the last 30 years, although large numbers of patients continue to be reported from the Mediterranean countries, eastern Europe, and Asia (Table I). This peculiar geographic distribution of the disease has never been explained.

Although some have questioned the existence of Buerger's disease,[3,4] there now appears little doubt that a clearly definable disease process does exist with a distinct clinical presentation, pathologic picture, and natural history quite distinct from atherosclerosis and the various forms of necrotizing arteritis. Well-defined diagnostic criteria for Buerger's disease have recently been described (Table II).

The active phase of Buerger's disease is characterized by an intensely cellular, inflammatory, segmental thrombotic occlusion of distal extremity arteries. In contrast to necrotizing arteritis, vascular wall architecture is well-preserved.

The etiology of Buerger's disease remains as unclear today as it was over 80 years ago when Leo Buerger described an extensive clinical series of patients with this condition.[5] Reports of cutaneous hypersensitivity to tobacco extracts in patients with Buerger's disease are unconfirmed.[6] Numerous, inconsistent, abnormal coagulation parameters have been described, more likely due to the underlying thrombotic process than the actual disease itself.[7] Considerable investigation is currently underway into possible autoimmune factors associated with Buerger's disease.[8,9] Indeed, some investigators have identified significantly elevated levels of anticollagen antibody in patients with Buerger's disease, as well as apparent cellular sensitivity to collagen abstracts.[10] Presently, neither the specificity nor reproducibility of these findings are known. An association of Buerger's disease with specific HLA subtypes A9 and B5 has been reported, but this has not been confirmed by others.[11]

Patients with Buerger's disease usually present with distal extremity ischemia. Raynaud's phenomenon and superficial thrombophlebitis are frequently associated conditions (Table III). Upper extremity involvement is strikingly frequent (Tables III and IV). Although Buerger's disease is generally confined to distal extremity vessels, well-documented cases in unusual anatomic sites have been reported occasionally (Table IV).

The cornerstone of any treatment plan for a patient with Buerger's disease is total abstinence from tobacco. Over the past 80 years, abundant evidence clearly indicates an indisputable relationship between continued smoking and disease progression. Patients rarely, if ever, develop persistent, ongoing, ischemic lesions when tobacco abstinence is complete.[11,12] Numerous investigators have reported a variety of medical therapies, including corticosteroids,[12,13] vasodilators,[14,15] anticoagulants and hemorrhealogic agents,[11] antiplatelet drugs,[16] antibiotics,[17] and antimalarials[12] without clear-cut benefit. There has been some anecdotal success with prostaglandin E1 infusion,[18,19,20] but this therapy is unproven.

Lumbar sympathectomy has been used frequently to treat Buerger's disease in patients with

From the Vascular Surgery Service, Wilford Hall USAF Medical Center, Lackland AFB, Tex., and the Division of Vascular Surgery, Oregon Health Sciences University, Portland, Ore.

The opinions expressed herein are those of the author and do not necessarily reflect the opinions of the United States Air Force or the Department of Defense.

persistent pain at rest or nonhealing lesions despite conservative management. There is, however, no prospective randomized trial of lumbar sympathectomy in such patients, and all reports of efficacy are anecdotal (Table V).

Since Buerger's disease affects predominately the infrapopliteal and pedal arteries, arterial bypass is rarely possible. Only a small percentage of patients have bypassable disease, and bypass patency rates clearly are inferior to those obtained in atherosclerotic or diabetic patients (Table V).

The tables that follow outline the available data with regard to natural history and outcome of Buerger's disease. It is interesting to note that even though Buerger's disease carries a significant risk to the patient of major lower extremity amputation, because of the relative sparing of cerebral, visceral, and coronary circulations, life expectancy of patients with Buerger's disease approaches that of the normal population (Table VI).

Table I. Incidence and demographics

Demographic parameters	Incidence	Ref.
General population (North America)	8-11.6/100,000	21,22
In patients with peripheral vascular disease		
U.S.	0.75%	23
Italy	0.46%	24
Poland	3.3%	25
Japan	16.6%	26
Median age at onset	34.5 yr	11,25, 27-38
Male/female	7.5:1	11,27-29, 31,36

Table II. Diagnostic criteria

A. Onset of distal extremity ischemic symptoms before 45 years of age
B. Normal arteries proximal to the popliteal or distal brachial level
C. Distal occlusive disease documented by distinctive plethysmographic, arteriographic, or pathologic findings
D. Absence of any of the following conditions:
    1. Proximal embolic source
    2. Trauma
    3. Autoimmune disease
    4. Diabetes
    5. Hyperlipidemia

References 11,26,27,31,39.

Table III. Associated conditions

	Incidence (%)	Ref.
Superficial thrombophlebitis	37	11,24-27,31, 32,38,39
Raynaud's phenomenon	34	11,24,27,29, 32,39
Upper extremity involvement	34	11,25,27,34, 35,37,39

Table IV. Anatomic distribution of disease

	Incidence (%)	Ref.
Lower extremity only	68	11,25,27,33, 34,37
Upper extremity only	14	
Both upper and lower extremity	18	
Unusual sites of involvement (histologically documented cases, compatible clinical histories)		
Femoral artery		34
Iliac artery		40
Visceral arteries		41-44
Spermatic artery		37,45,46
Disputable cases (lack complete histologic or arteriographic confirmation): cerebral arteries		47,48

Table V. Surgical treatment of Buerger's disease

	Percent	Ref.
Patients undergoing lower extremity sympathectomy for nonhealing foot lesions	18	11,25-27,29, 31,35,36
Patients with surgically-reconstructable, lower extremity arterial disease	6.4	11,26,28, 30,34
Initial success rates of arterial reconstruction	29	11,26,28,34

Table VI. Morbidity and mortality data: Amputation and survival rates

Amputation	Percentage of patients	Ref.
Toe/forefoot	19	11,25,27,38
Major lower extremity (below- or above-knee)	19	11,25,27,31, 35,38
Finger amputation	6.3	25,37,38
Major upper extremity	Almost never	11,25,27
Survival		
5 years	97	11,25,38
10 years	93.6	38

Table VI. Commonly used indications for arteriography

	Ref.
Absent pulse	6,30,31
Diminished pulse	30
Secondary signs	
Large or expanding hematoma	30-32
Pulsatile external bleeding	6,30,31
Unexplained hypotension	6,30,31
Acute anemia	6,30
Bruit	6,30
Peripheral nerve injury	6,30,31
Joint dislocation (knee)	30
Gross hematuria	6,30
Wide mediastinum	6,30
Pelvic fracture	
Ongoing bleeding	
Large hematoma	6
Neurologic deficit following blunt trauma or penetrating neck trauma	8,9
Hemodynamically stable patient with blunt or penetrating injury to the thoracic outlet	14-27,31

Patients with secondary signs may have a palpable pulse. Arteriography is reported to miss up to 2.8% of operatively proven injuries.[1,2,5,33,34]

Table VII. Correlation between clinical signs and vascular injuries seen on arteriography

Clinical signs	Vascular injury by arteriography (%)	Ref.
Absent pulse	90	30
Diminished pulse	49	30
Normal pulse	9	30
Pale, cool, or cyanotic extremity	71	30
Compartment syndrome	69	30
Dislocation (knee)	50	30
Peripheral nerve injury	60	30
Large hematoma	50	30
Enlarging hematoma	75	30
Pulsatile arterial bleeding	31	30
Gross hematuria	86	30
Wide mediastinum	20	30

Table VIII. Methods of repair

	Percentage	Ref.
Suture	13-43	1-6,29
Resection and anastomosis	16-49	1-6,29
Vein graft	5-60	1-6,29,35
Synthetic graft	3-30	1-6,29,36
Ligation	0-22	1-6,29

Although the indications used for fasciotomy are variable, the procedure is performed in many trauma centers. Of patients with vascular wounds in the extremities, 9% to 21% had adjunctive fasciotomies.[1-3,5,6]

Table IX. Results of surgery

	Percentage	Ref.
Mortality (all patients)	10-16	1-5
Amputation (major arteries: extremity)	2-4	1-6
Patency of repair	80-98	1-5
Wound sepsis	3-5	1,2,5,6
Postoperative bleeding	0-2	2,4

Table X. Commonly used indications for fasciotomy

Signs and symptoms	Ref.
Swollen, tense, and tender compartment	37,38
Ischemia >4-6 hr	39
Prolonged hypotension	40
Combined arterial and venous injury	40
Extensive soft tissue injury	39
Postreconstructive pulse deficit with arteriographically patent vessels (normal caliber, or thin and skinny)	40
Compartment pressure >45 mm Hg	37
Abnormal Doppler venous signal at ankle	37

Presence of a palpable pulse does not preclude a compartment syndrome.[37]

REFERENCES

1. Drapanas T, Hewitt RL, Weichert RF, et al. Civilian vascular injuries: A critical appraisal of three decades of management. Ann Surg 1970;172:351-360.
2. Perry MO, Thal ER, Shires GT. Management of arterial injuries. Ann Surg 1971;173:403-408.
3. Reynolds RR, McDowell HA, Diethelm AG. The surgical treatment of arterial injuries in the civilian population. Ann Surg 1979;189:700-708.
4. Feliciano DV, Bitondo CG, Mattox KL, et al. Civilian trauma in the 1980s: A one year experience with 456 vascular and cardiac injuries. Ann Surg 1984;199:717-724.
5. Richardson JD, Vitale GC, Flint LM. Penetrating arterial trauma: Analysis of missed vascular injuries. Arch Surg 1987;122:678-686.
6. Robbs JV, Baker LW. Vascular trauma. Curr Probl Surg 1984;21:1-75.
7. Wiedeman JE, Mills JL, Robinson JG. Special problems after iatrogenic vascular injuries. Surg Gynecol Obstet 1988;166:323-326.
8. Perry MO. Basic considerations in the diagnosis and management of carotid injuries. J Vasc Surg 1988;8:193-194.
9. Perry MO. The Management of Acute Vascular Injuries. Baltimore: Williams & Wilkins, 1981, pp 67-81.
10. Liekweg WG, Greenfield LJ. Management of penetrating carotid arterial injury. Ann Surg 1978;188:587-592.
11. Perry MO, Snyder WH, Thal ER. Carotid artery injuries caused by blunt trauma. Ann Surg 1980;192:74-77.
12. Krajewski LP, Hertzer NR. Blunt carotid artery trauma: Report of two cases and review of the literature. Ann Surg 1980;191:341-346.
13. Ledgerwood AM, Mullins RJ, Lucas CE. Primary repair vs ligation for carotid artery injuries. Arch Surg 1980;115:L88–L93.
14. Flint LM, Snyder WH, Perry MO, Shires GT. Management of major vascular injuries in the base of the neck. Arch Surg 1973;106:407-413.
15. Smith RF, Elliott JP, Hageman JH, et al. Acute penetrating arterial injuries of the neck and limbs. Arch Surg 1974;109:198-205.
16. Faro RS, Monson DO, Weinberg M, et al. Disruption of aortic arch branches due to nonpenetrating chest trauma. Arch Surg 1983;118:1333-1336.
17. Zelenock GB, Kazmers A, Graham L, et al. Nonpenetrating subclavian artery injuries. Arch Surg 1985;120:685-692.
18. Mozingo JR, Denton IC. The neurological deficit associated with sudden occlusion of abdominal aorta due to blunt trauma. Surgery 1975;77:118-125.
19. Lock JS, Huffman AD, Johnson RC. Blunt trauma to the abdominal aorta. J Trauma 1987;27:676-677.
20. Collins PS, Galocovsky M, Selander JM, et al. Intraabdominal vascular injury secondary to penetrating trauma. J Trauma 1988;28:5165-5170.
21. Millikan JS, Moore EE. Critical factors in determining mortality from abdominal aortic trauma. Surg Gynecol Obstet 1985;160:313-316.
22. Clark DE, Georgitis JW, Ray FS. Renal arterial injuries caused by blunt trauma. Surgery 1981;90:87-96.
23. Lucas AE, Richardson JD, Flint LM, et al. Traumatic injury of the proximal superior mesenteric artery. Ann Surg 1981;193:30-34.
24. Bornman KR, Snyder WH, Weigeit JA. Civilian arterial trauma of the upper extremity: An 11-year experience in 267 patients. Am J Surg 1986;148:794-799.
25. Graham JM, Mattox KL, Feliciano DV, et al. Vascular injuries of the axilla. Ann Surg 1982;195:232-237.
26. Shah DM, Carson JD, Karmody AM, et al. Optimal management of tibial arterial trauma. J Trauma 1988;28:228-234.
27. Meyer J, Wash J, Schuler JJ, et al. The early fate of venous repair after civilian vascular trauma. Ann Surg 1987;206:458-464.
28. Pasch AR, Bishara RA, Schuler JS, et al. Results of venous reconstruction after civilian vascular trauma. Arch Surg 1986;121:607-611.
29. Feliciano DV, Herskowitz K, O'Gorman RB, et al. Management of vascular injuries in the lower extremities. J Trauma 1988;28:319-327.
30. Rose SC, Moore EE. Trauma angiography: The use of clinical findings to improve patient selection and care preparation. J Trauma 1988;28:240-245.
31. Turcotte JK, Towne JB, Bernhard VM. Is arteriography necessary in the management of vascular trauma of the extremities? Surgery 1978;84:557-562.
32. Reid JDS, Weigelt JA, Thal ER, et al. Assessment of proximity of a wound to major vascular structures as an indication for arteriography. Arch Surg 1988;123:962-964.
33. Feliciano DV, Cruse PA, Burch JM, et al. Delayed diagnosis of arterial injuries. Am J Surg 1987;154:579-583.
34. Snyder WH, Thal ER, Bridges RA, et al. The validity of normal arteriography in penetrating trauma. Arch Surg 1978;113:424-428.
35. McCready RA, Hyde GL. Autogenous tissue in the revascularization of traumatic vascular injuries—its value and limitations. In Bergan JJ, Yao JST, eds. Vascular Surgical Emergencies. Orlando: Grune & Stratton, 1987, pp 179-189.
36. Feliciano DV. Use of prosthetic grafts in extensive arterial injuries. In Bergan JJ, Yao JST, eds. Vascular Surgical Emergencies. Orlando: Grune & Stratton, 1987, pp 191-202.
37. Perry MO. Compartment syndromes and reperfusion injury. Surg Clin North Am 1988;68:853-864.
38. Mubark SJ, Hargrens AR. Acute compartment syndromes. Surg Clin North Am 1983;63:539-565.
39. Rich NM, Spencer FC. Vascular Trauma. Philadelphia: WB Saunders, 1978, pp 376, 379, 539, 558.
40. Snyder WH, Watkins WL, Whidden LL, et al. Civilian popliteal artery trauma: An eleven-year experience with 83 injuries. Surgery 1979;85:101-108.

15

Arterial and Prosthetic Graft Infection

Richard A. Yeager, MD, John M. Porter, MD, Portland, Oregon

Primary arterial infections continue to be one of the most challenging clinical problems encountered by vascular surgeons, and postoperative graft infection is one of the most feared complications. Since vascular infections present grave risks to life and limb, vascular surgeons must be fully informed concerning prevention, early diagnosis, and prompt vigorous treatment.

Much new information is available in recent years about arterial infection. New culture techniques have revealed that a disturbingly high percentage of diseased arteries routinely harbor bacteria. Additionally, chronic intraaneurysmal thrombi are culture-positive in a significant number of patients. However, the relevance of these

findings to subsequent clinical arterial infection remains undetermined.

A host of new imaging techniques has markedly improved our ability to diagnose vascular infections. We have long recognized the role of computed tomographic (CT) scanning in early diagnosis of prosthetic graft infection. Preliminary data suggest that magnetic resonance imaging (MRI) may be a remarkable addition in this area. Both the indium-tagged leukocyte and immunoglobulin scans appear promising for early diagnosis.

Finally, in the area of treatment, one is faced with many choices. Some of these include preliminary versus delayed extraanatomic bypass, extraanatomic versus in situ graft replacement, and graft excision and remote bypass versus vigorous local care only. We hope vascular surgeons will find a useful summary of information in the following tables (Tables I-XV).

From the Department of Surgery, Oregon Health Sciences University and the Portland Veterans Administration Medical Center, Portland, Ore.

Table I. Incidence of bacteriology of positive cultures from grossly uninfected aneurysm contents or arterial wall

| | | Bacteriology | | |
	Positive (%)	Gram-positive isolates (%)	Gram-positive isolates that are coagulase-negative staphylococci (%)	Ref.
Abdominal aortic aneurysm (AAA) contents				
All reported cases (n = 872)	13	82	53	1-10
Elective	8	—	—	2,7-9
Symptomatic (urgent)	12	—	—	2,7-9
Ruptured	20	—	—	2,7-9
Elective arterial cases (culture technique included mechanical grinding of specimens)	36	93	69	10-12
Femoral pseudoaneurysms (sonication culture technique)	54	100	68	13

Table II. Relevance of culture results for predicting subsequent prosthetic graft infection*

| | Reported cases developing subsequent prosthetic graft infection (%) | | |
	Negative culture results	Positive culture results	Ref.
AAA cases	1	8	1-5,7-9
Elective arterial reconstructions	0	5	10,11,13

*Cultures from grossly uninfected aneurysm contents or arterial wall.

Table III. Prospective randomized studies documenting significant reduction in vascular surgery wound infection rates using intravenous antibiotics

Drug (dose)	Dosage interval and duration	Ref.
Cefazolin (1 g)	On-call and post-operatively every 6 hr for four doses	14
Cephradine (1 g)	1 hour preoperatively and every 6 hr for four doses	15*
Cefuroxime (1.5 g)	On-call and every 8 hr for three doses	16†
Methicillin (2 g) + Netilmicin (200 mg)	Pre-operatively at start of general anesthesia and at 8 and 16 hr after first dose	17
Cephradine (1 g)	At induction of anesthesia and post-operatively every 6 hr for three doses	18
Cefuroxime (1.5 g) or Cefotaxime (2 g)	At onset of anesthesia and two to three post-operative doses	19
Vancomycin (1 g)	1 hr before surgery and 4 hr after surgery	20

*No added benefit with topical antibiotic wound irrigation.
†No added benefit with 3-day regimen.

Table IV. Current reported incidence of prosthetic graft infection

Insertion site	Graft infection (%)	Ref.
Aortoiliac	<0.5	21-23
Aortofemoral	2	22,23
Axillofemoral/femorofemoral	1	23,24
Femoropopliteal/tibial	2.5	22-24

Table V. Sensitivity and specificity of testing for prosthetic graft infection*

Test modality	Sensitivity (%)	Specificity (%)	Ref.
CT scan†	57	100	25-27
Indium-labeled WBC scan	96	85	26,28-31
MRI scan	85	100	32
Indium-labeled immunoglobulin G scan	88	100	33

WBC = white blood cell.
*Compiled from patients with clinical suspicion of late prosthetic graft infection.
†Positive scan defined by presence of perigraft gas or fluid.

Table VI. Current bacteriology of primary aortic prosthetic graft infection*

Organism[†]	Isolates (%)
Staphylococcus aureus	24
S. epidermidis	17
Escherichia sp.	10
Pseudomonas sp.	8
Streptococcus	7
Klebsiella sp.	3
Enterococcus	3
Bacteroides sp.	3
Proteus sp.	3
Enterobacter sp.	3
Peptostreptococcus sp.	3
Proprionibacterium	2
Others (each 1% or less)	6
No growth	8

*Data based on selected reports since 1980 (see references 33-55).
[†]21% of patients had culture results that were positive for two or more organisms.

Table VII. Surgical mortality for graft-enteric fistula versus primary aortic graft infection*

	Mortality (%)	Ref.
Graft-enteric fistula	46	21,33,42,43,51, 56-65,67-74, 76-82
Primary prosthethic graft infection	21	21-23,33,34,38, 41-43,46,51,66, 75-77,80,82

*Inclusive data compiled from reports since 1980.

Table VIII. Surgical results related to method of management for aortic prosthetic graft infection*

Method of revascularization in conjunction with excision of aortic graft	Mortality (%)	Subsequent graft sepsis (%)
In situ prosthetic[†] graft replacement	32	11
Extraanatomical prosthetic bypass graft	38	15

*Inclusive data compiled from reports since 1980 (see references 21,22,33,38,42,43,46,48,51,52,55-68,70-74,76,78-82), including patients with prosthetic-enteric communication as well as primary aortic prosthetic graft infection.
[†]Data may be influenced by selective performance of in situ grafting for cases with minimal local aortic sepsis.

Table IX. Surgical results for management of aortic graft infection according to sequence and staging of extraanatomical bypass and aortic graft excision*

	Mortality (%)	Amputation (%)	Extraanatomical bypass graft sepsis
Extraanatomical bypass followed by graft excision	21	11	18
Graft excision followed by extra-anatomical bypass	26	46	23

*Data based on selected reports since 1980 (see references 21,51,55,76,81), including patients with graft-enteric fistula.

Table X. Current reported survival following surgical management of aortic prosthetic graft infection*

	1 mo	1 yr	5 yr
Patient survival (%)	75	60	50

*Data based on selected current reports (see references 21,42, 51,55,73,82), including patients with graft-enteric fistula.

Table XI. Surgical results for peripheral (nonaortic) prosthetic graft infection compared with primary aortic prosthetic graft infection*

	Surgical results	
	Mortality (%)	Amputation (%)
Peripheral (nonaortic)	17	41
Aortic[†]	24	21

*Data based on selected reports since 1980 (see references 22-24,34,42,43,46,83-86).
[†]Analysis excludes patients with graft-enteric fistula.

Table XII. Recent results reported for nonresectional therapy of prosthetic graft infection*

Graft salvage (%)	Mortality (%)
70	8

*Data inclusive of both aortic and nonaortic (peripheral) prosthetic grafts. Cases reported since 1980 (see references 24,35,37,39,40,42,45,49,50,54,78,87-89) managed with drainage and wound debridement, local and systemic antibiotics, and delayed wound coverage.

Table XIII. Current bacteriology of infected aortic aneurysms*

Organism	Isolates (%)
Salmonella sp.	38
Staphylococcus sp.	17
Streptococcus	8
Escherichia sp.	7
Campylobacter sp.	5
Bacteroides sp.	3
Histoplasma sp.	3
Mycobacterium sp.	2
Haemophilus sp.	2
Enterococcus	1
Klebsiella sp.	1
Listeria sp.	1
Pseudomonas sp.	1
S. arizona	1
Others (each less than 1%)	5
No growth	5

*Cases reported since 1980 (see references 79,90-144), including patients with embolomycotic and other types of infected aortic aneurysms.

Table XIV. Results of surgical management of infected infrarenal aortic aneurysms*

Type of revascularization in conjunction with resection of aortic aneurysm	Mortality (%)	Subsequent graft sepsis (%)
In situ prosthetic graft[†] replacement	15	9
Extraanatomical prosthetic bypass graft	30	< 1

*Data based on reports since 1980 (see references 34,61,65, 79,90,91,94,96-102,104,106-111,113-117,119-121,123,124,126,128, 130-134,142,145-150), including patients with embolomycotic and other types of infected infrarenal aortic aneurysms as well as primary aorto-enteric fistula cases.
[†]Data may be influenced by selective performance of in situ grafting for cases with minimal local aortic sepsis.

Table XV. Surgical results for infected femoral pseudoaneurysms due to parenteral drug abuse

Surgical treatment of pseudoaneurysm	Postoperative wound hemorrhage (%)	Prosthetic graft sepsis (%)	Amputation (%)	Ref.
Ligation and excision without revascularization	6	—	23	151-159
Excision with in situ autogenous revascularization	31	—	6	152,155-158,160,161
Excision with remote prosthetic bypass	1	18	9	151,154,157-159,161,162

93. Bardin JA, Collins GM, Devin JB, et al. Nonaneurysmal suppurative aortitis. Arch Surg 1981;116:954-956.

94. McIntyre KE Jr, Malone JM, Richards E, et al. Mycotic aortic pseudoaneurysm with aortoenteric fistula caused by *Arizona hinshawii*. Surgery 1982;91:173-177.

95. Ewart JM, Burke ML, Bunt TJ. Spontaneous abdominal aortic infections. Essentials of diagnosis and management. Am Surg 1983;49:37-50.

96. Blabey RG, Parry MF, Bull SM, et al. Mycotic aneurysm of the abdominal aorta: Successful management of *Campylobacter fetus* aortitis. Conn Med 1983;47:129-130.

97. Anolik JR, Mildvan D, Winter JW, et al. Mycotic aortic aneurysm—a complication of *Campylobacter fetus* septicemia. Arch Intern Med 1983;143:609-610.

98. Miller BM, Waterhouse G, Alford RH, et al. Histoplasma infection of abdominal aortic aneurysms. Ann Surg 1983;197:57-62.

99. Marty AT, Webb TA, Stubbs KG, et al. Inflammatory abdominal aortic aneurysm infected by *Campylobacter fetus*. JAMA 1983;249:1190-1192.

100. Parsons R, Gregory J, Palmer DL. Salmonella infections of the abdominal aorta. Rev Infect Dis 1983;5:227-231.

101. Trout HH III, Kozloff L, Giordano JM. Priority of revascularization in patients with graft enteric fistulas, infected arteries, or infected arterial prostheses. Ann Surg 1984;199:669-683.

102. Harvey MH, Strachan CJL, Thom BT. *Listeria monocytogenes:* a rare cause of mycotic aortic aneurysm. Br J Surg 1984;71:166-167.

103. Atlas SW, Vogelzang RL, Bressler EL, et al. CT diagnosis of a mycotic aneurysm of the thoracoabdominal aorta. J Comp Assist Tomogr 1984;8:1211-1212.

104. Brown SL, Busuttil RW, Baker JD, et al. Bacteriologic and surgical determinants of survival in patients with mycotic aneurysms. J Vasc Surg 1984;1:541-547.

105. Bergsland J, Kawaguchi A, Roland JM, et al. Mycotic aortic aneurysms in children. Ann Thorac Surg 1984;37:314-318.

106. Bednar DA, Jain AK, Scott HJ. Mycotic abdominal aortic aneurysm: A case report. Can J Surg 1985;28:23-24.

107. Righter J, Woods JM. Campylobacter and endovascular lesions. Can J Surg 1985;28:451-452.

108. Perry MO. Infected aortic aneurysms. J Vasc Surg 1985;2:597-599.

109. Bunt TJ, Wilson TG. Infected abdominal aortic aneurysm. South Med J 1985;78:419-422.

110. McNamara MF, Finnegan MO, Bakshi KR. Abdominal aortic aneurysms infected by *Escherichia coli.* Surgery 1985;98:87-92.

111. Harris RL, Lawrie GM, Wheeler TM, et al. Successful management of *Histoplasma capsulatum* infection of an abdominal aortic aneurysm. J Vasc Surg 1986;3:649-651.

112. Dean RH, Meacham PW, Weaver FA, et al. Mycotic embolism and embolomycotic aneurysms—neglected lessons of the past. Ann Surg 1986;204:300-307.

113. Cargile JS III, Fisher DF Jr, Burns DK, et al. Tuberculous aortitis with associated necrosis and perforation: Treatment and options. J Vasc Surg 1986;4:612-615.

114. Ljungberg B, Braconier JH. Abdominal aortitis and infected aneurysms due to Salmonella. Scand J Infect Dis 1986;18:401-406.

115. Humphrey RW, Nugent P, Abu-Dalu J, et al. The challenge of managing the infected abdominal aorta. Infect Surg 1987;6:25-34.

116. Wilde CC, Tan L, Cheong FW. Case report: Computed tomography and ultrasound diagnosis of mycotic aneurysm of the abdominal aorta due to salmonella. Clin Radiol 1987;38:325-326.

117. Bitseff EL, Edwards WH, Mulherin JL Jr, et al. Infected abdominal aortic aneurysms. South Med J 1987;80:309-312.

118. Yao JST, McCarthy WJ. Contained rupture of a thoracoabdominal aneurysm. Contemp Surg 1988;33:47-51.

119. Taylor LM Jr, Deitz DM, McConnell DB, et al. Treatment of infected abdominal aneurysms by extraanatomic bypass, aneurysm excision, and drainage. Am J Surg 1988;155:655-658.

120. Kolbeinsson ME, Okada F, Tsang D. Mycotic aortic aneurysm: A CT diagnosis. Contemp Surg 1988;33:11-15.

121. Woods JM IV, Schellack J, Stewart MT, et al. Mycotic abdominal aortic aneurysm induced by immunotherapy with bacille Calmette-Guerin vaccine for malignancy. J Vasc Surg 1988;7:808-810.

122. Chan FY, Crawford ES, Coselli JS, et al. In situ prosthetic graft replacement for mycotic aneurysm of the aorta. Ann Thorac Surg 1989;47:193-203.

123. Ala-Kulju K, Heikkinen L, Salo J. One-stage vascular surgery for abdominal aortic aneurysm infected by Salmonella. Eur J Vasc Surg 1989;3:173-175.

124. Blackett RL, Hill SF, Bowler I, et al. Mycotic aneurysm of the aorta due to Group B streptococcus *(Streptococcus agalactiae).* Eur J Vasc Surg 1989;3:177-179.

125. Borris LC, Nohr M, Petersen K. Rapid growth and early rupture of a primary mycotic aneurysm of the abdominal aorta. Eur J Vasc Surg 1989;3:461-463.

126. DuPont J-R, Bonavita JA, DiGiovanni RJ, et al. Acquired immunodeficiency syndrome and mycotic abdominal aortic aneurysms: A new challenge? Report of a case. J Vasc Surg 1989;10:254-257.

127. Semel L, Szmalc F, Bredenberg CE. Management of suspected mycotic suprarenal aortic aneurysm. Ann Vasc Surg 1989;3:380-383.

128. Oz MC, Brener BJ, Buda JA, et al. A ten-year experience with bacterial aortitis. J Vasc Surg 1989;10:439-449.

129. Atnip RG. Mycotic aneurysms of the suprarenal abdominal aorta: Prolonged survival after in situ aortic and visceral reconstruction. J Vasc Surg 1989;10:635-641.

130. Rutherford EJ, Eakins JW, Maxwell JG, et al. Abdominal aortic aneurysm infected with *Campylobacter fetus* subspecies *fetus.* J Vasc Surg 1989;10:193-197.

131. Trairatvorakul P, Sriphojanart S, Sathapatayavongs B. Abdominal aortic aneurysms infected with Salmonella: problems of treatment. J Vasc Surg 1990;12:16-19.

132. Reddy DJ, Shepard AD, Evans JR, et al. Management of infected aortoiliac aneurysms. Arch Surg 1991;126:873-879.

133. Rogers AJ, Rowlands BJ, Flynn TC. Infected aortic aneurysm after intraabdominal abscess. Texas Heart Inst J 1987;14:208-214.

134. Morrow C, Safi H, Beall AC, Jr. Primary aortoduodenal fistula caused by Salmonella aortitis. J Vasc Surg 1987;6:415-418.

135. Cohen JI, Bartlett JA, Corey GR. Extra-intestinal manifestations of Salmonella infections. Medicine 1987;66:349-388.

136. Smith EJ, Milligan SL, Filo RS. Salmonella mycotic aneurysm after renal transplantation. South Med J 1981;74:1399-1401.

137. Hammacher E, Bast T, DeGeest R, et al. Salmonella infection of the abdominal aorta. Neth J Surg 1984;36:86.

138. Jones E, Ballon H, Burton J, et al. Salmonella infection of an aortic aneurysm. Can Med Assoc J 1983;128:41-43.

139. Kwai A. Salmonellosis and ruptured abdominal aortic aneurysm: A case report. Mt Sinai J Med 1982;49:504-507.

140. Brooks DJ, Cant AJ, Lambert HP, et al. Recurrent Salmonella septicaemia with aortitis, osteomylitis and psoas abscess. J Infect 1983;7:156-158.

141. Sheehan JP. Bacteroides aortitis and aneurysm formation following arteriography. J Infect 1983;7:153-155.

142. McCready RA, Hyde GL, Mattingly SS. Infected abdominal aortic aneurysm following transfemoral arteriography: Case report. Contemp Surg 1988;32:37-44.

143. Kato R, Ohta T, Kazui H, et al. *Campylobacter fetus* infection of abdominal aortic aneurysm. J Cardiovasc Surg 1990;31:756-759.

144. Blumoff RL, McCartney W, Jaques P, et al. Diagnosis of mycotic abdominal aortic aneurysm using 67-gallium citrate. Am Surg 1982;48:601-603.

145. Benhamou G, Duron JJ. Aorto-digestive fistulae. Int Surg 1982;67:307-310.

146. Taheri SA, Kulaylat MN, Grippi J, et al. Surgical treatment of primary aortoduodenal fistula. Ann Vasc Surg 1991;5:265-270.

147. Mii S, Onohara T, Okadome K, et al. Surgical repair of primary aorto-jejunal fistula associated with non-specific inflammatory abdominal aortic aneurysm. Eur J Vasc Surg 1991;5:355-357.

148. Mollerup CL, Strand L. Gastrointestinal hemorrhage due to fistula from aortic aneurysm. Acta Chir Scand 1987;153:631-632.

149. Sweeney MS, Gadacz TR. Primary aortoduodenal fistula: Manifestation, diagnosis, and treatment. Surgery 1984;96:492-497.

150. Pfeiffer RB. Successful repair of three primary aortoduodenal fistulae. Arch Surg 1982;117:1098-1099.

151. Feldman AJ, Berguer R. Management of an infected aneurysm of the groin secondary to drug abuse. Surg Gynecol Obstet 1983;157:519-522.

152. Yeager RA, Hobson RW II, Padberg FT, et al. Vascular complications related to drug abuse. J Trauma 1987;27:305-308.

153. Huebl HC, Read RC. Aneurysmal abscess. Minn Med 1966;49:11-16.

154. Fromm SH, Lucas CE. Obturator bypass for mycotic aneurysm in the drug addict. Arch Surg 1970;100:82-83.

155. Anderson CB, Butcher HR Jr, Ballinger WF. Mycotic aneurysms. Arch Surg 1974;109:712-717.

156. Yellin AE. Ruptured mycotic aneurysm: A complication of parenteral drug abuse. Arch Surg 1977;112:981-986.

157. Johnson JR, Ledgerwood AM, Lucas CE. Mycotic aneurysm: New concepts in therapy. Arch Surg 1983;118:577-582.

158. Reddy DJ, Smith RF, Elliott JP Jr, et al. Infected femoral artery false aneurysms in drug addicts: Evolution of selective vascular reconstruction. J Vasc Surg 1986;3:718-724.

159. Patel KR, Semel L, Clauss RH. Routine revascularization with resection of infected femoral pseudoaneurysms from substance abuse. J Vasc Surg 1988;8:321-328.

160. Tuckson W, Anderson BB. Mycotic aneurysms in intravenous drug abuse: Diagnosis and management. J Nat Med Assoc 1985;77:99-102.

161. Welch GH, Reid DB, Pollock JG. Infected false aneurysms in the groin of intravenous drug abusers. Br J Surg 1990;70:330-333.

162. Patel KR, Semel L, Clauss RH. Routine revascularization with resection of infected femoral pseudoaneurysms from substance abuse. Letter to the editors. J Vasc Surg 1989;10:358.

25. Meyer AA, Ahlquist RE, Trunkey DD. Mortality from ruptured abdominal aortic aneurysms. Am J Surg 1986;152: 27-33.

26. Lawrie GM, Morris GJ Jr, Crawford ES, et al. Improved results of operation for ruptured abdominal aortic aneurysm. Surgery 1979;85:483-488.

27. Hoffman M, Avellone JC, Plecha FR, et al. Operation for ruptured abdominal aortic aneurysms: A community-wide experience. Surgery 1982;91:597-602.

28. Johnson G, McDevitt NB, Proctor HJ, et al. Emergent or selective operation for symptomatic abdominal aortic aneurysm. Arch Surg 1980;115:51-53.

29. McCabe CJ, Coleman WS, Brewster DC. The advantage of early operation for abdominal aortic aneurysm. Arch Surg 1981;116:1025-1029.

30. Chang FC, Smith JL, Rahbar A, et al. Abdominal aortic aneurysms: A comparative analysis of surgical treatment of symptomatic and asymptomatic patients. Am J Surg 1978; 136:705-708.

31. Baird RJ, Gurry JF, Kellam JF, et al. Abdominal aortic aneurysms: Recent experience with 210 patients. Can Med Assoc J 1978;118:1229-1235.

32. Thompson JE, Hollier LH, Putman RD, et al. Surgical management of abdominal aortic aneurysms. Ann Surg 1975;181: 654-660.

33. Crawford ES, Salwa SA, Babb JW, et al. Infra-abdominal aortic aneurysm. Ann Surg 1981;193:699-709.

34. Whittemore AD, Clowes AW, Hechtman HB, et al. Aortic aneurysm repair reduced operative mortality associated with maintenance of optimal cardiac performance. Ann Surg 1980; 120:414-421.

35. Hertzer NR. Myocardial ischemia. Surgery 1983;93:97-101.

36. Pilcher DB, Davis JH, Ashileoga T, et al. Treatment of abdominal aortic aneurysm in an entire state over 7½ years. Am J Surg 1980;139:487-494.

37. Hertzer NR, Avellone JC, Farrel CJ, et al. The risk of vascular surgery in a metropolitan community. J Vasc Surg 1984;1: 13-21.

38. O'Donnell TF, Darling RC, Linton RR. Is 80 years too old for aneurysmectomy? Arch Surg 1976;111:1250-1257.

39. Esselstyn CB, Humphries AW, Young JR, et al. Aneurysmectomy in the aged? Surgery 1970;67:34-39.

40. Hollier LH, Reigel MM, Kozmier FJ, et al. Conventional repair of abdominal aortic aneurysm in the high-risk patient: A plea for abandonment of nonresective treatment. J Vasc Surg 1986;3:712-717.

41. Inahora T, Beary GL, Mukherjee D, et al. The contrary position to the nonresective treatment for abdominal aortic aneurysm. J Vasc Surg 1985;2:42-48.

42. Karmody AM, Leather RP, Goldman M, et al. The current position of nonresective treatment for abdominal aortic aneurysm. Surgery 1983;94:591-597.

43. Cho SI, Johnson WC, Buch HL, Jr, et al. Lethal complications associated with nonresective treatment of abdominal aortic aneurysms. Arch Surg 1982;117:1214-1217.

44. Kwaan JHM, Khan RJ, Connolly JE. Total exclusion technique for the management of abdominal aortic aneurysms. Am J Surg 1983;146:93-97.

45. Schwarz RA, Nichols WK, Silver D. Is thrombosis of the infrarenal abdominal aortic aneurysm an acceptable alternative? J Vasc Surg 1986;3:448-455.

46. Johansen K, Koepsell T. Familial tendency for abdominal aortic aneurysms. JAMA 1986;256:1934-1936.

47. Buckels JAC, Fielding JWL, Black J, et al. Significance of positive bacterial cultures from aortic aneurysm contents. Br J Surg 1985;72:440-442.

48. Ernst CB, Campbell HC, Dougherty ME, et al. Incidence and significance of intraoperative cultures during abdominal aortic aneurysmectomy. Ann Surg 1977;185:626-633.

49. Sabiston DC Jr. Aortic abdominal aneurysms. In Sabiston DC Jr, ed. Textbook of Surgery, 13th ed. Philadelphia: WB Saunders, 1986, 1830-1838.

50. Pennel RC, Hollier LH, Lie JT, et al. Inflammatory abdominal aortic aneurysms: A thirty-year review. J Vasc Surg 1985;2: 859-869.

51. Johnson G Jr, Gurri JA, Burnham SJ. Life expectancy after abdominal aortic aneurysm repair. In Bergan JJ, Yao JST, eds. Aneurysms: Diagnosis and Treatment, New York: Grune and Stratton, 1982, pp. 279-285.

52. Hollier LH, Plate G, O'Brien PC, et al. Late survival after abdominal aortic aneurysm repair. J Vasc Surg 1984;1: 290-299.

53. Sreide O, Lillestl J, Christensen O, et al. Abdominal aortic aneurysms: Survival analysis of four hundred thirty-four patients. Surgery 1982;91:188-193.

Aorta and Visceral Branches

17

Renovascular Hypertension

Virginia Chiantella, MD, Richard H. Dean, MD, Winston-Salem, North Carolina

Review of accumulated data in the medical literature on renovascular hypertension underscores the lack of uniformity of opinion regarding important clinical characteristics, indications for evaluation, screening and definitive diagnostic tools, and choice of therapeutic options. Much of this lack of uniformity stems from the collection

From the Section on General Surgery, Wake Forest University Medical Center, Winston-Salem, N.C.

of data in preselected and screened subgroups of the hypertensive population, the lack of standardization of diagnostic methods, the continual introduction of new diagnostic tools, and the heterogenicity of results from respective methods of management. This review summarizes available data pertaining to renovascular hypertension and serves as a reference from which areas of controversy may be identified and subsequently resolved.

Table I. Incidence

	Hypertension from all causes (% of general population)	Ref.	Hypertension due to renovascular causes (% of hypertensive population)	Ref.
Adult	10-25	1,2	4-5	3-5
			67 male	3-5
			33 female	6
Adolescent	5	6	5	7
Child	1-2	6,8	56-95	7,9

Table II. Blood pressure levels in different kinds of hypertension

Diastolic blood pressure (no medications)	Total n (%)	Essential hypertension n (%)	Renovascular hypertension n (%)	Ref.
90-117	102 (100)	102 (100)	0 (0)	1
>117	35 (100)	26 (74)	9 (26)	1
Black	13 (37)	13 (100)	0 (0)	1
White	22 (63)	13 (59)	9 (41)	1
Accelerated or malignant hypertension	123 (100)		28 (23)	6

Table III. Characteristics of renovascular lesions

Type	Incidence (%)	Unilateral (%)	Bilateral (%)	Mean age (yr)	Sex distribution (%) Male	Sex distribution (%) Female
Atherosclerotic RAS	60-70[a]	62-75[b]	25[b]	40-55[c]	55-67[d]	33-45[d]
Focal	41[e]					
Diffuse	59[e]					
Fibromuscular dysplasia (FMD)	25[a]	21[f]	79[f]	30-38[c]	6-19[d]	81-94[d]
Intimal, percent of total FMD	5[g]					
Medial hyperplasia	1[g]					
Medial fibrodysplasia	70-85[h]					
Perimedial (subadventitial)	10[h]					
Other causes	5					

References: [a]10-12; [b]3,14,15; [c]13,16-18; [d]16-18; [e]13; [f]6,19; [g]10; [h]9,11.

Table IV. Natural history: Arteriographic progression of lesions

Lesion	Mean follow-up (mo)	n	Ipsilateral % exhibiting progression	Ipsilateral % progressing to occlusion	Contralateral % exhibiting progression	Ref.
Atherosclerosis	29-35	85	44	16		20,21
	28	35		12	17	22
Fibromuscular dysplasia	35	66	33	0		21

Table V. Natural history: Functional changes accompanying arteriographic progression

Parameter	Number (%) affected Atherosclerotic	Number (%) affected Fibromuscular dysplasia	Mean follow-up (mo)	Ref.
Serum creatinine (Cr)				
No change	17 (46%)	20 (91%)	45-52	20
New onset Cr >2	5 (12%)		31-74	21
>20% increase	20 (54%)	2 (9%)	45-52	21
>100% increase	2 (5%)		25	22
Decreased renal size				
By ≥1.5 cm	26 (70%)	6 (27%)	45-52	21
By ≥10%				
Ipsilateral	14 (37%)		17-36	22
Contralateral	5 (13%)		17-36	22
Glomerular filtration rate (GFR) or creatinine clearance				
Decreased by 25%-49%	11 (37%)		15-24	22
Decreased >50%	1 (3%)		15-24	22
No change	14 (47%)		15-24	22
Improved by ≥25%	4 (13%)		15-24	22

Table VI. Comparison of diagnostic studies

Study	Results (%)			Sensitivity (%)	Specificity (%)	Predictive value (%)
	True positive	False positive	False negative			
Hypertensive IVP in children	78-80[a]	11-13[a]	31[b]	69[b] 42[d]		31[c]
Radionuclide (GFR) scan[e]	70-80	25-30	25-30			
Renal vein renin (RVR) ratio ≥ 1.5:1						
Unilateral disease[f]				77	75	93
Bilateral disease[g]	71					
Single catheter technique	22-24[h]	22-24[h]	21[i]			
Simultaneous bilateral sampling	< 10[i]					
Peripheral plasma renin (PPR)			40[j]			
PPR-urine sodium index			50[i] 20[k]			
Renal vein-systemic renin index				74	100	
$\dfrac{(V - A)}{A} \geq 0.48$[k]						
Split renal function studies (SRFS) constant lateralization with decreased urine volume and increased urine para-amino-hippurate (PAH) and creatinine						
Unilateral disease[l]	90	10	8			
Bilateral disease[g]	69					
Combined +RVR and +SRFS, bilateral disease[g]	92					
Digital subtraction arteriography[m] overall		5	9			
Atherosclerotic lesions		16	3			
Fibromuscular dysplasia		0	20			

References: [a]17,23; [b]3; [c]18; [d]24; [e]10,23; [f]25; [g]26; [h]27; [i]10; [j]28; [k]23,29; [l]30; [m]31.

Table VII. Outcomes with percutaneous transluminal angioplasty (PCTA) versus surgery

	PCTA (%)	Surgery (%)
Mortality	0[a]	0-2[b]
Morbidity		
Procedure-related	5[a]	11[c]
Hematoma	3-4[d]	
Embolization	3[e]	
Kidney-related	10[a]	6[c]
Contrast nephropathy	2-5[d]	
Arterial dissection	5[f]	
Requiring second operative procedure	2-6[g]	
Early technical success, overall	89[h]	97[i]
Procedure technically unfeasible	3-6[j]	0[k]
Atherosclerotic, nonostial, nonoccluded	75[e]	
Ostial	20[e]	
Occluded vessel	20[e]	
Fibromuscular dysplasia, unilateral lesion	86[e]	

References: [a]32-34; [b]4,11,26,35-38; [c]38; [d]39,40; [e]40; [f]41; [g]41,48; [h]44,45,47,49,50; [i]51,52; [j]39,49; [k]37.

Table VIII. Early and late results with PCTA versus surgery

Early BP response	PCTA					Surgery				
	"Favorable"	Cured	Improved	Failed	n	"Favorable"	Cured	Improved	Failed	n
Atherosclerotic, unspecified	79%[a]					95%[b]				
Focal							37	45	18	1173[a]
Nonostial, non-occluded		20	45	35	20[c]		40	47	12	446[d]
Ostial		0	0	100	5[c]					
Occluded vessel		100	0	0	5[c]					
Diffuse							25	47	28	506[e]
FMD, unilateral lesion		54	41	5	338[f]	90%[g]	59	31	10	847[h]

Long-term results	PCTA (%)	Length of follow-up	n	Surgery (%)	Length of follow-up	n
Sustained BP benefit	44-65	1-52 mos	213[i]	90-93	6 mo-11 yr	308[j]
Saphenous vein patency				91-95	1-23 yr[k]	
Aneurysmal change				4		12/326[l]
Iliac arterial autograft patency				96-98	5 yr[m]	
Recurrent arterial atherosclerotic stenoses	10-100	1-22 mos[n]				
Reoperation rate				3		1038[o]
Reoperation success rate				82-85[o]		
Redilatation success rate	35			5-11[p]		
Loss of renal mass (% of patients)				13[q]		
Increase in renal mass (% of patients)				27[q]		
Serum creatinine						
Improved*				67	4-76 mo	34[r]
Unchanged				27	4-76 mo	14[r]
Worsened				6	4-76 mo	3[r]

*In atherosclerotic patients.

References: [a]2,10,38,53-60; [b]37; [c]40; [d]54,56,58-61; [e]38,54,56,58,60,62; [f]40,63-69; [g]50; [h]1,2,54-62; [i]31-33,45; [j]1,37,53; [k]1,12,70,71; [l]72,73; [m]74; [n]31,32,44,45,49,50,75; [o]76; [p]77; [q]21; [r]78.

REFERENCES

1. Dean RH. Surgical management of renovascular hypertension. In Bergan JJ, ed. Clinical Surgery International. vol. 8. Arterial Surgery. Edinburgh: Churchill Livingstone, 1984, 80-93.
2. Vidt DG. Advances in the medical management of renovascular hypertension. Urol Clin North Am 1984;11:417-424.
3. Foster JH, Dean RH, Pinkerton JA, et al. Ten years experience with the surgical management of renovascular hypertension. Ann Surg 1973;177:755-766.
4. Hunt JC, Strong CG. Renovascular hypertension: Mechanisms, natural history and treatment. In Laragh JH, ed. Hypertension Manual: Mechanisms, Methods, Management. New York: Dun-Donnelley, 1973, 509-536.
5. Rudnick KV, Sackett DL, Hirst S, et al. Hypertension in a family practice. Can Med Assoc J 1977;117:492-497.
6. Shapiro AP, Perez-Stable E, Scheib ET, et al. Renal artery stenosis and hypertension: Observations on current status of therapy from a study of 115 patients. Am J Med 1969;47:175-193.
7. Loggie JMH. Evaluation and management of childhood hypertension. Surg Clin North Am 1985;65:1623-1649.
8. Loggie JMH. Identification and management of juvenile hypertension. Postgrad Med 1979;65:103-111.
9. Clayman AS, Bookstein JJ. The role of renal arteriography in pediatric hypertension. Radiology 1973;108:107-110.
10. Dean RH. Renovascular hypertension. Curr Probl Surg 1985;22(2):1-67.
11. Dean RH. Operative management of renovascular hypertension. In Bergan JJ, Yao JST, eds. Surgery of the Aorta and Its Body Branches. New York: Grune & Stratton, 1979, 377-407.
12. Novick AC, Khauli RB, Vidt DG. Diminished operative risk and improved results following revascularization for atherosclerotic renovascular disease. Urol Clin North Am 1984;11:435-449.
13. Dean RH, Krueger TC, Whiteneck JM, et al. Operative management of renovascular hypertension: Results after a follow-up of fifteen to twenty-three years. J Vasc Surg 1984;1:234-242.
14. Starr DS, Lawrie GM, Morris GC Jr. Surgical treatment of renovascular hypertension: Long-term followup of 216 patients up to 20 years. Arch Surg 1980;115:494-496.
15. Davis BA, Crook JE, Vestal RE, et al. Prevalence of renovascular hypertension in patients with grade III or IV hypertensive retinopathy. N Engl J Med 1979;301:1273-1276.
16. Tucker RM, Labarthe DR. Frequency of surgical treatment for hypertension in adults at the Mayo Clinic from 1973 through 1975. Mayo Clin Proc 1977;52:549-555.

17. Thornbury JR, Stanley JC, Fryback DG. Hypertensive urogram: A nondiscriminatory test for renovascular hypertension. AJR 1982;138:43-49.

18. Barnes R, Berson A, Dean R, et al. Diagnosis and management of renovascular disease: Summary report. J Vasc Surg 1985;2:453-458.

19. Bookstein JJ, Abrams HL, Buenger RE, et al. Radiologic aspects of renovascular hypertension. Part 2: The role of urography in unilateral renovascular disease. JAMA 1972;9: 1225-1230.

20. Wollenweber J, Sheps SG, Davis GD. Clinical course of atherosclerotic renovascular disease. Am J Cardiol 1968;21: 60-71.

21. Schreiber MJ, Pohl MA, Novick AC. The natural history of atherosclerotic and fibrous renal artery disease. Urol Clin North Am 1984;11:383-392.

22. Dean RH, Kieffer RW, Smith BM, et al. Renovascular hypertension: Anatomic and renal function changes during drug therapy. Arch Surg 1981;116:1408-1415.

23. Vaughan ED Jr, Case DB, Pickering TG, et al. Clinical evaluation of renovascular hypertension and therapeutic decisions. Urol Clin North Am 1984;11:393-407.

24. Lawson JD, Boerth R, Foster JH, et al. Diagnosis and management of renovascular hypertension in children. Arch Surg 1977;112:1307-1316.

25. Marks LS, Maxwell MH, Varady PD, et al. Renovascular hypertension: Does the renal vein renin ratio predict operative results? J Urol 1976;115:365-368.

26. Dean RH. Indications for operative management of renovascular hypertension. Proceedings of the 8th International Congress of Nephrology 1981;1146-1153.

27. Whelton PK, Harrington DP, Russell RP, et al. Renal vein renin activity: A prospective study of sampling techniques and methods of interpretation. Johns Hopkins Med J 1977; 141:112-118.

28. Cohen EL, Rovner DR, Conn JW. Postural augmentation of plasma renin activity: Importance in diagnosis of renovascular hypertension. JAMA 1966;197:973-978.

29. Pickering TG, Sos TA, Vaughan ED Jr, et al. Predictive value and changes of renin secretion in hypertensive patients with unilateral renovascular disease undergoing successful renal angioplasty. Am J Med 1984;76:398-404.

30. Dean RH, Rhamy RK. Split renal function studies in renovascular hypertension. In Ernst C, Fry W, Stanley J, eds. Renovascular Hypertension. Philadelphia: WB Saunders, 1984, 135-145.

31. Zabbo A, Novick AC. Digital subtraction angiography for noninvasive imaging of the renal artery. Urol Clin North Am 1984;11:409-416.

32. Schwarten DE. Transluminal angioplasty of renal artery stenosis: 70 experiences. AJR 1980;135:969-974.

33. Grim CE, Weinberger MH, Yune HY. Balloon dilatation as a treatment of hypertension due to renal artery stenosis: Preliminary results in 25 patients. Proceedings of the First SCOR- Hypertension Conference, Cornell Medical Center, New York City. May 7-8, 1980, 125-129.

34. Tegtmeyer CJ, Teates CD, Crigler N, et al. Percutaneous transluminal angioplasty in patients with renal artery stenosis: Follow-up studies. Radiology 1981;140:323-330.

35. Hunt JC, Strong CG. Renovascular hypertension: Mechanisms, natural history and treatment. Am J Cardiol 1973;32: 562-574.

36. Dean RH. Comparison of medical and surgical treatment of renovascular hypertension. Nephron 1986;44(Suppl 1): 101-104.

37. Perry MO, Silane MF. Management of renovascular problems during aortic operations. Arch Surg 1984;119:681-685.

38. Dean RH. Surgery or transluminal dilatation for renal artery stenosis? Vasc Diagnost Treat 1983;4:27-34.

39. Pickering TG, Sos TA, Laragh JH. Role of balloon dilatation in the treatment of renovascular hypertension. Am J Med 1984; 77(Suppl 2A):61-66.

40. Martin LG, Casarella WJ, Alspaugh JP, et al. Renal artery angioplasty: Increased technical success and decreased complications in the second 100 patients. Radiology 1986;159: 631-634.

41. Sos TA, Pickering TG, Sniderman K, et al. Percutaneous transluminal renal angioplasty in renovascular hypertension due to atheroma or fibromuscular dysplasia. N Engl J Med 1983;309:274-279.

42. Martin LG, Price RB, Casarella WJ, et al. Percutaneous angioplasty in the clinical management of renovascular hypertension: Initial and long-term results. Radiology 1985;155: 629-633.

43. Löhr E, Weichert HC, Hartjes H, et al. Percutaneous transluminal angioplasty of renal arteries: A therapeutic principle. Case report of 128 patients with renovascular hypertension. In Dotter CT, Grüntzig AR, Schoop W, Zeitler E, eds. Percutaneous Transluminal Angioplasty. Berlin: Springer-Verlag, 1983, 281-285.

44. Colapinto RF, Stronell RD, Harries-Jones EP, et al. Percutaneous transluminal dilatation of the renal artery: Follow-up studies on renovascular hypertension. AJR 1982;139:727-732.

45. Tegtmeyer CJ, Kofler TJ, Ayers CA. Renal angioplasty: Current status. AJR 1984;142:17-21.

46. Tegtmeyer CJ, Dyer R, Teates CD, et al. Percutaneous transluminal dilatation of the renal arteries: Techniques and results. Radiology 1980;135:589-599.

47. Schwarten DE. Percutaneous transluminal renal angioplasty. Urol Radiol 1981;2:193-200.

48. Cohn DJ, Sos TA, Saddekni S, et al. Transluminal angioplasty for atherosclerotic renal artery stenosis. Semin Intervent Radiol 1984;1:279-287.

49. Katzen BT, Chang J, Knox WG. Percutaneous transluminal angioplasty with the Grüntzig balloon catheter: A review of 70 cases. Arch Surg 1979;114:1389-1399.

50. Puijlaert CBAJ, Boomsma JHB, Ruijs JHJ, et al. Transluminal renal artery dilatation in hypertension: Technique, results, and complications in 60 cases. Urol Radiol 1981;2:201-210.

51. Dean RH, Hollifield JW, Oates JA. Medical versus surgical treatment of renovascular hypertension. In Ernst CB, Stanley JC, Fry WJ, eds. Renovascular Hypertension. Philadelphia: WB Saunders, 1984, 354-362.

52. Dean RH. Aortorenal bypass for renovascular hypertension due to atherosclerosis. In Rutherford RB, ed. Vascular Surgery, 2nd ed. Philadelphia: WB Saunders, 1984, 1136-1144.

53. Dean RH. Renovascular hypertension. In Moore WS, ed. Vascular Surgery: A Comprehensive Review. New York: Grune & Stratton, 1983, 433-463.

54. Novick AC, Straffon RA, Stewart BH, et al. Diminished operative morbidity and mortality in renal revascularization. JAMA 1981;246:749-753.

55. Bergentz SE, Ericsson BF, Husberg B. Technique and complications in the surgical treatment of renovascular hypertension. Acta Chir Scand 1979;145(3):143-148.

56. Stanley JC. Renovascular hypertension: The surgical point of view. In van Schilfgaarde R, ed. Clinical Aspects of Renovascular Hypertension. Boston: Martinus Nijhoff, 1983, pp. 259-268.

57. Thevenet A, Mary H, Boennec M. Results following surgical correction of renovascular hypertension. J Cardiovasc Surg 1980;21:517-528.

Table IV. Etiology of acute intestinal ischemia*

Cause	Acute intestinal ischemia (%)	Ref.
Arterial embolism	29	1-3,7-9
Arterial thrombosis	23	1-3,7-9
Venous thrombosis	10	1-3,7-9
Nonocclusive ischemia	31	1-3,7-9
Miscellaneous[†]	7	1-3,7-9
Total	100	

*Pooled data from 388 patients described in the references.
[†]Miscellaneous category includes arteritis, postoperative athero-embolism, etc.

Table V. Mortality of acute intestinal ischemia

Category	Mortality rate (n)	Ref.
Mesenteric arterial embolization	70% (120)	2,3,9-15
Mesenteric arterial thrombosis	92% (86)	2,3,9-12,14,15
Nonocclusive intestinal ischemia	92% (93)	3,9-11,14,15

Table VI. Incidence of history of chronic abdominal pain in patients treated for acute intestinal ischemia

Patient source	No.	Chronic pain history (%)	Ref.
Patients dying of acute ischemia	12	58	16
Patients operated for mesenteric arterial thrombosis	8	100	17

Table VII. Normal values for mesenteric artery hemodynamics determined by noninvasive methods

Artery	Flow velocity* (syst/diast)	Volume flow[†] (mean)	Flow pattern	Ref.
SMA[‡]	125/21	378	High resistance	18,19
Celiac[‡]	123/41	—	Low resistance	
SMA[§]	173/84	1200	Low resistance	18,19
Celiac[§]	143/49	—	Low resistance	

SMA = superior mesenteric artery.
*In cm/sec.
[†]In ml/min.
[‡]Fasting values.
[§]Maximum changes values after test meals.

Table VIII. Accuracy of noninvasive diagnosis of mesenteric artery obstruction*

Artery	Criteria	Sensitivity (%)	Specificity (%)	PPV (%)	NPV (%)	Ref.
SMA	PSV >275 cm/sec	89	92	80	96	27
Celiac	PSV >200 cm/sec	75	89	85	80	27

PPV = positive predictive value; NPV = negative predictive value; PSV = peak systolic velocity.
*Obstruction defined as arteriographic stenosis of 70% or greater.

Table IX. Treatment of mesenteric artery obstruction using percutaneous balloon angioplasty[20]

Category	No. of patients	Patients (%)
Patients treated	35	100
Initially successful	28	80
Recurred within 12 mo*	7 of 18	39
Overall 12 mo success rate[†]	11 of 23	48

*Only patients with initially successful dilation and at least 12 mo follow-up considered.
[†]All patients with at least 12 mo follow-up considered.

Table X. Surgical treatment of chronic intestinal ischemia

Surgical technique	No.	Surgical mortality (%)	Early success (%)	Late success (%)	Ref.
SMA reimplant	60	3.5	94	80*	21
Prosthetic graft from supraceliac aorta	39	3	95	90[†]	17,22,23
Prosthetic graft from infrarenal aorta	39	5	95	90[§]	17
Aortomesenteric vein graft	61	4	75	—	15,24-26
Transaortic visceral endarterectomy	47	—	96	—	23
Total	246	4	91	85	

SMA = superior mesenteric artery
*Mean follow-up 8.5 yr.
[†]Mean follow-up about 4.5 yr.
[§]Mean follow-up 4.2 yr.

REFERENCES

1. Kairaluoma MI, Karkola P, Heikkinen E, et al. Mesenteric infarction. Am J Surg 1977;133:188-193.
2. Bergan JJ, McCarthy WJ III, Flinn WR, et al. Nontraumatic mesenteric vascular emergencies. J Vasc Surg 1987;5:903-909.
3. Ottinger LW, Austen WG. A study of 136 patients with mesenteric infarction. Surg Gynecol Obstet 1967;124:251-261.
4. Marston A. Diagnosis and management of intestinal ischemia. Ann R Coll Surg Engl 1972;50:29-41.
5. Croft RJ, Menon GP, Marston A. Does "intestinal angina" exist? A critical study of obstructed visceral arteries. Br J Surg 1981;68:316-318.
6. Bron KM, Redman HC. Splanchnic artery stenosis and occlusion. Radiology 1969;92:323-328.
7. Rivers SP. Acute nonocclusive intestinal ischemia. In Taylor LM Jr., guest ed, Rutherford RB, ed. Seminars in Vascular Surgery 1990;3:172-175.
8. Clavien PA, Muller C, Harder F. Treatment of mesenteric infarction. Br J Surg 1987;74:500-503.
9. Sachs SM, Morton JH, Schwartz SI. Acute mesenteric ischemia. Surgery 1982;92:646-653.
10. Slater H, Elliot DW. Primary mesenteric infarction. Am J Surg 1972;123:309-311.
11. Boley SJ, Sprayregen S, Siegelman SS, et al. Initial results from an aggressive roentgenological and surgical approach to acute mesenteric ischemia. Surgery 1977;82:848-855.
12. Krauz MM, Manny J. Acute superior mesenteric arterial occlusion: A plea for early diagnosis. Surgery 1978;83:482-485.
13. Boley SJ, Feinstein FR, Sammartano R, et al. New concepts in the management of emboli of the superior mesenteric artery. Surg Gynecol Obstet 1981;153:561-569.
14. Rogers DM, Thompson JE, Garrett WV, et al. Mesenteric vascular problems: A 26-year experience. Ann Surg 1982;195:554-565.
15. Bergan JJ, Dean RH, Conn J, et al. Revascularization in the treatment of mesenteric infarction. Ann Surg 1975;182:430-434.
16. Dunphy JE. Abdominal pain of vascular origin. Am J Med Sci 1936;192:109-113.
17. Taylor LM Jr, Porter JM. Treatment of chronic intestinal ischemia. In Taylor LM Jr, guest ed, Rutherford RB, ed. Seminars in Vascular Surgery 1990;3:186-199.
18. Jager K, Bollinger A, Valli C, et al. Measurement of mesenteric blood flow by duplex scanning. J Vasc Surg 1986;3:462-469.
19. Moneta GL, Taylor DC, Helton WS, et al. Duplex ultrasound measurement of postprandial intestinal blood flow: Effect of meal composition. Gastroenterology 1988;95:1294-1301.
20. Tegtmeyer CJ, Selby JB. Balloon angioplasty of the visceral arteries (renal and mesenteric circulation): Indications, results, and complications. In Moore WS, Ahn SS, eds. Endovascular Surgery. Philadelphia: WB Saunders, 1989; pp 223-257.
21. Kieny R, Batellier J, Kretz J. Aortic reimplantation of the superior mesenteric artery for atherosclerotic lesions of the visceral arteries: Sixty cases. Ann Vasc Surg 1990;4:122-125.
22. Beebe HG, MacFarlane S, Raker EJ. Supraceliac aortomesenteric bypass for intestinal ischemia. J Vasc Surg 1987;5:749-754.
23. Rapp JH, Reilly LM, Qvarfordt PG, et al. Durability of endarterectomy and antegrade grafts in the treatment of chronic visceral ischemia. J Vasc Surg 1986;3:799-806.
24. Zelenock GB, Graham LM, Whitehouse WM, et al. Splanchnic arteriosclerotic disease and intestinal angina. Arch Surg 1980;115:497-501.
25. Stoney RJ, Ehrenfeld WK, Wylie EJ. Revascularization methods in chronic visceral ischemia. Ann Surg 1977;186:468-476.
26. McCollum CH, Graham JM, DeBakey ME. Chronic mesenteric arterial insufficiency: Results of revascularization in 33 cases. South Med J 1976;69:1266-1268.
27. Moneta GL, Yeager RA, Dalman R, et al. Duplex ultrasound criteria for diagnosis of splanchnic artery stenosis or occlusion. J Vasc Surg 1991;14(4):511-518.
28. Clavien PA, Muller C, Harder F. Treatment of mesenteric infarction. Br J Surg 1987;74:500-503.
29. Lazaro T, Sierra L, Gesto R, et al. Embolization of the mesenteric arteries: Surgical treatment in twenty-three consecutive cases. Ann Vasc Surg 1986;1:311-315.
30. Sachs SM, Morton JH, Schwartz SI. Acute mesenteric ischemia. Surgery 1982;92:646-653.
31. Bergan JJ, McCarthy WJ III, Flinn WR, et al. Nontraumatic mesenteric vascular emergencies. J Vasc Surg 1987;5:903-909.
32. VanWay CW, Brockman SK, Rosenfeld L. Spontaneous thrombosis of the mesenteric veins. Ann Surg 1971;173:561-568.
33. Abdu RA, Zakhour BJ, Dallis DJ. Mesenteric venous thrombosis—1911 to 1984. Surgery 1987;101:383-388.
34. Anane-Sefah JC, Blair E, Reckler S. Primary mesenteric venous occlusive disease. Surg Gynecol Obstet 1975;141:740-742.

35. Mathews JE, White RR. Primary mesenteric venous occlusive disease. Am J Surg 1971;122:579-583.

36. Aldrete JS, Han SY, Laws HL, et al. Intestinal infarction complicating low cardiac output states. Surg Gynecol Obstet 1977;144:371-375.

37. Watt-Boolsen S. Non-occlusive intestinal infarction. Acta Chir Scand 1977;143:365-369.

38. Williams LF, Anastasia LF, Hasiotis CA, et al. Nonocclusive mesenteric infarction. Am J Surg 1967;114:376-381.

39. Rheudasil JM, Stewart MT, Schellach JV, et al. Surgical treatment of chronic mesenteric arterial insufficiency. J Vasc Surg 1988;8:495-500.

40. Hollier LH, Bernatz PE, Pairolero PC, et al. Surgical management of chronic intestinal ischemia: A reappraisal. Surgery 1981;90:940-946.

19

Colon Ischemia Following Aortic Reconstruction

David F.J. Tollefson, MD, Calvin B. Ernst, MD, Detroit, Michigan

Ischemic colitis following aortic reconstruction, although uncommon, has potentially devastating consequences. Although clinically apparent after only about 2% of aortic reconstructions, subclinical episodes undoubtedly occur much more frequently. The mortality associated with transmural colonic infarction can exceed 50%.

Colon ischemia is usually due to a watershed phenomenon, wherein the collateral blood flow to the sigmoid colon from the superior mesenteric artery (SMA) or hypogastric arteries (HGA) is inadequate after inferior mesenteric artery (IMA) occlusion occurring subsequent to aortic reconstruction. This collateral blood flow is through either the meandering mesenteric artery (for SMA to IMA flow) or the marginal artery of Drummond.

Certain criteria are useful in predicting individuals at risk for postoperative colon ischemia. Early postoperative diagnosis is crucial to minimize morbidity and mortality associated with ischemic colitis. Although diarrhea, fever, severe postoperative abdominal pain, or signs of sepsis and peritonitis all suggest colonic ischemia, flexible sigmoidoscopy is essential to establish the diagnosis and can be performed at the bedside.

Nonoperative management, including broad-spectrum antibiotics and careful attention to fluid and electrolyte administration, is the preferred treatment for mild cases of colon ischemia involving only the mucosa. However, at the first signs of advanced ischemia, whether noted endoscopically or clinically, resection of all necrotic bowel with colostomy and either mucous fistula or Hartmann's pouch is mandatory.

From the Department of Vascular Surgery, Henry Ford Hospital, Detroit, Mich.

The following tables summarize our review of ischemic colitis following aortic reconstruction. Although improvement in operative technique and perioperative care can diminish the occurrence of ischemic colitis, constant vigilance for detection of early signs of colon ischemia is essential to minimize the morbidity and mortality associated with this potentially lethal complication.

Table I. Clinically apparent incidence[1-30]

Condition	Percentage
Overall*	2.0 (range 0-50)
Elective AAA repair	1.8 (range 0-50)
Ruptured AAA repair	13.4 (range 2.1-32)
Occlusive disease	0.3 (range 0.1-2.4)

AAA = abdominal aortic aneurysm.
*Instances of ischemic colitis in 8125 patients following aortic reconstruction.

Table II. Colonoscopic (including subclinical) incidence[20,28]

Condition	Percentage
Overall	9.3
Elective AAA repair	5.8 (range 4.5-6.8)
Ruptured AAA repair	24.0 (range 17.6-35.3)
Occlusive disease	6.7

Table III. Mortality[1-30]

Condition	Percentage
Overall	51.0 (range 0-86)
With transmural involvement	84.0 (range 67-100)

Table IV. Classification/clinical course*

Type	Pathologic findings	Clinical findings	Clinical outcome
I	Mucosal ischemia, submucosal edema/hemorrhage; mucosal slough ulceration may follow	Diarrhea with or without blood; ± fever; onset usually 24-48 hr	Reversible; no sequelae; near zero mortality
II	As above with penetration of muscularis	Symptoms vary between Type I and Type II	Reversible; residual ischemic stricture possible
III	Transmural bowel involvement	Profound physiologic changes; sepsis, acidosis, cardiovascular collapse (May develop feculent peritonitis or late fecal fistula)	Irreversible; mortality = 70% ± 1%

*References 5,9,13,15,16,19,22,29,31,32.

Table V. Etiology[9]

Source	Incidence
Arterial ischemia	Almost all
Venous occlusion	Rare

Table VI. Predisposing factors*

Improper IMA ligation
Failure to restore IMA and/or hypogastric flow
Ruptured aneurysm with mesenteric compression
Congenitally inadequate mesenteric collateral communications
Injury to collateral vessels (including meandering mesenteric or artery of Drummond)
Colonic trauma caused by retractors
Persistent hypotension and hypoperfusion

*References 10,16,22,33,37-40.

Table VII. Colonic collateral blood supply[33,34,37]

Left colonic blood supply (from splenic flexure to rectosigmoid)
   Left colic artery
   Sigmoidal artery
   Superior rectal arteries
Key arterial collaterals
   Meandering mesenteric artery*
   Marginal artery of Drummond[†]

*Identified on preoperative aortography in 27% and 35% of patients with aneurysmal and occlusive disease, respectively. Carries blood flow from superior mesenteric artery to inferior mesenteric artery if inferior mesenteric artery blood flow occluded.
†Continuity lacking in area of ascending colon (5%), sigmoid colon (20%), and rectosigmoid even more often (see references 34,35,41,42).

Table VIII. Criteria for safe IMA ligation[19]

Pressure	Measurement
IMA pressure	>40 torr*
IMA/systemic pressure	>0.4

IMA = inferior mesenteric artery.
*IMA stump pressure.

Table IX. Inferior mesenteric aortic circulation: Contribution from collateral beds (hypogastric and SMA)[43]

IMA-SPI*	Patent IMA
0.61 ± 0.20	Open MCA and both HGA
0.56 ± 0.17	Open MCA and clamp right HGA
0.54 ± 0.17	Open MCA and clamp left HGA
0.54 ± 0.19	Open MCA and clamp both HGA
0.32 ± 0.15†	Clamp MCA and open HGA
0.30 ± 0.16	Clamp MCA and clamp right HGA
0.29 ± 0.16	Clamp MCA and clamp left HGA
0.26 ± 0.14	Clamp MCA and clamp both HGA

IMA-SPI	Chronically occluded
0.60 ± 0.11	Open MCA and both HGA
0.59 ± 0.12	Open MCA and clamp right HGA
0.58 ± 0.12	Open MCA and clamp left HGA
0.57 ± 0.11	Open MCA and clamp both HGA
0.34 ± 0.04†	Clamp MCA and open HGA
0.33 ± 0.03	Clamp MCA and right HGA
0.33 ± 0.03	Clamp MCA and left HGA
0.32 ± 0.04	Clamp MCA and both HGA

SMA = superior mesenteric artery; SPI = stump pressure index; MCA = middle colic artery (branch of SMA); HGA = hypogastric artery.
*IMA-SPI = ratio of mean IMA pressure divided by corresponding mean radial arterial pressure.
†Statistically significant drop in IMA-SPI with clamping of MCA in both patent and chronically occluded IMAs ($p < 0.01$).

Table X. Risk prediction for ischemic bowel following abdominal aortic reconstruction

Risk factors	Ref.
Greatest risk	
Symptoms of visceral ischemia	19,22,27,38,
Aortic aneurysm (ruptured)	39,44-46
Patent IMA	
Zero operative Doppler flow	
IMA stump pressure <40 mm Hg	
IMA to SMA flow in meandering	
mesenteric artery	
Least risk	
Thrombosed IMA	19,44-47
SMA to IMA flow in meandering	
mesenteric artery	
Operative Doppler flow present	
IMA stump pressure >40 mm Hg	
Reconstruction for occlusive disease	

Table XI. Clinical manifestations of ischemic colitis*

Diarrhea: most common, 24-48 hr (bloody or non-bloody)
Extraordinary postoperative lower abdominal pain
Progressive abdominal distention
Sepsis with WBC >20-30,000/mm³
Thrombocytopenia <90,000/mm³
Acidosis
Oliguria

WBC = white blood cells.
*References 2,7,9,13,15,16,24,31,47,48.

Table XII. Postoperative diagnosis of ischemic colitis*

Modality	Application
Barium contrast studies	Useful only for late diagnosis of bowel stricture
Arteriography	Only indirect evidence of ischemic colitis—no collaterals seen
Flexible sig-moidoscopy	Study of choice, performed early at bedside. Performed only to 40 cm or up to the first lesion seen

*References 7,9,13,19,20,30,51,52.

Table XIII. Flexible sigmoidoscopic appearance of ischemic colitis[19,20,30,51]

Stage	Appearance
Early	Circumferential petechial hemorrhages and edema
Advanced	Pseudomembranes, erosions, and ulcers
Transmural involvement	Yellowish-green necrotic noncontractile surface

Table XIV. Treatment of ischemic colitis[47]

Clinical condition	Management
Mild ischemia (no evidence of peritonitis/sepsis)	Broad spectrum antibiotics, optimal fluid and electrolyte status
	Reversible lesions resolve 7-10 days
Progressive ischemia worsening, symptoms, advancing endoscopic findings	Prompt operative intervention: resect nonviable bowel with colostomy and Hartmann's pouch
	Never perform primary anastomosis
	Protect aortic graft from contamination

20

EDITOR'S NOTE: In Chapters 20 and 21 an extensive review of data on primary communications between the aorta and the gastrointestinal tract will be presented. Dossa et al. have reviewed the available English language literature regarding these rare lesions and compiled the essential data. Part I discusses abdominal aortointestinal communications. Part II deals with communications in the thorax. It is hoped that surgeons who encounter these very rare lesions will find thie review helpful in clinical decision making.

Primary Aortoenteric Fistula: Part I

Christos D. Dossa, MD, Iraklis I. Pipinos, MD, Alexander D. Shepard, MD, and Calvin B. Ernst, MD, Detroit, Michigan

Primary aortoenteric fistula (AEF) is a rare but often lethal vascular catastrophe when it occurs. Because of the rarity of this lesion no individual surgeon or institution has had a large enough experience to provide clinically pertinent basic data. This is reflected by the literature on this topic over the past 15 years, which includes case reports and occasional small series. To better define the presentation, diagnosis, treatment and outcome of primary AEF and to derive a data base to aid in clinical decision making, all English language reports over the past 15 years were analyzed and the data tabulated.

From the Division of Vascular Surgery, Department of Surgery, Henry Ford Hospital, Detroit, Mich.

Table I. Demographics

		No. of patients	References
Male:female	2.8:1	65*	1-31, 33-44, 46-50
Mean age	61 yr	69	1-50
Age range	23-91 yr	69	1-50

*The gender of four patients was not identified.

Table II. Etiology

	%		No. of patients		References
Aortic pathology	77		53/69		
Aneurysm		[85]		[45/53]	
Nonspecific/degenerative		78		35/45	2-4, 7-9, 12, 13, 17, 19, 20, 24, 25, 29, 30, 33, 38, 41, 43, 45, 46, 48, 50
Mycotic		14		6/45	13, 16, 22, 37, 41
Inflammatory		4		2/45	5, 49
Posttraumatic		4		2/45	6, 32
Aortitis*		9		5/53	1, 3, 11, 28, 39
Ulcerative atherosclerosis		6		3/53	15, 18, 31
GI pathology	13		9/69		
Peptic ulcer		60		5/9	10, 26, 27, 35, 40
Cancer		20		2/9	14, 45
Duodenal diverticulum		10		1/9	36
Pancreatic pseudocyst		10		1/9	44
Foreign body	4		3/69		21, 23, 42
Radiation	6		4/69		13, 34, 47

*Includes both nonspecific and microbial varieties.

Table III. Site of bowel involvement

	%		No. of patients		References
Stomach	6		4/69		2, 26, 27, 35
Duodenum	82		57/69		1, 3, 4, 6-13, 15-20, 22-25, 28-34, 36-41, 43-46, 48-50
First part		0		0/57	
Second part		3		2/57	12, 44
Third part		51		29/57	1, 3, 4, 9, 10, 11, 13, 15, 20, 22, 23, 25, 28, 30, 33, 36, 37, 38, 40, 41, 43, 46, 50
Fourth part		18		10/57	3, 6, 15, 19, 22, 29, 31, 34, 39, 48
Unspecified		28		16/57	7, 8, 16, 17, 32, 45, 49
Jejunum	6		4/69		5, 13, 14, 42
Ileum	3		2/69		47
Colon	3		2/69		21, 46

Table IX. Interval from first hospital admission related to AEF to time of diagnosis and/or treatment

	%	No. of patients	References
No delay	15	8/55	3, 6, 13, 16, 27, 34, 36, 39
<24 hr	36	20/55	2, 3, 7, 12, 13, 15, 19, 22, 30-32, 38, 47, 50
1-9 days	20	11/55	3, 13, 20, 21, 28, 29, 43, 44, 46-48
10-30 days	15	8/55	1, 10, 18, 24, 33, 37, 40
>30 days	15	8/55	4, 5, 9, 11, 17, 25, 38, 49

Table X. Operative culture results

	%	No. of patients	References
Positive culture	79	22/28*	1-3, 7, 9, 10, 13, 15, 16, 22, 28, 36-41
Negative culture	21	6/28	5, 12, 18, 33
Streptococcus (non-group D)	23	5/22	1, 2, 7, 16
Salmonella	19	4/22	15, 22, 41
Mycobacterium tuberculosis	14	3/22	3, 28, 37
Mixed†	14	3/22	9, 38, 40
Staphylococcus aureus	9	2/22	7, 13
Klebsiella	9	2/22	3, 36
Arizona hinshawii	4	1/22	39
Candida species	4	1/22	10
Unidentified gram-positive organism	4	1/22	7

*Culture information available on only 28 of the patients reported.
†*Clostridium* and enterococcus,[9] *Klebsiella* and *Streptococcus*,[38] *Escherichia coli*, *Proteus*, enterococcus, *Peptostreptococcus*, and *Clostridium*.[40]

Table XI. Results of operation

	Mortality	References
In situ prosthetic grafting	28% (10/35)	2-5, 7-9, 12-14, 16, 22, 24, 28, 30-33, 35, 37, 38, 41, 45, 46, 48
Local repair	27% (3/11)	13, 19, 21, 23, 26, 34, 42, 44, 45, 47
Aortic ligation/extra-anatomic bypass	50% (3/6)	7, 17, 36, 39, 43, 49
Exploratory celiotomy alone	100% (5/5)	11, 15, 29, 40, 50
Operation	37% (21/57)	
No operation	100% (8/8)	13, 15, 18, 20, 25, 27, 32, 46
Overall	45% (29/65)	

Table XII. Factors affecting operative mortality

	Operative mortality	p Value	References
Age		0.527	
≤ 60 yr	42% (8/19)		1, 2, 5, 6, 11, 13, 17, 18, 20,
> 60 yr	33% (11/33)*		22, 29, 32, 40-42, 44-47
Abdominal aortic aneurysm		0.391	
Present	32% (11/34)		2, 4-6, 8, 9, 12, 14, 16-20, 22, 24, 29, 30, 33, 35-38, 41, 43, 46, 48-50
Absent	18% (8/18)		1, 3, 10, 11, 13, 15, 21, 23, 26-28, 31, 32, 34, 39, 40, 42, 44, 47
Sex		0.226	
Male	32% (12/38)		2-6, 8, 9, 11-20, 22-25, 28-31, 33, 37-39, 41, 42, 44, 47
Female	50% (7/14)		1, 7, 10, 15, 21, 22, 24, 26, 27, 34-36, 40, 41, 43, 47
Fistula to duodenum		0.634	
Yes	38% (16/42)		1, 3, 4, 6, 8-13, 15-20, 22-41, 43-44, 48-50
No	30% (3/10)		2, 5, 13, 14, 21, 26, 27, 35, 42, 46, 47
Shock		0.160	
Yes	31% (11/35)*		1-5, 8, 9, 11-15, 18-22, 26, 27, 29, 31, 33-35, 38, 40, 42-44, 47
No	54% (7/13)		6, 10, 16, 17, 23-25, 28, 30, 36, 37, 39, 46, 48, 50
Sepsis		0.296	
Yes	21% (3/14)*		1, 3, 5, 6, 9, 13, 15-17, 21, 28, 33, 34, 39, 43, 44
No	39% (7/18)		3, 12, 13, 15, 18-20, 22-25, 29-31, 37, 38
No. of diagnostic tests		0.059	
≤ 2	24% (6/25)		3, 6, 8, 12, 13, 15-17, 19, 20, 26, 27-32, 34, 35, 38, 39, 41-43, 46, 47, 50
> 2	50% (13/26)		1, 2, 4, 5, 9-11, 14, 18, 21-25, 28-31, 33, 36, 37, 40, 44, 48
Delay		0.192	
≤ 1 day	29% (5/17)		2, 3, 12, 13, 15, 19, 22, 30-32, 38, 47, 50
> 1 day	50% (12/24)		1, 3-5, 9-11, 13, 17, 18, 20, 21, 24, 25, 28, 29, 33, 37, 38, 40, 43, 44, 46, 47, 48, 49

*Although advanced age, shock, and sepsis appear to be paradoxically associated with better operative mortality, these outcomes are statistically insignificant.

REFERENCES

1. Calligaro KD, Bergen WS, Savarese RP, et al. Primary aortoduodenal fistula due to septic aortitis. J Cardiovasc Surg 1992;33:192-198.
2. Van Damme H, Belachew M, Damas P, et al. Mycotic aneurysm of the upper abdominal aorta ruptured into the stomach. Arch Surg 1992;127:478-482.
3. Wheeler WE, Hanks J, Raman VK. Primary aortoenteric fistulas. Am Surg 1992;58:53-54.
4. Barman AA, Kerr P. Primary and secondary aortoenteric fistula and thoracic aortic aneurysm. NY State J Med 1992; 92:156-158.
5. Shinsuke M, Onohara T, Okadome K, et al. Surgical repair of primary aorto-jejunal fistula associated with non-specific inflammatory abdominal aortic aneurysm. Eur J Vasc Surg 1991;5:335-357.
6. Mohan JC, Kumar P, Malik VK. Aortocaval and aorto-duodenal fistulae with a leaking abdominal aortic aneurysm. Indian Heart J 1991;43:53-54.
7. Hickey NC, Downing R, Hamer JD, et al. Abdominal aortic aneurysms complicated by spontaneous iliocaval or duodenal fistulae. J Cardiovasc Surg 1991;32:181-185.
8. Robinson JA, Johansen K. Aortic sepsis: Is there a role for in situ graft reconstruction? J Vasc Surg 1991;13:677-684.
9. Taheri SA, Kulaylat MN, Grippi J, et al. Surgical treatment of primary aortoduodenal fistula. Ann Vasc Surg 1991;5:265-270.
10. Odze RD, Begin LR. Peptic-ulcer-induced aortoenteric fistula: Report of a case and review of the literature. J Clin Gastroenterol 1991;13:682-686.
11. Frizelle FA, Hung NA, Heslop JH, et al. Obscure gastrointestinal bleeding: Idiopathic aortoduodenal fistula. J R Coll Surg Edinb 1991;36:331-333.
12. Koot HWJ, Veen HF. Haemorrhagic shock due to primary aortoduodenal fistula. Neth J Surg 1990;42-2:53-55.
13. Nohr M, Juul-Jensen KE, Balslev IB, et al. Primary aortoenteric fistula: A practicable curable condition? Pathogenetic and clinical aspects. Int Angiol 1990;9:278-281.
14. Armitage NC, Ballantyne KC. Primary aortoenteric fistula due to recurrent colorectal cancer: Report of a case. Dis Colon Rectum 1990;33:148-149.
15. Gad A. Aortoduodenal fistula revisited. Scand J Gastroenterol 1989;24(Suppl 167):97-100.
16. Gutman H, Russo I, Neuman-Levin M, et al. Computed tomography diagnosis of primary aorto-enteric fistula. Clin Imaging 1989;13:215-216.
17. Ibrahim IM, Raccuia JS, Micale J, et al. Primary aortoduodenal fistula: Diagnosis by computed tomography. Arch Surg 1989;124:870-871.
18. Perrott CA. Aortoenteric fistula without aortic dilatation: Case report. J Emerg Med 1989;7:349-351.
19. Pritchett DB, Dragutsky MS. Primary aortoduodenal fistula: Successful diagnosis and treatment. South Med J 1989;82: 393-394.
20. Aboh IFO, Ofili OP, Aghahowa JA. Primary aorto-duodenal fistula in a Nigerian. Ethiop Med J 198;26:105-109.
21. Caes F, Vierendeels T, Welch W, et al. Aortocolic fistula caused by an ingested chicken bone. Surgery 1988;103:481-483.
22. Morrow C, Safi H, Beall AC. Primary aortoduodenal fistula caused by salmonella aortitis. J Vasc Surg 1987;6:415-418.
23. D'Souza CR, Hebert RJ, Trautman AF, et al. Aortoenteric fistula: Case review and a new surgical technique. Can J Surg 1987;30:415-417.
24. Travis RC, Wattie WJ. Aorto-enteric fistula. Australas Radiol 1987;31:271-277.
25. Yano H, Jimi A, Kojiro M, et al. Primary aortoduodenal fistula—Report of an autopsy case. Gastroenterol Jap 1987; 22:218-221.
26. Jackman JSG, McDonald AM. Haematemesis due to an aorto-gastric fistula secondary to benign gastric ulceration. J R Coll Surg Edinb 1987;32:377.
27. Sternberg A, Nava HR, Isac AT, et al. Perforation of a benign gastric ulcer into the subdiaphragmatic aorta. Am J Gastroenterol 1987;82:579-581.
28. Goldbaum TS, Lindsay J Jr, Levy C, et al. Tuberculous aortitis presenting with an aortoduodenal fistula: A case report. Angiology 1986;37:519-523.
29. Grigsby WS, Eitzen EM, Boyle DJ. Aortoenteric fistula: A catastrophe waiting to happen. Ann Emerg Med 1986;15: 731-734.
30. Curran KB, Macmath T. Primary aortoduodenal fistula presenting as an upper gastrointestinal bleed. J Emerg Med 1985;3:201-204.
31. Jaroch MT, Diehl JT, Zippert AM. Primary aortoduodenal fistula without abdominal aortic aneurysm. Cleve Clin Q 1985;52:579-581.
32. Gozzetti G, Poggioli G, Spolaore R, et al. Aorto-enteric fistulae: Spontaneous and after aorto-iliac operations. J Cardiovasc Surg 1984;25:420-425.
33. Sweeney MS, Gadacz TR. Primary aortoduodenal fistula: Manifestation, diagnosis, and treatment. Surgery 1984;96: 492-497.
34. Estrada FP, Tachovscy TJ, Orr RM, et al. Primary aortoduodenal fistula following radiotherapy. Surg Gynecol Obstet 1983; 156:646-650.
35. Jensen MH, Dedichen H. Penetrating peptic ulcer and aortic aneurysm with aortogastric fistula. Surgery 1984;95:756-758.
36. Adinolfi MF, Hardin W, Kerstein MD. Aortic erosion by duodenal diverticulum: An unusual aortoenteric fistula. South Med J 1983;76:1069-1070.
37. Benhamou G, Duron JJ. Aorto-digestive fistulae. Int Surg 1982;67:307-310.
38. Pfeiffer RB. Successful repair of three primary aortoduodenal fistulae. Arch Surg 1982;117:1098-1099.
39. McIntyre KE, Malone JM, Richards E, et al. Mycotic aortic pseudoaneurysm with aortoenteric fistula caused by *Arizona hinshawii*. Surgery 1982;91:173-177.
40. Steffes BC, O'Leary P. Primary aortoduodenal fistula: A case report and review of the literature. Am Surg 1980;46:121-129.
41. Daugherty M, Shearer GR, Ernst CB. Primary aortoduodenal fistula: Extra-anatomic vascular reconstruction not required for successful management. Surgery 1979;86:399-401.
42. Hambrick E, Rao TR, Lim LT. Jejunoaortic fistula from ingested seamstress needle: Arch Surg 1979;114:732-733.
43. Lewis RT, Allan CM. Spontaneous aortoduodenal fistula: Successful treatment by extra-anatomic vascular bypass. Can J Surg 1979;22:234-236.
44. Sindelar WF, Mason GR. Aortocystoduodenal fistula: Rare complication of pancreatic pseudocyst. Arch Surg 1979;114: 953-955.

45. Florendo FT, Harmon HC. Aortoenteric fistula: A mandatory early operative diagnosis. South Med J 1989;72:1516-1518.

46. Graeber GM, Bredenberg CE, Gregg RO. Diagnosis and management of spontaneous aortoenteric fistulas. Am J Surg 1978;136:269-272.

47. Kwon TH, Boronow RC, Swan RW, et al. Arterio-enteric fistula following pelvic radiation: A case report. Gynecol Oncol 1978;6:474-478.

48. Mehta AI, McDowell DE, James EC. Treatment of massive gastrointestinal hemorrhage from aortoenteric fistula. Surg Gynecol Obstet 1978;146:59-62.

49. Olcott C, Holcroft JW, Stoney RJ, et al. Unusual problems of abdominal aortic aneurysms. Am J Surg 1978;135:426-431.

50. Reiner MA, Brau SA, Schanzer H. Primary aortoduodenal fistula: Case presentation and review of the literature. Am J Gastroenterol 1978;70:292-297.

21

Primary Aortoesophageal Fistula: Part II

Christos D. Dossa, MD, Iraklis I. Pipinos, MD, Alexander D. Shepard, MD, and Calvin B. Ernst, MD, Detroit, Michigan

Primary aortoesophageal fistula (AEsF) is a variant of aortoenteric fistula. Since this lesion primarily involves the thorax rather than the abdomen, there are different characteristic presenting symptoms, diagnostic modalities, and operative techniques. A 15-year review and analysis of all English language reports of this rare lesion yielded 79 patients with primary AEsF.

From the Division of Vascular Surgery, Department of Surgery, Henry Ford Hospital, Detroit, Mich.

Table I. Demographics

		No. of patients	References
Male:female	1.4:1	56*	1-39,41,42
Mean age	58 yr	56*	1-39,41,42
Median age	65 yr	56	1-39,41,42
Age range	3 mo to 87 yr	56	1-39,41,42

*Age and sex information available on only 56/79 patients.

Table II. Etiology

	%		No. of patients		References
Aortic pathology	63		50/79		
Aneurysm		92		46/50	
Nonspecific/degenerative		89		41/46	1,3,7,15,16,19,28-32,34-36,39,41
Associated with dissection		9		4/46	4,8,9,12
Associated with aortitis		2		1/46	24
Ulcerative atherosclerosis		4		2/50	22,40
Congenital anomalies*		4		2/50	26
Esophageal pathology	16		13/79		
Benign (ulcer)		46		6/13	14,26,31,35,40
Malignant		38		5/13	6,12,40
Infections†		16		2/13	17,23
Foreign body	15		12/79		
Bone (fish/chicken)		58		7/12	2,18,21,22,38
Nasogastric tube		17		2/12	10,13
Sharp metallic object		17		2/12	5,14
Celestin tube		8		1/12	40
Other	5		4/79		
Unknown				3/4	33,37,42
Bronchial cancer				1/4	40

*Right aortic arch with aortic diverticulum, aneurysm at origin of aberrant right subclavian artery.
†Tuberculosis,[17] postoperative esophagogastrectomy.[23]

Table III. Location of fistula

	%	No. of patients	References
Esophagus			Data available for 75/79 patients
Endoscopic location (distance from incisors)		Mean 28 cm	1-3,15,22,24,26,30,31,38,42 (data available on only 13 patients)
Thoracic portion	79	59/75	1,10-13,18,19,22,25,27-31,33,36,39,41
Hiatal portion	21	16/75	11,14,15,20,23,24,26,30-32,35-37
Aorta			Data available for 54/79 patients
Arch	17	9/54	3,4,10,27,28,36,42
Descending	83	45/54	1,2,5-9,12-26,29-31,33-39,41

Table IV. Presenting symptoms

	%		No. of patients		References
GI bleeding	96		54/56		1-11,13-41,42
Hematemesis		91		49/54	
Melena only		8		4/54	
Hemorrhagic shock		78		42/54	
Herald bleeding*		76		41/54	
Sepsis	21		12/56		2,5,6,8,12,14,22,25,28,38
Chest pain	45		25/56		2,6-8,12,16,18,19,21,22,25,26,30-33,36,39,41
Dysphagia	41		23/56		1,2,6,7,9,14,17-19,22,27,29-31,34,36,38,39
Upper back pain	18		10/56		3,16,17,25,29-31
Abdominal pain	13		7/56		4,11,15,34,37,39,41

*Initial bleeding that stops followed by period of stabilization.

27. Edwards BS, Edwards WD, Connolly DC, et al. Arterial-esophageal fistula developing in patients with anomalies of the aortic arch system. Chest 1984;86:732-735.

28. Livoni JP. Fatal gastrointestinal hemorrhage due to aorto-esophageal fistula. Ann Emerg Med 1983;12:518-519.

29. Snyder DM, Crawford ES. Successful treatment of primary aorto-esophageal fistula resulting from aortic aneurysm. J Thorac Cardiovasc Surg 1983;85:457-463.

30. Myers HS, Silber W. Oesophageal bleeding from aortoesophageal fistula due to aortic aneurysm: Case reports and review of the literature. S Afr Med J 1983;63:124-127.

31. Cronen P, Snow N, Nightingale D. Aortoesophageal fistula secondary to reflux esophagitis. Ann Thorac Surg 1982;33: 78-80.

32. Naschitz JE, Bassan H, Lazarov N, et al. Upper gastrointestinal bleeding, aneurismatic dilatation of the thoracic aorta and filling defect on the esophagogram. Radiology 1982;22: 283-285.

33. Baker MS, Baker BH. Aortoesophageal fistula. South Med J 1982;75:770-771.

34. Baron RL, Koehler RE, Gutierrez FR, et al. Clinical and radiographic manifestations of aortoesophageal fistulas. Radiology 1981;141:599-605.

35. Montgomery ACV, Chilvers AS. Oesophago-aortic fistula. Postgrad Med J 1981;57:380.

36. Han SY, Jander HP, Ho KJ. Aortoesophageal fistula. South Med J 1981;74:1260-1262.

37. Ferguson LJ, Goldin AR, Kench P. Fatal haematemesis from an aorto-oesophageal fistula of obscure aetiology: A case report. Aust NZ J Surg 1980;50:412-414.

38. Ctercteko G, Mok CK. Aorto-esophageal fistula induced by a foreign body. J Thorac Cardiovasc Surg 1980;80:233-235.

39. Braman R, Napoli VM. Exsanguination from esophageal rupture of an atherosclerotic aortic aneurysm in a patient with treated tuberculosis. South Med J 1979;79:892-893.

40. Carter R, Mulder GA, Snyder EN, et al. Aortoesophageal fistula. Am J Surg 1978;136:26-30.

41. Dale HT, Thompson K, DeWeese JA, et al. Aortic rupture into the esophagus during angiography. JAMA 1978;239:1880-1881.

42. Magnusson I, Notander A, Rieger A, et al. Massive hematemesis due to an aorto-esophageal fistula. Acta Chir Scand 1987;153:317-319.

Extremities

22

Natural History of Intermittent Claudication

Martha D. McDaniel, MD, Jack L. Cronenwett, MD, Hanover, New Hampshire, and White River Junction, Vermont

An accurate definition of the natural history of intermittent claudication is essential to evaluate the need for therapeutic intervention. Available data are imperfect, however, because they are biased by differences in disease severity, referral patterns, and important covariates, such as diabetes, gender, and smoking. Furthermore, some reports of the "natural history" of claudication have included patients treated operatively[1-9] or have analyzed arteriosclerosis per se without spe-

From the Section of Vascular Surgery, Dartmouth-Hitchcock Medical Center, Hanover, N.H., and the Veterans Administration Medical Center, White River Junction, Vt.
This study was supported in part by the Career Development program of the Veterans Administration.

cifically referring to associated symptoms.[10-20] We have summarized data from series that specifically identified claudicants without rest pain or tissue loss. Earlier studies relied on symptom evaluation and pulse palpation (Table I), whereas contemporary reports have added noninvasive measurements or arteriography (Table II). Natural history, epidemiology, effects of diabetes and smoking, outcome prediction factors, and miscellaneous aspects of intermittent claudication are outlined in Tables III, IV, and VIII. To derive comparable information from individual references, some extrapolation was required to calculate weighted means for the combined data. Our best estimate of the current natural history of intermittent claudication based on contemporary data is summarized in Table VII.

Table I. Diagnosis made by history and physical examination alone

Author	No.	Age (yr)*	Female (%)	Diabetic (%)	Follow-up (yr)*	Mortality (%)	Vascular deaths[†] (%)	Outcome[§] (% of survivors) Tissue loss/ operation	Ampu- tation	Continued claudi- cation
Juergens[21] (1960)	380	40-60	8	0	5	—	—	—	3	—
Bloor[22,23] (1961)	1476	58	11	4	4-10	46	84	18	8	74
Begg[24,25] (1962)	123	55	7	4	5-9	48	86	19	3	78
Peabody[26,27] (1974)	162	35-76	33	—	8.3	23[‖]	100	8	4.8	—
McAllister[28] (1976)	100	65	31	13	6	11	100	17	7	76
Lassila[29] (1986)	228	61	17	—	9-12	54	68	31[#]	—	69
Weighted mean**	2469 (total)	57	13	4	7	52 (7.4%/yr)	80 (5.9%/yr)	19 (2.7%/yr)	7 (1%/yr)	74

*Mean, if single figure; range, if two figures.
[†]Deaths definitely attributable to peripheral arterial, cardiac, or cerebrovascular causes.
[§]Each outcome mutually exclusive; only worst outcome tabulated (claudication < tissue loss/operation < amputation).
[‖]Minimal estimate since only cardiovascular deaths reported.
[#]Includes amputations.
**Weighted mean: $\Sigma x = 1$ to n $\dfrac{[(\text{mean value})(\text{no. of patients in study})]}{\text{total no. of patients with relevent data}}$, where n refers to the number of studies with relevent data.

Table VIII. Miscellaneous aspects of intermittent claudication

Parameter	Value	Ref.
Percent of patients with claudiation of nonarterial etiology	up to 38%	32,46
Percent of patients with arterial occlusive disease but no claudication	8%	15,41,46
Mean improvement in walking distance with exercise program	67%	47,48
Mean duration of symptoms before specialty referral	2.5 yr	18,24,42
Prevalence of bilateral claudication	63%	24,34
Symptom progression		
During first yr	16%	36,37
During subsequent yr	4%/yr	36,37
Distribution of lesions in claudicants >40 yr		
Aortoiliac	18%	25,33,34,38
Femoropopliteal	65%	9,25,33,34,38
Multilcvcl	17%	25,33,34,38
Distribution of lesions in claudicants <40 yr		
Aortoiliac	53%	4
Femoropopliteal	25%	4
Multilevel	22%	4
Development of rest pain at 5 yr		
With multilevel disease	25%	34
With single level disease	12%	34
Amputation rate at 2.5 yr according to number of patent below-knee outflow vessels		
2-3	2%	30
1-2	9%	30
0-1	2%	30
Amputation rate at 2.5 yr according to severity of initial claudication symptoms		
Mild	0%	30
Moderate	3%	30
Severe	15%	30

REFERENCES

1. Bollinger A, Simon HJ, Mahler F. The natural course of peripheral arteriosclerosis obliterans evaluated by flow measurements. Angiology 1969;20:414-421.
2. DeBakey ME, Crawford ES, Garrett HE, et al. Occlusive disease of the lower extremities in patients 16 to 37 years of age. Ann Surg 1964;159:873-890.
3. De Beacker G, Kornitzer M, Sobloski J, et al. Intermittent claudication—epidemiology and natural history. Acta Cardiologica 1979;34(3):115-124.
4. Hallett JW Jr, Greenwood LH, Robison JG. Lower extremity arterial disease in young adults: A systematic approach to early diagnosis. Ann Surg 1985;202:647-652.
5. Holmes DR Jr, Burbank MK, Fulton RE, et al. Arteriosclerosis obliterans in young women. Am J Med 1979;66:997-1000.
6. McCready RA, Vincent AE, Schwartz RW, et al. Atherosclerosis in the young: A virulent disease. Surgery 1984;96:863-869.
7. Nunn DB. Symptomatic peripheral arteriosclerosis of patients under age 40. Am Surg 1973;39:224-228.
8. Pairolero PC, Joyce JW, Skinner CR, et al. Lower limb ischemia in young adults: Prognostic implications. J Vasc Surg 1984;1:459-464.
9. Singer A, Rob C. The fate of the claudicator. Br Med J 1960;2:633-636.
10. Birkenstock WE, Louw JH, Terblanche J, et al. Smoking and other factors affecting the conservative management of peripheral vascular disease. South Afr Med J 1975;49:1129-1132.
11. Felix WR Jr, Sigel B, Gunther L. The significance for morbidity and mortality of Doppler-absent pedal pulses. J Vasc Surg 1987;5:849-855.
12. LeFevre FA, Corbacioglu C, Humphries AW, et al. Management of arteriosclerosis obliterans of the extremities. JAMA 1959;170:656-661.
13. Mathiesen FR, Larsen EE, Wulff M. Some factors influencing the spontaneous course of arterial vascular insufficiency. Acta Chir Scand 1970;136:303-308.
14. Rosen AJ, DePalma RG, Victor Y. Risk factors in peripheral atherosclerosis. Arch Surg 1973;107:303-308.
15. Schadt DC, Hines EA Jr, Juergens JL, et al. Chronic atherosclerotic occlusion of the femoral artery. JAMA 1961;175:937-940.
16. Silbert S, Zazeela H. Prognosis in arteriosclerotic peripheral vascular disease. JAMA 1958;166:1816-1821.
17. Taylor GW, Calo AR. Atherosclerosis of arteries of lower limbs. Br Med J 1962;1:507-510.
18. Tillgren C. Obliterative arterial disease of the lower limbs. II. A study of the course of the disease. Acta Med Scand 1965;178:103-119.
19. Ulrich J, Engell HC, Siggaard-Andersen J. A plethysmographic study of the spontaneous course of obliterative arterial disease in the lower leg. Scand J Clin Lab Invest 1973;31(Suppl 128):75-81.
20. Warren R, Gomez RL, Marston JAP, et al. Femoropopliteal arteriosclerosis obliterans—arteriographic patterns and rates of progression. Surgery 1966;55:135-143.

21. Juergens JL, Barker NW, Hines EA Jr. Arteriosclerosis obliterans: Review of 520 cases with special reference to pathogenic and prognostic factors. Circulation 1960;21:188-195.

22. Bloor K. Natural history of arteriosclerosis of the lower extremities. Ann R Coll Surg Engl 1961;28:36-52.

23. Boyd AM. The natural course of arteriosclerosis of the lower extremities. Angiology 1960;11:10-14.

24. Begg TB, Richards RL. The prognosis of intermittent claudication. Scot Med J 1962;7:341-352.

25. Richards RL. Prognosis of intermittent claudication. Br Med J 1957;2:1091-1093.

26. Peabody CN, Kannel WB, McNamara PM. Intermittent claudication: Surgical significance. Arch Surg 1974;109:693-697.

27. Kannel WB, Skinner JJ Jr, Schwartz MJ, et al. Intermittent claudication: Incidence in the Framingham study. Circulation 1970;41:875-883.

28. McAllister FF. The fate of patients with intermittent claudication managed nonoperatively. Am J Surg 1976;132:593-595.

29. Lassila R, LaPantalo M, Lindfors O. Peripheral arterial disease—natural outcome. Acta Med Scand 1986;220:295-301.

30. Imparato AM, Kim G-E, Davidson T, et al. Intermittent claudication: Its natural course. Surgery 1975;78:795-799.

31. Wilson SE, Schwartz I, Williams RA, et al. Occlusion of the superficial femoral artery: What happens without operation. Am J Surg 1980;140:112-118.

32. Kallero KS. Mortality and morbidity in patients with intermittent claudication as defined by venous occlusion plethysmography: A ten year follow-up study. J Chron Dis 1981;34:455-462.

33. Cronenwett JL, Warner KG, Zelenock GB, et al. Intermittent claudication: Current results of nonoperative management. Arch Surg 1984;119:430-436.

34. Jonason T, Ringqvist I. Factors of prognostic importance for subsequent rest pain in patients with intermittent claudication. Acta Med Scand 1985;218:27-33.

35. Jonason T, Ringqvist I. Diabetes mellitus and intermittent claudication: Relation between peripheral vascular complications and location of the occlusive atherosclerosis in the legs. Acta Med Scand 1985;218:217-221.

36. Jelnes R, Gaardsting O, Jensen KH, et al. Fate in intermittent claudication: Outcome and risk factors. Br Med J 1986;293:1137-1140.

37. Naschitz JE, Ambrosio DA, Chang JB. Intermittent claudication: Predictors and outcome. Angiology 1988;39(1 Pt 1):16-22.

38. Rosenbloom MS, Flanigan DP, Schuler JJ, et al. Risk factors affecting the natural history of intermittent claudication. Arch Surg 1988;123:867-870.

39. Reunanen A, Takkunen H, Aromaa A. Prevalence of intermittent claudication and its effect on mortality. Acta Med Scand 1982;211:249-256.

40. Samuelsson O, Wilhelmsen L, Pennert K, et al. Angina pectoris, intermittent claudication and congestive heart failure in middle-aged male hypertensives. Acta Med Scand 1987;221:23-32.

41. Criqui MH, Fronek A, Barrett-Conner E, et al. The prevalence of peripheral arterial disease in a defined population. Circulation 1985;71:510-515.

42. Hughson WG, Mann JI, Garron D. Intermittent claudication: Prevalence and risk factors. Br Med J 1978;1:1379-1381.

43. Jonason T, Bergstrom R. Cessation of smoking in patients with intermittent claudication: Effects on the risk of peripheral vascular complications, myocardial infarction and mortality. Acta Med Scand 1987;221:253-260.

44. Hughson WG, Mann JI, Tibbs DJ, et al. Intermittent claudication: Factors determining outcome. Br Med J 1978;1:1377-1379.

45. Jonason T, Ringqvist I. Changes in peripheral blood pressures after five years of follow-up in non-operated patients with intermittent claudication. Acta Med Scand 1986;220:127-132.

46. Widmer LK, Greensher A, Kannel WB. Occlusion of peripheral arteries: A study of 6,400 working subjects. Circulation 1964;30:836-842.

47. Dahllof A-G, Holm J, Schersten T, et al. Peripheral arterial insufficiency: Effect of physical training on walking tolerance, calf blood flow and blood flow resistance. Scand J Rehab Med 1976;8:19-26.

48. Ernst EEW, Matrai A. Intermittent claudication, exercise, and blood rheology. Circulation 1987;76:1110-1114.

23

Acute Limb Ischemia

Joseph L. Mills, MD, John M. Porter, MD, Lackland AFB, Texas, and Portland, Oregon

The tables that follow contain basic data concerning acute leg ischemia developing after peripheral embolization or thrombosis of native vessels secondary to underlying atherosclerotic occlusive disease. Patients with acute limb ischemia resulting from bypass graft thrombosis are a separate clinical entity beyond the scope of this review. Differences in patient selection account for some of the variability in the treatment outcome attributed to alternative therapeutic methods. Reports of the use of thrombolytic therapy are particularly difficult to analyze because patients with sudden onset of worsening claudication, thrombosed bypass grafts, and patients who also required operation or angioplasty are often included.

The data were derived by pooling information from the authoritative references cited with appropriate weighting for varying patient numbers.

From the Department of Vascular Surgery, Wilford Hall USAF Medical Center, Lackland AFB, Texas, and the Department of Vascular Surgery, Oregon Health Sciences University, Portland, Ore.

The opinions expressed herein are those of the authors and do not necessarily reflect the opinions of the United States Air Force or the Department of Defense.

Table I. Incidence and etiology

	Incidence (%)	Ref.
Incidence of peripheral arterial emboli		
Autopsy series	0.23	1
Following myocardial infarction	< 1	2
Etiology of acute limb ischemia		
Acute thrombosis	59	3-7
Embolization	41	3-7

Table II. Source of embolization

Source of embolization	Incidence (%)*	Ref.
Cardiac	75	2,4,8-14
Atrial fibrillation		15-17
Atherosclerotic heart disease	21	
Rheumatic heart disease	30	
Acute myocardial infarction	24	
Noncardiac	9.3	
Proximal atheroma	4.7	10,13,14, 16,17
Proximal aneurysm	4.6	
Postoperative cardiovascular procedure	6.7	2,11

*Note: Categories do not add to 100% because various referenced series do not include all embolic sources.

Table III. Distribution: Site of peripheral embolization

Site of embolization	Incidence (%)	Ref.
Series of peripheral emboli		
Aorta, saddle	15.5	2,8,9,11,12,14, 16,19-22
Iliac	17.6	2,9,11,12,16, 19,21,22
Femoral	43.4	2,8,9,11,12, 16,19-22
Popliteal	15	2,8,9,11,12,14, 16,19-22
Upper extremity	8.5	2,8,9,11,12,14, 16,19-22
All inclusive series		
Carotid	13	2,8,19
Visceral/renal	6.7	8,11,19

Table IV. Outcome of treatment of acute limb ischemia

	Surgical treatment of thrombotic acute limb ischemia		
	Mortality (%)	Limb salvage (%)	Ref.
	5	66	3,4

	Treatment of embolic acute limb ischemia		
Treatment	Mortality (%)	Limb salvage (%)	Ref.
Heparin therapy	12.6	78	5,10,23,24,28
Fogarty catheter thromboembolectomy	17	84	2,5,6,8,10,12,13,16, 17,20,25,26,27
Perioperative heparin and Fogarty catheter thromboembolectomy	10.2	92	2,4,18,24,28-30

Table V. Thrombolytic therapy for treatment of acute limb ischemia*

End point	Incidence (%)	Ref.[†]
Clot lysis	67	34-46
Limb salvage	82	35,37-45
Major bleeding[§]	12.2	34-39,42-46
Mortality	4.6	35,36,39,42,45
Subsequent operation	32	33-41,43-45
Subsequent percutaneous transluminal angioplasty	50	34-41,43,44,46

*Includes thrombotic and embolic cases, as well as patients with sudden worsening of preexisting claudication. An attempt was made to exclude cases in which the etiology of the ischemia was occlusion of a bypass graft.
[†]13 series reviewed include the use of various lytic agents: tissue plasminogen activator (1); urokinase (2); streptokinase (10).
[§]Requiring transfusion or operation.

Table VI. Miscellaneous

	Incidence (%)	Ref.
Incidence of recurrent embolization		
With routine anticoagulation	7	5,18,24
Without anticoagulation	21	2,10,15,16,19, 20,25,26,28
Incidence of myonephropathic metabolic syndrome	7.5	31,32
Percent of patients requiring fasciotomy	8.7	9,16,17,29,32

REFERENCES

1. Lerman J, Miller FN, Lund CC. Arterial embolism and embolectomy: Report of cases. JAMA 1930;94:1128-1133.
2. Panetta T, Thompson JE, Talkington CM. Arterial embolectomy: A 34-year experience with 400 cases. Surg Clin N Am 1986;66(2):339-353.
3. Cambria RP, Abbott WM. Acute arterial thrombosis of the lower extremity: Its natural history contrasted with arterial embolism. Arch Surg 1984;119:784-787.
4. Dale WA. Differential management of acute peripheral arterial ischemia. J Vasc Surg 1984;1(2):269-278.
5. Jivegard LE, Arfvidsson B, Holm J, et al. Selective conservative and routine early operative treatment in acute limb ischemia. Br J Surg 1987;74:798-801.
6. McPhail NV, Fratesi SJ, Barger GG. Management of acute thromboembolic limb ischemia. Surgery 1983;93(3):381-385.
7. Meier GH, Brewster DC. Acute arterial thrombosis. In Bergan JJ, ed. Vascular Surgical Emergencies. Orlando: Grune & Stratton, Inc., 1987, pp 499-515.
8. Abbott WM, Maloney RD, McCabe CC, et al. Arterial embolism: A 44 year perspective. Am J Surg 1982;143:460-464.
9. Barker CF, Rosato FE, Roberts B. Peripheral arterial embolism. Surg Gynecol Obstet 1966;123:22-26.
10. Baxter-Smith D, Ashton F, Slaney G. Peripheral arterial embolism. A 20-year review. J Cardiovasc Surg 1988;29:453-457.
11. Billig DM, Hallman GL, Cooley DA. Arterial embolism: Surgical treatment and results. Arch Surg 1967;95(1):1-6.
12. Caruana JA, Gutierrez IZ, Anderson MN, et al. Factors that affect the outcome of peripheral arterial embolization. Arch Surg 1981;116:423-425.
13. Connett MC, Murray DH, Wenneker WW. Peripheral arterial emboli. Am J Surg 1984;148:14-18.
14. Cranley JJ. Acute embolic occlusion of major arteries. In Bergan JJ, ed. Vascular Surgical Emergencies. Orlando: Grune & Stratton, Inc., 1987, pp 487-498.
15. Green RM, DeWeese JA, Rob CG. Arterial embolectomy before and after the Fogarty catheter. Surgery 1975;77(1):24-33.
16. Kendrick J, Thompson BW, Read RC, et al. Arterial embolectomy in the leg: Results in a referral hospital. Am J Surg 1981;142:739-743.
17. Lorentzen JE, Roder OC, Hansen HJB. Peripheral arterial embolism: A follow-up of 130 consecutive patients submitted to embolectomy. Acta Chir Scan 1980;111-116.
18. Campbell HC, Hubbard SG, Ernst CB. Continuous heparin anticoagulation in patients with arteriosclerosis and arterial emboli. Surg Gynecol Obstet 1980;150:54-56.
19. Darling RC, Austen WG, Linton RR. Arterial embolism. Surg Gynecol Obstet 1967;124:106-114.
20. Englund R, Magee HR. Peripheral arterial embolism: 1961-1985. Aust NZ J Surg 1987;57:27-31.
21. Hight DW, Tilney NL, Couch NP. Changing clinical trends in patients with peripheral arterial emboli. Surgery 1976;79(2):172-176.
22. MacGowan WAL, Mooneeram R. A review of 174 patients with arterial embolism. Brit J Surg 1973;60(11):894-898.
23. Blaisdell FW, Steele M, Allen RE. Management of acute lower extremity arterial ischemia due to embolism and thrombosis. Surgery 1978;84(6):822-834.
24. Tawes RL, Beare JP, Scribner RG. Value of postoperative heparin in peripheral arterial thromboembolism. Am J Surg 1983;146:213-215.
25. Busuttil RQ, Keehn G, Milliken J, et al. Aortic saddle embolus: A twenty-year experience. Ann Surg 1983;197(6):698-706.
26. Silvers LW, Royster TS, Mulcare RJ. Peripheral arterial emboli and factors in their recurrence rate. Ann Surg 1980;192(2):236-237.
27. Erikkson I, Holmberg JT. Analysis of factors affecting limb salvage and mortality after embolectomy. Acta Chir Scand 1977;143:232-240.
28. Elliott JP, Hageman JM, Szilagyi DE, et al. Arterial embolization: Problems of source, multiplicity, recurrence, and delayed treatment. Surgery 1980;88(6):833-845.
29. Satiani B, Gross WS, Evans WE. Improved limb salvage after arterial embolectomy. Ann Surg 1978;188(2):153-157.
30. Gregg RO, Chamberlain BE, Myers JK, et al. Embolectomy or heparin therapy for arterial emboli? Surgery 1983;93(3):377-380.
31. Haimovici H. Muscular, renal, and metabolic complications of acute arterial occlusions: Myonephropathic-metabolic syndrome. Surgery 1979;85(4):461-468.
32. Haimovici H. Acute atherosclerotic thrombosis. In Haimovici H, ed. Vascular Emergencies. New York: Appleton-Century-Crofts, 1982, pp 213-223.
33. Field T, Littooy FN, Baker WH. Immediate and long-term outcome of acute arterial occlusion of the extremities: The effect of added vascular reconstruction. Arch Surg 1982;117:1156-1160.
34. Belkin M, Belkin B, Bucknam C, et al. Intraarterial fibrinolytic therapy. Efficacy of streptokinase vs urokinase. Arch Surg 1986;121:769-773.
35. Berni GA, Bandyk DF, Zierler RE, et al. Streptokinase treatment of acute arterial occlusion. Ann Surg 1983;198(2):185-191.
36. Graor RA, Risius B, Yung JR, et al. Peripheral artery and bypass graft thrombolysis with recombinant human tissue-type plasminogen activator. J Vasc Surg 1986;3(1):115-124.
37. Hargrove WC, Barker CF, Berkowitz HD, et al. Treatment of acute peripheral arterial and graft thromboses with low-dose streptokinase. Surgery 1982;92(6):981-993.
38. Hamelink JK, Elliott BM. Localized intraarterial streptokinase therapy. Am J Surg 1986;152:252-256.
39. McNamara TO, Rischer JR. Thrombolysis of peripheral arterial and graft occlusions: Improved results using high-dose urokinase. AJR 1985;144:769-775.
40. Rush DS, Gewertz BL, Lu CT, et al. Selective infusion of streptokinase for arterial thrombosis. Surgery 1983;93(6):828-833.
41. Seeger JM, Flynn TC, Quintessenza JA. Intraarterial streptokinase in the treatment of acute arterial thrombosis. Surg Gynecol Obstet 1987;164(4):303-307.
42. Sicard GA, Schier JJ, Totty WG, et al. Thrombolytic therapy for acute arterial occlusion. J Vasc Surg 1985;2(1):65-78.
43. Kakkasseril JS, Cranley JJ, Arbaugh JJ, et al. Efficacy of low-dose streptokinase in acute arterial occlusion and graft thrombosis. Arch Surg 1985;120:427-429.
44. Wolfson RH, Kumpe DA, Rutherford RB. Role of intra-arterial streptokinase in treatment of arterial thromboembolism. Arch Surg 1984;119:697.
45. Kolts RL, Kuehner ME, Swanson MK, et al. Local intra-arterial streptokinase therapy for acute peripheral arterial occlusions: Should thrombolytic therapy replace embolectomy? Am Surg 1985;51(7):381-387.
46. Katzen BT, Edwards KC, Albert AS, et al. Low-dose direct fibrinolysis in peripheral vascular disease. J Vasc Surg 1984;1:718-722.
47. Fogarty TJ, Cranley JJ, Krause RJ. A method for extraction of arterial emboli and thrombi. Surg Gynecol Obstet 1963;116:241-244.

24

Peripheral Artery Aneurysms

Richard L. McCann, MD, Durham, North Carolina

Peripheral artery aneurysms obviously encompass a broad anatomic range. The following tables present basic data selected to define the clinical characteristics of each lesion.

For both femoral and popliteal aneurysms there is a marked male predominance; lesions in females are distinctly unusual. Most patients with these lesions have a general tendency toward aneurysm formation, and many harbor aneurysms at multiple sites. Over one third will have abdominal aortic aneurysms. Popliteal aneurysms seldom rupture, but they often cause ischemic symptoms by thrombosis or embolism.

Carotid aneurysms occur in younger patients with only about a 2:1 male-female ratio. Only about half of the lesions appear to be caused by atherosclerosis with the remainder divided among false aneurysms, surgical trauma, and connective tissue diseases. Although occasionally subject to rupture, carotid aneurysms are much more likely to cause thromboembolic stroke, and prevention of this complication is the most pressing indication for surgery.

Subclavian aneurysms are unusual and also occur in younger patients. They are more common on the right, and approximately half result from atherosclerosis. For unknown reasons, aberrant subclavian arteries are particularly prone to aneurysm development. About half of subclavian aneurysms require a transthoracic procedure. Another interesting and unusual lesion is the persistent sciatic artery. Although the incidence of this vascular anomaly is rare, the aberrant vessel has an unusual tendency to become aneurysmal. Because of general degeneration of the vascular tree in these cases, there is a high rate of amputation. Although Takayasu's arteritis is most firmly associated with obstructive lesions, some patients with this condition develop dilated and even aneurysmal arterial segments.

Femoral false aneurysms are common, especially if methodically sought by routine ultrasound or arteriography. Interestingly, most are associated with proximal inflow reconstructions rather than outflow procedures. Recurrence of femoral false aneurysms appears more common after repair by direct suture, compared with repair by placement of an interposition graft.

Table I. Clinical data related to atherosclerotic femoral artery aneurysms

		Ref.
Mean age at presentation	65 yr	1-3
Male:female	28:1	1-3
Percent bilateral	54%	1-3
Percent with AAA	75%	1-3
Risk to limb without repair to small asymptomatic FAA	5%	3
Ratio of risk of rupture to thrombo-embolic complications	2:13	3

AAA = abdominal aortic aneurysm; FAA = femoral artery aneurysm.

Table II. Clinical data related to popliteal aneurysms

		Ref.
Male:female	33:1	4-10
Mean age at presentation	63 yr	4-5,7-9
Percent asymptomatic	39%	4-10
Percent bilateral	56%	4-10
Percent with other aneurysm	50%	4-10
Percent with AAA	33%	4-10

From the Department of Surgery, Duke University Medical Center, Durham, N.C.

33. Mandell VS, Jaques PF, Delany DJ, et al. Persistent sciatic artery: Clinical, embryologic, and angiographic features. AJR 1985;144:245-249.

34. Loh FK. Embolization of a sciatic artery aneurysm: An alternative to surgery: a case report. Angiology—J Vasc Dis 1985;7:472-476.

35. Gerner T, Henjum A, Dedichten H. Persistent sciatic artery: Case report. Acta Chir Scand 1988;154:667-668.

36. Mayschak DT, Flye MW. Treatment of the persistent sciatic artery. Ann Surg 1984;199:69-74.

37. Williams LR, Flanigan DP, O'Connor RJA, et al. Persistent sciatic artery: Clinical aspects and operative management. Am J Surg 1983;145:687-693.

38. Becquemin JP, Gaston A, Coubret P, et al. Aneurysm of persistent sciatic artery: Report of a case treated by endovascular occlusion and femoropopliteal bypass. Surgery 1985;98: 605-611.

39. Martin KW, Hyde GL, McCready RA, et al. Sciatic artery aneurysms: Report of three cases and review of the literature. J Vasc Surg 1986;4:365-371.

40. Seko Y, Yazaki Y, Uchimura H, et al. A case of Takayasu's disease with ruptured carotid aneurysm. Jpn Heart J 1986; 27:523-531.

41. Lande A, LaPorta A. Takayasu arteritis: An arteriographic-pathological correlation. Arch Pathol Lab Med 1976;100: 437-440.

42. Dimarzo L, Strandness EL, Schultz RD, et al. Reoperation for femoral anastomotic false aneurysm: A 15 year experience. Ann Surg 1987;206:168-172.

43. Schellack J, Salam A, Abouzeid MA, et al. Femoral anastomotic aneurysms: A continuing change. J Vasc Surg 1987;6: 308-317.

44. Ernst CB, Elliott JP, Ryan CJ, et al. Recurrent femoral anastomotic aneurysm: A 30-year experience. Ann Surg 1988;208: 401-409.

45. Dennis JW, Littooy FN, Greisler HP, et al. Anastomotic pseudoaneurysm: A continuing late complication of vascular reconstructive procedures. Arch Surg 1986;121:314-317.

46. Sieswerda C, Skotnicki SH, Barentsz JO, et al. Anastomotic aneurysms—an underdiagnosed complication after aorto-iliac reconstructions. Eur J Vasc Surg 1989;3:233-238.

25

Infrainguinal Revascularization Procedures

Ronald L. Dalman, MD, Lloyd M. Taylor, Jr, MD, Portland, Oregon

A review of current reports on the results of infrainguinal revascularization procedures emphasizes the critical importance of strict adherence to the recommendations of the Ad Hoc Committee on Reporting Standards in Arterial Surgery of the Joint Vascular Societies.[1] Definitions of primary and secondary patency, level of distal anastomosis, what constitutes a "re-do" operation, etc., all must be clearly stated. The inclusion of life tables is critical.

From the Department of Surgery, Oregon Health Sciences University, Portland, Ore.

The tables that follow necessarily incorporate the uncertainty inherent in averaging results of multiple studies that, with rare exception, have not adhered meticulously to the recommended reporting standards. In them we describe expected patency, limb salvage rates, and survival rates for patients undergoing revascularization procedures, which have been determined by pooling information from the references cited with appropriate weighting for varying numbers and length of follow-up.

Table I. Above-knee femoropopliteal grafts

Primary patency*	1 mo	6 mo	1 yr	2 yr	3 yr	4 yr	Ref.
Reverse saphenous vein	99	91	84	82	73	69	7,10-12,17,19,20
Arm vein	99		82	65	60	60	18
Human umbilical vein	95	90	82	82	70	70	12,43
Polytetrafluoroethylene (PTFE)		89	79	74	66	60	7,11,12,17,20,21

*All patencies are expressed as percentages; all series published since 1981.

Table II. Below-knee femoropopliteal grafts

	1 mo	6 mo	1 yr	2 yr	3 yr	4 yr	Ref.
Patency*							
Primary							
Reverse saphenous vein	98	90	84	79	78	77	7-12,17,19,20
In situ vein bypass	95	87	80	76	73	68	8,12,14-16
Secondary							
In situ vein bypass	97	96	96	89	86	81	15,16
Arm vein	97		83	83	73	70	18
Human umbilical vein	88	82	77	70	61	60	12,43
PTFE	96	80	68	61	44	40	9,11,12,17,20,21
Limb salvage							
Reverse saphenous vein	100	92	90	88	86	75	7,8,10
In situ vein bypass	97	96	94	84	83		14,41,42

*All patencies are expressed as percentages; all series published since 1981.

Table III. Infrapopliteal grafts

	1 mo	6 mo	1 yr	2 yr	3 yr	4 yr	Ref.
Patency*							
Primary							
Reverse saphenous vein	92	81	77	70	66	62	2-13
In situ vein bypass	94	84	82	76	74	68	14-17
Secondary							
Reverse saphenous vein	93	89	84	80	8	76	2,5,10,13
In situ vein bypass	95	90	89	87	84	81	15,16
Arm vein	94		73	62	58		44
Human umbilical vein	80	65	52	46	40	37	12,43
PTFE	89	58	46	32		21	6,7,12,22
Limb salvage							
Reverse saphenous vein	95	88	85	83	82	82	3-7,9,37
In situ vein bypass	96		91	88	83	83	14,38
PTFE		76	68	60	56	48	6,7,9

*All patencies are expressed as percentages; all series published since 1981.

Table IV. At or below-ankle grafts

Patency*	1 mo	6 mo	1 yr	2 yr	3 yr	Ref.
Primary						
Reverse saphenous vein	95	85	81			30
Secondary						
Reverse saphenous vein	96	90	85	81	76	27
In situ vein bypass	93	93	92	82	72	27,28
Foot salvage	99	94	93	87	84	26-28

*All patencies are expressed as percentages; all series published since 1981.

Table V. Miscellaneous

Patency*	1 mo	6 mo	1 yr	2 yr	3 yr	4 yr	5 yr	Ref.
Grafts with proximal anastomosis at the common femoral artery								
Primary	93		83	80	78	78	78	8,10,12
Secondary	95		91	86	82	80	80	10,15
Grafts with proximal anastomosis distal to the common femoral artery								
Primary	97	89	83	79	75	74	73	3,10,26,29
Secondary	100	96	90	86	80			10,27
Reoperation								
All grafts†		90	80	65	55	45		32
Primary autogenous vein	96	82	79	71	62	57	57	34
Primary PTFE	100	62	42	28			34	
All autogenous grafts								
Patients with diabetes mellitus			90		82		77	10,40
Patients without diabetes mellitus			88		78		72	10,40
Foot salvage after grafting								
Patients with diabetes mellitus			87		85			6,10
Patients without diabetes mellitus			96		93			6,10
Common femoral endarterectomy and superficial femoral endarterectomy		86	78	73	70			23,24
Common femoral endarterectomy	97		97	97	97	94		25
Survival with bypass for claudication							88	45
Survival with bypass for limb salvage	97	97	92	86	76	68	64	5,9,13,32,38

*All patencies are expressed as percentages; all series published since 1981.
†All grafts, all conduits, irrespective of number of operations required to maintain patency.

REFERENCES

1. Ad Hoc Committee on Reporting Standards, SVS/ISCVS. Suggested standards for reports dealing with lower extremity ischemia. J Vasc Surg 1986;4:80-94.
2. Barry R, Satiani B, Mohan B, et al. Prognostic indicators in femoropopliteal and distal bypass grafts. Surg Gynecol Obstet 1985;161:129-132.
3. Cantelmo NL, Snow JR, Menzoian JO, et al. Successful vein bypass in patients with an ischemic limb and a palpable popliteal pulse. Arch Surg 1986;121:217-220.
4. Schuler JJ, Flanigan DP, Williams LR, et al. Early experience with popliteal to infrapopliteal bypass for limb salvage. Arch Surg 1983;118:472-476.
5. Berkowitz HD, Greenstein SM. Improved patency in reversed femoral infrapopliteal autogenous vein grafts by early detection and treatment of the failing graft. J Vasc Surg 1987;5: 755-761.
6. Dalsing MC, White JV, Yao JST, et al. Infrapopliteal bypass for established gangrene of the forefoot or toes. J Vasc Surg 1985;2:669-677.
7. Veith FJ, Gupta SK, Ascer E, et al. Six-year prospective multicenter randomized comparison of autologous saphenous vein and expanded polytetrafluoroethylene grafts in infrainguinal arterial reconstructions. J Vasc Surg 1986;3:104-114.
8. Veterans Administration Cooperative Study Group 141. Comparative evaluation of prosthetic, reversed, and in situ vein bypass grafts in distal popliteal and tibial-peroneal revascularization. Arch Surg 1988;123:434-438.
9. Hobson RW, Lynch TG, Jamil Z, et al. Results of revascularization and amputation in severe lower extremity ischemia: A five-year clinical experience. J Vasc Surg 1985;2:174-185.
10. Taylor LM, Edwards JM, Porter JM, et al. Present status of reversed vein bypass: Five year results of a modern series. J Vasc Surg 1990;11(2):193-205.
11. Bergan JJ, Veith FJ, Bernhard VM, et al. Randomization of autogenous vein and polytetrafluoroethylene grafts in femoro-distal reconstruction. Surgery 1982;92:921-929.
12. Rutherford RB, Jones DN, Bergentz SE, et al. Factors affecting the patency of infrainguinal bypass. J Vasc Surg 1988;8: 236-246.
13. Rosenbloom MS, Walsh JJ, Schuler JJ, et al. Long-term results of infragenicular bypasses with autogenous vein originating from the distal superficial femoral and popliteal arteries. J Vasc Surg 1988;7:691-696.
14. Harris RW, Andros G, Dulawa LB, et al. The transition to in situ vein bypass grafts. Surg Gynecol Obstet 1986;163:21-27.
15. Leather RP, Shah DM, Chang BB, et al. Resurrection of the in situ saphenous vein bypass. Ann Surg 1988;208:435-442.
16. Bandyk DF, Kaebnick HW, Stewart SW, et al. Durability of the in situ saphenous vein arterial bypass: A comparison of primary and secondary patency. J Vasc Surg 1987;5:256-268.
17. Kent KC, Whittemore AD, Mannick JA. Short-term and midterm results of an all-autogenous tissue policy for infrainguinal reconstruction. J Vasc Surg 1989;9:107-114.
18. Harris RW, Andros G, Salles-Cunha SX. Alternative autogenous vein grafts to the inadequate saphenous vein. Surgery 1986;100:822-827.
19. Brewster DC, Lasalle AJ, Darling RC, et al. Comparison of above-knee and below-knee anastomosis in femoropopliteal bypass grafts. Arch Surg 1981;116:1013-1018.
20. Hall RG, Coupland GAE, Lane R, et al. Vein, Gore-tex or a composite graft for femoropopliteal bypass. Surg Gynecol Obstet 1985;161:308-312.
21. Quiñones-Baldrich WJ, Busuttil RW, Baker JD, et al. Is the preferential use of polytetrafluoroethylene grafts for femoropopliteal bypass justified? J Vasc Surg 1988;8:219-222.
22. Flinn WR, Rohrer MJ, Yao JST, et al. Improved long-term patency of infragenicular polytetrafluoroethylene grafts. J Vasc Surg 1988;7:685-690.
23. Inahara T, Scott CM. Endarterectomy for segmental occlusive disease of the superficial femoral artery. Arch Surg 1981;116: 1547-1553.
24. Ouriel K, Smith CR, DeWeese JA. Endarterectomy for localized lesions of the superficial femoral artery at the adductor canal. J Vasc Surg 1986;3:531-534.
25. Mukherjee D, Inahara T. Endarterectomy as the procedure of choice for atherosclerotic occlusive lesions of the common femoral artery. Am J Surg 1989;157:498-500.
26. Buchbinder D, Pasch AR, Rollins DL, et al. Results of arterial reconstruction of the foot. Arch Surg 1986;121:673-677.
27. Andros G, Harris RW, Salles-Cunha SX, et al. Bypass grafts to the ankle and foot. J Vasc Surg 1988;7:785-794.
28. Corsoni JD, Karmody AM, Shah DM, et al. In situ vein bypasses to distal tibial and limited outflow tracts for limb salvage. Surgery 1984;96:756-763.
29. Veith FJ, Ascer E, Gupta SK, et al. Tibiotibial vein bypass grafts: A new operation for limb salvage. J Vasc Surg 1985; 2:552-557.
30. Ascer E, Veith FJ, et al. Bypasses to plantar arteries and other tibial branches: An extended approach to limb salvage. J Vasc Surg 1988;8:434-441.
31. Dennis JW, Littooy FN, Greisler HP, et al. Secondary vascular procedures with polytetrafluoroethylene grafts for lower extremity ischemia in a male veteran population. J Vasc Surg 1988;8:137-142.
32. Bartlett ST, Olinde AJ, Flinn WR, et al. The reoperative potential of infrainguinal bypass: Long-term limb and patient survival. J Vasc Surg 1987;5:170-179.
33. Veith FJ, Ascer E, et al. Management of the occluded and failing PTFE graft. Acta Chir Scand 1987;538:117-124.
34. Edwards JM, Taylor LM, Porter JM. Treatment of failed lower extremity bypass grafts with new autogenous vein bypass. J Vasc Surg 1990;11(1):136-144.
35. Watelet J, Cheysson E, et al. In situ vs. reversed saphenous vein for femoropopliteal bypass: A prospective randomized study of 100 cases. Ann Vasc Surg 1986;1:441-452.
36. Harris PL, How TV, Jones DR. Prospectively randomized clinical trial to compare in-situ and reversed saphenous vein grafts for femoropopliteal bypass. Br J Surg 1987;74:252-255.
37. Taylor LM, Edwards JM, Brant B, et al. Autogenous reversed vein bypass for lower extremity ischemia in patients with absent or inadequate greater saphenous vein. Am J Surg 1987;153:505-510.
38. Leather RP, Shah DM, Karmody AM. Infrapopliteal arterial bypass for limb salvage: Increased patency and utilization of the saphenous vein used "In Situ." Surgery 1981;90: 1000-1008.
39. Hurley JJ, Auer AI, Hershey FB, et al. Distal arterial reconstruction: Patency and limb salvage in diabetics. J Vasc Surg 1987;5:796-802.
40. Shah DM, Chang BB, Fitzgerald KM, et al. Durability of the tibial artery bypass in diabetic patients. Am J Surg 1988;156: 133-135.
41. Buchbinder D, Rollins DL, Verta MJ, et al. Early experience with in-situ saphenous vein bypass for distal arterial reconstruction surgery. Surgery 1986;99:350-357.
42. Bush HL, Nasbeth DC, Curl GR, et al. In-situ vein bypass grafts for limb salvage. Am J Surg 1985;149:477-480.
43. Dardik H, Miller N, Dardik A, et al. A decade of experience with the glutaraldehyde tanned human umbilical cord vein graft for revascularization of the lower limb. J Vasc Surg 1988;7:336-346.
44. Andros G, Harris RW, Salles-Cunha SX, et al. Arm veins for arterial revascularization of the leg: Arteriographic and clinical observations. J Vasc Surg 1986;4:416-427.
45. Kent KC, Donaldson MC, Attinger CE, et al. Femoropopliteal reconstruction for claudication. Arch Surg 1988;123: 1196-1198.

26

Results of Percutaneous Transluminal Angioplasty for Peripheral Vascular Occlusive Disease

Samuel E. Wilson, MD, Barry Sheppard, MD, Torrance, California

Percutaneous transluminal angioplasty (PTA) was first described in 1964 by Dotter and Judkins[1] who utilized a coaxial system of catheters to dilate the superficial femoral artery. Gruntzig introduced the balloon catheter for dilatation in 1974,[2] thus reducing the number of technical difficulties with the procedure and bringing PTA into wider acceptance as a practical alternative to reconstructive surgery in selected arterial occlusions.

Although early reports of results of PTA appeared to be comparable with those of surgery, these investigators often did not address the rate of initial failure and follow-up was short (Table I). Later studies, with observations from 3 to 5 years after the procedures, revealed patencies of PTA to be somewhat lower than those achieved surgically, with better results in aortoiliac occlusions than in femoropopliteal disease (Figs. 1 and 2).

A prospective, randomized cooperative study has compared PTA with surgery in patients who had lesions amenable to either therapy (Figs. 3 and 4). A higher technical failure rate occurred with PTA, but results between successful PTAs and reconstructive surgery were comparable up to 3 years. The patient group studied probably had a less advanced stage of disease than that seen in patients reported in surgical series since all lesions in both groups of patients were correctable with angioplasty.

Clinical variables proposed as predictors of good results with PTA have been site of occlusion (with the aortoiliac better than the femoropopliteal) and absence of diabetes mellitus (which has been consistent in all studies), as well as several more controversial variables such as length of lesion, runoff, indication for PTA, where claudication had better results than limb threat, and severity of lesion (Table II).

Complications from PTA have been inconsistently reported. Some studies have listed all hematomas in their complications, yielding rates as high as 8%–20%, whereas others list only complications requiring surgical intervention, yielding rates of 2%–3%. Reporting of complications should be standardized, perhaps including those that lengthen hospital stay or require surgery (Table III).

Six studies have analyzed the use of PTA for limb salvage in patients considered unfit for operation. Although the success rates in these patients are much lower, due to the severity of their vascular disease as well as their poor risk status, this application of PTA may be of limited value in a population with few alternatives other than amputation (Table IV).

Results of percutaneous transluminal angioplasty for peripheral vascular occlusive disease from other authors are indicated and can be found in references 24 to 40.

From the Department of Surgery, UCLA School of Medicine, Harbor-UCLA Medical Center, Torrance, Calif.

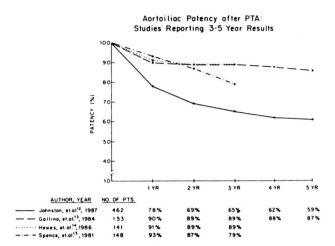

Fig. 1. Three- and 5-year patency rates for four series of patients undergoing PTA for aortoiliac arteriosclerotic vascular disease.

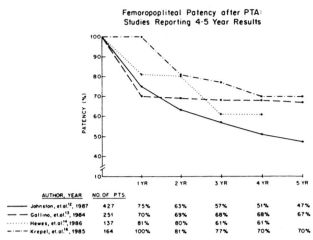

Fig. 2. Four- and 5-year patency rates for four series of patients undergoing PTA for femoropopliteal arteriosclerotic occlusive disease.

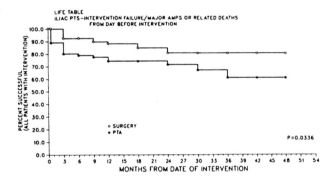

Fig. 3. Life-table analysis of intervention failures, related deaths, and amputations in patients randomized to receive either PTA or operations for aortoiliac arteriosclerotic occlusive disease.

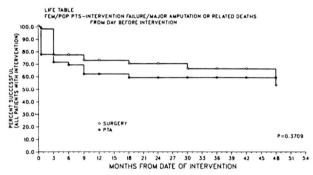

Fig. 4. Life-table analysis of intervention failures, related deaths, and amputations in patients randomized for femoropopliteal arteriosclerotic occlusive disease.

Table I. Initial failure and 1-year patency rates using PTA

Author/Institution	No. of patients	Site	Initial failure rate*	1-year patency rate (%)
Greenfield, Harvard (1980)[3]	70	FP & Tibial	13 (19%)	89
Tamura, et al., Cornell (1982)[4]	34	Popliteal	8 (23%)	85
Arfvidsson, et al., Karlstad, Sweden (1983)[5]	54	AI & FP	11 (20%)	98
Mosley, et al., Middlesex, UK (1984)[6]	23	AI	10 (43%)	100
	51	FP	34 (67%)	60
Campbell, Bristol, UK (1983)[7]	52	AI & FP	20 (38%)	93
Graor, et al., Cleveland Clinic Foundation (1984)[8]	35	AI	7 (20%)	79
	25	FP	5 (20%)	68
Cambria, et al., Yale (1987)[9]	142	AI & FP	32 (23%)	68

AI = Aortoiliac segment; FP = Femoropopliteal segment
*As addressed by Cambria, et al.,[9] Lally, et al.,[10] and Kumpe,[11] a technical success without evidence of clinical improvement should not be termed a clinical success; therefore failure rates include (1) technical failure, including inability to pass a lesion and inability to dilate a lesion, as well as (2) clinical failure, including no hemodynamic improvement as measured by noninvasive studies, need for operative intervention at same site within 2 weeks, or persistence of symptoms at the same level of severity.

Table II. Predictors of outcome for PTA

Author/Institution	Diabetes mellitus (present vs absent)	Site of lesion AI vs FP	Length of lesion (<3 cm vs >3 cm)	Runoff (3 vessel vs <3 vessel)	Indication (claudication vs rest pain)	Severity (occlusion vs stenosis)
Johnston, U. of Toronto (1987)[12]	Yes	Yes	Not stated	Yes	Yes	Not stated
Cambria, Yale (1987)[9]	Yes	Not stated	Yes	Yes	Yes	Yes
Spence, U. of Penn (1981)[15]	Yes	Yes	Not stated	No	No	Not stated
Gallino, U. of Bern, Switzerland (1984)[13]	Yes	Yes	Yes	Yes	Yes	Yes
Hewes, Johns-Hopkins (1986)[14]	Yes	Not stated	No	No	Not stated	No
Krepel, Eindhoven, The Netherlands (1985)[16]	Not stated	Not stated	Yes	Yes	Not stated	No

Table III. Reported complications of PTA in peripheral arteriosclerotic occlusive disease

Author	No. of procedures	Hematoma	Dissection/ extravasation	Embolism	Thrombosis	Urgent surgery	Death	Combined mortality and morbidity
Greenfield, et al (1980)[3]	70	4	8	4 (1)*	0	1	0	8 (11.4%)
Spence, et al (1981)[15]	251	Not reported	1	1	6	0	1	13 (4.6%)
Kadir, et al (1983)[18]	141	8	0	2 (2)*	2	2	0	14 (10.0%)
Rush, et al (1983)[20]	140	7 (2)*	2	1	0	2	3	13 (9.3%)
Campbell, et al (1983)[7]	40	Not reported	1	2	1 (1)*	1	1	4 (10.0%)
Gallino, et al (1984)[13]	482	16 (5)*	10 (4)*	11	0	9	0	39 (8.1%)
Krepel, et al (1985)[16]	164	3	0	4	2	2	0	10 (6.0%)
Murray, et al (1987)[19]	193	3	0	4 (1)*	3	1	0	13 (6.7%)
Cambria, et al (1987)[9]	142	Not reported	Not reported	Not reported	Not reported	Not reported	1	12 (8.5%)
Wilson, et al (1989)[17]	129	0	8	2	5	0	0	15 (11.6%)
Total	1752	41 (7)*	30 (4)*	31 (4)*	19 (1)*	18	6 (0.34%)	138 (7.8%)

*Numbers in parentheses indicate the number of cases requiring surgical intervention.

Table IV. Results of PTA for limb salvage in poor-risk patients

Author/ institution	Number of limbs	Technical failures	Ampu- tations	1-year salvage rate (%)*
Rush, et al, U. of Chicago (1983)[20]	97	10 (10%)	21 (22%)	68
Glover, et al, Indiana University (1983)[21]	83	11 (13%)	12 (14%)	34
Jones, et al, U. of Toronto (1985)[22]	85	16 (19%)	Not reported	69
Fletcher, et al, Westmead, New South Wales (1986)[23]	64	6 (9%)	15 (23%)	76
Hewes, et al, Johns Hop- kins (1986)[14]	21	Not reported	11 (52%)	43

*Salvage reported as salvage by PTA alone, as some failures went on to surgical intervention.

REFERENCES

1. Dotter CT, Judkins MP. Transluminal treatment of arteriosclerotic obstruction: Description of a new technique and a preliminary report of its application. Circulation 1964;30: 654-670.
2. Gruntzig A, Hopff H. Perkutane rekanalisation chronischer arterieller verschlusse mit einem neuen dilatation-skatheter: Modifikation der dotter-technik. Dtsch Med Wochenschr 1974;99:2502-2510.
3. Greenfield AJ. Femoral, popliteal and tibial arteries: Percutaneous transluminal angioplasty. AJR 1980;135:927-935.
4. Tamura S, Sniderman KW, Beinart C, et al. Percutaneous transluminal angioplasty of the popliteal artery and its branches. Radiology 1982;143(3):645-648.
5. Arfvidsson B, Davidsen JP, Persson B, et al. Percutaneous transluminal angioplasty (PTA) for lower extremity arterial insufficiency. Acta Chir Scand 1983;149(1):43-47.
6. Mosley JG, Gulati SM, Raphael M, et al. The role of percutaneous transluminal angioplasty for atherosclerotic disease of the lower extremities. Ann R Coll Surg Engl 1985;67(2): 83-86.
7. Campbell WB, Jeans WD, Cole SE, et al. Percutaneous transluminal angioplasty for lower limb ischaemia. Br J Surg 1983;70(12):736-739.
8. Graor RA, Young JR, McCandless M, et al. Percutaneous transluminal angioplasty: Review of iliac and femoral dilatations at the Cleveland Clinic. Clev Clin Q 1984;51(1):149-154.
9. Cambria RP, Faust G, Gusberg R, et al. Percutaneous angioplasty for peripheral arterial occlusive disease: Correlates of clinical success. Arch Surg 1987;122(3):283-287.
10. Lally ME, Johnston KW, Andrews D. Percutaneous transluminal dilatation of peripheral arteries: An analysis of factors predicting early success. J Vasc Surg 1984;1(5):704-709.
11. Kumpe DA, Jones DN. Percutaneous transluminal angioplasty: Radiological viewpoint. Vasc Diagn Ther 1982;3:19.
12. Johnston KW, Rae M, Hoss-Johnston SA, et al. Five-year results of a prospective study of percutaneous transluminal angioplasty. Ann Surg 1987;206(4):404-413.
13. Gallino A, Mahler F, Probst P, et al. Percutaneous transluminal angioplasty of the arteries of the lower limbs: A 5 year follow-up. Circulation 1984;70(4):619-623.
14. Hewes RC, White RI, Murray RR, et al. Long term results of superficial femoral artery angioplasty. AJR 1986;146:1025-1029.
15. Spence RK, Freiman DB, Gatenby R, et al. Long-term results of transluminal angioplasty of the iliac and femoral arteries. Arch Surg 1981;116:1377-1386.
16. Krepel VM, VanAndel GJ, VanErp WF, et al. Percutaneous transluminal angioplasty of the femoropopliteal artery: Initial and long term results. Radiology 1985;156:325-328.
17. Wilson SE, Wolf GL, Cross AP. Percutaneous transluminal angioplasty versus operation for peripheral arteriosclerosis: Report of a prospective randomized trial in a selected group of patients. J Vasc Surg 1989;9:1-9.
18. Kadir S, White R Jr, Kaufman S, et al. Long term results of aortoiliac angioplasty. Surgery 1983;94:10-14.
19. Murray RR, Hewes RC, White RI, et al. Long segment femoropopliteal stenosis: Is angioplasty a boon or a bust? Radiology 1987;162:473-476.
20. Rush DS, Gewertz BL, Lu CT, et al. Limb salvage in poor-risk patients using transluminal angioplasty. Arch Surg 1983; 118(10):1209-1212.
21. Glover JL, Bendick PJ, Dilley RS, et al. Balloon catheter dilation for limb salvage. Arch Surg 1983;118(5):557-560.
22. Jones BA, Maggisano R, Robb C, et al. Transluminal angioplasty: Results in high-risk patients with advanced peripheral vascular disease. Canacl J Surg 1985;28(2):150-152.
23. Fletcher JP, Little JM, Fermanis GG, et al. Percutaneous transluminal angioplasty for severe lower extremity ischaemia. Aust NZ J Surg 1986;56(2):121-125.
24. Roberts B, McLean GKP. Role of percutaneous angioplasty in the treatment of peripheral arterial disease. Adv Surg 1986; 19:329-354.
25. Reidy JF. Angioplasty in peripheral vascular disease. Postgrad Med J 1987;63(740):435-438.
26. Anderson JB, Wolinski AP, Wells IP, et al. The impact of percutaneous transluminal angioplasty on the management of peripheral vascular disease. Br J Surg 1986;73(1):17-19.
27. Doubilet P, Abrams HL. The cost of underutilization: Percutaneous transluminal angioplasty for peripheral vascular disease. N Engl J Med 1984;12:310(2):95-102.
28. Transluminal angioplasty for peripheral vascular disease (letter). N Engl J Med 1984;14:310(24):1607-1608.
29. Bergqvist D, Jonsson K, Weibull H. Complications after percutaneous transluminal angioplasty of peripheral and renal arteries. Acta Radiol 1987;28(1):3-12.
30. Kadir S, Smith GW, White RI Jr, et al. Percutaneous transluminal angioplasty as an adjunct to the surgical management of peripheral vascular disease. Ann Surg 1982;195(6): 786-795.
31. Percutaneous angioplasty for peripheral vascular disease (editorial). Lancet 1984;17;1(8377):606.
32. Zarins CK, Lu CT, McDonnell AE, et al. Limb salvage by percutaneous transluminal recanalization of the occluded superficial femoral artery. Surgery 1980;87(6):701-708.
33. Ford K, Braun SD, Moore AV Jr, et al. Percutaneous transluminal angioplasty in diabetic patients: An effective treatment modality. Cardiovasc Intervent Radiol 1984;7(5): 204-208.

34. Zeitler E. Primary and late results of percutaneous transluminal angioplasty (PTA) in iliac and femoropopliteal obliterations. Int Angiol 1985;4(1):81-85.

35. Wollenweber J, Henne W, Kiefer H, et al. Early and late results after percutaneous transluminal angioplasty in peripheral arterial occlusive disease. Vasa 1986;15(1):67-70.

36. Katzen BT. Percutaneous transluminal angioplasty for arterial disease of the lower extremities. AJR 1984;142(1):23-25.

37. Van Andel GJ. Transluminal iliac angioplasty: Long-term results. Radiology 1980;135:607-611.

38. Freiman DB, Ring EJ, Oleaga JA, et al. Transluminal angioplasty of the iliac, femoral and popliteal arteries. Radiology 1979;132:285-288.

39. Colapinto RF, Harries-Jones EP, Johnston KW. Percutaneous transluminal dilatation and recanalization in the treatment of peripheral vascular disease. Radiology 1980;135:583-587.

40. Lu CT, Zarins CK, Yang CF, et al. Percutaneous transluminal angioplasty for limb salvage. Radiology 1982;142:337-341.

27

Laser Angioplasty

James M. Seeger, MD, Gainesville, Florida

Systems have been developed that allow transmission of laser energy through fiberoptic catheters so that arterial obstructions can be treated without direct surgical exposure. However, arterial recanalization using current laser delivery systems produces only a small channel through an occluded artery, and laser recanalization must be used as an adjunct to balloon angioplasty. Treatment of infrainguinal arterial occlusions by balloon angioplasty alone is associated with a high rate of reocclusion in the first year of follow-up. Whether creation of a 2-mm channel with a thermal laser probe prior to balloon dilatation will reduce restenosis is unknown. Regardless, laser-assisted balloon angioplasty is being widely applied to patients with peripheral vascular disease.

Unlike standard arterial bypass surgery, the success of laser angioplasty appears to be dependent on the location and the length and type of the arterial lesion treated. In addition, the size and length of the vessels that are obstructed, the high incidence of diabetes mellitus in patients with peripheral vascular disease (which leads to calcified occlusions), and the response of diseased peripheral arteries to the injury of plaque removal by thermal laser energy appear to be significant limitations to this new therapy. Thus, though the use of laser energy to recanalize occluded peripheral arteries is appealing, careful patient selection is necessary for good results and limited risk.

The tables presented here review the currently available results of clinical trials using laser-assisted balloon angioplasty in patients with peripheral vascular disease. Results are presented in terms of clinical success, meaning alleviation of symptoms and an increased Doppler ankle/brachial systolic pressure index, rather than technical success, which means only that the laser probe could cross the lesion. The effect of lesion length, lesion location, and lesion type (stenosis versus occlusion) on initial clinical success is presented. In addition, the success rate of recanalization using laser energy of different wavelengths is shown. Finally, complications associated with laser angioplasty, available long-term results of laser angioplasty, and the percentage of patients with peripheral vascular disease likely to benefit from this new technology are summarized.

It is important to remember that this new technology is at the beginning of its development, and delivery catheters, guidance systems, and the understanding of laser tissue interaction are very primitive. In addition, results of laser angioplasty must be compared with the results of arterial bypass surgery, which have established a benchmark against which all new treatments of peripheral vascular disease must be judged.

From the Section of Vascular Surgery, Department of Surgery, University of Florida, Gainesville, Fla.

Table VI. One-year results* of laser-assisted balloon angioplasty

Author	Lesion location	Lesion type	Lesion length (cm)	Number followed	Clinical success at 1 year (%)*
Diethrich et al.[2]	Iliac	Stenosis		10	90
		Occlusion		20	85
	SFA	Stenosis		28	93
		Occlusion		69	90
	Popliteal	Stenosis		5	80
		Occlusion		8	63
	Tibial	Stenosis		10	70
		Occlusion		4	50
Perler et al.[9]	SFA/popliteal	Occlusion		22	35
Sanborn et al.[6]	SFA	Stenosis		21	95
		Occlusion	1-3	17	93
			4-7	26	76
			>7	35	58

*Continuing clinical success in patients who were successfully treated initially.

Table VII. Impact of laser thermal angioplasty on the treatment of peripheral vascular disease

Author	No. of patients examined	Patients successfully treated by LABA* not treatable by BA (%)[†]
Sanborn et al.[6,7]	219	18
Seeger et al.[10]	195	13.5

*Laser-assisted balloon angioplasty.
[†]Balloon angioplasty.

REFERENCES

1. Cumberland DC, Crue JR, Myler RK, et al. Clinical laser angioplasty experience at Northern General Hospital and the San Francisco Heart Institute. In Sanborn TA, ed. Laser Angioplasty. New York: Alan R. Liss, 1989.
2. Diethrich EB, Timbadia E, Bahadir I. Applications and limitations of laser-assisted angioplasty. Eur J Vasc Surg 1989; 3:61-70.
3. Lammer J, Karnel F. Percutaneous transluminal laser angioplasty with contact probes. Radiology 1988;168:733-737.
4. McCowan TC, Ferris EJ, Barnes RW, et al. Laser thermal angioplasty for the treatment of obstruction of the distal superficial femoral or popliteal arteries. Am J Radiol 1988; 150:1169-1173.
5. Nordstrom LA, Castaneda-Zuniga WR, Young EG, et al. Direct argon laser exposure for recanalization of peripheral arteries: Early results. Radiology 1988;168:359-364.
6. Sanborn TA, Cumberland DC, Greenfield AJ, et al. Percutaneous laser thermal angioplasty: Initial results and 1-year follow-up in 129 femoropopliteal lesions. Radiology 1988; 168:121-125.
7. Sanborn TA, Cumberland DC, Greenfield AJ, et al. Peripheral laser-assisted balloon angioplasty: Initial multicenter experience in 219 peripheral arteries. Arch Surg 1989;124:1099-1103.
8. Myler RK, Cumberland DA, Clark DA, et al. High and low power thermal laser angioplasty for total occlusions and restenosis in man. Circulation 1987;(76)Suppl IV:IV–230.
9. Perler BA, Osterman FA, White RI, et al. Percutaneous laser probe femoropopliteal angioplasty: A preliminary experience. J Vasc Surg 1989;10:351-357.
10. Seeger JM, Abela GS, Silverman SH, et al. Initial results of laser recanalization in lower extremity arterial reconstruction. J Vasc Surg 1989;9:10-17.
11. Barbeau GR, Abela GS, Seeger JM, et al. Laser thermal-optical angioplasty in totally occluded peripheral arteries: Immediate and intermediate results. Circulation 1989; 80(No.4):II–227.
12. Geschwind HJ, DuBois-Rande J, Shafton E, et al. Percutaneous pulsed laser-assisted balloon angioplasty guided by spectroscopy. Am Heart J 1989;117:1147-1152.
13. Litvack F, Grundfest WS, Adler L, et al. Percutaneous excimer-laser and excimer-laser-assisted angioplasty of the lower extremities: results of initial clinical trial. Radiology 1989;172:331-335.

28

Amputations

Robert D. De Frang, MD, Lloyd M. Taylor, Jr, MD, John M. Porter, MD, Portland, Oregon

The ability of well-performed vascular surgery to achieve a 5-year limb salvage rate in excess of 90% in patients presenting with limb-threatening ischemia has been documented in several recent series.[24,64] Presently, primary amputation is necessary in only 2% of patients in whom we perform arteriography in anticipation of limb bypass. Despite this, a large number of patients continue to require limb amputations for ischemia, currently

From the Division of Vascular Surgery, Oregon Health Sciences University, Portland, Ore.

estimated at greater than 115,000 per year in the United States alone.[106,122] A large number of patients who require limb amputation because of arterial ischemia have associated diabetes, end-stage renal disease, or severe neurologic impairment.

The following tables present basic data related to major lower extremity amputations, which we consider important for informed clinical decision making. The data were derived from the references listed, with appropriate weighting for patient numbers and length of follow-up.

Table I. Total amputations per year (USA)*

Type of amputation	No.	Percent
Phalangeal	36,800	32
Foot	11,500	10
Below-knee	33,350	29
Above-knee	33,350	29
Total	115,000	100

*References 2,4,31,70,71,72,80,86,87,106,122.

Table II. Amputee demographics

Category		No. of patients	Ref.
Male:female	1.8:1	2332	18,19,26,30,33,43,60,78,86,91,99,112,119
Diabetics (%)	54	1361/2532	18,33,55,60,70,86,98,102,107,112,117
Tobacco use (%)	65	414/639	33,44,52,69,98,99
Mean age	65 yr	2254	18,30,33,37,43,70,78,81,86,112,117
History			
Coronary artery disease (%)	44	772/1754	17,30,33,52,54,55,69,95,98,99,112
Prior myocardial infarction (%)	33	215/633	18,27,30,38,43,44
Hypertension (%)	47	951/2027	8,18,27,33,60,69,98,112
Cerebral vascular disease (%)	19	418/2200	18,44,54,55,78,98,99,107,112
Prior vascular surgery (%)	39	394/993	31,43,44,86,94,96,99
BKA:AKA ratio	2.2:1	588/257	20,34,96,102,106,117,119

BKA:AKA = below-knee amputation:above-knee amputation.

REFERENCES

1. Acton D, Hyland J, Nolan D, et al. In hospital rehabilitation of amputees: A prospective study. Irish Med J 1984;77: 131-133.

2. Barber GG, McPhail NV, Scobie TK, et al. A prospective study of lower limb amputations. Can J Surg 1983;26: 339-341.

3. Barnes RW, Slaymaker EE. Post-operative DVT in the lower extremity amputee: A prospective study with Doppler ultrasound. Ann Surg 1976;183:429-432.

4. Barnes RW, Thornhill B, Nix L, et al. Prediction of amputation wound healing. Arch Surg 1981;116:80-83.

5. Bartlett ST, Olinde AJ, Flinn WR, et al. The re-operative potential of infrainguinal bypass: Long-term limb and patient survival. J Vasc Surg 1987;5:170-179.

6. Bloom RJ, Stevick A. Amputation and distal bypass salvage of the limb. Surg Gynecol Obstet 1988,166:1-5.

7. Bodily KC, Burgess EM. Contralateral limb and patient survival after leg amputation. Am J Surg 1983;146:280-282.

8. Bongard O, Krahenbuhl B. Predicting amputation in severe ischemia—the value of transcutaneous PO_2. J Bone Joint Surg 1988;70B:465-467.

9. Britton JP, Barrie WW. Amputation in the diabetic: Ten years experience in a district general hospital. Ann R Coll Surg 1987;69:127-129.

10. Bunt TJ, Manship LL, Bynoe RPH, et al. Lower extremity amputation for peripheral vascular disease. Am Surg 1984; 50:581-584.

11. Burnham SJ, Wagner WH, Keagy BA, et al. Objective measurement of limb perfusion by dermal fluorometry. Arch Surg 1990;125:104-106.

12. Butler CM, Ham RO, Laffery K, et al. The effect of adjuvant oxygen therapy on transcutaneous PO_2 and healing in the below knee amputee. Prosthet Orthot Int 1987;11:10-16.

13. Callow AD, Mackey WC. Costs and benefits of prosthetic vascular surgery. Int Surg 1988;73:237-240.

14. Cederberg PA, Pritchard DJ, Joyce JW. Doppler determined segmental pressures and wound healing in amputations for vascular disease. J Bone Joint Surg 1983;65A:363-365.

15. Christensen KS, Klarke M. Transcutaneous oxygen measurement in peripheral occlusive disease. J Bone Joint Surg 1986;68B:423-426.

16. Clarke-Williams MJ. The elderly amputee. Physiotherapy 1969;55:368-371.

17. Colt JD, Lee PY. Mortality rate of above the knee amputation for arteriosclerotic gangrene: A critical evaluation. Angiology 1972;23:205-210.

18. Couch NP, David JK, Tilney NL, et al. Natural history of the leg amputee. Am J Surg 1977;133:469-473.

19. Cumming JGR, Jain AS, Walker WF, et al. Fate of the vascular patient after below knee amputation. Lancet 1987; September 12:613-615.

20. Cumming JGR, Spence VA, Jain AS, et al. Further experience in the healing rate of lower limb amputations. Eur J Vasc Surg 1988;2:383-385.

21. Dardik H, Kahn M, Dardik I, et al. Influence of failed vascular bypass procedures on conversion of below knee to above knee amputation levels. Surgery 1982;91:64-69.

22. DeCossart G, Randall P, Turner P, et al. The fate of the below knee amputee. Ann R Coll Surg 1983;65:230-232.

23. Dwars BJ, Rauwerda JA, Van Den Broek TAA, et al. A modified scintigraphic technique for amputation level selection in diabetics. Eur J Nucl Med 1989;15:38-41.

24. Edwards JM, Taylor LM Jr, Porter JM. Limb salvage in end-stage renal disease (ESRD): Comparison of modern results in patients with and without ESRD. Arch Surg 1988;123:1164-1168.

25. Eidemiller LR, Awe WC, Peterson CG. Amputation of the ischemic extremity. Am Surg 1968;34:491-493.

26. Epstein SB, Worth MH Jr, El Ferzli G. Level of amputation following failed vascular reconstruction for lower limb ischemia. Curr Surg 1989;May-June:185-192.

27. Evans WE, Hayes JP, Vermilion BD. Rehabilitation of the bilateral amputee. J Vasc Surg 1987;5:589-593.

28. Falkel JE. Amputation as a consequence of diabetes mellitus. Physical Therapy 1983;63:960-964.

29. Faxon HH. Major amputations for advanced peripheral arterial obliterative disease. JAMA 1939;113:1199.

30. Fearon J, Campbell DR, Hoar CS Jr, et al. Improved results with diabetic below knee amputations. Arch Surg 1985;120: 777-780.

31. Finch DRA, MacDougal M, Tibbs DJ, et al. Amputation for vascular disease: The experience of a peripheral vascular unit. Br J Surg 1980;67:233-237.

32. Fisher SV, Gullickson G Jr. Energy cost of ambulation in health and disability: A literature review. Arch Phys Med Rehabil 1978;59:124-133.

33. Fowl RJ, Patterson RB, Boienham RJ, et al. Functional failure of patent femorodistal in situ grafts. Ann Vasc Surg 1989;3:200-204.

34. Francis W, Renton CJC. Mobility after major limb amputation for arterial occlusive disease. Prosthet Orthot Int 1987; 11:85-89.

35. Gibbons GW, Wheelock FC Jr, Siembieda C, et al. Noninvasive prediction of amputation level in diabetic patients. Arch Surg 1979;114:1253-1257.

36. Gonzales EG, Corcoran PJ, Reyes RL. Energy expenditure in below knee amputees: Correlation with stump length. Arch Phys Med Rehabil 1974;55:111-119.

37. Gregg RO. Bypass or amputation? Am J Surg 1985;149: 397-402.

38. Gutman M, Kaplan O, Skornick Y, et al. Gangrene of the lower limbs in diabetic patients: A malignant complication. Am J Surg 1987;154:305-308.

39. Haimovici H. Failed grafts and level of amputation. J Vasc Surg 1985;2:371-374.

40. Hansson J. The leg amputee: A clinical follow-up study. Acta Orthop Scand 1964;69 (Suppl): 1-104.

41. Harper DR, Dhall DP, Woodruff PWH. Prophylaxis in iliofemoral venous thrombosis: The major amputee as a clinical research model. Br J Surg 1973;60:831.

42. Harris JP, McLaughlin AF, Quinn RJ, et al. Skin blood flow measurement with xenon 133 to predict healing of lower extremity amputations. Aust NZ J Surg 1986;56:413-415.

43. Harris PL, Read F, Eardley A, et al. The fate of elderly amputees. Br J Surg 1974;61:665-668.

44. High RM, McDowell DE, Savrin RA. A critical review of amputation in vascular patients. J Vasc Surg 1984;1: 653-655.

45. Honson RW II, Lynch TG, Jamil Z, et al. Results of revascularization and amputation in severe lower extremity ischemia: A 5 year clinical experience. J Vasc Surg 1984;2: 174-185.

46. Holloway GA, Burgess EM. Preliminary experiences with laser doppler velocimetry for the determination of amputation levels. Prosthet Orthot Int 1983;7:63-66.

47. Holstein P. Level selection in leg amputation for arterial occlusive disease. Acta Orthop Scand 1982;53:821-831.

48. Holstein P. Skin perfusion pressure measured by radioisotope washout for predicting wound healing in lower limb amputation for arterial occlusive disease. Acta Orthop Scand 1985;Suppl 213, 56:1-47.

49. Holstein P. Ischemic wound complications in above knee amputations in relation to skin perfusion pressure. Prosthet Orthot Int 1980;4:81-86.

50. Holstein P, Dovey H, Lassen NA. Wound healing in above knee amputation in relation to skin perfusion pressure. Acta Orthop Scand 1979;50:59-66.

51. Holstein P, Sager P, Lassen NA. Wound healing in below knee amputations in relation to skin perfusion pressure. Acta Orthop Scand 1979;50:49-58.

52. Huston CC, Bivins BA, Ernst CB, et al. Morbid implications of above knee amputations. Arch Surg 1980;115:165-167.

53. Hyland J, Nolan D, Browne H, et al. Factors influencing the outcome of major lower limb amputations. Irish Med J 1982;75:58-60.

54. Kahn D, Wagner W, Bessman AN. Mortality of diabetic patients treated surgically for lower limb infection/gangrene. Diabetes 1974;23:287-292.

55. Kald A, Carlsson R, Nilsson E. Major amputation in a defined population: Incidence, mortality, and results of treatment. Br J Surg 1989;76:308-310.

56. Kaplow M, Muroff K, Fish W, et al. The dysvascular amputee: Multidisciplinary management. Can J Surg 1983;26:368-369.

57. Katrak PH, Baggot JB. Rehabilitation of elderly lower extremity amputees. Med J Aust 1980;1:651-653.

58. Katsamouris A, Brewster DC, Megerman J, et al. Transcutaneous oxygen tension in selection of amputation level. Am J Surg 1984;147:510-517.

59. Kazmers M, Satiani B, Evans WE. Amputation level following unsuccessful distal limb salvage operations. Surgery 1980;87:683-687.

60. Keagy BA, Schwartz JA, Kotb M, et al. Lower extremity amputation: The control series. J Vasc Surg 1986;4:321-326.

61. Kihn RB, Warren R, Beebe GW. The geriatric amputee. Ann Surg 1972;176:305-314.

62. Kram HB, Appel PL, Shoemaker WC. Prediction of below knee amputation wound healing using noninvasive laser doppler velocimetry. Am J Surg 1989;158:29-31.

63. Kram HB, Appel PL, Shoemaker WC. Multisensor transcutaneous oximetric mapping to predict below knee amputation wound healing: Use of a critical PO_2. J Vasc Surg 1989;9:796-800.

64. Leather RP. In situ saphenous vein arterial bypass to the tibial arteries. J Vasc Surg 1984;1:912-913.

65. Lepantalo MJA, Haajanen J, Lindfors O, et al. Predictive value of preoperative segmental blood pressure measurements in below knee amputations. Acta Chir Scand 1982;148:581-584.

66. Lepantalo MIA, Isoniemi H, Kyllonen L. Can failure of a below knee amputation be predicted. Ann Chir Gynecol 1987;76:119-123.

67. Lexier RR, Harrington IJ, Woods JM. Lower extremity amputations: A 5 year review and comparative study. Can J Surg 1987;30:374-376.

68. Light JT, Rice JC, Kerstein MD. Sequelae of limited amputation. Surgery 1988;103:294-299.

69. Malone JM, Anderson GG, Lalka SG, et al. Prospective comparison of noninvasive techniques for amputation level selection. Am J Surg 1987;154:179-184.

70. Malone JM, Leal JM, Moore WS, et al. The gold standard for amputation level selection: Xenon 133 clearance. J Surg Res 1981;30:449-455.

71. Malone JM, Moore WS, Goldstone J, et al. Therapeutic and economic impact of a modern amputation program. Ann Surg 1979;189:798-802.

72. Malone JM, Moore WS, Leal JM, et al. Rehabilitation for lower extremity amputation. Arch Surg 1981;116:93-98.

73. McCollum PT, Spence VA, Walker WF. Amputation for peripheral vascular disease: The case for level selection. Br J Surg 1988;75:1193-1195.

74. McFarland DC, Lawrence PF. Skin fluorescence: A method to predict amputation site healing. J Surg Res 1982;32:410-415.

75. Moore WS. Determination of amputation level. Arch Surg 1973;107:798-802.

76. Moore WS, Henry RE, Malone JM, et al. Prospective use of xenon 133 clearance for amputation level selection. Arch Surg 1981;116:86-88.

77. Mueller MJ, Delitto A. Selective criteria for successful long term prosthetic use. Physical Therapy 1985;65:1037-1040.

78. Nagendran T, Johnson G Jr, McDaniel WJ, et al. Amputation of the leg: an improved outlook. Ann Surg 1972;175:994-999.

79. Nicholas GG, Myers JL, DeMuth WE Jr. The role of vascular laboratory criteria in the selection of patients for lower extremity amputation. Ann Surg 1982;195:469-473.

80. Oishi CS, Fronek A, Golbranson FL. The role of noninvasive vascular studies in determining levels of amputation. J Bone Joint Surg 1988;70A:1520-1530.

81. Ouriel K, Fiore WM, Geary JE. Limb-threatening ischemia in the medically compromised patient: Amputation or revascularization? Surgery 1988;104:667-672.

82. Oveson J, Stockel M. Measurement of skin perfusion by photoelectric technique—an aid to amputation level selection in arteriosclerotic disease. Prosthet Orthot Int 1984;8:39-42.

83. Parziale JR, Hahn KK. Functional considerations in partial foot amputations. Orthop Rev 1988;17:262-266.

84. Pohjolainen T, Alaranta H, Wikstrom J. Primary survival and prosthetic fitting of lower limb amputees. Prosthet Orthot Int 1989;13:63-69.

85. Pollock SB, Ernst CB. Use of Doppler pressure measurements in predicting success in amputation of the leg. Am J Surg 1980;139:303-309.

86. Porter JM, Baur GM, Taylor LM Jr. Lower-extremity amputations for ischemia. Arch Surg 1981;116:89-92.

87. Potts JR III, Wendelken JR, Elkins RC, et al. Lower extremity amputation: Review of 110 cases. Am J Surg 1979;138:924-928.

88. Ramsburgh SR, Lindenauer SM, Weber TR, et al. Femoropopliteal bypass for limb salvage. Surgery 1977;81:453-458.

89. Ratliff DA, Clyne CAC, Chant ADB, et al. Prediction of amputation wound healing: The role of transcutaneous PO_2 assessment. Br J Surg 1984;71:219-222.

90. Raviola CA, Nichter LS, Baker JD, et al. Cost of treating advanced leg ischemia. Arch Surg 1988;123:495-496.

91. Redhead RG. The place of amputation in the management of the ischemic lower limb in the dysvascular geriatric patient. Int Rehabil Med 1984;6:68-71.

92. Robbs JV, Human RR, Rajaruthnam P. Bypass versus primary major amputation in patients with femoropopliteal distal disease and a threatened limb. S Afr Med J 1984;66:809-812.

93. Robbs JV, Ray R. Clinical predictors of below knee stump healing following amputation for ischemia. S Afr J Surg 1982;20:305-310.

94. Roon AJ, Moore WS, Goldstone J. Below knee amputation: A modern approach. Am J Surg 1977;134:153-158.

95. Rosenberg N, Adiarte E, Bujdoso LJ, et al. Mortality factors in major limb amputations for vascular disease: A study of 176 procedures. Surgery 1970;67:437-441.

Table I. Distribution of arterial macroemboli to the upper extremity causing acute ischemia

	Incidence (%)	References
Upper extremity emboli in relation to all systemic embolic episodes	18.3	1,4,5,7,21,24, 25,27

Location of embolization	Incidence (%)	References
Subclavian artery	11.0	1,2,5,6,16,21,22, 25,26
Axillary artery	22.0	1,2,5,6,16,21,22 25,26
Brachial artery	60.5	1,2,5,6,16,21,22 25,26
Proximal to profunda brachii	23.0	1,2,21,22
Distal to profunda brachii	27.0	1,2,16,21,23
Radial artery	2.5	1,2,5,6,14,21,22, 25,26
Ulnar artery	1.2	1,2,5,21,22,25

NOTE: Categories do not total 100% as various references do not include all sites of embolization.

Table II. Source of arterial embolization to upper extremities

Source of embolization	Incidence (%)	References
Cardiac	87.0	1-3,6,7,10,21-23,26, 27,30
Atrial fibrillation	64.0	1-3,6,7,10,21-23,26, 27,30
Atherosclerotic heart disease	43.0	1,2,7,10,21,22,27,30
Acute myocardial infarction	14.0	1-3,21-33
Rheumatic heart disease	8.0	7,11,27,29
Ventricular aneurysm	7.0	1,3,21,23
Bacterial endocarditis	2.0	2,6,22,26
Noncardiac	13.0	1-3,6,7,21-23,26,27
Proximal aneurysm*	3.5	1-3,6,7,21-23,26,27
Proximal atheroma	4.5	3,7,11,23,27,31

NOTE: Categories do not total 100% as sources of embolization often overlap.
*Includes sources from arterial thoracic outlet syndrome.

Table III. Treatment outcome of acute embolic upper extremity ischemia

Treatment	Mortality*	Limb salvage (%) Residual dysfunction	No dysfunction	Total	References
Heparin therapy	25.0	56.5	21.5	78.0	21,22,24,26
Balloon catheter embolectomy	12.5	22.0	62.0	84.0	21-27
Arteriotomy outside of antecubital fossa		47.0	35.0	82.0	21
Antecubital arteriotomy		6.0	91.0	97.0	21

*Recurrent embolism to the cerebral and mesenteric arteries was the most frequent cause of death (46%), followed by cardiac failure (23%) and acute myocardial infarction (14%).[21,27]

Table IV. Etiology of chronic upper extremity ischemia classified according to anatomic location of large vessel arterial pathology

Anatomic location	Etiology	References
Arch arteries	Atherosclerotic disease	
	Occlusive arteriosclerosis	1-20
	Degenerative aneurysm with embolization	1-3,6,7,21-23,26,27
	Nonatherosclerotic disease	
	Giant cell arteritis	51-60
	Takayasu's arteritis	61-68
Subclavian axillary arteries	Atherosclerotic disease	
	Occlusive arteriosclerosis	1-20
	Degenerative aneurysm with embolization	1-3,6,7,21-23,26,27
	Nonatherosclerotic disease	
	Arterial thoracic outlet syndrome	3,9,10,15,17,32-50
	Giant cell arteritis	51-60
	Fibromuscular dysplasia	69-80
Brachial, radial, and ulnar arteries	Atherosclerotic disease	
	Occlusive arteriosclerosis	1-20
	Nonatherosclerotic disease	
	Arteritis	51-68
	Fibromuscular dysplasia	69-80
	Buerger's disease (thromboangiitis obliterans)*	
	Hypothenar hammer syndrome*	

*These entities are reviewed in Part II. "Small Vessel Arterial Occlusive Disease," as manifestations mimic distal palmar and digital small vessel disease.

Table V. Distribution of atherosclerotic occlusive disease causing symptomatic upper extremity ischemia

Arterial segment	Incidence (%)	References
Innominate	19.5	3,5-7,9
Subclavian	60.5	2,3,5-7,9,14
Proximal to vertebral artery	54.5	2,3,7,9
With steal syndrome	43.0	2,5,8
Without steal syndrome	57.0	2,5,8
Distal to vertebral artery	45.5	2,3,7,9
Right subclavian artery	36.0	2,3,6
Left subclavian artery	64.0	2,3,6
Axillary artery	6.0	2,3,7,14
Brachial artery	12.0	7,14
Radial/ulnar artery	2.0	2,3,14

Arterial segment	Incidence (%)	References
Subclavian disease in general population, both symptomatic and asymptomatic, detected by Doppler screening examination	1.15	8
Symptomatic upper extremity arterial insufficiency as % of total symptomatic extremities	4.7	5

REFERENCES

1. Gross WS, Flanigan P, Kraft RO, et al. Chronic upper extremity arterial insufficiency. Arch Surg 1978;113:419-423.
2. Harris RW, Andros G, Dulawa LB, et al. Large-vessel arterial occlusive disease in symptomatic upper extremity. Arch Surg 1984;119:1277-1282.
3. Bergqvist D, Ericsson BF, Konrad P, et al. Arterial surgery of the upper extremity. World J Surg 1983;7:786-791.
4. Holleman JH Jr, Hardy JD, Williamson JW, et al. Arterial surgery for arm ischemia. A survey of 136 patients. Ann Surg 1980;191:727-737.
5. Welling RE, Cranley JJ, Krause RJ, et al. Obliterative arterial disease of the upper extremity. Arch Surg 1981;116:1593-1596.
6. Crawford ES, DeBakey ME, Morris GC, et al. Surgical treatment of occlusion of the innominate, common carotid and subclavian arteries: A 10-year experience. Surgery 1969;65:17-28.
7. Laroche GP, Bernatz PE, Joyce JW, et al. Chronic arterial insufficiency of the upper extremity. Mayo Clin Proc 1976;51:180-186.
8. Ackermann H, Diener HC, Dichgans J. Stenosis and occlusion of the subclavian artery: Ultrasonographic and clinical findings. J Neurol 1987;234:396-400.
9. Rapp JH, Reilly LM, Goldstone J, et al. Ischemia of the upper extremity: Significance of proximal arterial disease. Am J Surg 1986;152:122-126.
10. Williams SJ. Chronic upper extremity ischemia: Current concepts in management. Surg Clin North Am 1986;66:355-375.
11. Rostad H, Hall K. Arterial occlusive disease of the upper extremity. Scand J Thorac Cardiovasc Surg 1980;14:223-226.
12. McCarthy WJ, Flinn WR, Yao JST, et al. Results of bypass grafting for upper limb ischemia. J Vasc Surg 1986;3:741-746.
13. Schmidt FE, Hewitt RL. Severe upper limb ischemia. Arch Surg 1980;115:1188-1191.
14. McNamara MF, Takaki HS, Yao JST, et al. A systematic approach to severe hand ischemia. Surgery 1978;83:1-11.
15. Whelan TJ Jr. Management of vascular disease of the upper extremity. Surg Clin North Am 1982;62:373-389.
16. Dale WA, Lewis MR. Management of ischemia of the hand and fingers. Surgery 1970;67:62-79.
17. Moore WS, Malone JM, Goldstone J. Extra-thoracic repair of branch occlusions of the aortic arch. Am J Surg 1976;132:249-257.
18. Raithel D. Our experience of surgery for innominate and subclavian lesions. J Cardiovasc Surg 1980;21:423-430.
19. Carlson RE, Ehrenfeld WK, Stoney RJ, et al. Innominate artery endarterectomy: A 16-year experience. Arch Surg 1977;1121:1389-1393.
20. Posner MP, Riles TS, Ramirez AA, et al. Axillo-axillary bypass for symptomatic stenosis of the subclavian artery. Am J Surg 1983;145:644-646.
21. Savelyev VS, Zatevakhin II, Stepanov NV. Artery embolism of the upper extremities. Surgery 1977;81:367-375.
22. Baird RJ, Lajos TZ. Emboli to the arm. Ann Surg 1964;160:905-909.
23. Sachatello CR, Ernst CB, Griffen WO. The acutely ischemic upper extremity: Selective management. Surgery 1974;76:1002-1009.
24. Champion HR, Gill W. Arterial embolus to the upper limb. Br J Surg 1973;60:505-508.
25. Haimovici H. Cardiogenic embolism of the upper extremity. J Cardiovasc Surg 1982;23:209-213.
26. Ricotta JJ, Scudder PA, McAndrew JA. Management of acute ischemia of the upper extremity. Am J Surg 1983;145:661-666.
27. James EC, Khuri NT, Fedde CW, et al. Upper limb ischemia resulting from arterial thromboembolism. Am J Surg 1979;137:739-744.
28. Banis JC, Rich N, Whelan TJ. Ischemia of the upper extremity due to non-cardiac emboli. Am J Surg 1977;134:131-139.
29. Raithel D. Surgical treatment of acute embolization and acute arterial thrombosis: A review of 342 cases. J Cardiovasc Surg, Barcelona Congress Vol, Sept 27-29,1973;61-72.
30. Kofoed H, Buchardt Hansen HJ. Arterial embolism in the upper limb. Acta Chir Scand 1976;472:113-115.
31. Bryan AJ, Hicks E, Lewis MH. Unilateral digital ischemia secondary to embolization from subclavian atheroma. Ann R Coll Surg Engl 1989;71:140-142.
32. Heymann RL, Whelan TJ. Vascular complications of the thoracic outlet syndrome: A case report. Milit Med 1970;135:793-796.
33. Mathes JJ, Salam AA. Subclavian artery aneurysms: Sequelae of thoracic outlet syndrome. Surgery 1974;76:506-510.
34. Judy KL, Heymann RL. Vascular complications of thoracic outlet syndrome. Am J Surg 1972;123:521-531.
35. Martin J, Gaspard NJ, Johnston PW. Vascular manifestations of the thoracic outlet syndrome. A surgical urgency. Arch Surg 1976;111:779-782.
36. Lee BY, Thoden WR, Maden JL, et al. Subclavian artery aneurysms secondary to thoracic outlet syndrome. Contemp Surg 1984;25:19-24.
37. Dorazio RA, Ezzet F. Arterial complications of the thoracic outlet syndrome. Am J Surg 1979;138:246-250.
38. Etheredge S, Wilbur B, Stoney RJ. Thoracic outlet syndrome. Am J Surg 1979;138:175-182.
39. Prior AL, Wilson LA, Gosling RG, et al. Retrograde cerebral embolism. Lancet 1979;2:1044-1047.
40. Pairolero PC, Walls JT, Payne WS, et al. Subclavian-axillary artery aneurysms. Surgery 1981;90:757-763.
41. Scher LA, Veith FJ, Haimovici H, et al. Staging of arterial complications of cervical rib: Guidelines for surgical management. Surgery 1984;95:644-649.
42. Sullivan KL, Minken SL, White RI Jr. Treatment of a case of thromboembolism resulting from thoracic outlet syndrome with intra-arterial urokinase infusion. J Vasc Surg 1988;7:568-571.
43. Al-Hassan HK, Sattar MH, Eklof B. Embolic brain infarction: A rare complication of thoracic outlet syndrome. A report of ten cases. J Cardiovasc Surg 1988;29:322-325.
44. Brown SCW, Charlesworth D. Results of excision of a cervical rib in patients with the thoracic outlet syndrome. Br J Surg 1988;75:431-433.
45. Salo JA, Varstela E, Ketonen P, et al. Management of vascular complications in thoracic outlet syndrome. Acta Chir Scand 1988;154:349-352.
46. Baumgartner F, Nelson RJ, Robertson JM. The rudimentary first rib. A cause of thoracic outlet syndrome with arterial compromise. Arch Surg 1989;124:1090-1092.
47. Cormier JM, Amrane M, Ward A, et al. Arterial complication of the thoracic outlet syndrome. Fifty-five operative cases. J Vasc Surg 1989;9:778-787.
48. Sanders RJ, Haug C. Review of arterial thoracic outlet syndrome with a report of five new instances. Surg Gynecol Obstet 1991;173:415-425.
49. Blank RH, Connar RG. Arterial complications associated with thoracic outlet compression syndrome. Ann Thorac Surg 1974;17:315-324.
50. Roos DB. Congenital anomalies associated with thoracic outlet syndrome: Anatomy, symptoms, diagnosis and treatment. Am J Surg 1976;132:771-778.

51. Klein RG, Hunder GG, Stanson AW, et al. Large artery involvement in giant cell (temporal) arteritis. Ann Intern Med 1975;83:806-812.

52. Ninet JP, Bachet P, Dumontet CM, et al. Subclavian and axillary involvement in temporal arteritis and polymyalgia rheumatica. Am J Med 1990;88:13-20.

53. Hamrin B. Stenosing arteritis of the subclavian-axillary arteries (polymyalgia rheumatica sive arteritica). Acta Chir Scand 1976;142(Suppl 465):80-83.

54. Ostberg G. Morphological changes in the large arteries in polymyalgia arteritica. Acta Med Scand 1972;164(Suppl 533): 135-164.

55. Bengtsson BA, Malmvall BE. Giant cell arteritis. Acta Med Scand 1982;212(Suppl 658):1-102.

56. Swinson DR, Goodwill CJ, Talbot JC. Giant cell arteritis presenting as subclavian artery occlusion. A report of two cases. Postgrad Med J 1976;52:525-529.

57. Royster TS, DiRe JJ. Polymyalgia rheumatica and giant cell arteritis with bilateral axillary artery occlusion. Am Surg 1971;37:421-426.

58. Rivers SP, Baur GM, Inahara T, et al. Arm ischemia secondary to giant cell arteritis. Am J Surg 1982;143:554-558.

59. Perruquet JL, Davis DE, Harrington TM. Aortic arch arteritis in the elderly. An important manifestation of giant cell arteritis. Arch Intern Med 1986;146:289-291.

60. Huston KA, Hunder GG, Lie JT, et al. Temporal arteritis: A 25-year epidemiologic, clinical, and pathologic study. Ann Intern Med 1978;88:162-167.

61. Lupi-Herrera E, Sanchez-Torres G, Marcushamer J, et al. Takayasu's arteritis: Clinical study of 107 cases. Am Heart J 1977;93:94-103.

62. Hall S, Barr W, Lie JT, et al. Takayasu's arteritis: A study of 32 North American patients. Medicine 1985;64:89-99.

63. Ishikawa K. Natural history and classification of occlusive thromboaortopathy (Takayasu's disease). Circulation 1978;57: 27-35.

64. Mishima Y. Arterial insufficiency of the upper extremity with special reference to Takayasu's arteritis and Buerger's disease. J Cardiovasc Surg 1982;23:105-108.

65. Inada K, Shimizu H, Kobayashi I, et al. Pulseless disease and atypical coarctation of the aorta. Arch Surg 1962;84:306-312.

66. Lande A, Rossi P. The value of total aortography in the diagnosis of Takayasu's arteritis. Radiology 1975;114:287-297.

67. Nakao K, Ikeda M, Kimata S, et al. Takayasu's arteritis: Clinical report of eighty-four cases and immunologic studies of seven cases. Circulation 1967;35:1141-1155.

68. Shelhamer JH, Volkman DJ, Parrillo JE. Takayasu's arteritis and its therapy. Ann Intern Med 1989;103:121-126.

69. Edwards JM, Antonius JM, Porter JM. Critical hand ischemia caused by forearm fibromuscular dysplasia. J Vasc Surg 1985;2: 459-563.

70. Janevski B. Fibromuscular dysplasia of the ulnar artery. Fortschr Rontgenstr 1985;143:238-239.

71. Iwai T, Konno S, Hiejima K, et al. Fibromuscular dysplasia of the extremities. J Cardiovasc Surg 1985;26:496-501.

72. Luscher TF, Keller HM, Imhof HA, et al. Fibromuscular hyperplasia: Extension of the disease and therapeutic outcome. Results of the University Hospital Zurich Cooperative Study on Fibromuscular hyperplasia. Nephron 1986;44(Suppl 1):109-114.

73. Price RA, Vanter GF. Arterial fibromuscular dysplasia in infancy and childhood. Arch Pathol 1972;93:419-426.

74. Esfahani F, Rocholamini SA, Azadeh B, et al. Arterial fibrodysplasia: A regional cause of peripheral occlusive vascular disease. Angiology 1989;40:108-113.

75. Olson LA, Faber DB, LeMar JV, et al. Fibromuscular hyperplasia of the brachial artery — failure of calcium antagonist therapy. Angiology 1984;35:790-796.

76. Garret HE, Hodosh S, DeBakey ME. Fibromuscular hyperplasia of the left axillary artery. Arch Surg 1967;94:737-738.

77. Saha SP, Goff RD, Stephenson SE. Arm ischemia due to fibromuscular hyperplasia of the axillary artery. South Med J 1975;68:645-646.

78. Cheu HW, Mills JL. Digital artery embolization as a result of fibromuscular dysplasia of the brachial artery. J Vasc Surg 1991;14:225-228.

79. Mettinger KL. Fibromuscular dysplasia and the brain. II. Current concepts of the disease. Stroke 1982;13:53-58.

80. McCready RA, Pairolero PC, Hollier LH, et al. Fibromuscular dysplasia of the right subclavian artery. Arch Surg 1982;117: 1243-1245.

Table III. Prevalence of Raynaud's syndrome in patients with specific predisposing factors

	Percent	References
Occupation involving use of vibrating tools	40-90	33
Scleroderma/CREST syndrome	86	15-17
Systemic lupus erythematosus (SLE)	34	19-21
in patients with Sm antibodies	70	22
Mixed cryoglobulinemia	25-31	27
Thromboangiitis obliterans (Buerger's disease)	34	39-44

Table IV. Finger gangrene caused by small artery occlusive disease

	Percent	References
Underlying diagnosis		
Autoimmune disease	55	3, 6, 11
Scleroderma/CREST syndrome	25	6
Mixed connective tissue disease	5	6
Undifferentiated connective tissue disease	5	6
Miscellaneous (see Table II)	<3 each	6
Hypersensitivity angiitis (rapid-onset vascular occlusion)	22	6
Buerger's disease	10	3, 6
Atherosclerosis	9	6
Malignancy	4	6
Patient's with obstructive Raynaud's syndrome who subsequently develop finger gangrene	17	6, 11
Outcome of treatment		
Healing		
Conservative treatment*	88	6
Sympathectomy + conservative treatment	83	60, 61
PGE infusion + conservative treatment	82	62
Recurrent finger ulceration	11	6, 61
Formal finger amputation required	15	6, 61, 62
Arm amputation required	<1	3, 6, 61

*See text for description of conservative treatment.

Table V. Results of surgery for Raynaud's syndrome and digital ischemia caused by small artery occlusive disease

Procedure	"Improved" (%)	References
Thoracic sympathectomy	65	60, 63
Digital sympathectomy*	80	64, 65

Procedure	12-month patency (%)	References
Arterial reconstruction distal to wrist		
For ulnar aneurysm (hypothenar hammer hand)	88	66-68
For occlusive disease (arteriosclerosis obliterans, diabetes, other)	70	64, 66, 69-71

*Duration of follow-up unspecified.

REFERENCES

1. Bergan JJ, Conn J Jr, Trippel OH. Severe ischemia of the hand. Ann Surg 1971;173:301-307.
2. McNamara MF, Takaki HS, Yao JST, et al. A systematic approach to severe hand ischemia. Surgery 1978;83:1-11.
3. Kadwa AM, Robbs JV. Gangrenous fingers: The tip of the iceberg. J R Coll Surg Edinb 1990;35:71-74.
4. Campbell PM, LeRoy EC. Raynaud phenomenon. Semin Arthritis Rheum 1986;16:92-103.
5. Porter JM, Friedman EI, Mills JL. Occlusive and vasospastic diseases involving distal upper extremity arteries – Raynaud's syndrome. In Rutherford R, ed. Vascular Surgery, vol I. Philadelphia: WB Saunders, p 853, 1989.
6. Mills JL, Friedman EI, Taylor LM Jr, et al. Upper extremity ischemia caused by small artery disease. Ann Surg 1987;206:521-528.
7. Porter JM. Upper extremity digital gangrene caused by small artery occlusion. In Machleder HI, ed. Vascular Disorders of the Upper Extremity, 1st ed. Mt. Kisko, N.Y.: Future, pp 107-135, 1983.
8. Cosgriff TM, Arnold WF. Digital vasospasm and infarction associated with hepatitis B antigenemia. JAMA 1976;235:1362-1363.
9. Porter JM, Bardana EJ Jr, Baur GM, et al. The clinical significance of Raynaud's syndrome. Surgery 1976;80:756-764.
10. Peller JS, Gabor GT, Porter JM, et al. Angiographic findings in mixed connective tissue disease. Arthritis Rheum 1985;28:768-774.
11. Taylor LM Jr, Baur GM, Porter JM. Finger gangrene caused by small artery occlusive disease. Ann Surg 1981;193:453-461.
12. Gresham GA, Phear DN. Gangrene of the fingers in periarteritis nodosa. Am J Med 1957;23:671-672.
13. Carroll GJ, Withers K, Bayliss CE. The prevalence of Raynaud's syndrome in rheumatoid arthritis. Ann Rheum Dis 1981;40:567-570.
14. Bywaters EGL. Peripheral vascular obstruction in rheumatoid arthritis and its relationship to other vascular lesions. Ann Rheum Dis 1957;16:84-103.
15. Farmer RG, Gifford RW Jr, Hines EA Jr. Prognostic significance of Raynaud's phenomenon and other clinical characteristics of systemic scleroderma. A study of 271 cases. Circulation 1960;21:1088-1095.
16. Masi AT, Rodnan GP, Medsger TA, et al. Preliminary criteria for the classification of systemic sclerosis (scleroderma). Arthritis Rheum 1980;23:581-590.
17. Tuffanelli DL, Winkelmann RK. Systemic scleroderma. A clinical study of 727 cases. Arch Dermatol 1961;84:49-61.
18. Kallenberg CGM, Wouda AA, Hoet MH, et al. Development of connective tissue disease in patients presenting with Raynaud's phenomenon: A six year follow-up with emphasis on the predictive value of antinuclear antibodies as detected by immunoblotting. Ann Rheum Dis 1988;47:634-641.
19. Ansari A, Larson PH, Bates HD. Vascular manifestations of systemic lupus erythematosus. Angiology 1986;37:423-432.
20. Dimant J, Ginzler E, Schlesinger M, et al. The clinical significance of Raynaud's phenomenon in systemic lupus erythematosus. Arthritis Rheum 1979;22:815-819.
21. Tan EM, Cohen AS, Fries JF, et al. The 1982 revised criteria for the classification of systemic lupus erythematosus. Arthritis Rheum 1982;25:1271-1277.
22. Winn DM, Wolfe F, Lindberg DA, et al. Identification of a clinical subset of systemic lupus erythematosus by antibodies to the SM antigen. Arthritis Rheum 1979;22:1334-1337.
23. Tsokos M, Lazarov SA, Moutsopoulos HM. Vasculitis in primary Sjögren's syndrome. Am J Clin Pathol 1987;88:26-31.
24. LeRoy EL, Maricq HR, Kahaleh MB. Undifferentiated connective tissue syndromes. Arthritis Rheum 1980;23:341-343.
25. Jepson RP. Widespread and sudden occlusion of the small arteries of the hands and feet. Circulation 1956;14:1084-1089.
26. Baur GM, Porter JM, Bardana EJ, et al. Rapid onset of hand ischemia of unknown etiology. Ann Surg 1977;186:184-189.
27. Gorevic PD, Kassab HJ, Levo Y, et al. Mixed cryoglobulinemia: Clinical aspects and long-term follow-up of 40 patients. Am J Med 1980;69:287-308.
28. Mitchel AB, Pegrum GD, Gill AM. Cold agglutinin disease with Raynaud's phenomenon. Proc R Soc Med 1974;67:113-114.
29. Andrasch RH, Bardana EJ, Porter JM, et al. Digital ischemia and gangrene preceding renal neoplasm. Arch Intern Med 1976;136:486-488.
30. Powell KR. Raynaud's phenomenon preceding acute lymphocytic leukemia. J Pediatr 1973;82:539-540.
31. Hawley PR, Johnston AW, Rankin JT. Association between digital ischemia and malignant disease. Br Med J 1967;3:208-212.
32. Hardy JD, Conn JH, Fain WR. Nonatherosclerotic occlusive lesions of small arteries. Surgery 1965;57:1-13.
33. Taylor W, Pelmear PL. Raynaud's phenomenon of occupational origin. An epidemiological survey. Acta Chir Scand Suppl 1976;465:27-32.
34. Chatterjee DS, Petrie A, Taylor W. Prevalence of vibration-induced white finger in flourspar mines in Weardale. Br J Indust Med 1978;35:208-218.
35. Mackiewisz A, Piskorz A. Raynaud's phenomenon following long-term repeated action of great differences of temperature. J Cardiovasc Surg 1977;18:151-154.
36. Dietrich EB, Koopot R, Kinard SA, et al. Treatment of microemboli of the upper extremity. Surg Gynecol Obstet 1979;148:584-586.
37. Cormier JM, Amrane M, Ward A, et al. Arterial complications of the thoracic outlet syndrome. Fifty-five operative cases. J Vasc Surg 1959;9:778-787.
38. Blank RH, Connar RG. Arterial complications associated with thoracic outlet compression syndrome. Ann Thorac Surg 1974;17:315-374.
39. Mills JL, Taylor LM Jr, Porter JM. Buerger's disease in the modern era. Am J Surg 1987;154:123-129.
40. Zannini G, Cotrulo M. Epidemiological, angiographic and clinical aspects of Buerger's disease. J Cardiovasc Surg 1973;14:17-20.
41. Olin JW, Young JR, Graor RA, et al. The changing clinical spectrum of thromboangiitis obliterans (Buerger's disease). Circulation 1990;82(Suppl IV):IV3-IV8.
42. Shionoya S. What is Buerger's disease? World J Surg 1983;7:544-551.
43. Allen EV, Brown CE. Thrombo-angiitis obliterans: A clinical study of 200 cases. Ann Intern Med 1928;1:535-549.
44. Mozes M, Cahansky G, Doitsch V, et al. The association of atherosclerosis and Buerger's disease: A clinical and radiological study. J Cardiovasc Surg 1970;11:52-59.
45. Brouet JC, Clauvel JP, Danon F, et al. Biologic and clinical significance of cryoglobulins. Am J Med 1974;57:775-781.
46. Conn J, Bergan JJ, Bell JL. Hypothenar hammer syndrome: Posttraumatic digital ischemia. Surgery 1970;68:1122-1128.
47. Middleton DS. Occupational aneurysm of the palmar arteries. Br J Surg 1933;21:215-218.
48. Koman LA, Urbaniak JR. Ulnar artery insufficiency: A guide to treatment. J Hand Surg 1981;6:16-24.
49. Little JM, Ferguson DA. The incidence of the hypothenar hammer syndrome. Arch Surg 1972;105:684-688.

Table I. Effect of route of administration on initial results

	Success rate			
	NV (%)	Grafts (%)	Complications (%)	Ref.
IV	35* (30-40)		26.6	1,2
IA	71.5 (61-82.6)	49.1 (0-75)	31.9 (6.8-53.8)	3-9
IT	61.8 (33.3-88)	67.3 (26-88)	21.9 (9-44)	10-25

NV = native vessels; IV = intravenous; IA = intra-arterial; IT = intrathrombus.
*Reports did not specify type.

Table II. Thrombolytic agent vs. initial results

	All series		
	Success rate (%)	Complications (%)	Ref.
SK	63.5 (26-85)	31.8 (9-70)	3-7, 14-16, 18-22, 26-31
UK	72 (0-100)	22 (8.7-60)	8, 10, 1, 21-23, 25, 28, 32
tPA	88	36	33

	Single series comparing UK and SK success rates		
	Success rate (%)	*p* Value	Ref.
SK	41-50		
		<0.05	22, 28
UK	77-100		

SK = streptokinase; UK = urokinase; tPA = tissue-type plasminogen activator.

Table III. Doses of intrathrombotic urokinase vs. initial results

	Success rate (%)	Complications (%)	Ref.
Native vessels			
>75,000 U/hr	73.7	23	8, 9, 19, 22, 32
≤60,000 U/hr	84.8	20.9	10, 21, 24, 25, 28
Grafts			
125,000 U/hr	70 83	37.1	
	p = NS	*p* <0.05	32
50,000 U/hr	65 85	16.2	

Table IV. Administration of heparin vs. initial results

	Success rate (%)	Complications (%)	Ref.
Streptokinase with heparin	72.9 (67.6-80)	16.6 (6.8-22.9)	4, 14, 20
Streptokinase without heparin	56.4 (38-69.8)	12.3 (6.8-14)	4, 16, 18, 24
Urokinase with heparin	76.9 (54.2-88)	17.8 (2.7-26.1)	9, 10, 19, 21, 22, 25, 32

Table V. Major complications

	Streptokinase (%)	Urokinase (%)	Ref.
Bleeding requiring transfusion or surgical evacuation	3.9-60	2.8-25	1, 5, 9, 16, 18, 22, 23, 28, 34-41
CV accident	0.5-8	3.7	1, 5, 9, 27, 30, 34
Catheter thrombosis	2.9-12	16.7	4, 28, 34
Renal failure	4-9	4.5	9, 21, 22, 28
Distal embolization	1.9-16	2-15	4, 9, 10, 15, 21, 22, 28, 34
Amputation	0.6-10	1.8	5, 16, 23, 25
Death	0.6-2.6	2.8	4, 16, 25
Myocardial infarction	4.5-5.2	4.5	22, 25
Arterial/graft thrombosis	5.7-10.4	1.8	18, 25
Brachial plexus palsy	5.2	—	25
Pseudoaneurysm	1.4	1.2	10, 16, 34
Arterial aneurysm/graft rupture	4.5	1.8	9, 22
Gastrointestinal bleeding	1.0-2.8	—	4, 18
Retroperitoneal hematoma	7.6-8.5	—	7, 18

Table VI. Potential factors influencing initial outcome

	Success rate (%)	p Value	Ref.
Thrombus age			
<30 days	78	0.0071	6
>30 days	37		
0-2 days	77.1		
3-12 days	68.4	0.01	9
>12 days	41		
Grade of ischemia			
ABI < 0.25	22	0.0009	13
ABI > 0.25	89		
Limb paralysis/sensation loss	33.3	0.001	27
Rest pain alone	90		
Run off			
Poor	0		
Good	72.7	0.001	40
Graft age			
<6 mo	57.7	NS	9
>6 mo	71		
<12 mo	44.4		
>12 mo	70.8	NS	22
Graft position			
Suprainguinal	88	0.003	9
Infrainguinal	59		

ABI = ankle-brachial index.

Table VII. Influence of type of occlusion on initial result

	All series	
	Initial success (%)	Ref.
Native vessels	68.3 (45-88)	3-5, 10-16, 18-20
Grafts	61.6 (0-88)	3-6, 9, 11-13, 18-25, 29-34
Popliteal aneurysms	90 (70-100)	4, 5, 42

	Series comparing results in native vessels vs. grafts		
	Success rate (%)	p Value	Ref.
Native vessels	52	<0.05	20
Grafts	11		
Native vessels			
Suprainguinal	89	NS	25
Infrainguinal	70		
Grafts			
Suprainguinal	91		
Infrainguinal	68		
Grafts	75		
Femoropopliteal vessels	80	<0.04	13
Tibial vessels	20		
PTFE grafts	53-72	NS	16
Vein grafts	64.5-83		9, 22

32

Extra-Anatomic Bypass

James I. Fann, MD, E. John Harris, Jr., MD, and Ronald L. Dalman, MD, Stanford, California

Extra-anatomic bypass as defined in this report includes axillofemoral and femorofemoral bypass procedures. Other forms of extra-anatomic bypass grafting, including obturator bypass and arch vessel bypass, are not addressed. Direct anatomic reconstruction for aortoiliac occlusive disease provides superior long-term graft patency and as a rule is preferable to extra-anatomic bypass in patients with severe lower extremity ischemia. Recently the indications for axillofemoral or femorofemoral reconstruction have been extended to include patients with cardiovascular or pulmonary risk factors that would preclude abdominal aortic surgery. Aortoiliac or aortofemoral graft

From the Department of Cardiothoracic Surgery and the Division of Vascular Surgery, Department of Surgery, Stanford University Medical Center, Stanford, Calif.

infections are now routinely treated by lower extremity revascularization using extra-anatomic bypass followed by removal of the infected graft.

The role of thrombectomy and other adjunctive procedures used to maintain graft patency has been overlooked and underreported. Recent reports distinguish primary from secondary patency rates, allowing an accurate appraisal not only of the value of the technique but also of the benefits associated with diligent graft surveillance and early therapeutic intervention. The following tables reflect weighted averaging of multiple independent series reporting surgical results, frequently in a nonstandard fashion, and thus introduce a degree of uncertainty into the absolute value of the patency and survival rates reported. Nonetheless, the aggregate experience derived benefits from the significant numbers of patients and procedures reported and we feel presents a substantive reference for clinicians considering revascularization in this difficult patient population.

Table I. Indications for extra-anatomic bypass

	Limb salvage	Severe claudication	Failed reconstruction	Aneurysm	Infection	References
Ax-fem (%)	63	27	14	6.6	12	1-20
Ax-bifem (%)	60	26	7	16	11	1-8,10-13
Ax-unifem (%)	57	26	27	2.5	15	1-5,9
Fem-fem (%)	43	52	23	2.3	–	1,4,21-31

Ax-fem = axillofemoral bypass graft including axillobifemoral and axillounifemoral bypass; Ax-bifem = axillobifemoral bypass graft; Ax-unifem = axillounifemoral bypass graft; Fem-fem = femorofemoral bypass graft.

Table II. Characteristics of patients undergoing axillofemoral bypass

Patient characteristics		References
Male:female	2.2 : 1	3-5,9,10,14-18,32-35
Mean age (yr)	66	3-5,8-12,15,16,18,20,29,32-36
Smoking (%)	77	5,6,13,16,18,34
Coronary artery disease (%)	54	5,6,8-13,15,16,18,29,32-34,36
Hypertension (%)	41	5,6,8-10,32,33
Chronic obstructive pulmonary disease (%)	32	5,8-10,15,16,29,32
Diabetes mellitus (%)	26	5,6,8,9,11,13,15,18,29,32-34
Cerebrovascular disease (%)	20	5,8,9,11-13,15,18,29,32-34

Table III. Characteristics of patients undergoing femorofemoral bypass

Patient characteristics		References
Male:female	3.1 : 1	22-28,30,31
Mean age (yr)	62	22-30
Smoking (%)	80	21,23-26,31,37
Coronary artery disease (%)	33	21,23-30,37,38
Hypertension (%)	31	21,23,25,26,28,30,37,38
Diabetes mellitus (%)	20	21-31,37,38
Chronic obstructive pulmonary disease (%)	19	21,25,27-29,38
Cerebrovascular disease (%)	14	21,23,27-29,37,38
Hyperlipidemia (%)	14	23,30,37

Table IV. Operative mortality of patients undergoing extra-anatomic bypass

	%	References
Ax-fem	6.4	1-12,14-18,32,33,38
Ax-fem (for infection)	24.0	2,3,9,14,39-42
Ax-bifem	9.0	1-3,5-7,10,14,17
Ax-unifem	6.8	1,2,5,7
Ax-pop	13.0	43-45
Fem-fem	3.4	1,4,21-31,37,38

Ax-pop = axillopopliteal bypass graft.

Table V. Cumulative primary patency rates for extra-anatomic bypass

	3	6	12	24	36	48	60 (mo)	References
Ax-fem	87	73	72	68	61	58	43	1,4,6,8,9,13,14,16,32,33
Ax-bifem	90	85	79	78	69	69	58	1,6,8,9,13,14,16,18,32
Ax-unifem	88	65	50	48	44	28	24	1,9,13,14,16,18,32,33
Ax-pop	87	80	62	44	41	40	40	43-45
Fem-fem	94	91	89	80	74	65	65	1,4,21-23,30

Data expressed as percent.

REFERENCES

1. Rutherford RB, Patt A, Pearce WH. Extra-anatomic bypass: A closer view. J Vasc Surg 1987;6:437-446.
2. Quiñones-Baldrich WJ, Hernandez JJ, Moore WS. Long-term results following surgical management of aortic graft infection. Arch Surg 1991;126:507-511.
3. Ward RE, Holcroft JW, Conti S, et al. New concepts in the use of axillofemoral bypass grafts. Arch Surg 1983;118:573-576.
4. Hepp W, deJonge K, Pallua N. Late results following extra-anatomic bypass procedures for chronic aortoiliac occlusive disease. J Cardiovasc Surg 1988;29:181-185.
5. Ray LI, O'Connor JB, Davis CC, et al. Axillofemoral bypass: A critical reappraisal of its role in the management of aortoiliac occlusive disease. Am J Surg 1979;138:117-128.
6. Harris EJ, Taylor LM, McConnell DB, et al. Clinical results of axillobifemoral bypass using externally supported polytetrafluoroethylene. J Vasc Surg 1990;12:416-421.
7. Johnson WC, LoGerfo FW, Vollman RW, et al. Is axillobilateral femoral graft an effective substitute for aortic-bilateral iliac/femoral graft? An analysis of ten years experience. Ann Surg 1977;186:123-129.
8. Burrell MJ, Wheeler JR, Gregory RT, et al. Axillofemoral bypass: A ten year review. Ann Surg 1982;195:796-799.
9. Donaldson MC, Louras JC, Bucknam CA. Axillofemoral bypass: A tool with a limited role. J Vasc Surg 1986;3:757-763.
10. Savrin RA, Record GT, McDowell DE. Axillofemoral bypass: Expectations and results. Arch Surg 1986;121:1016-1020.
11. LoGerfo FW, Johnson WC, Corson JD, et al. A comparison of the late patency rates of axillobilateral femoral and axillo-unilateral femoral grafts. Surgery 1977;81:33-40.
12. Christenson JT, Broome A, Norgren L, et al. The late results after axillo-femoral bypass grafts in patients with leg ischemia. J Cardiovasc Surg 1986;27:131-135.
13. Chang JB. Current state of extraanatomic bypasses. Am J Surg 1986;152:202-205.
14. Cina C, Ameli FM, Kalman P, et al. Indications and role of axillofemoral bypass in high-risk patients. Ann Vasc Surg 1988;2:237-241.
15. Kalman PG, Hosang M, Cina C, et al. Current indications for axillounifemoral and axillofemoral bypass grafts. J Vasc Surg 1987;5:828-832.
16. Allison HF, Terblanche J, Immelman EJ, et al. Axillofemoral bypass: A two-decade experience reviewed. S Afr Med J 1985;68:559-562.
17. Harris KA, Niesobska V, Carroll SE, et al. Extra-anatomic bypass grafting: A rational approach. Can J Surg 1989;32:113-116.
18. Ascer E, Veith FJ, Gupta SK, et al. Comparison of axillounifemoral and axillobifemoral bypass operations. Surgery 1985;97:169-174.
19. Kenney DA, Sauvage LR, Wood SJ, et al. Comparison of noncrimped, externally supported (EXS) and crimped, non-supported Dacron prostheses for axillofemoral and above-knee femoropopliteal bypass. Surgery 1982;92:931-946.
20. Johnson WC, Squires JW. Axillo-femoral (PTFE) and infrainguinal revascularization (PTFE and umbilical vein). J Cardiovasc Surg 1991;32:344-349.
21. Brouwer MHJ, Biemans RGM, Donders HPC. Long-term results of 44 cross-over bypasses. J Cardiovasc Surg 1988;29:290-295.
22. Self SB, Richardson JD, Klamer TW, et al. Utility of femorofemoral bypass. Am Surg 1991;57:602-606.
23. Francois F, Picard E, Nicaud P, et al. Femorofemoral crossover bypass for noninfective complications of aortoiliac surgery. Ann Vasc Surg 1991;5:46-49.
24. Fahal AH, McDonald AM, Marston A. Femorofemoral bypass in unilateral iliac artery occlusion. Br J Surg 1989;76:22-25.
25. Plecha FR, Plecha FM. Femorofemoral bypass grafts: Ten-year experience. J Vasc Surg 1984;1:555-561.
26. Mosley JG, Marston A. Long term results of 66 femoral-to-femoral bypass grafts: A 9 year follow-up. Br J Surg 1983;70:631-634.
27. Kalman PG, Hosang M, Johnston KW, et al. The current role for femorofemoral bypass. J Vasc Surg 1987;6:71-76.
28. DeVolfe C, Adeleine P, Henrie M, et al. Iliofemoral and femoro-femoral crossover grafting. J Cardiovasc Surg 1983;24:634-640.
29. Mason RA, Smirnov VB, Newton B, et al. Alternative procedures to aortobifemoral bypass grafting. J Cardiovasc Surg 1989;30:192-197.
30. Association Universitaire de Recherche en Chirurgie, Ricco JB. Unilateral iliac artery occlusive disease: A randomized multicenter trial examining direct revascularization versus crossover bypass. Ann Vasc Surg 1992;6:209-219.
31. Dick LS, Brief DK, Alpert J, et al. A 12-year experience with femorofemoral crossover grafts. Arch Surg 1980;115:1359-1365.
32. Schneider JR, McDaniel MD, Walsh DB, et al. Axillofemoral bypass: Outcome and hemodynamic results in high-risk patients. J Vasc Surg 1992;15:952-963.
33. Naylor AR, Ah-see AK, Engeset J. Axillofemoral bypass as a limb salvage procedure in high risk patients with aortoiliac disease. Br J Surg 1990;77:659-661.
34. Schultz GA, Sauvage LR, Mathisen SR, et al. A five- to seven-year experience with externally-supported Dacron prostheses in axillofemoral and femoropopliteal bypass. Ann Vasc Surg 1986;1:214-224.
35. Agee JM, Kron IL, Flanagan T, et al. The risk of axillofemoral bypass grafting for acute vascular occlusion. J Vasc Surg 1991;14:190-194.
36. Broome A, Christenson JT, Eklof B, et al. Axillofemoral bypass reconstructions in sixty-one patients with leg ischemia. Surgery 1980;88:673-676.
37. Lamerton AJ, Nicolaides AN, Eastcott HHG. The femorofemoral graft. Arch Surg 1985;120:1274-1278.
38. Schroe H, Nevelsteen A, Suy R. Extra-anatomical grafting for aorto-occlusive disease: The outcome in 133 procedures. Acta Chir Belg 1990;90:240-243.
39. Yeager RA, Moneta GL, Taylor LM, et al. Improving survival and limb salvage in patients with aortic graft infection. Am J Surg 1990;159:466-469.
40. Bacourt F, Koskas F. Axillobifemoral bypass and aortic exclusion for vascular septic lesions: A multicenter retrospective study of 98 cases. Ann Vasc Surg 1992;6:119-126.
41. Schmitt DD, Seabrok GR, Bandyk DF, et al. Graft excision and extra-anatomic revascularization: The treatment of choice for the septic aortic prosthesis. J Cardiovasc Surg 1990;31:327-332.
42. Ricotta JJ, Faggioli GL, Stella A, et al. Total excision and extra-anatomic bypass for aortic graft infection. Am J Surg 1991;162:145-149.

43. Keller MP, Hoch JR, Harding AD, et al. Axillopopliteal bypass for limb salvage. J Vasc Surg 1992;15:817-822.

44. Ascer E, Veith FJ, Gupta S. Axillopopliteal bypass grafting: Indications, late results, and determinants of long-term patency. J Vasc Surg 1989;10:285-291.

45. McCarthy WJ, McGee GS, Lin WW, et al. Axillary-popliteal artery bypass provides successful limb salvage after removal of infected aortofemoral grafts. Arch Surg 1992;127:974-978.

46. Gupta SK, Veith FJ, Ascer E, et al. Five-year experience with axillopopliteal bypasses for limb salvage. J Cardiovasc Surg 1985;26:321-324.

33

Carotid Endarterectomy

Lloyd M. Taylor, Jr, MD, John M. Porter, MD, Portland, Oregon

The tables that follow contain basic data describing expected occurrences of stroke and death in patients with cerebrovascular disease and in patients undergoing carotid endarterectomy. The data were derived by pooling information from the authoritative references as listed, with appropriate weighting for varying patient numbers, length of follow-up, etc.

From the Division of Vascular Surgery, Oregon Health Sciences University, Portland, Ore.

Table I. Natural history of carotid artery disease

Category	Annual risk of stroke (%)	Annual risk of death (%)	Stroke/death combined/yr (%)	Ref.
Unselected U.S. males, age 65-74	0.8	3.6	4.4	25,26,45
Unselected U.S. females, age 65-74	0.9	2.5	3.4	25,26,45
Persons with asymptomatic carotid bruit	2.3	6.6	8.9	11,13,22,43,46,50
Persons with asymptomatic nonstenotic carotid ulcer	4.0	6.3	10.3	12,19
Persons with asymptomatic carotid stenosis >50% by vascular lab	6.4	5.2	11.6	7,10,27,33,43
Persons with TIAs with carotid stenosis	8.5	5.8	14.3	9,17,25,38,48
Persons with completed stroke	14.4	14.6	29.0	1,3,31,42

TIA = Transient ischemic attack.

Table II. Complications of carotid endarterectomy performed for various indications

Indication for surgery	Combined operative stroke/death	
	Best individual series (%)*	Community-wide survey (%)†
Asymptomatic carotid stenosis	1.0	5.6
Transient ischemic attacks	2.6	9.6
Completed stroke	9.6	21.0

*References 29,37,47,49.
†References 5,14,41.

Table III. Prognosis following treatment of carotid artery disease

Treatment category	Annual risk of stroke (%)	Annual risk of death (%)	Stroke/death combined/yr (%)	Ref.
After uncomplicated carotid endarterectomy for asymptomatic carotid stenosis	1.0	6.5	7.5	6,33,34,46
After uncomplicated carotid endarterectomy for TIAs	2.3	5.2	7.5	4,23,35,36
Medical (aspirin) therapy for TIAs	5.9	4.3	10.2	2,8,16
After uncomplicated carotid endarterectomy for completed stroke	4.5	8.3	12.8	4,23,35

Table IV. Special categories

Category	Percent	Ref.
The incidence of surgically correctible carotid artery disease in persons with non-hemorrhagic stroke	45*	20,21,32
The incidence of appropriate sided, surgically correctible carotid artery disease in persons with hemispheric TIAs	72*	15,18,39,48
The annual risk of stroke with asymptomatic, hemodynamically significant carotid stenosis contralateral to successful carotid endarterectomy	0.5	24,30,40,44

*Note: Expressed percentages exclude carotid occlusions.

REFERENCES

1. Acheson J, Hutchinson EC. The natural history of focal cerebral vascular disease. Q J Med 1970;40:15-23.

2. The American Canadian Study Group. Persantine aspirin trial in cerebral ischemia. Part II. Endpoint results. Stroke 1985; 16:406-415.

3. Baker RN, Schwarz WS, Ranseyer JC. Prognosis among survivors of ischemic stroke. Neurology 1968;18:933-941.

4. Bernstein EF, Humber PB, Collins GM, et al. Life expectancy and late stroke following carotid endarterectomy. Ann Surg 1983;198:80-86.

5. Brott T, Thalinger K. The practice of carotid endarterectomy in a large metropolitan area. Stroke 1984;15:950-955.

6. Burke PA, Callow AD, O'Donnel TF, et al. Carotid endarterectomy for asymptomatic bruit. Arch Surg 1982;117:1222-1227.

7. Busuttil RW, Baker JD, Davidson RK, et al. Carotid artery stenosis—hemodynamic significance and clinical course. JAMA 1981;245:1438-1445.

8. The Canadian Cooperative Study Group. A randomized trial of aspirin and sulfinpyrazone in threatened stroke. N Engl J Med 1978;299:53-59.

9. Cartledge NEF, Whisnant JP, Elveback LR. Carotid and vertebral-basilar transient cerebral ischemic attacks. Mayo Clin Proc 1977;52:117-120.

10. Clagett GP, Youkey JR, Brigham RA, et al. Asymptomatic carotid bruit and abnormal ocular pneumoplethysmography: A prospective study comparing two approaches to management. Surgery 1984;76:823-830.

11. Cooperman M, Martin EW, Evans WE. Significance of asymptomatic carotid bruits. Arch Surg 1978;113:1339-1340.

12. Dixon S, Pais SD, Raviola C, et al. Natural history of nonstenotic asymptomatic ulcerative lesions of the carotid artery. Arch Surg 1982;117:1493-1498.

13. Dorazio RA, Ezzet F, Nesbitt NL. Long-term follow-up of asymptomatic carotid bruits. Am J Surg 1980;140:212-213.

14. Easton JD, Sherman DG. Stroke and mortality rate in carotid endarterectomy—228 consecutive operations. Stroke 1977;8: 565-568.

15. Eisenberg RL, Nemzek WR, Moore WS, et al. Relationship of transient ischemic attacks and angiographically demonstrable lesions of carotid artery. Stroke 1977;8:483-486.

16. Fields WS, Lemak NA, Frankowski RF, et al. Controlled trial of aspirin in cerebral ischemia. Circulation 1980;62:(suppl V)90-96.

17. Fields WS, Maslenikox V, Meyer JS, et al. Joint study of extracranial arterial occlusion. V. Progress report of prognosis following surgery or nonsurgical treatment for transient cerebral ischemic attacks and cervical carotid artery lesions. JAMA 1970;211:1993-2003.

18. Gomensoro JB, Maslenikox V, Azambuja N, et al. Joint study of extracranial arterial occlusion. VIII. Clinical-radiographic correlation of carotid bifurcation lesions in 177 patients with transient cerebral ischemic attacks. JAMA 1973;224:985-991.

19. Harward TRS, Kroener JM, Wickbom IG, et al. Natural history of asymptomatic ulcerative plaques of the carotid bifurcation. Am J Surg 1983;146:208-212.

20. Hass WK, Fields WS, North RR, et al. Joint study of extracranial arterial occlusion. II. Arteriography, techniques, sites, and complications. JAMA 1968;203:159-166.

21. Heyman A, Fields WS, Keating RD. Joint study of extracranial arterial occlusion. VI. Rapid differences in hospitalized patients with ischemic stroke. JAMA 1972;222:285-289.

22. Heyman A, Wilkinson W, Heyden S, et al. Risk of stroke in asymptomatic persons with cervical arterial bruits. N Engl J Med 1980;302:838-841.

23. Hertzer NR, Arison R. Cumulative stroke and survival ten years after carotid endarterectomy. J Vasc Surg 1985;2: 661-668.

24. Humphries AW, Young JR, Santilli RN, et al. Unoperated, asymptomatic significant internal carotid artery stenosis: A review of 182 instances. Surgery 1976;80:695-698.

25. Joint committees for stroke facilities. Transient focal cerebral ischemia: Epidemiological and clinical aspects. Stroke 1974; 5:277-287.

26. Kannel WB, Gordon T. Evaluation of cardiovascular risk in the elderly: The Framingham study. Bull NY Acad Med 1978;54:573-591.

27. Kartchner MM, McRae LP. Carotid occlusive disease as a risk factor in major cardiovascular surgery. Arch Surg 1982;117: 1086-1088.

28. Kartchner MM, McRae LP. Noninvasive evaluation and management of the "asymptomatic" carotid bruit. Surgery 1977; 82:840-847.

29. Lees CD, Hertzer NR. Postoperative stroke and late neurologic complications after carotid endarterectomy. Arch Surg 1981; 116:1561-1568.

30. Levin SM, Sondheimer FK, Levin JM. The contralateral diseased but asymptomatic carotid artery: To operate or not. Am J Surg 1980;140:203-205.

31. McCullough JL, Mentzer RM, Harmon PK, et al. Carotid endarterectomy after a completed stroke: Reduction in long-term neurologic deterioration. J Vasc Surg 1985;2:7-13.

32. Mohr JP, Caplan LR, Melski JW, et al. The Harvard cooperative stroke registry: A prospective study. Neurology 1978;28: 754-762.

33. Moore DJ, Miles RD, Gooley NA, et al. Noninvasive assessment of stroke risk in asymptomatic and nonhemispheric patients with suspected carotid disease. Ann Surg 1985;212: 491-503.

34. Moore WS, Boren C, Malone JM, et al. Asymptomatic carotid stenosis, immediate and long-term results after prophylactic endarterectomy. Am J Surg 1978;138:228-233.

35. Muuronen A. Outcome of surgical treatment of 110 patients with transient ischemic attacks. Stroke 1984;15:959-964.

36. Norrving B, Nilsson B, Olsson JE. Progression of carotid disease after carotid endarterectomy: A Doppler ultrasound study. Ann Neurol 1982;12:548-552.

37. Nunn DB. Carotid endarterectomy. Ann Surg 1975;182: 733-738.

38. Olsson JE, Muller R, Berneli S. Long-term anticoagulant therapy for TIAs and minor strokes with minimum residuum. Stroke 1976;7:444-451.

39. Pessin MS, Duncan GW, Mohr JP, et al. Clinical and angiographic features of carotid transient ischemic attacks. N Engl J Med 1977;296:358-362.

40. Podore PC, DeWeese JA, May AG, et al. Asymptomatic contralateral carotid artery stenosis: A five-year follow-up study following carotid endarterectomy. Surgery 1980;88: 748-752.

41. Prioleau WH, Aiken AF, Hairston P. Carotid endarterectomy: Neurologic complications as related to surgical techniques. Ann Surg 1977;185:678-683.

42. Robinson RW, DeMirel M, LeBeau RJ. Natural history of cerebral thrombosis nine to nineteen year follow-up. J Chronic Dis 1968;21:221-230.

43. Roederer GO, Langlois YE, Jager KA, et al. The natural history of carotid arterial disease in asymptomatic patients with cervical bruits. Stroke 1984;15:605-613.

44. Roederer GO, Langlois YE, Lusiani L, et al. Natural history of carotid artery disease on the side contralateral to endarterectomy. J Vasc Surg 1984;1:62-72.

45. Soltero I, Liu K, Cooper R, et al. Trends in mortality from cerebrovascular disease in the United States 1960 to 1975. Stroke 1978;9:549-558.

46. Thompson JE, Patman RD, Talkington CM. Asymptomatic carotid bruit: Long-term outcome of patients having endarterectomy compared with unoperated controls. Ann Surg 1978;188:308-316.

47. Thompson JE, Talkington CM. Carotid surgery for cerebral ischemia. Surg Clin North Am 1979;59:539-553.

48. Toole JF, Janeway R, Choi K, et al. Transient ischemic attacks due to atherosclerosis. Arch Neurol 1975;32:5-12.

49. Whitney DC, Kahn EM, Estes JW, et al. Carotid artery surgery without a temporary indwelling shunt. Arch Surg 1980;115:1393-1399.

50. Wolf PA, Kannel WB, Sorlie P, et al. Asymptomatic carotid bruit and risk of stroke: The Framingham study. JAMA 1981;245:1442-1445.

34

Vertebral Artery Reconstruction

Ronald A. Kline, MD, and Ramon Berguer, MD, PhD, Detroit, Michigan

Repair of the VA has evolved in the last decade. It began as an uncommon operation used in a minute percentage of patients with cerebrovascular disease. At that time many neurologists and vascular surgeons viewed these reconstructions with skepticism, doubting that they could influence the neurologic outcome of these patients or even if they were needed at all.

During the past decade experience was gained with diagnostic techniques such as dynamic selective arteriography to outline VA pathology. This technique provides an anatomic definition of the compression mechanism of positional VBI. Pathologic studies also showed that a third of patients with VBI previously had embolization from the vertebrobasilar artery. The advent of MRI has shown the end-organ effects of microembolization: small infarctions in the posterior fossa previously missed by CT scan techniques.

The reconstructive surgical techniques have been paired down to rather straightforward operations on the proximal VA, mostly transpositions to the common carotid artery and, in the distal VA, to bypasses or transpositions.

Longitudinal data after 10 years of follow-up on these patients has shown that stroke prevention and resolution of symptoms are remarkably good whereas cumulative patency rates equal those of other arterial reconstructions. In fact, life-table analysis suggests that patients undergoing VA reconstruction are a healthier group than those undergoing carotid reconstruction, perhaps because of the inclusion of a substantial number of patients with mechanical compression, usually in the young age bracket.

As practitioners become aware of the frequency of dynamic compression of this artery and of the relevance of microembolization as a cause of VBI, more of these patients will undergo special arteriography and MRI to pinpoint the lesion and define its consequences. A brief compilation of anatomic, functional, clinical, and epidemiologic data pertaining to surgical reconstruction of the VA is presented in the following tables.

From the Division of Vascular Surgery, Harper Hospital and Wayne State University, Detroit, Mich.

ABBREVIATIONS

CBF	Cerebral blood flow by xenon wash-out method
PICA	Posterior inferior cerebellar artery
TIA	Transient ischemic attack
ICA	Internal carotid artery
VA	Vertebral artery
V_1	The first portion of the vertebral artery—that portion extending from the ostium of the vertebral artery at its origin until it enters the bony process of the cervical spine
V_2	The second portion of the vertebral artery—the intraosseous portion of the vertebral artery as it ascends through the transverse foramina of the cervical vertebrae up to the top of C2
V_3	The third portion of the vertebral artery—from C2 to the point where it perforates the dura
V_4	The fourth portion of the vertebral artery—that portion from the dura to the point where it joins the contralateral vertebral artery to form the basilar artery
VBI	Vertebrobasilar ischemia

Table I. Vertebral artery anatomic and functional data

Diameter: distended	4.1 ± 1.1 mm	Refs. 1-13	Origin		
Left larger than right	63%		Medial (0.5 to 2 cm) to thyrocervical trunk	84%	
Right larger than left	24%		Common origin with thyrocervical trunk	3%	Refs. 3, 20-22
Flow: average intraoperative					
For normal arteries or following reconstruction	45-160 ml/min (mean 100)	Refs. 6-9	Left VA arising from right common carotid (mostly in individuals with right retroesophageal subclavian artery)	0.3%	Refs. 23-25
Flow-limiting compression with 45° neck rotation					
Unilateral occlusion	65%			5%	Refs. 26, 27
Bilateral occlusion	10%	Refs. 14-19	Hypoplastic or ending in PICA		

Table II. Level of entry of vertebral artery into vertebral column[1, 28-31]

Cervical level	C-7	C-6	C-5	C-4
Left	4.2%	87.6%	7.8%	0.4%
Right	2.3%	90.5%	6.3%	0.9%

Table III. Presenting symptoms of vertebral artery occlusive disease[32-40]

Dizziness	66%
Posterior headache	50%
Blurred vision	47%
Vertigo	38%
Ataxia	31%
Tinnitus	31%
Dysarthria	31%
Diplopia	28%
Nausea	25%
Syncope	22%
Perioral numbness & tingling	16%
Hemispheric TIAs	9%

Table IV. Causes of vertebrobasilar ischemia[41-46]

Emboli resulting in infarcts	21%
Hypotension of basilar territory (hemodynamic mechanism)	45%
Mixed	21%
Nonclassified	13%

Table V. Cardiac emboli of cerebral destination with posterior circulation lodgement[47-51]

PICA	14%
Vertebral or basilar artery	5%

Table VI. Dynamic arteriographic findings[52,53]

Compression of VA	
One level	89%
Two levels	11%
Occlusion of VA	13%
Narrowing of VA with delayed filling of basilar artery	79%
No filling of basilar artery or PICA	87%

Table VII. Anatomic cause of vertebral compression[2,41]*

V_1 compression by	
Longus colli	90%
Scalenus anticus	64%
Stellate ganglion	30%
Transverse bony foramen	17%
V_2 compression by	
Bony impingement	95%
V_3 compression by	
Second intervertebral nerve	46%
Atlantoaxial joint	35%
Edge foramen of axis	95%
Fibrous ridge	14%
Edge of occipital bone	13%
Atlanto-occipital joint	7%

*Many patients have more than one site of compression.

Table VIII. Empirical indications for reconstruction[54-57]

Clinical symptoms
Anatomic findings
> 75% loss of cross-sectional area of the only patent or dominant VA or of both VAs
Bilateral ICA occlusion & > 50% cross-sectional area loss of VA
Any lesion suspected to be embologenic, regardless of degree of stenosis or presence of normal contralateral VA

Table IX. Operative morbidity and mortality

Proximal VA operations	
Morbidity[58-60]	
Transient Horner's syndrome	33.0%
Transient dysphagia	1.9%
Phrenic nerve injury	1.1%
Chylothorax	0.4%
Lymphatic fistula	3.2%
Subclavian artery thrombosis	1.7%
Operative mortality	0.5%
Survival at 10 yr	83.0%
Patency at 10 yr	93.0%
Asymptomatic at 10 yr	62.0%
VBI better at 10 yr	15.0%
VBI same at 10 yr	13.0%
VBI worse at 10 yr	10.0%
Distal VA operations[33,36,39,57,58,61-71]	
Operative mortality	3.3%
Survival at 10 yr	83.0%
Patency (secondary)	85.0%
VBI free	85.0%

Table X. Reconstruction statistics (combined proximal plus distal data)[6,55-58,69-74]

Cure of symptoms	85%
Improvement of symptoms	7%
Stroke rate (operative + 30 days)	< 1%
Stroke rate (average 1 yr follow-up)	1.5%
Survival rate at 10 yr	71%
Percentage of cerebrovascular reconstructions	5.6%

Table XI. Results of combined carotid endarterectomy and proximal or distal operations[67,71,75-78]

Combined morbidity and mortality	5%
% Stroke free at 10 yr	79%
Survival at 10 yr	69%
VBI free at 10 yr	88%

Table XII. Effect of unilateral reconstruction on CBF[74]*

Patient group	Patients with > 10% increase in CBF (%)
Severe occlusive disease of both ICAs	88[†]
Unilateral or no occlusive disease of ICAs	31

*As determined by xenon wash-out method.
[†]$p < 0.05$.

REFERENCES

1. Cavdar S, Arisan E. Variations in the extracranial origin of the human vertebral artery. Acta Anat 1989;135:236-238.
2. Koskas F, Comizzoli I, Gobin YP, et al. Effects of spinal mechanics on the vertebral artery. In Berguer R, Caplan LR, eds. Vertebrobasilar Arterial Disease. St. Louis: Quality Medical Publishing, 1992, pp 15-28.
3. Arnold G, Lang J. Mabe des schadels, korrelation von leitungsbahnen and beispiele ihrer praktischen bedeutung. Acta Anat 1969;73:98-108.
4. Arnolds BJ, von Reutern G-M. Transcranial Doppler sonography examination technique and normal reference values. Ultrasound Med Biol 1986;12:115-123.
5. Gulisano M. Zecchi S, Pacini P, et al. The behaviour of some human arteries as regards the corrected circumference: A statistical research. Anat Anz 1982;152:341-357.
6. Berguer R, Andaya LV, Bauer RB. Vertebral artery bypass. Arch Surg 1976;111:976-979.
7. Ekestrom S, Retmal E. Haemodynamic condition in the subclavian steal syndrome. Scand J Thorac Cardiovasc Surg 1967;1:161-164..
8. Hardesty JA, Golding AL, Mazzei EA, et al. An experimental hemodynamic study of the subclavian steal syndrome. Surg Gynecol Obstet 1967;24:1212-1218.
9. Bohmfalk GL, Story JL, Brown WE , et al. Subclavian steal syndrome. Part 2. Intraoperative vertebral artery blood flow measurement. J Neurosurg 1979;51:641-643.
10. Salamon G. Arteries of the vertebrobasilar system. In Salamon G, Huang YP, eds. Radiologic Anatomy of the Brain. New York: Springer-Verlag, 1976, pp 303-331.
11. Stopford JSB. The arteries of the pons and medulla oblongata. J Anat 1916;50:131-164.
12. Fields WS. Collateral circulation in cerebrovascular disease. In Vinken P, Bruyn G, eds. Handbook of Clinical Neurology, vol 11. Amsterdam: Elsevier, 1972, pp 168-182.
13. Kazui S, Kuriyama Y, Naritomi H, et al. Estimation of vertebral arterial asymmetry by computed tomography. Neuroradiology 1989;31:237-239.
14. Lewis BD, James EM, Welch TJ. Current applications of duplex and color Doppler ultrasound imaging: Carotid and peripheral vascular system. Mayo Clin Proc 1989;64:1147-1157.
15. Trattnig S, Hubsch P, Schuster H, et al. Color-coded Doppler imaging of normal vertebral arteries. Stroke 1990;21:1222-1225.
16. Wood CPL, Meire HB. A technique for imaging the vertebral artery using pulsed Doppler ultrasound. Ultrasound Med Biol 1980;6:329-339.
17. Bendick PJ, Jackson VP. Evaluation of the vertebral arteries with duplex sonography. J Vasc Surg 1986;3:523-530.

18. Bendick PJ. A parametric study of the accuracy of quantitative blood flow measurements by duplex sonography. Proc AAMI Annu Mtg 1988;23:14.

19. Bendick PJ, Glover JL. Vertebrobasilar insufficiency. Evaluation by quantitative duplex flow measurements. J Vasc Surg 1987;5:594-600.

20. Toole JF. Effects of change of head, limb and body position on cephalic circulation. N Engl J Med 1968;279:307-310.

21. Toole JF. Positional effects of head and neck on vertebral artery blood flow. In Berguer R, Caplan LR, eds. Vertebrobasilar Arterial Disease. St. Louis: Quality Medical Publishing, 1992, pp 11-14.

22. Koskas F, Comizzoli I, Gobin YP, et al. Effects of spinal mechanics on the vertebral artery. Anatomic basis of positional postural compression of the cervical vertebral artery. In Berguer R, Caplan LR, eds. Vertebrobasilar Arterial Disease. St. Louis: Quality Medical Publishing, 1992, pp 15-28.

23. Daseler EH, Anson BJ. Surgical anatomy of the subclavian artery and its branches. Surg Gynecol Obstet 1959;108:149-174.

24. Schechter MM, Zingesser LH. The radiology of basilar thrombosis. Radiology 1965;85:23-29.

25. Takahashi M. Atlas of vertebral angiography. Berlin: Urban-Schwarzenberg, 1974.

26. George AE. A systematic approach to the interpretation of posterior fossa angiography. Radiol Clin North Am 1974;7: 371-400.

27. Bergman RA, Thompson SA, Afifi AK, et al. Compendium of Human Anatomic Variation. Text, Atlas and World Literature. Baltimore: Urban & Schwarzenberg, 1988, pp 336-345.

28. Anson BJ. An Atlas of Human Anatomy. Philadelphia: WB Saunders, 1950.

29. Bell RH, Swigart LL, Anson BJ. The relation of the vertebral artery to the cervical vertebrae. Based on a study of 200 specimens. Q Bull Northwestern Univ Med Sch 1950;24:184-185.

30. Stevens JM, Kendall BE. Vascular anatomy in the suboccipital region and lateral cervical puncture. Br J Radiol 1981;54: 572-575.

31. Daseler EH, Anson BJ. Surgical anatomy of the subclavian artery and its branches. Surg Gynecol Obstet 1959;108:149-174.

32. Elefteriades JA, Spencer DD, Gusberg RJ. Vertebral artery stenosis with brain stem ischemia: Anatomic and therapeutic implications. Conn Med 1982;46:628-632.

33. Imparato AM. Vertebral arterial reconstruction: A nineteen-year experience. J Vasc Surg 1985;2:626-634.

34. Berguer R, Bauer RB, eds. Vertebrobasilar Arterial Occlusive Disease. Medical and Surgical Management. New York: Raven Press, 1984.

35. Kieffer E. Nonatherosclerotic disease of the vertebral artery. In Berguer R, Caplan LR, eds. Vertebrobasilar Arterial Disease. St. Louis: Quality Medical Publishing, 1992, pp 29-82.

36. Branchereau A, Magan PE. Results of vertebral artery reconstruction. J Cardiovasc Surg 1990;31:320-326.

37. Naritoni H, Sakai F, Meyer JS. Pathogenesis of transient ischemic attacks within the vertebrobasilar arterial system. Arch Neurol 1979;36:121-128.

38. Habozit B. Vertebral artery reconstruction: Results in 106 patients. Ann Vasc Surg 1991;5:61-65.

39. Thevenet A, Ruotolo C. Surgical repair of vertebral artery stenosis. J Cardiovasc Surg 1984;25:101-109.

40. Moufarrij NA, Little JR, Furlan AJ, et al. Vertebral artery stenosis: Long-term follow-up. Stroke 1984;15:260-263

41. Rancurel G, Kieffer E, Arzimanoglou A, et al. Hemodynamic vertebrobasilar ischemia: Differentiation of hemodynamic and thromboembolic mechanisms. In Berguer R, Caplan LR, eds. Vertebrobasilar Arterial Disease. St. Louis: Quality Medical Publishing, 1992, pp 40-51.

42. Heyman A, Wilkinson WE, Hurwitz BJ. Clinical and epidemiologic aspects of vertebrobasilar and nonfocal cerebral ischemia. In Berguer R, Bauer RB, eds. Vertebrobasilar Arterial Occlusive Disease. New York: Raven Press, 1984, pp 27-36.

43. Caplan LR, Tetenborn B. Embolism in the posterior circulation. In Berguer R, Caplan LR, eds. Vertebrobasilar Arterial Disease. St. Louis: Quality Medical Publishing, 1992, pp 52-65.

44. Luxon LM. Signs and symptoms of vertebrobasilar insufficiency. In Offerberth B, Brune GG, Sitzger G, et al., eds. Vascular Brainstem Disease. Munich: S Karger, 1990.

45. Caplan LR, Sergay S. Positional and cerebral ischemia. J Neurol Neurosurg Psychiatry 1976;39:385-391.

46. Sakai F, Ishii K, Igarishi H. Regional cerebral blood flow during an attack of vertebrobasilar insufficiency. Stroke 1988;19:1427-1430.

47. Oder W, Siostrzonek P, Lang W, et al. Distribution of ischemic cerebrovascular events in cardiac embolism. Klin Wochenschr 1991;69:757-762.

48. Mohr JP, Caplan LR, Melski J, et al. The Harvard Cooperative Stroke Registry: A perspective registry. Neurology 1978;28: 754-762.

49. Caplan LR, Hier DB, D'Cruz I. Cerebral embolism in the Michael Reese Stroke Registry. Stroke 1083;14:530-536.

50. Foulkes MA, Wolf P, Price T, et al. The Stroke Data Bank: Design, method, and baseline characteristics. Stroke 1988;19: 547-554.

51. Kittner SJ, Sharkness CM, Price Tr, et al. Infarcts with a cardiac source of embolism in the NINCDA Stroke Data Bank: Historical features. Neurology 1990;40:281-284.

52. Ruotolo C, Hazan H, Rancurel G, et al. Dynamic arteriography. In Berguer R, Caplan LR, eds. Vertebrobasilar Arterial Diseases. St. Louis: Quality Medical Publishing, 1992, pp 116-123.

53. Bradac GB, Oberson R, eds. Angiography in Cerebro-Arterial Occlusive Diseases. New York: Springer-Verlag, 1979, pp 40-41.

54. Beven EG. Surgery for atherosclerosis of the extracranial arteries. Geriatrics 1973;28:156-162.

55. Berguer R, Feldman AJ. Surgical reconstruction of the vertebral artery. Surgery 1983;93:670-675.

56. Berguer R, Bauer RB. Vertebral artery reconstruction. A successful technique in selected patients. Ann Surg 1981;193: 441-447.

57. Berguer R. Distal vertebral artery bypass: Technique, the "occipital connection," and potential uses. J Vasc Surg 1985; 2:621-626.

58. Berguer R. Long-term results of reconstruction of the vertebral artery. In Yao JST, Pearce W, eds. Long-Term Results in Vascular Surgery. Norwalk, Conn.: Appleton & Lange, 1992.

59. Kieffer E, Rancurel G, Branchereau A. L'insuffisance vertebrobasilaire par lesion de l'artere vertebrale. J Mal Vasc 1985;10(Suppl C):253-309.

60. Branchereau A, Magan PE. Results of vertebral artery reconstruction. J Cardiovasc Surg 1990;31:320-326.

61. Branchereau A, Rosset ELD, Magnan P-E, et al. Proximal reconstructions. In Berguer R, Caplan LR, eds. Vertebrobasilar Arterial Disease. St. Louis: Quality Medical Publishing, 1992, pp 265-278.

62. Berguer R. Selection of patients, choice of surgical technique, and results with vertebral artery reconstruction. In Berguer R, Bauer RB, eds. Vertebrobasilar Arterial Occlusive Disease. New York: Raven Press, 1984, pp 297-302.

63. Edwards WH, Mulherin JL. The surgical reconstruction of the proximal subclavian and vertebral artery. J Vasc Surg 1985; 2:634-639.

64. Devin R, Branchereau A, Bordeaux J, et al. La Chirurgie de l'Artere Vertebrale. Complications et resultats. In Devin R, ed. La Chirurgie de l'Artere Vertebrale. Paris: Masson, 1984, pp 107-114.

65. Crawford ES, DeBakey ME, Fields WS. Roentgenographic diagnosis and surgical treatment of basilar artery insufficiency. JAMA 1958;168:509-514.

66. Cate WR, Scott HW. Cerebral ischemia of central origin: Relief by subclavian vertebral artery thromboendarterectomy. Surgery 1959;45:19-30.

67. Kieffer E, Rancurel G. Surgical management of combined carotid and vertebral disease. In Berguer R, Bauer RB, eds. Vertebrobasilar Arterial Occlusive Disease. New York: Raven Press, 1984, pp 305-311.

68. Moufarrij NA, Little JR, Furlan AJ, et al. Vertebral artery stenosis: Long-term follow-up. Stroke 1984;15:260-263.

69. Kieffer E, Rancurel G, Richard T. Reconstruction of the distal cervical vertebral artery. In Berguer R, Bauer RB, eds. Vertebrobasilar Arterial Occlusive Disease. New York: Raven Press, 1984, pp 265-290.

70. Heyman A. Joint Committee for Stroke Facilities. Stroke 1974;5:277-287.

71. Kieffer E, Bahnini A, Rancurel G. Surgery of vertebral artery insufficiency. In Bergan JJ, Yao JST, eds. Arterial Surgery: New Diagnostic and Operative Techniques. New York: Grune & Stratton, 1988, pp 187-214.

72. DeBakey ME, Crawford ES, Morris GC, et al. Surgical considerations of occlusive disease of the innominate, carotid, subclavian, and vertebral arteries. Ann Surg 1961;154:698-725.

73. Natali J, Maraval M, Kieffer E. Surgical treatment of stenosis and occlusion of the internal carotid and vertebral arteries. J Cardiovasc Surg 1972;13:4-15.

74. DeWeese JA, Rob CG, Satran R, et al. Results of carotid endarterectomies for transient ischemia attacks—five years later. Ann Surg 1973;178:258-264.

75. Malone JM, Moore W, Hamilton R, et al. Combined carotid-vertebral vascular disease: A new surgical approach. Arch Surg 1980;115:783-785.

76. Bahnini A, Koskas F, Kieffer E. Combined carotid and vertebral artery surgery. In Berguer R, Caplan LR, eds. Vertebrobasilar Arterial Disease. St. Louis: Quality Medical Publishing, 1992, pp 248-256.

77. McNamara MF, Berguer R. Simultaneous carotid-vertebral reconstruction. J Cardiovasc Surg 1989;30:161-164.

78. Bahnini A, Petitjean C, Koskas F, et al. Chirurgie simultanee de la bifurcation carotidiene et de lártére vertébrale: Tactique et technique. In Kieffer E, Natali J, eds. Aspects Techniques de la Chirurgie Carotidienne. Paris: AERCV, 1987, pp 287-298.

79. Kline R, Higgins R, Berguer R. Regional cerebral blood flow in vertebral artery reconstruction. In Berguer R, Caplan L, eds. Vertebrobasilar Arterial Disease. St. Louis: Quality Medical Publishing, 1992, pp 158-164.

Veins

35

Venous Thromboembolism

G. Patrick Clagett, MD, Dallas, Texas

The following tables contain basic data describing the incidence of venous thromboembolism under varying clinical circumstances; the clinical spectrum of venous thromboembolism relative to objective diagnostic tests; the frequency of adverse events with and without treatment (natural history); the incidence of perioperative venous thromboembolism in patients with varying risk

From the Department of Surgery, The University of Texas, Southwestern Medical Center, Dallas, Tex.

factors; and the effects of prophylaxis on venous thromboembolism in general surgery patients. The data were derived from either scientifically sound clinical trials, major reviews by authorities in the area, and meta-analyses. The most up-to-date information available has been used with the exception of older, "classic" studies that would be impossible to perform today (for example, a randomized, controlled trial of anticoagulant therapy in acute pulmonary embolism).

Table I. Incidence of pulmonary embolism in the United States/year[1-3]

	No. of patients	Incidence (%)
Total	630,000	—
Death within 1 hr	67,000	11
Survival >1 hr	563,000	89
Survivors in whom diagnosis is made and therapy started	163,000	29 (of immediate survivors)
Lived	150,000	92
Died	13,000	8
Survivors in whom diagnosis is not made, no treatment	400,000	71 (of immediate survivors)
Lived	280,000	70
Died	120,000	30
Total PE deaths	200,000	32 (of total)

PE = Pulmonary embolism.

Table II. Clinical spectrum of deep venous thrombosis

	Incidence (%)	Ref.
Population with evidence of prior episode of DVT	2.5-5	4,5
Population with chronic venous insufficiency	0.5-2	5,6
Patients presenting with signs and symptoms of DVT who actually have DVT	30-50	7,8
Proximal extension of calf DVT into popliteal and AK veins	20	9,10
Calf DVT that manifests signs and symptoms	5	10,11
AK DVT that manifests signs and symptoms	40-50	11
Patients with superficial thrombophlebitis who have DVT	20-30	12
Varicosities present	3	13
Varicosities absent	44	13

DVT = Deep venous thrombosis; AK = above-knee.

Table III. Clinical spectrum of pulmonary embolism

	Incidence (%)	Ref.
Patients with PE who have lower extremity DVT (silent and overt)	70-80	7,14,15
Patients with PE who have clinical signs and symptoms of DVT	30-40	7,15a
PE in *untreated* patients with calf DVT that does not extend into popliteal and AK veins	<1	16
PE in *untreated* patients with AK DVT	50	7,17,18
PE documented by arteriography in patients with clinically-suspected PE	50	7,19-21

Table IV. Results of treatment of venous thromboembolism

	Incidence (%)	Ref.
Heparin, standard intravenous therapy for acute phase		
Recurrent venous thromboembolism	<5	7,22-26
Major hemorrhage	5-10	7,22-26
Oral anticoagulation, long-term phase (3-4 mo)		
Recurrent venous thromboembolism	2	27-29
Major hemorrhage	4	27-29
After discontinuance of oral anticoagulant therapy		
Recurrent venous thromboembolism in 1 yr	5-10	7,22

Table V. Expected frequencies of deep venous thrombosis in patients of varying risk[30-32]

Diagnosis	Low risk: minor surgery in patients <40 yr and no other risk factor (%)	Moderately high risk: surgery in patients >40 yr, myocardial infarction or heart failure (%)	High risk: surgery in patients >40 yr with previous DVT, PE, malignant disease, major orthopedic surgery, or stroke (%)
DVT (+FUT)	2.0	10-40	40-80
AK DVT	0.4	2-8	10-20
Clinical PE	0.2	1-8	5-10
FPE	0.002	0.1-0.4	1-5

FUT = I^{125}-fibrinogen uptake test; FPE = fatal pulmonary embolism.

Table VI. Effect of prophylaxis of venous thromboembolism in general surgery* patients[33]

	No prophylaxis (%)	LDH (%)	Dextran (%)	HDHE (%)	IPC (%)	ES (%)	ASA (%)
DVT (+FUT)[†]	25	9	16	9	9	9	20
Confirmed DVT (+FUT, phlebogram)	19	6	NA[‡]	NA	NA	NA	NA
DVT (+FUT)(malignant disease)	29	13	23	NA	13	NA	NA
AK DVT	7	1.4	NA	NA	NA	NA	NA
Clinical DVT	3	NA	NA	NA	NA	NA	NA
PE	1.6	0.5	0.7	0.5	NA	NA	NA
FPE	0.9	0.2	0.3	NA	NA	NA	NA
Major hemorrhage	1	2	2	1	NA	NA	NA
Wound hematomas	2	6-8	3	3	NA	NA	NA

LDH = low dose heparin; HDHE = heparin-dehydroergotamine; IPC = intermittent pneumatic compression; ES = elastic stockings; ASA = aspirin.
*General surgery patient refers to an individual 40 yr or older undergoing major abdominal surgery.
[†]DVT (+FUT) = deep venous thrombosis + I^{125}-fibrinogen uptake test.
[‡]NA = reliable information not available.

REFERENCES

1. Alpert JS, Smith R, Carlson J, et al. Mortality in patients treated for pulmonary embolism. JAMA 1976;236:1477-1480.
2. Dalen JE, Alpert JS. Natural history of pulmonary embolism. Prog Cardiovasc Dis 1975;17:259-270.
3. Dalen JE, Paraskos JA, Ockene IS, et al. Venous thromboembolism: Scope of the problem. Chest 1986;89:370S–373S.
4. Carter C, Gent M, LeClerc JR. The epidemiology of venous thrombosis. In Colman RW, Hirsh J, Marder VJ, et al., eds. Hemostasis and thrombosis. Philadelphia: JB Lippincott, 1987, pp 1185-1198.
5. Coon WW, Willis PW, Keller JB. Venous thromboembolism and other venous disease in the Tecumseh community health study. Circulation 1973;48:839.
6. Gjores JE. The incidence of venous thrombosis and its sequelae in certain districts of Sweden. Acta Chir Scand 1956; 2061:(Suppl)88.
7. Hirsh J, Hull RD. Natural history and clinical features of venous thrombosis. In Colman RW, Hirsh J, Marder VJ, et al., eds. Hemostasis and thrombosis. Philadelphia: JB Lippincott, 1987, pp 1208-1219.
8. Stamatakis JO, Kakkar VV, Lawrence D, et al. The origin of thrombi in the deep veins of the lower limb: A venographic study. Br J Surg 1978;65(Suppl 7):449-451.
9. Kakkar VV, Flank C, Howe CT, et al. Natural history of postoperative deep vein thrombosis. Lancet 1969;2:230-233.
10. Lagerstedt CI, Fagher BO, Olsson C-G, et al. Need for long-term anticoagulant treatment in symptomatic calf-vein thrombosis. Lancet 1985;Sept:515-518.
11. Oster G, Tuden RL, Colditz GA. A cost-effectiveness analysis of prophylaxis against deep-vein thrombosis in major orthopedic surgery. JAMA 1987;257:203-208.
12. Adar R, Salzman EW. Treatment of thrombosis of veins of the lower extremities. New Engl J Med 1975;292:348-350.
13. Bergqvist D, Jaroszewski H. Deep vein thrombosis in patients with superficial thrombophlebitis of the leg. Br Med J 1986; 292(No. 6521):658-659.
14. Hull RD, Hirsh J, Carter CJ, et al. Pulmonary angiography, ventilation lung scanning and venography for clinically suspected pulmonary embolism with abnormal perfusion lung scan. Ann Intern Med 1983;98:[No.6] 891-899.
15. Browse NL, Clemenson G, Croft DN. Fibrinogen detectable thrombosis in the legs and pulmonary embolism. Br Med J 1974;1:603.
16. Corrigan TP, Fossard DP, Spindler J, et al. Phlebography in the management of pulmonary embolism. Br J Surg 1974; 61:484-488.
17. Hull RD, Hirsh J, Carter CJ, et al. Diagnostic efficacy of impedance plethysmography for clinically suspected deep-vein thrombosis. Ann Int Med 1985;102:21-28.
18. Gallus AS. Established venous thrombosis and pulmonary embolism. Clin Haematol 1981;10:583-611.
19. Kistner RL, Ball JJ, Nordyke RA, et al. Incidence of pulmonary embolism in the course of thrombophlebitis of the lower extremities. Am J Surg 1972;124:169-176.
20. Urokinase pulmonary embolism trial: A national co-operative study. Circulation 1973;47(Suppl 2):1.
21. Bell WR, Simon TL, Demets DL. The clinical features of submassive and massive pulmonary emboli. Am J Med 1977; 62:355.
22. Bell WR, Simon TL. A comparative analysis of pulmonary perfusion scans with pulmonary angiograms: From a national co-operative study. Am Heart J 1976;92:700.
23. Hirsh J, Marder VJ, Salzman EW, et al. Preventing complications of venous thromboembolism. In Colman RW, Hirsh J, Marder VJ, et al., eds., Hemostasis and Thrombosis. Philadelphia: JB Lippincott, 1987, pp 1266-1272.
24. Barritt DW, Jordon SC. Anticoagulant drugs in the treatment of pulmonary embolism: A controlled trial. Lancet 1960;1: 1309.
25. Basu D, Gallus A, Hirsh J, et al. A prospective study of the value of monitoring heparin treatment with the activated partial thromboplastin time. N Engl J Med 1972;287:324.
26. Kanis JA. Heparin in the treatment of pulmonary thromboembolism. Thromb Diath Haemorrh 1974;32:519.
27. Salzman EW, Deykin D, Shapiro RM, et al. Management of heparin therapy. N Engl J Med 1975;292:1046.
28. Hull R, Delmore T, Genton E, et al. Warfarin sodium versus low-dose heparin in the long-term treatment of venous thrombosis. N Engl J Med 1979;301:271-272.
29. Hull R, Delmore T, Carter C, et al. Adjusted subcutaneous heparin vs warfarin sodium in the long-term treatment of venous thrombosis. N Engl J Med 1982;306:189-194.
30. Hull R, Hirsh J, Jay R. Different intensities of anticoagulation in the long term treatment of proximal vein thrombosis. N Engl J Med 1982;307(27):1676-1681.
31. Salzman EW, Hirsh J. Prevention of venous thromboembolism chapter. In Colman RW, Hirsh J, Marder VJ, eds., Hemostasis and Thrombosis. Philadelphia: JB Lippincott, 1987, pp 1252-1265.
32. Hull RD, Raskob GE, Hirsh J. Prophylaxis of venous thromboembolism. Chest 1986;89:374S–383S.
33. Prevention of venous thrombosis and pulmonary embolism. NIH consensus conference. JAMA 1986;256:744-749.
34. Clagett GP, Reisch JS. Prevention of venous thromboembolism in general surgery patients: Results of meta-analysis. Ann Surg 1988;208(2):227-240.

36

Thrombolytic Therapy For Venous Thrombosis

Timothy Pilla, MD, and Anthony J. Comerota, MD, Philadelphia, Pennsylvania

Fibrinolytic therapy for acute venous thrombosis is a controversial technique to many physicians. Intuitively, they agree that a thrombus in the deep venous system is harmful and that elimination of the thrombus is beneficial. Deep venous thrombosis (DVT) leads to pulmonary embolism and the postthrombotic syndrome. There are some important questions to be considered. Can the incidence of pulmonary embolism be reduced? Can the postthrombotic syndrome be avoided? Can the risk of recurrent episodes of DVT be reduced? Is the cost-effectiveness ratio of therapy (both in dollars and avoidance of complications) favorable? Although the question regarding prevention of pulmonary emboli is unlikely to be answered due to the effective protection offered by anticoagulant therapy, answers to the other questions are currently being investigated.

From the Section of Vascular Surgery, Temple University School of Medicine, Philadelphia, Pa.

Clouding the data are studies that report data on patients at various times other than at the onset of DVT, incomplete follow-up, follow-up that obscures the influence of intercurrent events, and reports that fail to appreciate the physiologic benefit of lysis versus nonlysis.

The rapid advances in noninvasive vascular technology are allowing complete, accurate, and repetitive evaluations of the deep venous system. Ongoing studies promise to provide definitive information regarding the long-term function of the venous system in patients suffering deep vein thrombosis who are offered fibrinolytic therapy as compared with standard anticoagulation. Until these answers are obtained, the data provided in the tables that follow may assist the clinician in making therapeutic decisions. The basic data describing lysis rates, symptomatic consequences, and complications of fibrinolytic therapy for acute deep venous thrombosis are given. The tables also summarize the currently available literature.

Table I. Radiographic lysis, pulmonary embolism, and bleeding complications

Ref.	Duration of clot (days)	Significant or complete phlebographic clearance of DVT				Fatal/major pulmonary embolism		Major bleeding			
		Heparin	SK	UK	tPA	Heparin	SK	Heparin	SK	UK	tPA
1,2	<4	2/9	6/9			1/10			1/10		
3	<5	1/15	10/19			1/15			4/19		
4	<14	1/26	6/23					1/26	6/23		
4	<3	0/13	3/8								
5	<14	11/25	11/21								
6	<7	1/17	8/18			1/17	1/18				
7	<8	0/25	17/23			2/25			3/26		
8,13	<14	4/14	4/11					5/25	7/21		
8,13	<3	0/11	6/11								
9,15	<5	5/11	15/21					2/21	2/21		
10	<21	0/5	3/5								
11,34	<4	1/7	5/9					2/7	6/17		
12	>6	4/42	62/93			5/42	7/93				
14	mean >7	0/12	5/12						1/15		
16	0-14	7/24	17/25								
18	<14	2/7	7/14								
19*	<14	16/91	59/96					2/59	8/57		
20	<4	60/108				3/108	16/108				
21	<14		6/10						1/10		
22	<10	34/40				1/40		5/40			
23	0-7	15/19						3/19			
24	<5†	3/5	4/5			1/5					
25	mean 16		5/14						1/14‡		
26	<16		9/13						2/13		
27	<4	1/8	5/8								
28	<4	0/5§	0/6§					1/8	2/12		
29	<6	3/14	8/14								
30	>7	2/16‖	15/18				1/18		1/18		
31	<10		7/14								
32	>5		18/41						2/41		
35	<7	1/20	11/20								
36	2-21#		10/29			3/64			5/64		
37	0-7**	4/20	4/6	8/16						1/11	
38	≤7		24/30	25/30					5/30	0/30	
39	<1††			3/6							
40	mean 4		2/10	4/21							
41	<21			34/50‡‡						0/50	
42	<15			12/41						0/41	
42	<5			8/13						0/13	
49	<42				2/2						0/2
50				5/12							1/12

SK = streptokinase; UK = urokinase; tPA = tissue plaminogen activator.

*Pooled analysis.

†No initial phlebogram.

‡Jaundice, liver function tests.

§Subtherapeutic doses.

‖Ancrod.

#All initial therapy with heparin.

**Followed by impedance plethysmography.

††Post-thrombectomy rethrombosis.

‡‡Concurrent heparin.

Table II. Long-term results of thrombolytic therapy for DVT

	Ref.	Length of follow-up	Heparin	After therapy Streptokinase
Normal phlebogram				
	2	6-12 mo	1/18	4/7
	5,13	4-18 mo	1/12	6/15
	15	41-106 mo	8/18	7/17
	17	14-57 mo		0/28
	23	6-50 mo		8/15
Asymptomatic				
	7	19 mo mean	2/25	12/13
	15	41-106 mo	6/18	13/17
	17	6-51 mo		9/35
	18	8-10 yr	2/2	3/7
Normal phlebogram				
	16	24 mo	2/2	1/5
	17	6-51 mo		2/35
	18	8-10 yr		1/6
	31	8-53 mo		3/5
	35	5-10 yr		11/12

Table III. Significant or complete phlebographic clearance of subclavian-axillary DVT

Ref.	Duration of clot	Streptokinase	Urokinase	Major bleeding Streptokinase	Urokinase
43	?	7/9		0/9*	
44	?	4/7†			
45	<24 hr	2/2		0/2	
46,47	<9 days	0/4‡	11/11		0/11*
48	<7 days		15/18		

*Low dose, local therapy.
†All patients symptomatically improved.
‡Streptokinase stopped due to fever or rethrombosis.

Table IV. Pooled results: Significant or complete clearance with lytic therapy

	Ref.	Total patients	Percent	Comment
Lysis-DVT	1-42,49,50	995	58	All
	1-37,38,40	817	59	Streptokinase
	37-42	164	52	Urokinase
	49,50	14	50	Tissue plasminogen activator
	1-19,24,27,29,35	431	16	Heparin
Lysis—axillary-subclavian DVT	43-48	51	76	All
	46-48	29	90	Urokinase
	43-47	22	59	Streptokinase

Table V. Major bleeding complications*

Ref.	Total patients	Bleeding DVT (%)	Therapy
1-4,7-9,11,13,15, 19-23,26,28,30, 32,34,36,38	654	14	Streptokinase
4,8,9,11,13,15, 19,28,34	146	9	Heparin
49,50	14	7	Tissue plasminogen activator
37,38,41,42	132	0.8	Urokinase

		Bleeding axillary— subclavian DVT	Therapy
43,45,46,47	22	0	Low dose, local therapy (except for study in Reference 45)

*Resulting in discontinuance of therapy, blood transfusion, or death.

Table VI. Fatal or major pulmonary embolus during therapy

Ref.	Total patients	Fatal or major pulmonary embolism (%)	Therapy
1-3,6,7,12,24	114	10	Heparin
6,12,20,22,30,36	341	5	Streptokinase

Table VII. Long-term results following initial significant complete lysis

Ref.	Total patients	Normal follow-up phlebogram (%)	Therapy
2,5,13,15,17,23	82	30	Streptokinase
2,5,13,15	48	4	Heparin

		Normal clinical examination; patients asymptomatic (%)	Therapy
7,15,17,18	72	51	Streptokinase
7,15	43	19	Heparin

REFERENCES

1. Kakkar VV, Flanc C, Howe CT, et al. Treatment of deep vein thrombosis. A trial of heparin, streptokinase and arvin. Br J Med 1969;1:806-810.
2. Kakkar VV, Howe CT, Laws JW, et al. Late results of treatment of deep vein thrombosis. Br J Med 1969;1:810-811.
3. Tsapogas MJ, Peabody RA, Karmody AM, et al. Controlled study of thrombolytic therapy in deep vein thrombosis. Surgery 1973;74(6):973-984.
4. Porter JM, Seaman AJ, Common HH, et al. Comparison of heparin and streptokinase in the treatment of venous thrombosis. Am Surg 1975;41(9):511-519.

5. Rosch J, Dotter CT, Seaman AJ, et al. Healing of deep venous thrombosis: Venographic findings in a randomized study comparing streptokinase and heparin. Am J Roentgenol 1976;127:553-558.
6. Watz R, Savidge GF. Rapid thrombolysis and preservation of valvular venous function in high deep vein thrombosis. Acta Med Scand 1979;205:293-298.
7. Elliot MS, Immelman EJ, Jeffery P, et al. A comparative randomized trial of heparin versus streptokinase in the treatment of acute proximal venous thrombosis: An interim report of a prospective trial. Br J Surg 1979;66:838-843.

8. Seaman AJ, Common HH, Rosch J, et al. Deep vein thrombosis treated with streptokinase or heparin. Angiology 1976; 27(10):549-556.

9. Arnesen H, Heilo A, Jakobsen E, et al. A prospective study of streptokinase and heparin in the treatment of deep vein thrombosis. Acta Med Scand 1978;203:457-463.

10. Browse NL, Thomas ML, Pim HP. Streptokinase and deep vein thrombosis. Br Med J 1968;3:717-720.

11. Robertson BR, Nilsson IM, Nylander G. Thrombolytic effect of streptokinase as evaluated by phlebography of deep venous thrombi of the leg. Acta Chir Scand 1970;136: 173-180.

12. Duckert F, Mueller G, Nyman D. Treatment of deep vein thrombosis with streptokinase. Br Med J 1975;1:479-481.

13. Common HH, Seaman AJ, Rosch J. Deep vein thrombosis treated with streptokinase or heparin. Angiology 1986; 27(11):645-654.

14. Marder VJ, Soulen RL, Atichartakarn V, et al. Quantitative venographic assessment of deep vein thrombosis in the evaluation of streptokinase and heparin therapy. J Lab Clin Med 1977;89(5):1018-1029.

15. Arnesen H, Hoiseth A, Ly B. Streptokinase or heparin in the treatment of deep vein thrombosis. Acta Med Scand 1982; 211:65-68.

16. Kakkar VV, Lawrence D. Hemodynamic and clinical assessment after therapy for acute deep vein thrombosis. Am J Surg 1985;Oct:54-63.

17. Albrechtsson U, Anderson J, Einarsson E, et al. Streptokinase treatment of deep venous thrombosis and the post-thrombotic syndrome. Arch Surg 1981;116:33-37.

18. Johansson L, Nylander G, Hedner V, et al. Comparison of streptokinase with heparin: Late results in the treatment of deep venous thrombosis. Acta Med Scand 1979;206:93-98.

19. Goldhaber SZ, Buring JE, Lipnick RJ, et al. Pooled analysis of randomized trials of streptokinase and heparin in phlebographically documented acute deep venous thrombosis. Am J Med 1984;76:393-397.

20. Ott P, Eldrup E, Oxholm P, et al. Streptokinase therapy in the routine management of deep venous thrombosis in the lower extremities. Acta Med Scand 1986;219:295-300.

21. Mavor GE, Bennett B, Galloway JMD, et al. Streptokinase in iliofemoral venous thrombosis. Br J Surg 1969;56(8):564-570.

22. Mavor GE, Dhall DR, Dawson JS, et al. Streptokinase therapy in deep vein thrombosis. Br J Surg 1973;60(6):468-474.

23. Johansson E, Ericson K, Zetterquist S. Streptokinase treatment of deep venous thrombosis of the lower extremity. Acta Med Scand 1976;199:89-94.

24. Bieger R, Boekhout-Mussert RJ, Hohmann F, et al. Is streptokinase useful in the treatment of deep vein thrombosis? Acta Med Scand 1976;199:81-88.

25. Tibbutt DA, Chesterman CW, Williams WE, et al. Controlled trial of the sequential use of streptokinase and ancrod in the treatment of deep vein thrombosis of lower limb. Thromb & Haemostas 1977;37:222-231.

26. Olow B, Johnson C, Anderson J. Deep venous thrombosis treated with a standard dosage of streptokinase. Acta Chir Scand 1970;136:181-189.

27. Robertson BR, Nilsson IM, Nylander G. Value of streptokinase and heparin in treatment of acute deep venous thrombosis. Acta Chir Scand 1968;134:203-208.

28. Robertson BR, Nilsson IM, Nylander G, et al. Effect of streptokinase and heparin on patients with deep venous thrombosis. Acta Chir Scand 1967;133:205-215.

29. Gormsen J, Laursen B. Treatment of acute phlebothrombosis with streptase. Acta Med Scand 1967;181:373-383.

30. Tibbutt DA, Williams EW, Walker MW, et al. Controlled trial of ancrod and streptokinase in the treatment of deep vein thrombosis of lower limb. Br J Haematol 1974;27:407-414.

31. Norgren L, Gjores JE. Venous function in previously thrombosed legs. Acta Chir Scand 1977;143:421-424.

32. Astedt B, Robertson B, Haeger K. Experience with standardized streptokinase therapy of deep venous thrombosis. Surg Gynecol Obstet 1974;139:387-388.

33. Dhall DP, Dawson AA, Mavor GE. Problems of resistant thrombolysis and early recurrent thrombosis in streptokinase therapy. Surg Gynecol Obstet 1978;46:15-20.

34. Robertson BR. On thrombosis, thrombolysis and fibrinolysis. Acta Chir Scand Suppl 1971;421:1-51.

35. Jeffrey P, Immelman E, Amoore J. Treatment of deep vein thrombosis with heparin or streptokinase: Long-term venous function assessment. London, Second International Vascular Symposium, Abstract S20.3, 1986.

36. Meissner AJ, Misiak A, Ziemski JM, et al. Hazards of thrombolytic therapy in deep vein thrombosis. Br J Surg 1987;74: 991-993.

37. Sharma GVRK, O'Connell DJ, Belko JS. Thrombolytic therapy in deep vein thrombosis. In Poclett R, Sherry S, eds. Thrombosis and Urokinase, New York: Headline Press, 1977;9: 181-184.

38. Graor RA, Young JR, Risius B, et al. Comparison of cost effectiveness of streptokinase and urokinase in the treatment of deep vein thrombosis. Ann Vasc Surg 1987;1:524-528.

39. Mavor GE, Ogston D, Galloway JMW, et al. Urokinase in iliofemoral venous thrombosis. Br J Surg 1969;56(8):571-574.

40. Van De Loo JCW, Kriessmann H, Trubestein G, et al. Controlled multicenter pilot study of urokinase-heparin and streptokinase in deep vein thrombosis. Thromb & Haemostas 1983;50:660-663.

41. Halser K, Magdalinski D. Urokinase therapy of deep vein thrombosis. Munch Med Wochenschr 1984;126:122-124.

42. D'Angelo A, Mannucci PM. Outcome of treatment of deep vein thrombosis with urokinase: Relationship to dosage, duration of therapy age of the thrombus and laboratory changes. Thromb & Haemostas 1984;51:236-239.

43. Huey H, Morris DC, Nichols DM. Low-dose streptokinase thrombolysis of axillary-subclavian vein thrombosis. Cardiovasc Intervent Radiol 1987;10:92-95.

44. Steed DL, Teodori MF, Peitzman AB. Streptokinase in the treatment of subclavian vein thrombosis. J Vasc Surg 1986; 4:28-32.

45. Taylor LM, McAllister WR, Dennis DL, et al. Thrombolytic therapy followed by first rib resection for spontaneous ("effort") subclavian vein thrombosis. Am J Surg 1985;149: 644-648.

46. Becker GJ, Holden RW, Mail JT, et al. Local thrombolytic therapy for "thoracic inlet syndrome." Semin Interven Radiol 1985;2:349.

47. Becker GJ, Holden RW, Rabe FE, et al. Local thrombolytic therapy for subclavian and axillary vein thrombosis. Radiol 1983;149:419-423.

48. Zimmerman R, Morl H, Harenberg J. Urokinase therapy of subclavian axillary vein thrombosis. Klin Wochenschr 1981; 59:851.

49. Weimar W, Stibbe J, Van Seyen AJ, et al. Specific lysis of an iliofemoral thrombus by administration of extrinsic (tissue-type) plasminogen activator. Lancet 1981;2:1018.

50. Turpie AGG, Jay RM, Carter CJ, et al. A randomized trial of recombinant tissue plasminogen activator for the treatment of proximal deep vein thrombosis. Abstract Circulation 1985; III-193.